Course   ENGL200

Course Number   **Composition and Literature**

American Public University
American Military University

www.apus.edu

http://create.mcgraw-hill.com

ISBN-10: 1121239269   ISBN-13: 9781121239265

Contents

Unit 4: Reading & Writing About Drama 275

Unit 5: Reading & Writing About Essays 385

Unit 6: Research Essay 447

General Reference 519

Credits

Unit 4: Reading & Writing About Drama 275

Unit 5: Reading & Writing About Essays 385

Unit 6: Research Essay 447

General Reference 519

Unit 1: Introduction to Literature

CHAPTER 1

Reading and Responding to Literature and Film

"The art of writing has for backbone a fierce attachment to an idea."

Virginia Woolf

Writing essays for college English courses—indeed for most courses—is a challenge. You must generate thoughts and opinions; harness and organize them; and transform these ideas into effective papers. The end product of this process should be an essay that reads clearly and expresses your insights and discoveries about a topic in a clear and convincing way. To facilitate this process, *Ways In,* a brief guide to writing about literature and film, will show you how to develop ideas and support them with evidence drawn from literary and visual texts and also from research. In the end, you will discover the wisdom of Virginia Woolf's observation that you need "a fierce attachment to an idea" to produce writing that will make a positive impression on your audience.

WHAT IS LITERATURE?

Although critics argue over the definition, what has come to be known as *literature* is writing in prose or verse that contains complex yet coherent ideas and meanings; deals with significant or universal issues; contains original and imaginative writing; and interests a large number of educated readers. As the celebrated Peruvian novelist Mario Vargas Llosa states, "Literature has been, and will continue to be, as long as it exists, one of the common denominators of human experience through which human beings may recognize themselves and converse with each other." Who decides if a work—whether fiction, poetry, drama, film script, or essay—meets these criteria? Admittedly, experts often decide the quality of any endeavor. But anyone can learn to study, analyze, discuss, and apply the specialized vocabulary of criticism to literature and also film.

Of course, there is also a subjective element in literary criticism. For instance, in eighteenth-century England, a definition of "literature" would have included philosophy, history, letters, and essays as well as such standard forms as poetry. Literary judgments are based on the age's personal taste and various cultural assumptions, even though such tastes have been molded by conventional standards. This is a bit different from being an expert in a less subjective field like sports. A sprinter who can run the 100-meter dash in 10.0 seconds is obviously top-notch while another who runs the same distance in 12.0 seconds would not be considered a world-class competitor. With literature, it is more difficult to be certain of your opinions about what is good or mediocre. However, if a work stands the test of time like Sophocles' *Oedipus Rex* or *Othello* by Shakespeare or Tolstoy's *War and Peace,* you may assume that generations of readers have returned to these works and found them personally meaningful and of literary merit. This quality of literature to endure is what the writer Ezra Pound was referring to when he stated that "Literature is news that stays news."

Today, however, there is much debate over the idea of the *canon,* that is, the body of work we believe to be deemed literature. Many argue that what is considered literature is merely the narrow-minded view of a group of like-minded individuals from a more-or-less similar social class, with homogeneous values, who share a similar outlook on life and art. In other words, why have certain literary works been accepted, read, and taught over centuries, while others have either vanished or have been ignored? This argument embraces cultures, genres, and social classes. Nonetheless, newly discovered or rediscovered works often make for exciting and provocative reading; only the future will tell us whether they will enter the body of writing we call literature. Take the work of Kate Chopin. Her short stories, for example "A Respectable Woman," and novels like *The Awakening* were neglected for many years; however, a couple of decades ago, critics began to view her work as explorations of feminism that were ahead of their time, so that now her fiction is read and discussed widely. Or consider the case of Emily Dickinson. Virtually unknown while she was alive, today she is considered to be one of America's greatest poets.

READING AND THINKING CRITICALLY

To write intelligently about literature, you must first read actively and think critically about it. But why does literature require such reading and reflection? Good literature forces you to enter into a dialogue with it. The themes, style, content, meanings, and structure of true literature challenge you intellectually and imaginatively. Other forms of writing usually do not.

You *can* read a story or novel straight through for entertainment, sensing that you have easily extracted all its meaning, derived from it all its pleasure. This is popular literature—crime fiction, romance novels, westerns, science fiction—and you *consume* these forms. When you are done, you find yourself satisfied for the time being. You put the book down, often not to pick it up again. Conversely, with truly significant literature, you not only read it, but also think about it, ask questions about it. How do you know if what you are reading requires such an effort? If you find yourself thinking about what you have read; if you feel the need to review some or all of it for deeper comprehension; if there are elements such as character, theme, plot, style, and other literary components that have you curious or perplexed, the work is more likely to be literary.

Informed readers of literature usually automatically ask themselves certain basic, key questions about what they are reading. The following questions can help you grasp the significant elements of what you are reading and serve as springboards to pursue further and more detailed issues in the text.

1. What is the author's purpose?

A Raisin in the Sun has been viewed as one of the first plays that simultaneously brought the weakness and strength of the African-American family to light for mainstream America. Was that the purpose of Lorraine Hansberry, the playwright? Was the play's purpose to evoke sympathy, outrage, or was it meant to engage its audience in an evening of riveting theater, one that would make them raise issues about their own attitudes toward racism? Or did the playwright have in mind breaking racial stereotypes that many white Americans had about African-American families? All these would be valid purposes. But without the author directly stating his or her purpose, we must infer it. The value of inquiring about purpose is that it can assist you in understanding the *theme* of what you read.

2. What is the author's theme or main idea?

The theme of Raymond Carver's frequently anthologized short story "Cathedral" is that an individual whose perception is limited psychologically can be blind to reality while a truly blind person may have a rich experience of reality. If that statement seems emphatic, it was meant to be. It is one person's summing up of his interpretation of a work of fiction. The term "theme" is sometimes referred to as an author's main idea or major statement or "what the author is trying to say." Regardless of what term you use, you should be cautious in assuming that the theme *you* have determined to be the correct one is the only valid one. Of course, common sense and rational thought will prevent one from accepting *any* theme as possible; still, there may be more than one acceptable one. Stating your interpretation of a theme of a work of literature and then writing about it is an important step toward understanding what you read. It is often the starting and end point for making sense of a work of literature. Discovering a theme gives your reading clarity so that all the elements of what you read are more easily and succinctly comprehended.

3. What is the emotional effect of the writing?

Critics and philosophers have been concerned with the emotional effect of literature since the Greek philosopher Aristotle discussed the issue in his

Poetics some 2,500 years ago. He referred to the concept of *catharsis* as that emotion one experiences when watching a drama that purges one of pent-up emotions. Identification, anger, glee, sadness are all emotions that may be evoked by literature. In fact, tragedy and comedy, two modes of dramatic literature, are often defined by them. Your emotional response to literature will most probably be tempered by your own personality and life experience, perhaps even your gender. For years, critics called Hemingway a "man's writer" because his work portrayed stoic men who endured life without complaint. His story "A Clean, Well-Lighted Place" and novels like *The Old Man and the Sea* are fine examples of this tone of stoicism. Do you identify with the older waiter in "A Clean, Well-Lighted Place" or the old, solitary fisherman in Hemingway's novella? If so, how much has it to do with whether you are a man or woman? How much does it have to do with whether you yourself feel lonely or not and how you regard your loneliness? Raising questions about the emotional effect of writing helps you understand what you read and can assist you in understanding yourself as well.

4. What biases or ideological viewpoints do you detect?

Many students of literature claim that *all* authors have a personal bias and/or an ideological viewpoint that bears on their writing. For example, the mere fact that a writer has had a college education places him or her in a certain class, and therefore places that writer in a particular educational class. For your purposes, it is probably better to consider the bias or ideological leanings of a writer based on his or her gender, economic class, racial and ethnic background, and political viewpoint. Some authors present such viewpoints in more obvious ways than others. For example, Langston Hughes, an African American, was often critical of American society; if you read his poetry, plays like *Soul Gone Home,* and his short fiction, you will discover a humorous, lucid, and straightforward critique of class and caste. Similarly, when we apply such terms as Orwellian, Kafkaesque, quixotic, or Rabelaisian to literature, we use these words to capture certain characteristics of the human condition that Orwell, Kafka, Cervantes, and Rabelais reveal to us. Good literature often poses radical questions about the world in which we live.

5. What personal experiences and/or biases do you bring to the work?

The flip side of the author's bias is your own. You should not necessarily consider the word "bias" in this context a negative one. Rather, it is meant to denote your own perspective based upon your social, economic, and ethnic background. For example, if you are an African American and read the fiction of John A. Williams or August Wilson's plays, you are more likely to have a personal response based upon your racial heritage than if you are a white American.

Raising these questions (merely a sampling of the many you could ask) about what you read should demonstrate how literature challenges you, makes you wonder and question. True literature *requires* that you do this in order to derive full appreciation of it.

LEARNING TO ANALYZE LITERATURE

To illustrate the need to read literature critically, examine the following two passages. The first is a fictive episode; the second is a very brief story entitled "Girl" by Jamaica Kincaid. As you read the two passages, think about how they differ:

> "You should be more tidy in your everyday habits," Janine's mother said sternly, as she examined her daughter's messy room.
>
> Janine averted her eyes from her mother's severe gaze and uttered a deep sigh, as if to communicate that she had heard it all before.
>
> "I want you to pay attention to me. I am your mother, and I set the rules for conduct in this house," her mother continued.
>
> "Mother, why are you always lecturing me? The way I keep my room is my business. Patricia's mother lets her keep her room any way she likes. Besides that, she lets her stay out late, and gives her plenty of spending money." Janine was getting more and more frustrated.
>
> Janine's mother was wishing her daughter would stop this endless comparison. She felt it undermined her authority.
>
> "I'm not Patricia's mother. I'm your mother. And you're not Patricia, you're Janine, my daughter. Now I expect you to start following the rules around here."

• • •

> Wash the white clothes on Monday and put them on the stone heap; wash the color clothes on Tuesday and put them on the clothesline to dry; don't walk barehead in the hot sun; cook pumpkin fritters in very hot sweet oil; soak your little cloths right after you take them off; when buying cotton to make yourself a nice blouse, be sure that it doesn't have gum on it, because that way it won't hold up well after a wash; soak salt fish overnight before you cook it; is it true that you sing benna[1] in Sunday school?; always eat your food in such a way that it won't turn someone else's stomach; on Sundays try to walk like a lady and not like the slut you are so bent on becoming; don't sing benna in Sunday school; you musn't speak to wharf-rat boys, not even to give directions; don't eat fruits on the street—flies will follow you; *but I don't sing benna on Sundays at all and never in Sunday school*; this is how to sew on a button; this is how to make a buttonhole for the button you have just sewed on; this is how to hem a dress when you see the hem coming down and so to prevent yourself from looking like the slut I know you are so bent on becoming; this is how you iron your father's khaki shirt so that it doesn't have a crease; this is how you iron your father's khaki pants so that they don't have a crease; this is how you grow okra—far from the house, because okra tree harbors red ants; when you are growing dasheen, make sure it gets plenty of water or else it makes your throat itch when you are eating it; this is how you sweep a corner; this is how you sweep a whole house; this is how

[1]Calypso or rock and roll.

you sweep a yard; this is how you smile to someone you don't like at all; this is how you smile to someone you like completely; this is how you set a table for tea; this is how you set a table for dinner; this is how you set a table for dinner with an important guest; this is how you set a table for lunch; this is how you set a table for breakfast; this is how to behave in the presence of men who don't know you very well, and this way they won't recognize immediately the slut I have warned you against becoming; be sure to wash every day, even if it is with spit; don't squat down to play marbles—you are not a boy, you know; don't pick people's flowers—you might catch something; don't throw stones at blackbirds, because it might not be a blackbird at all; this is how to make a bread pudding; this is how to make doukona; this is how to make pepper pot; this is how to make a good medicine for a cold; this is how to make a good medicine to throw away a child before it even becomes a child; this is how to catch a fish; this is how to throw back a fish you don't like, and that way something bad won't fall on you; this is how to bully a man; this is how a man bullies you; this is how to love a man, and if this doesn't work there are other ways, and if they don't work don't feel too bad about giving up; this is how to spit up in the air if you feel like it, and this is how to move quick so that it doesn't fall on you; this is how to make ends meet; always squeeze the bread to make sure it's fresh; *but what if the baker won't let me feel the bread?*; you mean to say that after all you are really going to be the kind of woman who the baker won't let near the bread?

Now ask yourself a few questions.

- Which of the two excerpts is more challenging to you, the reader?
- Which one is more intriguing and more original?
- Which one requires more thought, more *critical thinking?*
- Which requires a second reading?
- Which seems to have a unique style?
- Which has an authorial voice, something special that makes it stand out from other things you've read?

If you review the two selections, only "Girl" *requires* you to think in order to appreciate and understand it. For example, who is speaking and who is being spoken to in the second excerpt? In the first, it is all clear and obvious. The dialogue sounds familiar, and has probably been echoed in numerous stories to be found in magazines and in the drawers of would-be authors. In the second, however, things are not as transparent upon first glance. You must infer certain meanings based on what the author has provided in the way of tone, diction, and voice. In the first selection, the author is "telling" the reader how the character feels with such indicators as "Janine's mother said sternly" and "Janine was getting more and more frustrated." In the latter, the author is "showing" you. What is she showing? That is the key to the meaning of the short story. The fact that the story is written in the imperative mode, that its tone is stern, didactic, and commanding should indicate that the author is demonstrating what strategies are needed for survival among women who live in a specific culture, and how these strategies are transmitted from generation to generation. By figuring out how the speaker is feeling and what her relationship is to the person being spoken to, you arrive at an understanding of the selection.

Another critical issue an educated reader might pose is what *formal* aspects make "Girl" special. What is there about its style that sets it apart from other writing? For example, consider the issue of person. The latter excerpt is written in the second-person narrative or "you" form (implied but not stated since it is in the imperative mode). This in itself adds a bit of originality to the work, for it is probable that most if not all fiction you have read has been written in the first-person or "I" form, or the third-person or "he/she" form. (A complete discussion of this subject appears in the "point of view" section in Chapter 3.) But it is not enough merely to be original. You should also consider the purpose or effect of using the second person. Perhaps it provides a way for the writer to more directly imitate true conversation. If you compare the two excerpts, you will probably agree that the latter does seem to mirror the vibrant, continuous quality of speech, while the former seems a bit stilted and contrived, and perhaps worst of all, generic.

Yet another element of active reading is recognizing the author's use of language. Like spoken language, written language has rhythm, sound, tone, diction, imagery, and syntax. In the second selection, you may have noted the music-like quality of the speaker. This may be attributed to the Caribbean dialect and its intonations. For example, if you review the selection by Kincaid, you will notice the author employs such literary devices as alliteration (repetition of consonant sounds), assonance (repetition of vowel sounds), and inventive use of punctuation (the string of clauses held together by semicolons to keep up the movement of the language).

Originality, subtlety, concerns with the aesthetics of language: all three are good indicators that what you are reading is literature, and not just standard prose. Notable writers like Jamaica Kincaid are aware of and incorporate these aspects of language into their writing. And the more you read, think critically about, and write about literature, the more mastery you will acquire in identifying these and other components that enable literary artists to make significant and memorable statements about human experience.

DEVELOPING A CRITICAL PERSPECTIVE

The more you read literature, the easier it will be for you to spot those elements that are worthy of critical analysis and further study. If you read a poem, for example, you can base your reading and understanding of it on your past experience of thinking critically about texts you have already mastered. Reading the short poem "Wild Nights–Wild Nights!" by Emily Dickinson—after having read and analyzed "Girl"—should provide you with the skills to scrutinize and "decode" the poem as a more informed and educated reader. Take a few moments to read the "Wild Nights–Wild Nights!" in its entirety and reflect upon it:

> Wild Nights–Wild Nights!
> Were I with thee
> Wild Nights should be
> Our Luxury!

Futile–the Winds–
To a Heart in port–
Done with the Compass–
Done with the Chart–

Rowing in Eden–
Ah, the Sea!
Might I but moor–Tonight–
In Thee!

Thinking critically about the poem should now come easier. You should be able to raise and answer for yourself questions of narrator, voice, style, language, and syntax. An important aspect of being an educated reader is being able to ask appropriate questions on your own. You may ask yourself such things as what is the tone (emotional tenor) of the poem? Who is speaking? How is syntax used to contribute to the poem's effect? Note, for example, how Dickinson's use of dashes breaches the conventions of customary punctuation. Mentally rearrange the lines in a more typical way and compare the two renderings. What do you discover? Examine the phrase "Rowing in Eden." What does it imply? How does it fit into the overall message of the poem? What is the effect of the nautical imagery? It should be clear to you now that the more you know the method and "language" of literary criticism (a subject treated fully in Part Two of this text), the richer your experience of it will be, and the more discriminating a reader you will become. Ultimately, when the time comes to write about literature, you will have the critical tools necessary to forge your ideas and thoughts into a well-crafted essay.

WRITING ABOUT LITERATURE

Writing about literature adds a unique variable to the equation of an assignment for English class. In order to write about a poem, short story, novel, or play, you must read critically and understand the unique and peculiar aspects of literature. With such an understanding, the analysis, interpretation, and decoding of literature can become a more organized and often more rewarding activity for you.

When you write, you write for a reason or a purpose. The well-known British essayist, journalist, and novelist George Orwell addressed this issue in his famous essay, "Why I Write." In it, he enumerated the reasons he wrote. Among them were "the desire to seem clever," the "desire to share an experience which one feels is valuable and ought not to be missed," "to find out true facts," and the "desire to push the world in a certain direction." Perhaps the reason this essay has become a classic is that it articulates an important issue about writers themselves. Orwell was addressing the reason for and purpose of his own essays and fiction, but it may be just as fruitful to ask the same question of the type of writing you will be doing in this course (and perhaps in future courses and careers). While your motives for writing may not be as ambitious as Orwell's, an understanding of the purposes of writing about literature may help you address the challenge with more clarity and understanding.

Since the times of classical Greece, philosophers have created taxonomies to identify the various forms and purposes of writing. While these systems vary from theorist to theorist, the following list provides convenient categories and sample selections from your literature anthology to elucidate them.

Writing to Summarize

Summarizing requires that you distill the major aspects of a work of literature, for example, its theme, characterization, setting, tone, and the like. Summarizing is helpful in formulating what you believe to be the essential elements of what you have read, and communicating them to others. You may also think of summarizing as an exercise for the mind. It challenges you to think about and express succinctly what you have read. Thus, in writing an essay tracing the developments of African-American drama in the twentieth century, you might begin your discussion of August Wilson's *Ma Rainey's Black Bottom* to include its basic characters, setting, theme, tone, and mood. A summarizing paragraph might go something like this:

> *Ma Rainey's Black Bottom,* set in a makeshift recording studio during the 1930s, depicts the economic and artistic control of black artists by white producers through a series of vignettes that show the resentment felt by black musicians toward their employers and to each other, despite the fact that they have been selected to play backup for a leading singer of the period by the name of Ma Rainey. Their banter reveals feelings of oppression, hopelessness, self-deprecation, and desperation, and culminates in a violent and ultimately deadly confrontation between two of the musicians: one who advocates that the black man take greater control of his destiny; the other attempting to exploit the issue by devising music more to the white man's taste.

Writing to summarize is often an intermediate step in the writing process in that it can be a preparation to writing an essay comparing and contrasting different works of literature or classifying a particular work of literature for inclusion into a particular school or genre.

WRITING TO RESPOND PERSONALLY

Perhaps the very first way we responded to writing as children was emotionally, before we had criteria established for us as to *how* we were to respond or *what* we were to seek out in a text to respond to. When you respond personally, you are actually developing a thesis about what you have read, even if it is merely to demonstrate how you feel about a particular work of literature. Responding to a text personally puts you directly in touch with what affects you about a work of literature.

Writing to Analyze

Writing is a process where feedback plays a crucial role. When you analyze what you read, you can more succinctly express on paper the significance of what you have read. By the same token, writing itself often helps stimulate ideas that had not occurred to you or were existing in only an inchoate state. Writing to analyze often enables you to zero in on a particular aspect or feature of a work of literature. For example, reading, then writing an analysis of sexual and religious imagery in the poem "Wild Nights–Wild Nights!" by Emily Dickinson can make the experience of reading and understanding the poem a more profound one. Like all forms of analysis, writing an analysis of a work of literature broadens and deepens your understanding.

Writing to Compare and Contrast

You gather knowledge about a field of inquiry through study. The more you study, the more you are likely to gain expertise in your field of endeavor. Comparing and contrasting works of literature is perhaps one of the most salient ways of developing your ability to discriminate between what is good and bad; understand what is unique about an author's work; and discern differences between authors, literary styles, genres, and different periods of literary history. You may compare many different aspects of literature. Perhaps the most fruitful forms of comparison are those that you spontaneously or instinctively become aware of through your reading. For instance, you may discover common themes between two poems, two short stories, or two plays, and to enrich your discovery, choose to write about what you see are the essential similarities and/or differences between the two. For example, the poems, "Photograph of My Father in His Twenty-Second Year" by Raymond Carver and "My Papa's Waltz" by Theodore Roethke, relate the memory of a father by his son. Neither memory is positive, and much sadness and betrayal seem to be expressed by both authors toward their respective fathers. But on closer examination, Carver's portrait seems to have the more pathos and sympathy. Thus, in contrasting the two poems, you might generate a theme such as the following: "While both 'Photograph of My Father in His Twenty-Second Year' by Carver and 'My Papa's Waltz' by Roethke portray a father/son relationship absent of healthy emotional affiliation, Carver's portrait is the more tender, sympathetic, and kind." An essay presenting this thesis would be one that compares tone; however, comparison/contrast essays can also address style, ideology, theme, and culture.

Writing to Classify

You probably spend much of your waking life classifying: classifying types of professors, types of food, types of jobs, and so forth. The ability to classify is a vital part of your intelligence. It helps you to see connections, understand relationships, and hone your skills at discerning similarities and differences between people and objects. Classifying literature provides you with a means of organizing your readings and coming to conclusions about what you have read in terms of where it fits in to a particular style, genre, historical period, ideology, or theme. For example, your anthology is classified around genres: fiction, poetry, and drama. As an exercise in classification, see if you can derive a meaningful classification from some of the works you have read in your anthology. Remember, however, that there are innumerable ways to classify, but the fruitful ones provide you with a means of gaining insights and helping to appreciate more fully what you have read.

Writing to Present an Argument

When you see the term "argument" in a writing assignment, it usually means something similar to "prove" or "demonstrate." You do this in writing about literature through developing your main point, and then providing supporting evidence to prove your point. Presenting an argument when writing about literature is very similar to the way a lawyer argues a case in court. He or she presents the thesis—that his or her client is innocent—then provides the proof to demonstrate the truth of the argument. Take, for example, the well-known short story "The Lottery" by Shirley Jackson. Since its publication, critics and students have tackled its meaning through analyzing the nature of the community it depicts, the behavior of its characters, its setting, social relationships in the town, and other elements. Some critics say it demonstrates blind adherence to ritual, the evils of fascism, communism, and the deadly consequences of conservatism. Perhaps your reading of the story can provide a new argumentative approach.

Writing to Evaluate

You are probably familiar with writing that evaluates if you have ever read a movie review or a book review in your favorite paper or magazine. Many people turn to these reviews in helping them plan their entertainment if they feel they can safely rely on the judgment of the reviewer. When you write to evaluate, you are judging what you are reading. You are considering whether what you have read has merit or not. Evaluation, however, is a complex matter, and much personal bias goes into an evaluation. Perhaps the best way to write a competent evaluation of literature is to read as much of it as possible. For example, if you critically and carefully read selections in any literature anthology, you will probably come up with a few favorites. You can then return to these selections and ask yourself, "Why do I favor this selection over these others?" Writing to evaluate will help you understand what qualities are considered meritorious in literature, and at the same time help you understand yourself. Through analyzing which works of literature you prefer and why, you can discover your own literary tastes. To substantiate any evaluation, the writer must show through example how the work possesses various positive and/or negative attributes.

We shall continue to deal with some of these approaches in subsequent chapters. For now, it is important for you to know that writing about literature enjoys a long tradition. After all, Aristotle, the Greek philosopher, provided us with a study of dramatic literature in his *Poetics* over 2,000 years ago. From the age of classic Greece to the present, we have been writing about literature. The concerns and approaches of literary critics and interpreters have been greatly influenced and shaped by the political, social, religious, and ideological forces of their times. Given these variables, we can agree that there is no single meaning in a text. When you read a text, you interact with it to create those meanings that you plan to write about.

APPROACHES TO LITERATURE

Thus far, you may have noticed that we have discussed literature in general and several works in particular by focusing on the works themselves. A school of literary criticism that had its roots in the 1920s and flourished in the 1950s, often referred to as "The New Criticism," popularized the approach of centering all meaning of a work of literature based on what was written on the page. But if you think for a moment, it should be obvious that there are many other ways to examine a poem, a short story, or a play. For example, you could examine the biographical elements of a work of literature by studying the writer's life. Or, if you're interested in the works of Freud or Jung or Lacan, you might apply a psychological perspective to a work, trying to understand, perhaps, the unconscious meanings of a play or story. Actually, for the past quarter of a century, many approaches to studying and thinking critically about literature have emerged. Some have remained popular; others have diminished in their influence. Nevertheless, a brief cross section of these various methods can enrich the way you look at literature and expand the ways you think about it. The following summary is provided to give you a basic understanding of these different methods. If any of them intrigue you, it is easy to follow up your interest by asking your instructor or by referring to the literary criticism of your library or on an Internet site.

Psychological Criticism

You are probably familiar with the concept of interpreting dreams. You may relate a dream to a close friend, and together try to figure out what the symbolism might signify. This activity is similar to the methods used in psychological criticism. This form of criticism attempts to apply modern psychological theories, primarily Freudian (and more recently Lacanian), to understanding literature. Freud, after all, in *The Interpretation of Dreams* explains what he terms the Oedipal complex by analyzing Sophocles' play *Oedipus Rex.* There are various ways that you may critique a work of literature from a psychological perspective. As noted above, you may take a work that has obvious symbolism and interpret what each image means. Another use of psychological criticism in literature is to attempt to understand the underlying motivations of a character in a short story or novel. What are the unconscious wishes of the characters in a play or work of fiction? Or what desires lie hidden in the relationship between Hamlet and his mother? Psychological criticism has also proved fruitful in examining so-called stream of consciousness writing, where we purportedly are entering into the mind of a literary work's narrator, as for example, we seem to do in the poem "The Love Song of J. Alfred Prufrock" by T. S. Eliot. Authors who have used this device in novels include such notables as James Joyce, Virginia Woolf, and William Faulkner. A third function of psychological criticism may be to understand an author's psyche through a study of his or her works. For example, many critics claim you can infer Hemingway's psychological makeup by reading his stories. If you have read his "A Clean, Well-Lighted Place," what sort of man would you believe had written it, and what are his values?

Historical Criticism

Historical criticism attempts to study literature by placing it within the context of the time in which it was written. Thus, styles and forms of writing may be historically based. Much of Shakespearean drama is written in blank verse, as in *Othello*. However, you would be hard-pressed to find a contemporary play written in verse today. Most likely, we would think the author was being either old-fashioned or naive. Content as well as style is greatly influenced by historical forces. If you read Matthew Arnold's "Dover Beach" without a knowledge of the changes in European culture at the turn of the twentieth century, you cannot hope to understand many of the poem's references. The same holds true for William Butler Yeats' "Easter 1916." You must not only be aware of the Irish Liberation Movement to appreciate the poem, but you must have some inkling of the personages referred to throughout the poem.

The New Historicism

New Historicist critics take the concept of history and give it a new perspective. These critics argue that indeed literature can be studied from a historical point of view, but you must be careful not to inject your own historical perspective into a text that was written in another century. For example, the issues of jealousy raised in *Othello*, the issues of incest raised in *Oedipus Rex*, or the issues of the American dream addressed in *Death of a Salesman* may seem familiar and obvious to us. They might appear typical subjects for an afternoon TV show, in fact. However, the significance of the themes in these plays must be considered within the social, economic, political, and aesthetic contexts of the time they were written. *Death of a Salesman*, for example, opened the eyes of a generation to the reductionist, distorted view that the goal in life was to make a good impression on others, and to the need to make as much money as possible to prove your self-worth.

Biographical Criticism

Biographical criticism bears some similarities to historical criticism, only its concerns focus more on the particular life of the author, rather than the time he or she was writing in. Knowing that Wilfred Owen witnessed the horrors of World War I can help us understand the motivation behind the subject matter and themes in his poems, for example, "Anthem for Doomed Youth" and "Dulce et Decorum Est." Many poems cry out for biographical understanding of the author, for example Raymond Carver's poem "Photograph of My Father in His Twenty-Second Year" or Sylvia Plath's "Daddy" or Dylan Thomas's "Fern Hill." Prose fiction too lends itself to biographical criticism, as with "Girl" by Jamaica Kincaid. This is not to suggest that a work of fiction is a direct transcription of an author's life, but many authors use their experiences as sources of their richest work.

Marxist and Social Criticism

Although the philosopher Karl Marx wrote his major works in the nineteenth century, many literary critics have used his analysis of class conflict to examine even the earliest forms of literature. Perhaps because issues of class conflict seem to have existed at all times in human history (there were strong class divisions among the Greeks, for example), and since literature is often about people in conflict with one another and with society-at-large, Marxist criticism lends itself quite readily to explanations of literature. Although issues of race and ethnicity are implicated in much modern literature, many stories and plays can simultaneously be interpreted using a Marxist paradigm. Even if the theories of Marx are not applied directly, the importance of power between and among individuals and groups, and the powerful influences of the conventions of society over our behavior tend to have at least some relevance to a Marxist reading. Much of Richard Wright's fiction subtly shows the potentially insidious effects of class and racism on the future of one young man. Just as graphically, Bertolt Brecht's plays can be read as studies in the effects of sanctioned economic inequality on human beings and entire societies.

Structuralism

The literary method of structuralism takes its inspiration from the work of Ferdinand de Saussure, a Swiss linguist whose major ideas were transcribed by his students at the beginning of the twentieth century. The basic thesis of structuralism is that language is a system, a code of communication with its own rules and regulations. For example, sentences in English have a particular syntax which, if broken, ruptures the sense of the language. Literary critics have taken this basic idea and applied it to literature, primarily in their attempt to raise the importance of genre as an explanatory principle in discussing works of literature. For example, a structuralist might read a detective story, and rather than discuss merits of the style or the symbolic significance of the locale, use the story as a tool to understand the conventions of detective story type. Therefore, structuralist critics are often interested in examining works of literature to understand literature as a whole. So, for example, reading "The South" by Jorge Luis Borges, a structuralist might be more interested in discussing the concept of initiation and relating this concept to other works where initiation plays a significant role. Many advocates of structuralism have claimed that the idea of quality in literature must be reconsidered. Rather than ask whether a poem or story or play is well-written, the question a structuralist might ask is, "How well does this work of fiction fulfill the conventions of the genre it is a member of?"

Reader-Response Criticism

If a tree falls in the forest and no ones sees or hears it, has it really fallen? This old riddle bears considerable significance to the school of reader-response criticism. People who advocate this approach to literature claim that a play or story or poem only exists in its relationship to the reader. Without the reader, it is not literature. The one who reads fulfills an essential aspect of the literary process. While this may seem rather obvious, reader-response criticism was an important reaction to the strong tendency of some critics—particularly the New Critics mentioned earlier—to consider the text in isolation, as though it were an immutable thing whose essence could be uncovered if one simply had the right tools and perspicuity. But reader-response critics hold that we construct meanings from what we read based upon our own individual experience, our cultural background, and the "community" within which we operate. You are a college student, for example, and you constitute with your peers a community. Your study of literature is obviously being influenced by the views that the academic community holds in so far as the way literature should be examined. Even your class itself may have its own biases toward interpretation (most likely controlled by the instructor or perhaps the philosophical perspective of your English department). That a text is incomplete in itself, and that reading it makes it come to life, gives more power to the reader, and some reader-response critics place as much if not more importance on the role of the reader as they do that of the author. Suppose, for example, your father works as a traveling salesman. This may have quite a bearing on your response to the play *Death of a Salesman*. Your response to any of the selections in any anthology may be strongly determined by your own class, racial, and ethnic background. Or take something even more basic: your gender. Chances are that male and female students may see a work of literature quite differently. After reading the story "The Lady with the Pet Dog" by Chekhov, your focus on character might be a result of how you identify with the characters, and that identification may well be based on your sex.

Feminist Criticism

Feminist criticism is an outgrowth of the feminist movement that began in the 1960s, but has been used retroactively to examine works wherein gender issues are prominent. In fact, feminist critics often uncover issues of gender in older texts that previously may not have been considered literature that had feminist implications. One major and legitimate complaint of feminist critics has been that women writers have been ignored since it has been mainly men who have ruled on what is considered literature and what is not. Feminist critics have adopted many writers that have lived in obscurity, so that today authors like Kate Chopin and Charlotte Perkins Gilman and Zora Neale Hurston have been recognized as major writers where formerly their works went unread. Feminist critics often look for and find themes of women's oppression, and stories by such writers as Kay Boyle, Alice Walker, and Nadine Gordimer are seen as works that not only examine women's lives but advocate for them.

INTERPRETING LITERATURE

In a class full of literature students, there is a strong possibility that there will be many interpretations of the same literary work. At the same time, the teacher's interpretation may differ from the students'. Who determines which is the correct interpretation? Or is it safe to say that there is more than one correct interpretation? Literature is open to so many readings, interpretations, and opinions that readers seldom agree on *every* aspect of a literary work. One may say that there are various competent readings, but not *all* readings are valid. You may even change your mind over an interpretation of a particular poem or story depending on when you read it, how often, and in what context.

Regardless of your personal interpretation of a story, it is most probable that the more carefully you read a work of literature, the more likely your interpretation will be valid. If you believe you understand the theme of a work, the particulars of it must back up your comprehension of it. The theme or meaning of a work is a generalization; the elements in it are the particulars. Put another way, your interpretation of a theme is your argument; its various elements are your proofs. If the proofs don't follow, then chances are you have a weak argument.

Some works are easier to interpret than others, however. The play *Krapp's Last Tape* by Samuel Beckett, for example, has been analyzed, studied, debated, and interpreted over and over. On the other hand, a play like *Suppressed Desires* by Susan Glaspell is fairly direct in its presentation of its theme, and few major arguments over its meaning are likely to be forthcoming. There are quite a few factors that influence the difficulty of interpretation of a work of literature. Two major ones are the degree to which the work breaks the conventions of genre; the other is the degree to which the motivations and/or the actions of a character are ambiguous. There have been many classroom arguments over whether the main character in Richard Wright's "The Man Who Was Almost a Man" actually becomes a man by escaping the provincial town he is living in or whether he is merely running away from his problems and therefore remaining a boy.

EVALUATING LITERATURE

"That was a really good movie!" "I couldn't stand the play we read in class." "I hate poetry." These common assertions are all evaluations. However, they are not particularly articulate ones. To evaluate or judge a work of literature requires that you have a set of guidelines. Guidelines for evaluation are not etched in stone and, depending upon your philosophical bent, can vary greatly. For example, a social critic might evaluate a work of literature based on whether it reflects the individual's own world view. If you've gone to the movies and have seen the "good guys" win, you may decide it's a good movie because it ended the way you wanted it to or anticipated.

In most English classes, however, evaluation is usually focused on the integrity of the work itself:

- Do all the elements seem to fit together in a cohesive unit?
- Do the characters seem plausible?
- Are the language, tone, and diction consistent, or if they aren't has the author provided a good reason for the inconsistency?
- Does the work seem to have an original voice, or like the example of "Janine and Her Mother," does it seem to be generic?
- Are the ideas in the work consistent?
- Does each element seem to contribute to the overall theme?
- Is the language vivid, appropriate, and accurate for what the author is trying to convey?

These are only some of the questions you should ask yourself when evaluating literature. For example, if you read poetry by Langston Hughes, ask yourself whether the diction and tone seem to ring true. Perhaps one way to summarize these questions about evaluation is to ask yourself the question, "Does the author of this work seem to have an intimate grasp of the universe of the poem or story or play?"

The more you read and ask questions like these, the more you will develop your own evaluative skills and not have to rely on the views of others. We will return to these issues of interpretation and evaluation in several subsequent chapters.

6 CHAPTER

Navigating the Writing Process

L et's look at an average weekend for a couple of college students.
The first weekend is Carrie's. Carrie lives at home, commutes to college, and has a younger sister and parents who work multiple jobs in order to pay the rent. She babysits her sister all day Saturday and Sunday so her parents can work, and she goes to her job at a local pizza parlor at night. Between family duties, work, and the few hours she manages to steal away with her friends on Saturday night, she hasn't much time to think about schoolwork.

How about Antonio's weekend? Antonio works forty hours a week tending bar, has a son, and hasn't been to school in more than six years. He's decided to return to college to get his business degree, but he can't afford day care, so he watches his son by day. He works at the bar all night, and when he does get some down time, he tries to spend it with his girlfriend and son. This schedule means he typically takes courses on the weekends and online, and he seldom has time to devote himself to school because his everyday life gets in the way.

These weekends may be like yours (they may even be less stressful). Somewhere in between friends, family, children, dating, work, sports, rehearsal, and everything else, those pesky professors also expect you to complete major assignments. This is the reality of college life. When a professor assigns a paper, you may be tempted to sit on the assignment for several busy weekends before finally writing it the day before it's due. We've all done writing like this, but it's not the best way to write. In fact, it's a horrible way to write; the end product you submit for a grade will simply be a rough draft, full of mistakes and lost chances to improve.

As you will learn in this chapter, writing is a *process*. It takes time to craft a top-notch paper, and no matter how good a writer you are, understanding and following helpful steps in the process of writing will help you become a great writer. Though you'll often feel like time is against you during your college days, the steps outlined here can be accomplished in a matter of hours and can help you create a paper you can be proud of. Although ideally you should devote several days or at least several hours to each step in the process, even cramming all the steps into one evening may improve your final product.

PROCRASTINATION

We would like to offer a few words about procrastination, a subject that years of experience have made us experts on. Almost everyone procrastinates in some areas of life. Some of us even accept it as inevitable, but knowing the underlying psychological reasons behind some types of writing assignment procrastination can help us deal with the problem. Without being entirely conscious of it, some people set themselves up to procrastinate as a way of protecting their self-esteem. Consider the grade ranges below, and then look at a typical student's response to getting these grades:

> B or C: This isn't bad at all—I didn't put nearly enough time into this. In fact, it shows I'm pretty smart—I got this grade even though I really had to rush. Imagine the kind of grade I would have gotten if I'd really put all the time I should have into this! I'm a better writer than I thought!

> D or F: Wow. This is terrible. But it doesn't really reflect my real talents. I just didn't put enough time into this. I'm a lot better writer than this!

Sometimes procrastinators are perfectionists in disguise. They want everything they do to be perfect, but who can be perfect? By sabotaging themselves through procrastination, they have an excuse for not achieving perfection. Wouldn't it be better to accept that you aren't perfect, but no one else is, either, so you may as well get the very best grade that you are capable of getting with proper time management.

LEARNING STYLES

Before getting into the steps of the process every writer must go through, you should know a little something about the way your brain works. If you can come to understand how people think and learn, you'll also understand how important it is to write your paper in different steps, each separate from the others. Many of the steps of the writing process detailed next have been followed by professional writers for generations. Recent studies in psychology, sociology, neurology, and many other fields are giving scientific reasons why these steps have always worked so well.

Cognitive scientists have categorized three separate styles of learners: **kinesthetic** learners (those who learn best by touch or by doing), **auditory** learners (those who learn best by hearing), and **visual** learners (those who learn best by seeing). Every one of us utilizes a mix of the three categories, and most of us are dominant in one of the styles, using it more than the other two. However, those of us who can use all three styles equally well, will have an easier time learning in every situation.

As you read about the steps of the writing process throughout this chapter, keep these learning styles in mind. If you understand how your own brain works, what styles of learning and even what side of the brain you use most, then every step of the writing process will make more sense to you. Let's take a closer look at the styles.

Kinesthetic Learners

Kinesthetic learners process and remember information best by taking an active role in the subject matter. Many athletes are primarily kinesthetic learners because of untold

Century

hours practicing the same moves over and over. The goal of many athletes is to reach a place where there is no thought involved in the action; the body has its own kind of "memory," and this is what kinesthetic learners rely on. For example, a baseball player may get two strikes in a row because he's thinking too much—wondering what pitch is coming next, thinking about his grip on the bat, worrying about his foot placement. After he lets his body take over, he nails the ball. In karate, the same concept is called *mu shin,* which means "no mind," or "nothingness." You practice *katas* and rehearsed movements endlessly, so that eventually, your body remembers how to block and punch without your conscious mind ever coming into it.

How does all of this sports talk help us in the classroom and the writing process? It shows you a possible strength and weakness in your learning style. If you are a kinesthetic learner, you probably find yourself taking copious notes; your hand may even take notes in class while your mind is wondering what to pick up for dinner on your way home. A great way for kinesthetic learners to study is to simply rewrite their own notes a few times. A few rounds of this rewriting, and when you start your midterm, your body will almost remember the information itself once you start writing the answers for the essay question. You may find that the physical feel of drafting an essay with pencil and paper helps you more than typing at a keyboard. You may also find yourself regularly using note cards during the research process or taking notes in the margins of your books because underlining and engaging in the text helps you remember the content.

Whereas you may enjoy lectures because they give you something solid to write down, you may have trouble working in study groups because the conversational atmosphere doesn't give you any content to copy. You may get very little from overheads or information on chalk boards, but you may thrive on writing on the board and even making collages.

KINESTHETIC LEARNERS

- Learn by doing.
- Are often athletes, martial artists, dancers, or sculptors.
- Study by rewriting class notes, using note cards, and taking notes in books to stay involved in the information.
- Have as strengths in-class writing, essay drafting, note taking, sculpting, sports.

Auditory Learners

Auditory learners process and remember information best by listening to what is presented to them. Musicians, music lovers, and actors are often auditory learners because those tasks require listening. A musician's brain is trained to hear minute differences in tone or pitch and can "hear" and translate the symbols on a sheet of music into sounds that will entertain us. Even if you're simply a lover of music, you'll probably find that your ability to distinguish between the subtle differences of your favorite guitarists indicates that you are a strong auditory learner. Similarly, if you are an actor or an orator, you have to memorize long speeches and monologues, and you train yourself to listen for your cues. When another actor says, "Is someone at the door?" you know it's your time to come on to stage and say your next line.

This translates to some very helpful skill sets in the classroom setting. If you are a strong auditory learner, you'll do well to listen to lectures. Attending study groups or tutorials and talking to friends about the day's lecture will be very helpful because remembering the conversations you have will be easier than remembering the pages of a book or the contents of a classroom overhead projection. Auditory learners may have an uncanny knack for recalling details the professor says during lectures and will excel in a class based on class discussions. Tape recorders are often the best tool to help auditory learners study. Record the day's lecture and replay it the night before the test; hearing the information will help you to recall it the next day. Similarly, when you're doing research, taking notes on a tape recorder (or, preferably, a digital recorder with separate file folders to sort your notes) may be more helpful than note cards or comments written on paper.

AUDITORY LEARNERS

- Learn by listening and talking.
- Are often musicians, music lovers, actors, or orators.
- Study by attending study sessions and listening to a taped version of class lectures or taped notes during the research process.
- Have as strengths recalling lectures, talking about the subject matter.

Visual Learners

Visual learners are best able to process and remember information that they've seen. Painters grasp the fundamentals of perspective, shading, color, and painting to create abstract or representational images to create a variety of effects. Photographers can look at commonplace objects or scenes and create art through an ability to see the beauty or drama in images that other people may overlook. Architects, while relying heavily on math and geometry, have to be able to translate the lines on a blueprint into a real building that will some day exist. Fashion designers (even just people with a strong fashion sense) need to understand how every piece of clothing, every cloth type, color choice, and accessory will come together to produce a fabulous outfit.

In the classroom, a visual learner would do well with a professor who utilizes the board, overheads, and even PowerPoint presentations. You'll remember images you've seen more than notes or lectures, and you may even find yourself doodling a lot in your notebook. (Contrary to what your grammar school teachers may have said, doodling in class is actually a good thing; it proves your brain is still "on"). When you read a textbook, you may find that you visually recall a certain photo or graphic on a page, and only then do you remember what the words on the page said. To study for this type of visualization, skim over the chapter several times after you've read it; this will make you familiar with the book and remind you of materials in association with pictures and obvious visuals in the book. While taking a test, you may find yourself closing your eyes to remember what your page of notes looked like in order to dig up

118   CHAPTER 6   Navigating the Writing Process

that memory. Often, your notes will simply be a graphic representation of exactly what the professor put on the board, and you may study by using a lot of different colored highlighters and pens to visually separate different bits of information.

VISUAL LEARNERS

- Learn by seeing.
- Are often painters, photographers, architects, or fashion designers.
- Study by using various colors of ink and highlighters to give notes distinct visual presences; skim over chapters/notes to become familiar with visuals.
- Have as strengths remembering what's on the board, recalling books, benefiting from highlighters.

Left- and Right-Brain Thinking

Aside from the three modes of learning previously discussed, another major distinction between learning styles (and a major factor in the steps of the writing process) comes from the biology of the brain. The human brain has two hemispheres, a left one and a right one. Recent research suggests that each hemisphere of the brain is responsible for different types of thought. Thus, each side of the brain is responsible for different steps of the writing process. People are generally more dominant in one hemisphere of the brain than in the other. The closer you are to a fifty-fifty "brain mix" (or an "orbital" brain function), the better off you'll be. Read the different brain functions described next and try to figure out which side of the brain you may favor.

First, let's look at the left side of the brain. This lobe of the brain is said to be responsible for logical functions. It keeps track of time, and it views the world very much like a computer, separating everything you perceive into parts and bits of data (it may see an eyeball, a nose, black hair, and a mouth, but it may not put it all together as belonging to a face). This side of the brain controls all functions that require systems and organization, such as logic, mathematics, geometry, chemistry formulas, grammar, spelling, and all the formulaic rules of writing.

If you are left-brain dominant, you may find that you excel at math, and complicated formulae that baffle your friends make sense to you. Blueprints and schematics may be easy for you to understand, as well as logic, Boolean logic, and computer languages. In writing, this side of the brain controls all the mechanical issues: grammar, spelling, MLA and APA documentation rules, outlining, structure, and so on. If you ever turn in papers and have your teacher tell you that your grammar is strong, but you need better content, you may be left-brain dominant.

The right side of the brain controls the opposite functions. Whereas the left controls logic, the right controls emotion. The saying "Time flies when you're having fun" reflects this side of the brain; it controls pleasure, and it has no concept of time. On a basic level, while the left side of the brain assembles the parts of the world, the right side puts them together into a comprehensive whole (all those features I'm seeing are actually a face . . . my mom's face!). If you are right-brain dominant, you may excel at the humanities. Art, music, theater, literature, even aspects of philosophy or the imagination to truly understand history all come from this side of the brain.

In writing, your ability to generate imaginative and innovative content as well as the sense that something just *sounds good* is linked to the right side of the brain. Similarly, if you've written a paper, and your instructor says that it flows well and your arguments are creative, but you need help with grammar and punctuation, the right side of the brain was probably taking over.

The distinctions between left- and right-brain thinking are perhaps the most important reason for the separate stages of the writing process. Each step of the process requires that a different side of the brain take over. Think about starting a car in the winter. You can turn on the ignition, but if you drive right away, your car will not be very efficient—no heat, poor visibility due to frosted windows, and you may even keep stalling out. If you let it run for a few minutes, however, you'll find a smoothly running, efficient engine. This is how your brain works, as well. If the proper side of the brain isn't given time to warm up before being used, you will be inefficient in your thought processes.

If you complete a right-brain task, then switch to a left and back again, neither side of the brain ever gets a chance to fully warm up. This means both types of thought process will be slow and foggy. If you separate the steps of the process, however, you'll find that each one will get all the brain power it deserves. For a good example of how one side of the brain gets fired up and takes over whatever task you're doing, think of a time you've been enjoying a hobby (playing or listening to music, painting, playing video games, writing, even gossiping on the phone) and completely lost track of time. This "lost time" is because the right side of your brain took over and the left side "powered down." Let each step of the writing process fire up the appropriate portion of your brain before proceeding.

LEFT BRAIN	RIGHT BRAIN
Logic	Emotion
Time	No Time
Parts	Whole Picture
Systems/Math	Art/Beauty
Grammar	Content
Spelling	Poetics

THE WRITING PROCESS

There are several steps to the process of writing a research paper: prewriting, research and note taking, generating a research proposal, outlining, drafting, and revising/editing. The steps are listed next in an order that many students find logical and natural. If you have never written a research paper and are intimidated by all the work that lies ahead, you may want to follow the steps in the linear order they are described here. However, you may find that you perform these steps in a different order—you may even perform some of them simultaneously, such as generating a rough outline as you generate your research proposal to see if your topic is workable before you have to commit yourself. Writing tends to be a very organic, messy, and recursive activity. ("Recursive" means that you move back and forth from earlier to later stages.) You may feel like you are going in circles at times, bouncing back and forth between these steps in order to write. That doesn't mean that you aren't making progress—writing a paper can be a lot like painting a portrait. Artists don't start at the top of the canvas and move down. They do some quick sketches to stimulate ideas. After they are happy with a basic idea of organization, they sketch on the canvas itself. Then they start applying the brushstrokes of paint, working on different sections of the canvas that seem to need their attention the most, then moving on to other sections. They often come back to areas that have already been painted to add some extra touches. They may even paint over sections of the canvas if they don't like an area or get a better idea.

The point is to learn what type of writing style best suits you. Just don't slight any of the steps that you need simply to save time. We know that your time as a college or university student is limited and valuable, and some of these steps may seem unnecessary and time consuming, but even briefly focusing on each step will help you create a stronger paper.

PREWRITING

Prewriting is a means to help generate your actual topic and refine a working thesis statement for your paper-writing process. It is a crucial first step of anyone's writing process. For more information and examples, prewriting is fully discussed in detail in Chapter 1.

RESEARCHING AND NOTE TAKING

After you have done some prewriting to generate ideas, the next step in the process is gathering information on the topic you've chosen to write about. Every argument you make in support of your thesis in your research papers needs to have a substantial fact or piece of evidence to help prove your point. This step in the prewriting process is the point when you gather those bits of information. Think of the notes you take at this stage as little time capsules for your future self, who will be busy writing the paper and won't have time to do any more research or dig through disorganized stacks of information. Always have your thesis in mind while taking notes. When you sit down to write your paper, it will be easier if most of your notes relate directly to your thesis.

The process of research, if done properly, typically takes more time than it will take to write the actual paper. You may find yourself spending several entire weekends at the library to generate research for a paper that you can draft in one evening. Researching is a painstaking process, and many writers make mistakes early on that hinder their progress. Some of these errors include the following:

1. You lose data. While researching, you may find a perfect passage to quote in a book, but a week later when you start writing your paper, this passage is impossible to find. Similarly, you may find a great source on a database, but when it's time to collect that source in the library, your limited notes prevent you from

getting your hands on the actual book or journal. Even the most simple fact, quotation, or bit of information is easy to forget when you're under a deadline and trying to write a good paper quickly. Trust us on that.

2. You lose citation information. Often, in a rush to get out of the library or speed up the research process, students cut corners when taking notes on the bibliographic and citation information for sources. This loss is often disastrous. You may find yourself using materials from a book to prove some major arguments in your paper, only to realize at the end that you have to take these ideas out of the paper because you can't properly attribute their sources with in-text citations and on your works-cited page—and you don't want to get a failing grade because of plagiarism.

3. You don't have regular access to a source. Some of the best sources in a library are found in the reference section (they typically have the code "REF" before the call numbers). These sources cannot be checked out of the library; they are meant to be accessible to any student at any time. Because you can't take these books home with you, good note taking is essential. Also, the typical academic library lets you borrow a source only for a very limited number of days. You'll need the information longer than that, so you need to master the skills of taking notes thorough enough so that you can complete your paper without having the actual book in hand.

These research perils, however, are very easy to overcome if you develop a good system of note taking. The system detailed below is just one way to organize your notes. Try it out, and then experiment with variations and differences as your college career continues. Modify your note-taking system to suit your needs and your own learning style. The key to any note-taking system you develop, however, is consistency. Don't use one system for taking notes and saving bibliographic information for one source and another system for another source. That type of variation will cause you to miss key information and lead to more work (and headaches) for you later.

Electronic or Paper Research "Cards"

In research writing, the traditional way to take notes on your sources is to use paper note cards. In fact, many professors require you to use note cards and submit them with your final paper to show how you gathered your data; others may have you submit them throughout the term to make sure that you are making progress in your research. Note cards are very handy because you can easily store them for use later in the class. They're small and easy to transport, and they're relatively durable, so they don't get wrinkled and ripped while you're transporting them from library to home and back again.

Alternatively, you may choose to create electronic "cards" on your computer. Many students have access to computers or even laptops they can take right into the library while doing research, and, of course, they can access library databases on their home computers. Electronic "cards," which can also be called source sets, information sets, or e-notes, have certain advantages over paper cards—for example, the information stored on your computer is easily integrated into your paper when you are at the drafting stage. Your professor may accept these sets submitted electronically, or you can print out the appropriate sections and paste them onto cards, enabling you to meet your professor's requirements and still have all your notes stored on your computer (and, we hope, a backup flash drive).

Paper cards have their own advantages. They are more portable, they force you to be more concise (you may have only one main idea or quotation to a card), and they can enable you to spread cards out in front of you on a table and move ideas around like puzzle pieces. This can be a lot easier than cutting and pasting information in a computer document. Arranging physical cards on a table can let you see the "big picture." You may even decide to combine the two types of note taking to suit your own purposes. Even though you may end up not using physical paper cards at all, we are going to refer to the source information sets as card sets for simplicity's sake.

A typical set contains two types: bibliography (works cited) cards and note cards. Your instructor may also require other types, such as evaluations that you have created using reference sources like *Book Review Digest*, *Contemporary Authors,* and *Magazines for Libraries*. (For a more complete discussion of evaluating sources, see Chapter 4.)

Bibliography Cards

The bibliography (work cited) card should be the first card you fill out whenever you find a source you plan to use. It needs to be thorough and accurate—don't cut corners to save a few minutes. The following bibliography card is an example.

Note the following key elements to this card:

A is the full bibliographic entry for the source in either proper MLA or APA format. This entry should be done *exactly* how it will be reprinted in the works-cited page of your paper. It is a bit time consuming to do it this way, but it will save you a lot of time during your paper draft, and it virtually eliminates any mistakes you'd make while compiling the works-cited list at a later date.

B is an annotation (brief explanation) of the source. On larger papers, you'll read so many sources that it will be hard to tell the difference between them later on. You will probably end up reading more sources than you actually use. Later on, when you are preparing to write your paper, the annotation should help you recall exactly what source you're dealing with. It could include a brief description of the major arguments you're drawing on and what made the source good enough for you to use. If you are a visual learner, you may even want to include a physical description, like "the blue book with all the good graphs in the back."

C is a source number. Every source you pick up should have its own number assigned to it. The first book you pick up is number 1. Finish the bibliography card and start taking notes from this source. The next source is number 2. Finish that bibliography card and take all the notes out of that source next. This seems very simple at this stage, but the source numbers become a life saver when we get to the note cards.

In Chapter 4, we discussed a variety of techniques for evaluating sources and reading critically, such as annotating texts, the SASE (Summarize, Analyze, Synthesize, and Evaluate) method, and writing a rhetorical précis. If you used any or all of these techniques, they are fertile ground for your research paper notes.

Note Cards

Note cards contain the actual notes themselves. Every bit of information you have from a source needs to be documented. As a general rule, with paper cards, you should make only one note per card, and you should try whenever possible to keep the entire note on the front side of the card. Don't forget to cite the source's page numbers. There are several sizes of note cards to choose from. The 3×5-inch note cards are small—it can be hard to squeeze a lot of information on one card, so you may prefer to use a larger card for your notes. The 4×6-inch note cards are fairly standard. If you're a visual learner, you may even want different colored note cards to help you make an association between colors and content. If your cards are electronic, try to think in terms of how much information you could get on a physical note card (especially useful if you will be pasting your typed notes on regular cards). Even if you don't have to turn physical cards in, you want to make sure that your e-notes are distinct and concise. It will make organizing your information a lot easier later on when you are writing your paper.

Types of Notes

DIRECT QUOTATIONS

You should use direct quotations sparingly. In fact, a general rule is to keep direct quotations to ten percent or less of your total paper (check with your instructor). When you find a quotation that you think you may use in your paper, it should do two things for you. First, it should contain information that is critical to the argument you are making. If the content of the quotation does not help you support your own thesis in some way, you shouldn't use it. Second, a direct quotation should express an idea in an especially lively, arresting, or otherwise interesting way. The content is important, obviously, but you could always paraphrase the information, so the quality of the prose is a key to deciding whether to use a direct quotation. Try to quote only passages that sound better than anything you could have phrased yourself. Of course, sometimes you have to use direct quotations instead of paraphrasing, because the information may be very technical and impossible to paraphrase.

When you copy a quotation onto a note card, you'll need to be careful to copy it verbatim (word for word). You can also photocopy a passage and glue it to the note card if you use physical cards. Students often copy passages too quickly or sloppily and later inadvertently misquote their sources without even realizing it. Although it is possible to use too many quotations in your paper, it is not possible to have too many quotations in your note cards when you start your paper. You will be better off deciding which quotations to keep, paraphrase, or cut while you are drafting than trying to find more information at the last minute. Make your notes accurate, and you'll be saving yourself time when it comes time to write your first draft.

SUMMARIES AND PARAPHRASES

Most often, when you find good information that you want to use in your paper, it's better just to say it in your own words instead of using a direct quotation. When you do this, you are either summarizing or paraphrasing. Summarizing is when you take only the main points of a passage and put them into your own words. Paraphrasing is when you restate all the ideas of the original passage in your own words, which means the paraphrase will be roughly the same length as the original. (For a more complete discussion of summarizing and paraphrasing, see Chapter 8.) Why not just use direct quotations instead? Perhaps the original source material is very formal and wordy, full of vocabulary that is more formal—or informal—than the language you're using in your paper. In the sciences, for example, your source could be highly technical and full of jargon. You may want to keep the content but make it more "reader friendly." Also, you don't want to have a greater percentage of direct quotations than what your instructor specifies.

Remember, these notes are for your own use as your write the paper. If you have a hard time understanding something, take the notes in a way that will be easier for you to digest later as you write. When you put a summary or paraphrase on a note card, keep in mind that you'll still need to include a page number for the source material. You should be just as careful with these types of notes as with direct quotation notes.

It is a good idea to keep a photocopy (or electronic copy, when possible) of the original passages that you quote or paraphrase. Why? So that later, as you polish your paper, you don't accidentally "improve" your own writing back to the original wording without even realizing it.

STATISTIC/DATE/HISTORICAL FACT

Many times you will find a simple fact, date, or statistic in a source that you will want to use. The language is not beautiful or provocative enough for a direct quotation, and the information is too brief to bother trying to paraphrase. Nevertheless, such facts and details will help bolster your arguments (and prove to your professor that you did your research). If you were writing a paper on the singer Kurt Cobain for a course on the history of rock and roll, for example, you may need to cite a statistic (one album sold three million copies in less than three months), a specific date (he committed suicide on April 8, 1994), or a biographical fact about him (he was born in Hoquiam, Washington).

For note-taking purposes, quickly summarizing these types of facts is just fine for your note card or e-card. As suggested earlier, it is wise to keep a copy of a summarized passage to refer back to. As always, include the page number(s) where you originally found any of these facts when you use print sources.

PERSONAL THOUGHTS AND IDEAS

Finally, some of the sources you're reading may bring up memories from past classes or give you a new insight. Always make time to take these notes, as well. If a source led you to some conclusion of your own, be sure that you write it down right away. It's a good idea to jot down your idea in either paper note card or e-card format because consistency is important—keep your own ideas cataloged using the same format you use for all note taking. You might misplace the insight unless you preserve it and know where to look for it. Also, you may want to mention the original source material that led you to this conclusion, so citing that source alongside your own thoughts might not be a bad idea.

Sample Paper Cards and E-Cards

Take a look at the following sample quotation note card:

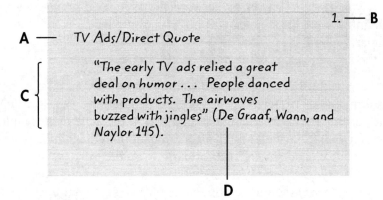

Note the following elements on this note card:

A is the topic heading for the note card. The topic heading lets you know at a glance exactly what type of information is on this card. Here it says, "TV Ads/Direct Quote" to let you know the type of information on the card and whether the card contains a quotation, paraphrase, or summary. The topic heading should ultimately correspond to specific points on your outline. Your card could even have a topic heading, such as "II.B.2 TV History/Direct Quote." The "II.B.2" tells you that this will ultimately be used in that specific point of the outline (see the outlining section of this chapter for more details).

B is the source number. This number corresponds to the source number of the bib card for the source the note comes from. By using this simple system of source numbers, you'll never have to write any bibliographic information on your note cards. If you see the number 7 in that corner, just flip to the bib card with a number 7 on it for the corresponding bibliographic information. This system will save you hours of copying the same bib notes repeatedly.

126   CHAPTER 6   Navigating the Writing Process

C is the note itself. This is the most important part of the note-taking process, obviously. You will need to take different types of notes: direct quotes, paraphrases, statistics, dates/historical facts, and personal thoughts. (For more on types of notes, see pages 123–125.)

D is the citation information, in proper MLA or APA format. Note that you've included the author's last name (or an abbreviation of the title if no name is given), just as you would in the body of your paper. Following proper documentation format at this stage will make citing sources easier when you write your paper. The most important detail on this part of the note card is the page number. Get in the habit of always including page numbers in your note cards. Note cards will probably become your primary method of taking notes while researching, so if the page number isn't part of your note, you will not be able to provide an accurate in-text citation.

Tips for Electronic Note Taking

The key to electronic note taking, as with paper note cards, is to remain as organized as possible. If you have dozens of saved word files sprawled around your desktop or on several thumb drives, these notes will be difficult to access when it comes time to draft your paper.

Consider the following tips while taking notes on a computer:

1. *Organize:* You must decide how you want to organize your e-notes before you begin taking them. We recommend a single, separate word-processing document for each source you use. For example, if you take ten notes out of one book you're using, save all of that as one file, complete with the work-cited entry, annotation, and any other information you recorded, such as a source evaluation. Later, you simply open that book's note file, and you'll find all the information you thought to copy down. Make sure your document names are clear, like "Set 1, *Affluenza*." (Beginning each document name with the same word, like "set," "card," or "e-card," will help you to keep them organized in your computer files.) Later, when you are writing your paper, you can start blending all the e-card sections you choose to use into one document.

   On the opposite page is an example of the first section of a single-document e-card set. This is the sort of set a professor might ask a student to turn in, so all the elements are in MLA format. If you are keeping electronic cards for your own purposes only, you don't need to double-space or have your name and course identification information in the upper-left corner. In fact, you might even choose to use the last name of the author of your source in the upper-right header.

2. *Track the Original Location:* The author and page number (when available) of every note you take must be tracked during your note taking. (If there is no author, use the first important word or words of the title; also, nonprint sources will not have page numbers unless they are PDF files.) You could use MLA or APA style parenthetical citations to track the author and page number, or you could use a system more akin to the note cards mentioned previously.

Dianne Jeffries

Professor Rupert Giles

English 1A: 12:30 MW

17 October 2009

Research Information Set #7

Work-Cited

McChesney, Robert W. *Corporate Media and the Threat to Democracy.* Ed. Greg
Ruggiero and Stuart Sahulka. New York: Seven Stories, 1997. Print. Open Media
Pamphlet Series.

Annotation

This book examines the media conglomerate corporations that own the majority of the
public airwaves throughout America (and the world). One of the book's main arguments
is that corporate control of mass media is a threat to self-governance and democracy.
McChesney's research should be helpful to my paper because he provides many examples
of corporate media control and a lot of historical facts about the media and journalism.

Author Evaluation

McChesney is a well known author, research professor, and the president and co-founder
of The Free Press, an organization which informs the public about corporate controlled
media. According to *Contemporary Authors*, McChesney "has devoted his professional
career to understanding the media, educating others about his findings, and working to
reform it."

Note #1

<u>Historical Journalism. Paraphrase:</u> The 1820s and 1830s were a golden age of journalism
when newspapers existed simply to inform the masses and get them involved in the political process. In the 1840s, many newspapers changed their format when they realized they
could make a profit from their work (McChesney 12).

Note #2

<u>Political Journalism. Quotation:</u> "The press was closely linked to the political culture of
the day; any given city might have several newspapers providing very different interpretations of public issues. Some modern scholars term this era the 'Dark Ages of American
Journalism'" (11).

3. *Bibliographic Information:* Just as note cards start with detailed work-cited cards, your electronic notes must begin with electronic bibliographic information. Every bit of information you may need for a works-cited page should be copied down during note taking. The way you take down this information depends on how you took your e-notes: A) If you decided to take all your notes in one large file, you could use the bibliographic information as a way to organize your notes visually. Each time you start a new source in this large file, you begin that section with a full works-cited entry for that source. B) If every note is its own saved file, you could organize them all in one "folder" along with a separate saved file that contains nothing but the bibliographic information. This way, each folder contains all the notes and works-cited information you'll need. C) If you opt to make each source its own file, the top of that document should contain the bibliographic information.

4. *Backups:* Make backup copies of all your notes. Data loss and computer crashes are very commonplace events, and a fried hard drive would be catastrophic if it cost you all of your notes. Email the notes to yourself, so they're sitting on a server somewhere, and don't delete them until after the end of the term. Put them on separate thumb drives. You can even store them on a friend's computer until the paper is finished. You are never too paranoid when it comes to protecting electronic data.

Copies and Printouts

Another way to keep track of your sources is to make full copies. Virtually every library will give you access to a photocopier, so you can make copies of the sources you're using. This is especially important for print versions of journal articles and reference books, which can't be checked out. You'll still want to keep good notes using one of the methods previously discussed, but having the source on hand can be very important during the writing process. Many databases now allow you to email yourself whole articles and files, so you can save on print costs (and trees) by keeping electronic versions of the sources you're using.

After your note cards or e-cards are all completed, you'll need to organize them in some fashion. The most logical way to do this is to create an outline (see "Outline," p. 131). After your outline is complete, go through your cards. Set aside paper cards that you don't think you'll need and put all the rest in the order you'll probably end up using in the paper. Paste e-cards you think you'll use into a document that can become your first draft. Remember, this type of logical organization is a left-brain activity, whereas writing the draft of your paper is a right-brain activity. If all the organizing is done in advance, you'll be free to write without distraction, pulling information from cards in the order that you need it.

Another type of note taking that can be useful is called "double-column note taking" or the "double-entry journal." See page 85 for an explanation and example.

RESEARCH PROPOSAL

At some point in the writing process, you may be asked to propose your ideas to your instructor, so she can give you feedback and guidance on what you plan to include. The research proposal has many applications later in life as well: in your jobs you may be asked to submit such proposals to secure funding for a project or to get a cash grant; in graduate school you will be asked to write a prospectus of your thesis or dissertation before you start working on it. The proposal you write should let the audience know exactly what you plan to research and write about. You may want to submit a proposal after you've done some preliminary research (so you know what you are talking about), but before you fully commit to your ideas and gather your final sources. Even if nobody assigns a research proposal, you may wish to complete one anyway. The action of putting your plans down on paper will help to clarify your process and what actions you need to take to complete your paper. Consider writing yourself a proposal using the steps detailed next, just to explore your own ideas and assumptions.

There are two types of proposal you can write. The first is an informal proposal that is brief and to the point. The second is a formal prospectus that goes into much greater detail. Your instructor should clarify which type of proposal she is interested in.

Informal Proposal

The informal proposal is typically brief (often only a paragraph long) and gives a quick overview of your thoughts and plans for this project. Within this paragraph, you should include the following elements and any others you think important:

- The purpose of the paper (to inform, persuade, critique, etc.).
- The audience of the paper (a general audience, your peers, instructor, professionals in the field, etc.).
- The topic you have chosen (and possibly why you chose this topic).
- Your working thesis statement.
- Major arguments you plan to include.
- Any other key challenges that are ahead of you, your original research question(s), your title, a timeline, or reactions you hope to get from the audience.

Following is an example of a research proposal for Dianne Jeffries's sample paper found in Chapter 11. This does not contain the final thesis she used in the actual paper; this was a much rougher working thesis that was refined as her writing process continued. Finally, notice that she uses the term "in this paper, I plan to . . . ." This statement is perfectly acceptable in a proposal—after all, the whole point is to tell the instructor what you plan to do. However, it should generally be avoided in the actual paper itself because many instructors find such phrases redundant and tedious.

Freedom of speech is not just something that lets us sit in a coffee shop and talk bad about the government. Instead, it is a fundamental right to accurate and free information that is important to our world and safety. With the current system of corporate media ownership, however, there is no free speech. As media companies own more and

130   CHAPTER 6   Navigating the Writing Process

more of the airwaves and websites we rely upon for information, information starts to cost us money and get distorted. In this paper, I plan to inform an audience of my peers about the nature of modern-day media cartels and then convince them that these corporations are hurting the values we need to keep America strong. Major arguments will include a look at how free speech is crucial for democracy as well as opinions from several media experts who think this system is harmful to our society. My working thesis will be this: American media corporations are hurting free speech and the very nature of democracy.

Formal Prospectus

A formal prospectus is a much longer endeavor than the informal proposal. It is still designed to help you decide how to proceed in the writing of your paper, but it is a much more thorough piece of work. It is often several pages long and could include many of the following elements. Often, the nature of your paper and research will determine which elements you will ultimately include in your prospectus, but before starting, you should find out from your instructor exactly which elements she may prefer.

TITLE PAGE

This would be an MLA or APA style title page that gives the planned title of your project.

INTRODUCTION

Because this is a longer project, you will need an introduction, just as you would with a short paper. This introduction should include your preliminary thesis statement as well as a quick rationale of why you have chosen this topic. If you started with an informal proposal like the preceding one, you could adapt that paragraph as the introduction of your prospectus.

ABSTRACT

An abstract is a brief summary of your overall plan. It should encapsulate all the major arguments and research you plan to include and should neatly sum up your entire paper in 50–150 words. An abstract is very popular in the sciences and in papers written in APA format.

REVIEW OF LITERATURE

Here you briefly review the major sources, documents, and research that exists on this subject (also called the "literature" of a subject). You should discuss the major sources you found in your early research and tell the audience about the major arguments and scholarly camps that exist in this field of study.

BIBLIOGRAPHY (OR ANNOTATED BIBLIOGRAPHY)

This is a working bibliography of all sources. It could easily be merged with the Review of Literature to get an Annotated Bibliography, or it can be a standalone list of bibliographic entries in your documentation style (MLA, APA, etc.) to serve as a quick reference list for you and your audience.

RESEARCH METHODS

Here you discuss the overall plan for your research. Research encompasses many types of information gathering, so for this portion of the prospectus, you will determine the nature of the research you will be conducting. Here are some questions you may ask: What types of sources will you be using, and will you need help from colleagues, professors, or library staff to gather them? Will you be using traditional library research, or will you need to conduct surveys and experiments to support your final thesis? Will you need funding and, if so, where will you secure it? What is your timeline for the research?

OUTLINE

The next step in the paper-writing process is crucial, whether you're writing an extended research project, a personal narrative, or even an in-class essay. It's the outline. This is the step that most students skip and consider a waste of time, whereas, ironically, it is the biggest time saver and tool for quality assurance in writing. Many writers find that while facing an immediate due date, the simple act of scrawling several major points they intend to cover and in what order they intend to cover them makes a significant difference in the quality of the final paper and actually makes writing it faster.

Think of your outline as the blueprint for your paper. Just as an architect would never turn the construction of a house over to the contractors without perfect blueprints detailing every aspect of construction, you should never start your draft until you have a blueprint of your own. Similar to note taking, your outline is a message to your future self. You're doing this work now so you don't have to do even more work later. Consider when you're six pages into writing the draft of a ten-page paper, and you have just run out of things to say. You can either panic and spend another hour pouring over note cards and wondering what you originally had in mind, or—if you've done some planning—you can look at a well-developed outline. That outline will tell you exactly what point you should make next and exactly what quotation or paraphrase to use, and you can keep writing without interruption. It's a very secure feeling knowing that you have that blueprint to fall back on.

Next we show several ways to construct an outline.

Casual/Scratch Outline

The first type of outline, a **casual or scratch outline,** is simply a brief sketch of what you'd like to put in your paper. If an instructor asks you for a formal outline (see the section "Formal Outline"), a casual outline might even be your first step in constructing that type of outline. Creating a casual outline is a great way to plan for quick in-class writing for short essay answers on tests. A casual outline may consist of a quick list or a series of keywords, but it seldom consists of complete sentences (or even complete thoughts).

Casual outlines are commonly used before or during the research process. You might want a quick overview of your major ideas, so you know what to start researching. Similarly, this type of outline may be the result of a solid afternoon at a library. Outside sources may have given you these ideas in the first place, so you draft a quick outline to help you continue your research and your thought-generation process. Following is

132   CHAPTER 6   Navigating the Writing Process

an example of a casual outline. (This outline was used in researching the sample MLA format research paper beginning on page 255.)

RESEARCH PAPER: CORPORATE MASS MEDIA OWNERSHIP

- History of American corporations
- Early American corporations
- Modern American corporate mergers
- Federal Communications Commission
- Mergers of communications corporations
- Freedom of speech
- Examples of faulty news reporting

Informal Outline

An **informal outline** is the intermediate step between the casual and formal outlines. It has far more detail and structure than a casual outline, but it's still largely intended to be seen only by the writer. The informal outline is still a sketch at times, leaving out some of the minor points that will be in the paper and focusing instead on the major arguments you intend to make. You might use a series of numbers to delineate your points, and you might even include some major quotations or your initial thesis statement. This is a good choice when you don't have to turn an outline in, but you still need those blueprints to base your draft on. You may still have questions about your topic, specific arguments, and thesis at the outlining stage. Don't worry, the answers will come when you write the draft. Informal outlines are likely to change significantly during the writing process. Ultimately, they can provide either the final outline you use for a brief paper or the early draft of a formal outline that will come together later in the writing process.

Following is an example of an informal outline. Note that, like a casual outline, an informal outline doesn't require complete sentences or correct grammar: fragments and incomplete thoughts are fine, as long as you'll understand them later. This is still a somewhat vague outline at times, but it's plenty to sink your teeth into while you're still doing research or preparing a very rough draft. (This outline was used early in the writing process of the sample MLA format research paper found on page 255.)

INFORMAL OUTLINE

Thesis: Today, modern corporations' power over the media has damaged democracy by limiting public exposure to a diverse and comprehensive range of information, perspectives, and analyses, even resulting in lies and misinformation in the news media.

- Introduction with thesis
  - Quote from Madison
  - Brief overview of issues
- History of American corporations
  - Early American Corporations
  - Corporations becoming legal "people"

- Modern corporations
- Mergers of communication corporations
■ Federal Communications Commission
  - Define the FCC
  - Commissioners' statements
■ Effects of mergers
  - Harm to freedom of speech
  - Harm to diverse viewpoints
  - Harm to trustworthy news and information
■ Examples of faulty news reporting
  - Mass media that promotes corporate agendas
  - Celebrity scandals instead of real news
■ Conclusion
  - Reiteration of thesis and major arguments
  - Remind reader of opening quote

Formal Outline

The **formal outline** has a rigid structure; it is incredibly detailed, and it includes every single point that will make its way into the paper. This level of formality is often reserved for outlines that are part of an assignment; they are typically intended for an audience of some sort (even if it's only your professor, a tutor/proofreader, or partners in a class peer group) who need to get a strong sense of your paper before they even read it. Formal outlines are the ultimate writing blueprints because every single argument and fact from your paper, no matter how minor, shows up in it. They take time and dedication, but they definitely pay off in the end.

Below is the typical form for a formal outline. The following series of heading and subheadings, letters, and numerals is used at almost every college and university. The major headings are listed with Roman numerals. Here are the first twenty Roman numerals: I, II, III, IV, V, VI, VII, VIII, IX, X, XI, XII, XIII, XIV, XV, XVI, XVII, XVIII, XIX, XX.

I. First Major Heading
 A. First Sub-heading (level 1)
  1. First Sub-heading (level 2)
  2. Second Sub-heading (level 2)
   a. First Sub-heading (level 3)
   b. Second Sub-heading (level 3)
    (1) First Sub-heading (level 4)
    (2) Second Sub-heading (level 4)
     (a) First Sub-heading (level 5)
     (b) Second Sub-heading (level 5)
 B. Second Sub-heading (level 1)
II. Second Major Heading

A variation on the formal outline is listed below. It is often used in the sciences, business, and even computer studies, and it's based on decimals instead of the Roman numeral structure shown previously.

1. First Major Heading
   1.1 First Sub-heading (level 1)
      1.1.1 First Sub-heading (level 2)
      1.1.2 Second Sub-heading (level 2)
         1.1.1.1 First Sub-heading (level 3)
         1.1.1.2 Second Sub-heading (level 3)
   1.2 Second Sub-heading (level 1)
      1.2.1 First Sub-heading (level 2)
      1.2.2 Second Sub-heading (level 2)

2. Second Major Heading

Topic Outlines and Full-Sentence Outlines

There are two options for formal outlines: the topic outline and the full-sentence outline. The topic outline lists all the major topics as you will include them in your paper, but as phrases instead of as complete sentences. The full-sentence outline, however, uses only complete sentences. You should aim for parallel structure in both types of outlines: don't phrase some sentences as assertions and others as questions, and don't switch back and forth between passive and active voice (active voice is preferable).

TOPIC OUTLINE

Although a **topic outline** shows the general structure of the paper, it is possible for gaps or flaws in the argument to go undetected because it is still rather skeletal and just a brief sketch of the final paper. The main points will be clear, however, and the outline will be a great help as you draft. Following is an example of a topic outline. (This is the outline that was used while the student wrote the sample MLA format research paper beginning on page 255.)

FORMAL TOPIC OUTLINE

Thesis: Today, modern corporations' power over the media has damaged democracy by limiting public exposure to a diverse and comprehensive range of information, perspectives, and analyses, even resulting in lies and misinformation in the news media.

   I. Introduction
      A. Quote from Madison—reader "hook"
      B. Importance of communication on democracy
      C. Thesis statement
   II. History of American corporations
      A. Early American Corporations
      B. Boston Tea Party
         a. Quote from Lasn
         b. Critical discussion of Lasn's quote

Century

C. Corporations becoming legal "people"
III. Modern Corporations
A. Recession of the 1980s
B. Branding
a. Quote Klein
b. Critical discussion of Klein's quote
C. Mergers of communication corporations
a. Quote Bagdikian
b. Critical discussion of Bagdikian's quotes
D. The threat to democracy
a. Quote McChesney
b. Critical discussion of McChesney's quote

IV. Federal Communications Commission
A. Define the FCC
B. Commissioner Adalstein's statements
C. Commissioner Copps's statements

V. Effects of mergers

VI. Examples of faulty news reporting
A. *Project Censored*
B. Sunny Lewis article
1. Quote Lewis article
2. Critical discussion of Lewis's quote
C. Bovine Growth Hormone news story
1. Background of news story
2. Quote from *Project Censored*
3. Critical discussion of quote
D. Celebrity Scandals
1. Information from Halpern's *Fame Junkies*
2. Critical discussion of Halpern's information
3. Pew Research Center's study
4. Real News replaced by celebrity scandals
a. For ratings
b. Low cost

VII. Conclusion
A. Reiteration of thesis and major arguments
B. Remind reader of Madison's quote

FULL-SENTENCE OUTLINE

A **full-sentence** outline takes considerably more time to create than any of the other options, but preparing one is a major step toward completing your first draft. This type of outline is likely to reveal any problems in your argument. If you are not spending enough time developing one specific point, or if a flaw exists in the logical organization of your paper, you'll probably see the problem with this full-sentence outline. Similarly,

136   CHAPTER 6   Navigating the Writing Process

with a little editing, many of the sentences you use in the outline can serve as topic sentences in your body paragraphs and transitional statements helping to wrap up major arguments. Cut and paste these sentences from outline to draft as you write.

Also, although the example that follows does not do so, many writers type or cut and paste all their quotes and paraphrases directly into their full-sentence outline. Again, this step will be time consuming up front, but when you're actually drafting your paper, a simple cut and paste will keep your writing flow going, in contrast to fishing for quotations and typing in someone else's words and then having to recover your writing flow. The following is a formal, full-sentence outline. (This is the outline that was used while the student wrote the sample MLA format research paper beginning on page 255.)

FULL-SENTENCE FORMAL OUTLINE

I.   Introduce the paper by discussing key notions of democracy as connected to free communications.
  A.   Madison proves that reliable information is a key component to a true self-governing democracy.
  B.   The growth and power of the modern corporation limits the ability of Americans to receive quality information.
  C.   Thesis Statement: Today, modern corporations' power over the media has damaged democracy by limiting public exposure to a diverse and comprehensive range of information, perspectives, and analyses, even resulting in lies and misinformation in the news media.

II.   The history of the American corporation provides a background for the discussion of media control.
  A.   Corporate corruption in the early colonies leads to the Boston Tea Party.
  B.   The spirit of the American Revolution kept corporations small for years.
  C.   The Santa Clara legal decision gives corporations the same rights as an individual person.

III.   The modern corporation grows in stature and power, eventually dominating the American airwaves.
  A.   The recession of the 1980s forces corporations to develop new models of business to keep operating.
  B.   Marketing and slick "branding" techniques give corporations more wealth and power than before.
  C.   Mergers of communication corporations create six major media conglomerates that own the bulk of all means of mass communication.
  D.   These media conglomerates care about profit more than anything else, and this harms several key components to American democracy.

IV.   The Federal Communications Commission's primary function is to manage and safeguard the American airwaves, ensuring that they are still owned and run by citizens and that free speech is strong and viable.
  A.   Chairman Adalstein thinks the airwaves should promote an "uninhibited marketplace of ideas," but they fail to.

    B. Commissioner Copps believes that though the public airwaves belong to the citizenry, they are entirely dominated by corporate interests bent on gaining advertising revenue, not serving the needs of the people.

V. In spite of this corporate stranglehold on information, however, watchdog groups can still provide us with reliable information.

VI. Several examples of faulty news reporting exist that will show the misinformation caused by corporate media ownership.

    A. Every year, *Project Censored* creates a list of twenty-five significant news stories that have not properly been reported.

        1. Sunny Lewis's article shows mass pollution in American water that is never reported in the mainstream media.

        2. Fox News cuts a story on Bovine Growth Hormone being found in American milk.

    B. Corporate news media is increasingly looking more like entertainment than news.

        1. The book *Fame Junkies* shows that celebrity news was more important than major stories like the genocide in Darfur or the war in Iraq.

        2. The Pew Research Center study shows that the people are tired of watching the same tired stories about celebrities in trouble, but it dominates the airwaves because these stories are cheap, easy, and help fill the need for 24 hours of information being broadcast on cable networks.

VII. Conclude by discussing the truth in Madison's quote about American democracy merely being a farce or a tragedy.

Outlining is an inherently left-brain activity. It requires logic, sequential order, and a focus on the system you'll use to convince your audience of your thesis. This is perhaps the most important time in all of the writing process to separate left- and right-brain functions. If you attempt to skip this step and move straight to writing your paper, you're really hampering your own creativity. For most writers, every time their left brain gets warmed up, and they are thinking of their next logical step in the paper (figuring out what comes next), they have to switch gears and start getting creative. By the time their right brain is hot, and they're starting to lose themselves in the writing, they run out of things to say and have to toggle back to left-brain, sequential thought. However, you need to realize that your individual writing process will be unique. For example, you might discover that your organization is not working and decide to reorganize while you are in the middle of drafting your paper. There is nothing wrong with that, even though drafting is a right-brain activity and organizing is a left-brain one. Learn to become conscious of what works best for you.

Do yourself a favor and prepare your outline ahead of time in one shot. This will let your left brain do its thing and then allow your right brain to really cook when you have to get creative in the next step of the process. Even a brief sketch outline on the back of a paper napkin will help you keep your mental states separate. Finally, keep in mind that most word processing programs have an outline feature built in to them. However, you should experiment with this option in the software before starting your outlines.

Many people find the software's automatic formatting in this type of outlining to be confusing and hard to control.

DRAFTING

As you can see by now, there are several steps to the process of writing a good paper that should be completed before you begin your first draft. Many students simply write a draft, run a spell check, and call it a paper. This method may get you a passing grade, but starting with the drafting step and ignoring the others will seriously diminish the quality of your paper. Professional writers of all types—reporters, novelists, screenwriters, even bloggers—complete all the steps of the writing process and often double back and redo them. These writers realize that they can't produce a top-quality final product that they can be satisfied with by taking one stab at a draft and then submitting it for publication.

When you write your first draft, remember that it's a *rough* draft. It doesn't need to be perfect. In fact, it doesn't even need to be grammatically correct at this point. You should turn off your spell check and grammar check while you're drafting. Don't second guess yourself or correct things as you go. Writing is a right-brain process, and worrying about spelling and rules will take you away from your right brain and give control to the left. You need to stay creative, let your imagination flow, and just write. All mistakes can be corrected in the edits you do later. Rely on the outline at all times. Every time you have to worry about what comes next, you're hurting your creativity. Focus on creativity, and when you're not sure what comes next, look at your outline, refer to your well-documented note cards or e-cards, and keep writing.

If you're having writer's block and struggling to get started, try skipping the introduction. You already have an idea of the thesis by now, and you have an outline waiting to be fleshed out, so just start with the first part of your body. Often the opening of a paper is the most difficult part to write; however, by starting with the body and then coming back later, you'll discover that the introduction may seem to write itself. After all, how can you effectively introduce something that doesn't exist yet? The introduction is the first thing that your audience will read, but there is no reason that it should be the first section that you write. In fact, if you still have writer's block while trying to begin the body of your paper, try writing several paragraphs on the part of your paper that you personally find most interesting and the easiest to write about. Because you are probably using a word processor, it doesn't really matter where you start. Your outline will be your blueprint when you finally put all the parts together.

REVISING AND EDITING

As you complete the process of crafting the perfect paper, you will need to do a series of edits and revisions. Notice that we say a *series* of edits and revisions, not simply one edit and revision. Yet again, recognizing how our left and right brain hemispheres function is valuable here. **Revising** (which is rereading for content, personal style, and "flow") is mainly a right-brain activity. **Editing** (correcting style, mechanics, punctuation, grammar, and spelling) is mainly a left-brain activity. Another word for editing that you are probably familiar with is "proofreading." Keep these processes separate. Think of revision as a continual process of writing and rewriting, with editing focusing more on style, punctuation, grammar, word choice, and spelling after you have produced a draft with evidence, organization, and ideas that you are happy with. (See Chapter 10 for guidelines.)

Revision

Revision is global. Look at your entire essay or research paper and pay attention to your organization, the integration of your sources, your overall argument, supporting arguments, the logical flow of your ideas, and the quality of your evidence. Ask yourself how well you are using rhetorical appeals (see *Ethos, Logos,* and *Pathos* in Chapter 5). Be prepared to ruthlessly cut out any sentences or even paragraphs that you wrote that don't add to the overall impact of your paper, and ask yourself what you may need to add to bolster any weak sections. Be prepared to cut and paste and rearrange. Revise anything larger than a paragraph on a hard copy of your work before you do any major rearranging. If you do everything on the computer screen, you can have difficulty seeing the "big picture" of your paper.

Visualize the audience you are trying to reach. Try to look at your work as if you are a member of the audience and you have never seen the paper before. Another way to look at it is in the persona of an editor who is reading a paper that has been submitted to your periodical for publication. You have high standards, and you accept only top-notch work.

Following is a checklist of questions to ask yourself when you are revising. These questions are designed for the typical college essay or research paper, so we assume a certain level of formality.

REVISION CHECKLIST

- Does my introduction include a thesis statement that clearly states, in one sentence, the assertion that my paper will prove? Is it a debatable point, not merely a statement of fact?

- Do all my body paragraphs support my thesis in some way? Do they create a unified effect? Are they presented in the most logical order?

- Have I kept in mind a broad audience of people representing a spectrum of ages, cultural backgrounds, sexual preferences, religious choices (including no religion), political viewpoints, economic and social classes, and places of national origin?

- Have I put myself in the shoes of my audience and asked myself what my readers will need to know to understand the points that I am making?

- Have I been fair to my subject and audience? Have I avoided logical fallacies or other instances of shaky reasoning? Have I anticipated any arguments that people who might disagree with me could raise, and have I answered them?

- Have I avoided unnecessary references to myself and my feelings? (Are my personal emotional reactions relevant to my audience?)

- Does my conclusion provide a sense of closure, highlighting the key points that I have made and showing how they have supported my thesis?

- Do I have in-text citations for ideas from every source I used, whether paraphrased, summarized, or quoted? Have I introduced my sources to my audience, letting my readers know why they are credible? Do I have works-cited entries for each source? Do I have the correct number of sources that my instructor requires?

140 CHAPTER 6 Navigating the Writing Process

Editing

After you have revised to your satisfaction—which should take several rereadings—you can engage a different part of your brain and go over your paper at the "micro" level, looking for problems in style, punctuation, and grammar. Chapter 10's "Twenty-Five Common Punctuation and Grammar Errors to Avoid" and the "Commonly Confused Words and Phrases" can help you with this part of the process.

EDITING CHECKLIST

- Have I checked my paper for errors in format (MLA, APA, etc.)? Have I made sure my identification information is in the correct order and placed on the first page? Are all titles formatted correctly by type of source (article titles enclosed in quotation marks, periodical and book titles italicized or underlined, etc.)?

- Have I avoided dry, formulaic sentences like "This essay will prove . . . ," "This paper will be about . . . ," and "I will discuss . . ." in my introduction and "In conclusion . . . ," "To sum up all of my main points . . . ," and "As this paper has proved . . ." in my conclusion?

- Have I been clear, effective, and concise in my word choice?

- Is the tone of my writing appropriate for my situation? Have I avoided slang and idioms?

- Have I avoided sexist or exclusionary language of any kind? (Changing singulars to plurals is a graceful way to avoid problems.)

- Have I used pronouns appropriate for formal writing, avoiding second person ("you" and "your") completely, avoiding first person ("I," "me") unless it is absolutely necessary, and avoiding using plural pronouns ("they," "their") with singular nouns?

- Have I eliminated any fused sentences and sentence fragments?

- Do my sentences vary in structure, rhythm, and length?

- Have I looked for typical grammar problems? Have I used a consistent verb tense? Do my subjects and verbs agree? Do my pronouns and antecedents agree?

- Have I looked for typical punctuation problems, such as comma splices?

- Have I used—but not solely relied on—a spelling and grammar check?

- Have I checked my own error portfolio? (See page 141.)

OTHER TIPS FOR REVISING AND EDITING

Get a Second Opinion

A second pair of eyes can catch errors that you won't notice. You may know exactly what you mean in a sentence that doesn't come out the way you think it does. Sometimes a sentence that makes perfect sense to the writer is totally confusing to the audience. Another reader can also catch spelling errors that spell-check programs don't. (For example, you wrote "there" when you meant to write the pronoun "their"; when you read your own draft, your brain saw what you meant to write, not the error, and the spell checker can't tell the difference.) When at all possible, get your paper done early, and see if your instructor will look at it with you to give you some overall notes about the strength of your essay's logic, content, critical thought, and so on. Your school should have a tutoring center, as well; tutors are hired to read essays, and they'll be able to point out at least some of your errors and show you how to correct them on future drafts. Don't stop there, though: teaching assistants, friends, relatives, roommates, classmates, and even professors from previous terms can all help you. Every reader can give you some type of feedback you can use.

Read Aloud

Another way to identify errors and improve your writing is to read your own paper aloud. You can read your paper aloud to someone else and get their feedback, but reading it aloud to yourself is still a very helpful practice. We are all much better at speaking and listening than writing (we speak and listen approximately sixteen hours a day, but we may write only sixteen or so hours a semester). Reading a paper aloud will reveal flaws in syntax and sentence structure. If you can't get through a sentence as you're trying to read it aloud, you should highlight it and keep reading. Go back later and revise the sentences you got snagged on—they probably have serious problems.

Read Backwards

As mentioned earlier, your brain often sees what you meant to write instead of what you actually did write. Reading your paper backwards, sentence by sentence, interrupts the flow of your thoughts and makes it easier to catch errors, especially sentence fragments.

Keep an Error Portfolio

Keep track of errors from earlier papers in a portfolio from the current and even recent semesters. (Don't keep them too long, or you'll be looking for error types you've already mastered.) Watch for these recurring errors specifically during your revisions. It is also helpful to keep a list of words you know you regularly misspell. This way, you already know what to look for (and can even program your spell checker to autocorrect them for you). The error portfolio takes dedication on your part, but it will make you a much better writer as time goes on.

Edit Multiple Times for Multiple Error Types

Another great way to edit is to hunt down specific errors in a single edit. If you keep an error portfolio, this step is particularly helpful because you'll know exactly what to look for. If you know, for example, that you always make mistakes with comma usage, mark each comma in your paper with a yellow highlighter, then check later to make sure each is used correctly. Next, if you have your list of commonly misspelled words, go through with a blue highlighter, looking for those errors. If you have trouble with your parenthetical citations, highlight those with an orange highlighter. Later, you can rewrite to correct these problems, and the use of different colored highlighters will help you in your organization. This is a great way to edit your paper because you can search for one type of sentence error and then look up the rules for correcting that error specifically. You won't get bogged down with every error type under the sun.

KNOW THYSELF

The processes that we have discussed in this chapter are useful for most writers in most situations. This discussion has been one that addresses different learning styles, writing approaches, and typical difficulties. However, understanding your own unique thought processes is infinitely more important. As you think about the writing process, consider your own process. Discover what type of learner you are (kinesthetic, auditory, or visual), and figure out what hemisphere of the brain is dominant for you. More specifically, you need to understand what makes you become creative. What will help you ignore distractions and focus on the writing task before you?

Start by reflecting on some previous writing sessions. Was there something that distracted you constantly and kept you from writing? Many students claim that for some reason, whenever they write, they have to do so in a completely clean house. The cleanliness of the house probably isn't really the issue. What's happening is that the house cleaning has somehow become part of their writing process. The hour or more they spend picking up clothes, magazines, and other belongings and putting them away (probably listening to music and being alone the whole time) may be just what they need to collect themselves and get ready to write. In fact, they often find that they have unconsciously begun drafting sections of the paper—they seem to flow almost automatically after they sit down at the keyboard.

If you're trying to write and you keep thinking about a cup of coffee, get it. If you're longing for a candy bar or an ice cream cone or some peanuts, go get them. The distraction will only get worse, and in the meantime your body may be telling you it needs certain proteins, sugar, or caffeine before it feels like writing. Those little nagging distractions may be your brain telling you it needs another few minutes before it starts writing, or that it's hungry for some specific fuel it needs before getting creative.

Also, although all the steps outlined previously are good for most people, be prepared to adapt them. Your instructor will probably want a certain set of prewriting steps submitted for part of your grade, so obviously you need to follow those instructions. If you need to take note cards in a different manner than the one outlined earlier, or if you have a very innovative way to outline your paper on your computer, do it your way. If you are a new writer, you'd be wise to try out the exact techniques listed previously. However, as time goes by, and you've written more frequently, stick with what works. Above all else, "to thine own self be true."

Unit 2: Reading & Writing About Short Fiction

CHAPTER 3

Writing about Fiction

Writing about fiction is your chance to enter a house that from the outside looks forbiddingly large and mysterious. But having entered, you find many interesting and delightfully arranged rooms filled with sunlight to explore, all really yours alone to enjoy, examine, and describe.

Although the instructor may review for you formal literary criticism (a large, well-appointed room with great oak beams and stained-glass windows), the points to be covered in your paper should reflect your thoughts and feelings about the literary work at hand.

Think of fiction at the outset of our discussion as a counterfeiting, a making up and manipulation of a series of events and characters and their thoughts. We first encountered fiction as children when we read or had read to us the classic stories assigned to children from Grimm's *Fairy Tales,* Aesop's *Fables,* and other similar works. Children's fiction, whether classic or contemporary, does not completely help us to understand fiction, but it does indicate that we are familiar with it.

As you write about fiction, you should next ask yourself if you like or dislike the work you read and why. Did you like what happened and the way it happened? In addition, you might consider the possibility that other readers liked the work as much as you did. Why would this be so? What elements of a Chekhov story could be as important to you as to a student in Russia or India or France? Which elements in Dickens' novels have made them so universally acclaimed? You may be intrigued by the plot, the events that lead you deeper and deeper into the story. You may share the same emotions as a character, and would do the same thing he or she would do in similar situations. You may have discovered yourself enveloped in a certain mood as you read. Was that an accident?

Great fiction resonates with universal human experience. The rules of human conduct tend to be informally agreed on in many diverse cultures, including primitive ones even before there were ten commandments. Earlier peoples had been inclined to behave morally before such conduct became codified by law. The writer often reflects what is already deeply rooted in humankind. It may be these abiding universal truths that make us like a work of fiction.

As you know from the first chapter, there are several schools of literary criticism, some old, some new. Authors, however, rarely write to the beat of such criticism; they are assigned to a particular school after the fact. They may write at a specific time and be influenced by the style and events of that period. However, writers such as Nathaniel Hawthorne, James Joyce, Franz Kafka, Richard Wright, and Flannery O'Connor were innovators of narrative styles, and found ways to write that differed from those of writers who came before them.

Consequently, you'd do well to think of the uniqueness of the writer before you write about the work. When did the author live and where? What was going on at the time that the writer *may* have been influenced by? Where did the writer travel and what happened when she or he got there? What kind of work did the writer do in addition to writing? (Many writers have held a variety of jobs before and while writing; several of them were journalists like Hemingway or physicians like Chekhov.) What books did the writer read? What unusual experiences, if any, did the writer have? Consider that the writer, like those cited above, discovered something new to write about or a new way of writing about something often written before, some aspect of characterization or narrative that illustrates an unusual perception of the human condition.

Remember that the blank page for the writer is like a new world about to be discovered—just as it is for you. You and the writer are heirs to the oldest means of communication exclusive of voice sounds and hand signs. (The telephone is only 125 years old; television is barely 65.) In the life of humankind writing itself is a relatively recent means of making communications visible— perhaps something over 7,500 years old. And at the very start of this literary history there was fiction. The Egyptian *Tales of the Magicians,* a collection of stories from about 4000 B.C., naturally supposes even earlier beginnings. Other narrative works have come from India, ancient Israel, the kingdoms of the Euphrates, the Greeks, the Arabs, and from many other peoples and places.

The creative urge to tell stories is universally one of the strongest emotions in human beings. Fiction, of course, is not all pure creation; sometimes it is the reworking of experience or communal history—that is, making reality fit fictional needs, which then often go beyond reality to make specific points. Our earliest fiction consisted of moral writing; good things happened to good people (or animals) and bad things happened to bad people (or animals). Perhaps this is as it should be, but it is not what most of us understand about reality today. The drive to write fiction that in part or whole is didactic (morally instructive) is still obvious in the work of many contemporary writers of fiction.

Writing about fiction should be something of both challenge and opportunity, exploration and discovery. What does *this* writer have to say—and how does he or she say it? you might ask yourself. A story or a novel is a special room in the house you are visiting. Unlike television where you see the story, fiction makes you envision it, stretch your knowledge and imagination to match the author's. Understand, though, that most writers *are* writers because writing is for them the most lasting, perhaps even the most natural way they can reach out to others. "Writing," of course, is a combination of thinking *and* writing, as we shall see.

THE ELEMENTS OF FICTION

Once you sense the uniqueness of an author and the significance of his or her work, you should be able to write critically about it. Critical writing requires you to deal with key elements of fiction. These elements are discussed in the section that follows.

Plot

Plot is the arrangement of related events, however simple or complex, in the narrative of a work of fiction with the result that subsequently some conflict around which the story revolves will be concluded. (All fiction does not contain the same degree of conflict, and there is fiction in which there is very little conflict.) Plotting a story is the ordering of a world and the lives of the characters who inhabit it. William Faulkner wrote: "I like to think of the world I created as being a kind of keystone in the universe; that small as the keystone is, if it were ever taken away the universe itself would collapse."

The real world is rarely within our ability to control. But fiction offers a "splendid economy" an artistic ordering to counteract what Henry James' observation that life is splendid waste, "all is conclusion and confusion."

Aristotle in his *Poetics* calls plot the first element of drama or epic, which is composed of three elements: (1) a beginning that presumes additional action, (2) a middle that considers previous action and presumes succeeding action, and (3) an end that requires attention to earlier events but anticipates no further action.

Over the years Aristotle's three elements have been increased to five, more clearly defined fundamentals of plot. They are: (1) the beginning and exposition, which set the plot (or plots) in motion; (2) rising action, a series of actions, each of which causes another to begin and which considers the importance of tension and conflict (earlier critics used "conflict" and "crisis" interchangeably); (3) the climax, the most critical section of the narrative; (4) falling action, a lessening of tension, during which time some degree of tension (or suspension) is still maintained together with the explanation of the related events, sometimes called the denouement; (5) the resolution of the conflict—the happy or unhappy ending.

Whether you prefer the pure Aristotelian formula for plot or its expanded contemporary version, remember that plot in fiction is the structuring or ordering of the narrative. How does Kate Chopin plot a story in a brief moment of time, while Kafka seems to embrace all of time in a story like "A Hunger Artist"? How does any writer create and heighten conflict and how is it resolved? Why does Leslie Marmon Silko divide "The Man to Send Rain Clouds" into sections? And does Arna Bontemps' "A Summer Tragedy" conform to Aristotle's definition of plot? These are some of the questions you might want to consider as you write about fiction. (Plot is in the map room of the house.)

Character

The people you come to know in stories or novels are characters; they create action in the narrative. They tend to be the focus of the work. John Dryden believed that "the story is the least part" of a work, the character the most important. The writer creates the characters and supplies us with the information that allows us to identify, positively or negatively, with them. We know something about how the characters look, live, and think; often we know about their jobs and their social status, their aspirations and problems. We enter their heads—as we cannot with real people in real life—and share their emotions; we have access to the most secret and intimate corridors of their being. It is here where character motivation originates and plot commences. If the writer has done well, the character is revealed to the reader, act by act, spoken word by spoken word, thought by thought, like a flower unfolding petal by petal in the summer sun.

Not infrequently you will find characters so strongly drawn that they become the titles of the works they are in, for example, Charles Dickens' *Martin Chuzzlewit*, or Henry James' *Daisy Miller*, or Herman Melville's *Billy Budd, Foretopman: An Inside Narrative*, or Stephen Crane's *Maggie: A Girl of the Streets*. Short stories like Hawthorne's "Young Goodman Brown" and Gloria Naylor's "Kiswana Browne" indicate the continuing popularity of character titles involving people of all kinds of stations who function as fictional heroes and heroines.

Good characters must have dimension—that is, not merely inhabit the narrative for the sake of being there. The character must function; plot must turn on the character's actions; dialogue between characters must move plot as well as enlarge the character. It is crucial that we know everything about a character that is pertinent to the story, and perhaps that knowledge will resonate beyond the bounds of fiction. For example, we *want* to know what happens to the hero and heroine in "The Lady with the Pet Dog," for we invest in them as people and wonder about their destinies. That is what good writing and vivid characterization do. (Character can be found in the screening room.)

Point of View

Point of view is the position in which the writer places the character, around whom move all the elements of fiction. Point of view, like the defined area seen through a camera lens, is the frame or boundary of a work of fiction. Frequently it is through the point of view that we discover different ways of telling a story.

Traditionally there are three basic points of view: the first person or "I"; the somewhat experimental second person or "you"; and the third person "he," "she," "it," or "they."

First-person point of view is the method by which the author centrally positions one person through whom the story is told. Every detail of the work is filtered through that character who cannot intimately know others; he or she is the "I" character of the first-person singular. This is a limiting, but often effective way of writing, but that may be precisely what the author desires. This might be called a high-intensity point of view, providing the author with a special and perhaps unique voice in a strictly circumscribed world. Joyce's "Araby" and Louise Erdrich's "Snares" are two examples of the use of the internal or "I" voice.

Daniel Defoe's *Robinson Crusoe*, Joseph Conrad's *Lord Jim*, and Herman Melville's *Moby Dick* are but three of many novels in which writers have used the first-person voice effectively. The first-person point of view dictates that the protagonist can examine himself inside out, but most constantly decipher the acts and words of others to examine himself. (Untraditionally, however, there can be more than one "I" character in the same work. For example, if there are three people at the scene of a crime—the perpetrator, the victim, and a witness—the crime can be related by each character in turn, therefore bringing different first-person points of view to the story.)

The use of the third-person or external voice gives writers far more leeway—though they may not use it. The "I" becomes "he" or "she" and this lets the writer use the *limited* or *pseudo* third person, focusing not on several characters, but one, as in Wright's "The Man Who Was Almost a Man." From this point of view, the writer moves that character from a distance, and does not become one with the "I." No other character is really penetrated, or certainly not to the degree the protagonist has been. Sometimes, as in Bontemps' "A Summer Tragedy," two characters, Jennie and Jeff Patton, can become the third person of a story. Third person can be compared to a camera that has been focused between closeup and wide-angle, and it is this point of view many authors use to make us see a resemblance between fiction and the real world. The interior experiences of a singular major character are such that we can readily share them. Nothing stands between the writer and reader but the manipulated distance provided by the third person. Gone is the intrusive authorial voice of past use of the point of view (often opinionated, or editorializing and addressing the reader directly by the pronoun "you"). In modern fiction the characters speak; no authors are allowed.

Readers tend to identify more readily with one major character, though they seem to prefer the larger reality offered by the third-person voice over the first-person. Both, however, are widely used in the short story.

Unlimited third-person and omniscient or objective points of view are essentially the same. Herein, the author views all characters from an equal, objective stance; she can enter all their minds or none; the writer can share knowledge of one or more characters with every other character in the work. With the omniscient or unlimited third person and a large number of characters, through the use of the *interior monologue*, much like the dramatic soliloquy, the author can let us know how much one character knows about another. This achieves dynamic progress in the same way film is used to create anticipation and tension through montage. But sacrificed by this point of view is the sense of closeness to character found in the first person or limited third person. Here the author is truly a god, aiming characters at each other, constructing plots, establishing settings, issuing subjects and themes couched in a variety of styles, all conveyed through a team of characters.

Leo Tolstoy's *War and Peace* is a great model for the use of the omniscient point of view. The novel is a vibrant animism that conveys the movements of people and history. Tolstoy uses more than 500 characters ranging from peasant to Napoleon, with the key players meeting or crossing paths at crucial times after earlier being introduced in alternating chapters. The distance between author and characters is not always equal, since the major actors are only three of the multitude: Natasha Rostova, Prince Andrei Bolkonski, and Pierre Bezukhov.

Shifts in point of view may be indicated by a new paragraph, a space break in the narrative, or nothing at all. E. M. Forster declared that with an effective shift of viewpoint the writer has the power "to bounce the reader into accepting what he says." Dickens' *Bleak House*, Stevenson's *Dr. Jekyll and Mr. Hyde*, as well as Tolstoy's epic, present examples of shifting points of view. Shifting points of view may come as relief to some readers, a change of pace. For the writer, they expand or contract perception, allow a closeup or telephoto angle.

Tense usage combined with point of view offers tempting avenues for experimentation. Present tense makes narrative seem as though events are occurring as you read them; past tense is more leisurely and is used with greater frequency. A writer might shift point of view between first person, third person, and omniscient for certain specific effects (closeness or distance) and at the same time shift from past to present tense for certain other effects, for instance, pacing—speeding or slowing down the action. Traditionally, however, fiction is usually presented in only one tense and one point of view.

Setting

Setting is the physical place and time where action occurs in a narrative. Place and time are of immense importance in establishing the mood of a work of fiction.

Just as characters often are the titles of novels and stories they are in, places, too, are frequently titles—for example, Langston Hughes' "On the Road," Eudora Welty's "A Worn Path," and Ernest Hemingway's "A Clean, Well-Lighted Place." In Welty's "A Worn Path," for example, an elderly black woman wills her aching body across fields and woods to secure medicine for her sick grandchild. Welty's setting, rich in imagery and symbolism, grows to almost epic proportions, an odyssey of sorts, expressing the greatness of the human spirit.

We feel a sense of comfort with the familiar. When we read a book whose settings are known to us, or see a film set in a city that we either live in or have visited, we feel closer to the story. Yet, we are also curious about places and times we know little about. Edgar Allan Poe's "The Masque of the Red

Death," considered one of his greatest stories, has a setting that is as much in Prince Prospero's mind as it is in the castle to which he retires to escape the plague. We are drawn into the story to ricochet between the "real" and another level of imagination, terror.

As we know, a setting in fiction is not fixed as in many plays—is not real, but a construction of words designed to give the reader a sense of place through description. But settings can also be deceptive. Shirley Jackson's "The Lottery" begins in a small American town (like the one in "Young Goodman Brown" quite possibly) on a day that is "clear and sunny," but ends with a character screaming, "It isn't fair, it isn't right." (Jackson, like Poe, is a fine writer of Gothic horror.)

Settings can be physical as well as symbolic, as Welty's title suggests. In short, setting is where the fiction lives.

Tone

Tone, which we also find in poetry and drama, is the "attitude" of the author in a work of fiction. When we speak of a story as being happy or sad, comic or tragic, ironic or satiric, we are trying to establish the writer's attitude toward his or her materials. Sometimes it is easy to establish the tone of a story. For example, the very title of Arna Bontemps' "A Summer Tragedy" indicates the author's perspective on the action. At other times, we have a sudden shift in tone that turns the title into an ironic commentary. Tone can also be a complex subject, embracing matters of setting and mood, characterization, narrative action, and style. Consider Amy Tan's story "Two Kinds." The story presents a young, somewhat rebellious girl who knows she doesn't have the talents her mother ascribes to her. Yet, there are moments when, briefly, she thinks she does. Then comes the moment when she deliberately—though this might not altogether be the case—performs badly enough to make her mother have doubts. As behavior shifts, the tone also shifts from small hope to failure and to guilt because Jing-mei has failed to keep alive the immigrant's dream of becoming "anything you wanted to be in America." The "voice" changes, becomes more reflective and mellow when Jing-mei reaches thirty and looks back on her childhood. Moreover, there is another voice in the story, the mother's, which lends tension to the story, heightens the conflict between mother and daughter and between reality and possibility. Here the tone is at first hopeful, then desperate, and finally, defeated. The reconciliation when Jing-mei is an adult is sad and touching, and this is the final tonality in an admittedly complex tale.

Symbolism

A symbol is a representation of a reality on one level that has a corresponding reality on another level; symbols are things that represent other things by habit, association, or convention. Symbols in fiction, poetry, and drama possess specific points of reference created by the writer to lead you to and inside the work. *Symbols* are most often associated with *allegory* (Greek: "to speak other"). Allegory has two levels of meaning, but the second meaning is to be read beneath and concurrent with the surface story and may well itself be an extended story. In Kay Boyle's "The Astronomer's Wife," symbolism and allegory are relatively easy to discern. You may wish to discuss the symbolism expressed by the occupations of Mrs. Ames' husband and the plumber, or the allegory that further describes *where* they work, or the similarities between a plumber's pipe and an astronomer's telescope. In Franz Kafka's "A Hunger Artist," a more complex story, you can find several meanings that can be read as ironic or tragic, as well as allegorical. Edgar Allan Poe's "The Masque of the Red Death" abounds in allegory. A critical reading of these works should help you understand the various levels of meaning they contain.

Style

Style is found in the way a work of fiction is written. George Henry Lewes, who lived with Marian Evans (whose pen name was George Eliot), listed five rules of style: (1) economy (conciseness with precision); (2) simplicity; (3) sequential development of plot; (4) the inevitability of climax; and (5) variety.

These rules seem to still be valid even though language has changed tremendously since Lewes' time. But modern applications also see style as the way certain rhythms are employed in fiction writing; the way authors choose their words and use abstract, concrete, and figurative language; and the way they handle all the traditional elements of fiction—plot, character, point of view, setting, and theme. These, too, have been modified by time, and as these have been altered, so too has the heading under which more recent works fall: post-modernism.

But for many writers style is simply the way they write, the way words occur to them while shaping their fiction. For others, style may have developed over time through studying, consciously or subconsciously, the work of still other writers.

Writers who have journalism backgrounds, like Hemingway or Martha Gellhorn, may write in a style quite different from the one used by writers who also write or have written poetry, like Robert Penn Warren. Few poets, Walt Whitman being one of the exceptions, emerge from a background in journalism. There are many factors that may help to shape a style. And of course there are writers without any writing background who love language and ultimately find themselves to be writers.

Hemingway, whose style a generation of writers tried to copy, is known for his Spartan prose which is almost devoid of adjectives and adverbs, and for his use of plain language. These helped to make him clearly understandable and accessible. Ford Madox Ford said, "Hemingway's words strike you, each one, as if they were pebbles fetched from a brook."

William Faulkner's style is rotund, full-blown, expansive, and not very accessible—which led Hemingway to say of him, "Poor Faulkner. Does he really think big emotions come from big words?"

But then critic Max Eastman said Hemingway had "a literary style . . . of wearing false hair on the chest." Both Faulkner and Hemingway are Nobel laureates in literature.

Theme

To some readers theme and subject mean the same thing. They are quite different. Matthew Arnold wrote that "all depends on subject: choose a fitting action, penetrate yourself with the feeling of its situations; this done, everything will follow."

Theme, however, really is the distillation of subject; it makes relevant all the words that are used to frame the theme, which is the fine print of subject. The following brief dialogue examines the difference between subject and theme.

STUDENT A: "What's the book about?"
STUDENT B: "War." [Subject]
STUDENT A: "War?"
STUDENT B: "Actually, the horrors experienced by soldiers at the Battle of the Bulge. [Theme]

The subject is general; the theme is a specific statement about the subject. The same principle might be applied to Tolstoy, who wrote about *armies* in *War and Peace* and Hemingway, whose writings included pieces on the *units* of armies in three wars. The poet Wilfred Owen once said, "My subject is War, and the pity of War. The poetry is in the pity." Owen thus defines the difference between subject and theme in his own work.

INTERPRETING FICTION

Your interpretation of a literary work begins with accepting its theme, its diction and construction, what the work conveys to you, and your reaction to it. You accept the writing as a complete entity, a work of art, that possesses values you and other readers respect.

That done, you will find it worthwhile to review the elements of fiction to see if they are present or mostly present in the story you are interpreting. Then it may be expedient to note the theme of the story. If we took Chekhov's "The Lady with the Pet Dog," would we be seeing another "star-crossed lovers" theme or quite some other theme?

You might try to describe the kind of man Gurov is and decide whether or not there is irony in how he has changed by the end of the story. How has his openness to the "encounters of life" contributed to the plot? How effective are plot and character in support of theme? Point of view? With the questions and your answers digested, you can then move to the author's motive, if any, for writing the story. Chekhov is very good at detail that is important to his stories, so it will help if you read this (or any other story) more than once.

There are not, really, as many kinds of fiction as there are poetry, but it would be unfair to poetry to say that it does not require as much analysis as fiction; the amount of analysis depends on the work under study, not because it is one genre or the other. Most stories, however, are longer than most poems, and will require longer, more analytical reading. Some poems provide clues to their meanings by the way they are structured on the page, with some lines indented, very brief stanzas, or the use of punctuation: colons, for instance, or dashes. In a poem, these clues tend to leap out.

Such is not the case with most fiction. Outward appearances on the printed page reveal nothing. Reading is the only way to dig out the elements necessary for you to write about fiction. A first reading of a story may reveal its plot and then its theme. Plots generally come to life first, but not the theme within, so it may take a second or third reading before theme emerges. Plot, as you know, is the element in fiction where tension and conflict are found.

Once you have a good idea of what the story is about you can gather the characters on stage to see how well they have carried and moved plot, if their motivations, inner thoughts, dialogues and actions support your possible conclusions about the theme. You will want to describe the function of each character as part of your analysis.

Anton Chekhov said, "Cut a good story anywhere and it will bleed." (He was a doctor, remember.) Would the story you're reading lose anything if it had not been written the way it is? Could you cross out a paragraph and still have the story make sense, or eliminate a character without disturbing the plot? Imagine Philip Roth's "The Conversion of the Jews" without the janitor, Yakov Blotnik; would the story still work? Is the protagonist, Ozzie Freedman, unreasonable? Can you find, subtly located, the reason for Ozzie's behavior, which explains the nature of the conflict? Crucial differences between Itzie and Ozzie arise early in the story. How do they become manifest at the climax of the story?

Notice the shifts in points of view. Do they help you to understand the story, and in which ways? How do the breaks in the story add to its tension? These are the kinds of questions you should ask yourself and find answers to in order to write cogently about any story.

Remember that interpretations of fiction are not engraved in stone. Unless an author tells us of her intention in writing the story, or what the theme most assuredly is, or why a character does this or says that, we simply cannot know for sure why a story is the way it is. We just examine what has been given to us and come to the best interpretation we can which is, as it can only be, your opinion.

EVALUATING FICTION

A famous painter said, "A painting is valuable to you if *you* like it." In the same light, a work of fiction is valuable to you if you appreciate it for what it is. But that is only the beginning. Almost none of us is comfortable being alone in an evaluative process.

Students of literature can take heart: There is a proven track record of great fiction, whether we agree with it or not. In any case, the record is always changing. Herman Melville may be on the record for a number of years, and then he is off it; the same with Henry James and Virginia Woolf. The record may showcase at a given time some of the great Russian writers—Dostoyevski, Chekhov, and Tolstoy, for example—but never cite Leonid Andreyev. Some astoundingly good writers have never been on the record, like Martha Gellhorn. It would be a serious mistake not to read the record for information and assistance.

The following questions can help to guide you in your evaluation of a story or novel:

- Is the plot predictable or original?
- Do the characters have unique and well-developed dimensions or are they simply flat or stock types?
- Is the setting strikingly conveyed or are time, place, and atmosphere underdeveloped?
- Does the symbolism, if present, enhance the story or does it merely seem tacked on or confusing?
- Is the theme provocative and consequential or relatively unimportant or trite?
- Is the author's use of language original or not at all memorable?
- Which critical approach seems most useful in evaluating this work of fiction, and why?

Great fiction engages the universe and millions of readers, each of whom relates to it differently, yet somehow the same. And that is the way we really are. Great fiction has the ability to draw us into it as individuals and as members of a community called humanity stuck in space. We can find knowledge and comfort in fiction, pride and sorrow. Fiction is, after all, merely a reflection of what we are, have been, and perhaps may be.

CHAPTER 7

Organizing the Essay

The number one student complaint when faced with writing a paper is, "I don't know how to get started!" You've probably made this complaint a couple of times in your own academic career, and if you haven't, you will. There's an old Chinese adage that says the hardest part of any journey is taking the first step. This is especially true with writing papers.

No matter how much prewriting and research a student does, no matter how strong the outline, the actual task of launching the paper is almost always a tough one. Every step until the first keystroke on the keyboard or the first ink scrawl on the page is preparation. Your paper is still in the theoretical stage. But when you sit down to begin drafting that introduction, it's all too real. If you've never written a research paper or documented essay before (and plenty of incoming college students have not), starting the first draft can often seem so frightening that it produces writer's block (a mental state which temporarily "blocks" people from being able to write).

However, if you know some tips and tricks about what to include in introductions and how to structure them to have maximum impact, this knowledge will make your paper-writing process much less daunting. The same is true about drafting your body paragraphs and conclusions: the more you know about how to structure an essay, including research papers, the more you can reduce the stress associated with writing your first draft. The first part of the equation is a solid thesis statement (see Chapter 1 for more details on what a thesis statement is and isn't, as well as tips for generating a working thesis). The second part is a strong introduction designed to showcase your thesis statement and to let your audience know what to expect from your paper. The third part is a well-developed body that supports your thesis statement, and the last part is your conclusion, which reminds your audience of how you have supported your thesis. If you look at the process of generating a first draft as a matter of completing manageable individual steps, getting started will be easier.

We begin our discussion of the writing process with the introduction because that is the first part of your work that your audience will read, but we don't recommend trying to write a fully developed introduction as your first step. How well could you introduce a person you'd barely met to an audience eager for meaningful information? Introductions to papers work much the same way. You need to know your paper well before you can introduce it well, so you will only frustrate yourself (and make your writer's block more severe) if you try to complete the entire introduction first.

INTRODUCTIONS

In many ways, your **introduction** is the most important part of the entire paper. In just a few sentences, you suggest the topic and scope of your paper, set your tone, demonstrate your writing style, and provide your thesis; you may even set up some of the major arguments the audience will encounter. (Even though your literal audience is your instructor, imagine yourself as a professional who is writing for a wider, general audience.) If you write a flat, generic introduction, the audience is already expecting an uninspired paper. However, if you present your readers with an introduction that's full of insight, strong development, and even wit, they will already be pleased with their decision to read the upcoming paper, and they will want to continue reading what you have to say.

Before getting into the elements that make an introduction effective, let's take a look at the introduction to an actual paper. This paper's broad topic is the media, but as you can see by the end of the introduction, the student has gotten specific and focuses on the negative aspects of corporate media ownership. Using this eleven-sentence example, let's look at the key ingredients and functions of an introduction. (This is the introduction to the sample student paper found in Chapter 11 on page 255.)

1) James Madison once said that a "popular government without popular information, or the means to acquiring it, is but a prologue to a farce or a tragedy, or perhaps both" (qtd. in McChesney 6). 2) With this, Madison—America's fourth president, often called the father of the Constitution—establishes an important aspect of democracy. 3) The people must be informed about world events in order to be able to make informed decisions during any democratic election. 4) If people are misinformed, their votes for or against candidates, bills, and propositions are based on false information. 5) In nondemocratic countries, history shows a pattern of misinformation and media manipulation emphasizing propaganda, suppression of the truth, and even mass brainwashing. 6) The ideal of American journalism and freedom of speech is supposed to protect us from governmental influences over the mass media, ensuring us reliable news and information. 7) However, with the recent and steady rise in power of the modern corporation, the media is no longer as free as many would think. 8) Instead of the kinds of governmental intrusions on the news media that nondemocratic countries endure, we face a system of corporate ownership, which dominates news media instead. 9) As corporations have grown over the last one hundred years, they slowly acquired more and more aspects of the "mediascape," and now a few corporations own the majority of television stations, movie studios, publishing houses, and newspaper and magazine printing presses. 10) Over time, the American corporation has transformed from being just a business model to the nation's most powerful force. 11) Today, modern corporations' power over the media has damaged democracy by limiting public exposure to a diverse and comprehensive range of information, perspectives, and analyses, even resulting in lies and misinformation in the news media.

Gradual Buildup

Notice that this introduction doesn't start right away with dates, data, or a thesis. Introductions that start that way fail in their basic function: to introduce. An effective introduction should gradually "walk" a reader into the topic. The audience has no idea what is coming up in a paper when they first pick it up. Their minds could be on anything from what to eat for dinner to what time the party starts. Only through the introduction does the reader finally understand what the topic is. To just start your introduction "cold" and pack the opening sentence with a lot of information and facts is like waking people up by throwing cold water on their faces. It's harsh.

A successful introduction will take into consideration the fact that your readers have no idea what's coming just yet. (The only clue your audience has about the topic is what they've gleaned from the paper's title.) Thus, your introduction will gradually provide information, bit by bit, and by the time the thesis statement is revealed, your readers will have anticipated it and will be prepared to consider the often complex concepts you're presenting.

The preceding sample introduction begins with a quotation from James Madison (sentence 1). A quotation such as this one is a great way to begin an introduction. First, it is a good hook for the audience (see "Hooks" later in the chapter). Second, it begins to introduce the topic gradually. Readers now have a hint about the content of the paper: it will be about information, or government, or James Madison himself. As the introduction builds, the topic moves away from Madison, though. Sentences 2–5 use Madison's quote as a sounding board to open up a broader discussion of the media and democracy. By sentences 6 and 7, readers know they are reading a paper about corporate media and democracy. Starting with sentence 8, the writer gives readers some specific details they are likely to find in the paper, and by the final sentence—the thesis statement—the audience is fully aware of all the major ideas to be presented in the body of the paper.

PAPER TITLES

The title of your paper is an important part of introducing your audience to the specifics of your paper. Don't give your paper bland or vague titles like "Research Paper Number One," "Television," or even "Television History." Instead, give some specific details about your topic and argument. A title such as "Television History and the Evolution of Information Control" provides some key phrases and ideas. The reader now knows to look for history, the evolution of the technology, and the concept of information control.

You can even make your title a catchy phrase followed by a subtitle containing the important details, such as "The Boob Tube: A History of the Evolution of the Most Important Communications Device on Earth."

Hooks

Not only does a good introduction need to gradually build up to the major points you'll make, it also needs to make an audience interested in reading the paper. Consider our sample introduction again. What if the opening line of the paper was actually the thesis? Would you want to read a paper that began with the following sentence?

> The rapid spread of advertising that penetrates most aspects of public life is both desensitizing and angering to the American population, so we need to consider legislation to limit the amount and frequency of advertisements that we are exposed to on television, following the model of European Union countries that limit product placement in programs and allow commercials to interrupt shows only at designated intervals.

To most people, that introduction would sound dull, and they'd anticipate a dull paper. That is not a good way to start your relationship with your audience. After you've hooked the audience with an interesting introduction, it is easy for the readers to stay on track even through less interesting parts of the writing. The techniques that follow will help you hook your audience and make them want to read your paper instead of considering it a chore.

QUOTATIONS

You can always open a paper with an interesting **quotation.** Many papers written for literature classes open this way, but it is a technique that you can use in many other disciplines. You should stick with quotations that have some substance. Here are some suggestions to consider while picking an opening quotation:

a. Consider using a famous quotation. Reference works like *Bartlett's Familiar Quotations* and the *Oxford Dictionary of Quotations* are great resources available in most libraries and bookstores, and the Literature Network provides selections from *Bartlett's Familiar Quotations* online in a free, searchable database (http://www.online-literature.com/). Interesting and pertinent quotations are also very easy to find with a quick Web search, but there are dangers associated with this searching method. You can't always trust the site you're getting the quotation from (there could be typos, missing words, false information, or false attribution), and you can't always find reliable citation information for later inclusion in your works-cited page through these online sources. You are better off with reference works like the ones mentioned.

b. Consider quoting someone famous. Whether you turn to the classics or more modern sources, even if the quotation itself isn't familiar, the fact that it came from a well-known person will help "sell" the quotation. Consider the quotation in our sample introduction. Madison was one of the founding fathers and was largely credited as one of the authors of the Constitution. If he has something to say about democracy or government, an audience will trust that he knows what he's talking about. If you were writing a paper about quantum physics, you could turn to a prominent physicist like Stephen Hawking. Some students even have success finding quotes from famous films or television shows, especially when writing on popular culture.

    c. Look for observations that are beautifully or powerfully stated. You may find a perfect quotation from someone who is not particularly famous. It could be from a scholar, a poet, or even a songwriter, but if the wording will grab your audience and make them think about your topic and your slant on it, it can be just as effective as a famous saying from a famous person.

Make sure that you properly attribute any quotation that you use. Many quotations are famous enough to be public information—for example, a quotation from the Declaration of Independence or from a famous speech, such as John F. Kennedy's "Ask not what your country can do for you, but what you can do for your country." These meet common knowledge guidelines (because the quotes are very well known to almost everyone, they don't need to be cited) and do not need entries on works-cited pages; however, you should clearly identify the sources in your paper—never assume your audience knows where even very well-known quotations come from. Many of Shakespeare's most famous lines, for example, are often mistakenly attributed to the Bible. Most quotations do not meet common knowledge guidelines and will need full citations on your works-cited page, as well as identifying information in the paper itself.

BACKGROUND INFORMATION OR INTERESTING FACT

Another effective way to hook your audience is to provide them with some background on your topic. Often you will need to provide a great deal of explanation to set up your thesis statement. This technique also shows the audience right away that you've done enough research to become an expert on the subject you've chosen to discuss, so it helps to establish your authority. If you are writing about a certain television show, for example, you could open with some interesting facts about the stars of the show, the director, or how long it was on the air. If you are writing a paper about local businesses, you could start with a brief sketch about the history of the major businesses in your hometown.

Similarly, you can start with interesting theories or facts about your subject. If you have found assertions that surprised you when you first read them, consider opening with them. Your audience is also likely to be surprised by these ideas and then be intrigued to see what your take on this information is as they continue to read your paper.

In the example that follows, we've replaced the Madison quotation from the earlier introduction with the suggestion that the news media have possibly contributed to the conditions that led to some of the world's worst atrocities. The writer may consider this information to be too insignificant for the body of the paper, but it may be such an unfamiliar idea that it will grab a reader's attention right away. The highlighted portions are the new hook and are just as effective at drawing the attention of the audience as the Madison quote they've replaced.

1) Many people wonder how the horrors of the Second World War came to pass and how the atrocities of Hitler and Stalin were ever tolerated. 2) Some people think it was due to the lack of perspectives and the one-sided nature of their news media (McChesney 11). 3) With only one side of every argument being aired, entire schools of thought and whole truths were buried under lies and propaganda; shockingly, this type of information control could some day happen in America. 4) The people must

be informed about world events in order to be able to make informed decisions during any democratic election. 5) If people are misinformed, their votes for or against candidates, bills, and propositions are based on false information. 6) In nondemocratic countries, history shows a pattern of misinformation and media manipulation emphasizing propaganda, suppression of the truth, and even mass brainwashing. 7) The ideal of American journalism and freedom of speech is supposed to protect us from governmental influences over the mass media, ensuring us reliable news and information. 8) However, with the recent and steady rise in power of the modern corporation, the media is no longer as free as many would think. 9) Instead of the kinds of governmental intrusions on the news media that nondemocratic countries endure, we face a system of corporate ownership, which dominates news media instead. 10) As corporations have grown over the last one hundred years, they slowly acquired more and more aspects of the "mediascape," and now a few corporations own the majority of television stations, movie studios, publishing houses, and newspaper and magazine printing presses. 11) Over time, the American corporation has transformed from being just a business model to the nation's most powerful force. 12) Today, modern corporations' power over the media has damaged democracy by limiting public exposure to a diverse and comprehensive range of information, perspectives, and analyses, even resulting in lies and misinformation in the news media.

The notion that the media may be partially to blame for the horrors of the war should grab people's attention, especially when compared to our own media. The author here didn't provide a direct quote because it wasn't a *great* quote; the facts were very interesting, but the wording of the original didn't merit inclusion in the paper. The author simply wanted to include this information right away and didn't think this data was suited for the body of the paper. Any material that needs to be part of your argument should come later as support for your thesis. The introduction is a good place for information that will pique the audience's interest and make them want to learn more.

RHETORICAL QUESTIONS

Another great way to hook an audience, a **rhetorical question** is asked not to prompt an actual response but to inspire thought, conversation, or an argument. It makes the reader think for a moment about an issue for which there may be no final answer, but instead an ongoing debate. Such a device is good to use for an introduction. If you can get your audience to think about a pressing question right away, you've interested them in your subject matter.

Here's a warning, though: too many rhetorical questions in the body of a paper can leave your readers with a sense that you haven't done enough research. Questions don't have much of a place in a paper after the thesis has been revealed. The body of your paper is supposed to provide answers to questions, not raise more questions. The introduction, however, is a great place to ask questions that your thesis, body, and conclusion will set out to prove or disprove.

The following example shows how to open with a rhetorical question.

1) How do podcasts of nightly news anchor Katie Couric ensure that we have a healthy, working democracy? 2) Why would Benjamin Franklin sleep better at night watching a politician squirm and try to defend herself while Jon Stewart makes fun of her on *The Daily Show?* 3) These questions may seem frivolous, but they actually help establish important aspects of democracy. 4) The people must be informed about world events in order to be able to make informed decisions during any democratic election. 5) If people are misinformed, their votes for or against candidates, bills, and propositions are based on false information. 6) In nondemocratic countries, history shows a pattern of misinformation and media manipulation emphasizing propaganda, suppression of the truth, and even mass brainwashing. 7) The ideal of American journalism and freedom of speech is supposed to protect us from governmental influences over the mass media, ensuring us reliable news and information. 8) However, with the recent and steady rise in power of the modern corporation, the media is no longer as free as many would think. 9) Instead of the kinds of governmental intrusions on the news media that nondemocratic countries endure, we face a system of corporate ownership, which dominates news media instead. 10) As corporations have grown over the last one hundred years, they slowly acquired more and more aspects of the "mediascape," and now a few corporations own the majority of television stations, movie studios, publishing houses, and newspaper and magazine printing presses. 11) Over time, the American corporation has transformed from being just a business model to the nation's most powerful force. 12) Today, modern corporations' power over the media has damaged democracy by limiting public exposure to a diverse and comprehensive range of information, perspectives, and analyses, even resulting in lies and misinformation in the news media.

Notice that the questions really do get you thinking. References to TV personalities and podcasts may at first seem silly and irrelevant, but in the context of the rest of the introduction, they make sense. They also add a bit of humor, which can be a way to get your audience interested, as well (see "Humor" on page 151). Such questions are too casual and speculative to include in your paper's formal body, but they work nicely as an introductory hook.

PERSONAL ANECDOTE

Another great way to hook a reader is to tell a **personal anecdote.** An anecdote is simply a brief, amusing, or interesting personal story. Everyone has stories to tell, and often these stories pertain directly to essays you may be writing. Using a personal story is often a great way to hook the reader. Such a narrative may let the audience know that there's more to this paper than just clinical facts—there's a personal angle as well.

Caution: Personal anecdotes should be used carefully because they can lead to problems with your paper if not used properly. Many college professors insist that you not use "I" in your writing because statements such as "I think" or "I feel" or even "I agree" downgrade your writing from a discussion of facts to an airing of personal opinion. They are also usually redundant because readers fully understand that the views in a paper are yours. Solid research papers are based on empirical evidence and facts, and including too many personal opinions hurts your argument.

150   CHAPTER 7   Organizing the Essay

Personal anecdotes are inevitably "I" pieces of writing, and in a true research paper, they have very little place. Thesis statements in such essays should be supported by research and data, not emotional appeals and personal stories. However, using a personal narrative to open a piece of academic writing can be a clever way to introduce a topic, as long as you don't overdo it. Eventually, your introduction will end up with a focus on the thesis, and you will avoid using stories as evidence in the body of your paper.

If we opened our sample introduction with an anecdote instead of Madison's quote, it would look something like this:

1) When I was still in my junior high government class, I remember we studied freedom of speech. 2) We spent weeks studying the importance of information to our government, and I remember being bored to tears and not understanding how the ability to simply talk and listen actually equaled democracy. 3) Recently, however, I noticed how trivial and repetitive televised news is, and I started to wonder if communication and free speech do indeed have an impact on our lives as the founding fathers seemed to have thought. 4) I realized that in a true democracy, the people must be informed about world events in order to be able to make informed decisions during any democratic election. 5) If people are misinformed, their votes for or against candidates, bills, and propositions are based on false information. 6) In nondemocratic countries, history shows a pattern of misinformation and media manipulation emphasizing propaganda, suppression of the truth, and even mass brainwashing. 7) The ideal of American journalism and freedom of speech is supposed to protect us from governmental influences over the mass media, ensuring us reliable news and information. 8) However, with the recent and steady rise in power of the modern corporation, the media is no longer as free as many would think. 9) Instead of the kinds of governmental intrusions on the news media that nondemocratic countries endure, we face a system of corporate ownership, which dominates news media instead. 10) As corporations have grown over the last one hundred years, they slowly acquired more and more aspects of the "mediascape," and now a few corporations own the majority of television stations, movie studios, publishing houses, and newspaper and magazine printing presses. 11) Over time, the American corporation has transformed from being just a business model to the nation's most powerful force. 12) Today, modern corporations' power over the media has damaged democracy by limiting public exposure to a diverse and comprehensive range of information, perspectives, and analyses, even resulting in lies and misinformation in the news media.

This personal story about the author's experiences in junior high ties directly to the concept of how important communication and information are to democracy. This simple story will make others think about what the author is pausing to think about. Everyone has heard the term "freedom of speech" thrown about, but how many people have really pondered its importance? This narrative successfully hooks readers. Notice how the introduction gets more professional and scholarly in tone, though, as it moves toward the thesis. This story is not referred to in the body of the paper. It's purely a means of appealing to the audience and drawing them in.

HUMOR

Like the personal anecdote, **humor** should usually be avoided in academic writing, especially in the body of your paper, where you need to maintain an academic tone. However, striking a witty or quirky note in the opening lines of an introduction may be a good way to grab your audience's attention.

The previous rhetorical question example uses a bit of humor to lure in the reader; the question is strange and unexpected, somehow linking podcasts, Katie Couric, and Jon Stewart to Benjamin Franklin having a good night's sleep. This simple bit of humor lets the audience smile a bit before getting into the more scholarly tone of the rest of the introduction and the paper that follows it. The humor here isn't always laugh-out-loud funny, but it's witty and quirky enough to lighten the mood or bring a smile to the reader's face.

Additional Tips on Writing the Introduction

THESIS PLACEMENT

Remember that an introduction should introduce your topic to your audience as interestingly as possible, give the topic a sense of context, and clearly state your thesis—the point about your topic that you support with arguments in the body of your paper. Unless your instructor specifically asks for you to put the thesis first (this may happen in science classes—in fact, you may be asked to open your paper with a brief abstract), you should always consider placing the thesis toward the end of the introduction. In fact, the very last sentence is ideal. It makes a strong impact there; it serves as a marker that the introduction is done and the body is about to begin, and your audience will know what to look for as they continue reading your paper. You don't want readers to wonder what you are trying to prove. You want them to leave the introduction with a clear idea of your purpose. However, always check with your instructor for his or her personal preference. (For more detail on the thesis statement, see Chapter 1.)

KNOW YOUR AUDIENCE

When choosing the information you need to include in a paper and when constructing your arguments, you should imagine a general audience of intelligent people who may not be the experts that you are on a particular topic. Don't forget that you have a reader who is not imaginary—the person who will be grading your work. Before choosing an introduction hook, find out your instructor's requirements, which will help you determine the proper tone for your paper. Don't try to guess—ask.

One professor may have an active sense of humor and love to crack jokes during lectures, so a humor hook could be great, but it could also fall flat if he or she wants students' papers to have a strictly academic tone. Another professor may strike everyone as a consummate professional and scientist, but this person may actually enjoy an introduction that begins with a funny story. Still another professor may cultivate a daring, edgy persona in the classroom but expect a traditional style of writing, so attempting a daring, edgy gimmick in your introduction could backfire. If your professor doesn't explicitly address tone and level of formality when talking about an

152 CHAPTER 7 Organizing the Essay

assigned paper, you should assume that your paper should be written in a formal, academic tone (or you should raise your hand and ask). Use a hook that is appropriate for your overall writing purpose and your audience.

LENGTH

Introductions can—and should—be different lengths for different papers. Many writers think that the introduction must be one paragraph long, period. If you're writing a three-page paper, the introduction should be about a paragraph long, but this is not an established rule of academic prose. Longer papers require longer introductions. You may find that in a ten-page paper, your introduction may be two paragraphs long or even a full page long (or longer). Let your argument, and what you need to say in order to prove it, determine how many paragraphs you need to introduce your topic.

CONTRACT WITH YOUR AUDIENCE

One way to think of your introduction is as a contract between you and your audience. The introduction tells the audience exactly what to expect from the upcoming paper, in form and content as well as style. Go back and review the first example introduction for this section (page 147) one last time.

Did you notice the essay structure that this introduction suggests? Sentences 9–11 show major ideas we now expect to see in the paper (corporate domination of the media, media saturation, and so on). If any of these main points of your argument are missing from the body of the paper, you have broken your contract with the reader. In fact, even if you present your points in a different order than the order you presented them in the introduction, you've already started to break your contract. Always read your introduction again after you've finished your paper. Writers often end up cutting a section or adding a new argument, and these changes need to be reflected in your introduction and your thesis. It's silly to go back and change your whole paper to reflect your introduction; change a sentence or two in your introduction to reflect a new element in your paper instead.

Also, if you use sophisticated vocabulary and sentence structure in your introduction, your readers will expect that style for the entire paper. In our sample introduction, notice the use of terms like "flippant," "proliferation," "antagonisms," and "psychological." If the paper stops using this level of diction, the audience will notice a shift in your style—another violation of the contract.

FIRST IMPRESSIONS

Remember that your introduction is your audience's first impression of you and your ideas. If your introduction is full of typographical errors, punctuation mistakes, and weak sentence construction, the audience will expect that your entire paper will be full of the same types of errors. Your readers will need several well-crafted pages to forget what they noticed in the introduction, be it good or bad. Think about how strong first impressions are when you are introduced to someone. At a party you can meet a very bright, witty person who is having a bad day, and you will walk away from that person feeling unimpressed, with no idea of how intellectually stimulating he or she actually can be. In fact, you may want to avoid having to listen to that person ever again. A poor introduction to a paper can have the same effect. Make your introduction count!

WRITER'S BLOCK

Starting an introduction can be very difficult. Perhaps you've got so many ideas and information that even with your outline, you truly don't know where to begin. Those first few words can be the hardest of your entire paper. You think you'd be fine if you could just start with the body of your paper—then go ahead! If you're having trouble starting, skip the introduction for now and proceed with the

INTRODUCTIONS FOR SCIENTIFIC DISCIPLINES

Writing a scientific paper is significantly different from writing a report or an argumentative paper in the humanities. You typically have an audience of experts in scientific writing, and you will be more concerned with providing data and interpreting it than compiling a research-based argument. One of your major goals in this type of writing is to present the information clearly but concisely so that your experiments are easy to interpret and possible to duplicate. Introductions in this scientific format are far more structured, data driven, and formal. Following is a list of some of the elements your professor may expect in an introduction to this type of paper:

Hypothesis

Your entire scientific paper will revolve around a hypothesis, a working assumption that you plan to prove or disprove through your study. You will clearly identify your hypothesis here and let the readers know whether your hypothesis was proved or disproved in your paper (both results are equally valid and desirable in scientific writing).

Abstract

Here you provide a brief discussion/summary of your entire paper. You will probably include the primary reason for writing this paper and conducting this research. It will include a brief discussion of the results and conclusions you've drawn.

Methods

Your introduction may include a discussion of the methods you've used to support your hypothesis and how you conducted your study. It will include a discussion of the data collection and statistical analysis portion of the paper as well as how you designed the experiments you conducted.

Results

For this portion, you tell the reader what you found in your study. Summarize your data here, using tables, charts, and graphs as well as text if necessary. Do not try to interpret the meaning of the data or extrapolate on how they support your hypothesis in this portion; simply report on the basic findings.

first paragraph of the paper's body. Start with facts and move on from there. The introduction is often the last section that experienced writers will write. Having the entire body and the conclusion finished can liberate you when writing your introduction. If you already know exactly what's coming up in the paper itself, introducing it can be easier. Give this method a try if you're stuck; it might just break your writer's block.

THE BODY OF THE ESSAY

Normally, students have the easiest time writing the body. It's based upon research you've already spent a considerable amount of time on, so by this stage of the writing process, you know your material fairly well. You've also completed an outline, so you know the order and logic of your arguments. It's just a matter of writing them down. However, to successfully support your thesis, the body of a well-crafted research paper should do much more than state a lot of facts, give a lot of quotes, and list a lot of dates. The outside evidence you've compiled and your own ideas and conclusions need to come together as an integrated whole.

You, as the writer, need to do more than state facts; you need to interpret the facts and use them to support your paper. You also need to prove to the audience that you've critically examined your sources and that you fully understand the ramifications they have for your thesis statement and your own arguments. (For more on how to integrate source material, see Chapter 8.) Following is a sample body paragraph from the student essay found on page 255. It is a body paragraph in support of the sample introduction used previously.

1) Instead of making money by selling a quality product, corporations started to practice "branding." 2) Branding is when a corporation makes the identity of a certain brand name (such as Coke, Nike, or the Gap) become synonymous with high quality, luxury, or just "being cool." 3) This branding worked better than anyone could have ever hoped and seemed to end the financial woes that the recession brought to corporate America. 4) Naomi Klein, media activist and author of the influential book on advertising, *No Logo*, discusses this corporate success story:

> The astronomical growth in the wealth and cultural influence of multinational corporations over the last fifteen years can arguably be traced back to a single, seemingly innocuous idea developed by management theorists in the mid-1980s: that successful corporations must primarily produce brands, as opposed to products. (1) Until that time . . . the primary concern of every manufacturer was the production of goods.

5) When corporations focused on enhancing their brands instead of manufacturing products, as Klein suggests, they started making record earnings and grew in power and stature. 6) Making a high-quality burger that tasted good did not sell nearly as well as selling the notion of "cool" or by convincing the audience that they are indeed "loving it," as McDonald's suggests in their highly successful ad campaign. 7) Brand loyalty proved far more successful for the corporation than high-quality products seemed to, and the corporation was able to grow in wealth and stature as a result.

Topic Sentence

The first element to note in this sample body paragraph is the **topic sentence,** which tells the reader what the paragraph is about. Some instructors prefer that you begin every paragraph in your body with a topic sentence, which can work especially well when the final sentence in the previous paragraph is used as part of a transition. Many writers prefer to embed the topic sentence somewhere in the paragraph. For example, they may introduce ideas that build up to the topic sentence, then give the topic sentence, and follow it with extra examples or supporting ideas. Some writers' topic sentences may be implicit (not directly stated), but this can be risky in student writing, so we don't recommend it. Being able to clearly state your topic sentences helps to keep you on track. It's a great idea to come up with them before you even begin the paper—they can serve as the main points in the outline you create. Wherever you place each topic sentence, you should consider it a miniature thesis statement. Where the thesis is in effect the controlling argument for the whole of the paper, the topic sentence is the controlling argument or idea for the individual paragraph. Often, you may use one topic sentence to set up a few paragraphs if they are all closely related, but make sure that you have a topic sentence before every argument.

Here is the sample topic sentence for the sample body paragraph:

> Instead of making money by selling a quality product, corporations started to practice "branding."

This topic sentence tells the reader that the focus for the upcoming paragraph is the notion of branding. As you read through the rest of the paragraph, every sentence, including the quotation, supports this assertion.

In your own writing, when you reread a paragraph and notice that one of the sentences does not directly support the topic sentence, you should either cut or revise it. Otherwise, you risk wandering off topic and losing the paragraph's **coherence,** the quality of writing in which all of the elements relate to one another and to a central idea. Similarly, after you've finished your rough draft, if you find any topic sentences that fail to support the thesis directly, you should cut or revise them (and their corresponding paragraphs) as well.

Support

The body paragraph should introduce, provide, and examine evidence to support the point made in your topic sentence. This support can be a logical argument you generate yourself or evidence drawn from sources such as a quotation, paraphrase, statistic, or fact. Notice that in the sample body paragraph on page 154, sentences 2 and 3 gradually set up the evidence the author later presents us with. Sentence 4 directly introduces the source, complete with the author's names and background and the title of the book. Sentence 4 contains the actual quotation, and sentences 5 through 7 discuss the importance and meaning of the quotation. We learn here that the writer thinks this quotation is accurate, and she provides more examples to give further support to her thesis.

156   CHAPTER 7   Organizing the Essay

Transitions

When you have made one point, whether it is one paragraph or one page long, you always need to provide a logical **transition** to your next main point. A **transition sentence** helps readers move from one paragraph to the next. One of the goals of great writing is to make the reading of your words an effortless task. When you leave out transitions, your readers don't know they need to shift mental gears from Point A to Point B. They finish with one point and get several sentences into the next one before they realize there's been a shift. This makes following the details of your individual arguments difficult, and it forces your readers to have to continually reread sections of your paper to stay on track. Transitions help readers stay on track by announcing shifts in advance. A transition should subtly tell readers, "I'm done with Point A and moving on to Point B now." Transition words such as *although, finally, however, in conclusion, moreover, nevertheless, on the one hand, therefore,* and *though* let your readers know how one idea relates to another within a paragraph.

Transitions also give your essay continuity. When you use transitions to connect paragraphs, the audience knows that your essay is written according to a logical plan and that it all works together seamlessly. If you're writing a longer paper, and you have points going on for several paragraphs or even several pages, don't feel that you need a transition at the end of each paragraph. You should make sure they happen at the end of every point you make. If you have a longer or shorter point, you should adjust the placement and frequency of your transitions accordingly.

Here is another excerpt found in the sample student paper. Look at the bottom of this paragraph to see the transition:

1) In fact, in his book (appropriately titled *Corporate Media and the Threat to Democracy*), McChesney suggests that

> the commercial basis of U.S. media has negative implications for the exercise of political democracy: it encourages a weak political culture that makes depoliticization, apathy and selfishness rational choices for the citizenry, and it permits the business and commercial interests that actually rule U.S. society to have inordinate influence over media content . . . for those committed to democracy, it is imperative to reform the media system. (7)

2) In this quotation, McChesney not only shows the negative impact of the media conglomerates, he even posits that someone who is truly dedicated to democracy and free speech must explore ways to change things. 3) One government body is indeed doing some fact finding to try to find a way to change things in favor of the citizens, and that is the Federal Communications Commission.

In this paragraph, the first two sentences introduce, provide, and discuss a bit of evidence. Sentence 3 shows us a solid transition. It begins by addressing the issues of this paragraph—someone needs to look for a way to change the current media system—but it ends up introducing the Federal Communications Commission. The next paragraph is entirely about the FCC, and this transition sentence serves to not only wrap up the current point, but let the reader know what the next point will be about. This transition sentence does a great job of leading the audience from one topic to the next.

Thesis Reminders

Your readers are never as familiar with your topic or your specific arguments as you are, so you should make a conscious effort to remind them of your original thesis statement at various points throughout your paper. You don't want to simply cut and paste the same sentence over and over, but you need to keep nudging the audience back toward your controlling argument. These reminders may seem redundant, but because your goal is to make your readers understand what you write and agree with your points, reminding them about your specific thesis is always a good idea.

More practically, your professor is your true audience, and he or she will be reading a *lot* of papers before and after yours. Suppose everyone in the class is writing about television. The instructor will be reading arguments about television for hours, and your individual voice might easily be drowned out. With solid reminders of your thesis throughout the body of your paper, however, your instructor (or any reader) will always remember exactly where your paper started and exactly what your paper is constructed to prove. Often, it can be part of a transition or some other part of the body of your essay. Like a transition, you don't need to add a thesis reminder after every paragraph in a longer argument. In fact, you don't need them in every point you make. It's possible to add too many. There is no rule for how many to provide, or how often to provide them, but think about including one after every page or two. If you have rather complex points with a lot of facts or tangents, you will need to remind your audience of your thesis a bit more often.

Remember the thesis from the sample introduction:

Today, modern corporations' power over the media has damaged democracy by limiting public exposure to a diverse and comprehensive range of information, perspectives, and analyses, even resulting in lies and misinformation in the news media.

Consider the following paragraph from the student essay and how it supports this thesis. The last sentence of the paragraph (highlighted in yellow) serves not only to wrap up the current argument, but to remind the audience of the specifics of the thesis sentence:

Indeed, in 2003, these five corporations were controlled by just five men: Richard Parsons, head of Time Warner; Michael Eisner, head of Disney; Sumner Redstone, head of Viacom; Rupert Murdoch, head of News Corps (and current owner of the *Wall Street Journal*); and Reinhard Mohn, a man who had deceived the public about his company's Nazi history (Bagdikian, New 27–28). These conglomerates have merged and bought out every type of information technology possible—magazines, newspapers, websites, cable networks, even Internet service providers and the physical infrastructure of satellite systems and phone lines. If there is a way to get information about our world, odds are these conglomerates own it, and that is where free speech—and its corollary, free, accurate, and uncensored information—becomes limited for citizens.

158   CHAPTER 7   Organizing the Essay

Additional Tips on Writing the Body of Your Paper

PARAGRAPH LENGTH

Just like the introduction and the conclusion, there is no standard length for the body of your essay. More to the point, there is no set length for a body paragraph. You should play around with the size of your paragraphs, but understand that paragraphs are constructed to contain distinct units of information. If you have a lot to say, you can easily spread one point (thus one transition and one topic sentence) over two or three separate paragraphs, making one larger point. The first paragraph could introduce the point, the second could provide concrete supporting examples, and the third could offer a conclusion. Conversely, some points may be briefer, with all these elements occurring in one paragraph. Instead of thinking about your paragraphs in terms of word count, think about the clearest way of presenting your information and ideas.

THESIS

While you revise your paper, always keep your thesis in mind. If you read a paragraph during revision, and you decide it has no bearing on the thesis, cut that paragraph or revise it to apply directly to your thesis.

MINI-PAPERS

Often, the thought of writing a ten- or fifteen-page paper is enough to make a student drop a class. Don't panic! The best way to think of longer papers is simply as a collection of smaller papers strung together. Instead of obsessing about writing a fifteen-page paper, divide your points up into major sections. Perhaps you're making four distinct points in your paper, and each one will be three pages long. You'll start with a topic sentence (instead of a thesis), then give the evidence/argument (which is like the body), and end with a transitional or closing statement (like a micro conclusion). If you break the writing up into several two- to four-page mini papers, in no time, you'll find that you've just written a fifteen-page paper, and you have done it by breaking the process into smaller, more manageable tasks. After these shorter papers are complete, all you'll have left to do is to write a full introduction and conclusion and tie the papers together with thesis reminders and transitions.

YOUR IDEAS MATTER

In a research paper, your ideas are important. If you provide only facts and quotations, you haven't written a research paper—you've strung together other people's ideas and information. For this reason, you should usually avoid opening and closing a body paragraph with a quotation. If you open with a quotation that will be a major part of a point you're making, then you fail to introduce the source, and you fail to provide a topic sentence to help guide that paragraph. You need that topic sentence to give a sense of transition. Similarly, you typically don't want to end on a quotation or paraphrase; the paper is supposed to be your own interpretation of outside evidence, so you need to end with your ideas, not those of other scholars. End your body paragraphs with a critical look at how the quotations or paraphrases you've presented apply to your thesis.

CONCLUSIONS

The final part of any paper is, of course, the **conclusion.** Traditionally, this is the place for an author to make his or her final statements about all the evidence he or she has just presented. It is the final chance to shore up the argument so that the thesis is fully developed and proven. The conclusion serves several other functions as well, though. Much as the introduction eases readers into the paper's topic, the conclusion should ease the readers back out, leaving them with a clear sense that the paper is finished.

Here is the conclusion to the sample paper from which the sample introduction and body paragraph from earlier in this chapter were taken:

1) Serving the needs of the people should be of paramount importance to every citizen in our mediated world, however, not simply the financial bottom line of corporate America. 2) Corporations used to be manageable and closely monitored by the people and the government. 3) The current corporate dominance of the airwaves, though, undermines our ability to stay well informed, feel a sense of community, and therefore fully participate in our own democratic government. 4) We cannot let corporations control and limit what we know about our own country and the rest of the world. 5) As President Madison, one of the fathers of this democracy, said, "popular government without popular information, or the means to acquiring it, is but a prologue to a farce or a tragedy, or perhaps both" (qtd. in McChesney 6). 6) If the corporations become the ultimate gatekeepers of the powers of mass communication, our own ability to engage in true free speech and to have complete access to the information we need to make truly informed decisions about everything from our health to the leaders we elect will be only a farce or a tragedy as Madison predicted.

Thesis Finality

If there is any place in your paper where your audience needs to be fully reminded of your thesis statement, it is in the conclusion. You've said all you have to say—all the citations and evidence and all the points you've made—but remember that the audience has just digested a lot of information. After you've presented your research and findings, the audience may make its own interpretations and come to its own conclusions about the evidence. Your final words need to clarify your conclusion. Don't make the mistake of assuming that the reader will necessarily understand what all of your evidence just proved. This is your job as a writer.

Often, the first sentence or two of a conclusion are a concise attempt to remind the audience of exactly what your thesis was and how you just proved it, as sentences 2 and 3 do in the previous example. They sum up the thesis (which is less boring if it is worded differently from the original). They also manage to briefly encapsulate all the major points made in this paper. Opening your conclusion this way gives your readers a reminder of all the pertinent details from your paper as well as a solid topic sentence for the concluding paragraph.

You may have a much longer conclusion than the one shown earlier. It could even be several paragraphs long, and you may go over several of the key points of your paper in more detail. A more detailed conclusion is useful for a longer project or a paper filled with scientific or mathematical findings.

Century

160   CHAPTER 7   Organizing the Essay

Conclusion Structure

There is no set pattern for writing a conclusion; just remember the main goal is to give readers a sense of finality about your thesis and your essay. Naturally, some writers end up with a conclusion that mirrors their introduction. When you remind the reader of the thesis in your first sentence, you've already mirrored your introduction to some extent, of course. You open the conclusion with the thesis, just as you closed the introduction with it.

In your introduction, your second step is to gradually walk the reader into your topic; alternatively, in the conclusion, your second step is to gradually walk the reader away from your topic and back out of your paper. Finally, your introduction probably started with a fairly general statement and some kind of hook; true to its mirror form, your conclusion will end with a general statement or hook.

In this sample conclusion, notice that sentences 4, 5, and 6 all depart from the specifics of the thesis and end up with more general ideas about Madison's opening quote and what we have learned about it since the paper started.

Hooks

Just as the introduction needs a hook to entice readers to *want* to read a paper, you need to end your paper with a hook that will make them remember it. It is often effective to end your paper with the same hook you opened with. The reader will remember how you hooked him or her in the beginning of this paper; ending with the same hook creates a good sense of closure.

A concluding hook needs to engage the readers. It needs to let them ponder the future or think of ways to confront issues in the present. Try to make an impact with your closing statement.

Different Hooks

QUOTATIONS

If you opened with a quotation, you can end with the same quotation, or at least a continuation of it. You can revisit the quotation and reaffirm it in light of the evidence you've presented, or discuss how it doesn't hold up to what you've actually revealed in your paper. You can remind the audience of your opening quotation and then reflect on it to show how you (therefore, they) have changed in the course of your research. In the sample conclusion, the author ends by reminding the audience of the Madison quotation and by hoping the sentiments expressed in that quotation haven't come true in modern America.

BACKGROUND INFORMATION/INTERESTING FACT

Discussing the background of a topic in your introduction always gives you a great opportunity to discuss the future of the same topic in your conclusion. Take the ideas you opened with and project them into the future; the audience will enjoy the ride.

Here is a final conclusion-closing hook for the preceding conclusion example. The final sentence is revised to reflect the essay's original introduction hook. Revisit the

"Background Information" sample introduction on page 147 to see how it all comes full circle.

1) Serving the needs of the people should be of paramount importance to every citizen in our mediated world, however, not simply the financial bottom line of corporate America. 2) Corporations used to be manageable and closely monitored by the people and the government. 3) The current corporate dominance of the airwaves, though, undermines our ability to stay well informed, feel a sense of community, and therefore fully participate in our own democratic government. 4) We cannot let corporations control and limit what we know about our own country and the rest of the world. 5) Stalin and Hitler were infinitely worse than the modern corporation, but they did manage to control all information and thus their people. 6) Although the tragedies visited upon the world under their rule will hopefully never occur again, we cannot let a different set of tragedies come to pass in our modern age through corporate manipulation of the media.

RHETORICAL QUESTION

A writer who opens with a rhetorical question owes it to the audience to give a final reflection on the opening question by the end of the paper. This doesn't need to be an actual answer to the question (there may not even be such a thing), but the readers will need to be taken past this original question. You could also end with deeper questions; good research often leads to the need for more research. Let your audience know that you aren't finished with your quest for answers, and let them know they shouldn't be done with their own quest, either.

Here is a closing hook for the sample conclusion. It poses even deeper questions—ones that couldn't be answered in the limited number of pages of this research paper.

1) As advertising continues to grow and spread, then, and as consumers continue to grow either deadened or angry at the constant onslaught, something must be done. 2) There must be a call for more legislation against spam, bulk mailing, and telemarketing; similarly, we as consumers must let the corporations themselves know that we want ads to be limited. 3) Though this message could be sent through activism or boycotts, the corporations must be sent a message or they will not change, and this message could be as simple as purchasing goods and services only from corporations whose business methods you support. 4) After all, most corporations aren't trying to annoy us; they simply want to make money and satisfy customers and shareholders. 5) If these corporations are made aware that the populace is tired of advertising, they may willingly change just to keep customers happy. 6) If legislation and activism fail to work, how can we change American advertising? 7) What can we do to make sure future generations can see a blue sky at a park instead of miles of billboards hawking beer, sex, and cologne?

1) Serving the needs of the people should be of paramount importance to every citizen in our mediated world, however, not simply the financial bottom line of corporate America. 2) Corporations used to be manageable and closely monitored by the people and the government. 3) The current corporate dominance of the airwaves, though, undermines our ability to stay well informed, feel a sense of community, and therefore fully participate in our own democratic government. 4) We cannot let corporations control and limit what we

Century

162 CHAPTER 7 Organizing the Essay

know about our own country and the rest of the world. 5) But if we do nothing to stop the mergers and power of the modern media corporations, how much of the truth will they eventually own? 6) Will we one day reach a point where all information is owned and traded like commodities? 7) Or will we simply reach a day where, like the novel 1984, the truth becomes indistinguishable from the lies?

PERSONAL ANECDOTE

If you opened with a personal anecdote, you can also use this same anecdote to close your paper. Follow it through to its conclusion. If the story in your introduction brought up a problem, make sure you present a solution or at least a resolution of some kind (even if it means revealing a deeper problem) in your conclusion. You could even tell an alternative version of the tale where events happened differently, and the hypothetical outcome was better.

Here is the sample intro with the final sentences revised to reflect on the opening anecdote found in the introduction on page 149.

1) When I was still in my junior high government class, I remember we studied freedom of speech. 2) We spent weeks studying the importance of information on our government, and I remember being bored to tears and not understanding how the ability to simply talk and listen actually equaled democracy. 3) Recently, however, I noticed how trivial and repetitive televised news is, and I started to wonder if communication and free speech do indeed have an impact on our lives as the founding fathers seemed to have thought. 4) I realized that in a true democracy, the people must be informed about world events in order to be able to make informed decisions during any democratic election.

1) Serving the needs of the people should be of paramount importance to every citizen in our mediated world, however, not simply the financial bottom line of corporate America. 2) Corporations used to be manageable and closely monitored by the people and the government. 3) The current corporate dominance of the airwaves, though, undermines our ability to stay well informed, feel a sense of community, and therefore fully participate in our own democratic government. 4) We cannot let corporations control and limit what we know about our own country and the rest of the world. 5) When I think back on my apathy toward freedom of speech when I was still in junior high, it makes me wonder if anyone else even cares about the media and free speech. 6) Perhaps the disinterest I felt back then is what has allowed corporations to grow as much as they have. 7) Perhaps if enough of us realize that communication and information are the true cornerstones of a democracy, more people will start to concern themselves with who owns our airwaves.

Additional Tips on Writing the Conclusion

LENGTH

Like the introduction and the body of a paper, there is no set length for a conclusion. Let the requirements of the assignment and your writing situation dictate the length of your conclusion. If you've written a fifteen-page paper, your conclusion may very well be a page or more in length. Similarly, if you have written a shorter paper full of dense facts and data, you may need to summarize these in your concluding paragraph before you sum up your own arguments or revisit your thesis statement.

NEW EVIDENCE AND POINTS

Your conclusion is not the place to introduce new material. If you find that you're using your conclusion to squeeze in new information or one last fact, you haven't really finished writing the body of your paper yet. A conclusion should sum up the main points you have developed in the body of your paper to support your thesis, not make a few more points. Any new material you present in the conclusion will distract your readers and weaken the impact of your paper, so fold all such information into your body paragraphs instead.

VISUAL PAPER STRUCTURE

One way to imagine your paper as a graphic image is to picture a martini glass. At the top is an upside-down pyramid, at the bottom is a smaller pyramid (normal side up), and in the middle is a solid line. This image doesn't represent the size or even the importance of the different sections of your paper—your body contains your arguments and your evidence—but it does show how your audience moves through your paper.

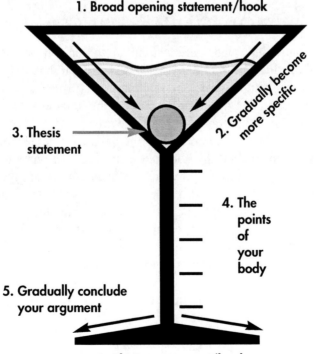

1. Broad opening statement/hook

2. Gradually become more specific

3. Thesis statement

4. The points of your body

5. Gradually conclude your argument

6. Closing statement/hook

164   CHAPTER 7   Organizing the Essay

An introduction is intended to move your audience from the general to the specific (as found in your thesis). Because you need to walk your audience into the topic gradually, you begin with a generic statement or a hook—nothing too specific. As the introduction continues, you slowly close in on your thesis, revealing more and more details to your audience. As the inverted pyramid narrows, it focuses on a sharp point: your final thesis statement.

Next is the body. The body is a column, a straight line of points, one after the other, all in an orderly, organized row. In architecture, a column can support a great deal of weight, and this column of evidence here will support and ultimately prove your thesis.

Finally, you arrive at the conclusion, which is almost the mirror image of the introduction. You start with a reminder of your thesis statement to help readers recall what you've just accomplished. You then walk readers away from your specific topic and thesis, just as you brought them gradually into your paper in your introduction. You end the paper with a broad statement that lets readers "out" of the paper and returns them to the world around them (you may want to bring your readers full circle by reemphasizing the hook in your introduction).

You may even try drawing this shape on a piece of paper before you prepare your outline. You could sketch key ideas and points next to or inside this glass. It's a great way for visual learners to see their outline and a great way for kinesthetic learners to get to interact with the form of their paper. For more help on essay structure, you can also look at our discussion of the Toulmin Method on pages 94–97 in Chapter 5. First designed as a model for dissecting arguments that we read or hear, it also shows an effective way to structure our own arguments and argumentative papers.

RHETORICAL MODES OF WRITING

The organization that we have been talking about up to this point covers the chronological presentation of the different sections in essays and research papers. Writing also has different types of organization of information relating to different purposes for writing. We refer to the categories that differ by purpose as the "modes of writing." Rhetorical modes are patterns of organization aimed at achieving a particular effect in the reader. The following four are usually categorized as the basic modes: description (describing a person, place, or event so that the audience can "see" it), narration (telling a non-fiction or fiction story), exposition (providing information), and argument/persuasion (asserting and supporting an opinion). These modes can be further subdivided into the following nine rhetorical modes, which are the ones generally taught in English classes: **exemplification, extended definition, comparison/contrast, description, narration, cause/effect, classification/division, process analysis,** and **argument.** You may be asked to read or write essays that exemplify individual modes, but most writing relies on creating effective combinations of different modes. Thus, the content of your essays and research papers must also be organized with an eye toward your overall purpose and the purposes of different sections.

Exemplification is "the giving of an example." The purpose of an exemplification is to give an extended example or a series of shorter examples to illustrate a main idea, which can be an abstraction. An essay in this mode typically draws on the modes of *extended definition* and *comparison/contrast*.

Extended definition consists of defining a subject at length (rather than briefly, like a dictionary). An essay in this mode typically starts with a term to be defined, may follow with a dictionary definition, and then elaborates. An essay in this mode typically draws on the modes of *exemplification* and *comparison/contrast*.

Comparison/contrast essays show how two or more subjects are alike and/or different. This mode can be applied to any number of subjects, including people, organizations, values, and viewpoints. The writer can take different points and alternate between comparing and contrasting the subjects on these points, or have one section listing all the similarities and another that lists all the differences. An essay in this mode typically draws on the modes of *exemplification* and *description*.

Description is also sometimes called "illustration," and one definition of "illustrate" is "to describe with pictures." A description essay can take a person or object to describe in great detail, including details that involve other senses besides sight. Most writers choose specific organizational plans. An essay that describes how a person looks could start from the feet and work up, or start at the head and work down, for instance (direction is less important than consistency).

Narration provides the details of an event. Like a description, it should have an organizational plan, and chronological order is logical and the most common. It is like a list of events written in paragraph form. Newspaper articles are often narrations, and narration is often used in *cause/effect* essays.

Cause/effect essays start with a subject, such as an event, and then show the causes (reasons) for it or the effects (results) of it. These could involve a simple single cause, a single effect relationship, or an entire chain of events leading up to a particular outcome or even series of outcomes. Cause and effect essays often employ *narration*.

Classification/division essays divide a whole into parts or sort related items into categories. Classification places items into different groups according to specific criteria, and division breaks one item into parts and then examines the parts in relationship to the whole. This is especially helpful with broad and complicated subjects because they make the subjects more manageable. An essay in this mode typically draws on the modes of *exemplification* and *description*.

Process analysis explores how to do something or how something works. (This could cover the range from how to change a light bulb to how Arctic ice melts.) An essay in this mode typically draws on the modes of *exemplification* and *description*.

Argumentation is also called "persuasion" because arguments are often about persuading people to believe something or to take some action. The writer

166   CHAPTER 7   Organizing the Essay

offers a debatable opinion (not a simple fact) and then provides support through evidence and logic. The best argumentative essays also provide opposing viewpoints to explain and rebut. Argumentation papers typically draw on most, even all, of the other modes. Important terms must be defined, examples should be given, cause and effect relationships may need to be explained, and so on.

Sometimes essays can use one pattern of organization to support a larger purpose. The following table shows the main rhetorical modes. Any one of them can be the main point of a piece of writing, but, with an argumentative paper, all the other modes are likely to be drawn upon in service of making the main point that you are trying to prove clear to your audience. Most college research papers are supposed to be argumentative.

Exemplification	Extended Definition	Description
Narration	**Argumentation**	Process Analysis
Comparison/ Contrast	Classification/ Division	Cause/Effect

The table shows the centrality of argument in a research paper, but it does not indicate the proportions of other modes represented in the paper. The proportions will be determined by need. In different types of writing, this can also be dictated by situation.

Suppose you decide that you want to write a letter to the editor about some issue you feel strongly about. Your main point is to support an argument so that you can persuade your audience—other people in your community—to see the issue the way you do or even to act upon it. You sit down and type furiously, and in just half an hour you have come up with a terrific letter. You have named the problem, given examples, talked about the effects that will occur if something isn't done, and identified and rebutted arguments made by people on the other side of the issue. You proofread the letter, make some organizational changes, make your opening sentence a stronger "hook" to grab people's attention, and then you go to the paper's website and look at the guidelines for submitting letters to the opinion page. They tell you that letters must be 250 words or fewer. You do a quick word count. You have 598!

In this situation, you have to make some hard choices about your own writing. You have to get rid of a lot of sentences you really love. What do you get rid of, and what do you keep? You realize that you need to focus on the argument, and you start to think about what examples, definitions, and other sections of your letter you can cut out without ruining your points. You realize that lots of examples and information in your paper are common knowledge to people who have been following the issue that you are addressing, and that helps you. You finally get your letter down to exactly 250 words. As far as the modes of writing are concerned, the ratio looks like what you see in the following pie chart:

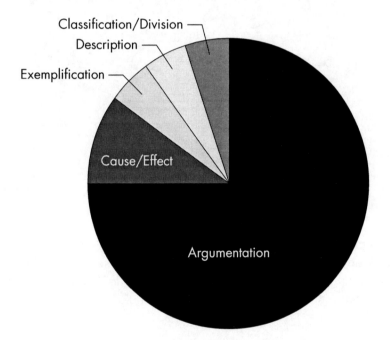

You submit your letter and contact information and mention that you are a student at the local college. A couple of days later, you are contacted by the editor of the opinion page. She liked your letter, and she wants to know if you would consider writing an extended version for the Community Voices section, which is used to give people in the community the chance to have editorial-length pieces published. She likes the idea of presenting a college student's perspective on the subject. She wants to know if you can expand your letter to between 750 and 1,000 words. You agree, and you go back to your original letter (it's a good thing you saved the original version before you started revising it to a much shorter length). Now you need to think of what to add to make your arguments stronger and your letter more compelling. After all, you can't convince anyone unless they are willing to read your opinion piece all the way through.

168   CHAPTER 7   Organizing the Essay

You decide that you can begin with a couple of examples that are really vivid, and in your conclusion you warn about what could be coming in the future if there aren't any changes. If you were to create a pie chart that showed the modes of writing you employed in this longer letter, it might look like the following:

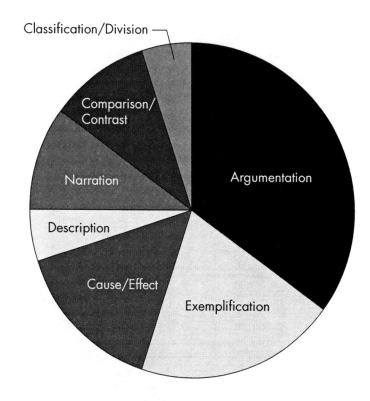

When you write essays and research papers for classes, the proportions of the modes that you draw on should shift with your needs. Keep these modes in mind along with your audience and purpose as you write to make sure that you don't spend too much time in some modes and too little in others.

►◄ SHERMAN ALEXIE ►◄

What You Pawn I Will Redeem

Noon

One day you have a home and the next you don't, but I'm not going to tell you my particular reasons for being homeless, because it's my secret story, and Indians have to work hard to keep secrets from hungry white folks

I'm a Spokane Indian boy, an Interior Salish, and my people have lived within a one-hundred-mile radius of Spokane, Washington, for at least ten thousand years. I grew up in Spokane, moved to Seattle twenty-three years ago for college, flunked out within two semesters, worked various blue- and bluer-collar jobs for many years, married two or three times, fathered two or three kids, and then went crazy. Of course, "crazy" is not the official definition of my mental problem, but I don't think "asocial disorder" fits it, either, because that makes me sound like I'm a serial killer or something. I've never hurt another human being, or at least not physically. I've broken a few hearts in my time, but we've all done that, so I'm nothing special in that regard. I'm a boring heartbreaker, at that, because I've never abandoned one woman for another. I never dated or married more than one woman at a time. I didn't break hearts into pieces overnight. I broke them slowly and carefully. And I didn't set any land-speed records running out the door. Piece by piece, I disappeared. And I've been disappearing ever since. But I'm not going to tell you any more about my brain or my soul.

I've been homeless for six years. If there's such a thing as being an effective homeless man, I suppose I'm effective. Being homeless is probably the only thing I've ever been good at. I know where to get the best free food. I've made friends with restaurant and convenience-store managers who let me use their bathrooms. And I don't mean the public bathrooms, either. I mean the employees' bathrooms, the clean ones hidden in the back of the kitchen or the pantry or the cooler. I know it sounds strange to be proud of, but it means a lot to me, being trustworthy enough to piss in somebody else's clean bathroom. Maybe you don't understand the value of a clean bathroom, but I do.

Probably none of this interests you. I probably don't interest you much. Homeless Indians are everywhere in Seattle. We're common and boring, and you walk right on by us, with maybe a look of anger or disgust or even sadness at the terrible fate of the noble savage. But we have dreams and families. I'm friends with a homeless Plains Indian man whose son is the editor of a big-time newspaper back east. That's his story, but we Indians are great storytellers and liars and mythmakers, so maybe that Plains Indian hobo is a plain old everyday Indian. I'm kind of suspicious of him, because he describes himself only as Plains Indian, a generic term, and not by a specific tribe. When I asked him why he wouldn't tell me exactly what he is, he said, "Do any of us know exactly what we are?" Yeah, great, a philosophizing Indian. "Hey," I said, "you got to have a home to be that homely." He laughed and flipped me the eagle and walked away. But you probably want to know more about the story I'm really trying to tell you.

I wander the streets with a regular crew, my teammates, my defenders, and my posse. It's Rose of Sharon,[1] Junior, and me. We matter to one another if we don't matter to anybody else. Rose of Sharon is a big woman, about seven feet tall if you're measuring overall effect, and about five feet tall if you're talking about the physical. She's a Yakama Indian of the Wishram variety. Junior is a Colville, but there are about 199 tribes that make up the Colville, so he could be anything. He's good-looking, though, like he just stepped out of some "Don't Litter the Earth" public-service advertisement. He's got those great big cheekbones that are like planets, you know, with little moons orbiting around them. He gets me jealous, jealous, and jealous. If you put Junior and me next to each other, he's the Before Columbus Arrived Indian and I'm the After Columbus Arrived Indian. I am living proof of the horrible damage that colonialism has done to us Skins. But I'm not going to let you know how scared I sometimes get of history and its ways. I'm a strong man, and I know that silence is the best way of dealing with white folks.

This whole story started at lunchtime, when Rose of Sharon, Junior, and I were panning the handle down at Pike Place Market. After about two hours of negotiating, we earned five dollars, good enough for a bottle of fortified courage from the most beautiful 7-Eleven in the world. So we headed over that way, feeling like warrior drunks, and we walked past this pawnshop I'd never noticed before. And that was strange, because we Indians have built-in pawnshop radar. But the strangest thing was the old powwow-dance regalia I saw hanging in the window.

"That's my grandmother's regalia," I said to Rose of Sharon and Junior.

"How do you know for sure?" Junior asked.

I didn't know for sure, because I hadn't seen that regalia in person ever. I'd seen only photographs of my grandmother dancing in it. And that was before somebody stole it from her fifty years ago. But it sure looked like my memory of it, and it had all the same colors of feathers and beads that my family always sewed into their powwow regalia.

"There's only one way to know for sure," I said.

So Rose of Sharon, Junior, and I walked into the pawnshop and greeted the old white man working behind the counter.

"How can I help you?" he asked.

"That's my grandmother's powwow regalia in your window," I said. "Somebody stole it from her fifty years ago, and my family has been looking for it ever since."

The pawnbroker looked at me like I was a liar. I understood. Pawnshops are filled with liars.

"I'm not lying," I said. "Ask my friends here. They'll tell you."

"He's the most honest Indian I know," Rose of Sharon said.

"All right, honest Indian," the pawnbroker said. "I'll give you the benefit of the doubt. Can you prove it's your grandmother's regalia?"

Because they don't want to be perfect, because only God is perfect, Indian people sew flaws into their powwow regalia. My family always sewed one yellow bead somewhere on their regalia. But we always hid it where you had to search hard to find it.

---

1. An allusion to a character of that name in John Steinbeck's *The Grapes of Wrath* (1939).

"If it really is my grandmother's," I said, "there will be one yellow bead hidden somewhere on it."

"All right, then," the pawnbroker said. "Let's take a look."

He pulled the regalia out of the window, laid it down on his glass counter, and we searched for that yellow bead and found it hidden beneath the armpit.

"There it is," the pawnbroker said. He didn't sound surprised. "You were right. This is your grandmother's regalia."

"It's been missing for fifty years," Junior said.

"Hey, Junior," I said. "It's my family's story. Let me tell it."

"All right," he said. "I apologize. You go ahead."

"It's been missing for fifty years," I said.

"That's his family's sad story," Rose of Sharon said. "Are you going to give it back to him?"

"That would be the right thing to do," the pawnbroker said. "But I can't afford to do the right thing. I paid a thousand dollars for this. I can't give away a thousand dollars."

"We could go to the cops and tell them it was stolen," Rose of Sharon said.

"Hey," I said to her, "don't go threatening people."

The pawnbroker sighed. He was thinking hard about the possibilities.

"Well, I suppose you could go to the cops," he said. "But I don't think they'd believe a word you said."

He sounded sad about that. Like he was sorry for taking advantage of our disadvantages.

"What's your name?" the pawnbroker asked me.

"Jackson," I said.

"Is that first or last?" he asked

"Both."

"Are you serious?"

"Yes, it's true. My mother and father named me Jackson Jackson. My family nickname is Jackson Squared. My family is funny."

"All right, Jackson Jackson," the pawnbroker said. "You wouldn't happen to have a thousand dollars, would you?"

"We've got five dollars total," I said.

"That's too bad," he said and thought hard about the possibilities. "I'd sell it to you for a thousand dollars if you had it. Heck, to make it fair, I'd sell it to you for nine hundred and ninety-nine dollars. I'd lose a dollar. It would be the moral thing to do in this case. To lose a dollar would be the right thing."

"We've got five dollars total," I said again.

"That's too bad," he said again and thought harder about the possibilities. "How about this? I'll give you twenty-four hours to come up with nine hundred and ninety-nine dollars. You come back here at lunchtime tomorrow with the money, and I'll sell it back to you. How does that sound?"

"It sounds good," I said.

"All right, then," he said. "We have a deal. And I'll get you started. Here's twenty bucks to get you started."

He opened up his wallet and pulled out a crisp twenty-dollar bill and gave it to me. Rose of Sharon, Junior, and I walked out into the daylight to search for nine hundred and seventy-four more dollars.

1:00 P.M.

Rose of Sharon, Junior, and I carried our twenty-dollar bill and our five dollars in loose change over to the 7-Eleven and spent it to buy three bottles of imagination. We needed to figure out how to raise all that money in one day. Thinking hard, we huddled in an alley beneath the Alaska Way Viaduct and finished off those bottles one, two, and three.

2:00 P.M.

Rose of Sharon was gone when I woke. I heard later that she had hitchhiked back to Toppenish and was living with her sister on the reservation.

Junior was passed out beside me, covered in his own vomit, or maybe somebody else's vomit, and my head hurt from thinking, so I left him alone and walked down to the water. I loved the smell of ocean water. Salt always smells like memory.

When I got to the wharf, I ran into three Aleut cousins, who sat on a wooden bench and stared out at the bay and cried. Most of the homeless Indians in Seattle come from Alaska. One by one, each of them hopped a big working boat in Anchorage or Barrow or Juneau, fished his way south to Seattle, jumped off the boat with a pocketful of cash to party hard at one of the highly sacred and traditional Indian bars, went broke and broker, and has been trying to find his way back to the boat and the frozen north ever since.

These Aleuts smelled like salmon, I thought, and they told me they were going to sit on that wooden bench until their boat came back.

"How long has your boat been gone?" I asked.

"Eleven years," the elder Aleut said.

I cried with them for a while.

"Hey," I said. "Do you guys have any money I can borrow?"

They didn't.

3:00 P.M.

I walked back to Junior. He was still passed out. I put my face down near his mouth to make sure he was breathing. He was alive, so I dug around in his blue-jean pockets and found half a cigarette. I smoked it all the way down and thought about my grandmother.

Her name was Agnes, and she died of breast cancer when I was fourteen. My father thought Agnes caught her tumors from the uranium mine on the reservation. But my mother said the disease started when Agnes was walking back from the powwow one night and got run over by a motorcycle. She broke three ribs, and my mother said those ribs never healed right, and tumors always take over when you don't heal right.

Sitting beside Junior, smelling the smoke and salt and vomit, I wondered if my grandmother's cancer had started when somebody stole her powwow regalia. Maybe the cancer started in her broken heart and then leaked out into her breasts. I know it's crazy, but I wondered if I could bring my grandmother back to life if I bought back her regalia.

I needed money, big money, so I left Junior and walked over to the Real Change office.

4:00 P.M.

"Real Change is a multifaceted organization that publishes a newspaper, supports cultural projects that empower the poor and homeless, and mobilizes the public around poverty issues. Real Change's mission is to organize, educate, and build alliances to create solutions to homelessness and poverty. They exist to provide a voice to poor people in our community."

I memorized Real Change's mission statement because I sometimes sell the newspaper on the streets. But you have to stay sober to sell it, and I'm not always good at staying sober. Anybody can sell the newspaper. You buy each copy for thirty cents and sell it for a dollar and keep the net profit.

"I need one thousand four hundred and thirty papers," I said to the Big Boss.

"That's a strange number," he said. "And that's a lot of papers."

"I need them."

The Big Boss pulled out the calculator and did the math. "It will cost you four hundred and twenty-nine dollars for that many," he said.

"If I had that kind of money, I wouldn't need to sell the papers."

"What's going on, Jackson-to-the-Second-Power?" he asked. He is the only one who calls me that. He is a funny and kind man.

I told him about my grandmother's powwow regalia and how much money I needed to buy it back.

"We should call the police," he said.

"I don't want to do that," I said. "It's a quest now. I need to win it back by myself."

"I understand," he said. "And to be honest, I'd give you the papers to sell if I thought it would work. But the record for most papers sold in a day by one vendor is only three hundred and two."

"That would net me about two hundred bucks," I said.

The Big Boss used his calculator. "Two hundred and eleven dollars and forty cents," he said.

"That's not enough," I said.

"The most money anybody has made in one day is five hundred and twenty-five. And that's because somebody gave Old Blue five hundred-dollar bills for some dang reason. The average daily net is about thirty dollars."

"This isn't going to work."

"No."

"Can you lend me some money?"

"I can't do that," he said. "If I lend you money, I have to lend money to everybody."

"What can you do?"

"I'll give you fifty papers for free. But don't tell anybody I did it."

"O.K.," I said.

He gathered up the newspapers and handed them to me. I held them to my chest. He hugged me. I carried the newspapers back toward the water.

5:00 P.M.

Back on the wharf, I stood near the Bainbridge Island Terminal and tried to sell papers to business commuters walking onto the ferry

I sold five in one hour, dumped the other forty-five into a garbage can, and walked into the McDonald's, ordered four cheeseburgers for a dollar each, and slowly ate them.

After eating, I walked outside and vomited on the sidewalk. I hated to lose my food so soon after eating it. As an alcoholic Indian with a busted stomach, I always hope I can keep enough food in my stomach to stay alive.

6:00 P.M.

With one dollar in my pocket, I walked back to Junior. He was still passed out, so I put my ear to his chest and listened for his heartbeat. He was alive, so I took off his shoes and socks and found one dollar in his left sock and fifty cents in his right sock. With two dollars and fifty cents in my hand, I sat beside Junior and thought about my grandmother and her stories.

When I was sixteen, my grandmother told me a story about World War II. She was a nurse at a military hospital in Sydney, Australia. Over the course of two years, she comforted and healed U.S. and Australian soldiers.

One day, she tended to a wounded Maori soldier. He was very dark-skinned. His hair was black and curly, and his eyes were black and warm. His face was covered with bright tattoos.

"Are you Maori?" he asked my grandmother.

"No," she said. "I'm Spokane Indian. From the United States."

"Ah, yes," he said. "I have heard of your tribes. But you are the first American Indian I have ever met."

"There's a lot of Indian soldiers fighting for the United States," she said. "I have a brother still fighting in Germany, and I lost another brother on Okinawa."

"I am sorry," he said. "I was on Okinawa as well. It was terrible." He had lost his legs to an artillery attack.

"I am sorry about your legs," my grandmother said.

"It's funny, isn't it?" he asked.

"What's funny?"

"How we brown people are killing other brown people so white people will remain free."

"I hadn't thought of it that way."

"Well, sometimes I think of it that way. And other times, I think of it the way they want me to think of it. I get confused."

She fed him morphine.

"Do you believe in Heaven?" he asked.

"Which heaven?" she asked.

"I'm talking about the heaven where my legs are waiting for me."

They laughed.

"Of course," he said, "my legs will probably run away from me when I get to heaven. And how will I ever catch them?"

"You have to get your arms strong," my grandmother said. "So you can run on your hands."

They laughed again.

Sitting beside Junior, I laughed with the memory of my grandmother's story. I put my hand close to Junior's mouth to make sure he was still breathing. Yes, Junior was alive, so I took his two dollars and fifty cents and walked to the Korean grocery store over in Pioneer Square.

7:00 P.M.

In the Korean grocery store, I bought a fifty-cent cigar and two scratch lottery tickets for a dollar each. The maximum cash prize was five hundred dollars a ticket. If I won both, I would have enough money to buy back the regalia.

I loved Kay, the young Korean woman who worked the register. She was the daughter of the owners and sang all day.

"I love you," I said when I handed her the money.

"You always say you love me," she said.

"That's because I will always love you."

"You are a sentimental fool."

"I'm a romantic old man."

"Too old for me."

"I know I'm too old for you, but I can dream."

"Okay," she said. "I agree to be a part of your dreams, but I will only hold your hand in your dreams. No kissing and no sex. Not even in your dreams."

"Okay," I said. "No sex. Just romance."

"Good-bye, Jackson Jackson, my love, I will see you soon."

I left the store, walked over to Occidental Park, sat on a bench, and smoked my cigar all the way down.

Ten minutes after I finished the cigar, I scratched my first lottery ticket and won nothing. So I could win only five hundred dollars now, and that would be just half of what I needed.

Ten minutes later, I scratched my other lottery ticket and won a free ticket, a small consolation and one more chance to win money.

I walked back to Kay.

"Jackson Jackson," she said. "Have you come back to claim my heart?"

"I won a free ticket," I said.

"Just like a man," she said. "You love money and power more than you love me."

"It's true," I said. "And I'm sorry it's true."

She gave me another scratch ticket, and I carried it outside. I liked to scratch my tickets in private. Hopeful and sad, I scratched that third ticket and won real money. I carried it back inside to Kay.

"I won a hundred dollars," I said.

She examined the ticket and laughed. "That's a fortune," she said and counted out five twenties. Our fingertips touched as she handed me the money. I felt electric and constant.

"Thank you," I said and gave her one of the bills.

"I can't take that," she said. "It's your money."

"No, it's tribal. It's an Indian thing. When you win, you're supposed to share with your family."

"I'm not your family."

"Yes, you are."

She smiled. She kept the money. With eighty dollars in my pocket, I said good-bye to my dear Kay and walked out into the cold night air.

8:00 P.M.

I wanted to share the good news with Junior. I walked back to him, but he was gone. I later heard he had hitchhiked down to Portland, Oregon, and died of exposure in an alley behind the Hilton Hotel.

9:00 P.M.

Lonely for Indians, I carried my eighty dollars over to Big Heart's in South Downtown. Big Heart's is an all-Indian bar. Nobody knows how or why Indians migrate to one bar and turn it into an official Indian bar. But Big Heart's has been an Indian bar for twenty-three years. It used to be way up on Aurora Avenue, but a crazy Lummi Indian burned that one down, and the owners moved to the new location, a few blocks south of Safeco Field.

I walked inside Big Heart's and counted fifteen Indians, eight men and seven women. I didn't know any of them, but Indians like to belong, so we all pretended to be cousins.

"How much for whiskey shots?" I asked the bartender, a fat white guy.

"You want the bad stuff or the badder stuff?"

"As bad as you got."

"One dollar a shot."

I laid my eighty dollars on the bar top.

"All right," I said. "Me and all my cousins here are going to be drinking eighty shots. How many is that apiece?"

"Counting you," a woman shouted from behind me, "that's five shots for everybody."

I turned to look at her. She was a chubby and pale Indian sitting with a tall and skinny Indian man.

"All right, math genius," I said to her and then shouted for the whole bar to hear. "Five drinks for everybody!"

All of the other Indians rushed the bar, but I sat with the mathematician and her skinny friend. We took our time with our whiskey shots.

"What's your tribe?" I asked them.

"I'm Duwamish," she said. "And he's Crow."

"You're a long way from Montana," I said to him.

"I'm Crow," he said. "I flew here."

"What's your name?" I asked them.

"I'm Irene Muse," she said. "And this is Honey Boy."

She shook my hand hard, but he offered his hand like I was supposed to kiss it. So I kissed it. He giggled and blushed as well as a dark-skinned Crow can blush.

"You're one of them two-spirits, aren't you?" I asked him.

"I love women," he said. "And I love men."

"Sometimes both at the same time," Irene said.

We laughed.

"Man," I said to Honey Boy. "So you must have about eight or nine spirits going on inside of you, enit?"

"Sweetie," he said, "I'll be whatever you want me to be."

"Oh, no," Irene said. "Honey Boy is falling in love."

"It has nothing to do with love," he said.

We laughed.

"Wow," I said. "I'm flattered, Honey Boy, but I don't play on your team."

"Never say never," he said.

"You better be careful," Irene said. "Honey Boy knows all sorts of magic. He always makes straight boys fall for him."

"Honey Boy," I said, "you can try to seduce me. And Irene, you can try with him. But my heart belongs to a woman named Kay."

"Is your Kay a virgin?" Honey Boy asked.

We laughed.

We drank our whiskey shots until they were gone. But the other Indians bought me more whiskey shots because I'd been so generous with my money. Honey Boy pulled out his credit card, and I drank and sailed on that plastic boat.

After a dozen shots, I asked Irene to dance. And she refused. But Honey Boy shuffled over to the jukebox, dropped in a quarter, and selected Willie Nelson's "Help Me Make It Through the Night." As Irene and I sat at the table and laughed and drank more whiskey, Honey Boy danced a slow circle around us and sang along with Willie.

"Are you serenading me?" I asked him.

He kept singing and dancing.

"Are you serenading me?" I asked him again.

"He's going to put a spell on you," Irene said.

I leaned over the table, spilling a few drinks, and kissed Irene hard. She kissed me back.

10:00 P.M.

Irene pushed me into the women's bathroom, into a stall, shut the door behind us, and shoved her hand down my pants. She was short, so I had to lean over to kiss her. I grabbed and squeezed her everywhere I could reach, and she was wonderfully fat, and every part of her body felt like a large, warm, and soft breast.

MIDNIGHT

Nearly blind with alcohol, I stood alone at the bar and swore I'd been standing in the bathroom with Irene only a minute ago.

"One more shot!" I yelled at the bartender.

"You've got no more money!" he yelled.

"Somebody buy me a drink!" I shouted.

"They've got no more money!"

"Where's Irene and Honey Boy?"

"Long gone!"

2:00 A.M.

"Closing time!" the bartender shouted at the three or four Indians still drinking hard after a long hard day of drinking. Indian alcoholics are either sprinters or marathon runners.

"Where's Irene and Honey Bear?" I asked.

"They've been gone for hours," the bartender said.

"Where'd they go?"

"I told you a hundred times, I don't know."

"What am I supposed to do?"

"It's closing time. I don't care where you go, but you're not staying here."

"You are an ungrateful bastard. I've been good to you."

"You don't leave right now, I'm going to kick your ass."

"Come on, I know how to fight."

He came for me. I don't remember what happened after that.

4:00 A.M.

I emerged from the blackness and discovered myself walking behind a big ware-house. I didn't know where I was. My face hurt. I touched my nose and decided it might be broken. Exhausted and cold, I pulled a plastic tarp from a truck bed, wrapped it around me like a faithful lover, and fell asleep in the dirt.

6:00 A.M.

Somebody kicked me in the ribs. I opened my eyes and looked up at a white cop.

"Jackson," said the cop. "Is that you?"

"Officer Williams," I said. He was a good cop with a sweet tooth. He'd given me hundreds of candy bars over the years. I wonder if he knew I was diabetic.

"What the hell are you doing here?" he asked.

"I was cold and sleepy," I said. "So I laid down."

"You dumb-ass, you passed out on the railroad tracks."

I sat up and looked around. I was lying on the railroad tracks. Dockworkers stared at me. I should have been a railroad-track pizza, a double Indian pepperoni with extra cheese. Sick and scared, I leaned over and puked whiskey.

"What the hell's wrong with you?" Officer Williams asked. "You've never been this stupid."

"It's my grandmother," I said. "She died."

"I'm sorry, man. When did she die?"

"1972."

"And you're killing yourself now?"

"I've been killing myself ever since she died."

He shook his head. He was sad for me. Like I said, he was a good cop.

"And somebody beat the hell out of you," he said. "You remember who?"

"Mr. Grief and I went a few rounds."

"It looks like Mr. Grief knocked you out."

"Mr. Grief always wins."

"Come on," he said, "let's get you out of here."

He helped me stand and led me over to his squad car. He put me in the back. "You throw up in there," he said, "and you're cleaning it up."

"That's fair," I said.

He walked around the car and sat in the driver's seat. "I'm taking you over to detox," he said.

"No, man, that place is awful," I said. "It's full of drunk Indians."

We laughed. He drove away from the docks.

"I don't know how you guys do it," he said.

"What guys?" I asked.

"You Indians. How the hell do you laugh so much? I just picked your ass off the railroad tracks, and you're making jokes. Why the hell do you do that?"

"The two funniest tribes I've ever been around are Indians and Jews, so I guess that says something about the inherent humor of genocide."

We laughed.

"Listen to you, Jackson. You're so smart. Why the hell are you on the streets?"

"Give me a thousand dollars, and I'll tell you."

"You bet I'd give you a thousand dollars if I knew you'd straighten up your life."

He meant it. He was the second-best cop I'd ever known.

"You're a good cop," I said.

"Come on, Jackson," he said. "Don't blow smoke up my ass."

"No, really, you remind me of my grandfather."

"Yeah, that's what you Indians always tell me."

"No, man, my grandfather was a tribal cop. He was a good cop. He never arrested people. He took care of them. Just like you."

"I've arrested hundreds of scumbags, Jackson. And I've shot a couple in the ass."

"It don't matter. You're not a killer."

"I didn't kill them. I killed their asses. I'm an ass-killer."

We drove through downtown. The missions and shelters had already released their overnighters. Sleepy homeless men and women stood on corners and stared up at the gray sky. It was the morning after the night of the living dead.

"Do you ever get scared?" I asked Officer Williams.

"What do you mean?"

"I mean, being a cop, is it scary?"

He thought about that for a while. He contemplated it. I liked that about him.

"I guess I try not to think too much about being afraid," he said. "If you think about fear, then you'll be afraid. The job is boring most of the time. Just driving and looking into dark corners, you know, and seeing nothing. But then things get heavy. You're chasing somebody or fighting them or walking around a dark house and you just know some crazy guy is hiding around a corner, and hell yes, it's scary."

"My grandfather was killed in the line of duty," I said.

"I'm sorry. How'd it happen?"

I knew he'd listen closely to my story.

"He worked on the reservation. Everybody knew everybody. It was safe. We aren't like those crazy Sioux or Apache or any of those other warrior tribes. There's only been three murders on my reservation in the last hundred years."

"That is safe."

"Yeah, we Spokane, we're passive, you know? We're mean with words. And we'll cuss out anybody. But we don't shoot people. Or stab them. Not much, anyway."

"So what happened to your grandfather?"

"This man and his girlfriend were fighting down by Little Falls."

"Domestic dispute. Those are the worst."

"Yeah, but this guy was my grandfather's brother. My great-uncle."

"Oh, no."

"Yeah, it was awful. My grandfather just strolled into the house. He'd been there a thousand times. And his brother and his girlfriend were all drunk and beating on each other. And my grandfather stepped between them just like he'd done a hundred times before. And the girlfriend tripped or something. She fell down and hit her head and started crying. And my grandfather knelt down beside her to make sure she was all right. And for some reason, my great-uncle reached down, pulled my grandfather's pistol out of the holster, and shot him in the head."

"That's terrible. I'm sorry."

"Yeah, my great-uncle could never figure out why he did it. He went to prison forever, you know, and he always wrote these long letters. Like fifty pages of tiny little handwriting. And he was always trying to figure out why he did it. He'd write and write and write and try to figure it out. He never did. It's a great big mystery."

"Do you remember your grandfather?"

"A little bit. I remember the funeral. My grandmother wouldn't let them bury him. My father had to drag her away from the grave."

"I don't know what to say."

"I don't, either."

We stopped in front of the detox center.

"We're here," Officer Williams said.

"I can't go in there," I said.

"You have to."

"Please, no. They'll keep me for twenty-four hours. And then it will be too late."

"Too late for what?"

I told him about my grandmother's regalia and the deadline for buying it back.

"If it was stolen," he said, "then you need to file reports. I'll investigate it myself. If that thing is really your grandmother's, I'll get it back for you. Legally."

"No," I said. "That's not fair. The pawnbroker didn't know it was stolen. And besides, I'm on a mission here. I want to be a hero, you know? I want to win it back like a knight."

"That's romantic crap."

"It might be. But I care about it. It's been a long time since I really cared about something."

Officer Williams turned around in his seat and stared at me. He studied me.

"I'll give you some money," he said. "I don't have much. Only thirty bucks. I'm short until payday. And it's not enough to get back the regalia. But it's something."

"I'll take it," I said.

"I'm giving it to you because I believe in what you believe. I'm hoping, and I don't know why I'm hoping it, but I hope you can turn thirty bucks into a thousand somehow."

"I believe in magic."

"I believe you'll take my money and get drunk on it."

"Then why are you giving it to me?"

"There ain't no such thing as an atheist cop."

"Sure there is."

"Yeah, well, I'm not an atheist cop."

He let me out of the car, handed me two fives and a twenty, and shook my hand. "Take care of yourself, Jackson," he said. "Stay off the railroad tracks."

"I'll try," I said.

He drove away. Carrying my money, I headed back toward the water.

8:00 A.M.

On the wharf, those three Aleut men still waited on the wooden bench.

"Have you seen your ship?" I asked.

"Seen a lot of ships," the elder Aleut said. "But not our ship."

I sat on the bench with them. We sat in silence for a long time. I wondered whether we would fossilize if we sat there long enough.

I thought about my grandmother. I'd never seen her dance in her regalia. More than anything, I wished I'd seen her dance at a powwow.

"Do you guys know any songs?" I asked the Aleuts.

"I know all of Hank Williams," the elder Aleut said.

"How about Indian songs?"

"Hank Williams is Indian."

"How about sacred songs?"

"Hank Williams is sacred."

"I'm talking about ceremonial songs, you know, religious ones. The songs you sing back home when you're wishing and hoping."

"What are you wishing and hoping for?"

"I'm wishing my grandmother was still alive."

"Every song I know is about that."

"Well, sing me as many as you can."

The Aleuts sang their strange and beautiful songs. I listened. They sang about my grandmother and their grandmothers. They were lonely for the cold and snow. I was lonely for everybody.

10:00 A.M.

After the Aleuts finished their last song, we sat in silence. Indians are good at silence.

"Was that the last song?" I asked.

"We sang all the ones we could," the elder Aleut said. "All the others are just for our people."

I understood. We Indians have to keep our secrets. And these Aleuts were so secretive that they didn't refer to themselves as Indians.

"Are you guys hungry?" I asked.

They looked at one another and communicated without talking.

"We could eat," the elder Aleut said.

11:00 A.M.

The Aleuts and I walked over to Mother's Kitchen, a greasy diner in the International District. I knew they served homeless Indians who'd lucked in to money.

"Four for breakfast?" the waitress asked when we stepped inside.

"Yes, we're very hungry," the elder Aleut said.

She sat us in a booth near the kitchen. I could smell the food cooking. My stomach growled.

"You guys want separate checks?" the waitress asked.

"No, I'm paying for it," I said.

"Aren't you the generous one," she said.

"Don't do that," I said.

"Do what?" she asked.

"Don't ask me rhetorical questions. They scare me."

She looked puzzled, and then she laughed.

"Okay, Professor," she said. "I'll only ask you real questions from now on."

"Thank you."

"What do you guys want to eat?"

"That's the best question anybody can ask anybody," I said.

"How much money you got?" she asked.

"Another good question," I said. "I've got twenty-five dollars I can spend. Bring us all the breakfast you can, plus your tip."

She knew the math.

"All right, that's four specials and four coffees and fifteen percent for me."

The Aleuts and I waited in silence. Soon enough, the waitress returned and poured us four coffees, and we sipped at them until she returned again with four plates of food. Eggs, bacon, toast, hash-brown potatoes. It's amazing how much food you can buy for so little money.

Grateful, we feasted.

NOON

I said farewell to the Aleuts and walked toward the pawnshop. I later heard the Aleuts had waded into the saltwater near Dock 47 and disappeared. Some Indians said the Aleuts walked on the water and headed north. Other Indians saw the Aleuts drown. I don't know what happened to them.

I looked for the pawnshop and couldn't find it. I swear it wasn't located in the place where it had been before. I walked twenty or thirty blocks looking for the pawnshop, turned corners and bisected intersections, looked up its name in the phone books, and asked people walking past me if they'd ever heard of it. But that pawnshop seemed to have sailed away from me like a ghost ship. I wanted to cry. Right when I'd given up, when I turned one last corner and thought I might die if I didn't find that pawnshop, there it was, located in a space I swore it hadn't been filling up a few minutes before.

I walked inside and greeted the pawnbroker, who looked a little younger than he had before.

"It's you," he said.

"Yes, it's me," I said.

"Jackson Jackson."

"That is my name."

"Where are your friends?"

"They went traveling. But it's okay. Indians are everywhere."

"Do you have my money?"

"How much do you need again?" I asked and hoped the price had changed.

"Nine hundred and ninety-nine dollars."

It was still the same price. Of course it was the same price. Why would it change?

"I don't have that," I said.

"What do you have?"

"Five dollars."

I set the crumpled Lincoln on the countertop. The pawnbroker studied it.

"Is that the same five dollars from yesterday?"

"No, it's different."

He thought about the possibilities.

"Did you work hard for this money?" he asked.

"Yes," I said.

He closed his eyes and thought harder about the possibilities. Then he stepped into his back room and returned with my grandmother's regalia.

"Take it," he said and held it out to me.

"I don't have the money."

"I don't want your money."

"But I wanted to win it."

"You did win it. Now, take it before I change my mind."

Do you know how many good men live in this world? Too many to count!

I took my grandmother's regalia and walked outside. I knew that solitary yellow bead was part of me. I knew I was that yellow bead in part. Outside, I wrapped myself in my grandmother's regalia and breathed her in. I stepped off the sidewalk and into the intersection. Pedestrians stopped. Cars stopped. The city stopped. They all watched me dance with my grandmother. I was my grandmother, dancing.

2003

◆◄ ANN BEATTIE ►◆

Janus

The bowl was perfect. Perhaps it was not what you'd select if you faced a shelf of bowls, and not the sort of thing that would inevitably attract a lot of attention at a crafts fair, yet it had real presence. It was as predictably admired as a mutt who has no reason to suspect he might be funny. Just such a dog, in fact, was often brought out (and in) along with the bowl.

Andrea was a real-estate agent, and when she thought that some prospective buyers might be dog lovers, she would drop off her dog at the same time she placed the bowl in the house that was up for sale. She would put a dish of water in the kitchen for Mondo, take his squeaking plastic frog out of her purse and drop it on the floor. He would pounce delightedly, just as he did every day at home, batting around his favorite toy. The bowl usually sat on a coffee table, though recently she had displayed it on top of a pine blanket chest and on a lacquered table. It was once placed on a cherry table beneath a Bonnard[1] still life, where it held its own.

Everyone who has purchased a house or who has wanted to sell a house must be familiar with some of the tricks used to convince a buyer that the house is quite special: a fire in the fireplace in early evening; jonquils in a pitcher on the kitchen counter, where no one ordinarily has space to put flowers; perhaps the slight aroma of spring, made by a single drop of scent vaporizing from a lamp bulb.

The wonderful thing about the bowl, Andrea thought, was that it was both subtle and noticeable—a paradox of a bowl. Its glaze was the color of cream and seemed to glow no matter what light it was placed in. There were a few bits of color in it—tiny geometric flashes—and some of these were tinged with flecks of silver. They were as mysterious as cells seen under a microscope; it was difficult not to study them, because they shimmered, flashing for a split second, and then resumed their shape. Something about the colors and their random placement suggested motion. People who liked country furniture always commented on the bowl, but then it turned out that people who felt comfortable with Biedermeier[2] loved it just as much. But the bowl was not at all ostentatious, or even so noticeable that anyone would suspect that it had been put in place deliberately. They might notice the height of the ceiling on first entering a room, and only when their eye moved down from that, or away from the refraction of sunlight on a pale wall, would they see the bowl. Then they would go immediately to it and comment. Yet they always faltered when they tried to say something. Perhaps it was because they were in the house for a serious reason, not to notice some object.

Once Andrea got a call from a woman who had not put in an offer on a house she had shown her. That bowl, she said—would it be possible to find out where the owners had bought that beautiful bowl? Andrea pretended that she did not

---

1. Pierre Bonnard (1867–1947), French painter.
2. A style of furniture originally popular in Germany in the early nineteenth century.

know what the woman was referring to. A bowl, somewhere in the house? Oh, on a table under the window. Yes, she would ask, of course. She let a couple of days pass, then called back to say that the bowl had been a present and the people did not know where it had been purchased.

When the bowl was not being taken from house to house, it sat on Andrea's coffee table at home. She didn't keep it carefully wrapped (although she transported it that way, in a box); she kept it on the table, because she liked to see it. It was large enough so that it didn't seem fragile or particularly vulnerable if anyone sideswiped the table or Mondo blundered into it at play. She had asked her husband to please not drop his house key in it. It was meant to be empty.

When her husband first noticed the bowl, he had peered into it and smiled briefly. He always urged her to buy things she liked. In recent years, both of them had acquired many things to make up for all the lean years when they were graduate students, but now that they had been comfortable for quite a while, the pleasure of new possessions dwindled. Her husband had pronounced the bowl "pretty," and he had turned away without picking it up to examine it. He had no more interest in the bowl than she had in his new Leica.

She was sure that the bowl brought her luck. Bids were often put in on houses where she had displayed the bowl. Sometimes the owners, who were always asked to be away or to step outside when the house was being shown, didn't even know that the bowl had been in their house. Once—she could not imagine how—she left it behind, and then she was so afraid that something might have happened to it that she rushed back to the house and sighed with relief when the woman owner opened the door. The bowl, Andrea explained—she had purchased a bowl and set it on the chest for safekeeping while she toured the house with the prospective buyers, and she . . . She felt like rushing past the frowning woman and seizing her bowl. The owner stepped aside, and it was only when Andrea ran to the chest that the lady glanced at her a little strangely. In the few seconds before Andrea picked up the bowl, she realized that the owner must have just seen that it had been perfectly placed, that the sunlight struck the bluer part of it. Her pitcher had been moved to the far side of the chest, and the bowl predominated. All the way home, Andrea wondered how she could have left the bowl behind. It was like leaving a friend at an outing—just walking off. Sometimes there were stories in the paper about families forgetting a child somewhere and driving to the next city. Andrea had only gone a mile down the road before she remembered.

In time, she dreamed of the bowl. Twice, in a waking dream—early in the morning, between sleep and a last nap before rising—she had a clear vision of it. It came into sharp focus and startled her for a moment—the same bowl she looked at every day.

She had a very profitable year selling real estate. Word spread, and she had more clients than she felt comfortable with. She had the foolish thought that if only the bowl were an animate object she could thank it. There were times when she wanted to talk to her husband about the bowl. He was a stockbroker, and sometimes told people that he was fortunate to be married to a woman who had such a fine aesthetic sense and yet could also function in the real world. They were a lot alike, really—they had agreed on that. They were both quiet people—reflective, slow to make value judgments, but almost intractable once they had come to a conclusion. They both liked details, but while ironies attracted her, he was more impatient and dismissive when matters became many-sided or unclear. They both knew this, and it was the kind of thing they could talk about when they were alone in the car together, coming home from a party or after a weekend with friends. But she never talked to him about the bowl. When they were at dinner, exchanging their news of the day, or while they lay in bed at night listening to the stereo and murmuring sleepy disconnections, she was often tempted to come right out and say that she thought that the bowl in the living room, the cream-colored bowl, was responsible for her success. But she didn't say it. She couldn't begin to explain it. Sometimes in the morning, she would look at him and feel guilty that she had such a constant secret.

Could it be that she had some deeper connection with the bowl—a relationship of some kind? She corrected her thinking: how could she imagine such a thing, when she was a human being and it was a bowl? It was ridiculous. Just think of how people lived together and loved each other . . . But was that always so clear, always a relationship? She was confused by these thoughts, but they remained in her mind. There was something within her now, something real, that she never talked about.

The bowl was a mystery, even to her. It was frustrating, because her involvement with the bowl contained a steady sense of unrequited good fortune; it would have been easier to respond if some sort of demand were made in return. But that only happened in fairy tales. The bowl was just a bowl. She did not believe that for one second. What she believed was that it was something she loved.

In the past, she had sometimes talked to her husband about a new property she was about to buy or sell—confiding some clever strategy she had devised to persuade owners who seemed ready to sell. Now she stopped doing that, for all her strategies involved the bowl. She became more deliberate with the bowl, and more possessive. She put it in houses only when no one was there, and removed it when she left the house. Instead of just moving a pitcher or a dish, she would remove all the other objects from a table. She had to force herself to handle them carefully, because she didn't really care about them. She just wanted them out of sight.

She wondered how the situation would end. As with a lover, there was no exact scenario of how matters would come to a close. Anxiety became the operative force. It would be irrelevant if the lover rushed into someone else's arms, or wrote her a note and departed to another city. The horror was the possibility of the disappearance. That was what mattered.

She would get up at night and look at the bowl. It never occurred to her that she might break it. She washed and dried it without anxiety, and she moved it often, from coffee table to mahogany corner table or wherever, without fearing an accident. It was clear that she would not be the one who would do anything to the bowl. The bowl was only handled by her, set safely on one surface or another; it was not very likely that anyone would break it. A bowl was a poor conductor of electricity: it would not be hit by lightning. Yet the idea of damage persisted. She did not think beyond that—to what her life would be without the bowl. She only continued to fear that some accident would happen. Why not, in a world where people set plants where they did not belong, so that visitors touring a house would be fooled into thinking that dark corners got sunlight—a world full of tricks?

She had first seen the bowl several years earlier, at a crafts fair she had visited half in secret, with her lover. He had urged her to buy the bowl. She didn't *need* any more things, she told him. But she had been drawn to the bowl, and they had lingered near it. Then she went on to the next booth, and he came up behind her, tapping the rim against her shoulder as she ran her fingers over a wood carving. "You're still insisting that I buy that?" she said. "No," he said. "I bought it for you." He had bought her other things before this—things she liked more, at first— the child's ebony-and-turquoise ring that fitted her little finger; the wooden box, long and thin, beautifully dovetailed, that she used to hold paper clips; the soft gray sweater with a pouch pocket. It was his idea that when he could not be there to hold her hand she could hold her own—clasp her hands inside the lone pocket that stretched across the front. But in time she became more attached to the bowl than to any of his other presents. She tried to talk herself out of it. She owned other things that were more striking or valuable. It wasn't an object whose beauty jumped out at you; a lot of people must have passed it by before the two of them saw it that day.

Her lover had said that she was always too slow to know what she really loved. Why continue with her life the way it was? Why be two-faced, he asked her. He had made the first move toward her. When she would not decide in his favor, would not change her life and come to him, he asked her what made her think she could have it both ways. And then he made the last move and left. It was a decision meant to break her will, to shatter her intransigent ideas about honoring previous commitments.

Time passed. Alone in the living room at night, she often looked at the bowl sitting on the table, still and safe, unilluminated. In its way, it was perfect: the world cut in half, deep and smoothly empty. Near the rim, even in dim light, the eye moved toward one small flash of blue, a vanishing point on the horizon.

1986

Kate Chopin (1850–1904), the daughter of a well-to-do businessman, was educated at the Academy of the Sacred Heart in St. Louis, Missouri. She was fluent in French and German and well versed in music, reading, and writing. In 1870 she married Oscar Chopin and moved to his home state of Louisiana, living first in New Orleans and later on their plantation in Cloutierville, north of the city, where her husband was a prosperous cotton factor. In 1882 Oscar died of fever; at first, Chopin ran the plantation herself, but in 1884 she moved with her six children back to St. Louis where she began teaching herself biology and anthropology. She also began writing fiction, publishing her first two stories in 1889. Over the course of her life she wrote nearly 100 stories and sketches, most of which are set in Louisiana. The stories were published in two collections, *Banyon Folk* (1894) and *A Night in Acadie* (1897). Though her stories were published in national as well as regional magazines, she was never considered more than a regional writer, and since she had no correspondence with other writers, she had no real influence upon them. As a result, she was never studied or read much after her early death in 1904. The critical reaction to her (now) best-known novel, *The Awakening*, may have added to that lack of academic interest. When *The Awakening* was published in 1899, critics condemned the book for being immoral and not a fit subject for women to write about or read. Libraries banned it, and the book got such bad press that Chopin wrote only five stories after its publication. Though interest in Chopin languished for decades, in the late 1950s scholars began to reappraise her. In 1963, the scholar Per Seyersted wrote a biography of her that convinced others of Chopin's place in literary history.

The Story of an Hour

Kate Chopin

Knowing that Mrs. Mallard was afflicted with a heart trouble, great care was taken to break to her as gently as possible the news of her husband's death.   1

It was her sister Josephine who told her, in broken sentences, veiled hints that revealed in half concealing. Her husband's friend Richards was there, too, near her. It was he who had been in the newspaper office when intelligence of the railroad disaster was received, with Brently Mallard's name leading the list of "killed." He had only taken the time to assure himself of its truth by a second telegram, and had hastened to forestall any less careful, less tender friend in bearing the sad message.   2

She did not hear the story as many women have heard the same, with a paralyzed inability to accept its significance. She wept at once, with sudden, wild abandonment, in her sister's arms. When the storm of grief had spent itself she went away to her room alone. She would have no one follow her.   3

There stood, facing the open window, a comfortable, roomy armchair. Into this she sank, pressed down by a physical exhaustion that haunted her body and seemed to reach into her soul.   4

She could see in the open square before her house the tops of trees that were all aquiver with the new spring life. The delicious breath of rain was in the air. In the street below a peddler was crying his wares. The notes of a distant song which some one was singing reached her faintly, and countless sparrows were twittering in the eaves.   5

There were patches of blue sky showing here and there through the clouds that   6
had met and piled above the other in the west facing her window.

She sat with her head thrown back upon the cushion of the chair, quite motion-   7
less, except when a sob came up into her throat and shook her, as a child who has
cried itself to sleep continues to sob in its dreams.

She was young, with a fair, calm face, whose lines bespoke repression and even   8
a certain strength. But now there was a dull stare in her eyes, whose gaze was fixed
away off yonder on one of those patches of blue sky. It was not a glance of reflection, but rather indicated a suspension of intelligent thought.

There was something coming to her and she was waiting for it, fearfully. What   9
was it? She did not know; it was too subtle and elusive to name. But she felt it, creeping out of the sky, reaching toward her through the sounds, the scents, the color that
filled the air.

Now her bosom rose and fell tumultuously. She was beginning to recognize   10
this thing that was approaching to possess her, and she was striving to beat it back
with her will—as powerless as her two white slender hands would have been.

When she abandoned herself a little whispered word escaped her slightly parted   11
lips. She said it over and over under her breath: "Free, free, free!" The vacant stare
and the look of terror that had followed it went from her eyes. They stayed keen and
bright. Her pulses beat fast, and the coursing blood warmed and relaxed every inch
of her body.

She did not stop to ask if it were or were not a monstrous joy that held her. A   12
clear and exalted perception enabled her to dismiss the suggestion as trivial.

She knew that she would weep again when she saw the kind, tender hands folded   13
in death; the face that had never looked save with love upon her, fixed and gray
and dead. But she saw beyond that bitter moment a long procession of years to come
that would belong to her absolutely. And she opened and spread her arms out to them
in welcome.

There would be no one to live for her during those coming years; she would live   14
for herself. There would be no powerful will bending her in that blind persistence
with which men and women believe they have a right to impose a private will upon
a fellow-creature. A kind intention or a cruel intention made the act seem no less
a crime as she looked upon it in that brief moment of illumination.

And yet she had loved him—sometimes. Often she had not. What did it matter!   15
What could love, the unsolved mystery, count for in the face of this possession of self-
assertion which she suddenly recognized as the strongest impulse of her being!

"Free! Body and soul free!" she kept whispering.   16

Josephine was kneeling before the closed door with her lips to the keyhole,   17
imploring for admission. "Louise, open the door! I beg; open the door—you will make
yourself ill. What are you doing, Louise? For heaven's sake open the door."

"Go away. I am not making myself ill." No; she was drinking in a very elixir of   18
life through that open window.

Her fancy was running riot along those days ahead of her. Spring days, and sum-   19
mer days, and all sorts of days that would be her own. She breathed a quick prayer

that life might be long. It was only yesterday she had thought with a shudder that life might be long.

She arose at length and opened the door to her sister's importunities. There was 20 a feverish triumph in her eyes, and she carried herself unwittingly like a goddess of Victory. She clasped her sister's waist, and together they descended the stairs. Richards stood waiting for them at the bottom.

Some one was opening the front door with a latchkey. It was Brently Mallard 21 who entered, a little travel-stained, composedly carrying his grip-sack and umbrella. He had been far from the scene of accident, and did not even know there had been one. He stood amazed at Josephine's piercing cry; at Richards' quick motion to screen him from the view of his wife.

But Richards was too late. 22

When the doctors came they said she had died of heart disease—of joy that kills. 23

Questions for Discussion

1. What goes through Louise Mallard's mind as she sits in her room alone, adjusting to the news of her husband's death? What is the process of her thinking?
2. What was the "subtle and elusive" (paragraph 9) thing that comes to Louise as she gazes out the window?
3. What are Louise's feelings toward her husband? What are her feelings toward marriage and men in general?
4. What is the "joy that kills" (paragraph 23)? Why is this phrase ironic?
5. Why is the time of year (early spring) and the setting (Louise Mallard's room with a window) important to the story? What do the room, window, and spring symbolize?
6. Why is it important that readers see into Louise Mallard's thoughts? How might the story have been told without this knowledge of what she was thinking?
7. In what ways would this story be different if it were told from the point of view of one of the male characters?

Questions for Reflection and Writing

1. Write a story with a sudden, ironic twist at the end. What techniques did you use to show readers what your main character was thinking and to create irony?
2. Look up "irony," "cosmic irony," and "dramatic irony" in a dictionary of literary terms. Discuss Chopin's use of irony in this story.
3. Compare "The Story of an Hour" with another of Chopin's stories, such as "The Storm" or "A Pair of Silk Stockings," or if you have time to read it, her novel, *The Awakening*. What themes are present in both or all of the stories? What character types are common?

Harlan Ellison (1934–) is the author of numerous works of science fiction, horror, and fantasy as well as short stories, novellas and criticism. Born in Ohio, Ellison has never led a traditional life. He left home as a teenager and drifted around the country, working at various odd jobs. He returned to Ohio and sporadically attended Ohio State University. In the mid-1950s he began to sell short works of science fiction and was then drafted into the Army where he served from 1957 to 1959. After his discharge, Ellison published more short stories and began selling scripts to television, to some of the most popular science-fiction series ever to air on television, including the original Outer Limits series and the original Star Trek series. In addition to his popular television work, Ellison is also a respected editor. *Dangerous Visions* (1967) is considered to be the best and most influential science-fiction anthology of all time. Despite his success, Ellison has a reputation for being a difficult and abrasive person. Isaac Asimov once remarked that Ellison has "no sense of tact whatsoever." Personality aside, Ellison remains a force in science-fiction writing, both in print and in television and movies. Some of his most famous works include *Spider Kiss* (1961), *The Glass Teat: Essays of Opinion on Television* (1970), and the screenplay (with Isaac Asimov) *I, Robot* written in the late 1970s.

"Repent, Harlequin!" Said the Ticktockman

Harlan Ellison

There are always those who ask, what is it all about? For those who need to ask,   1
for those who need points sharply made, who need to know "where it's at," this:

> The mass of men serve the state thus, not as men mainly, but as machines, with their bodies. They are the standing army, and the militia, jailors, constables, *posse comitatus*, etc. In most cases there is no free exercise whatever of the judgment or of the moral sense; but they put themselves on a level with wood and earth and stones; and wooden men can perhaps be manufactured that will serve the purpose as well. Such command no more respect than men of straw or a lump of dirt. They have the same sort of worth only as horses and dogs. Yet such as these even are commonly esteemed good citizens. Others—as most legislators, politicians, lawyers, ministers, and office-holders—serve the state chiefly with their heads; and, as they rarely make any moral distinctions, they are as likely to serve the Devil, without intending it, as God. A very few, as heroes, patriots, martyrs, reformers in the great sense, and men, serve the state with their consciences also and so necessarily resist it for the most part; and they are commonly treated as enemies by it.

> Henry David Thoreau
> *Civil Disobedience*

That is the heart of it. Now begin in the middle, and later learn the begin-   2
ning; the end will take care of itself.

But because it was the very world it was, the very world they had allowed it   3
to *become*, for months his activities did not come to the alarmed attention of The
Ones Who Kept The Machine Functioning Smoothly, the ones who poured the

very best butter over the cams and mainsprings of the culture. Not until it had become obvious that somehow, someway, he had become a notoriety, a celebrity, perhaps even a hero for (what Officialdom inescapably tagged) "an emotionally disturbed segment of the populace," did they turn it over to the Ticktockman and his legal machinery. But by then, because it was the very world it was, and they had no way to predict he would happen—possibly a strain of disease long-defunct, now, suddenly, reborn in a system where immunity had been forgotten, had lapsed—he had been allowed to become too real. Now he had form and substance.

He had become a *personality,* something they had filtered out of the system 4 many decades before. But there it was, and there *he* was, a very definitely imposing personality. In certain circles—middle-class circles—it was thought disgusting. Vulgar ostentation. Anarchistic. Shameful. In others, there was only sniggering: those strata where thought is subjugated to form and ritual, niceties, proprieties. But down below, ah, down below where the people always needed their saints and sinners, their bread and circuses, their heroes and villains, he was considered a Bolivar; a Napoleon; a Robin Hood; a Dick Bong (Ace of Aces); a Jesus; a Jomo Kenyatta.

And at the top—where, like socially-attuned Shipwreck Kellys, every tremor 5 and vibration threatening to dislodge the wealthy, powerful and titled from their flagpoles—he was considered a menace; a heretic; a rebel; a disgrace; a peril. He was known down the line, to the very heart-meat core, but the important reactions were high above and far below. At the very top, at the very bottom.

So his file was turned over, along with his time-card and his cardioplate, to 6 the office of the Ticktockman.

The Ticktockman: very much over six feet tall, often silent, a soft purring man 7 when things went timewise. The Ticktockman.

Even in the cubicles of the hierarchy, where fear was generated, seldom suf- 8 fered, he was called the Ticktockman. But no one called him that to his mask.

You don't call a man a hated name, not when that man, behind his mask, is 9 capable of revoking the minutes, the hours, the days and nights, the years of your life. He was called the Master Timekeeper to his mask. It was safer that way.

"This is *what* he is," said the Ticktockman with genuine softness, "but not *who* 10 he is. This time-card I'm holding in my left hand has a name on it, but it is the name of *what* he is, not *who* he is. The cardioplate here in my right hand is also named, but not *whom* named, merely *what* named. Before I can exercise proper revocation, I have to know *who* this *what* is."

To his staff, all the ferrets, all the loggers, all the finks, all the commex, even 11 the mineez, he said, "Who is this Harlequin?"

He was not purring smoothly. Timewise, it was jangle. 12

However, it *was* the longest speech they had ever heard him utter at one time, 13 the staff, the ferrets, the loggers, the finks, the commex, but not the mineez, who usually weren't around to know, in any case. But even they scurried to find out.

Who is the Harlequin? 14

High above the third level of the city, he crouched on the humming   15
aluminum-frame platform of the air-boat (foof! air-boat, indeed! swizzleskid is
what it was, with a tow-rack jerry-rigged) and he stared clown at the neat
Mondrian arrangement of the buildings.

Somewhere nearby, he could hear the metronomic left-right-left of the   16
2:47 PM shift, entering the Timkin roller-bearing plant in their sneakers. A minute
later, precisely, he heard the softer right-left-right of the 5:00 AM formation, going
home.

An elfin grin spread across his tanned features, and his dimples appeared for a   17
moment. Then, scratching at his thatch of auburn hair, he shrugged within his
motley, as though girding himself for what came next, and threw the joystick forward, and bent into the wind as the air-boat dropped. He skimmed over a slidewalk, purposely dropping a few feet to crease the tassels of the ladies of fashion,
and—inserting thumbs in large ears—he stuck out his tongue, rolled his eyes and
went wugga-wugga-wugga. It was a minor diversion. One pedestrian skittered and
tumbled, sending parcels everywhichway, another wet herself, a third keeled slant-
wise and the walk was stopped automatically by the servitors till she could be
resuscitated. It was a minor diversion.

Then he swirled away on a vagrant breeze, and was gone. Hi-ho. As he   18
rounded the cornice of the Time-Motion Study Building, he saw the shift, just
boarding the slidewalk. With practiced motion and an absolute conservation of
movement, they sidestepped up onto the slow-strip and (in a chorus line reminis-
cent of a Busby Berkeley film of the antediluvian 1930s) advanced across the strips
ostrich-walking till they were lined up on the expresstrip.

Once more, in anticipation, the elfin grin spread, and there was a tooth miss-   19
ing back there on the left side. He dipped, skimmed, and swooped over them; and
then, scrunching about on the air-boat, he released the holding pins that fastened
shut the ends of the home-made pouring troughs that kept his cargo from dumping prematurely. And as he pulled the trough-pins, the air-boat slid over the factory workers and one hundred and fifty thousand dollars' worth of jelly beans
cascaded down on the expresstrip.

Jelly beans! Millions and billions of purples and yellows and greens and   20
licorice and grape and raspberry and mint and round and smooth and crunchy outside and soft-mealy inside and sugary and bouncing jouncing tumbling Clittering
clattering skittering fell on the heads and shoulders and hard hats and carapaces
of the Timkin workers, tinkling on the slidewalk and bouncing away and rolling
about underfoot and filling the sky on their way down with all the colors of joy
and childhood and holidays, coming down in a steady rain, a solid wash, a torrent
of color and sweetness out of the sky from above, and entering a universe of san-
ity and metronomic order with quite-mad coocoo newness. Jelly beans!

The shift workers howled and laughed and were pelted, and broke ranks, and   21
the jelly beans managed to work their way into the mechanism of the slidewalks
after which there was a hideous scraping as the sound of a million fingernails
rasped down a quarter of a million blackboards, followed by a coughing and a sput-
tering, and then the slidewalks all stopped and everyone was dumped this-

awayandthataway in a jackstraw tumble, still laughing and popping little jelly bean eggs of childish color into their mouths. It was a holiday, and a jollity, an absolute insanity, a giggle. But . . .

The shift was delayed seven minutes. 22

They did not get home for seven minutes. 23

The master schedule was thrown off by seven minutes. 24

Quotas were delayed by inoperative slidewalks for seven minutes. 25

He had tapped the first domino in the line, and one after another, like chik 26 chik chik, the others had fallen.

The System had been seven minutes' worth of disrupted. It was a tiny matter, 27 one hardly worthy of note, but in a society where the single driving force was order and unity and equality and promptness and clocklike precision and attention to the clock, reverence of the gods of the passage of time, it was a disaster of major importance.

So he was ordered to appear before the Ticktockman. It was broadcast across 28 every channel of the communications web. He was ordered to be *there* at 7:00 dammit on time. And they waited, and they waited, but he didn't show up till almost ten-thirty, at which time he merely sang a little song about moonlight in a place no one had ever heard of, called Vermont, and vanished again. But they had all been waiting since seven, and it wrecked *hell* with their schedules. So the question remained: Who is the Harlequin?

But the *unasked* question (more important of the two) was: how did we get *into* 29 this position, where a laughing, irresponsible japer of jabberwocky and jive could disrupt our entire economic and cultural life with a hundred and fifty thousand dollars' worth of jelly beans . . .

Jelly for God's sake *beans!* This is madness! Where did he get the money to buy 30 a hundred and fifty thousand dollars' worth of jelly beans? (They knew it would have cost that much, because they had a team of Situation Analysts pulled off another assignment, and rushed to the slidewalk scene to sweep up and count the candies, and produce findings, which disrupted *their* schedules and threw their entire branch at least a day behind.) Jelly beans! Jelly . . . *beans?* Now wait a second—a second accounted for—no one has manufactured jelly beans for over a hundred years. Where did he get jelly beans?

That's another good question. More than likely it will never be answered to 31 your complete satisfaction. But then, how many questions ever are?

The middle you know. Here is the beginning. How it starts: 32

A desk pad. Day for day, and turn each day. 9:00—open the mail. 9:45— 33 appointment with planning commission board. 10:30—discuss installation progress charts with J.L. 11:45—pray for rain. 12:00—lunch. And so it goes.

"I'm sorry, Miss Grant, but the time for interviews was set at 2:30, and it's 34 almost five now. I'm sorry you're late, but those are the rules. You'll have to wait till next year to submit application for this college again." *And so it goes.*

The 10:10 local stops at Cresthaven, Galesville, Tonawanda Junction, Selby 35 and Farnhurst, but not at Indiana City, Lucasville and Cotton, except on Sunday.

The 10:35 express stops at Galesville, Selby and Indiana City, except on Sundays & Holidays, at which time it stops at . . . *and so it goes.*

"I couldn't wait, Fred. I had to be at Pierre Cartain's by 3:00, and you said you'd   36
meet me under the clock in the terminal at 2:45, and you weren't there, so I had to go on. You're always late, Fred. If you'd been there, we could have sewed it up together, but as it was, well, I took the order alone . . . And so it goes.

Dear Mr. and Mrs. Atterley: In reference to your son Gerold's constant tardi-   37
ness, I am afraid we will have to suspend him from school unless some more reliable method can be instituted guaranteeing he will arrive at his classes on time. Granted he is an exemplary student, and his marks are high, his constant flouting of the schedules of this school makes it impractical to maintain him in a system where the other children seem capable of getting where they are supposed to be on time *and so it goes.*

YOU CANNOT VOTE UNLESS YOU APPEAR AT 8:45 AM.   38

"I DON'T CARE IF THE SCRIPT IS GOOD, I NEED IT THURSDAY!"   39

CHECK-OUT TIME IS 2:00 PM.   40

"You got here late. The job's taken. Sorry"   41

YOUR SALARY HAS BEEN DOCKED FOR TWENTY MINUTES   42
TIME LOST.

"God, what time is it, I've gotta run!"   43

And so it goes. And so it goes. And so it goes. And so it goes goes goes goes   44
goes tick tock tick tock tick tock and one day we no longer let time serve us, we serve time and we are slaves of the schedule, worshippers of the sun's passing, bound into a life predicated on restrictions because the system will not function if we don't keep the schedule tight.

Until it becomes more than a minor inconvenience to be late. It becomes a   45
sin. Then a crime. Then a crime punishable by this:

> **EFFECTIVE 15 JULY 2389 12:00:00 midnight, the office of the Master
> Timekeeper will require all citizens to submit their timecards and cardio-
> plates for processing. In accordance with Statute 555-7-SGH-999 govern-
> ing the revocation of time per capita, all cardioplates will be keyed to the
> individual holder and—**

What they had done was devise a method of curtailing the amount of life a   46
person could have. If he was ten minutes late, he lost ten minutes of his life. An hour was proportionately worth more revocation. If someone was consistently tardy, he might find himself, on a Sunday night, receiving a communique from the Master Timekeeper that his time had run out, and he would be "turned off" at high noon on Monday, please straighten your affairs, sir, madame or bisex.

And so, by this simple scientific expedient (utilizing a scientific process held   47
dearly secret by the Ticktockman's office) the System was maintained. It was the only expedient thing to do. It was, after all, patriotic. The schedules had to be met. After all, there *was* a war on!

But, wasn't there always?   48

"Now that is really disgusting," the Harlequin said, when Pretty Alice showed   49
him the wanted poster. "Disgusting and *highly* improbable. After all, this isn't the
Day of the Desperado. A *wanted* poster!"

"You know," Pretty Alice noted, "you speak with a great deal of inflection."   50

"I'm sorry," said the Harlequin, humbly.   51

"No need to be sorry. You're always saying 'I'm sorry.' You have such massive   52
guilt, Everett, it's really very sad."

"I'm sorry," he said again, then pursed his lips so the dimples appeared   53
momentarily. He hadn't wanted to say that at all. "I have to go out again. I have
to *do* something."

Pretty Alice slammed her coffee-bulb down on the counter. "Oh for God's   54
sake, Everett, can't you stay home just *one* night! Must you always be out in that
ghastly clown suit, running around *annoying* people?"

"I'm—" he stopped, and clapped the jester's hat onto his auburn thatch with   55
a tiny tinkling of bells. He rose, rinsed out his coffee-bulb at the spray, and put it
into the dryer for a moment. "I have to go."

She didn't answer. The faxhox was purring, and she pulled a sheet out, read it,   56
threw it toward him on the counter. "It's about you. Of course. You're ridiculous."

He read it quickly. It said the Ticktockman was trying to locate him. He did-   57
n't care, he was going out to be late again. At the door, dredging for an exit line,
he hurled back petulantly, "Well, *you* speak with inflection, *too!*"

Pretty Alice rolled her pretty eyes heavenward. "You're ridiculous."   58

The Harlequin stalked out, slamming the door, which sighed shut softly, and   59
locked itself.

There was a gentle knock, and Pretty Alice got up with an exhalation of exas-   60
perated breath, and opened the door. He stood there. "I'll be back about ten-thirty,
okay?"

She pulled a rueful face. "Why do you tell me that? Why? You *know* you'll be   61
late! You *know* it. You're *always* late, so why do you tell me these dumb things?"
She closed the door.

On the other side, the Harlequin nodded to himself. *She's right. She's always*   62
right. I'll be late. I'm always late. Why do I tell her these dumb things?

He shrugged again, and went off to be late once more.   63

He had fired off the firecracker rockets that said: I will attend the 115th   64
annual International Medical Association Invocation at 8:00 PM precisely I do
hope you will all be able to join me.

The words had burned in the sky, and of course the authorities were there,   65
lying in wait for him. They assumed, naturally, that he would be late. He arrived
twenty minutes early, while they were setting up the spiderwebs to trap and hold
him. Blowing a large bullhorn, he frightened and unnerved them so, their own
moisturized encirclement webs sucked closed, and they were hauled up, kicking
and shrieking, high above the amphitheater's floor. The Harlequin laughed and
laughed, and apologized profusely. The physicians, gathered in solemn conclave,
roared with laughter, and accepted the Harlequin's apologies with exaggerated

bowing and posturing, and a merry time was had by all, who thought the Harlequin was a regular foofaraw in fancy pants; all, that is, but the authorities, who had been sent out by the office of the Ticktockman; they hung there like so much dockside cargo, hauled up above the floor of the amphitheater in a most unseemly fashion.

(In another part of the same city where the Harlequin carried on his "activi- 66 ties," totally unrelated in every way to what concerns us here, save that it illustrates the Ticktockman's power and import, a man named Marshall Delahanty received his turn-off notice from the Ticktockman's office. His wife received the notification from the gray-suited mince who delivered it, with the traditional "look of sorrow" plastered hideously across his face. She knew what it was, even without unsealing it. It was a billet-doux of immediate recognition to everyone these days. She gasped, and held it as though it were a glass slide tinged with botulism, and prayed it was not for her. Let it be for Marsh, she thought, brutally, realistically, or one of the kids, but not for me, please dear God, not for me. And then she opened it, and it *was* for Marsh, and she was at one and the same time horrified and relieved. The next trooper in the line had caught the bullet. "Marshall," she screamed, "Marshall! Termination, Marshall! OhmiGod, Marshall, whattl we do, whattl we do, Marshall omigodmarshall . . ." and in their home that night was the sound of tearing paper and fear, and the stink of madness went up the flue and there was nothing, absolutely nothing they could do about it.

(But Marshall Delahanty tried to run. And early the next day, when turn-off 67 time came, he was deep in the Canadian forest two hundred miles away, and the office of the Ticktockman blanked his cardioplate, and Marshall Delahanty keeled over, running, and his heart stopped, and the blood dried up on its way to his brain, and he was dead that's all. One light went out on the sector map in the office of the Master Timekeeper, while notification was entered for fax reproduction, and Georgette Delahanty's name was entered on the dole roles till she could remarry. Which is the end of the footnote, and all the point that need be made, except don't laugh, because that is what would happen to the Harlequin if ever the Ticktockman found out his real name. It isn't funny.)

The shopping level of the city was thronged with the Thursday-colors of the 68 buyers. Women in canary yellow chitons and men in pseudo-Tyrolean outfits that were jade and leather and fit very tightly, save for the balloon pants.

When the Harlequin appeared on the still-being-constructed shell of the new 69 Efficiency Shopping Center, his bullhorn to his elfishly-laughing lips, everyone pointed and stared, and he berated them:

"Why let them order you about? Why let them tell you to hurry and scurry 70 like ants or maggots? Take your time! Saunter a while! Enjoy the sunshine, enjoy the breeze, let life carry you at your own pace! Don't be slaves of time, it's a helluva way to die, slowly, by degrees . . . down with the Ticktockman!"

Who's the nut? most of the shoppers wanted to know. Who's the nut oh wow 71 I'm gonna be late I gotta run . . .

And the construction gang on the Shopping Center received an urgent order 72
from the office of the Master Timekeeper that the dangerous criminal known as
the Harlequin was atop their spire, and their aid was urgently needed in appre-
hending him. The work crew said no, they would lose time on their construction
schedule, but the Ticktockman managed to pull the proper threads of governmental webbing, and they were told to cease work and catch that nitwit up thereon
the spire; up there with the bullhorn. So a dozen and more burly workers began
climbing into their construction platforms, releasing the a-grav plates, and rising
toward the Harlequin.

After the debacle (in which, through the Harlequin's attention to personal 73
safety, no one was seriously injured), the workers tried to reassemble, and assault
him again, but it was too late. He had vanished. It had attracted quite a crowd,
however, and the shopping cycle was thrown off by hours, simply hours. The purchasing needs of the system were therefore falling behind, and so measures were
taken to accelerate the cycle for the rest of the day, but it got bogged down and
speeded up and they sold too many float-valves and not nearly enough wegglers,
which meant that the popli ratio was off, which made it necessary to rush cases
and cases of spoiling Smash-O to stores that usually needed a case only every three
or four hours. The shipments were bollixed, the transshipments were misrouted,
and in the end, even the swizzleskid industries felt it.

"Don't come back till you have him!" the Ticktockman said, very quietly, very 74
sincerely, extremely dangerously.

They used dogs. They used probes. They used cardioplate crossoffs. They used 75
teepers. They used bribery. They used stiktytes. They used intimidation. They used
torment. They used torture. They used finks. They used cops. They used search&
seizure. They used fallaron. They used betterment incentive. They used finger-
prints. They used the Bertillon system. They used cunning. They used guile. They
used treachery. They used Raoul Mitgong, but he didn't help much. They used
applied physics. They used techniques of criminology.

And what the hell: they caught him. 76

After all, his name was Everett C. Marm, and he wasn't much to begin with, 77
except a man who had no sense of time.

"Repent, Harlequin!" said the Ticktockman. 78

"Get stuffed!" the Harlequin replied, sneering. 79

"You've been late a total of sixty-three years, five months, three weeks, two 80
days, twelve hours, forty-one minutes, fifty-nine seconds, point oh three six one
one one microseconds. You've used up everything you can, and more. I'm going to
turn you off."

"Scare someone else. I'd rather be dead than live in a dumb world with a 81
bogeyman like you."

"It's my job." 82

"You're full of it. You're a tyrant. You have no right to order people around and   83
kill them if they show up late."

"You can't adjust. You can't fit in."   84

"Unstrap me, and I'll fit my fist into your mouth."   85

"You're a nonconformist."   86

"That didn't used to be a felony."   87

"It is now. Live in the world around you."   88

"I hate it. It's a terrible world."   89

"Not everyone thinks so. Most people enjoy order."   90

"I don't, and most of the people I know don't."   91

"That's not true. How do you think we caught you?"   92

"I'm not interested."   93

"A girl named Pretty Alice told us who you were."   94

"That's a lie."   95

"It's true. You unnerve her. She wants to belong; she wants to conform; I'm   96
going to turn you off."

"Then do it already, and stop arguing with me."   97

"I'm not going to turn you off."   98

"You're an idiot!"   99

"Repent, Harlequin!" said the Ticktockman.   100

"Get stuffed."   101

So they sent him to Coventry. And in Coventry they worked him over. It was   102
just like what they did to Winston Smith in *Nineteen Eighty-Four*, which was a
book none of them knew about, but the techniques are really quite ancient, and
so they did it to Everett C. Marm; and one day, quite a long time later, the
Harlequin appeared on the communications web, appearing elfin and dimpled and
bright-eyed, and not at all brainwashed, and he said he had been wrong, that it
was a good, a very good thing indeed, to belong, to be right on time hip-ho and
away we go, and everyone stared up at him on the public screens that covered an
entire city block, and they said to themselves, well, you see, he was just a nut after
all, and if that's the way the system is run, then let's do it that way, because it
doesn't pay to fight city hall, or in this case, the Ticktockman. So Everett C. Marm
was destroyed, which was a loss, because of what Thoreau said earlier, but you can't
make an omelet without breaking a few eggs, and in every revolution a few die
who shouldn't, but they have to, because that's the way it happens, and if you
make only a little change, then it seems to be worthwhile. Or, to make the point
lucidly:

"Uh, excuse me, sir, I, uh, don't know how to uh, to uh, tell you this, but you   103
were three minutes late. The schedule is a little, uh, bit off."

He grinned sheepishly.   104

"That's ridiculous!" murmured the Ticktockman behind his mask. "Check   105
your watch." And then he went into his office, going *mrmee, mrmee, mrmee,
mrmee*.

Questions for Discussion

1. A "harlequin" can be defined in the following two ways: either as a masked comic character dressed in multicolored diamond-patterned tights, often depicted with either a magic wand or wooden sword; or as a buffoon. In what ways does the protagonist, Everett Marm, meet or diverge from these definitions?

2. Why do you think Ellison decided to include so many nonsense words like "swizzlekid," "wugga-wugga-wugga," and "mineez"? What is the purpose of combining nonsense names of people, places, and things with real ones?

3. Do you ever feel that you are a "slave to time"?

4. Why does the Harlequin choose to disrupt the pace of time by throwing thousands of jellybeans? What might the jellybeans symbolize?

5. Notice how frequently the number seven appears: "The shift was delayed by seven minutes." "The master schedule was thrown off by seven minutes." "He was ordered to be *there* at 7:00." Seven is frequently a symbolic of perfection. Why might the number seven be ironic in this story?

6. Why do you think the Ticktockman is unable to "turn off" Everett the way he had done with Marshall Delahanty?

7. Discuss the names of the characters and what they might symbolize or allude to: Everett Marm, Pretty Alice, Ticktockman, and Marshall Delahanty.

8. Why is the Ticktockman so insistent on "repentance"?

Questions for Reflection and Writing

1. Carefully review the excerpt from Thoreau's "Civil Disobedience" that begins this short story. How does Ellison's dystopian world follow Thoreau's assessment of society in its own bizarre way?

2. Consider the allusions in Paragraph 4 to Simon Bolivar, Napoleon Bonaparte, Robin Hood, Dick Bong, Jesus, and Jomo Kenyatta. How does the Harlequin embody aspects of each of these historical figures?

3. Think about the conclusion of the story. Is there any point in fighting the system?

F. Scott Fitzgerald (1896–1940) is best known for his novel *The Great Gatsby* (1925), which for many epitomized the "Jazz Age" (Fitzgerald's half-affectionate coinage for the decade of the 1920s). Together with his wife, Zelda, Fitzgerald for a time achieved the kind of celebrity status now typically accorded to rock stars; their wildly extravagant lifestyle eventually ended in Zelda's institutionalization and Fitzgerald's breakdown and a losing lifelong battle with alcoholism. Though Fitzgerald wrote many of his short stories simply to make ends meet, reserving his profoundly "creative" efforts for his novels, several of them, including "Winter Dreams" are generally ranked among the finest that the twentieth century has produced. "Winter Dreams" was first published in *Metropolitan Magazine* in 1922 and collected in *All the Sad Young Men* (1926). Fitzgerald died while writing the novel *The Last Tycoon* (1941). Though it remains unfinished, some critics consider it his best.

Winter Dreams

F. Scott Fitzgerald

I

Some of the caddies were poor as sin and lived in one-room houses with a neuras-   1
thenic cow in the front yard, but Dexter Green's father owned the second best grocery-store in Black Bear—the best one was "The Hub," patronized by the wealthy people from Sherry Island—and Dexter caddied only for pocket-money.

In the fall when the days became crisp and gray, and the long Minnesota win-   2
ter shut down like the white lid of a box, Dexter's skis moved over the snow that hid the fairways of the golf course. At these times the country gave him a feeling of profound melancholy—it offended him that the links should lie in enforced fal-lowness, haunted by ragged sparrows for the long season. It was dreary, too, that on the tees where the gay colors fluttered in summer there were now only the desolate sand-boxes knee-deep in crusted ice. When he crossed the hills the wind blew cold as misery, and if the sun was out he tramped with his eyes squinted up against the hard dimensionless glare.

In April the winter ceased abruptly. The snow ran down into Black Bear Lake   3
scarcely tarrying for the early golfers to brave the season with red and black balls. Without elation, without an interval of moist glory, the cold was gone.

Dexter knew that there was something dismal about this Northern spring, just   4
as he knew there was something gorgeous about the fall. Fall made him clinch his hands and tremble and repeat idiotic sentences to himself, and make brisk abrupt gestures of command to imaginary audiences and armies. October filled him with hope which November raised to a sort of ecstatic triumph, and in this mood the fleeting brilliant impressions of the summer at Sherry Island were ready grist to his mill. He became a golf champion and defeated Mr. T. A. Hedrick in a marvellous match played a hundred times over the fairways of his imagination, a match each detail of which he changed about untiringly—sometimes he won with almost laugh-able ease, sometimes he came up magnificently from behind. Again, stepping from

a Pierce-Arrow automobile, like Mr. Mortimer Jones, he strolled frigidly into the lounge of the Sherry Island Golf Club—or perhaps, surrounded by an admiring crowd, he gave an exhibition of fancy diving from the spring-board of the club raft. . . . Among those who watched him in open-mouthed wonder was Mr. Mortimer Jones.

And one day it came to pass that Mr. Jones—himself and not his ghost—came 5
up to Dexter with tears in his eyes and said that Dexter was the——best caddy in the club, and wouldn't he decide not to quit if Mr. Jones made it worth his while, because every other——caddy in the club lost one ball a hole for him—regularly—

"No, sir," said Dexter decisively, "I don't want to caddy any more." Then, after 6
a pause: "I'm too old."

"You're not more than fourteen. Why the devil did you decide just this morning 7
that you wanted to quit? You promised that next week you'd go over to the State tournament with me."

"I decided I was too old." 8

Dexter handed in his "A Class" badge, collected what money was due him from 9
the caddy master, and walked home to Black Bear Village.

"The best——caddy I ever saw," shouted Mr. Mortimer Jones over a drink that 10
afternoon. "Never lost a ball! Willing! Intelligent! Quiet! Honest! Grateful!"

The little girl who had done this was eleven—beautifully ugly as little girls are 11
apt to be who are destined after a few years to be inexpressibly lovely and bring no end of misery to a great number of men. The spark, however, was perceptible. There was a general ungodliness in the way her lips twisted down at the corners when she smiled, and in the—Heaven help us!—in the almost passionate quality of her eyes. Vitality is born early in such women. It was utterly in evidence now, shining through her thin frame in a sort of glow.

She had come eagerly out on to the course at nine o'clock with a white linen 12
nurse and five small new golf-clubs in a white canvas bag which the nurse was carrying. When Dexter first saw her she was standing by the caddy house, rather ill at ease and trying to conceal the fact by engaging her nurse in an obviously unnatural conversation graced by startling and irrelevant grimaces from herself.

"Well, it's certainly a nice day, Hilda," Dexter heard her say. She drew down the 13
corners of her mouth, smiled, and glanced furtively around, her eyes in transit falling for an instant on Dexter.

Then to the nurse: 14

"Well, I guess there aren't very many people out here this morning, are there?" 15

The smile again—radiant, blatantly artificial—convincing. 16

"I don't know what we're supposed to do now," said the nurse looking nowhere 17
in particular.

"Oh, that's all right. I'll fix it up." 18

Dexter stood perfectly still, his mouth slightly ajar. He knew that if he moved 19
forward a step his stare would be in her line of vision—if he moved backward he would lose his full view of her face. For a moment he had not realized how young she was. Now he remembered having seen her several times the year before—in bloomers.

Suddenly, involuntarily, he laughed, a short abrupt laugh—then, startled by him- 20
self, he turned and began to walk quickly away.

"Boy!"   21

Dexter stopped.   22

"Boy—"   23

Beyond question he was addressed. Not only that, but he was treated to that   24
absurd smile, that preposterous smile—the memory of which at least a dozen men
were to carry into middle age.

"Boy, do you know where the golf teacher is?"   25

"He's giving a lesson."   26

"Well, do you know where the caddy-master is?"   27

"He isn't here yet this morning."   28

"Oh." For a moment this baffled her. She stood alternately on her right and   29
left foot.

"We'd like to get a caddy," said the nurse. "Mrs. Mortimer Jones sent us out to   30
play golf, and we don't know how without we get a caddy."

Here she was stopped by an ominous glance from Miss Jones, followed imme-   31
diately by the smile.

"There aren't any caddies here except me," said Dexter to the nurse, "and I got   32
to stay here in charge until the caddy-master gets here."

"Oh."   33

Miss Jones and her retinue now withdrew, and at a proper distance from Dexter   34
became involved in a heated conversation, which was concluded by Miss Jones
taking one of the clubs and hitting it on the ground with violence. For further emphasis she raised it again and was about to bring it down smartly upon the nurse's bosom,
when the nurse seized the club and twisted it from her hands.

"You damn little mean old *thing!*" cried Miss Jones wildly.   35

Another argument ensued. Realizing that the elements of comedy were implied   36
in the scene, Dexter several times began to laugh, but each time restrained the laugh
before it reached audibility. He could not resist the monstrous conviction that the
little girl was justified in beating the nurse.

The situation was resolved by the fortuitous appearance of the caddy-master,   37
who was appealed to immediately by the nurse.

"Miss Jones is to have a little caddy, and this one says he can't go."   38

"Mr. McKenna said I was to wait here till you came," said Dexter quickly.   39

"Well, he's here now." Miss Jones smiled cheerfully at the caddy-master. Then   40
she dropped her bag and set off at a haughty mince toward the first tee.

"Well?" The caddy-master turned to Dexter. "What you standing there like a   41
dummy for? Go pick up the young lady's clubs."

"I don't think I'll go out to-day," said Dexter.   42

"You don't—"   43

"I think I'll quit."   44

The enormity of his decision frightened him. He was a favorite caddy, and the   45
thirty dollars a month he earned through the summer were not to be made elsewhere
around the lake. But he had received a strong emotional shock, and his perturbation
required a violent and immediate outlet.

It is not so simple as that, either. As so frequently would be the case in the future, 46
Dexter was unconsciously dictated to by his winter dreams.

II

Now, of course, the quality and the seasonability of these winter dreams varied, but 47
the stuff of them remained. They persuaded Dexter several years later to pass up a
business course at the State university—his father, prospering now, would have
paid his way—for the precarious advantage of attending an older and more famous
university in the East, where he was bothered by his scanty funds. But do not get the
impression, because his winter dreams happened to be concerned at first with musings on the rich, that there was anything merely snobbish in the boy. He wanted not
association with glittering things and glittering people—he wanted the glittering
things themselves. Often he reached out for the best without knowing why he wanted
it—and sometimes he ran up against the mysterious denials and prohibitions in which
life indulges. It is with one of those denials and not with his career as a whole that
this story deals.

He made money. It was rather amazing. After college he went to the city from 48
which Black Bear Lake draws its wealthy patrons. When he was only twenty-three
and had been there not quite two years, there were already people who liked to say:
"Now *there's* a boy—" All about him rich men's sons were peddling bonds precariously, or investing patrimonies precariously, or plodding through the two dozen
volumes of the "George Washington Commercial Course," but Dexter borrowed a
thousand dollars on his college degree and his confident mouth, and bought a part-
nership in a laundry.

It was a small laundry when he went into it, but Dexter made a specialty of learn- 49
ing how the English washed fine woolen golfstockings without shrinking them, and
within a year he was catering to the trade that wore knickerbockers. Men were insisting that their Shetland hose and sweaters go to his laundry, just as they had insisted
on a caddy who could find golf-balls. A little later he was doing their wives' lin-
gerie as well—and running five branches in different parts of the city. Before he
was twenty-seven he owned the largest string of laundries in his section of the country. It was then that he sold out and went to New York. But the part of his story
that concerns us goes back to the days when he was making his first big success.

When he was twenty-three Mr. Hart—one of the gray-haired men who liked to 50
say "Now there's a boy"—gave him a guest card to the Sherry Island Golf Club for
a week-end. So he signed his name one day on the register, and that afternoon played
golf in a foursome with Mr. Hart and Mr. Sandwood and Mr. T. A. Hedrick. He did
not consider it necessary to remark that he had once carried Mr. Hart's bag over
this same links, and that he knew every trap and gully with his eyes shut—but he
found himself glancing at the four caddies who trailed them, trying to catch a gleam
or gesture that would remind him of himself, that would lessen the gap which lay
between his present and his past.

It was a curious day, slashed abruptly with fleeting, familiar impressions. One 51
minute he had the sense of being a trespasser—in the next he was impressed by the

tremendous superiority he felt toward Mr. T. A. Hedrick, who was a bore and not even a good golfer any more.

Then, because of a ball Mr. Hart lost near the fifteenth green, an enormous thing happened. While they were searching the stiff grasses of the rough there was a clear call of "Fore!" from behind a hill in their rear. And as they all turned abruptly from their search a bright new ball sliced abruptly over the hill and caught Mr. T. A. Hedrick in the abdomen. 52

"By Gad!" cried Mr. T. A. Hedrick, "they ought to put some of these crazy women off the course. It's getting to be outrageous." 53

A head and a voice came up together over the hill: 54

"Do you mind if we go through?" 55

"You hit me in the stomach!" declared Mr. Hedrick wildly. 56

"Did I?" The girl approached the group of men. "I'm sorry. I yelled 'Fore!'" 57

Her glance fell casually on each of the men—then scanned the fairway for her ball. 58

"Did I bounce into the rough?" 59

It was impossible to determine whether this question was ingenuous or malicious. In a moment, however, she left no doubt, for as her partner came up over the hill she called cheerfully: 60

"Here I am! I'd have gone on the green except that I hit something." 61

As she took her stance for a short mashie shot, Dexter looked at her closely. She wore a blue gingham dress, rimmed at throat and shoulders with a white edging that accentuated her tan. The quality of exaggeration, of thinness, which had made her passionate eyes and down-turning mouth absurd at eleven, was gone now. She was arrestingly beautiful. The color in her cheeks was centred like the color in a picture—it was not a "high" color, but a sort of fluctuating and feverish warmth, so shaded that it seemed at any moment it would recede and disappear. This color and the mobility of her mouth gave a continual impression of flux, of intense life, of passionate vitality—balanced only partially by the sad luxury of her eyes. 62

She swung her mashie impatiently and without interest, pitching the ball into a sand-pit on the other side of the green. With a quick, insincere smile and a careless "Thank you!" she went on after it. 63

"That Judy Jones!" remarked Mr. Hedrick on the next tee, as they waited—some moments—for her to play on ahead. "All she needs is to be turned up and spanked for six months and then to be married off to an old-fashioned cavalry captain." 64

"My God, she's good-looking!" said Mr. Sandwood, who was just over thirty. 65

"Good-looking!" cried Mr. Hedrick contemptuously, "She always looks as if she wanted to be kissed! Turning those big cow-eyes on every calf in town!" 66

It was doubtful if Mr. Hedrick intended a reference to the maternal instinct. 67

"She'd play pretty good golf if she'd try," said Mr. Sandwood. 68

"She has no form," said Mr. Hedrick solemnly. 69

"She has a nice figure," said Mr. Sandwood. 70

"Better thank the Lord she doesn't drive a swifter ball," said Mr. Hart, winking at Dexter. 71

Later in the afternoon the sun went down with a riotous swirl of gold and vary-   72
ing blues and scarlets, and left the dry, rustling night of Western summer. Dexter
watched from the veranda of the Golf Club, watched the even overlap of the waters
in the little wind, silver molasses under the harvest-moon. Then the moon held a
finger to her lips and the lake became a clear pool, pale and quiet. Dexter put on
his bathing-suit and swam out to the farthest raft, where he stretched dripping on
the wet canvas of the spring-board.

There was a fish jumping and a star shining and the lights around the lake were   73
gleaming. Over on a dark peninsula a piano was playing the songs of last summer and
of summers before that—songs from "Chin-Chin" and "The Count of Luxemburg"
and "The Chocolate Soldier"—and because the sound of a piano over a stretch of
water had always seemed beautiful to Dexter he lay perfectly quiet and listened.

The tune the piano was playing at that moment had been gay and new five years   74
before when Dexter was a sophomore at college. They had played it at a prom once
when he could not afford the luxury of proms, and he had stood outside the gym-
nasium and listened. The sound of the tune precipitated in him a sort of ecstasy
and it was with that ecstasy he viewed what happened to him now. It was a mood
of intense appreciation, a sense that, for once, he was magnificently attuned to life
and that everything about him was radiating a brightness and a glamour he might
never know again.

A low, pale oblong detached itself suddenly from the darkness of the Island, spit-   75
ting forth the reverberated sound of a racing motorboat. Two white streamers of cleft
water rolled themselves out behind it and almost immediately the boat was beside
him, drowning out the hot tinkle of the piano in the drone of its spray. Dexter raising himself on his arms was aware of a figure standing at the wheel, of two dark
eyes regarding him over the lengthening space of water—then the boat had gone
by and was sweeping in an immense and purposeless circle of spray round and round
in the middle of the lake. With equal eccentricity one of the circles flattened out and
headed back toward the raft.

"Who's that?" she called, shutting off her motor. She was so near now that Dexter   76
could see her bathing suit, which consisted apparently of pink rompers.

The nose of the boat bumped the raft, and as the latter tilted rakishly he was   77
precipitated toward her. With different degrees of interest they recognized each
other.

"Aren't you one of those men we played through this afternoon?" she demanded.   78
He was.   79
"Well, do you know how to drive a motor-boat? Because if you do I wish you'd   80
drive this one so I can ride on the surf-board behind. My name is Judy Jones"—she
favored him with an absurd smirk—rather, what tried to be a smirk, for, twist her
mouth as she might, it was not grotesque, it was merely beautiful—"and I live in a
house over there on the Island, and in that house there is a man waiting for me. When
he drove up at the door I drove out of the dock because he says I'm his ideal."

There was a fish jumping and a star shining and the lights around the lake were   81
gleaming. Dexter sat beside Judy Jones and she explained how her boat was driven.
Then she was in the water, swimming to the floating surf-board with a sinuous crawl.

Watching her was without effort to the eye, watching a branch waving or a sea-gull flying. Her arms, burned to butternut, moved sinuously among the dull platinum ripples, elbow appearing first, casting the forearm back with a cadence of falling water, then reaching out and down, stabbing a path ahead.

They moved out into the lake; turning, Dexter saw that she was kneeling on the   82
low rear of the now uptilted surf-board.

"Go faster," she called, "fast as it'll go."   83

Obediently he jammed the lever forward and the white spray mounted at the   84
bow. When he looked around again the girl was standing up on the rushing board,
her arms spread wide, her eyes lifted toward the moon.

"It's awful cold," she shouted. "What's your name?"   85

He told her.   86

"Well, why don't you come to dinner to-morrow night?"   87

His heart turned over like a fly-wheel of the boat, and, for the second time,   88
her casual whim gave a new direction to his life.

III

Next evening while he waited for her to come down-stairs, Dexter peopled the soft   89
deep summer room and the sun-porch that opened from it with the men who had
already loved Judy Jones. He knew the sort of men they were—the men who when
he first went to college had entered from the great prep schools with graceful clothes
and the deep tan of healthy summers. He had seen that, in one sense, he was better
than these men. He was newer and stronger. Yet in acknowledging to himself that
he wished his children to be like them he was admitting that he was but the rough,
strong stuff from which they eternally sprang.

When the time had come for him to wear good clothes, he had known who were   90
the best tailors in America, and the best tailors in America had made him the suit
he wore this evening. He had acquired that particular reserve peculiar to his university, that set it off from other universities. He recognized the value to him of
such a mannerism and he had adopted it; he knew that to be careless in dress and
manner required more confidence than to be careful. But carelessness was for his children. His mother's name had been Krimslich. She was a Bohemian of the peasant
class and she had talked broken English to the end of her days. Her son must keep to
the set patterns.

At a little after seven Judy Jones came down-stairs. She wore a blue silk after-   91
noon dress, and he was disappointed at first that she had not put on something more
elaborate. This feeling was accentuated when, after a brief greeting, she went to
the door of a butler's pantry and pushing it open called: "You can serve dinner,
Martha." He had rather expected that a butler would announce dinner, that there
would be a cocktail. Then he put these thoughts behind him as they sat down side
by side on a lounge and looked at each other.

"Father and mother won't be here," she said thoughtfully.   92

He remembered the last time he had seen her father, and he was glad the par-   93
ents were not to be here to-night—they might wonder who he was. He had been
born in Keeble, a Minnesota village fifty miles farther north, and he always gave

Keeble as his home instead of Black Bear Village. Country towns were well enough to come from if they weren't inconveniently in sight and used as footstools by fashionable lakes.

They talked of his university, which she had visited frequently during the past two years, and of the near-by city which supplied Sherry Island with its patrons, and whither Dexter would return next day to his prospering laundries. **94**

During dinner she slipped into a moody depression which gave Dexter a feeling of uneasiness. Whatever petulance she uttered in her throaty voice worried him. Whatever she smiled at—at him, at a chicken liver, at nothing—it disturbed him that her smile could have no root in mirth, or even in amusement. When the scarlet corners of her lips curved down, it was less a smile than an invitation to a kiss. **95**

Then, after dinner, she led him out on the dark sun-porch and deliberately changed the atmosphere. **96**

"Do you mind if I weep a little?" she said. **97**

"I'm afraid I'm boring you," he responded quickly. **98**

"You're not. I like you. But I've just had a terrible afternoon. There was a man I cared about, and this afternoon he told me out of a clear sky that he was poor as a church-mouse. He'd never even hinted it before. Does this sound horribly mundane?" **99**

"Perhaps he was afraid to tell you." **100**

"Suppose he was," she answered. "He didn't start right. You see, if I'd thought of him as poor—well, I've been mad about loads of poor men, and fully intended to marry them all. But in this case, I hadn't thought of him that way, and my interest in him wasn't strong enough to survive the shock. As if a girl calmly informed her fiancé that she was a widow. He might not object to widows, but— **101**

"Let's start right," she interrupted herself suddenly. "Who are you, anyhow?" **102**

For a moment Dexter hesitated. Then: **103**

"I'm nobody," he announced. "My career is largely a matter of futures." **104**

"Are you poor?" **105**

"No," he said frankly, "I'm probably making more money than any man my age in the Northwest. I know that's an obnoxious remark, but you advised me to start right." **106**

There was a pause. Then she smiled and the corners of her mouth drooped and an almost imperceptible sway brought her closer to him, looking up into his eyes. A lump rose in Dexter's throat, and he waited breathless for the experiment, facing the unpredictable compound that would form mysteriously from the elements of their lips. Then he saw—she communicated her excitement to him, lavishly, deeply, with kisses that were not a promise but a fulfillment. They aroused in him not hunger demanding renewal but surfeit that would demand more surfeit . . . kisses that were like charity, creating want by holding back nothing at all. **107**

It did not take him many hours to decide that he had wanted Judy Jones ever since he was a proud, desirous little boy. **108**

IV

It began like that—and continued, with varying shades of intensity, on such a note right up to the dénouement. Dexter surrendered a part of himself to the most direct **109** and unprincipled personality with which he had ever come in contact. Whatever Judy wanted, she went after with the full pressure of her charm. There was no divergence of method, no jockeying for position or premeditation of effects—there was a very little mental side to any of her affairs. She simply made men conscious to the highest degree of her physical loveliness. Dexter had no desire to change her. Her deficiencies were knit up with a passionate energy that transcended and justified them.

When, as Judy's head lay against his shoulders that first night, she whispered, "I don't know what's the matter with me. Last night I thought I was in love with a man and to-night I think I'm in love with you—"—it seemed to him a beautiful and romantic thing to say. It was the exquisite excitability that for the moment he controlled and owned. But a week later he was compelled to view this same quality in a different light. She took him in her roadster to a picnic supper, and after supper she disappeared, likewise in her roadster, with another man. Dexter became enormously upset and was scarcely able to be decently civil to the other people present. When she assured him that she had not kissed the other man, he knew she was lying—yet he was glad that she had taken the trouble to lie to him.   110

He was, as he found before the summer ended, one of a varying dozen who circulated about her. Each of them had at one time been favored above all others—about half of them still basked in the solace of occasional sentimental revivals. Whenever one showed signs of dropping out through long neglect, she granted him a brief honeyed hour, which encouraged him to tag along for a year or so longer. Judy made these forays upon the helpless and defeated without malice, indeed half unconscious that there was anything mischievous in what she did.   111

When a new man came to town every one dropped out—dates were automatically cancelled.   112

The helpless part of trying to do anything about it was that she did it all herself. She was not a girl who could be "won" in the kinetic sense—she was proof against cleverness, she was proof against charm; if any of these assailed her too strongly she would immediately resolve the affair to a physical basis, and under the magic of her physical splendor the strong as well as the brilliant played her game and not their own. She was entertained only by the gratification of her desires and by the direct exercise of her own charm. Perhaps from so much youthful love, so many youthful lovers, she had come, in self-defense, to nourish herself wholly from within.   113

Succeeding Dexter's first exhilaration came restlessness and dissatisfaction. The helpless ecstasy of losing himself in her was opiate rather than tonic. It was fortunate for his work during the winter that those moments of ecstasy came infrequently. Early in their acquaintance it had seemed for a while that there was a deep and spontaneous mutual attraction—that first August, for example—three days of long evenings on her dusky veranda, of strange wan kisses through the late afternoon, in shadowy alcoves or behind the protecting trellises of the garden arbors, of mornings when she was fresh as a dream and almost shy at meeting him in the clarity of the rising day. There was all the ecstasy of an engagement about it, sharpened by his realization that there was no engagement. It was during those three days that, for the first time, he   114 had asked her to marry him. She said "Maybe some day," she said "kiss me," she said "I'd like to marry you," she said "I love you"—she said—nothing.

The three days were interrupted by the arrival of a New York man who visited 115 at her house for half September. To Dexter's agony, rumor engaged them. The man was the son of the president of a great trust company. But at the end of a month it was reported that Judy was yawning. At a dance one night she sat all evening in a motor-boat with a local beau, while the New Yorker searched the club for her frantically. She told the local beau that she was bored with her visitor, and two days later he left. She was seen with him at the station, and it was reported that he looked very mournful indeed.

On this note the summer ended. Dexter was twenty-four, and he found him- 116 self increasingly in a position to do as he wished. He joined two clubs in the city and lived at one of them. Though he was by no means an integral part of the stag-lines at these clubs, he managed to be on hand at dances where Judy Jones was likely to appear. He could have gone out socially as much as he liked—he was an eligible young man, now, and popular with down-town fathers. His confessed devotion to Judy Jones had rather solidified his position. But he had no social aspirations and rather despised the dancing men who were always on tap for the Thursday or Saturday parties and who filled in at dinners with the younger married set. Already he was playing with the idea of going East to New York. He wanted to take Judy Jones with him. No disillusion as to the world in which she had grown up could cure his illusion as to her desirability.

Remember that—for only in the light of it can what he did for her be 117 understood.

Eighteen months after he first met Judy Jones he became engaged to another 118 girl. Her name was Irene Scheerer, and her father was one of the men who had always believed in Dexter. Irene was light-haired and sweet and honorable, and a little stout, and she had two suitors whom she pleasantly relinquished when Dexter formally asked her to marry him.

Summer, fall, winter, spring, another summer, another fall—so much he had 119 given of his active life to the incorrigible lips of Judy Jones. She had treated him with interest, with encouragement, with malice, with indifference, with contempt. She had inflicted on him the innumerable little slights and indignities possible in such a case—as if in revenge for having ever cared for him at all. She had beckoned him and yawned at him and beckoned him again and he had responded often with bitterness and narrowed eyes. She had brought him ecstatic happiness and intolerable agony of spirit. She had caused him untold inconvenience and not a little trouble. She had insulted him, and she had ridden over him, and she had played his interest in her against his interest in his work—for fun. She had done everything to him except to criticise him—this she had not done—it seemed to him only because it might have sullied the utter indifference she manifested and sincerely felt toward him.

When autumn had come and gone again it occurred to him that he could not 120 have Judy Jones. He had to beat this into his mind but he convinced himself at last. He lay awake at night for a while and argued it over. He told himself the trouble and the pain she had caused him, he enumerated her glaring deficiencies as a wife. Then he said to himself that he loved her, and after a while he fell asleep. For a week, lest he imagine her husky voice over the telephone or her eyes opposite him at lunch, he worked hard and late, and at night he went to his office and plotted out his years.

At the end of a week he went to a dance and cut in on her once. For almost 121 the first time since they had met he did not ask her to sit out with him or tell her that she was lovely. It hurt him that she did not miss these things—that was all. He was not jealous when he saw that there was a new man to-night. He had been hardened against jealousy long before.

He stayed late at the dance. He sat for an hour with Irene Scheerer and talked 122 about books and about music. He knew very little about either. But he was beginning to be master of his own time now, and he had a rather priggish notion that he— the young and already fabulously successful Dexter Green—should know more about such things.

That was in October, when he was twenty-five. In January, Dexter and Irene 123 became engaged. It was to be announced in June, and they were to be married three months later.

The Minnesota winter prolonged itself interminably, and it was almost May when 124 the winds came soft and the snow ran down into Black Bear Lake at last. For the first time in over a year Dexter was enjoying a certain tranquility of spirit. Judy Jones had been in Florida, and afterward in Hot Springs, and somewhere she had been engaged, and somewhere she had broken it off. At first, when Dexter had definitely given her up, it had made him sad that people still linked them together and asked for news of her, but when he began to be placed at dinner next to Irene Scheerer people didn't ask him about her any more—they told him about her. He ceased to be an authority on her.

May at last. Dexter walked the streets at night when the darkness was damp as 125 rain, wondering that so soon, with so little done, so much of ecstasy had gone from him. May one year back had been marked by Judy's poignant, unforgivable, yet forgiven turbulence—it had been one of those rare times when he fancied she had grown to care for him. That old penny's worth of happiness he had spent for this bushel of content. He knew that Irene would be no more than a curtain spread behind him, a hand moving among gleaming teacups, a voice calling to children . . . fire and loveliness were gone, the magic of nights and the wonder of the varying hours and seasons . . . slender lips, down-turning, dropping to his lips and bearing him up into a heaven of eyes. . . . The thing was deep in him. He was too strong and alive for it to die lightly.

In the middle of May when the weather balanced for a few days on the thin 126 bridge that led to deep summer he turned in one night at Irene's house. Their engagement was to be announced in a week now—no one would be surprised at it. And to-night they would sit together on the lounge at the University Club and look on for an hour at the dancers. It gave him a sense of solidity to go with her—she was so sturdily popular, so intensely "great."

He mounted the steps of the brownstone house and stepped inside. 127

"Irene," he called. 128

Mrs. Scheerer came out of the living-room to meet him. 129

"Dexter," she said, "Irene's gone up-stairs with a splitting headache. She wanted 130
to go with you but I made her go to bed."

"Nothing serious, I—" 131

"Oh, no. She's going to play golf with you in the morning. You can spare her 132
for just one night, can't you, Dexter?"

Her smile was kind. She and Dexter liked each other. In the living-room he 133
talked for a moment before he said good-night.

Returning to the University Club, where he had rooms, he stood in the door- 134
way for a moment and watched the dancers. He leaned against the door-post, nodded at a man or two—yawned.

"Hello, darling." 135

The familiar voice at his elbow startled him. Judy Jones had left a man and 136
crossed the room to him—Judy Jones, a slender enameled doll in cloth of gold: gold
in a band at her head, gold in two slipper points at her dress's hem. The fragile glow
of her face seemed to blossom as she smiled at him. A breeze of warmth and light
blew through the room. His hands in the pockets of his dinner-jacket tightened spasmodically. He was filled with a sudden excitement.

"When did you get back?" he asked casually. 137

"Come here and I'll tell you about it." 138

She turned and he followed her. She had been away—he could have wept at the 139
wonder of her return. She had passed through enchanted streets, doing things that
were like provocative music. All mysterious happenings, all fresh and quickening
hopes, had gone away with her, come back with her now.

She turned in the doorway. 140

"Have you a car here? If you haven't, I have." 141

"I have a coupé." 142

In then, with a rustle of golden cloth. He slammed the door. Into so many cars 143
she had stepped—like this—like that—her back against the leather, so—her elbow
resting on the door—waiting. She would have been soiled long since had there been
anything to soil her—except herself—but this was her own self outpouring.

With an effort he forced himself to start the car and back into the street. This 144
was nothing, he must remember. She had done this before, and he had put her behind
him, as he would have crossed a bad account from his books.

He drove slowly down-town and, affecting abstraction, traversed the deserted 145
streets of the business section, peopled here and there where a movie was giving
out its crowd or where consumptive or pugilistic youth lounged in front of pool halls.
The clink of glasses and the slap of hands on the bars issued from saloons, cloisters
of glazed glass and dirty yellow light.

She was watching closely and the silence was embarrassing, yet in this crisis 146
he could find no casual word with which to profane the hour. At a convenient turning he began to zigzag back toward the University Club.

"Have you missed me?" she asked suddenly. 147

"Everybody missed you." 148

He wondered if she knew of Irene Scheerer. She had been back only a day—her 149
absence had been almost contemporaneous with his engagement.

"What a remark!" Judy laughed sadly—without sadness. She looked at him 150
searchingly. He became absorbed in the dashboard.

"You're handsomer than you used to be," she said thoughtfully. "Dexter, you have 151
the most rememberable eyes."

He could have laughed at this, but he did not laugh. It was the sort of thing that 152
was said to sophomores. Yet it stabbed at him.

"I'm awfully tired of everything, darling." She called everyone darling, endow- 153
ing the endearment with careless, individual comraderie. "I wish you'd marry me."

The directness of this confused him. He should have told her now that he was 154
going to marry another girl, but he could not tell her. He could as easily have sworn
that he had never loved her.

"I think we'd get along," she continued, on the same note, "unless probably 155
you've forgotten me and fallen in love with another girl."

Her confidence was obviously enormous. She had said, in effect, that she found 156
such a thing impossible to believe, that if it were true he had merely committed a
childish indiscretion—and probably to show off. She would forgive him, because it
was not a matter of any moment but rather something to be brushed aside lightly.

"Of course you could never love anybody but me," she continued, "I like the way 157
you love me. Oh, Dexter, have you forgotten last year?"

"No, I haven't forgotten." 158

"Neither have I!" 159

Was she sincerely moved—or was she carried along by the wave of her own acting? 160

"I wish we could be like that again," she said, and he forced himself to answer: 161

"I don't think we can." 162

"I suppose not. . . . I hear you're giving Irene Scheerer a violent rush." 163

There was not the faintest emphasis on the name, yet Dexter was suddenly 164
ashamed.

"Oh, take me home," cried Judy suddenly; "I don't want to go back to that idi- 165
otic dance—with those children."

Then, as he turned up the street that led to the residence district, Judy began 166
to cry quietly to herself. He had never seen her cry before.

The dark street lightened, the dwellings of the rich loomed up around them, 167
he stopped his coupé in front of the great white bulk of the Mortimer Joneses' house,
somnolent, gorgeous, drenched with the splendor of the damp moonlight. Its solidity startled him. The strong walls, the steel of the girders, the breadth and beam
and pomp of it were there only to bring out the contrast with the young beauty beside
him. It was sturdy to accentuate her slightness—as if to show what a breeze could
be generated by a butterfly's wing.

He sat perfectly quiet, his nerves in wild clamor, afraid that if he moved he would 168
find her irresistibly in his arms. Two tears had rolled down her wet face and trembled
on her upper lip.

"I'm more beautiful than anybody else," she said brokenly, "why can't I be happy?" 169
Her moist eyes tore at his stability—her mouth turned slowly downward with an

exquisite sadness: "I'd like to marry you if you'll have me, Dexter. I suppose you think I'm not worth having, but I'll be so beautiful for you, Dexter."

A million phrases of anger, pride, passion, hatred, tenderness fought on his 170 lips. Then a perfect wave of emotion washed over him, carrying off with it a sediment of wisdom, of convention, of doubt, of honor. This was his girl who was speaking, his own, his beautiful, his pride.

"Won't you come in?" He heard her draw in her breath sharply.   171

Waiting.   172

"All right," his voice was trembling, "I'll come in."   173

V

It was strange that neither when it was over nor a long time afterward did he regret 174 that night. Looking at it from the perspective of ten years, the fact that Judy's flare for him endured just one month seemed of little importance. Nor did it matter that by his yielding he subjected himself to a deeper agony in the end and gave serious hurt to Irene Scheerer and to Irene's parents, who had befriended him. There was nothing sufficiently pictorial about Irene's grief to stamp itself on his mind.

Dexter was at bottom hard-minded. The attitude of the city on his action was 175 of no importance to him, not because he was going to leave the city, but because any outside attitude on the situation seemed superficial. He was completely indifferent to popular opinion. Nor, when he had seen that it was no use, that he did not possess in himself the power to move fundamentally or to hold Judy Jones, did he bear any malice toward her. He loved her, and he would love her until the day he was too old for loving—but he could not have her. So he tasted the deep pain that is reserved only for the strong, just as he had tasted for a little while the deep happiness.

Even the ultimate falsity of the grounds upon which Judy terminated the 176 engagement—that she did not want to "take him away" from Irene—Judy, who had wanted nothing else—did not revolt him. He was beyond any revulsion or any amusement.

He went East in February with the intention of selling out his laundries and set- 177 tling in New York—but the war came to America in March and changed his plans. He returned to the West, handed over the management of the business to his partner, and went into the first officers' training-camp in late April. He was one of those young thousands who greeted the war with a certain amount of relief, welcoming the liberation from webs of tangled emotion.

VI

This story is not his biography, remember, although things creep into it which have 178 nothing to do with those dreams he had when he was young. We are almost done with them and with him now. There is only one more incident to be related here, and it happens seven years farther on.

It took place in New York, where he had done well—so well that there were 179 no barriers too high for him. He was thirty-two years old, and, except for one flying trip immediately after the war, he had not been West in seven years. A man named

Devlin from Detroit came into his office to see him in a business way, and then and there this incident occurred, and closed out, so to speak, this particular side of his life.

"So you're from the Middle West," said the man Devlin with careless curiosity. 180
"That's funny—I thought men like you were probably born and raised on Wall Street. You know—wife of one of my best friends in Detroit came from your city. I was an usher at the wedding."

Dexter waited with no apprehension of what was coming. 181

"Judy Simms," said Devlin with no particular interest; "Judy Jones she was once." 182

"Yes, I knew her." A dull impatience spread over him. He had heard, of course, 183
that she was married—perhaps deliberately he had heard no more.

"Awfully nice girl," brooded Devlin meaninglessly, "I'm sort of sorry for her." 184

"Why?" Something in Dexter was alert, receptive, at once. 185

"Oh, Lud Simms has gone to pieces in a way. I don't mean he ill-uses her, but he 186
drinks and runs around—"

"Doesn't she run around?" 187

"No. Stays at home with her kids." 188

"Oh." 189

"She's a little too old for him," said Devlin. 190

"Too old!" cried Dexter. "Why, man, she's only twenty-seven." 191

He was possessed with a wild notion of rushing out into the streets and taking 192
a train to Detroit. He rose to his feet spasmodically.

"I guess you're busy," Devlin apologized quickly. "I didn't realize—" 193

"No, I'm not busy," said Dexter, steadying his voice. "I'm not busy at all. Not 194
busy at all. Did you say she was—twenty-seven? No, I said she was twenty-seven."

"Yes, you did," agreed Devlin dryly. 195

"Go on, then. Go on." 196

"What do you mean?" 197

"About Judy Jones." 198

Devlin looked at him helplessly. 199

"Well, that's—I told you all there is to it. He treats her like the devil. Oh, they're 200
not going to get divorced or anything. When he's particularly outrageous she forgives him. In fact, I'm inclined to think she loves him. She was a pretty girl when she first came to Detroit."

A pretty girl! The phrase struck Dexter as ludicrous. 201

"Isn't she—a pretty girl, any more?" 202

"Oh, she's all right." 203

"Look here," said Dexter, sitting down suddenly. "I don't understand. You say she 204
was a 'pretty girl' and now you say she's 'all right.' I don't understand what you mean—Judy Jones wasn't a pretty girl, at all. She was a great beauty. Why, I knew her, I knew her. She was—"

Devlin laughed pleasantly. 205

"I'm not trying to start a row," he said. "I think Judy's a nice girl and I like her. 206
I can't understand how a man like Lud Simms could fall madly in love with her, but he did." Then he added: "Most of the women like her."

Dexter looked closely at Devlin, thinking wildly that there must be a reason 207
for this, some insensitivity in the man or some private malice.

"Lots of women fade just like *that*," Devlin snapped his fingers. "You must have 208
seen it happen. Perhaps I've forgotten how pretty she was at her wedding. I've seen
her so much since then, you see. She has nice eyes."

A sort of dullness settled down upon Dexter. For the first time in his life he 209
felt like getting very drunk. He knew that he was laughing loudly at something Devlin
had said, but he did not know what it was or why it was funny. When, in a few minutes, Devlin went he lay down on his lounge and looked out the window at the New
York sky-line into which the sun was sinking in dull lovely shades of pink and gold.

He had thought that having nothing else to lose he was invulnerable at last— 210
but he knew that he had just lost something more, as surely as if he had married Judy
Jones and seen her fade away before his eyes.

The dream was gone. Something had been taken from him. In a sort of panic he 211
pushed the palms of his hands into his eyes and tried to bring up a picture of the waters
lapping on Sherry Island and the moon-lit veranda, and gingham on the golf-links
and the dry sun and the gold color of her neck's soft down. And her mouth damp
to his kisses and her eyes plaintive with melancholy and her freshness like a new fine
linen in the morning. Why, these things were no longer in the world! They had
existed and they existed no longer.

For the first time in years the tears were streaming down his face. But they were 212
for himself now. He did not care about mouth and eyes and moving hands. He wanted
to care, and he could not care. For he had gone away and he could never go back any
more. The gates were closed, the sun was gone down, and there was no beauty but
the gray beauty of steel that withstands all time. Even the grief he could have borne
was left behind in the country of illusion, of youth, of the richness of life, where his
winter dreams had flourished.

"Long ago," he said, "long ago, there was something in me, but now that thing 213
is gone. Now that thing is gone, that thing is gone. I cannot cry. I cannot care. That
thing will come back no more."

Questions for Discussion, Reflection, and Writing

1. Why does the story begin by distinguishing Dexter's economic class from that of "some
   of the [other] caddies"? What does class have to do with it?

2. Can you explain why a story that begins by identifying its protagonist as a caddy would
   then proceed to describe him on the links—in winter? What draws Dexter there?

3. Compare the way "Miss Jones" is described as a girl to the way Dexter has so far been
   described. What kinds of things do we know about each? (Do we, for example, know
   what Dexter looks like? Do we know what the girl looks like?) Abstract from this to
   a provisional analysis of how Fitzgerald builds character in his fiction.

4. What is the significance of the description of Dexter's "winter dreams" in the first paragraph of Part II? What *are* "winter dreams"?

5. Why should Dexter want to "lessen the gap which lay between his present and his past"
   (par. 50)? What role does the past play in his life—and in the story?

6. How does Irene compare to Judy, in Dexter's eyes? Do we have any basis for challenging his judgment?

7. The observation that opens Part VI makes it seem as if what we learn next about Dexter is an afterthought. Is it? How important is what we learn next to a full understanding of why the story was told in the first place?

8. What is the effect on Dexter of Devlin's statement (in paragraph 200) that Judy was "a pretty girl"? What effect does it have on Dexter?

9. Paragraph 211 begins, "The dream was gone." What was this dream? What happened to it?

§ Connect the readings: Compare Dexter's ambitions—and his achievement—to those of Paul in Willa Cather's "Paul's Case." Does one protagonist win more of the reader's sympathy than the other? If so, why?

Nathaniel Hawthorne (1804–1864) was born in Salem, Massachusetts, into a prominent and old family; one of the founding families of Salem. His family's history sparked his interest in colonial New England, which became the setting of many of his stories and novels. Hawthorne's father was a ship captain who died when Hawthorne was just four years old; the boy was sent to live with relatives who recognized his talent and sent him to good schools and later to Bowdoin College. They even supported him at various times during his writing career. Hawthorne graduated from Bowdoin in 1825; in 1828 he published *Fanshawe*, a romance that Hawthorne later considered so poorly written that he tried to destroy all copies. Developing a new format for his stories, a format that limited stories to just one scene with a tightly controlled plot, he began writing the stories for which he is known today. The stories began with *The Hollow of the Three Hills* (1830), published in the *Salem Gazette*. This was followed by other stories published at first separately and then in a single book, *Twice-Told Tales* (1837). In 1836, Hawthorne moved to Boston, hoping to make his reputation as an editor; however, the owners of the magazine (*The American Magazine of Useful and Entertaining Knowledge*), never paid his salary, so Hawthorne was forced to quit after just a few months. For two years he worked as a measurer in the Boston customhouse; he liked the job, but it gave him no time for writing. At that time he also became interested in Transcendentalism and quit his job to join the Brook Farm commune in April 1841. Unfortunately, this venture also did not give him enough time to write, and he left in November. When he married soon after leaving Brook Farm, he and his wife lived near Ralph Waldo Emerson in Concord; *Mosses from an Old Manse* (1846) describes their time there. In 1846, Hawthorne again worked as a customs agent, this time as the surveyor of the port of Salem. However, in 1849, with a new party in the presidential office, he lost that job. Several of his novels published soon afterward gave him a degree of financial security; those novels are his famous *The Scarlet Letter* (1850); *The House of the Seven Gables* (1851); *The Snow-Image*, and *Other Twice-Told Tales* (1852); and *The Blithedale Romance* (1852). In 1852, his college friend Franklin Pierce, was elected president and Hawthorne was given a short-term job in Liverpool, England, as American consul. He was finally able to travel in Europe and lived in Italy until 1862 when the Civil War compelled him to return to the United States. A last novel, *The Marble Faun* (1860), was inspired by his time in Italy.

The Birthmark

Nathaniel Hawthorne

In the latter part of the last century there lived a man of science, an eminent profi-   1
cient in every branch of natural philosophy, who not long before our story opens had made experience of a spiritual affinity more attractive than any chemical one. He had left his laboratory to the care of an assistant, cleared his fine countenance from the furnace smoke, washed the stain of acids from his fingers, and persuaded a beautiful woman to become his wife. In those days, when the comparatively recent discovery of electricity and other kindred mysteries of Nature seemed to open paths into the region of miracle, it was not unusual for the love of science to rival the love of woman in its depth and absorbing energy. The higher intellect, the imagination, the spirit, and even the heart might all find their congenial ailment in pursuits which, as some of their ardent votaries believed, would ascend from one step of powerful intelligence to another, until the philosopher should lay his hand on the secret of creative force and perhaps make new worlds for himself. We know not whether

Aylmer possessed this degree of faith in man's ultimate control over Nature. He had devoted himself, however, too unreservedly to scientific studies ever to be weaned from them by any second passion. His love for his young wife might prove the stronger of the two; but it could only be by intertwining itself with his love of science and uniting the strength of the latter to his own.

Such a union accordingly took place, and was attended with truly remarkable consequences and a deeply impressive moral. One day, very soon after their marriage, Aylmer sat gazing at his wife with a trouble in his countenance that grew stronger until he spoke.

2

"Georgiana," said he, "has it never occurred to you that the mark upon your cheek might be removed?"

3

"No, indeed," said she, smiling; but, perceiving the seriousness of his manner, she blushed deeply. "To tell you the truth, it has been so often called a charm that I was simple enough to imagine it might be so."

4

"Ah, upon another face perhaps it might," replied her husband; "but never on yours. No, dearest Georgiana, you came so nearly perfect from the hand of Nature that this slightest possible defect, which we hesitate whether to term a defect or a beauty, shocks me, as being the visible mark of earthly imperfection."

5

"Shocks you, my husband!" cried Georgiana, deeply hurt; at first reddening with momentary anger, but then bursting into tears. "Then why did you take me from my mother's side? You cannot love what shocks you!"

6

To explain this conversation, it must be mentioned that in the centre of Georgiana's left cheek there was a singular mark, deeply interwoven, as it were, with the texture and substance of her face. In the usual state of her complexion—a healthy though delicate bloom—the mark wore a tint of deeper crimson, which imperfectly defined its shape amid the surrounding rosiness. When she blushed it gradually became more indistinct, and finally vanished amid the triumphant rush of blood that bathed the whole cheek with its brilliant glow. But if any shifting motion caused her to turn pale there was the mark again, a crimson stain upon the snow, in what Aylmer sometimes deemed an almost fearful distinctness. Its shape bore not a little similarity to the human hand, though of the smallest pygmy size. Georgiana's lovers were wont to say that some fairy at her birth hour had laid her tiny hand upon the infant's cheek, and left this impress there in token of the magic endowments that were to give her such sway over all hearts. Many a desperate swain would have risked life for the privilege of pressing his lips to the mysterious hand. It must not be concealed, however, that the impression wrought by this fairy sign manual varied exceedingly according to the difference of temperament in the beholders. Some fastidious persons—but they were exclusively of her own sex—affirmed that the bloody hand, as they chose to call it, quite destroyed the effect of Georgiana's beauty and rendered her countenance even hideous. But it would be as reasonable to say that one of those small blue stains which sometimes occur in the purest statuary marble would convert the Eve of Powers to a monster. Masculine observers, if the birthmark did not heighten their admiration, contented themselves with wishing it away, that the world might possess one living specimen of ideal loveliness without the semblance of a flaw.

7

After his marriage,—for he thought little or nothing of the matter before,—Aylmer discovered that this was the case with himself.

Had she been less beautiful,—if Envy's self could have found aught else to sneer   8
at,—he might have felt his affection heightened by the prettiness of this mimic hand, now vaguely portrayed, now lost, now stealing forth again and glimmering to and fro with every pulse of emotion that throbbed within her heart; but, seeing her otherwise so perfect, he found this one defect grow more and more intolerable with every moment of their united lives. It was the fatal flaw of humanity which Nature, in one shape or another, stamps ineffaceably on all her productions, either to imply that they are temporary and finite, or that their perfection must be wrought by toil and pain. The crimson hand expressed the ineludible gripe in which mortality clutches the highest and purest of earthly mould, degrading them into kindred with the lowest, and even with the very brutes, like whom their visible frames return to dust. In this manner, selecting it as the symbol of his wife's liability to sin, sorrow, decay, and death, Aylmer's sombre imagination was not long in rendering the birthmark a frightful object, causing him more trouble and horror than ever Georgiana's beauty, whether of soul or sense, had given him delight.

At all the seasons which should have been their happiest he invariably, and with-   9
out intending it, nay, in spite of a purpose to the contrary, reverted to this one disastrous topic. Trifling as it at first appeared, it so connected itself with innumerable trains of thought and modes of feeling that it became the central point of all. With the morning twilight Aylmer opened his eyes upon his wife's face and recognized the symbol of imperfection; and when they sat together at the evening hearth his eyes wandered stealthily to her cheek, and beheld, flickering with the blaze of the wood fire, the spectral hand that wrote mortality where he would fain have worshipped. Georgiana soon learned to shudder at his gaze. It needed but a glance with the peculiar expression that his face often wore to change the roses of her cheek into a deathlike paleness, amid which the crimson hand was brought strongly out, like a bas relief of ruby on the whitest marble.

Late one night, when the lights were growing dim so as hardly to betray the stain   10
on the poor wife's cheek, she herself, for the first time, voluntarily took up the subject.

"Do you remember, my dear Aylmer," said she, with a feeble attempt at a smile,   11
"have you any recollection, of a dream last night about this odious hand?"

"None! none whatever!" replied Aylmer, starting; but then he added, in a dry,   12
cold tone, affected for the sake of concealing the real depth of his emotion, "I might well dream of it; for, before I fell asleep, it had taken a pretty firm hold of my fancy."

"And you did dream of it?" continued Georgiana, hastily; for she dreaded lest   13
a gush of tears should interrupt what she had to say. "A terrible dream! I wonder that you can forget it. Is it possible to forget this one expression?—'It is in her heart now; we must have it out!' Reflect, my husband; for by all means I would have you recall that dream."

The mind is in a sad state when Sleep, the all-involving, cannot confine her   14
spectres within the dim region of her sway, but suffers them to break forth, affrighting this actual life with secrets that perchance belong to a deeper one. Aylmer now

remembered his dream. He had fancied himself with his servant Aminadab, attempting an operation for the removal of the birthmark; but the deeper went the knife, the deeper sank the hand, until at length its tiny grasp appeared to have caught hold of Georgiana's heart; whence, however, her husband was inexorably resolved to cut or wrench it away.

When the dream had shaped itself perfectly in his memory Aylmer sat in his wife's presence with a guilty feeling. Truth often finds its way to the mind close muffled in robes of sleep, and then speaks with uncompromising directness of matters in regard to which we practise an unconscious self-deception during our waking moments. Until now he had not been aware of the tyrannizing influence acquired by one idea over his mind, and of the lengths which he might find in his heart to go for the sake of giving himself peace. 15

"Aylmer," resumed Georgiana, solemnly, "I know not what may be the cost to both of us to rid me of this fatal birthmark. Perhaps its removal may cause cureless deformity; or it may be the stain goes as deep as life itself. Again: do we know that there is a possibility, on any terms, of unclasping the firm grip of this little hand which was laid upon me before I came into the world?" 16

"Dearest Georgiana, I have spent much thought on the subject," hastily interrupted Aylmer. "I am convinced of the perfect practicability of its removal." 17

"If there be the remotest possibility of it," continued Georgiana, "let the attempt be made, at whatever risk. Danger is nothing to me; for life, while this hateful mark makes me the object of your horror and disgust—life is a burden which I would fling down with joy. Either remove this dreadful hand, or take my wretched life! You have deep science. All the world bears witness of it. You have achieved great wonders. Cannot you remove this little, little mark, which I cover with the tips of two small fingers? Is this beyond your power, for the sake of your own peace, and to save your poor wife from madness?" 18

"Noblest, dearest, tenderest wife," cried Aylmer, rapturously, "doubt not my power. I have already given this matter the deepest thought—thought which might almost have enlightened me to create a being less perfect than yourself. Georgiana, you have led me deeper than ever into the heart of science. I feel myself fully competent to render this dear cheek as faultless as its fellow; and then, most beloved, what will be my triumph when I shall have corrected what Nature left imperfect in her fairest work! Even Pygmalion, when his sculptured woman assumed life, felt not greater ecstasy than mine will be." 19

"It is resolved, then," said Georgiana, faintly smiling. "And, Aylmer, spare me not, though you should find the birthmark take refuge in my heart at last." 20

Her husband tenderly kissed her cheek—her right cheek—not that which bore the impress of the crimson hand. 21

The next day Aylmer apprised his wife of a plan that he had formed whereby he might have opportunity for the intense thought and constant watchfulness which the proposed operation would require; while Georgiana, likewise, would enjoy the perfect repose essential to its success. They were to seclude themselves in the extensive apartments occupied by Aylmer as a laboratory, and where, during his toilsome youth, he had made discoveries in the elemental powers of Nature that had roused 22 the admiration of all the learned societies in Europe. Seated calmly in this laboratory, the pale philosopher had investigated the secrets of the highest cloud region and of the profoundest mines; he had satisfied himself of the causes that kindled and kept alive the fires of the volcano; and had explained the mystery of fountains, and how it is that they gush forth; some so bright and pure, and others with such rich medicinal virtues, from the dark bosom of the earth. Here, too, at an earlier period, he had studied the wonders of the human frame, and attempted to fathom the very process by which Nature assimilates all her precious influences from earth and air, and from the spiritual world, to create and foster man, her masterpiece. The latter pursuit, however, Aylmer had long laid aside in unwilling recognition of the truth— against which all seekers sooner or later stumble—that our great creative Mother, while she amuses us with apparently working in the broadest sunshine, is yet severely careful to keep her own secrets, and, in spite of her pretended openness, shows us nothing but results. She permits us, indeed, to mar, but seldom to mend, and, like a jealous patentee, on no account to make. Now, however, Aylmer resumed these half-forgotten investigations; not, of course, with such hopes or wishes as first suggested them; but because they involved much physiological truth and lay in the path of his proposed scheme for the treatment of Georgiana.

As he led her over the threshold of the laboratory, Georgiana was cold and tremulous. Aylmer looked cheerfully into her face, with intent to reassure her, but was so startled with the intense glow of the birthmark upon the whiteness of her cheek that he could not restrain a strong convulsive shudder. His wife fainted.   23

"Aminadab! Aminadab!" shouted Aylmer, stamping violently on the floor.   24

Forthwith there issued from an inner apartment a man of low stature, but bulky frame, with shaggy hair hanging about his visage, which was grimed with the vapors of the furnace. This personage had been Aylmer's underworker during his whole scientific career, and was admirably fitted for that office by his great mechanical readiness, and the skill with which, while incapable of comprehending a single principle, he executed all the details of his master's experiments. With his vast strength, his shaggy hair, his smoky aspect, and the indescribable earthiness that incrusted him, he seemed to represent man's physical nature; while Aylmer's slender figure, and pale, intellectual face, were no less apt a type of the spiritual element.   25

"Throw open the door of the boudoir, Aminadab," said Aylmer, "and burn a pastil."   26

"Yes, master," answered Aminadab, looking intently at the lifeless form of Georgiana; and then he muttered to himself, "If she were my wife, I'd never part with that birthmark."   27

When Georgiana recovered consciousness she found herself breathing an atmosphere of penetrating fragrance, the gentle potency of which had recalled her from her deathlike faintness. The scene around her looked like enchantment. Aylmer had converted those smoky, dingy, sombre rooms, where he had spent his brightest years in recondite pursuits, into a series of beautiful apartments not unfit to be the secluded abode of a lovely woman. The walls were hung with gorgeous curtains, which imparted the combination of grandeur and grace that no other species of adornment can achieve; and, as they fell from the ceiling to the floor, their rich and ponderous   28 folds, concealing all angles and straight lines, appeared to shut in the scene from infinite space. For aught Georgiana knew, it might be a pavilion among the clouds. And Aylmer, excluding the sunshine, which would have interfered with his chemical processes, had supplied its place with perfumed lamps, emitting flames of various hue, but all uniting in a soft, impurpled radiance. He now knelt by his wife's side, watching her earnestly, but without alarm; for he was confident in his science, and felt that he could draw a magic circle round her within which no evil might intrude.

"Where am I? Ah, I remember," said Georgiana, faintly; and she placed her hand   29
over her cheek to hide the terrible mark from her husband's eyes.

"Fear not, dearest!" exclaimed he. "Do not shrink from me! Believe me,   30
Georgiana, I even rejoice in this single imperfection, since it will be such a rapture to remove it."

"O, spare me!" sadly replied his wife. "Pray do not look at it again. I never can   31
forget that convulsive shudder."

In order to soothe Georgiana, and, as it were, to release her mind from the bur-   32
den of actual things, Aylmer now put in practice some of the light and playful secrets which science had taught him among its profounder lore. Airy figures, absolutely bodiless ideas, and forms of unsubstantial beauty came and danced before her, imprinting their momentary footsteps on beams of light. Though she had some indistinct idea of the method of these optical phenomena, still the illusion was almost perfect enough to warrant the belief that her husband possessed sway over the spiritual world. Then again, when she felt a wish to look forth from her seclusion, immediately, as if her thoughts were answered, the procession of external existence flitted across a screen. The scenery and the figures of actual life were perfectly represented, but with that bewitching yet indescribable difference which always makes a picture, an image, or a shadow so much more attractive than the original. When wearied of this, Aylmer bade her cast her eyes upon a vessel containing a quantity of earth. She did so, with little interest at first; but was soon startled to perceive the germ of a plant shooting upward from the soil. Then came the slender stalk; the leaves gradually unfolded themselves; and amid them was a perfect and lovely flower.

"It is magical!" cried Georgiana. "I dare not touch it."   33

"Nay, pluck it," answered Aylmer,—"pluck it, and inhale its brief perfume while   34
you may. The flower will wither in a few moments and leave nothing save its brown seed vessels; but thence may be perpetuated a race as ephemeral as itself."

But Georgiana had no sooner touched the flower than the whole plant suf-   35
fered a blight, its leaves turning coal-black as if by the agency of fire.

"There was too powerful a stimulus," said Aylmer, thoughtfully.   36

To make up for this abortive experiment, he proposed to take her portrait by a   37
scientific process of his own invention. It was to be effected by rays of light striking upon a polished plate of metal. Georgiana assented; but, on looking at the result, was affrighted to find the features of the portrait blurred and indefinable; while the minute figure of a hand appeared where the cheek should have been. Aylmer snatched the metallic plate and threw it into a jar of corrosive acid.

Soon, however, he forgot these mortifying failures. In the intervals of study   38
and chemical experiment he came to her flushed and exhausted, but seemed invig-

orated by her presence, and spoke in glowing language of the resources of his art. He gave a history of the long dynasty of the alchemists, who spent so many ages in quest of the universal solvent by which the golden principle might be elicited from all things vile and base. Aylmer appeared to believe that, by the plainest scientific logic, it was altogether within the limits of possibility to discover this long-sought medium; "but," he added, "a philosopher who should go deep enough to acquire the power would attain too lofty a wisdom to stoop to the exercise of it." Not less singular were his opinions in regard to the elixir vitae. He more than intimated that it was at his option to concoct a liquid that should prolong life for years, perhaps interminably; but that it would produce a discord in Nature which all the world, and chiefly the quaffer of the immortal nostrum, would find cause to curse.

"Aylmer, are you in earnest?" asked Georgiana, looking at him with amazement and fear. "It is terrible to possess such power, or even to dream of possessing it." 39

"O, do not tremble, my love," said her husband. "I would not wrong either you or myself by working such inharmonious effects upon our lives; but I would have you consider how trifling, in comparison, is the skill requisite to remove this little hand." 40

At the mention of the birthmark, Georgiana, as usual, shrank as if a red hot iron had touched her cheek. 41

Again Aylmer applied himself to his labors. She could hear his voice in the distant furnace room giving directions to Aminadab, whose harsh, uncouth, misshapen tones were audible in response, more like the grunt or growl of a brute than human speech. After hours of absence, Aylmer reappeared and proposed that she should now examine his cabinet of chemical products and natural treasures of the earth. Among the former he showed her a small vial, in which, he remarked, was contained a gentle yet most powerful fragrance, capable of impregnating all the breezes that blow across a kingdom. They were of inestimable value, the contents of that little vial; and, as he said so, he threw some of the perfume into the air and filled the room with piercing and invigorating delight. 42

"And what is this?" asked Georgiana, pointing to a small crystal globe containing a gold-colored liquid. "It is so beautiful to the eye that I could imagine it the elixir of life." 43

"In one sense it is," replied Aylmer; "or rather, the elixir of immortality. It is the most precious poison that ever was concocted in this world. By its aid I could apportion the lifetime of any mortal at whom you might point your finger. The strength of the dose would determine whether he were to linger out years, or drop dead in the midst of a breath. No king on his guarded throne could keep his life if I, in my private station, should deem that the welfare of millions justified me in depriving him of it." 44

"Why do you keep such a terrific drug?" inquired Georgiana in horror. 45

"Do not mistrust me, dearest," said her husband, smiling; "its virtuous potency is yet greater than its harmful one. But see! here is a powerful cosmetic. With a few drops of this in a vase of water, freckles may be washed away as easily as the hands are cleansed. A stronger infusion would take the blood out of the cheek, and leave the rosiest beauty a pale ghost." 46

"Is it with this lotion that you intend to bathe my cheek?" asked Georgiana, 47 anxiously.

"O, no," hastily replied her husband; "this is merely superficial. Your case 48 demands a remedy that shall go deeper."

In his interviews with Georgiana, Aylmer generally made minute inquiries as to 49 her sensations, and whether the confinement of the rooms and the temperature of the atmosphere agreed with her. These questions had such a particular drift that Georgiana began to conjecture that she was already subjected to certain physical influences, either breathed in with the fragrant air or taken with her food. She fancied likewise, but it might be altogether fancy, that there was a stirring up of her system—a strange, indefinite sensation creeping through her veins, and tingling, half painfully, half pleasurably, at her heart. Still, whenever she dared to look into the mirror, there she beheld herself pale as a white rose and with the crimson birthmark stamped upon her cheek. Not even Aylmer now hated it so much as she.

To dispel the tedium of the hours which her husband found it necessary to devote 50 to the processes of combination and analysis, Georgiana turned over the volumes of his scientific library. In many dark old tomes she met with chapters full of romance and poetry. They were the works of the philosophers of the middle ages, such as Albertus Magnus, Cornelius Agrippa, Paracelsus, and the famous friar who created the prophetic Brazen Head. All these antique naturalists stood in advance of their centuries, yet were imbued with some of their credulity, and therefore were believed, and perhaps imagined themselves to have acquired from the investigation of Nature a power above Nature, and from physics a sway over the spiritual world. Hardly less curious and imaginative were the early volumes of the Transactions of the Royal Society, in which the members, knowing little of the limits of natural possibility, were continually recording wonders or proposing methods whereby wonders might be wrought.

But to Georgiana, the most engrossing volume was a large folio from her hus- 51 band's own hand, in which he had recorded every experiment of his scientific career, its original aim, the methods adopted for its development, and its final success or failure, with the circumstances to which either event was attributable. The book, in truth, was both the history and emblem of his ardent, ambitious, imaginative, yet practical and laborious life. He handled physical details as if there were nothing beyond them; yet spiritualized them all and redeemed himself from materialism by his strong and eager aspiration towards the infinite. In his grasp the veriest clod of earth assumed a soul. Georgiana, as she read, reverenced Aylmer and loved him more profoundly than ever, but with a less entire dependence on his judgment than heretofore. Much as he had accomplished, she could not but observe that his most splendid successes were almost invariably failures, if compared with the ideal at which he aimed. His brightest diamonds were the merest pebbles, and felt to be so by himself, in comparison with the inestimable gems which lay hidden beyond his reach. The volume, rich with achievements that had won renown for its author, was yet as melancholy a record as ever mortal hand had penned. It was the sad confession and continual exemplification of the shortcomings of the composite man, the spirit burdened with clay and working in matter, and of the despair that assails the higher nature at finding itself so miserably thwarted by the earthly part. Perhaps every man of genius, in whatever sphere, might recognize the image of his own experience in Aylmer's journal.

So deeply did these reflections affect Georgiana that she laid her face upon the open volume and burst into tears. In this situation she was found by her husband. 52

"It is dangerous to read in a sorcerer's books," said he with a smile, though his countenance was uneasy and displeased. "Georgiana, there are pages in that volume which I can scarcely glance over and keep my senses. Take heed lest it prove detrimental to you." 53

"It has made me worship you more than ever," said she. 54

"Ah, wait for this one success," rejoined he, "then worship me if you will. I shall deem myself hardly unworthy of it. But come, I have sought you for the luxury of your voice. Sing to me, dearest." 55

So she poured out the liquid music of her voice to quench the thirst of his spirit. He then took his leave with a boyish exuberance of gayety, assuring her that her seclusion would endure but a little longer, and that the result was already certain. Scarcely had he departed when Georgiana felt irresistibly impelled to follow him. She had forgotten to inform Aylmer of a symptom which for two or three hours past had begun to excite her attention. It was a sensation in the fatal birthmark, not painful, but which induced a restlessness throughout her system. Hastening after her husband, she intruded for the first time into the laboratory. 56

The first thing that struck her eye was the furnace, that hot and feverish worker, with the intense glow of its fire, which by the quantities of soot clustered above it seemed to have been burning for ages. There was a distilling apparatus in full operation. Around the room were retorts, tubes, cylinders, crucibles, and other apparatus of chemical research. An electrical machine stood ready for immediate use. The atmosphere felt oppressively close, and was tainted with gaseous odors which had been tormented forth by the process of science. The severe and homely simplicity of the apartment, with its naked walls and brick pavement, looked strange, accustomed as Georgiana had become to the fantastic elegance of her boudoir. But what chiefly, indeed almost solely, drew her attention, was the aspect of Aylmer himself. 57

He was pale as death, anxious and absorbed, and hung over the furnace as if it depended upon his utmost watchfulness whether the liquid which it was distilling should be the draught of immortal happiness or misery. How different from the sanguine and joyous mien that he had assumed for Georgiana's encouragement! 58

"Carefully now, Aminadab; carefully, thou human machine; carefully, thou man of clay," muttered Aylmer, more to himself than his assistant. "Now, if there be a thought too much or too little, it is all over." 59

"Ho! ho!" mumbled Aminadab. "Look, master! look!" 60

Aylmer raised his eyes hastily, and at first reddened, then grew paler than ever, on beholding Georgiana. He rushed towards her and seized her arm with a grip that left the print of his fingers upon it. 61

"Why do you come hither? Have you no trust in your husband?" cried he, impetuously. "Would you throw the blight of that fatal birthmark over my labors? It is not well done. Go, prying woman! Go!" 62

"Nay, Aylmer," said Georgiana with the firmness of which she possessed no 63
stinted endowment, "it is not you that have a right to complain. You mistrust your
wife; you have concealed the anxiety with which you watch the development of this
experiment. Think not so unworthily of me, my husband. Tell me all the risk we run,
and fear not that I shall shrink; for my share in it is far less than your own."

"No, no, Georgiana!" said Aylmer, impatiently; "it must not be." 64

"I submit," replied she, calmly. "And, Aylmer, I shall quaff whatever draught you 65
bring me; but it will be on the same principle that would induce me to take a dose
of poison if offered by your hand."

"My noble wife," said Aylmer, deeply moved, "I knew not the height and depth 66
of your nature until now. Nothing shall be concealed. Know, then, that this crimson
hand, superficial as it seems, has clutched its grasp into your being with a strength of
which I had no previous conception. I have already administered agents powerful
enough to do aught except to change your entire physical system. Only one thing
remains to be tried. If that fail us we are ruined."

"Why did you hesitate to tell me this?" asked she. 67

"Because, Georgiana," said Aylmer, in a low voice, "there is danger." 68

"Danger? There is but one danger—that this horrible stigma shall be left upon 69
my cheek!" cried Georgiana. "Remove it, remove it, whatever be the cost, or we shall
both go mad!"

"Heaven knows your words are too true," said Aylmer, sadly. "And now, dearest, 70
return to your boudoir. In a little while all will be tested."

He conducted her back and took leave of her with a solemn tenderness which 71
spoke far more than his words how much was now at stake. After his departure
Georgiana became rapt in musings. She considered the character of Aylmer and
did it completer justice than at any previous moment. Her heart exulted, while it
trembled, at his honorable love—so pure and lofty that it would accept nothing
less than perfection nor miserably make itself contented with an earthlier nature than
he had dreamed of. She felt how much more precious was such a sentiment than that
meaner kind which would have borne with the imperfection for her sake, and have
been guilty of treason to holy love by degrading its perfect idea to the level of the
actual; and with her whole spirit she prayed that, for a single moment, she might satisfy his highest and deepest conception. Longer than one moment she well knew it
could not be; for his spirit was ever on the march, ever ascending, and each instant
required something that was beyond the scope of the instant before.

The sound of her husband's footsteps aroused her. He bore a crystal goblet con- 72
taining a liquor colorless as water, but bright enough to be the draught of immortality. Aylmer was pale; but it seemed rather the consequence of a highly-wrought
state of mind and tension of spirit than of fear or doubt.

"The concoction of the draught has been perfect," said he, in answer to 73
Georgiana's look. "Unless all my science have deceived me, it cannot fail."

"Save on your account, my dearest Aylmer," observed his wife, "I might wish 74
to put off this birthmark of mortality by relinquishing mortality itself in preference
to any other mode. Life is but a sad possession to those who have attained precisely
the degree of moral advancement at which I stand. Were I weaker and blinder, it

might be happiness. Were I stronger, it might be endured hopefully. But, being what I find myself, methinks I am of all mortals the most fit to die."

"You are fit for heaven without tasting death!" replied her husband. "But why do we speak of dying? The draught cannot fail. Behold its effect upon this plant." 75

On the window seat there stood a geranium diseased with yellow blotches which had overspread all its leaves. Aylmer poured a small quantity of the liquid upon the soil in which it grew. In a little time, when the roots of the plant had taken up the moisture, the unsightly blotches began to be extinguished in a living verdure. 76

"There needed no proof," said Georgiana, quietly. "Give me the goblet. I joyfully stake all upon your word." 77

"Drink, then, thou lofty creature!" exclaimed Aylmer, with fervid admiration. "There is no taint of imperfection on thy spirit. Thy sensible frame, too, shall soon be all perfect." 78

She quaffed the liquid and returned the goblet to his hand. 79

"It is grateful," said she, with a placid smile. "Methinks it is like water from a heavenly fountain; for it contains I know not what of unobtrusive fragrance and deliciousness. It allays a feverish thirst that had parched me for many days. Now, dearest, let me sleep. My earthly senses are closing over my spirit like the leaves around the heart of a rose at sunset." 80

She spoke the last words with a gentle reluctance, as if it required almost more energy than she could command to pronounce the faint and lingering syllables. Scarcely had they loitered through her lips ere she was lost in slumber. Aylmer sat by her side, watching her aspect with the emotions proper to a man the whole value of whose existence was involved in the process now to be tested. Mingled with this mood, however, was the philosophic investigation characteristic of the man of science. Not the minutest symptom escaped him. A heightened flush of the cheek, a slight irregularity of breath, a quiver of the eyelid, a hardly perceptible tremor through the frame,—such were the details which, as the moments passed, he wrote down in his folio volume. Intense thought had set its stamp upon every previous page of that volume; but the thoughts of years were all concentrated upon the last. 81

While thus employed, he failed not to gaze often at the fatal hand, and not without a shudder. Yet once, by a strange and unaccountable impulse, he pressed it with his lips. His spirit recoiled, however, in the very act; and Georgiana, out of the midst of her deep sleep, moved uneasily and murmured as if in remonstrance. Again Aylmer resumed his watch. Nor was it without avail. The crimson hand, which at first had been strongly visible upon the marble paleness of Georgiana's cheek, now grew more faintly outlined. She remained not less pale than ever; but the birthmark, with every breath that came and went lost somewhat of its former distinctness. Its presence had been awful; its departure was more awful still. Watch the stain of the rainbow fading out of the sky, and you will know how that mysterious symbol passed away. 82

"By Heaven! It is well nigh gone!" said Aylmer to himself, in almost irrepressible ecstasy. "I can scarcely trace it now. Success! Success! And now it is like the faintest rose color. The lightest flush of blood across her cheek would overcome it. But she is so pale!" 83

He drew aside the window curtain and suffered the light of natural day to fall   84
into the room and rest upon her cheek. At the same time he heard a gross, hoarse
chuckle, which he had long known as his servant Aminadab's expression of delight.

"Ah, clod! Ah, earthly mass!" cried Aylmer, laughing in a sort of frenzy, "you   85
have served me well! Matter and spirit—earth and heaven—have both done their
part in this! Laugh, thing of the senses! You have earned the right to laugh."

These exclamations broke Georgiana's sleep. She slowly unclosed her eyes and   86
gazed into the mirror which her husband had arranged for that purpose. A faint smile
flitted over her lips when she recognized how barely perceptible was now that crimson hand which had once blazed forth with such disastrous brilliancy as to scare away
all their happiness. But then her eyes sought Aylmer's face with a trouble and anxiety that he could by no means account for.

"My poor Aylmer!" murmured she.   87

"Poor? Nay, richest, happiest, most favored!" exclaimed he. "My peerless bride,   88
it is successful! You are perfect!"

"My poor Aylmer," she repeated, with a more than human tenderness, "you have   89
aimed loftily; you have done nobly. Do not repent that, with so high and pure a
feeling, you have rejected the best the earth could offer. Aylmer, dearest Aylmer, I
am dying!"

Alas! it was too true! The fatal hand had grappled with the mystery of life, and   90
was the bond by which an angelic spirit kept itself in union with a mortal frame.
As the last crimson tint of the birthmark—that sole token of human imperfection—
faded from her cheek, the parting breath of the now perfect woman passed into the
atmosphere, and her soul, lingering a moment near her husband, took its heavenward flight. Then a hoarse, chuckling laugh was heard again! Thus ever does the gross
fatality of earth exult in its invariable triumph over the immortal essence which, in
this dim sphere of half development, demands the completeness of a higher state.
Yet, had Aylmer reached a profounder wisdom, he need not thus have flung away the
happiness which would have woven his mortal life of the selfsame texture with the
celestial. The momentary circumstance was too strong for him; he failed to look
beyond the shadowy scope of time, and, living once for all in eternity, to find the perfect future in the present.

Questions for Discussion

1. What does the birthmark symbolize? Why does Georgiana die when it is removed?
2. Why does Aylmer desire so ardently to get rid of Georgiana's birthmark?
3. How does Aylmer's obsession destroy his marriage, his wife, and his happiness? What
   should we learn from his actions?
4. What type of person does Aylmer represent? How much of yourself do you see in
   him?
5. Why does Georgiana go along with her husband's plan? In what ways is she wiser
   than he?
6. Hawthorne intersperses throughout the story comments about Man's relationship with
   Nature, comments such as, "It was the fatal flaw of humanity which Nature, in one
   shape or another, stamps ineffaceably on all her productions" (Paragraph 8), ". . . our

great creative Mother, while she amuses us with apparently working in the broadest sunshine, is yet severely careful to keep her own secrets" (Paragraph 22), or "Thus ever does the gross fatality of earth exult in its invariable triumph over the immortal essence" (Paragraph 90). What do these comments add to the story?

7. What is Aminadab spelled backwards? What does his name mean? What does he represent?

Questions for Reflection and Writing

1. Explain how this story can be read as a moral tale and applied to our own times.

2. Starting with question 6 above, find other comments about humans and nature in this story. Discuss what these comments mean and what relevance they have in the story. Do they have any relevance today?

3. Research alchemy. What was alchemy, and what were the goals of an alchemist? What kind of person was an alchemist supposed to be? Is Aylmer a good alchemist?

Zora Neale Hurston (1891?–1960), novelist, short story writer, journalist, and folklorist, was born in Eatonville, Florida, and educated at Howard University and Barnard College. Hurston's writing is frank and original and tends to focus on the lives of Southern blacks. Hurston's career went into eclipse in the 1940s, in part because of her conflict with eminent black literary figures, in part because of charges (apparently baseless) that she had molested a child. When she died, she had been working as a maid. In the early 1970s her reputation and her work were revived, in large part through the efforts of Alice Walker. "Sweat" first appeared in the avant-garde literary magazine *Fire!* in 1926 and was collected in *Spunk: The Selected Stories of Zora Neale Hurston* (1985).

Sweat

Zora Neale Hurston

I

It was eleven o'clock of a Spring night in Florida. It was Sunday. Any other night, Delia Jones would have been in bed for two hours by this time. But she was a wash-woman, and Monday morning meant a great deal to her. So she collected the soiled clothes on Saturday when she returned the clean things. Sunday night after church, she sorted and put the white things to soak. It saved her almost a half-day's start. A great hamper in the bedroom held the clothes that she brought home. It was so much neater than a number of bundles lying around.

She squatted on the kitchen floor beside the great pile of clothes, sorting them into small heaps according to color, and humming a song in a mournful key, but wondering through it all where Sykes, her husband, had gone with her horse and buck-board.°

Just then something long, round, limp, and black fell upon her shoulders and slithered to the floor beside her. A great terror took hold of her. It softened her knees and dried her mouth so that it was a full minute before she could cry out or move. Then she saw that it was the big bull whip her husband liked to carry when he drove.

She lifted her eyes to the door and saw him standing there bent over with laughter at her fright. She screamed at him.

"Sykes, what you throw dat whip on me like dat? You know it would skeer me—looks just like a snake, an' you knows how skeered Ah is of snakes."

"Course Ah knowed it! That's how come Ah done it." He slapped his leg with his hand and almost rolled on the ground in his mirth. "If you such a big fool dat you got to have a fit over a earth worm or a string, Ah don't keer how bad Ah skeer you."

"You ain't got no business doing it. Gawd knows it's a sin. Some day Ah'm goin-tuh drop dead from some of yo' foolishness. 'Nother thing, where you been wid mah rig? Ah feeds dat pony. He ain't fuh you to be drivin' wid no bull whip."

1

2

3

4

5

6

7

---

buckboard carriage

"You sho' is one aggravatin' nigger woman!" he declared and stepped into the room. She resumed her work and did not answer him at once. "Ah done tole you time and again to keep them white folks' clothes outa dis house." 8

He picked up the whip and glared at her. Delia went on with her work. She went out into the yard and returned with a galvanized tub and set it on the wash-bench. She saw that Sykes had kicked all of the clothes together again, and now stood in her way truculently, his whole manner hoping, *praying,* for an argument. But she walked calmly around him and commenced to re-sort the things. 9

"Next time, Ah'm gointer kick 'em outdoors," he threatened as he struck a match along the leg of his corduroy breeches. 10

Delia never looked up from her work, and her thin, stooped shoulders sagged further. 11

"Ah ain't for no fuss t'night Sykes. Ah just come from taking sacrament at the church house." 12

He snorted scornfully. "Yeah, you just come from de church house on a Sunday night, but heah you is gone to work on them clothes. You ain't nothing but a hypocrite. One of them amen-corner Christians—sing, whoop, and shout, then come home and wash white folks' clothes on the Sabbath." 13

He stepped roughly upon the whitest pile of things, kicking them helter-skelter as he crossed the room. His wife gave a little scream of dismay, and quickly gathered them together again. 14

"Sykes, you quit grindin' dirt into these clothes! How can Ah git through by Sat'day if Ah don't start on Sunday?" 15

"Ah don't keer if you never git through. Anyhow, Ah done promised Gawd and a couple of other men, Ah ain't gointer have it in mah house. Don't gimme no lip neither, else Ah'll throw 'em out and put mah fist up side yo' head to boot." 16

Delia's habitual meekness seemed to slip from her shoulders like a blown scarf. She was on her feet; her poor little body, her bare knuckly hands bravely defying the strapping hulk before her. 17

"Looka heah, Sykes, you done gone too fur. Ah been married to you fur fifteen years, and Ah been takin' in washin' fur fifteen years. Sweat, sweat, sweat! Work and sweat, cry and sweat, pray and sweat!" 18

"What's that got to do with me?" he asked brutally. 19

"What's it got to do with you, Sykes? Mah tub of suds is filled yo' belly with vittles more times than yo' hands is filled it. Mah sweat is done paid for this house and Ah reckon Ah kin keep on sweatin' in it." 20

She seized the iron skillet from the stove and struck a defensive pose, which act surprised him greatly, coming from her. It cowed him and he did not strike her as he usually did. 21

"Naw you won't," she panted, "that ole snaggle-toothed black woman you runnin' with ain't comin' heah to pile up on *mah* sweat and blood. You ain't paid for nothin' on this place, and Ah'm gointer stay right heah till Ah'm toted out foot foremost." 22

"Well, you better quit gittin' me riled up, else they'll be totin' you out sooner   23 than you expect. Ah'm so tired of you Ah don't know whut to do. Gawd! How Ah hates skinny wimmen!"

A little awed by this new Delia, he sidled out of the door and slammed the   24 back gate after him. He did not say where he had gone, but she knew too well. She knew very well that he would not return until nearly daybreak also. Her work over, she went on to bed but not to sleep at once. Things had come to a pretty pass!

She lay awake, gazing upon the debris that cluttered their matrimonial trail. Not   25 an image left standing along the way. Anything like flowers had long ago been drowned in the salty stream that had been pressed from her heart. Her tears, her sweat, her blood. She had brought love to the union and he had brought a longing after the flesh. Two months after the wedding, he had given her the first brutal beating. She had the memory of his numerous trips to Orlando with all of his wages when he had returned to her penniless, even before the first year had passed. She was young and soft then, but now she thought of her knotty, muscled limbs, her harsh knuckly hands, and drew herself up into an unhappy little ball in the middle of the big feather bed. Too late now to hope for love, even if it were not Bertha it would be someone else. This case differed from the others only in that she was bolder than the others. Too late for everything except her little home. She had built it for her old days, and planted one by one the trees and flowers there. It was lovely to her, lovely.

Somehow, before sleep came, she found herself saying aloud: "Oh well, what-   26 ever goes over the Devil's back, is got to come under his belly. Sometime or ruther, Sykes, like everybody else, is gointer reap his sowing." After that she was able to build a spiritual earthworks against her husband. His shells could no longer reach her. AMEN. She went to sleep and slept until he announced his presence in bed by kicking her feet and rudely snatching the covers away.

"Gimme some kivah heah, an' git yo' damn foots over on yo' own side! Ah   27 oughter mash you in yo' mouf fuh drawing dat skillet on me."

Delia went clear to the rail without answering him. A triumphant indifference   28 to all that he was or did.

II

The week was full of work for Delia as all other weeks, and Saturday found her behind   29 her little pony, collecting and delivering clothes.

It was a hot, hot day near the end of July. The village men on Joe Clarke's porch   30 even chewed cane listlessly. They did not hurl the cane-knots as usual. They let them dribble over the edge of the porch. Even conversation had collapsed under the heat.

"Heah come Delia Jones," Jim Merchant said, as the shaggy pony came 'round   31 the bend of the road toward them. The rusty buckboard was heaped with baskets of crisp, clean laundry.

"Yep," Joe Lindsay agreed. "Hot or col', rain or shine, jes'ez reg'lar ez de weeks   32 roll roun' Delia carries 'em an' fetches 'em on Sat'day."

"She better if she wanter eat," said Moss. "Syke Jones ain't wuth de shot an'   33 powder hit would tek tuh kill 'em. Not to *huh* he ain't."

"He sho' ain't," Walter Thomas chimed in. "It's too bad, too, cause she wuz a right pretty li'l trick when he got huh. Ah'd uh mah'ied huh mahself if he hadnter beat me to it." 34

Delia nodded briefly at the men as she drove past. 35

"Too much knockin' will ruin *any* 'oman. He done beat huh 'nough tuh kill three women, let 'lone change they looks," said Elijah Moseley. "How Syke kin stommuck dat big black greasy Mogul he's layin' roun' wid, gits me. Ah swear dat eight-rock couldn't kiss a sardine can Ah done throwed out de back do' 'way las' yeah." 36

"Aw, she's fat, thass how come. He's allus been crazy 'bout fat women," put in Merchant. "He'd a' been tied up wid one long time ago if he could a' found one tuh have him. Did Ah tell yuh 'bout him come sidlin' roun' *mah* wife—bringin' her a basket uh peecans outa his yard fuh a present? Yessir, mah wife! She tol' him tuh take 'em right straight back home, 'cause Delia works so hard ovah dat washtub she reckon everything on de place taste lak sweat an' soapsuds. Ah jus' wisht Ah'd a' caught 'im 'roun' dere! Ah'd a' made his hips ketch on fiah down dat shell road." 37

"Ah know he done it, too. Ah sees 'im grinnin' at every 'oman dat passes," Walter Thomas said. "But even so, he useter eat some mighty big hunks uh humble pie tuh git dat li'l 'oman he got. She wuz ez pritty ez a speckled pup! Dat wuz fifteen years ago. He useter be so skeered uh losin' huh, she could make him do some parts of a husband's duty. Dey never wuz de same in de mind." 38

"There oughter be a law about him," said Lindsay. "He ain't fit tuh carry guts tuh a bear." 39

Clarke spoke for the first time. "Tain't no law on earth dat kin make a man be decent if it ain't in 'im. There's plenty men dat takes a wife lak dey do a joint uh sugarcane. It's round, juicy, an' sweet when dey gits it. But dey squeeze an' grind, squeeze an' grind an' wring tell dey wring every drop uh pleasure dat's in 'em out. When dey's satisfied dat dey is wrung dry, dey treats 'em jes' lak dey do a cane-chew. Dey throws 'em away. Dey knows whut dey is doin' while dey is at it, an' hates theirselves fuh it but they keeps on hangin' after huh tell she's empty. Den dey hates huh fuh bein' a cane-chew an' in de way." 40

"We oughter take Syke an' dat stray 'oman uh his'n down in Lake Howell swamp an' lay on de rawhide till they cain't say Lawd a' mussy. He allus wuz uh ovahbearin niggah, but since dat white 'oman from up north done teached 'im how to run a automobile, he done got too beggety to live—an' we oughter kill 'im," Old Man Anderson advised. 41

A grunt of approval went around the porch. But the heat was melting their civic virtue and Elijah Moseley began to bait Joe Clarke. 42

"Come on, Joe, git a melon outa dere an' slice it up for yo' customers. We'se all sufferin' wid de heat. De bear's done got *me!*" 43

"Thass right, Joe, a watermelon is jes' whut Ah needs tuh cure de eppizudicks," Walter Thomas joined forces with Moseley. "Come on dere, Joe. We all is steady customers an' you ain't set us up in a long time. Ah chooses dat long, bowlegged Floridy favorite." 44

"A god, an' be dough. You all gimme twenty cents and slice away," Clarke   45
retorted. "Ah needs a col' slice m'self. Heah, everybody chip in. Ah'll lend y'all
mah meat knife."

The money was all quickly subscribed and the huge melon brought forth. At that   46
moment, Sykes and Bertha arrived. A determined silence fell on the porch and the
melon was put away again.

Merchant snapped down the blade of his jackknife and moved toward the store   47
door.

"Come on in, Joe, an' gimme a slab uh sow belly an' uh pound uh coffee—almost   48
fuhgot 'twas Sat'day. Got to git on home." Most of the men left also.

Just then Delia drove past on her way home, as Sykes was ordering magnificently   49
for Bertha. It pleased him for Delia to see.

"Git whutsoever yo' heart desires, Honey. Wait a minute, Joe. Give huh two   50
bottles uh strawberry soda-water, uh quart parched ground-peas, an' a block uh
chewin' gum."

With all this they left the store, with Sykes reminding Bertha that this was his   51
town and she could have it if she wanted it.

The men returned soon after they left, and held their watermelon feast.   52

"Where did Syke Jones git da 'oman from nohow?" Lindsay asked.   53

"Ovah Apopka. Guess dey musta been cleanin' out de town when she lef'. She   54
don't look lak a thing but a hunk uh liver wid hair on it."

"Well, she sho' kin squall," Dave Carter contributed. "When she gits ready tuh   55
laff, she jes' opens huh mouf an' latches it back tuh de las' notch. No ole granpa
alligator down in Lake Bell ain't got nothin' on huh."

III

Bertha had been in town three months now. Sykes was still paying her room-rent   56
at Dela Lewis'—the only house in town that would have taken her in. Sykes took
her frequently to Winter Park to "stomps." He still assured her that he was the swellest
man in the state.

"Sho' you kin have dat li'l ole house soon's Ah git dat 'oman outa- dere.   57
Everything b'longs tuh me an' you sho' kin have it. Ah sho' 'bominates uh skinny
'oman. Lawdy, you sho' is got one portly shape on you! You kin git *anything* you wants.
Dis is *mah* town an' you sho' kin have it."

Delia's work-worn knees crawled over the earth in Gethsemane and up the rocks   58
of Calvary many, many times during these months. She avoided the villagers and
meeting places in her efforts to be blind and deaf. But Bertha nullified this to a degree,
by coming to Delia's house to call Sykes out to her at the gate.

Delia and Sykes fought all the time now with no peaceful interludes. They slept   59
and ate in silence. Two or three times Delia had attempted a timid friendliness, but
she was repulsed each time. It was plain that the breaches must remain agape.

The sun had burned July to August. The heat streamed down like a million   60
hot arrows, smiting all things living upon the earth. Grass withered, leaves browned,
snakes went blind in shedding, and men and dogs went mad. Dog days!

Delia came home one day and found Sykes there before her. She wondered,   61
but started to go on into the house without speaking, even though he was standing
in the kitchen door and she must either stoop under his arm or ask him to move.
He made no room for her. She noticed a soap box beside the steps, but paid no particular attention to it, knowing that he must have brought it there. As she was stoop-
ing to pass under his outstretched arm, he suddenly pushed her backward, laughingly.

"Look in de box dere Delia, Ah done brung yuh somethin'!"   62

She nearly fell upon the box in her stumbling, and when she saw what it held,   63
she all but fainted outright.

"Syke! Syke, mah Gawd! You take dat rattlesnake 'way from heah! You *gottuh*.   64
Oh, Jesus, have mussy!"

"Ah ain't got tuh do nuthin' uh de kin'—fact is Ah ain't got tuh do nothin'   65
but die. Tain't no use uh you puttin' on airs makin' out lak you skeered uh dat snake—
he's gointer stay right heah tell he die. He wouldn't bite me cause Ah knows how tuh
handle 'im. Nohow he wouldn't risk breakin' out his fangs 'gin yo' skinny laigs."

"Naw, now Syke, don't keep dat thing 'round tryin' tuh skeer me tuh death. You   66
knows Ah'm even feared uh earth worms. Thass de biggest snake Ah evah did see.
Kill 'im Syke, please."

"Doan ast me tuh do nothin' fuh yuh. Goin' 'round tryin' tuh be so damn aster-   67
perious.° Naw, Ah ain't gonna kill it. Ah think uh damn sight mo' uh him dan you!
Dat's a nice snake an' anybody doan lak 'im kin jes' hit de grit."

The village soon heard that Sykes had the snake, and came to see and ask   68
questions.

"How de hen-fire did you ketch dat six-foot rattler, Syke?" Thomas asked.   69

"He's full uh frogs so he cain't hardly move, thass how Ah eased up on 'm. But   70
Ah'm a snake charmer an' knows how tuh handle 'em. Shux, dat aint nothin'. Ah
could ketch one eve'y day if Ah so wanted tuh."

"Whut he needs is a heavy hick'ry club leaned real heavy on his head. Dat's de   71
bes' way tuh charm a rattlesnake."

"Naw, Walt, y'all jes' don't understand dese diamon' backs lak Ah do," said Sykes   72
in a superior tone of voice.

The village agreed with Walter, but the snake stayed on. His box remained by   73
the kitchen door with its screen wire covering. Two or three days later it had digested
its meal of frogs and literally came to life. It rattled at every movement in the kitchen
or the yard. One day as Delia came down the kitchen steps she saw his chalky-
white fangs curved like scimitars hung in the wire meshes. This time she did not run
away with averted eyes as usual. She stood for a long time in the doorway in a red
fury that grew bloodier for every second that she regarded the creature that was her
torment.

That night she broached the subject as soon as Sykes sat down to the table.   74

"Syke, Ah wants you tuh take dat snake 'way fum heah. You done starved me   75
an' Ah put up widcher, you done beat me an Ah took dat, but you done kilt all mah
insides bringin' dat varmint heah."

---

asterperious   dialect: possibly a blending of obstreperous (unruly; loudly aggressive) and imperious (haughty)

Sykes poured out a saucer full of coffee and drank it deliberately before he answered her. 76

"A whole lot Ah keer 'bout how you feels inside uh out. Dat snake ain't goin' no damn wheah till Ah gits ready fuh 'im tuh go. So fur as beatin' is concerned, yuh ain't took near all dat you gointer take ef yuh stay 'round *me*." 77

Delia pushed back her plate and got up from the table. "Ah hates you, Sykes," she said calmly. "Ah hates you tuh de same degree dat Ah useter love yuh. Ah done took an' took till mah belly is full up tuh mah neck. Dat's de reason Ah got mah letter fum de church an' moved mah membership tuh Woodbridge—so Ah don't haf-tuh take no sacrament wid yuh. Ah don't wantuh see yuh 'round me atall. Lay 'round wid dat 'oman all yuh wants tuh, but gwan 'way fum me an' mah house. Ah hates yuh lak uh suck-egg dog." 78

Sykes almost let the huge wad of corn bread and collard greens he was chewing fall out of his mouth in amazement. He had a hard time whipping himself up to the proper fury to try to answer Delia. 79

"Well, Ah'm glad you does hate me. Ah'm sho' tiahed uh you hangin' ontuh *me*. Ah don't want yuh. Look at yuh stringey ole neck! Yo' rawbony laigs an' arms is enough tuh cut uh man tuh death. You looks jes' lak de devvul's doll-baby tuh *me*. You cain't hate me no worse dan Ah hates you. Ah been hatin' *you* fuh years." 80

"Yo' ole black hide don't look lak nothin' tuh me, but uh passle uh wrinkled up rubber, wid yo' big ole yeahs flappin' on each side lak uh paih uh buzzard wings. Don't think Ah'm gointuh be run 'way fum mah house neither. Ah'm goin' tuh de white folks 'bout *you*, mah young man, de very nex' time you lay yo' han's on me. Mah cup is done run ovah." Delia said this with no signs of fear and Sykes departed from the house, threatening her, but made not the slightest move to carry out any of them. 81

That night he did not return at all, and the next day being Sunday, Delia was glad she did not have to quarrel before she hitched up her pony and drove the four miles to Woodbridge. 82

She stayed to the night service—"love feast"—which was very warm and full of spirit. In the emotional winds her domestic trials were borne far and wide so that she sang as she drove homeward, 83

Jurden water, black an col'
Chills de body, not de soul
An' Ah wantah cross Jurden in uh calm time.

She came from the barn to the kitchen door and stopped.

"Whut's de mattah, ol' Satan, you ain't kickin' up yo' racket?" She addressed the snake's box. Complete silence. She went on into the house with a new hope in its birth struggles. Perhaps her threat to go to the white folks had frightened Sykes! Perhaps he was sorry! Fifteen years of misery and suppression had brought Delia to the place where she would hope *anything* that looked towards a way over or through her wall of inhibitions. 84

She felt in the match-safe behind the stove at once for a match. There was only 85 one there.

"Dat niggah wouldn't fetch nothin' heah tuh save his rotten neck, but he kin 86 run thew whut Ah brings quick enough. Now he done toted off nigh on tuh haff uh box uh matches. He done had dat 'oman heah in mah house, too."

Nobody but a woman could tell how she knew this even before she struck the 87 match. But she did and it put her into a new fury.

Presently she brought in the tubs to put the white things to soak. This time 88 she decided she need not bring the hamper out of the bedroom; she would go in there and do the sorting. She picked up the pot-bellied lamp and went in. The room was small and the hamper stood hard by the foot of the white iron bed. She could sit and reach through the bedposts—resting as she worked.

"*Ah wantah cross Jurden in a calm time.*" She was singing again. The mood of the 89 "love feast" had returned. She threw back the lid of the basket almost gaily. Then, moved by both horror and terror, she sprang back toward the door. *There lay the snake in the basket!* He moved sluggishly at first, but even as she turned round and round, jumped up and down in an insanity of fear, he began to stir vigorously. She saw him pouring his awful beauty from the basket upon the bed, then she seized the lamp and ran as fast as she could to the kitchen. The wind from the open door blew out the light and the darkness added to her terror. She sped to the darkness of the yard, slamming the door after her before she thought to set down the lamp. She did not feel safe even on the ground, so she climbed up in the hay barn.

There for an hour or more she lay sprawled upon the hay a gibbering wreck. 90

Finally she grew quiet, and after that came coherent thought. With this stalked 91 through her a cold, bloody rage. Hours of this. A period of introspection, a space of retrospection, then a mixture of both. Out of this an awful calm.

"Well, Ah done de bes' Ah could. If things ain't right, Gawd knows tain't mah 92 fault."

She went to sleep—a twitch sleep—and woke up to a faint gray sky. There was 93 a loud hollow sound below. She peered out. Sykes was at the wood-pile, demolishing a wire-covered box.

He hurried to the kitchen door, but hung outside there some minutes before 94 he entered, and stood some minutes more inside before he closed it after him.

The gray in the sky was spreading. Delia descended without fear now, and 95 crouched beneath the low bedroom window. The drawn shade shut out the dawn, shut in the night. But the thin walls held back no sound.

"Dat ol' scratch° is woke up now!" She mused at the tremendous whirr inside, 96 which every woodsman knows, is one of the sound illusions. The rattler is a ventriloquist. His whirr sounds to the right, to the left, straight ahead, behind, close under foot—everywhere but where it is. Woe to him who guesses wrong unless he is prepared to hold up his end of the argument! Sometimes he strikes without rattling at all.

Dat ol' Scratch the Devil

Inside, Sykes heard nothing until he knocked a pot lid off the stove while try- 97
ing to reach the match-safe in the dark. He had emptied his pockets at Bertha's.

The snake seemed to wake up under the stove and Sykes made a quick leap into 98
the bedroom. In spite of the gin he had had, his head was clearing now.

"Mah Gawd!" he chattered, "ef Ah could on'y strack uh light!" 99

The rattling ceased for a moment as he stood paralyzed. He waited. It seemed 100
that the snake waited also.

"Oh, fuh de light! Ah thought he'd be too sick"—Sykes was muttering to him- 101
self when the whirr began again, closer, right underfoot this time. Long before this,
Sykes' ability to think had been flattened down to primitive instinct and he leaped—
onto the bed.

Outside Delia heard a cry that might have come from a maddened chimpanzee, 102
a stricken gorilla. All the terror, all the horror, all the rage that man possibly could
express, without a recognizable human sound.

A tremendous stir inside there, another series of animal screams, the intermit- 103
tent whirr of the reptile. The shade torn violently down from the window, letting
in the red dawn, a huge brown hand seizing the window stick, great dull blows upon
the wooden floor punctuating the gibberish of sound long after the rattle of the snake
had abruptly subsided. All this Delia could see and hear from her place beneath
the window, and it made her ill. She crept over to the four o'clocks and stretched
herself on the cool earth to recover.

She lay there. "Delia, Delia!" She could hear Sykes calling in a most despair- 104
ing tone as one who expected no answer. The sun crept on up, and he called. Delia
could not move—her legs had gone flabby. She never moved, he called, and the
sun kept rising.

"Mah Gawd!" She heard him moan, "Mah Gawd fum Heben!" She heard him 105
stumbling about and got up from her flower-bed. The sun was growing warm. As
she approached the door she heard him call out hopefully, "Delia, is dat you Ah
heah?"

She saw him on his hands and knees as soon as she reached the door. He crept 106
an inch or two toward her—all that he was able, and she saw his horribly swollen
neck and his one open eye shining with hope. A surge of pity too strong to support
bore her away from that eye that must, could not, fail to see the tubs. He would see
the lamp. Orlando with its doctors was too far. She could scarcely reach the chin-
aberry tree, where she waited in the growing heat while inside she knew the cold
river was creeping up and up to extinguish that eye which must know by now that
she knew.

Questions for Discussion, Reflection, and Writing

1. What methods of characterization does Hurston use? How, in the first paragraphs, does she introduce us to Delia and Sykes?

2. What is Sykes's objection to "white folks' clothes" being in the house? How are we readers supposed to feel about Delia's work?

3. Whose point of view is expressed in paragraph 25 ("She lay awake, gazing upon the debris . . .)? How can you account for the sudden shift in diction?

4. How does the group of townsmen gathered at the local store function in the story? What, if anything, do they do to help the plot advance?

5. What is the significance of the Biblical allusions in the story? With what Biblical figure(s) is Delia identified? Sykes? The rattlesnake?

6. What happens, exactly, at the end of the story? What must Sykes "know by now"— and why must this knowledge be terrible for him?

§ **Connect the readings:** Compare "Sweat" with Kate Chopin's "The Storm." You might want to look at some or all of the following:

- use of dialect;
- portrayals of the female protagonists;
- portrayal of social conventions regarding marriage;
- role of social class/economic necessity;
- treatment of sexuality;
- role of nature.

Rudyard Kipling (1865–1936) was born in Bombay, India, of English parents. His parents sent him to England to be educated. After school, Kipling returned to India, working there from 1882 to 1889 as a journalist for the Anglo-Indian newspaper, *Civil and Military Gazette*, and as assistant editor and overseas correspondent for the Allahabad *Pioneer*. In 1889, he returned to London. An extremely prolific writer, Kipling had published eight books of poems and stories by the time he was twenty-three. In London he continued to write, publishing the books for which he is remembered by modern readers, the children's books *The Jungle Books* (1894 and 1895), *Captains Courageous: A Story of the Grand Banks* (1897), and *Just So Stories* (1902); the novel *Kim* (1901); and the short story "The Man Who Would Be King" (1898). He also wrote the now famous poem, *Gunga Din*, published in several periodicals in 1890 but not published as a separate work until 1987. Kipling traveled widely, covering the Boer War in 1900 as a journalist and traveling to Japan and North America. *Letters from Japan* (1962) and *American Notes* (1891) chronicle his travels. Kipling was immensely popular in his time, even receiving the Nobel Prize for literature in 1907. He has since been passed over by critics, however, who contend that his writing is not sophisticated enough to merit serious study.

The Gardener

Rudyard Kipling

> One grave to me was given,
> One watch till Judgment Day;
> And God looked down from Heaven
> and rolled the stone away.

> *One day in all the years,*
> *One hour in that one day,*
> *His Angel saw my tears,*
> *And rolled the stone away!*

Every one in the village knew that Helen Turrell did her duty by all her world, and   1
by none more honourably than by her only brother's unfortunate child. The village knew, too, that George Turrell had tried his family severely since early youth, and were not surprised to be told that, after many fresh starts given and thrown away, he, an Inspector of Indian Police, had entangled himself with the daughter of a retired non-commissioned officer, and had died of a fall from a horse a few weeks before his child was born. Mercifully, George's father and mother were both dead, and though Helen, thirty-five and independent, might well have washed her hands of the whole disgraceful affair, she most nobly took charge, though she was, at the time, under threat of lung trouble which had driven her to the South of France. She arranged for the passage of the child and a nurse from Bombay, met them at Marseilles, nursed the baby through an attack of infantile dysentery due to the carelessness of the nurse,

whom she had had to dismiss, and at last, thin and worn but triumphant, brought the boy late in the autumn, wholly restored, to her Hampshire home.

All these details were public property, for Helen was as open as the day, and held that scandals are only increased by hushing them up. She admitted that George had always been rather a black sheep, but things might have been much worse if the mother had insisted on her right to keep the boy. Luckily, it seemed that people of that class would do almost anything for money, and, as George had always turned to her in his scrapes, she felt herself justified—her friends agreed with her—in cutting the whole non-commissioned officer connection, and giving the child every advantage. A christening, by the Rector, under the name of Michael, was the first step. So far as she knew herself, she was not, she said, a child-lover, but, for all his faults, she had been very fond of George, and she pointed out that little Michael had his father's mouth to a line; which made something to build upon. 2

As a matter of fact, it was the Turrell forehead, broad, low, and well-shaped, with the widely-spaced eyes beneath it, that Michael had most faithfully reproduced. His mouth was somewhat better cut than the family type. But Helen, who would concede nothing good to his mother's side, vowed he was a Turrell all over, and, there being no one to contradict, the likeness was established. 3

In a few years Michael took his place, as accepted as Helen had always been—fearless, philosophical, and fairly good-looking. At six, he wished to know why he could not call her "Mummy," as other boys called their mothers. She explained that she was only his auntie, and that aunties were not quite the same as mummies, but that, if it gave him pleasure, he might call her "Mummy" at bedtime, for a pet-name between themselves. 4

Michael kept his secret most loyally, but Helen, as usual, explained the fact to her friends; which when Michael heard, he raged. 5

"Why did you tell? *Why* did you tell?" came at the end of the storm. 6

"Because it's always best to tell the truth," Helen answered, her arm round him as he shook in his cot. 7

"All right, but when the troof's ugly I don't think it's nice." 8

"Don't you, dear?" 9

"No, I don't, and"—she felt the small body stiffen—"now you've told, I won't call you 'Mummy' any more—not even at bedtimes." 10

"But isn't that rather unkind?" said Helen, softly. 11

"I don't care! I don't care! You hurted me in my insides and I'll hurt you back. I'll hurt you as long as I live!" 12

"Don't, oh, don't talk like that, dear! You don't know what—" 13

"I will! And when I'm dead I'll hurt you worse!" 14

"Thank goodness, I shall be dead long before you, darling." 15

"Huh! Emma says, ' 'Never know your luck.' " (Michael had been talking to Helen's elderly, flat-faced maid.) "Lots of little boys die quite soon. So'll I. *Then* you'll see!" 16

Helen caught her breath and moved towards the door, but the wail of "Mummy! Mummy!" drew her back again, and the two wept together. 17

At ten years old, after two terms at a prep. school, something or somebody gave   18
him the idea that his civil status was not quite regular. He attacked Helen on the subject, breaking down her stammered defences with the family directness.

" 'Don't believe a word of it," he said, cheerily, at the end. "People wouldn't have   19
talked like they did if my people had been married. But don't you bother, Auntie.
I've found out all about my sort in English Hist'ry and the Shakespeare bits. There
was William the Conqueror to begin with, and—oh, heaps more, and they all got on
first-rate. 'Twon't make any difference to you, my being *that*—will it?"

"As if anything could—" she began.   20

"All right. We won't talk about it any more if it makes you cry." He never men-   21
tioned the thing again of his own will, but when, two years later, he skilfully managed to have measles in the holidays, as his temperature went up to the appointed
one hundred and four he muttered of nothing else, till Helen's voice, piercing at
last his delirium, reached him with assurance that nothing on earth or beyond could
make any difference between them.

The terms at his public school and the wonderful Christmas, Easter, and Summer   22
holidays followed each other, variegated and glorious as jewels on a string; and as jewels Helen treasured them. In due time Michael developed his own interests, which
ran their courses and gave way to others; but his interest in Helen was constant
and increasing throughout. She repaid it with all that she had of affection or could
command of counsel and money; and since Michael was no fool, the War took him
just before what was like to have been a most promising career.

He was to have gone up to Oxford, with a scholarship, in October. At the end   23
of August he was on the edge of joining the first holocaust of public-school boys who
threw themselves into the Line; but the captain of his O.T.C., where he had been
sergeant for nearly a year, headed him off and steered him directly to a commission
in a battalion so new that half of it still wore the old Army red, and the other half
was breeding meningitis through living over-crowdedly in damp tents. Helen had
been shocked at the idea of direct enlistment.

"But it's in the family," Michael laughed.   24

"You don't mean to tell me that you believed that old story all this time?" said   25
Helen. (Emma, her maid, had been dead now several years.) "I gave you my word
of honour—and I gave it again—that—that it's all right. It is indeed."

"Oh, *that* doesn't worry me. It never did," he replied valiantly. "What I meant   26
was, I should have got into the show earlier if I'd enlisted—like my grandfather."

"Don't talk like that! Are you afraid of it's ending so soon, then?"   27

"No such luck. You know what K. says."   28

"Yes. But my banker told me last Monday it couldn't *possibly* last beyond   29
Christmas—for financial reasons."

" 'Hope he's right, but our Colonel—and he's a Regular—says it's going to be a   30
long job."

Michael's battalion was fortunate in that, by some chance which meant sev-   31
eral "leaves," it was used for coast-defence among shallow trenches on the Norfolk
coast; thence sent north to watch the mouth of a Scotch estuary, and, lastly, held for
weeks on a baseless rumour of distant service. But, the very day that Michael was

to have met Helen for four whole hours at a railway junction up the line, it was hurled out, to help make good the wastage of Loos, and he had only just time to send her a wire of farewell.

In France luck again helped the battalion. It was put down near the Salient, where it led a meritorious and unexacting life, while the Somme was being manufactured; and enjoyed the peace of the Armentières and Laventie sectors when that battle began. Finding that it had sound views on protecting its own flanks and could dig, a prudent Commander stole it out of its own Division, under pretence of helping to lay telegraphs, and used it round Ypres at large. 32

A month later, and just after Michael had written Helen that there was nothing special doing and therefore no need to worry, a shell-splinter dropping out of a wet dawn killed him at once. The next shell uprooted and laid down over the body what had been the foundation of a barn wall, so neatly that none but an expert would have guessed that anything unpleasant had happened. 33

By this time the village was old in experience of war, and, English fashion, had evolved a ritual to meet it. When the postmistress handed her seven-year-old daughter the official telegram to take to Miss Turrell, she observed to the Rector's gardener: "It's Miss Helen's turn now." He replied, thinking of his own son: "Well, he's lasted longer than some." The child herself came to the front-door weeping aloud, because Master Michael had often given her sweets. Helen, presently, found herself pulling down the house-blinds one after one with great care, and saying earnestly to each: "Missing *always* means dead." Then she took her place in the dreary procession that was impelled to go through an inevitable series of unprofitable emotions. The Rector, of course, preached hope and prophesied word, very soon, from a prison camp. Several friends, too, told her perfectly truthful tales, but always about other women, to whom, after months and months of silence, their missing had been miraculously restored. Other people urged her to communicate with infallible Secretaries of organisations who could communicate with benevolent neutrals, who could extract accurate information from the most secretive of Hun prison commandants. Helen did and wrote and signed everything that was suggested or put before her. 34

Once, on one of Michael's leaves, he had taken her over a munition factory, where she saw the progress of a shell from blank-iron to the all but finished article. It struck her at the time that the wretched thing was never left alone for a single second; and "I'm being manufactured into a bereaved next-of-kin," she told herself, as she prepared her documents. 35

In due course, when all the organisations had deeply or sincerely regretted their inability to trace, etc., something gave way within her and all sensation—save of thankfulness for the release—came to an end in blessed passivity. Michael had died and her world had stood still and she had been one with the full shock of that arrest. Now she was standing still and the world was going forward, but it did not concern her—in no way or relation did it touch her. She knew this by the ease with which she could slip Michael's name into talk and incline her head to the proper angle, at the proper murmur of sympathy. 36

In the blessed realisation of that relief, the Armistice with all its bells broke over   37
her and passed unheeded. At the end of another year she had overcome her physical loathing of the living and returned young, so that she could take them by the hand and almost sincerely wish them well. She had no interest in any aftermath, national or personal, of the War, but, moving at an immense distance, she sat on various relief committees and held strong views—she heard herself delivering them— about the site of the proposed village War Memorial.

Then there came to her, as next of kin, an official intimation, backed by a page   38
of a letter to her in indelible pencil, a silver identity-disc, and a watch, to the effect that the body of Lieutenant Michael Turrell had been found, identified, and re-interred in Hagenzeele Third Military Cemetery—the letter of the row and the grave's number in that row duly given.

So Helen found herself moved on to another process of the manufacturer—to   39
a world full of exultant or broken relatives, now strong in the certainty that there was an altar upon earth where they might lay their love. These soon told her, and by means of time-tables made clear, how easy it was and how little it interfered with life's affairs to go and see one's grave.

"*So different,*" as the Rector's wife said, "if he'd been killed in Mesopotamia, or   40
even Gallipoli."

The agony of being waked up to some sort of second life drove Helen across   41
the Channel, where, in a new world of abbreviated titles, she learnt that Hagenzeele Third could be comfortably reached by an afternoon train which fitted in with the morning boat, and that there was a comfortable little hotel not three kilometers from Hagenzeele itself, where one could spend quite a comfortable night and see one's grave next morning. All this she had from a Central Authority who lived in a board and tarpaper shed on the skirts of a razed city full of whirling lime-dust and blown papers.

"By the way," said he, "you know your grave, of course?"   42

"Yes, thank you," said Helen, and showed its row and number typed on Michael's   43
own little typewriter. The officer would have checked it, out of one of his many books; but a large Lancashire woman thrust between them and bade him tell her where she might find her son, who had been corporal in the A.S.C. His proper name, she sobbed, was Anderson, but, coming of respectable folk, he had of course enlisted under the name of Smith; and had been killed at Dickiebush, in early 'Fifteen. She had not his number nor did she know which of his two Christian names he might have used with his alias; but her Cook's tourist ticket expired at the end of Easter week, and if by then she could not find her child she should go mad. Whereupon she fell forward on Helen's breast; but the officer's wife came out quickly from a little bed-room behind the office, and the three of them lifted the woman on to the cot.

"They are often like this," said the officer's wife, loosening the tight bonnet-   44
strings. "Yesterday she said he'd been killed at Hooge. Are you sure you know your grave? It makes such a difference."

"Yes, thank you," said Helen, and hurried out before the woman on the bed   45
should begin to lament again.

Tea in a crowded mauve and blue striped wooden structure, with a false front, 46 carried her still further into the nightmare. She paid her bill beside a stolid, plain-featured Englishwoman, who, hearing her inquire about the train to Hagenzeele, volunteered to come with her.

"I'm going to Hagenzeele myself," she explained. "Not to Hagenzeele Third; 47 mine is Sugar Factory, but they call it La Rosière now. It's just south of Hagenzeele Three. Have you got your room at the hotel there?"

"Oh yes, thank you. I've wired." 48

"That's better. Sometimes the place is quite full, and at others there's hardly a 49 soul. But they've put bathrooms into the old Lion d'Or—that's the hotel on the west side of Sugar Factory—and it draws off a lot of people, luckily."

"It's all new to me. This is the first time I've been over." 50

"Indeed! This is my ninth time since the Armistice. Not on my own account. 51 *I* haven't lost any one, thank God—but, like every one else, I've a lot of friends at home who have. Coming over as often as I do, I find it helps them to have some one just look at the—the place and tell them about it afterwards. And one can take photos for them, too. I get quite a list of commissions to execute." She laughed nervously and tapped her slung Kodak. "There are two or three to see at Sugar Factory this time, and plenty of others in the cemeteries all about. My system is to save them up, and arrange them, you know. And when I've got enough commissions for one area to make it worth while, I pop over and execute them. It *does* comfort people."

"I suppose so," Helen answered, shivering as they entered the little train. 52

"Of course it does. (Isn't it lucky we've got window-seats?) It must do or they 53 wouldn't ask one to do it, would they? I've a list of quite twelve or fifteen commissions here"—she tapped the Kodak again—"I must sort them out to-night. Oh, I forgot to ask you. What's yours?"

"My nephew," said Helen. "But I was very fond of him." 54

"Ah yes! I sometimes wonder whether *they* know after death? What do you 55 think?"

"Oh, I don't—I haven't dared to think much about that sort of thing," said 56 Helen, almost lifting her hands to keep her off.

"Perhaps that's better," the woman answered. "The sense of loss must be enough, 57 I expect. Well, I won't worry you any more."

Helen was grateful, but when they reached the hotel Mrs. Scarsworth (they had 58 exchanged names) insisted on dining at the same table with her, and after the meal, in the little, hideous salon full of low-voiced relatives, took Helen through her "commissions" with biographies of the dead, where she happened to know them, and sketches of their next of kin. Helen endured till nearly half-past nine, ere she fled to her room.

Almost at once there was a knock at her door and Mrs. Scarsworth entered; 59 her hands, holding the dreadful list, clasped before her.

"Yes—yes—*I* know," she began. "You're sick of me, but I want to tell you something. You—you aren't married are you? Then perhaps you won't. . . . But it doesn't matter. I've *got* to tell some one. I can't go on any longer like this." 60

"But please—" Mrs. Scarsworth had backed against the shut door, and her mouth   61
worked dryly.

"In a minute," she said. "You—you know about these graves of mine I was telling   62
you about downstairs, just now? They really *are* commissions. At least several of them
are." Her eye wandered round the room. "What extraordinary wall-papers they have
in Belgium, don't you think? . . . Yes. I swear they are commissions. But there's *one*,
d'you see, and—and he was more to me than anything else in the world. Do you
understand?"

Helen nodded.   63

"More than any one else. And, of course, he oughtn't to have been. He ought   64
to have been nothing to me. But he *was*. He *is*. That's why I do the commissions, you
see. That's all."

"But why do you tell me?" Helen asked desperately.   65

"Because I'm *so* tired of lying. Tired of lying—always lying—year in and year out.   66
When I don't tell lies I've got to act 'em and I've got to think 'em, always. *You* don't
know what that means. He was everything to me that he oughtn't to have been—
the one real thing—the only thing that ever happened to me in all my life; and
I've had to pretend he wasn't. I've had to watch every word I said, and think out what
lie I'd tell next, for years and years!"

"How many years?" Helen asked.   67

"Six years and four months before, and two and three-quarters after. I've gone   68
to him eight times, since. To-morrow'll make the ninth, and—and I can't—I *can't*
go to him again with nobody in the world knowing. I want to be honest with some
one before I go. Do you understand? It doesn't matter about *me*. I was never truthful, even as a girl. But it isn't worthy of *him*. So—so I—I had to tell you. I can't
keep it up any longer. Oh, I can't!"

She lifted her joined hands almost to the level of her mouth, and brought them   69
down sharply, still joined, to full arms' length below her waist. Helen reached forward, caught them, bowed her head over them, and murmured: "Oh, my dear! My
dear!" Mrs. Scarsworth stepped back, her face all mottled.

"My God!" said she. "Is *that* how you take it?"   70

Helen could not speak, the woman went out; but it was a long while before Helen   71
was able to sleep.

Next morning Mrs. Scarsworth left early on her round of commissions, and Helen   72
walked alone to Hagenzeele Third. The place was still in the making, and stood some
five or six feet above the metalled road, which it flanked for hundreds of yards.
Culverts across a deep ditch served for entrances through the unfinished boundary
wall. She climbed a few wooden-faced earthen steps and then met the entire crowded
level of the thing in one held breath. She did not know that Hagenzeele Third
counted twenty-one thousand dead already. All she saw was a merciless sea of black
crosses, bearing little strips of stamped tin at all angles across their faces. She could
distinguish no order or arrangement in their mass; nothing but a waist-high wilderness as of weeds stricken dead, rushing at her. She went forward, moved to the left
and the right hopelessly, wondering by what guidance she should ever come to her
own. A great distance away there was a line of whiteness. It proved to be a block of

some two or three hundred graves whose headstones had already been set, whose flowers were planted out, and whose new-sown grass showed green. Here she could see clear-cut letters at the ends of the rows, and, referring to her slip, realised that it was not here she must look.

A man knelt behind a line of headstones—evidently a gardener, for he was firm- 73 ing a young plant in the soft earth. She went towards him, her paper in her hand. He rose at her approach and without prelude or salutation asked: "Who are you look- ing for?"

"Lieutenant Michael Turrell—my nephew," said Helen slowly and word for word, 74 as she had many thousands of times in her life.

The man lifted his eyes and looked at her with infinite compassion before he 75 turned from the fresh-sown grass towards the naked black crosses.

"Come with me," he said, "and I will show you where your son lies." 76

When Helen left the Cemetery she turned for a last look. In the distance she 77 saw the man bending over his young plants; and she went away, supposing him to be the gardener.

Questions for Discussion

1. Why does Helen think of Michael's mother's family as she does? On what is her snob- bery founded?
2. What is the "*that*" to which Michael refers in Paragraph 19?
3. In your opinion, should Helen have always been so truthful with Michael about his parentage?
4. Were you prepared for the news of Michael's death? Why might Kipling have sprung this information on us?
5. Why is the Rector not truthful with Helen (Paragraph 34)?
6. Who is the gardener of the title? Why is he not a central figure in the story? Is the man really a gardener? Who else could he be?
7. Why does the gardener tell Helen that he will show her where her son, not her nephew, lies?

Questions for Reflection and Writing

1. Reflect on the nature of truth and lies. What is the relationship between them? Is it always best to tell the truth, or do circumstances dictate whether one should lie or tell the truth?
2. Do you think that Michael's mother and grandfather (the non-commissioned offi- cer) gave up the child only for the money? Reread the beginning few paragraphs of the story and pay attention to what is said and not said. Write a brief answer to the ques- tion, defending your answer.
3. Research the life of soldiers in World War I and report on one aspect to your class- mates. What was daily life like in the trenches?

Bharati Mukherjee (1940–), born in Calcutta, India, has written seven novels, two short story collections, and is an English professor at the University of California, Berkeley.

A Wife's Story

Bharati Mukherjee

Imre says forget it, but I'm going to write David Mamet. So Patels are hard to sell   1
real estate to. You buy them a beer, whisper Glengarry Glen Ross, and they smell
swamp instead of sun and surf. They work hard, eat cheap, live ten to a room,
stash their savings under futons in Queens, and before you know it they own half
of Hoboken. You say, where's the sweet gullibility that made this nation great?

Polish jokes, Patel jokes: that's not why I want to write Mamet.   2

Seen their women?   3

Everybody laughs. Imre laughs. The dozing fat man with the Barnes &   4
Noble sack between his legs, the woman next to him, the usher, everybody. The
theater isn't so dark that they can't see me. In my red silk sari I'm conspicuous.
Plump, gold paisleys sparkle on my chest.

The actor is just warming up. *Seen their women?* He plays a salesman, he's had   5
a bad day and now he's in a Chinese restaurant trying to loosen up. His face is
pink. His wool-blend slacks are creased at the crotch. We bought our tickets at
half-price, we're sitting in the front row, but at the edge, and we see things we
shouldn't be seeing. At least I do, or think I do. Spittle, actors goosing each
other, little winks, streaks of makeup.

Maybe they're improvising dialogue too. Maybe Mamet's provided them   6
with insult kits, Thursdays for Chinese, Wednesdays for Hispanics, today for
Indians. Maybe they get together before curtain time, see an Indian woman set-
tling in the front row off to the side, and say to each other: "Hey, forget Friday.
Let's get *her* today. See if she cries. See if she walks out." Maybe, like the salesmen they play, they have a little bet on.

Maybe I shouldn't feel betrayed.   7

Their women, he goes again. *They look like they've just been fucked by a dead*   8
cat.

The fat man hoots so hard he nudges my elbow off our shared armrest.   9

"Imre. I'm going home." But Imre's hunched so far forward he doesn't hear.   10
English isn't his best language. A refugee from Budapest, he has to listen hard. "I
didn't pay eighteen dollars to be insulted."

I don't hate Mamet. It's the tyranny of the American dream that scares me.   11
First, you don't exist. Then you're invisible. Then you're funny. Then you're disgusting. Insult, my American friends will tell me, is a kind of acceptance. No

instant dignity here. A play like this, back home, would cause riots. Communal, racist, and antisocial. The actors wouldn't make it off stage. This play, and all these awful feelings, would be safely locked up.

I long, at times, for clear-cut answers. Offer me instant dignity, today, and I'll take it. 12

"What?" Imre moves toward me without taking his eyes off the actor. "Come again?" 13

Tears come. I want to stand, scream, make an awful scene. I long for ugly, nasty rage. 14

The actor is ranting, flinging spittle. *Give me a chance. I'm not finished, I can get back on the board. I tell that asshole, give me a real lead. And what does that asshole give me? Patels. Nothing but Patels.* 15

This time Imre works an arm around my shoulders. "Panna, what is Patel? Why are you taking it all so personally?" 16

I shrink from his touch, but I don't walk out. Expensive girls' schools in Lausanne and Bombay have trained me to behave well. My manners are exquisite, my feelings are delicate, my gestures refined, my moods undetectable. They have seen me through riots, uprootings, separation, my son's death. 17

"I'm not taking it personally." 18

The fat man looks at us. The woman looks too, and shushes. 19

I stare back at the two of them. Then I stare, mean and cool, at the man's elbow. Under the bright blue polyester Hawaiian shirt sleeve, the elbow looks soft and runny. "Excuse me," I say. My voice has the effortless meanness of well-bred displaced Third World women, though my rhetoric has been learned elsewhere. "You're exploiting my space." 20

Startled, the man snatches his arm away from me. He cradles it against his breast. By the time he's ready with comebacks, I've turned my back on him. I've probably ruined the first act for him. I know I've ruined it for Imre. 21

It's not my fault; it's the *situation*. Old colonies wear down. Patels—the new pioneers—have to be suspicious. Idi Amin's lesson is permanent. AT&T wires move good advice from continent to continent. Keep all assets liquid. Get into 7-11S, get out of condos and motels. I know how both sides feel, that's the trouble. The Patel sniffing out scams, the sad salesmen on the stage: postcolonialism has made me their referee. It's hate I long for; simple, brutish, partisan hate. 22

After the show Imre and I make our way toward Broadway. Sometimes he holds my hand; it doesn't mean anything more than that crazies and drunks are crouched in doorways. Imre's been here over two years, but he's stayed very old-world, very courtly, openly protective of women. I met him in a seminar on special ed. last semester. His wife is a nurse somewhere in the Hungarian country-side. There are two sons, and miles of petitions for their emigration. My husband manages a mill two hundred miles north of Bombay. There are no children. 23

"You make things tough on yourself," Imre says. He assumed Patel was a Jewish name or maybe Hispanic; everything makes equal sense to him. He found the play tasteless, he worried about the effect of vulgar language on my sensitive ears. "You have to let go a bit." And as though to show me how to let go, he breaks 24 away from me, bounds ahead with his head ducked tight, then dances on amazingly jerky legs. He's a Magyar, he often tells me, and deep down, he's an Asian too. I catch glimpses of it, knife-blade Attila cheekbones, despite the blondish hair. In his faded jeans and leather jacket, he's a rock video star. I watch MTV for hours in the apartment when Charity's working the evening shift at Macy's. I listen to WPLJ on Charity's earphones. Why should I be ashamed? Television in India is so uplifting.

Imre stops as suddenly as he'd started. People walk around us. The summer 25 sidewalk is full of theatergoers in seersucker suits; Imre's year-round jacket is out of place. European. Cops in twos and threes huddle, lightly tap their thighs with night sticks and smile at me with benevolence. I want to wink at them, get us all in trouble, tell them the crazy dancing man is from the Warsaw Pact. I'm too shy to break into dance on Broadway. So I hug Imre instead.

The hug takes him by surprise. He wants me to let go, but he doesn't really 26 expect me to let go. He staggers, though I weigh no more than 104 pounds, and with him, I pitch forward slightly. Then he catches me, and we walk arm in arm to the bus stop. My husband would never dance or hug a woman on Broadway. Nor would my brothers. They aren't stuffy people, but they went to Anglican boarding schools and they have a well-developed sense of what's silly.

"Imre." I squeeze his big, rough hand. "I'm sorry I ruined the evening for you." 27

"You did nothing of the kind." He sounds tired. "Let's not wait for the bus. 28 Let's splurge and take a cab instead."

Imre always has unexpected funds. The Network, he calls it, Class of '56. 29

In the back of the cab, without even trying, I feel light, almost free. Memories 30 of Indian destitutes mix with the hordes of New York street people, and they float free, like astronauts, inside my head. I've made it. I'm making something of my life. I've left home, my husband, to get a Ph.D. in special ed. I have a multiple-entry visa and a small scholarship for two years. After that, we'll see. My mother was beaten by her mother-in-law, my grandmother, when she'd registered for French lessons at the Alliance Française. My grandmother, the eldest daughter of a rich zamindar, was illiterate.

Imre and the cabdriver talk away in Russian. I keep my eyes closed. That way 31 I can feel the floaters better. I'll write Mamet tonight. I feel strong, reckless. Maybe I'll write Steven Spielberg too; tell him that Indians don't eat monkey brains.

We've made it. Patels must have made it. Mamet, Spielberg: they're not con- 32 descending to us. Maybe they're a little bit afraid.

Charity Chin, my roommate, is sitting on the floor drinking Chablis out of a 33 plastic wineglass. She is five foot six, three inches taller than me, but weighs a kilo and a half less than I do. She is a "hands" model. Orientals are supposed to have a monopoly in the hands-modelling business, she says. She had her eyes fixed eight or nine months ago and out of gratitude sleeps with her plastic surgeon every third Wednesday.

"Oh, good," Charity says. "I'm glad you're back early. I need to talk." 34

She's been writing checks. MCI, Con Ed, Bonwit Teller. Envelopes, already 35 stamped and sealed, form a pyramid between her shapely, knee-socked legs. The checkbook's cover is brown plastic, grained to look like cowhide. Each time Charity flips back the cover, white geese fly over sky-colored checks. She makes good money, but she's extravagant. The difference adds up to this shared, rent-controlled Chelsea one-bedroom.

"All right. Talk." 36

When I first moved in, she was seeing an analyst. Now she sees a nutritionist. 37

"Eric called. From Oregon." 38

"What did he want?" 39

"He wants me to pay half the rent on his loft for last spring. He asked me to 40
move back, remember? He *begged* me."

Eric is Charity's estranged husband. 41

"What does your nutritionist say?" Eric now wears a red jumpsuit and tills the 42
soil in Rajneeshpuram.

"You think Phil's a creep too, don't you? What else can he be when creeps are 43
all I attract?"

Phil is a flutist with thinning hair. He's very touchy on the subject of *flautists* 44
versus *flutists*. He's touchy on every subject, from music to books to foods to
clothes. He teaches at a small college upstate, and Charity bought a used blue
Datsun ("Nissan," Phil insists) last month so she could spend weekends with him.
She returns every Sunday night, exhausted and exasperated. Phil and I don't have
much to say to each other—he's the only musician I know; the men in my family
are lawyers, engineers, or in business—but I like him. Around me, he loosens up.
When he visits, he bakes us loaves of pumpernickel bread. He waxes our kitchen
floor. Like many men in this country, he seems to me a displaced child, or even a
woman, looking for something that passed him by, or for something that he can
never have. If he thinks I'm not looking, he sneaks his hands under Charity's
sweater, but there isn't too much there. Here, she's a model with high ambitions.
In India, she'd be a flat-chested old maid.

I'm shy in front of the lovers. A darkness comes over me when I see them 45
horsing around.

"It isn't the money," Charity says. Oh? I think. "He says he still loves me. 46
Then he turns around and asks me for five hundred."

What's so strange about that, I want to ask. She still loves Eric, and Eric, red 47
jumpsuit and all, is smart enough to know it. Love is a commodity, hoarded like
any other. Mamet knows. But I say, "I'm not the person to ask about love." Charity
knows that mine was a traditional Hindu marriage. My parents, with the help of a
marriage broker, who was my mother's cousin, picked out a groom. All I had to do
was get to know his taste in food.

It'll be a long evening, I'm afraid. Charity likes to confess. I unpleat my silk 48
sari—it no longer looks too showy—wrap it in muslin cloth and put it away in a
dresser drawer. Saris are hard to have laundered in Manhattan, though there's a
good man in Jackson Heights. My next step will be to brew us a pot of chrysan-
themum tea. It's a very special tea from the mainland. Charity's uncle gave it to
us. I like him. He's a humpbacked, awkward, terrified man. He runs a gift store on
Mott Street, and though he doesn't speak much English, he seems to have done

well. Once upon a time he worked for the railways in Chengdu, Szechwan Province, and during the Wuchang Uprising, he was shot at. When I'm down, when I'm lonely for my husband, when I think of our son, or when I need to be held, I think of Charity's uncle. If I hadn't left home, I'd never have heard of the Wuchang Uprising. I've broadened my horizons.

Very late that night my husband calls me from Ahmadabad, a town of textile   49
mills north of Bombay. My husband is a vice president at Lakshmi Cotton Mills. Lakshmi is the goddess of wealth, but LCM (Priv.), Ltd., is doing poorly. Lockouts, strikes, rock-throwings. My husband lives on digitalis, which he calls the food for our *yuga* of discontent.

"We had a bad mishap at the mill today." Then he says nothing for seconds.   50

The operator comes on. "Do you have the right party, sir? We're trying to   51
reach Mrs. Butt."

"Bhatt," I insist. "B for Bombay, H for Haryana, A for Ahmadabad, double T   52
for Tamil Nadu." It's a litany. "This is she."

"One of our lorries was firebombed today. Resulting in three deaths. The   53
driver, old Karamchand, and his two children."

I know how my husband's eyes look this minute, how the eye rims sag and   54
the yellow corneas shine and bulge with pain. He is not an emotional man—the Ahmadabad Institute of Management has trained him to cut losses, to look on the bright side of economic catastrophes—but tonight he's feeling low. I try to remember a driver named Karamchand, but can't. That part of my life is over, the way *trucks* have replaced *lorries* in my vocabulary, the way Charity Chin and her lurid love life have replaced inherited notions of marital duty. Tomorrow he'll come out of it. Soon he'll be eating again. He'll sleep like a baby. He's been trained to believe in turnovers. Every morning he rubs his scalp with cantharidine oil so his hair will grow back again.

"It could be your car next." Affection, love. Who can tell the difference in a   55
traditional marriage in which a wife still doesn't call her husband by his first name?

"No. They know I'm a flunky, just like them. Well paid, maybe. No need for   56
undue anxiety, please."

Then his voice breaks. He says he needs me, he misses me, he wants me to   57
come to him damp from my evening shower, smelling of sandalwood soap, my braid decorated with Jasmines.

"I need you too."   58

"Not to worry, please," he says. "I am coming in a fortnight's time. I have   59
already made arrangements."

Outside my window, fire trucks whine, up Eighth Avenue. I wonder if he can   60
hear them, what he thinks of a life like mine, led amid disorder.

"I am thinking it'll be like a honeymoon. More or less."   61

When I was in college, waiting to be married, I imagined honeymoons were   62
only for the more fashionable girls, the girls who came from slightly racy families, smoked Sobranies in the dorm lavatories and put up posters of Kabir Bedi, who was supposed to have made it as a big star in the West. My husband wants us to go to

Niagara. I'm not to worry about foreign exchange. He's arranged for extra dollars through the Gujarati Network, with a cousin in San Jose. And he's bought four hundred more on the black market. "Tell me you need me. Panna, please tell me again."

I change out of the cotton pants and shirt I've been wearing all day and put on a sari to meet my husband at JFK. I don't forget the jewelry; the marriage necklace of *mangalsutra*, gold drop earrings, heavy gold bangles. I don't wear them every day. In this borough of vice and greed, who knows when, or whom, desire will overwhelm. 63

My husband spots me in the crowd and waves. He has lost weight, and changed his glasses. The arm, uplifted in a cheery wave, is bony, frail, almost opalescent. 64

In the Carey Coach, we hold hands. He strokes my fingers one by one. "How come you aren't wearing my mother's ring?" 65

"Because muggers know about Indian women," I say. They know with us it's 24-karat. His mother's ring is showy, in ghastly taste anywhere but India: a blood-red Burma ruby set in a gold frame of floral sprays. My mother-in-law got her guru to bless the ring before I left for the States. 66

He looks disconcerted. He's used to a different role. He's the knowing, suspicious one in the family. He seems to be sulking, and finally he comes out with it. "You've said nothing about my new glasses." I compliment him on the glasses, how chic and Western-executive they make him look. But I can't help the other things, necessities until he learns the ropes. I handle the money, buy the tickets. I don't know if this makes me unhappy. 67

Charity drives her Nissan upstate, so for two weeks we are to have the apartment to ourselves. This is more privacy than we ever had in India. No parents, no servants, to keep us modest. We play at housekeeping. Imre has lent us a hibachi, and I grill saffron chicken breasts. My husband marvels at the size of the Perdue hens. "They're big like peacocks, no? These Americans, they're really something!" He tries out pizzas, burgers, McNuggets. He chews. He explores. He judges. He loves it all, fears nothing, feels at home in the summer odors, the clutter of Manhattan streets. Since he thinks that the American palate is bland, he carries a bottle of red peppers in his pocket. I wheel a shopping cart down the aisles of the neighborhood Grand Union, and he follows, swiftly, greedily. He picks up hair rinses and high-protein diet powders. There's so much I already take for granted. 68

One night, Imre stops by. He wants us to go with him to a movie. In his work shirt and red leather tie, he looks arty or strung out. It's only been a week, but I feel as though I am really seeing him for the first time. The yellow hair worn very short at the sides, the wide, narrow lips. He's a good-looking man, but self-conscious, almost arrogant. He's picked the movie we should see. He always tells me what to see, what to read. He buys the *Voice*. He's a natural avant-gardist. For tonight he's chosen *Numero Deux*. 69

"Is it a musical?" my husband asks. The Radio City Music Hall is on his list of sights to see. He's read up on the history of the Rockettes. He doesn't catch Imre's sympathetic wink. 70

Guilt, shame, loyalty. I long to be ungracious, not ingratiate myself with both   71
men.

That night my husband calculates in rupees the money we've wasted on   72
Godard. "That refugee fellow, Nagy, must have a screw loose in his head. I paid
very steep price for dollars on the black market."

Some afternoons we go shopping. Back home we hated shopping, but now it   73
is a lovers' project. My husband's shopping list startles me. I feel I am just getting
to know him. Maybe, like Imre, freed from the dignities of old-world culture, he
too could get drunk and squirt Cheez Whiz on a guest. I watch him dart into stores
in his gleaming leather shoes. Jockey shorts on sale in outdoor bins on Broadway
entrance him. White tube socks with different bands of color delight him. He
looks for microcassettes, for anything small and electronic and smuggleable. He
needs a garment bag. He calls it a "wardrobe," and I have to translate.

"All of New York is having sales, no?"   74

My heart speeds watching him this happy. It's the third week in August,   75
almost the end of summer, and the city smells ripe, it cannot bear more heat, more
money, more energy.

"This is so smashing! The prices are so excellent!" Recklessly, my prudent   76
husband signs away traveller's checks. How he intends to smuggle it all back I
don't dare ask. With a microwave, he calculates, we could get rid of our cook.

This has to be love, I think. Charity, Eric, Phil: they may be experts on sex.   77
My husband doesn't chase me around the sofa, but he pushes me down on
Charity's battered cushions, and the man who has never entered the kitchen of our
Ahmadabad house now comes toward me with a dish tub of steamy water to mas-
sage away the pavement heat.

Ten days into his vacation my husband checks out brochures for sightseeing   78
tours. Shortline, Grayline, Crossroads: his new vinyl briefcase is full of schedules
and pamphlets. While I make pancakes out of a mix, he comparison-shops. Tour
number one costs $10.95 and will give us the World Trade Center, Chinatown,
and the United Nations. Tour number three would take us both uptown *and* downtown for $14.95, but my husband is absolutely sure he doesn't want to see Harlem.
We settle for tour number four: Downtown and the Dame. It's offered by a new
tour company with a small, dirty office at Eighth and Forty-eighth.

The sidewalk outside the office is colorful with tourists. My husband sends me   79
in to buy the tickets because he has come to feel Americans don't understand his
accent.

The dark man, Lebanese probably, behind the counter comes on too friendly.   80
"Come on, doll, make my day!" He won't say which tour is his. "Number four?
Honey, no! Look, you've wrecked me! Say you'll change your mind." He takes two
twenties and gives back change. He holds the tickets, forcing me to pull. He leans
closer. "I'm off after lunch."

My husband must have been watching me from the sidewalk. "What was the   81
chap saying?" he demands. "I told you not to wear pants. He thinks you are Puerto
Rican. He thinks he can treat you with disrespect."

The bus is crowded and we have to sit across the aisle from each other. The   82
tour guide begins his patter on Forty-sixth. He looks like an actor, his hair
bleached and blow-dried. Up close he must look middle-aged, but from where I sit
his skin is smooth and his cheeks faintly red.

"Welcome to the Big Apple, folks." The guide uses a microphone. "Big Apple.   83
That's what we native Manhattan degenerates call our city. Today we have guests
from fifteen foreign countries and six states from this U.S. of A. That makes the
Tourist Bureau real happy. And let me assure you that while we may be the richest city in the richest country in the world, it's okay to tip your charming and talented attendant." He laughs. Then he swings his hip out into the aisle and sings a
song.

"And it's mighty fancy on old Delancey Street, you know. . . ."   84

My husband looks irritable. The guide is, as expected, a good singer. "The   85
bloody man should be giving us histories of buildings we are passing, no?" I pat his
hand, the mood passes. He cranes his neck. Our window seats have both gone to
Japanese. It's the tour of his life. Next to this, the quick business trips to
Manchester and Glasgow pale.

"And tell me what street compares to Mott Street, in July. . . ."   86

The guide wants applause. He manages a derisive laugh from the Americans   87
up front. He's working the aisles now. "I coulda been somebody, right? I coulda
been a star!" Two or three of us smile, those of us who recognize the parody. He
catches my smile. The sun is on his harsh, bleached hair. "Right, your highness?
Look, we gotta maharani with us! Couldn't I have been a star?"

"Right!" I say, my voice coming out a squeal. I've been trained to adapt; what   88
else can I say?

We drive through traffic past landmark office buildings and churches. The   89
guide flips his hands. "Art deco," he keeps saying. I hear him confide to one of the
Americans: "Beats me. I went to a cheap guide's school." My husband wants to
know more about this Art Deco, but the guide sings another song.

"We made a foolish choice," my husband grumbles. "We are sitting in the bus   90
only. We're not going into famous buildings." He scrutinizes the pamphlets in his
jacket pocket. I think, at least it's air-conditioned in here. I could sit here in the
cool shadows of the city forever.

Only five of us appear to have opted for the "Downtown and the Dame" tour.   91
The others will ride back uptown past the United Nations after we've been
dropped off at the pier for the ferry to the Statue of Liberty.

An elderly European pulls a camera out of his wife's designer tote bag. He   92
takes pictures of the boats in the harbor, the Japanese in kimonos eating popcorn,
scavenging pigeons, me. Then, pushing his wife ahead of him, he climbs back on
the bus and waves to us. For a second I feel terribly lost. I wish we were on the bus
going back to the apartment. I know I'll not be able to describe any of this to
Charity, or to Imre. I'm too proud to admit I went on a guided tour.

The view of the city from the Circle Line ferry is seductive, unreal. The sky-   93
line wavers out of reach, but never quite vanishes. The summer sun pushes
through fluffy clouds and dapples the glass of office towers. My husband looks

thrilled, even more than he had on the shopping trips down Broadway. Tourists and dreamers, we have spent our life's savings to see this skyline, this statue.

"Quick, take a picture of me!" my husband yells as he moves toward a gap of 94 railings. A Japanese matron has given up her position in order to change film. "Before the Twin Towers disappear!"

I focus, I wait for a large Oriental family to walk out of my range. My husband 95 holds his pose tight against the railing. He wants to look relaxed, an international businessman at home in all the financial markets.

A bearded man slides across the bench toward me. "Like this," he says and 96 helps me get my husband in focus. "You want me to take the photo for you?" His name, he says, is Goran. He is Goran from Yugoslavia, as though that were enough for tracking him down. Imre from Hungary. Panna from India. He pulls the old Leica out of my hand, signaling the Orientals to beat it, and clicks away. "I'm a photographer," he says. He could have been a camera thief. That's what my husband would have assumed. Somehow, I trusted. "Get you a beer?" he asks.

"I don't. Drink, I mean. Thank you very much." I say those last words very 97 loud, for everyone's benefit. The odd bottles of Soave with Imre don't count.

"Too bad." Goran gives back the camera. 98

"Take one more!" my husband shouts from the railing. "Just to be sure!" 99

The island itself disappoints. The Lady has brutal scaffolding holding her in. 100 The museum is closed. The snack bar is dirty and expensive. My husband reads out the prices to me. He orders two french fries and two Cokes. We sit at picnic tables and wait for the ferry to take us back.

"What was that hippie chap saying?" 101

As if I could say. A day-care center has brought its kids, at least forty of them, 102 to the island for the day. The kids, all wearing name tags, run around us. I can't help noticing how many are Indian. Even a Patel, probably a Bhatt if I looked hard enough. They toss hamburger bits at pigeons. They kick styrofoam cups. The pigeons are slow, greedy, persistent. I have to shoo one off the table top. I don't think my husband thinks about our son.

"What hippie?" 103

"The one on the boat. With the beard and the hair." 104

My husband doesn't look at me. He shakes out his paper napkin and tries to 105 protect his french fries from pigeon feathers.

"Oh, him. He said he was from Dubrovnik." It isn't true, but I don't want 106 trouble.

"What did he say about Dubrovnik?" 107

I know enough about Dubrovnik to get by. Imre's told me about it. And about 108 Mostar and Zagreb. In Mostar white Muslims sing the call to prayer. I would like to see that before I die: white Muslims. Whole peoples have moved before me; they've adapted. The night Imre told me about Mostar was also the night I saw my first snow in Manhattan. We'd walked down to Chelsea from Columbia. We'd walked and talked and I hadn't felt tired at all.

"You're too innocent," my husband says. He reaches for my hand. "Panna," he 109
cries with pain in his voice, and I am brought back from perfect, floating memories of snow, "I've come to take you back. I have seen how men watch you."

"What?" 110

"Come back, now. I have tickets. We have all the things we will ever need. I 111
can't live without you."

A little girl with wiry braids kicks a bottle cap at his shoes. The pigeons wheel 112
and scuttle around us. My husband covers his fries with spread-out fingers. "No
kicking," he tells the girl. Her name, Beulah, is printed in green ink on a heart-
shaped name tag. He forces a smile, and Beulah smiles back. Then she starts to flap
her arms. She flaps, she hops. The pigeons go crazy for fries and scraps.

"Special ed. course is two years," I remind him. "I can't go back." 113

My husband picks up our trays and throws them into the garbage before I can 114
stop him. He's carried disposability a little too far. "We've been taken," he says,
moving toward the dock, though the ferry will not arrive for another twenty minutes. "The ferry costs only two dollars round-trip per person. We should have chosen tour number one for $10.95 instead of tour number four for $14.95."

With my Lebanese friend, I think. "But this way we don't have to worry about 115
cabs. The bus will pick us up at the pier and take us back to midtown. Then we
can walk home."

"New York is full of cheats and whatnot. Just like Bombay." He is not accus- 116
ing me of infidelity. I feel dread all the same.

That night, after we've gone to bed, the phone rings. My husband listens, 117
then hands the phone to me. "What is this woman saying?" He turns on the pink
Macy's lamp by the bed. "I am not understanding these Negro people's accents."

The operator repeats the message. It's a cable from one of the directors of 118
Lakshmi Cotton Mills. "Massive violent labor confrontation anticipated. Stop.
Return posthaste. Stop. Cable flight details. Signed Kantilal Shah."

"It's not your factory," I say. "You're supposed to be on vacation. " 119

"So, you are worrying about me? Yes? You reject my heartfelt wishes but you 120
worry about me?" He pulls me close, slips the straps of my nightdress off my shoulder. "Wait a minute."

I wait, unclothed, for my husband to come back to me. The water is running 121
in the bathroom. In the ten days he has been here he has learned American rites:
deodorants, fragrances. Tomorrow morning he'll call Air India; tomorrow evening
he'll be on his way back to Bombay. Tonight I should make up to him for my years
away, the gutted trucks, the degree I'll never use in India. I want to pretend with
him that nothing has changed.

In the mirror that hangs on the bathroom door, I watch my naked body turn, 122
the breasts, the thighs glow. The body's beauty amazes. I stand here shameless, in
ways he has never seen me. I am free, afloat, watching somebody else.

Questions for Discussion

1. How is the story's opening disconcerting or disorienting? Why might Mukherjee desire this effect, given what the narrator experiences?

2. List the stereotypes of Indians represented in the David Mamet play. Are you familiar with these? How does Panna react, and how does she wish she could react? What keeps her from doing so? Do you believe insults are a kind of acceptance?

3. How do Panna, Imre, and Charity represent different kinds of outsiders in American society? Do Imre and Charity face similar prejudices as Panna does?

4. Why is Panna in New York, and how has she escaped the gender expectations of her homeland? How does the phone conversation with her husband communicate Panna's changes since being in the United States? What is significant about how she dresses to meet her husband? Have you dressed for similar motives?

5. What kind of unrest is happening in her husband's town north of Bombay in the story, and how does Panna's description of his reaction to it develop his character? How does his behavior in New York affect Panna? Does the author encourage readers to sympathize with him?

6. How does Panna's vulnerability to men's sexual advances and her reaction to these advances develop her characterization? How does the story's emphasis on the issue of Panna's wifely role and fidelity point to the larger struggle she seems to be experiencing?

7. How is the narrator's nudity at the end symbolic? What does her attitude toward her reflection indicate about the changes she has experienced? To what extent is the last scenario a "happy ending"?

Questions for Reflection and Writing

1. After reading Judith Ortiz Cofer's "The Myth of the Latin Woman," explain how her experiences with stereotypes compare to what Panna encounters. How does the traditional Latin American "island" treatment of women compare to that of the patriarchal Indian culture Mukherjee describes?

2. Analyze this story for its messages about the effects of cultural alienation: what it can inspire or inflict. How can it make an individual more vulnerable or stronger? Is experiencing cultural change more complicated for women? Explain your thoughts, blending quotations from the story for support.

3. Evaluate the effectiveness of this story in a brief essay. How effective are the characterizations, use of detail, pace, and dialogue? Is the overall message realistically complex or confusingly vague? Support your points with evidence from the story.

Tim O'Brien (1947–   ) was born in a small town in Minnesota, attended Macalester College, and, after graduation, served a tour of duty in Vietnam (1969–1970). After O'Brien returned, he attended graduate school at Harvard for a time and later worked as a reporter for *The Washington Post*. In 1973, O'Brien published his memoir *If I Die in a Combat Zone, Box Me Up and Send Me Home*, which launched his writing career. Since then, he has published five works of fiction, many of which portray his Vietnam War experience. "The Things They Carried" was first published in *Esquire* in 1986 and subsequently in a collection of stories of the same name published in 1990.

The Things They Carried

Tim O'Brien

First Lieutenant Jimmy Cross carried letters from a girl named Martha, a junior at   1
Mount Sebastian College in New Jersey. They were not love letters, but Lieutenant
Cross was hoping, so he kept them folded in plastic at the bottom of his rucksack. In
the late afternoon, after a day's march, he would dig his foxhole, wash his hands under
a canteen, unwrap the letters, hold them with the tips of his fingers, and spend the
last hour of light pretending. He would imagine romantic camping trips into the
White Mountains in New Hampshire. He would sometimes taste the envelope flaps,
knowing her tongue had been there. More than anything, he wanted Martha to love
him as he loved her, but the letters were mostly chatty, elusive on the matter of love.
She was a virgin, he was almost sure. She was an English major at Mount Sebastian,
and she wrote beautifully about her professors and roommates and midterm exams,
about her respect for Chaucer and her great affection for Virginia Woolf. She often
quoted lines of poetry; she never mentioned the war, except to say, Jimmy, take
care of yourself. The letters weighed ten ounces. They were signed "Love, Martha,"
but Lieutenant Cross understood that "Love" was only a way of signing and did not
mean what he sometimes pretended it meant. At dusk, he would carefully return the
letters to his rucksack. Slowly, a bit distracted, he would get up and move among
his men, checking the perimeter, then at full dark he would return to his hole and
watch the night and wonder if Martha was a virgin.

The things they carried were largely determined by necessity. Among the neces-   2
sities or near necessities were P-38 can openers, pocket knives, heat tabs, wrist
watches, dog tags, mosquito repellant, chewing gum, candy, cigarettes, salt tablets,
packets of Kool-Aid, lighters, matches, sewing kits, Military Payment Certificates,
C rations, and two or three canteens of water. Together, these items weighed between
fifteen and twenty pounds, depending upon a man's habits or rate of metabolism.
Henry Dobbins, who was a big man, carried extra rations; he was especially fond of
canned peaches in heavy syrup over pound cake. Dave Jensen, who practiced field
hygiene, carried a toothbrush, dental floss, and several hotel-size bars of soap he'd

stolen on R&R in Sydney, Australia. Ted Lavender, who was scared, carried tranquilizers until he was shot in the head outside the village of Than Khe in mid-April. By necessity, and because it was SOP,° they all carried steel helmets that weighed five pounds including the liner and camouflage cover. They carried the standard fatigue jackets and trousers. Very few carried underwear. On their feet they carried jungle boots—2.1 pounds—and Dave Jensen carried three pairs of socks and a can of Dr. Scholl's foot powder as a precaution against trench foot. Until he was shot, Ted Lavender carried six or seven ounces of premium dope, which for him was a necessity. Mitchell Sanders, the RTO,° carried condoms. Norman Bowker carried a diary. Rat Kiley carried comic books. Kiowa, a devout Baptist, carried an illustrated New Testament that had been presented to him by his father, who taught Sunday school in Oklahoma City, Oklahoma. As a hedge against bad times, however, Kiowa also carried his grandmother's distrust of the white man, his grandfather's old hunting hatchet. Necessity dictated. Because the land was mined and booby-trapped, it was SOP for each man to carry a steel-centered, nylon-covered flak jacket, which weighed 6.7 pounds, but which on hot days seemed much heavier. Because you could die so quickly, each man carried at least one large compress bandage, usually in the helmet band for easy access. Because the nights were cold, and because the monsoons were wet, each carried a green plastic poncho that could be used as a raincoat or ground sheet or makeshift tent. With its quilted liner, the poncho weighed almost two pounds, but it was worth every ounce. In April, for instance, when Ted Lavender was shot, they used his poncho to wrap him up, then to carry him across the paddy, then to lift him into the chopper that took him away.

They were called legs or grunts.   3

To carry something was to "hump" it, as when Lieutenant Jimmy Cross humped   4 his love for Martha up the hills and through the swamps. In its intransitive form, "to hump" meant "to walk," or "to march," but it implied burdens far beyond the intransitive.

Almost everyone humped photographs. In his wallet, Lieutenant Cross carried   5 two photographs of Martha. The first was a Kodachrome snapshot signed "Love," though he knew better. She stood against a brick wall. Her eyes were gray and neutral, her lips slightly open as she stared straight-on at the camera. At night, sometimes, Lieutenant Cross wondered who had taken the picture, because he knew she had boyfriends, because he loved her so much, and because he could see the shadow of the picture taker spreading out against the brick wall. The second photograph had been clipped from the 1968 Mount Sebastian yearbook. It was an action shot—women's volleyball—and Martha was bent horizontal to the floor, reaching, the palms of her hands in sharp focus, the tongue taut, the expression frank and competitive. There was no visible sweat. She wore white gym shorts. Her legs, he thought, were almost certainly the legs of a virgin, dry and without hair, the left knee cocked and carrying her entire weight, which was just over one hundred pounds. Lieutenant Cross remembered touching that left knee. A dark theater, he remembered, and the movie

---

SOP *Standard Operating Procedure.*
RTO *Radiotelephone operator.*

was *Bonnie and Clyde,* and Martha wore a tweed skirt, and during the final scene, when he touched her knee, she turned and looked at him in a sad, sober way that made him pull his hand back, but he would always remember the feel of the tweed skirt and the knee beneath it and the sound of the gunfire that killed Bonnie and Clyde, how embarrassing it was, how slow and oppressive. He remembered kissing her good night at the dorm door. Right then, he thought, he should've done something brave. He should've carried her up the stairs to her room and tied her to the bed and touched that left knee all night long. He should've risked it. Whenever he looked at the photographs, he thought of new things he should've done.

What they carried was partly a function of rank, partly of field specialty.   6

As a first lieutenant and platoon leader, Jimmy Cross carried a compass, maps,   7
code books, binoculars, and a .45-caliber pistol that weighed 2.9 pounds fully loaded.
He carried a strobe light and the responsibility for the lives of his men.

As an RTO, Mitchell Sanders carried the prc-25 radio, a killer, twenty-six pounds   8
with its battery.

As a medic, Rat Kiley carried a canvas satchel filled with morphine and plasma   9
and malaria tablets and surgical tape and comic books and all the things a medic must
carry, including M&M's for especially bad wounds, for a total weight of nearly twenty
pounds.

As a big man, therefore a machine gunner, Henry Dobbins carried the M-60,   10
which weighed twenty-three pounds unloaded, but which was almost always loaded.
In addition, Dobbins carried between ten and fifteen pounds of ammunition draped
in belts across his chest and shoulders.

As PFCs or Spec 4s, most of them were common grunts and carried the standard   11
M-16 gas-operated assault rifle. The weapon weighed 7.5 pounds unloaded, 8.2
pounds with its full twenty-round magazine. Depending on numerous factors, such
as topography and psychology, the riflemen carried anywhere from twelve to twenty
magazines, usually in cloth bandoliers, adding on another 8.4 pounds at minimum,
fourteen pounds at maximum. When it was available, they also carried M-16
maintenance gear—rods and steel brushes and swabs and tubes of LSA oil—all of
which weighed about a pound. Among the grunts, some carried the M-79 grenade
launcher, 5.9 pounds unloaded, a reasonably light weapon except for the ammunition, which was heavy. A single round weighed ten ounces. The typical load was
twenty-five rounds. But Ted Lavender, who was scared, carried thirty-four rounds
when he was shot and killed outside Than Khe, and he went down under an excep-
tional burden, more than twenty pounds of ammunition, plus the flak jacket and helmet and rations and water and toilet paper and tranquilizers and all the rest, plus the
unweighed fear. He was dead weight. There was no twitching or flopping. Kiowa,
who saw it happen, said it was like watching a rock fall, or a big sandbag or something—just boom, then down—not like the movies where the dead guy rolls around
and does fancy spins and goes ass over teakettle—not like that, Kiowa said, the
poor bastard just flat-fuck fell. Boom. Down. Nothing else. It was a bright morning
in mid-April. Lieutenant Cross felt the pain. He blamed himself. They stripped off
Lavender's canteens and ammo, all the heavy things, and Rat Kiley said the obvious,

the guy's dead, and Mitchell Sanders used his radio to report one U.S. KIA° and to request a chopper. Then they wrapped Lavender in his poncho. They carried him out to a dry paddy, established security, and sat smoking the dead man's dope until the chopper came. Lieutenant Cross kept to himself. He pictured Martha's smooth young face, thinking he loved her more than anything, more than his men, and now Ted Lavender was dead because he loved her so much and could not stop thinking about her. When the dust-off arrived, they carried Lavender aboard. Afterward they burned Than Khe. They marched until dusk, then dug their holes, and that night Kiowa kept explaining how you had to be there, how fast it was, how the poor guy just dropped like so much concrete. Boom-down, he said. Like cement.

In addition to the three standard weapons—the M-60, M-16, and M-79—they   12
carried whatever presented itself, or whatever seemed appropriate as a means of killing or staying alive. They carried catch-as-catch-can. At various times, in various situations, they carried M-14s and CAR-15s and Swedish Ks and grease guns and captured AK-47s and Chi-Coms and RPGs and Simonov carbines and black-market Uzis and .38-caliber Smith & Wesson handguns and 66 mm LAWs and shotguns and silencers and blackjacks and bayonets and C-4 plastic explosives. Lee Strunk carried a slingshot; a weapon of last resort, he called it. Mitchell Sanders carried brass knuckles. Kiowa carried his grandfather's feathered hatchet. Every third or fourth man carried a Claymore antipersonnel mine—3.5 pounds with its firing device. They all carried fragmentation grenades—fourteen ounces each. They all carried at least one M-18 colored smoke grenade—twenty-four ounces. Some carried CS or tear-gas grenades. Some carried white-phosphorus grenades. They carried all they could bear, and then some, including a silent awe for the terrible power of the things they carried.

In the first week of April, before Lavender died, Lieutenant Jimmy Cross received   13
a good-luck charm from Martha. It was a simple pebble, an ounce at most. Smooth to the touch, it was a milky-white color with flecks of orange and violet, oval-shaped, like a miniature egg. In the accompanying letter, Martha wrote that she had found the pebble on the Jersey shoreline, precisely where the land touched water at high tide, where things came together but also separated. It was this separate-but-together quality, she wrote, that had inspired her to pick up the pebble and to carry it in her breast pocket for several days, where it seemed weightless, and then to send it through the mail, by air, as a token of her truest feelings for him. Lieutenant Cross found this romantic. But he wondered what her truest feelings were, exactly, and what she meant by separate-but-together. He wondered how the tides and waves had come into play on that afternoon along the Jersey shoreline when Martha saw the pebble and bent down to rescue it from geology. He imagined bare feet. Martha was a poet, with the poet's sensibilities, and her feet would be brown and bare, the toenails unpainted, the eyes chilly and somber like the ocean in March, and though it was painful, he wondered who had been with her that afternoon. He imagined a pair of shadows moving along the strip of sand where things came together but also separated. It was phantom jealousy, he knew, but he couldn't help himself. He loved

---

KIA Killed in Action.

her so much. On the march, through the hot days of early April, he carried the pebble in his mouth, turning it with his tongue, tasting sea salts and moisture. His mind wandered. He had difficulty keeping his attention on the war. On occasion he would yell at his men to spread out the column, to keep their eyes open, but then he would slip away into daydreams, just pretending, walking barefoot along the Jersey shore, with Martha, carrying nothing. He would feel himself rising. Sun and waves and gentle winds, all love and lightness.

What they carried varied by mission.   14

When a mission took them to the mountains, they carried mosquito netting,   15
machetes, canvas tarps, and extra bug juice.

If a mission seemed especially hazardous, or if it involved a place they knew to   16
be bad, they carried everything they could. In certain heavily mined AOs,° where
the land was dense with Toe Poppers and Bouncing Betties, they took turns humping a twenty-eight-pound mine detector. With its headphones and big sensing plate,
the equipment was a stress on the lower back and shoulders, awkward to handle, often
useless because of the shrapnel in the earth, but they carried it anyway, partly for
safety, partly for the illusion of safety.

On ambush, or other night missions, they carried peculiar little odds and ends.   17
Kiowa always took along his New Testament and a pair of moccasins for silence. Dave
Jensen carried night-sight vitamins high in carotin. Lee Strunk carried his slingshot;
ammo, he claimed, would never be a problem. Rat Kiley carried brandy and M&M's.
Until he was shot, Ted Lavender carried the starlight scope, which weighed 6.3
pounds with its aluminum carrying case. Henry Dobbins carried his girlfriend's panty-
hose wrapped around his neck as a comforter. They all carried ghosts. When dark
came, they would move out single file across the meadows and paddies to their
ambush coordinates, where they would quietly set up the Claymores and lie down
and spend the night waiting.

Other missions were more complicated and required special equipment. In mid-   18
April, it was their mission to search out and destroy the elaborate tunnel complexes
in the Than Khe area south of Chu Lai. To blow the tunnels, they carried one-pound
blocks of pentrite high explosives, four blocks to a man, sixty-eight pounds in all.
They carried wiring, detonators, and battery-powered clackers. Dave Jensen carried earplugs. Most often, before blowing the tunnels, they were ordered by higher
command to search them, which was considered bad news, but by and large they just
shrugged and carried out orders. Because he was a big man, Henry Dobbins was
excused from tunnel duty. The others would draw numbers. Before Lavender died
there were seventeen men in the platoon, and whoever drew the number seventeen would strip off his gear and crawl in head first with a flashlight and Lieutenant
Cross's .45-caliber pistol. The rest of them would fan out as security. They would
sit down or kneel, not facing the hole, listening to the ground beneath them, imag-
ining cobwebs and ghosts, whatever was down there—the tunnel walls squeezing
in—how the flashlight seemed impossibly heavy in the hand and how it was tunnel

---

AOs Areas of Operation.

vision in the very strictest sense, compression in all ways, even time, and how you had to wiggle in—ass and elbows—a swallowed-up feeling—and how you found yourself worrying about odd things—will your flashlight go dead? Do rats carry rabies? If you screamed, how far would the sound carry? Would your buddies hear it? Would they have the courage to drag you out? In some respects, though not many, the waiting was worse than the tunnel itself. Imagination was a killer.

On April 16, when Lee Strunk drew the number seventeen, he laughed and muttered something and went down quickly. The morning was hot and very still. Not good, Kiowa said. He looked at the tunnel opening, then out across a dry paddy toward the village of Than Khe. Nothing moved. No clouds or birds or people. As they waited, the men smoked and drank Kool-Aid, not talking much, feeling sympathy for Lee Strunk but also feeling the luck of the draw. You win some, you lose some, said Mitchell Sanders, and sometimes you settle for a rain check. It was a tired line and no one laughed.   19

Henry Dobbins ate a tropical chocolate bar. Ted Lavender popped a tranquilizer and went off to pee.   20

After five minutes, Lieutenant Jimmy Cross moved to the tunnel, leaned down, and examined the darkness. Trouble, he thought—a cave-in maybe. And then suddenly, without willing it, he was thinking about Martha. The stresses and fractures, the quick collapse, the two of them buried alive under all that weight. Dense, crushing love. Kneeling, watching the hole, he tried to concentrate on Lee Strunk and the war, all the dangers, but his love was too much for him, he felt paralyzed, he wanted to sleep inside her lungs and breathe her blood and be smothered. He wanted her to be a virgin and not a virgin, all at once. He wanted to know her. Intimate secrets—why poetry? Why so sad? Why the grayness in her eyes? Why so alone? Not lonely, just alone—riding her bike across campus or sitting off by herself in the cafeteria. Even dancing, she danced alone—and it was the aloneness that filled him with love. He remembered telling her that one evening. How she nodded and looked away. And how, later, when he kissed her, she received the kiss without returning it, her eyes wide open, not afraid, not a virgin's eyes, just flat and uninvolved.   21

Lieutenant Cross gazed at the tunnel. But he was not there. He was buried with Martha under the white sand at the Jersey shore. They were pressed together, and the pebble in his mouth was her tongue. He was smiling. Vaguely, he was aware of how quiet the day was, the sullen paddies, yet he could not bring himself to worry about matters of security. He was beyond that. He was just a kid at war, in love. He was twenty-two years old. He couldn't help it.   22

A few moments later Lee Strunk crawled out of the tunnel. He came up grinning, filthy but alive. Lieutenant Cross nodded and closed his eyes while the others clapped Strunk on the back and made jokes about rising from the dead.   23

Worms, Rat Kiley said. Right out of the grave. Fuckin' zombie.   24

The men laughed. They all felt great relief.   25

Spook City, said Mitchell Sanders.   26

Lee Strunk made a funny ghost sound, a kind of moaning, yet very happy, and right then, when Strunk made that high happy moaning sound, when he want *Ahhooooo*, right then Ted Lavender was shot in the head on his way back from peeing.   27

He lay with his mouth open. The teeth were broken. There was a swollen black bruise under his left eye. The cheekbone was gone. Oh shit, Rat Kiley said, the guy's dead. The guy's dead, he kept saying, which seemed profound—the guy's dead. I mean really.

The things they carried were determined to some extent by superstition. 28
Lieutenant Cross carried his good-luck pebble. Dave Jensen carried a rabbit's foot. Norman Bowker, otherwise a very gentle person, carried a thumb that had been presented to him as a gift by Mitchell Sanders. The thumb was dark brown, rubbery to the touch, and weighed four ounces at most. It had been cut from a VC° corpse, a boy of fifteen or sixteen. They'd found him at the bottom of an irrigation ditch, badly burned, flies in his mouth and eyes. The boy wore black shorts and sandals. At the time of his death he had been carrying a pouch of rice, a rifle, and three magazines of ammunition.

You want my opinion, Mitchell Sanders said, there's a definite moral here. 29

He put his hand on the dead boy's wrist. He was quiet for a time, as if counting 30
a pulse, then he patted the stomach, almost affectionately, and used Kiowa's hunting hatchet to remove the thumb.

Henry Dobbins asked what the moral was. 31

Moral? 32

You know. *Moral.* 33

Sanders wrapped the thumb in toilet paper and handed it across to Norman 34
Bowker. There was no blood. Smiling, he kicked the boy's head, watched the flies scatter, and said, It's like that old TV show—Paladin. Have gun, will travel.

Henry Dobbins thought about it. 35

Yeah, well, he finally said. I don't see no moral. 36

There it *is*, man. 37

Fuck off. 38

They carried uso stationery and pencils and pens. They carried Sterno, safety 39
pins, trip flares, signal flares, spools of wire, razor blades, chewing tobacco, liberated joss sticks and statuettes of the smiling Buddha, candles, grease pencils, *The Stars and Stripes*, fingernail clippers, Psy Ops° leaflets, bush hats, bolos, and much more. Twice a week, when the resupply choppers came in, they carried hot chow in green Mermite cans and large canvas bags filled with iced beer and soda pop. They carried plastic water containers, each with a two-gallon capacity. Mitchell Sanders carried a set of starched tiger fatigues for special occasions. Henry Dobbins carried Black Flag insecticide. Dave Jensen carried empty sandbags that could be filled at night for added protection. Lee Strunk carried tanning lotion. Some things they carried in common. Taking turns, they carried the big PRC-77 scrambler radio, which weighed thirty pounds with its battery. They shared the weight of memory. They took up what others could no longer bear. Often, they carried each other, the wounded or weak. They carried infections. They carried chess sets, basketballs, Vietnamese-English dictionaries, insignia of rank, Bronze Stars and Purple Hearts, plastic cards

VC Vietcong.
Psy Ops Psychological Operations.

imprinted with the Code of Conduct. They carried diseases, among them malaria and dysentery. They carried lice and ringworm and leeches and paddy algae and various rots and molds. They carried the land itself—Vietnam, the place, the soil—a powdery orange-red dust that covered their boots and fatigues and faces. They carried the sky. The whole atmosphere, they carried it, the humidity, the monsoons, the stink of fungus and decay, all of it, they carried gravity. They moved like mules. By daylight they took sniper fire, at night they were mortared, but it was not battle, it was just the endless march, village to village, without purpose, nothing won or lost. They marched for the sake of the march. They plodded along slowly, dumbly, leaning forward against the heat, unthinking, all blood and bone, simple grunts, soldiering with their legs, toiling up the hills and down into the paddies and across the rivers and up again and down, just humping, one step and then the next and then another, but no volition, no will, because it was automatic, it was anatomy, and the war was entirely a matter of posture and carriage, the hump was everything, a kind of inertia, a kind of emptiness, a dullness of desire and intellect and conscience and hope and human sensibility. Their principles were in their feet. Their calculations were biological. They had no sense of strategy or mission. They searched the villages without knowing what to look for, not caring, kicking over jars of rice, frisking children and old men, blowing tunnels, sometimes setting fires and sometimes not, then forming up and moving on to the next village, then other villages, where it would always be the same. They carried their own lives. The pressures were enormous. In the heat of early afternoon, they would remove their helmets and flak jackets, walking bare, which was dangerous but which helped ease the strain. They would often discard things along the route of march. Purely for comfort, they would throw away rations, blow their Claymores and grenades, no matter, because by nightfall the resupply choppers would arrive with more of the same, then a day or two later still more, fresh watermelons and crates of ammunition and sunglasses and woolen sweaters—the resources were stunning—sparklers for the Fourth of July, colored eggs for Easter. It was the great American war chest—the fruits of science, the smokestacks, the canneries, the arsenals at Hartford, the Minnesota forests, the machine shops, the vast fields of corn and wheat—they carried like freight trains; they carried it on their backs and shoulders—and for all the ambiguities of Vietnam, all the mysteries and unknowns, there was at least the single abiding certainty that they would never be at a loss for things to carry.

After the chopper took Lavender away, Lieutenant Jimmy Cross led his men into   40
the village of Than Khe. They burned everything. They shot chickens and dogs, they trashed the village well, they called in artillery and watched the wreckage, then they marched for several hours through the hot afternoon, and then at dusk, while Kiowa explained how Lavender died, Lieutenant Cross found himself trembling.

He tried not to cry. With his entrenching tool, which weighed five pounds, he   41
began digging a hole in the earth.

He felt shame. He hated himself. He had loved Martha more than his men, and   42
as a consequence Lavender was now dead, and this was something he would have to carry like a stone in his stomach for the rest of the war.

All he could do was dig. He used his entrenching tool like an ax, slashing, feeling both love and hate, and then later, when it was full dark, he sat at the bottom of his foxhole and wept. It went on for a long while. In part, he was grieving for Ted Lavender, but mostly it was for Martha, and for himself, because she belonged to another world, which was not quite real, and because she was a junior at Mount Sebastian College in New Jersey, a poet and a virgin and uninvolved, and because he realized she did not love him and never would.   43

Like cement, Kiowa whispered in the dark. I swear to God—boom-down. Not a word.   44

I've heard this, said Norman Bowker.   45

A pisser, you know? Still zipping himself up. Zapped while zipping.   46

All right, fine. That's enough.   47

Yeah, but you had to see it, the guy just—   48

I *heard*, man. Cement. So why not shut the fuck *up?*   49

Kiowa shook his head sadly and glanced over at the hole where Lieutenant Jimmy Cross sat watching the night. The air was thick and wet. A warm, dense fog had settled over the paddies and there was the stillness that precedes rain.   50

After a time Kiowa sighed.   51

One thing for sure, he said. The Lieutenant's in some deep hurt. I mean that crying jag—the way he was carrying on—it wasn't fake or anything, it was real heavy-duty hurt. The man cares.   52

Sure, Norman Bowker said.   53

Say what you want, the man does care.   54

We all got problems.   55

Not Lavender.   56

No, I guess not, Bowker said. Do me a favor, though.   57

Shut up?   58

That's a smart Indian. Shut up.   59

Shrugging, Kiowa pulled off his boots. He wanted to say more, just to lighten up his sleep, but instead he opened his New Testament and arranged it beneath his head as a pillow. The fog made things seem hollow and unattached. He tried not to think about Ted Lavender, but then he was thinking how fast it was, no drama, down and dead, and how it was hard to feel anything except surprise. It seemed un-Christian. He wished he could find some great sadness, or even anger, but the emotion wasn't there and he couldn't make it happen. Mostly he felt pleased to be alive. He liked the smell of the New Testament under his cheek, the leather and ink and paper and glue, whatever the chemicals were. He liked hearing the sounds of night. Even his fatigue, it felt fine, the stiff muscles and the prickly awareness of his own body, a floating feeling. He enjoyed not being dead. Lying there, Kiowa admired Lieutenant Jimmy Cross's capacity for grief. He wanted to share the man's pain, he wanted to care as Jimmy Cross cared. And yet when he closed his eyes, all he could think was Boom-down, and all he could feel was the pleasure of having his boots off and the fog curling in around him and the damp soil and the Bible smells and the plush comfort of night.   60

After a moment Norman Bowker sat up in the dark.   61

What the hell, he said. You want to talk, *talk*. Tell it to me.   62

Forget it.   63

No, man, go on. One thing I hate, it's a silent Indian.   64

For the most part they carried themselves with poise, a kind of dignity. Now and   65
then, however, there were times of panic, when they squealed or wanted to squeal
but couldn't, when they twitched and made moaning sounds and covered their heads
and said Dear Jesus and flopped around on the earth and fired their weapons blindly
and cringed and sobbed and begged for the noise to stop and went wild and made stupid promises to themselves and to God and to their mothers and fathers, hoping
not to die. In different ways, it happened to all of them. Afterward, when the firing
ended, they would blink and peek up. They would touch their bodies, feeling shame,
then quickly hiding it. They would force themselves to stand. As if in slow motion,
frame by frame, the world would take on the old logic—absolute silence, then the
wind, then sunlight, then voices. It was the burden of being alive. Awkwardly, the
men would reassemble themselves, first in private, then in groups, becoming soldiers
again. They would repair the leaks in their eyes. They would check for casualties, call
in dust-offs, light cigarettes, try to smile, clear their throats and spit and begin cleaning their weapons. After a time someone would shake his head and say, No lie, I
almost shit my pants, and someone else would laugh, which meant it was bad, yes,
but the guy had obviously not shit his pants, it wasn't that bad, and in any case nobody
would ever do such a thing and then go ahead and talk about it. They would squint
into the dense, oppressive sunlight. For a few moments, perhaps, they would fall silent,
lighting a joint and tracking its passage from man to man, inhaling, holding in the
humiliation. Scary stuff, one of them might say. But then someone else would grin
or flick his eyebrows and say, Roger-dodger, almost cut me a new asshole, *almost*.

There were numerous such poses. Some carried themselves with a sort of wist-   66
ful resignation, others with pride or stiff soldierly discipline or good humor or macho
zeal. They were afraid of dying but they were even more afraid to show it.

They found jokes to tell.   67

They used a hard vocabulary to contain the terrible softness. *Greased*, they'd say.   68
Offed, lit up, zapped while zipping. It wasn't cruelty, just stage presence. They were
actors and the war came at them in 3-D. When someone died, it wasn't quite dying,
because in a curious way it seemed scripted, and because they had their lines mostly
memorized, irony mixed with tragedy, and because they called it by other names, as
if to encyst and destroy the reality of death itself. They kicked corpses. They cut off
thumbs. They talked grunt lingo. They told stories about Ted Lavender's supply of
tranquilizers, how the poor guy didn't feel a thing, how incredibly tranquil he was.

There's a moral here, said Mitchell Sanders.   69

They were waiting for Lavender's chopper, smoking the dead man's dope.   70

The moral's pretty obvious, Sanders said, and winked. Stay away from drugs. No   71
joke, they'll ruin your day every time.

Cute, said Henry Dobbins.   72

Mind-blower, get it? Talk about wiggy—nothing left, just blood and brains.   73

They made themselves laugh. 74

There it is, they'd say, over and over, as if the repetition itself were an act of poise, 75
a balance between crazy and almost crazy, knowing without going. There it is, which
meant be cool, let it ride, because oh yeah, man, you can't change what can't be
changed, there it is, there it absolutely and positively and fucking well *is*.

They were tough. 76

They carried all the emotional baggage of men who might die. Grief, terror, love, 77
longing—these were intangibles, but the intangibles had their own mass and specific
gravity, they had tangible weight. They carried shameful memories. They carried the
common secret of cowardice barely restrained, the instinct to run or freeze or hide,
and in many respects this was the heaviest burden of all, for it could never be put
down, it required perfect balance and perfect posture. They carried their reputations.
They carried the soldier's greatest fear, which was the fear of blushing. Men killed,
and died, because they were embarrassed not to. It was what had brought them to
the war in the first place, nothing positive, no dreams of glory or honor, just to avoid
the blush of dishonor. They died so as not to die of embarrassment. They crawled
into tunnels and walked point and advanced under fire. Each morning, despite the
unknowns, they made their legs move. They endured. They kept humming. They
did not submit to the obvious alternative, which was simply to close the eyes and fall.
So easy, really. Go limp and tumble to the ground and let the muscles unwind and
not speak and not budge until your buddies picked you up and lifted you into the
chopper that would roar and dip its nose and carry you off to the world. A mere matter of falling, yet no one ever fell. It was not courage, exactly; the object was not valor.
Rather, they were too frightened to be cowards.

By and large they carried these things inside, maintaining the masks of com- 78
posure. They sneered at sick call. They spoke bitterly about guys who had found
release by shooting off their own toes or fingers. Pussies, they'd say. Candyasses. It
was fierce, mocking talk, with only a trace of envy or awe, but even so, the image
played itself out behind their eyes.

They imagined the muzzle against flesh. They imagined the quick, sweet pain, 79
then the evacuation to Japan, then a hospital with warm beds and cute geisha nurses.

They dreamed of freedom birds. 80

At night, on guard, staring into the dark, they were carried away by jumbo jets. 81
They felt the rush of takeoff. *Gone!* they yelled. And then velocity, wings and engines,
a smiling stewardess—but it was more than a plane, it was a real bird, a big sleek
silver bird with feathers and talons and high screeching. They were flying. The
weights fell off, there was nothing to bear. They laughed and held on tight, feeling
the cold slap of wind and altitude, soaring, thinking *It's over, I'm gone!*—they were
naked, they were light and free—it was all lightness, bright and fast and buoyant,
light as light, a helium buzz in the brain, a giddy bubbling in the lungs as they were
taken up over the clouds and the war, beyond duty, beyond gravity and mortification
and global entanglements—*Sin loi!*° they yelled, *I'm sorry, motherfuckers, but I'm*

Sin loi! *"Sorry about that!"*

out of it, I'm goofed, I'm on a space cruise, I'm gone!—and it was a restful, disencumbered sensation, just riding the light waves, sailing that big silver freedom bird over the mountains and oceans, over America, over the farms and great sleeping cities and cemeteries and highways and the golden arches of McDonald's. It was flight, a kind of fleeing, a kind of falling, falling higher and higher, spinning off the edge of the earth and beyond the sun and through the vast, silent vacuum where there were no burdens and where everything weighed exactly nothing. *Gone!* they screamed, *I'm sorry but I'm gone!* And so at night, not quite dreaming, they gave themselves over to lightness, they were carried, they were purely borne.

On the morning after Ted Lavender died, First Lieutenant Jimmy Cross crouched at the bottom of his foxhole and burned Martha's letters. Then he burned the two photographs. There was a steady rain falling, which made it difficult, but he used heat tabs and Sterno to build a small fire, screening it with his body, holding the photographs over the tight blue flame with the tips of his fingers.   82

He realized it was only a gesture. Stupid, he thought. Sentimental, too, but mostly just stupid.   83

Lavender was dead. You couldn't burn the blame.   84

Besides, the letters were in his head. And even now, without photographs, Lieutenant Cross could see Martha playing volleyball in her white gym shorts and yellow T-shirt. He could see her moving in the rain.   85

When the fire died out, Lieutenant Cross pulled his poncho over his shoulders and ate breakfast from a can.   86

There was no great mystery, he decided.   87

In those burned letters Martha had never mentioned the war, except to say, Jimmy, take care of yourself. She wasn't involved. She signed the letters "Love," but it wasn't love, and all the fine lines and technicalities did not matter.   88

The morning came up wet and blurry. Everything seemed part of everything else, the fog and Martha and the deepening rain.   89

It was a war, after all.   90

Half smiling, Lieutenant Jimmy Cross took out his maps. He shook his head hard, as if to clear it, then bent forward and began planning the day's march. In ten minutes, or maybe twenty, he would rouse the men and they would pack up and head west, where the maps showed the country to be green and inviting. They would do what they had always done. The rain might add some weight, but otherwise it would be one more day layered upon all the other days.   91

He was realistic about it. There was that new hardness in his stomach.   92

No more fantasies, he told himself.   93

Henceforth, when he thought about Martha, it would be only to think that she belonged elsewhere. He would shut down the daydreams. This was not Mount Sebastian, it was another world, where there were no pretty poems or midterm exams, a place where men died because of carelessness and gross stupidity. Kiowa was right. Boom-down, and you were dead, never partly dead.   94

Briefly, in the rain, Lieutenant Cross saw Martha's gray eyes gazing back at him.   95

He understood.   96

It was very sad, he thought. The things men carried inside. The things men   97
did or felt they had to do.

He almost nodded at her, but didn't.   98

Instead he went back to his maps. He was now determined to perform his duties   99
firmly and without negligence. It wouldn't help Lavender, he knew that, but from
this point on he would comport himself as a soldier. He would dispose of his good-
luck pebble. Swallow it, maybe, or use Lee Strunk's slingshot, or just drop it along
the trail. On the march he would impose strict field discipline. He would be careful
to send out flank security, to prevent straggling or bunching up, to keep his troops
moving at the proper pace and at the proper interval. He would insist on clean
weapons. He would confiscate the remainder of Lavender's dope. Later in the day,
perhaps, he would call the men together and speak to them plainly. He would accept
the blame for what had happened to Ted Lavender. He would be a man about it.
He would look them in the eyes, keeping his chin level, and he would issue the
new SOPs in a calm, impersonal tone of voice, an officer's voice, leaving no room for
argument or discussion. Commencing immediately, he'd tell them, they would no
longer abandon equipment along the route of march. They would police up their
acts. They would get their shit together, and keep it together, and maintain it neatly
and in good working order.

He would not tolerate laxity. He would show strength, distancing himself.   100

Among the men there would be grumbling, of course, and maybe worse, because   101
their days would seem longer and their loads heavier, but Lieutenant Cross reminded
himself that his obligation was not to be loved but to lead. He would dispense with
love; it was not now a factor. And if anyone quarreled or complained, he would
simply tighten his lips and arrange his shoulders in the correct command posture. He
might give a curt little nod. Or he might not. He might just shrug and say Carry
on, then they would saddle up and form into a column and move out toward the
villages of Than Khe.

.

Edgar Allan Poe (1809–1849) published his first volume of poems at the age of 18. Orphaned early in life, Poe led a peripatetic existence, entering and leaving a series of schools (including West Point), enlisting in the Army, and writing for a series of newspapers and magazines in Richmond, Philadelphia, and New York. He first won a national reputation with the publication of his poem "The Raven" in 1845. Poe thought of himself primarily as a poet, though he is now perhaps better known for tales of horror such as "The Cask of Amontillado," first published in *Godey's Lady's Book* (1846) and later collected in Poe's *Works* (1850). In 1847 Poe was devastated by the death of his cousin and wife, Virginia, whom he had married when she was 13, and to whom he addressed the poem "Annabel Lee." Two years later, Poe, acutely alcoholic, died in Baltimore after a brief illness.

The Cask of Amontillado

Edgar Allan Poe

The thousand injuries of Fortunato I had borne as I best could; but when he ventured upon insult, I vowed revenge. You, who so well know the nature of my soul, will not suppose, however, that I gave utterance to a threat. *At length* I would be avenged; this was a point definitively settled—but the very definitiveness with which it was resolved, precluded the idea of risk. I must not only punish, but punish with impunity. A wrong is unredressed when retribution overtakes its redresser. It is equally unredressed when the avenger fails to make himself felt as such to him who has done the wrong. 1

It must be understood, that neither by word nor deed had I given Fortunato cause to doubt my good will. I continued, as was my wont, to smile in his face, and he did not perceive that my smile *now* was at the thought of his immolation. 2

He had a weak point—this Fortunato—although in other regards he was a man to be respected and even feared. He prided himself on his connoisseurship in wine. Few Italians have the true virtuoso spirit. For the most part their enthusiasm is adopted to suit the time and opportunity—to practice imposture upon the British and Austrian *millionnaires*. In painting and gemmary, Fortunato, like his countrymen, was a quack—but in the matter of old wines he was sincere. In this respect I did not differ from him materially: I was skillful in the Italian vintages myself, and bought largely whenever I could. 3

It was about dusk, one evening during the supreme madness of the carnival season, that I encountered my friend. He accosted me with excessive warmth, for he had been drinking much. The man wore motley. He had on a tight-fitting parti-striped dress, and his head was surmounted by the conical cap and bells. I was so pleased to see him, that I thought I should never have done wringing his hand. 4

I said to him—"My dear Fortunato, you are luckily met. How remarkably well you are looking to-day! But I have received a pipe° of what passes for Amontillado, and I have my doubts." 5

---

pipe *a cask*

"How?" said he. "Amontillado? A pipe? Impossible! And in the middle of the carnival!" 6

"I have my doubts," I replied; "and I was silly enough to pay the full Amontillado price without consulting you in the matter. You were not to be found, and I was fearful of losing a bargain." 7

"Amontillado!" 8

"I have my doubts." 9

"Amontillado!" 10

"And I must satisfy them." 11

"Amontillado!" 12

"As you are engaged, I am on my way to Luchesi. If any one has a critical turn, it is he. He will tell me—" 13

"Luchesi cannot tell Amontillado from Sherry." 14

"And yet some fools will have it that his taste is a match for your own." 15

"Come, let us go." 16

"Whither?" 17

"To your vaults." 18

"My friend, no; I will not impose upon your good nature. I perceive you have an engagement. Luchesi—" 19

"I have no engagement;—come." 20

"My friend, no. It is not the engagement, but the severe cold with which I perceive you are afflicted. The vaults are insufferably damp. They are encrusted with nitre." 21

"Let us go, nevertheless. The cold is merely nothing. Amontillado! You have been imposed upon. And as for Luchesi, he cannot distinguish Sherry from Amontillado." 22

Thus speaking, Fortunato possessed himself of my arm. Putting on a mask of black silk, and drawing a *roquelaire* closely about my person, I suffered him to hurry me to my palazzo. 23

There were no attendants at home; they had absconded to make merry in honor of the time. I had told them that I should not return until the morning, and had given them explicit orders not to stir from the house. These orders were sufficient, I well knew, to insure their immediate disappearance, one and all, as soon as my back was turned. 24

I took from their sconces two flambeaux, and giving one to Fortunato, bowed him through several suites of rooms to the archway that led into the vaults. I passed down a long and winding staircase, requesting him to be cautious as he followed. We came at length to the foot of the descent, and stood together on the damp ground of the catacombs of the Montresors. 25

The gait of my friend was unsteady, and the bells upon his cap jingled as he strode. 26

"The pipe," said he. 27

"It is farther on," said I; "but observe the white web-work which gleams from these cavern walls." 28

He turned toward me, and looked into my eyes with two filmy orbs that distilled   29
the rheum of intoxication.

"Nitre?" he asked, at length.   30

"Nitre," I replied. "How long have you had that cough?"   31

"Ugh! ugh! ugh!—ugh! ugh! ugh!—ugh! ugh! ugh!—ugh! ugh! ugh!—ugh!   32
ugh! ugh!"

My poor friend found it impossible to reply for many minutes.   33

"It is nothing," he said, at last.   34

"Come," I said, with decision, "we will go back; your health is precious. You   35
are rich, respected, admired, beloved; you are happy, as once I was. You are a man
to be missed. For me it is no matter. We will go back; you will be ill, and I cannot
be responsible. Besides, there is Luchesi—"

"Enough," he said; "the cough is a mere nothing; it will not kill me. I shall not   36
die of a cough."

"True—true," I replied; "and, indeed, I had no intention of alarming you unnec-   37
essarily—but you should use all proper caution. A draught of this Medoc will defend
us from the damps."

Here I knocked off the neck of a bottle which I drew from a long row of its fel-   38
lows that lay upon the mould.

"Drink," I said, presenting him the wine.   39

He raised it to his lips with a leer. He paused and nodded to me familiarly, while   40
his bells jingled.

"I drink," he said, "to the buried that repose around us."   41

"And I to your long life."   42

He again took my arm, and we proceeded.   43

"These vaults," he said, "are extensive."   44

"The Montresors," I replied, "were a great and numerous family."   45

"I forget your arms."   46

"A huge human foot d'or, in a field azure; the foot crushes a serpent rampant   47
whose fangs are imbedded in the heel."

"And the motto?"   48

"Nemo me impune lacessit."   49

"Good!" he said.   50

The wine sparkled in his eyes and the bells jingled. My own fancy grew warm   51
with the Medoc. We had passed through walls of piled bones, with casks and pun-
cheons intermingling, into the inmost recesses of the catacombs. I paused again, and
this time I made bold to seize Fortunato by an arm above the elbow.

"The nitre!" I said; "see, it increases. It hangs like moss upon the vaults. We   52
are below the river's bed. The drops of moisture trickle among the bones. Come,
we will go back ere it is too late. Your cough—"

"It is nothing," he said; "let us go on. But first, another draught of the Medoc."   53

I broke and reached him a flagon of De Grâve. He emptied it at a breath. His   54
eyes flashed with a fierce light. He laughed and threw the bottle upwards with a
gesticulation I did not understand.

I looked at him in surprise. He repeated the movement—a grotesque one.   55

"You do not comprehend?" he said.   56

"Not I," I replied.   57

"Then you are not of the brotherhood."   58

"How?"   59

"You are not of the masons."   60

"Yes, yes," I said, "yes, yes."   61

"You? Impossible! A mason?"   62

"A mason," I replied.   63

"A sign," he said.   64

"It is this," I answered, producing a trowel from beneath the folds of my   65
roquelaire.

"You jest," he exclaimed, recoiling a few paces. "But let us proceed to the   66
Amontillado."

"Be it so," I said, replacing the tool beneath the cloak, and again offering him   67
my arm. He leaned upon it heavily. We continued our route in search of the
Amontillado. We passed through a range of low arches, descended, passed on, and
descending again, arrived at a deep crypt, in which the foulness of the air caused
our flambeaux rather to glow than flame.

At the most remote end of the crypt there appeared another less spacious. Its   68
walls had been lined with human remains, piled to the vault overhead, in the fashion
of the great catacombs of Paris. Three sides of this interior crypt were still ornamented
in this manner. From the fourth the bones had been thrown down, and lay promis-
cuously upon the earth, forming at one point a mound of some size. Within the
wall thus exposed by the displacing of the bones, we perceived a still interior recess,
in depth about four feet, in width three, in height six or seven. It seemed to have
been constructed for no especial use in itself, but formed merely the interval between
two of the colossal supports of the roof of the catacombs, and was backed by one of
their circumscribing walls of solid granite.

It was in vain that Fortunato, uplifting his dull torch, endeavored to pry into the   69
depth of the recess. Its termination the feeble light did not enable us to see.

"Proceed," I said; "herein is the Amontillado. As for Luchesi—"   70

"He is an ignoramus," interrupted my friend, as he stepped unsteadily forward,   71
while I followed immediately at his heels. In an instant he had reached the extrem-
ity of the niche, and finding his progress arrested by the rock, stood stupidly bewildered. A moment more and I had fettered him to the granite. In its surface were
two iron staples, distant from each other about two feet, horizontally. From one of
these depended a short chain, from the other a padlock. Throwing the links about
his waist, it was but the work of a few seconds to secure it. He was too much astounded
to resist. Withdrawing the key I stepped back from the recess.

"Pass your hand," I said, "over the wall; you cannot help feeling the nitre. Indeed   72
it is *very* damp. Once more let me *implore* you to return. No? Then I must positively
leave you. But I must first render you all the little attentions in my power."

"The Amontillado!" ejaculated my friend, not yet recovered from his   73
astonishment.

"True," I replied; "the Amontillado." 74

As I said these words I busied myself among the pile of bones of which I have 75
before spoken. Throwing them aside, I soon uncovered a quantity of building stone
and mortar. With these materials and with the aid of my trowel, I began vigorously
to wall up the entrance of the niche.

I had scarcely laid the first tier of my masonry when I discovered that the intox- 76
ication of Fortunato had in a great measure worn off. The earliest indication I had of
this was a low moaning cry from the depth of the recess. It was *not* the cry of a drunken
man. There was then a long and obstinate silence. I laid the second tier, and the third,
and the fourth; and then I heard the furious vibrations of the chain. The noise lasted
for several minutes, during which, that I might hearken to it with the more satisfaction, I ceased my labors and sat down upon the bones. When at last the clanking subsided, I resumed the trowel, and finished without interruption the fifth, the
sixth, and the seventh tier. The wall was now nearly upon a level with my breast.
I again paused, and holding the flambeaux over the mason-work, threw a few feeble rays upon the figure within.

A succession of loud and shrill screams, bursting suddenly from the throat of the 77
chained form, seemed to thrust me violently back. For a brief moment I hesitated—
I trembled. Unsheathing my rapier, I began to grope with it about the recess; but the
thought of an instant reassured me. I placed my hand upon the solid fabric of the catacombs, and felt satisfied. I reapproached the wall. I replied to the yells of him who
clamored. I re-echoed—I aided—I surpassed them in volume and in strength. I did
this, and the clamorer grew still.

It was now midnight, and my task was drawing to a close. I had completed the 78
eighth, the ninth, and the tenth tier. I had finished a portion of the last and the
eleventh; there remained but a single stone to be fitted and plastered in. I struggled
with its weight; I placed it partially in its destined position. But now there came from
out the niche a low laugh that erected the hairs upon my head. It was succeeded by
a sad voice, which I had difficulty in recognising as that of the noble Fortunato. The
voice said—

"Ha! ha! ha!—he! he!—a very good joke indeed—an excellent jest. We will 79
have many a rich laugh about it at the palazzo—he! he! he!—over our wine—he!
he! he!"

"The Amontillado!" I said. 80

"He! he! he!—he! he! he!—yes, the Amontillado. But is it not getting late? Will 81
not they be awaiting us at the palazzo, the Lady Fortunato and the rest? Let us be
gone."

"Yes," I said, "let us be gone." 82

"For the love of God, Montresor!" 83

"Yes," I said, "for the love of God!" 84

But to these words I hearkened in vain for a reply. I grew impatient. I called 85
aloud—

"Fortunato!" 86

No answer. I called again— 87

"Fortunato!" 88

No answer still. I thrust a torch through the remaining aperture and let it fall   89
within. There came forth in return only a jingling of the bells. My heart grew sick—
on account of the dampness of the catacombs. I hastened to make an end of my labor.
I forced the last stone into its position; I plastered it up. Against the new masonry I
re-erected the old rampart of bones. For the half of a century no mortal has disturbed
them. *In pace requiescat!*

Kurt Vonnegut (1922–2007), one of the most esteemed American novelists of the twentieth century, penned fifteen novels, five collections of short stories, eight plays, and various essays published in collections and in periodicals such as *Cosmopolitan*, the *Ladies' Home Journal*, and the *Saturday Evening Post*. Vonnegut was born in Indianapolis, Indiana, and attended Cornell University from 1940–1942 before enlisting in the U.S. Army. The army sent him to the Carnegie Institute of Technology (now Carnegie-Mellon University) in 1943 to study engineering, but the next year he left for Europe and fought in the Battle of the Bulge. He was taken prisoner of war, was wounded, and received the Purple Heart. From 1945–1947, he studied at the University of Chicago but left due to a lack of money after drafting three theses. The university granted him an M.A. in 1971, accepting his novel *Cat's Cradle* in place of a thesis.

His work is known for combining science fiction, philosophy, and humor, and for its pessimism about the possibility of a meaningful life, with human kindness as perhaps the only saving grace. His style stood out for its informal voice, its long sentences, and its minimal punctuation. His most famous work was his first best-selling novel, *Slaughterhouse Five* (1969), which was based on his experience as a prisoner of war surviving the Allied firebombing of Dresden, Germany. It was especially popular because it spoke to issues increasingly important to Americans at the time, including war, the environment, and materialism. Among his many honors, he won a Guggenheim Fellowship (1967), the Literary Lion Award from the New York Public Library (1981), an Emmy Award for Outstanding Children's Program (1985), and was named New York's State Author by the New York State Writers' Institute (2001). His most recently published work is the novel *Armageddon in Retrospect* (April 2008). In "Harrison Bergeron," Vonnegut pessimistically envisions an America where a Constitutional amendment enforces "equality" via the disabling of all citizens into physical and mental mediocrity.

Harrison Bergeron

Kurt Vonnegut

1   The year was 2081, and everybody was finally equal. They weren't only equal before God and the law. They were equal every which way. Nobody was smarter than anybody else. Nobody was better looking than anybody else. Nobody was stronger or quicker than anybody else. All this equality was due to the 211th, 212th, and 213th Amendments to the Constitution, and to the unceasing vigilance of agents of the United States Handicapper General.

2   Some things about living still weren't quite right, though. April, for instance, still drove people crazy by not being springtime. And it was in that clammy month that the H-G men took George and Hazel Bergeron's fourteen-year-old son, Harrison, away.

3   It was tragic, all right, but George and Hazel couldn't think about it very hard. Hazel had a perfectly average intelligence, which meant she couldn't think about anything except in short bursts. And George, while his intelligence was way above normal, had a little mental handicap radio in his ear. He was required

by law to wear it at all times. It was tuned to a government transmitter. Every twenty seconds or so, the transmitter would send out some sharp noise to keep people like George from taking unfair advantage of their brains.

George and Hazel were watching television. There were tears on Hazel's cheeks, but she'd forgotten for the moment what they were about.   4

On the television screen were ballerinas.   5

A buzzer sounded in George's head. His thoughts fled in panic, like bandits from a burglar alarm.   6

"That was a real pretty dance, that dance they just did," said Hazel.   7

"Huh?" said George.   8

"That dance—it was nice," said Hazel.   9

"Yup," said George. He tried to think a little about the ballerinas. They weren't really very good—no better than anybody else would have been, anyway. They were burdened with sashweights and bags of birdshot, and their faces were masked, so that no one, seeing a free and graceful gesture or a pretty face, would feel like something the cat drug in. George was toying with the vague notion that maybe dancers shouldn't be handicapped. But he didn't get very far with it before another noise in his ear radio scattered his thoughts.   10

George winced. So did two out of the eight ballerinas.   11

Hazel saw him wince. Having no mental handicap herself she had to ask George what the latest sound had been.   12

"Sounded like somebody hitting a milk bottle with a ball peen hammer," said George.   13

"I'd think it would be real interesting, hearing all the different sounds," said Hazel, a little envious. "All the things they think up."   14

"Um," said George.   15

"Only, if I was Handicapper General, you know what I would do?" said Hazel. Hazel, as a matter of fact, bore a strong resemblance to the Handicapper General, a woman named Diana Moon Glampers. "If I was Diana Moon Glampers," said Hazel, "I'd have chimes on Sunday—just chimes. Kind of in honor of religion."   16

"I could think, if it was just chimes," said George.   17

"Well—maybe make 'em real loud," said Hazel. "I think I'd make a good Handicapper General."   18

"Good as anybody else," said George.   19

"Who knows better'n I do what normal is?" said Hazel.   20

"Right," said George. He began to think glimmeringly about his abnormal son who was now in jail, about Harrison, but a twenty-one-gun salute in his head stopped that.   21

"Boy!" said Hazel, "that was a doozy, wasn't it?"   22

It was such a doozy that George was white and trembling and tears stood on the rims of his red eyes. Two of the eight ballerinas had collapsed to the studio floor, were holding their temples.   23

"All of a sudden you look so tired," said Hazel. "Why don't you stretch out on the sofa, so's you can rest your handicap bag on the pillows, honeybunch."   24

She was referring to the forty-seven pounds of birdshot in canvas bag, which was padlocked around George's neck. "Go on and rest the bag for a little while," she said. "I don't care if you're not equal to me for a while."

George weighed the bag with his hands. "I don't mind it," he said. "I don't   25 notice it any more. It's just a part of me."

"You been so tired lately—kind of wore out," said Hazel. "If there was just   26 some way we could make a little hole in the bottom of the bag, and just take out a few of them lead balls. Just a few."

"Two years in prison and two thousand dollars fine for every ball I took out,"   27 said George. "I don't call that a bargain."

"If you could just take a few out when you came home from work," said Hazel.   28 "I mean—you don't compete with anybody around here. You just set around."

"If I tried to get away with it," said George, "then other people'd get away with   29 it and pretty soon we'd be right back to the dark ages again, with everybody competing against everybody else. You wouldn't like that, would you?"

"I'd hate it," said Hazel.   30

"There you are," said George. "The minute people start cheating on laws,   31 what do you think happens to society?"

If Hazel hadn't been able to come up with an answer to this question, George   32 couldn't have supplied one. A siren was going off in his head.

"Reckon it'd fall all apart," said Hazel.   33

"What would?" said George blankly.   34

"Society," said Hazel uncertainly. "Wasn't that what you just said?"   35

"Who knows?" said George.   36

The television program was suddenly interrupted for a news bulletin. It   37 wasn't clear at first as to what the bulletin was about, since the announcer, like all announcers, had a serious speech impediment. For about half a minute, and in a state of high excitement, the announcer tried to say, "Ladies and gentlemen—"

He finally gave up, handed the bulletin to a ballerina to read.   38

"That's all right—" Hazel said of the announcer, "he tried. That's the big   39 thing. He tried to do the best he could with what God gave him. He should get a nice raise for trying so hard."

"Ladies and gentlemen" said the ballerina, reading the bulletin. She must   40 have been extraordinarily beautiful, because the mask she wore was hideous. And it was easy to see that she was the strongest and most graceful of all the dancers, for her handicap bags were as big as those worn by two-hundred-pound men.

And she had to apologize at once for her voice, which was a very unfair voice   41 for a woman to use. Her voice was a warm, luminous, timeless melody. "Excuse me—"she said, and she began again, making her voice absolutely uncompetitive.

"Harrison Bergeron, age fourteen," she said in a grackle squawk, "has just   42 escaped from jail, where he was held on suspicion of plotting to overthrow the government. He is a genius and an athlete, is under-handicapped, and should be regarded as extremely dangerous."

A police photograph of Harrison Bergeron was flashed on the screen upside   43 down, then sideways, upside down again, then right side up. The picture showed the full length of Harrison against a background calibrated in feet and inches. He was exactly seven feet tall.

The rest of Harrison's appearance was Halloween and hardware. Nobody had 44 ever worn heavier handicaps. He had outgrown hindrances faster than the H-G men could think them up. Instead of a little ear radio for a mental handicap, he wore a tremendous pair of earphones, and spectacles with thick wavy lenses. The spectacles were intended to make him not only half blind, but to give him whanging headaches besides.

Scrap metal was hung all over him. Ordinarily, there was a certain symmetry, 45 a military neatness to the handicaps issued to strong people, but Harrison looked like a walking junkyard. In the race of life, Harrison carried three hundred pounds.

And to offset his good looks, the H-G men required that he wear at all times 46 a red rubber ball for a nose, keep his eyebrows shaved off, and cover his even white teeth with black caps at snaggle-tooth random.

"If you see this boy," said the ballerina, "do not—I repeat, do not—try to rea- 47 son with him."

There was the shriek of a door being torn from its hinges. 48

Screams and barking cries of consternation came from the television set. The 49 photograph of Harrison Bergeron on the screen jumped again and again, as though dancing to the tune of an earthquake.

George Bergeron correctly identified the earthquake, and well he might 50 have—for many was the time his own home had danced to the same crashing tune. "My God—" said George, "that must be Harrison!"

The realization was blasted from his mind instantly by the sound of an auto- 51 mobile collision in his head.

When George could open his eyes again, the photograph of Harrison was 52 gone. A living, breathing Harrison filled the screen.

Clanking, clownish, and huge, Harrison stood in the center of the studio. The 53 knob of the uprooted studio door was still in his hand. Ballerinas, technicians, musicians, and announcers cowered on their knees before him, expecting to die.

"I am the Emperor!" cried Harrison. "Do you hear? I am the Emperor! 54 Everybody must do what I say at once!" He stamped his foot and the studio shook.

"Even as I stand here—" he bellowed, "crippled, hobbled, sickened—I am a 55 greater ruler than any man who ever lived! Now watch me become what I *can* become!"

Harrison tore the straps of his handicap harness like wet tissue paper, tore 56 straps guaranteed to support five thousand pounds.

Harrison's scrap-iron handicaps crashed to the floor. 57

Harrison thrust his thumbs under the bar of the padlock that secured his head 58 harness. The bar snapped like celery. Harrison smashed his headphones and spectacles against the wall.

He flung away his rubber-ball nose, revealed a man that would have awed 59 Thor, the god of thunder.

"I shall now select my Empress!" he said, looking down on the cowering peo- 60
ple. "Let the first woman who dares rise to her feet claim her mate and her
throne!"

A moment passed, and then a ballerina arose, swaying like a willow. 61

Harrison plucked the mental handicap from her ear, snapped off her physical 62
handicaps with marvelous delicacy. Last of all, he removed her mask.

She was blindingly beautiful. 63

"Now" said Harrison, taking her hand, "shall we show the people the mean- 64
ing of the word dance? Music!" he commanded.

The musicians scrambled back into their chairs, and Harrison stripped them 65
of their handicaps, too. "Play your best," he told them, "and I'll make you barons
and dukes and earls."

The music began. It was normal at first—cheap, silly, false. But Harrison snatched 66
two musicians from their chairs, waved them like batons as he sang the music as
he wanted it played. He slammed them back into their chairs.

The music began again and was much improved. 67

Harrison and his Empress merely listened to the music for a while—listened 68
gravely, as though synchronizing their heartbeats with it.

They shifted their weights to their toes. 69

Harrison placed his big hands on the girl's tiny waist, letting her sense the 70
weightlessness that would soon be hers.

And then, in an explosion of joy and grace, into the air they sprang! 71

Not only were the laws of the land abandoned, but the law of gravity and the 72
laws of motion as well.

They reeled, whirled, swiveled, flounced, capered, gamboled, and spun. 73

They leaped like deer on the moon. 74

The studio ceiling was thirty feet high, but each leap brought the dancers 75
nearer to it.

It became their obvious intention to kiss the ceiling. 76

They kissed it. 77

And then, neutralizing gravity with love and pure will, they remained sus- 78
pended in air inches below the ceiling, and they kissed each other for a long, long
time.

It was then that Diana Moon Glampers, the Handicapper General, came into 79
the studio with a double-barreled ten-gauge shotgun. She fired twice, and the
Emperor and the Empress were dead before they hit the floor.

Diana Moon Glampers loaded the gun again. She aimed it at the musicians 80
and told them they had ten seconds to get their handicaps back on.

It was then that the Bergerons' television tube burned out. 81

Hazel turned to comment about the blackout to George.

But George had gone out into the kitchen for a can of beer.

George came back in with the beer, paused while a handicap signal shook him 82
up. And then he sat down again.

"You been crying?" he said to Hazel. 83

"Yup," she said.   84

"What about?" he said.   85

"I forget," she said. "Something real sad on television."   86

"What was it?" he said.   87

"It's all kind of mixed up in my mind," said Hazel.   88

"Forget sad things," said George.   89

"I always do," said Hazel.   90

"That's my girl," said George. He winced. There was the sound of a riveting   91
gun in his head.

"Gee—I could tell that one was a doozy," said Hazel.   92

"You can say that again," said George.   93

"Gee—" said Hazel, "I could tell that one was a doozy."   94

Questions for Discussion

1. What has allowed for the "equality" of citizens? How does Vonnegut cast a questioning light on the word "equality" from the first paragraph? How effective and economical is the opening paragraph?

2. Of George and Hazel, for whom does Vonnegut seem to inspire more sympathy? How so? Why do you think Vonnegut has Hazel speak in the manner she does?

3. Where does Vonnegut use humor in this story? Why employ humor if the topic is so serious? Does the humor make the story more or less effective?

4. What is Vonnegut's main message about "equality," government intervention, and human abilities in this story? How is this story a warning of what may come or of what already is? Do you see any evidence of American society heading in the direction of this fictional one?

5. How sympathetic a character is Harrison? What choices seem strange in his characterization? Does his characterization enhance the story's warning or undercut it?

6. Is the description of the shooting tragic, comic, or both? How could Vonnegut have written the scene differently to enhance or change the story's message?

Questions for Reflection and Writing

1. Write an essay in which you connect this story's message to that of Dylan Thomas's poem, "Do Not Go Gentle into That Good Night." What might be similar in Vonnegut's implicit message and Thomas's explicit one? Which writer seems more optimistic?

2. In a brief essay, explain your definition of social equality. If a totalitarian state adopted your definition, what might it do to enforce that equality?

3. In at least a few paragraphs, compare the portrait of humans in Vonnegut's story to Mark Twain's vision of humans in "The Lowest Animal." Use the texts for support in each point you make.

ALICE WALKER

Everyday Use

for your grandmama

I will wait for her in the yard that Maggie and I made so clean and wavy yester-day afternoon. A yard like this is more comfortable than most people know. It is not just a yard. It is like an extended living room. When the hard clay is swept clean as a floor and the fine sand around the edges lined with tiny, irregular grooves, anyone can come and sit and look up into the elm tree and wait for the breezes that never come inside the house.

Maggie will be nervous until after her sister goes: she will stand hopelessly in corners, homely and ashamed of the burn scars down her arms and legs, eyeing her sister with a mixture of envy and awe. She thinks her sister has held life always in the palm of one hand, that "no" is a word the world never learned to say to her.

You've no doubt seen those TV shows where the child who has "made it" is confronted, as a surprise, by her own mother and father, tottering in weakly from backstage. (A pleasant surprise, of course: What would they do if parent and child came on the show only to curse out and insult each other?) On TV mother and child embrace and smile into each other's faces. Sometimes the mother and father weep, the child wraps them in her arms and leans across the table to tell how she would not have made it without their help. I have seen these programs.

Sometimes I dream a dream in which Dee and I are suddenly brought together on a TV program of this sort. Out of a dark and soft-seated limousine I am ush-ered into a bright room filled with many people. There I meet a smiling, gray, sporty man like Johnny Carson who shakes my hand and tells me what a fine girl I have. Then we are on the stage and Dee is embracing me with tears in her eyes. She pins on my dress a large orchid, even though she has told me once that she thinks orchids are tacky flowers.

In real life I am a large, big-boned woman with rough, man-working hands. In the winter I wear flannel nightgowns to bed and overalls during the day. I can kill and clean a hog as mercilessly as a man. My fat keeps me hot in zero weather. I can work outside all day, breaking ice to get water for washing; I can eat pork liver cooked over the open fire minutes after it comes steaming from the hog. One winter I knocked a bull calf straight in the brain between the eyes with a sledge hammer and had the meat hung up to chill before nightfall. But of course all this does not show on television. I am the way my daughter would want me to be: a hundred pounds lighter, my skin like an uncooked barley pancake. My hair glis-tens in the hot bright lights. Johnny Carson has much to do to keep up with my quick and witty tongue.

But that is a mistake. I know even before I wake up. Who ever knew a John-son with a quick tongue? Who can even imagine me looking a strange white man

---

in the eye? It seems to me I have talked to them always with one foot raised in flight, with my head turned in whichever way is farthest from them. Dee, though. She would always look anyone in the eye. Hesitation was no part of her nature.

"How do I look, Mama?" Maggie says, showing just enough of her thin body enveloped in pink skirt and red blouse for me to know she's there, almost hidden by the door.

"Come out into the yard," I say.

Have you ever seen a lame animal, perhaps a dog run over by some careless person rich enough to own a car, sidle up to someone who is ignorant enough to be kind to him? That is the way my Maggie walks. She has been like this, chin on chest, eyes on ground, feet in shuffle, ever since the fire that burned the other house to the ground.

Dee is lighter than Maggie, with nicer hair and a fuller figure. She's a woman now, though sometimes I forget. How long ago was it that the other house burned? Ten, twelve years? Sometimes I can still hear the flames and feel Maggie's arms sticking to me, her hair smoking and her dress falling off her in little black papery flakes. Her eyes seemed stretched open, blazed open by the flames reflected in them. And Dee. I see her standing off under the sweet gum tree she used to dig gum out of; a look of concentration on her face as she watched the last dingy gray board of the house fall in toward the red-hot brick chimney. Why don't you do a dance around the ashes? I'd wanted to ask her. She had hated the house that much.

I used to think she hated Maggie, too. But that was before we raised the money, the church and me, to send her to Augusta to school. She used to read to us without pity; forcing words, lies, other folks' habits, whole lives upon us two, sitting trapped and ignorant underneath her voice. She washed us in a river of make-believe, burned us with a lot of knowledge we didn't necessarily need to know. Pressed us to her with the serious way she read, to shove us away at just the moment, like dimwits, we seemed about to understand.

Dee wanted nice things. A yellow organdy dress to wear to her graduation from high school; black pumps to match a green suit she'd made from an old suit somebody gave me. She was determined to stare down any disaster in her efforts. Her eyelids would not flicker for minutes at a time. Often I fought off the temptation to shake her. At sixteen she had a style of her own: and knew what style was.

I never had an education myself. After second grade the school was closed down. Don't ask me why: in 1927 colored asked fewer questions than they do now. Sometimes Maggie reads to me. She stumbles along good-naturedly but can't see well. She knows she is not bright. Like good looks and money, quickness passed her by. She will marry John Thomas (who has mossy teeth in an earnest face) and then I'll be free to sit here and I guess just sing church songs to myself. Although I never was a good singer. Never could carry a tune. I was always better at a man's job. I used to love to milk till I was hooked in the side in '49. Cows are soothing and slow and don't bother you, unless you try to milk them the wrong way.

I have deliberately turned my back on the house. It is three rooms, just like the one that burned, except the roof is tin; they don't make shingle roofs any more. There are no real windows, just some holes cut in the sides, like the portholes in a ship, but not round and not square, with rawhide holding the shutters up on the outside. This house is in a pasture, too, like the other one. No doubt when Dee sees it she will want to tear it down. She wrote me once that no matter where we "choose" to live, she will manage to come see us. But she will never bring her friends. Maggie and I thought about this and Maggie asked me, "Mama, when did Dee ever *have* any friends?"

She had a few. Furtive boys in pink shirts hanging about on washday after school. Nervous girls who never laughed. Impressed with her they worshiped the well-turned phrase, the cute shape, the scalding humor that erupted like bubbles in lye. She read to them.

When she was courting Jimmy T she didn't have much time to pay to us, but turned all her faultfinding power on him. He *flew* to marry a cheap city girl from a family of ignorant flashy people. She hardly had time to recompose herself.

When she comes I will meet—but there they are!

Maggie attempts to make a dash for the house, in her shuffling way, but I stay her with my hand. "Come back here," I say. And she stops and tries to dig a well in the sand with her toe.

It is hard to see them clearly through the strong sun. But even the first glimpse of leg out of the car tells me it is Dee. Her feet were always neat-looking, as if God himself had shaped them with a certain style. From the other side of the car comes a short, stocky man. Hair is all over his head a foot long and hanging from his chin like a kinky mule tail. I hear Maggie suck in her breath. "Uhnnnh," is what it sounds like. Like when you see the wriggling end of a snake just in front of your foot on the road. "Uhnnnh."

Dee next. A dress down to the ground, in this hot weather. A dress so loud it hurts my eyes. There are yellows and oranges enough to throw back the light of the sun. I feel my whole face warming from the heat waves it throws out. Earrings gold, too, and hanging down to her shoulders. Bracelets dangling and making noises when she moves her arm up to shake the folds of the dress out of her armpits. The dress is loose and flows, and as she walks closer, I like it. I hear Maggie go "Uhnnnh" again. It is her sister's hair. It stands straight up like the wool on a sheep. It is black as night and around the edges are two long pigtails that rope about like small lizards disappearing behind her ears.

"Wa-su-zo-Tean-o!" she says, coming on in that gliding way the dress makes her move. The short stocky fellow with the hair to his navel is all grinning and he follows up with "Asalamalakim, my mother and sister!" He moves to hug Maggie but she falls back, right up against the back of my chair. I feel her trembling there and when I look up I see the perspiration falling off her chin.

"Don't get up," says Dee. Since I am stout it takes something of a push. You can see me trying to move a second or two before I make it. She turns, showing white heels through her sandals, and goes back to the car. Out she peeks next with a Polaroid. She stoops down quickly and lines up picture after picture of me sitting there in front of the house with Maggie cowering behind me. She never takes a shot without making sure the house is included. When a cow comes nibbling around the edge of the yard she snaps it and me and Maggie *and* the house. Then she puts the Polaroid in the back seat of the car, and comes up and kisses me on the forehead.

Meanwhile Asalamalakim is going through motions with Maggie's hand. Maggie's hand is as limp as a fish, and probably as cold, despite the sweat, and she keeps trying to pull it back. It looks like Asalamalakim wants to shake hands but wants to do it fancy. Or maybe he don't know how people shake hands. Anyhow, he soon gives up on Maggie.

"Well," I say. "Dee."

"No, Mama," she says. "Not 'Dee,' Wangero Leewanika Kemanjo!"

"What happened to 'Dee'?" I wanted to know.

"She's dead," Wangero said. "I couldn't bear it any longer, being named after the people who oppress me."

"You know as well as me you was named after your aunt Dicie," I said. Dicie is my sister. She named Dee. We called her "Big Dee" after Dee was born.

"But who was *she* named after?" asked Wangero.

"I guess after Grandma Dee," I said.

"And who was she named after?" asked Wangero.

"Her mother," I said, and saw Wangero was getting tired. "That's about as far back as I can trace it," I said. Though, in fact, I probably could have carried it back beyond the Civil War through the branches.

"Well," said Asalamalakim, "there you are."

"Uhnnnh," I heard Maggie say.

"There I was not," I said, "before 'Dicie' cropped up in our family, so why should I try to trace it that far back?"

He just stood there grinning, looking down on me like somebody inspecting a Model A car. Every once in a while he and Wangero sent eye signals over my head.

"How do you pronounce this name?" I asked.

"You don't have to call me by it if you don't want to," said Wangero.

"Why shouldn't I?" I asked. "If that's what you want us to call you, we'll call you."

"I know it might sound awkward at first," said Wangero.

"I'll get used to it," I said. "Ream it out again."

Well, soon we got the name out of the way. Asalamalakim had a name twice as long and three times as hard. After I tripped over it two or three times he told me to just call him Hakim-a-barber. I wanted to ask him was he a barber, but I didn't really think he was, so I didn't ask.

"You must belong to those beef-cattle peoples down the road," I said. They said "Asalamalakim" when they met you, too, but they didn't shake hands. Always too busy: feeding the cattle, fixing the fences, putting up salt-lick shelters, throwing down hay. When the white folks poisoned some of the herd the men stayed up all night with rifles in their hands. I walked a mile and a half just to see the sight.

Hakim-a-barber said, "I accept some of their doctrines, but farming and raising cattle is not my style." (They didn't tell me, and I didn't ask, whether Wangero (Dee) had really gone and married him.)

We sat down to eat and right away he said he didn't eat collards and pork was unclean. Wangero, though, went on through the chitlins and corn bread, the greens and everything else. She talked a blue streak over the sweet potatoes. Everything delighted her. Even the fact that we still used the benches her daddy made for the table when we couldn't afford to buy chairs.

"Oh, Mama!" she cried. Then turned to Hakim-a-barber. "I never knew how lovely these benches are. You can feel the rump prints," she said, running her hands underneath her and along the bench. Then she gave a sigh and her hand closed over Grandma Dee's butter dish. "That's it!" she said. "I knew there was something I wanted to ask you if I could have." She jumped up from the table and went over in the corner where the churn stood, the milk in it clabber by now. She looked at the churn and looked at it.

"This churn top is what I need," she said. "Didn't Uncle Buddy whittle it out of a tree you all used to have?"

"Yes," I said.

"Uh huh," she said happily. "And I want the dasher, too."

"Uncle Buddy whittle that, too?" asked the barber.

Dee (Wangero) looked up at me.

"Aunt Dee's first husband whittled the dash," said Maggie so low you almost couldn't hear her. "His name was Henry, but they called him Stash."

"Maggie's brain is like an elephant's," Wangero said, laughing. "I can use the churn top as a centerpiece for the alcove table," she said, sliding a plate over the churn, "and I'll think of something artistic to do with the dasher."

When she finished wrapping the dasher the handle stuck out. I took it for a moment in my hands. You didn't even have to look close to see where hands pushing the dasher up and down to make butter had left a kind of sink in the wood. In fact, there were a lot of small sinks; you could see where thumbs and fingers had sunk into the wood. It was beautiful light yellow wood, from a tree that grew in the yard where Big Dee and Stash had lived.

After dinner Dee (Wangero) went to the trunk at the foot of my bed and started rifling through it. Maggie hung back in the kitchen over the dishpan. Out came Wangero with two quilts. They had been pieced by Grandma Dee and then Big Dee and me had hung them on the quilt frames on the front porch and quilted them. One was in the Lone Star pattern. The other was Walk Around the Mountain. In both of them were scraps of dresses Grandma Dee had worn fifty and more years ago. Bits and pieces of Grandpa Jarrell's Paisley shirts. And one teeny faded blue piece, about the size of a penny matchbox, that was from Great Grandpa Ezra's uniform that he wore in the Civil War.

"Mama," Wangero said sweet as a bird. "Can I have these old quilts?"

I heard something fall in the kitchen, and a minute later the kitchen door slammed.

"Why don't you take one or two of the others?" I asked. "These old things was just done by me and Big Dee from some tops your grandma pieced before she died."

"No," said Wangero. "I don't want those. They are stitched around the borders by machine."

"That'll make them last better," I said.

"That's not the point," said Wangero. "These are all pieces of dresses Grandma used to wear. She did all this stitching by hand. Imagine!" She held the quilts securely in her arms, stroking them.

"Some of the pieces, like those lavender ones, come from old clothes her mother handed down to her," I said, moving up to touch the quilts. Dee (Wangero) moved back just enough so that I couldn't reach the quilts. They already belonged to her.

"Imagine!" she breathed again, clutching them closely to her bosom.

"The truth is," I said, "I promised to give them quilts to Maggie, for when she marries John Thomas."

She gasped like a bee had stung her.

"Maggie can't appreciate these quilts!" she said. "She'd probably be backward enough to put them to everyday use."

"I reckon she would," I said. "God knows I been saving 'em for long enough with nobody using 'em. I hope she will!" I didn't want to bring up how I had offered Dee (Wangero) a quilt when she went away to college. Then she had told me they were old-fashioned, out of style.

"But they're *priceless!*" she was saying now, furiously; for she has a temper. "Maggie would put them on the bed and in five years they'd be in rags. Less than that!"

"She can always make some more," I said. "Maggie knows how to quilt."

Dee (Wangero) looked at me with hatred. "You just will not understand. The point is these quilts, *these* quilts!"

"Well," I said, stumped. "What would *you* do with them?"

"Hang them," she said. As if that was the only thing you *could* do with quilts.

Maggie by now was standing in the door. I could almost hear the sound her feet made as they scraped over each other.

"She can have them, Mama," she said, like somebody used to never winning anything, or having anything reserved for her. "I can 'member Grandma Dee without the quilts."

I looked at her hard. She had filled her bottom lip with checkerberry snuff and it gave her face a kind of dopey, hangdog look. It was Grandma Dee and Big Dee who taught her how to quilt herself. She stood there with her scarred hands hidden in the folds of her skirt. She looked at her sister with something like fear but she wasn't mad at her. This was Maggie's portion. This was the way she knew God to work.

When I looked at her like that something hit me in the top of my head and ran down to the soles of my feet. Just like when I'm in church and the spirit of God touches me and I get happy and shout. I did something I never had done before: hugged Maggie to me, then dragged her on into the room, snatched the quilts out of Miss Wangero's hands and dumped them into Maggie's lap. Maggie just sat there on my bed with her mouth open.

"Take one or two of the others," I said to Dee.

But she turned without a word and went out to Hakim-a-barber.

"You just don't understand," she said, as Maggie and I came out to the car.

"What don't I understand?" I wanted to know.

"Your heritage," she said. And then she turned to Maggie, kissed her, and said, "You ought to try to make something of yourself, too, Maggie. It's really a new day for us. But from the way you and Mama still live you'd never know it."

She put on some sunglasses that hid everything above the tip of her nose and her chin.

Maggie smiled; maybe at the sunglasses. But a real smile, not scared. After we watched the car dust settle I asked Maggie to bring me a snuff. And then the two of us sat there enjoying, until it was time to go in the house and go to bed.

1973

◄ MARY E. WILKINS FREEMAN ►

The Revolt of "Mother"[1]

"Father!"

"What is it?"

"What are them men diggin' over there in the field for?"

There was a sudden dropping and enlarging of the lower part of the old man's face, as if some heavy weight had settled therein; he shut his mouth tight, and went on harnessing the great bay mare. He hustled the collar on to her neck with a jerk.

"Father!"

The old man slapped the saddle upon the mare's back.

"Look here, father, I want to know what them men are diggin' over in the field for, an' I'm goin' to know."

"I wish you'd go into the house, mother, an' 'tend to your own affairs," the old man said then. He ran his words together, and his speech was almost as inarticulate as a growl.

But the woman understood; it was her most native tongue. "I ain't goin' into the house till you tell me what them men are doin' over there in the field," said she.

Then she stood waiting. She was a small woman, short and straight-waisted like a child in her brown cotton gown. Her forehead was mild and benevolent between the smooth curves of gray hair; there were meek downward lines about her nose and mouth; but her eyes, fixed upon the old man, looked as if the meekness had been the result of her own will, never of the will of another.

They were in the barn, standing before the wide open doors. The spring air, full of the smell of growing grass and unseen blossoms, came in their faces. The deep yard in front was littered with farm wagons and piles of wood; on the edges, close to the fence and the house, the grass was a vivid green, and there were some dandelions.

The old man glanced doggedly at his wife as he tightened the last buckles on the harness. She looked as immovable to him as one of the rocks in his pastureland, bound to the earth with generations of blackberry vines. He slapped the reins over the horse, and started forth from the barn.

"*Father!*" said she.

The old man pulled up. "What is it?"

"I want to know what them men are diggin' over there in that field for."

"They're diggin' a cellar, I s'pose, if you've got to know."

"A cellar for what?"

"A barn."

"A barn? You ain't goin' to build a barn over there where we was goin' to have a house, father?"

The old man said not another word. He hurried the horse into the farm wagon, and clattered out of the yard, jouncing as sturdily on his seat as a boy.

---

1. From *A New England Nun and Other Stories*, 1891.

The woman stood a moment looking after him, then she went out of the barn across a corner of the yard to the house. The house, standing at right angles with the great barn and a long reach of sheds and out-buildings, was infinitesimal compared with them. It was scarcely as commodious for people as the little boxes under the barn eaves were for doves.

A pretty girl's face, pink and delicate as a flower, was looking out of one of the house windows. She was watching three men who were digging over in the field which bounded the yard near the road line. She turned quietly when the woman entered.

"What are they digging for, mother?" said she. "Did he tell you?"

"They're diggin' for—a cellar for a new barn."

"Oh, mother, he ain't going to build another barn?"

"That's what he says."

A boy stood before the kitchen glass combing his hair. He combed slowly and painstakingly, arranging his brown hair in a smooth hillock over his forehead. He did not seem to pay any attention to the conversation.

"Sammy, did you know father was going to build a new barn?" asked the girl.

The boy combed assiduously.

"Sammy!"

He turned, and showed a face like his father's under his smooth crest of hair. "Yes, I s'pose I did," he said, reluctantly.

"How long have you known it?" asked his mother.

"'Bout three months, I guess."

"Why didn't you tell of it?"

"Didn't think 'twould do no good."

"I don't see what father wants another barn for," said the girl, in her sweet, slow voice. She turned again to the window, and stared out at the digging men in the field. Her tender, sweet face was full of a gentle distress. Her forehead was as bald and innocent as a baby's, with the light hair strained back from it in a row of curl-papers. She was quite large, but her soft curves did not look as if they covered muscles.

Her mother looked sternly at the boy. "Is he goin' to buy more cows?" said she.

The boy did not reply; he was tying his shoes.

"Sammy, I want you to tell me if he's goin' to buy more cows."

"I s'pose he is."

"How many?"

"Four, I guess."

His mother said nothing more. She went into the pantry, and there was a clatter of dishes. The boy got his cap from a nail behind the door, took an old arithmetic from the shelf, and started for school. He was lightly built, but clumsy. He went out of the yard with a curious spring in the hips, that made his loose home-made jacket tilt up in the rear.

The girl went to the sink, and began to wash the dishes that were piled up there. Her mother came promptly out of the pantry, and shoved her aside. "You wipe 'em," said she; "I'll wash. There's a good many this mornin'."

The mother plunged her hands vigorously into the water, the girl wiped the plates slowly and dreamily. "Mother," said she, "don't you think it's too bad father's going to build that new barn, much as we need a decent house to live in?"

Her mother scrubbed a dish fiercely. "You ain't found out yet we're women-folks, Nanny Penn," said she. "You ain't seen enough of men-folks yet to. One of these days you'll find it out, an' then you'll know that we know only what men-folks think we do, so far as any use of it goes, an' how we'd ought to reckon men-folks in with Providence, an' not complain of what they do any more than we do of the weather."

"I don't care; I don't believe George is anything like that, anyhow," said Nanny. Her delicate face flushed pink, her lips pouted softly, as if she were going to cry.

"You wait an' see. I guess George Eastman ain't no better than other men. You hadn't ought to judge father, though. He can't help it, 'cause he don't look at things jest the way we do. An' we've been pretty comfortable here, after all. The roof don't leak—ain't never but once—that's one thing. Father's kept it shingled right up."

"I do wish we had a parlor."

"I guess it won't hurt George Eastman any to come to see you in a nice clean kitchen. I guess a good many girls don't have as good a place as this. Nobody's ever heard me complain."

"I ain't complained either, mother."

"Well, I don't think you'd better, a good father an' a good home as you've got. S'pose your father made you go out an' work for your livin'? Lots of girls have to that ain't no stronger an' better able to than you be."

Sarah Penn washed the frying-pan with a conclusive air. She scrubbed the outside of it as faithfully as the inside. She was a masterly keeper of her box of a house. Her one living-room never seemed to have in it any of the dust which the friction of life with inanimate matter produces. She swept, and there seemed to be no dirt to go before the broom; she cleaned, and one could see no difference. She was like an artist so perfect that he has apparently no art. To-day she got out a mixing bowl and a board, and rolled some pies, and there was no more flour upon her than upon her daughter who was doing finer work. Nanny was to be married in the fall, and she was sewing on some white cambric and embroidery. She sewed industriously while her mother cooked, her soft milk-white hands and wrists showed whiter than her delicate work.

"We must have the stove moved out in the shed before long," said Mrs. Penn. "Talk about not havin' things, it's been a real blessin' to be able to put a stove up in that shed in hot weather. Father did one good thing when he fixed that stove-pipe out there."

Sarah Penn's face as she rolled her pies had that expression of meek vigor which might have characterized one of the New Testament saints. She was making mince-pies. Her husband, Adoniram Penn, liked them better than any other kind. She baked twice a week. Adoniram often liked a piece of pie between meals. She hurried this morning. It had been later than usual when she began, and she wanted to have a pie baked for dinner. However deep a resentment she might be forced to hold against her husband, she would never fail in sedulous attention to his wants.

Nobility of character manifests itself at loop-holes when it is not provided with large doors. Sarah Penn's showed itself to-day in flaky dishes of pastry. So she made the pies faithfully, while across the table she could see, when she glanced up from her work, the sight that rankled in her patient and steadfast soul—the digging of the cellar of the new barn in the place where Adoniram forty years ago had promised her their new house should stand.

The pies were done for dinner. Adoniram and Sammy were home a few minutes after twelve o'clock. The dinner was eaten with serious haste. There was never much conversation at the table in the Penn family. Adoniram asked a blessing, and they ate promptly, then rose up and went about their work.

Sammy went back to school, taking soft sly lopes out of the yard like a rabbit. He wanted a game of marbles before school, and feared his father would give him some chores to do. Adoniram hastened to the door and called after him, but he was out of sight.

"I don't see what you let him go for, mother," said he. "I wanted him to help me unload that wood."

Adoniram went to work out in the yard unloading wood from the wagon. Sarah put away the dinner dishes, while Nanny took down her curl-papers and changed her dress. She was going down to the store to buy some more embroidery and thread.

When Nanny was gone, Mrs. Penn went to the door. "Father!" she called.

"Well, what is it!"

"I want to see you jest a minute, father."

"I can't leave this wood nohow. I've got to git it unloaded an' go for a load of gravel afore two o'clock. Sammy had ought to helped me. You hadn't ought to let him go to school so early."

"I want to see you jest a minute."

"I tell ye I can't, nohow, mother."

"Father, you come here." Sarah Penn stood in the door like a queen; she held her head as if it bore a crown; there was that patience which makes authority royal in her voice. Adoniram went.

Mrs. Penn led the way into the kitchen, and pointed to a chair. "Sit down, father," said she; "I've got somethin' I want to say to you."

He sat down heavily; his face was quite stolid, but he looked at her with restive eyes. "Well, what is it, mother?"

"I want to know what you're buildin' that new barn for, father?"

"I ain't got nothin' to say about it."

"It can't be you think you need another barn?"

"I tell ye I ain't got nothin' to say about it, mother; an' I ain't goin' to say nothin'."

"Be you goin' to buy more cows?"

Adoniram did not reply; he shut his mouth tight.

"I know you be, as well as I want to. Now, father, look here"—Sarah Penn had not sat down; she stood before her husband in the humble fashion of a Scripture woman—"I'm goin' to talk real plain to you; I never have sence I married you, but I'm goin' to now. I ain't never complained, an' I ain't goin' to complain now, but I'm goin' to talk plain. You see this room here, father; you look at it well. You see there ain't no carpet on the floor, an' you see the paper is all dirty, an' droppin' off the walls. We ain't had no new paper on it for ten year, an' then I put it on myself, an' it didn't cost but ninepence a roll. You see this room, father; it's all the one I've had to work in an' eat in an' sit in sence we was married. There ain't another woman in the whole town whose husband ain't got half the means you have but what's got better. It's all the room Nanny's got to have her company in; an' there ain't one of her mates but what's got better, an' their fathers not so able as hers is. It's all the room she'll have to be married in. What would you have thought, father, if we had had our weddin' in a room no better than this? I was married in my mother's parlor, with a carpet on the floor, an' stuffed furniture, an' a mahogany card-table. An' this is all the room my daughter will have to be married in. Look here, father!"

Sarah Penn went across the room as though it were a tragic stage. She flung open a door and disclosed a tiny bedroom, only large enough for a bed and bureau, with a path between. "There, father," said she—"there's all the room I've had to sleep in forty year. All my children were born there—the two that died, an' the two that's livin'. I was sick with a fever there."

She stepped to another door and opened it. It led into the small, ill-lighted pantry. "Here," said she, "is all the buttery I've got—every place I've got for my dishes, to set away my victuals in, an' to keep my milk-pans in. Father, I've been takin' care of the milk of six cows in this place, an' now you're goin' to build a new barn, an' keep more cows, an' give me more to do in it."

She threw open another door. A narrow crooked flight of stairs wound upward from it. "There, father," said she, "I want you to look at the stairs that go up to them two unfinished chambers that are all the places our son an' daughter have had to sleep in all their lives. There ain't a prettier girl in town nor a more ladylike one than Nanny, an' that's the place she has to sleep in. It ain't so good as your horse's stall; it ain't so warm an' tight."

Sarah Penn went back and stood before her husband. "Now, father," said she, "I want to know if you think you're doin' right an' accordin' to what you profess. Here, when we was married, forty year ago, you promised me faithful that we should have a new house built in that lot over in the field before the year was out. You said you had money enough, an' you wouldn't ask me to live in no such place as this. It is forty year now, an' you've been makin' more money, an' I've been savin' of it for you ever since, an' you ain't built no house yet. You've built sheds an' cow-houses an' one new barn, an' now you're goin' to build another. Father, I want to know if you think it's right. You're lodgin' your dumb beasts better than you are your own flesh an' blood. I want to know if you think it's right."

"I ain't got nothin' to say."

"You can't say nothin' without ownin' it ain't right, father. An' there's another thing—I ain't complained; I've got along forty year, an' I s'pose I should forty more, if it wa'n't for that—if we don't have another house. Nanny she can't live with us after she's married. She'll have to go somewheres else to live away from us, an' it don't seem as if I could have it so, noways, father. She wa'n't ever strong. She's got considerable color, but there wa'n't never any backbone to her. I've always took the heft of everything off her, an' she ain't fit to keep house an' do everything herself. She'll be all worn out inside of a year. Think of her doin' all the washin' an' ironin' an' bakin' with them soft white hands an' arms, an' sweepin'! I can't have it so, noways, father."

Mrs. Penn's face was burning; her mild eyes gleamed. She had pleaded her little cause like a Webster; she had ranged from severity to pathos; but her opponent employed that obstinate silence which makes eloquence futile with mocking echoes. Adoniram arose clumsily.

"Father, ain't you got nothin' to say?" said Mrs. Penn.

"I've got to go off after that load of gravel. I can't stan' here talkin' all day."

"Father, won't you think it over, an' have a house built there instead of a barn?"

"I ain't got nothin' to say."

Adoniram shuffled out. Mrs. Penn went into her bedroom. When she came out, her eyes were red. She had a roll of unbleached cotton cloth. She spread it out on the kitchen table, and began cutting out some shirts for her husband. The men over in the field had a team to help them this afternoon; she could hear their halloos. She had a scanty pattern for the shirts; she had to plan and piece the sleeves.

Nanny came home with her embroidery, and sat down with her needlework. She had taken down her curl-papers, and there was a soft roll of fair hair like an aureole over her forehead; her face was as delicately fine and clear as porcelain. Suddenly she looked up, and the tender red flamed all over her face and neck. "Mother," said she.

"What say?"

"I've been thinking—I don't see how we're goin' to have any—wedding in this room. I'd be ashamed to have his folks come if we didn't have anybody else."

"Mebbe we can have some new paper before then; I can put it on. I guess you won't have no call to be ashamed of your belongin's."

"We might have the wedding in the new barn," said Nanny, with gentle pettishness. "Why, mother, what makes you look so?"

Mrs. Penn had started, and was staring at her with a curious expression. She turned again to her work, and spread out a pattern carefully on the cloth. "Nothin'," said she.

Presently Adoniram clattered out of the yard in his two-wheeled dump cart, standing as proudly upright as a Roman charioteer. Mrs. Penn opened the door and stood there a minute looking out; the halloos of the men sounded louder.

It seemed to her all through the spring months that she heard nothing but the halloos and the noises of saws and hammers. The new barn grew fast. It was a fine edifice for this little village. Men came on pleasant Sundays, in their meeting suits and clean shirt bosoms, and stood around it admiringly. Mrs. Penn did not speak of it, and Adoniram did not mention it to her, although sometimes, upon a return from inspecting it, he bore himself with injured dignity.

"It's a strange thing how your mother feels about the new barn," he said, confidentially, to Sammy one day.

Sammy only grunted after an odd fashion for a boy; he had learned it from his father.

The barn was all completed ready for use by the third week in July. Adoniram had planned to move his stock in on Wednesday; on Tuesday he received a letter which changed his plans. He came in with it early in the morning. "Sammy's been to the post-office," said he, "an' I've got a letter from Hiram." Hiram was Mrs. Penn's brother, who lived in Vermont.

"Well," said Mrs. Penn, "what does he say about the folks?"

"I guess they're all right. He says he thinks if I come up country right off there's a chance to buy jest the kind of a horse I want." He stared reflectively out of the window at the new barn.

Mrs. Penn was making pies. She went on clapping the rolling-pin into the crust, although she was very pale, and her heart beat loudly.

"I dun' know but what I'd better go," said Adoniram. "I hate to go off jest now, right in the midst of hayin', but the ten-acre lot's cut, an' I guess Rufus an' the others can git along without me three or four days. I can't get a horse round here to suit me, nohow, an' I've got to have another for all that wood-haulin' in the fall. I told Hiram to watch out, an' if he got wind of a good horse to let me know. I guess I'd better go."

"I'll get out your clean shirt an' collar," said Mrs. Penn calmly.

She laid out Adoniram's Sunday suit and his clean clothes on the bed in the little bedroom. She got his shaving-water and razor ready. At last she buttoned on his collar and fastened his black cravat.

Adoniram never wore his collar and cravat except on extra occasions. He held his head high, with a rasped dignity. When he was all ready, with his coat and hat brushed, and a lunch of pie and cheese in a paper bag, he hesitated on the threshold of the door. He looked at his wife, and his manner was defiantly apologetic. "*If* them cows come to-day, Sammy can drive 'em into the new barn," said he; "an' when they bring the hay up, they can pitch it in there."

"Well," replied Mrs. Penn.

Adoniram set his shaven face ahead and started. When he had cleared the doorstep, he turned and looked back with a kind of nervous solemnity. "I shall be back by Saturday if nothin' happens," said he.

"Do be careful, father," returned his wife.

She stood in the door with Nanny at her elbow and watched him out of sight. Her eyes had a strange, doubtful expression in them; her peaceful forehead was contracted. She went in, and about her baking again. Nanny sat sewing. Her wedding-day was drawing nearer, and she was getting pale and thin with her steady sewing. Her mother kept glancing at her.

"Have you got that pain in your side this mornin'?" she asked.

"A little."

Mrs. Penn's face, as she worked, changed, her perplexed forehead smoothed, her eyes were steady, her lips firmly set. She formed a maxim for herself, although incoherently with her unlettered thoughts. "Unsolicited opportunities are the guide-posts of the Lord to the new roads of life," she repeated in effect, and she made up her mind to her course of action.

"S'posin' I *had* wrote to Hiram," she muttered once, when she was in the pantry—"s'posin' I had wrote, an' asked him if he knew of any horse? But I didn't, an' father's goin' wa'n't none of my doin'. It looks like a providence." Her voice rang out quite loud at the last.

"What you talkin' about, mother?" called Nanny.

"Nothin'."

Mrs. Penn hurried her baking; at eleven o'clock it was all done. The load of hay from the west field came slowly down the cart track, and drew up at the new barn. Mrs. Penn ran out. "Stop!" she screamed—"stop!"

The men stopped and looked; Sammy upreared from the top of the load, and stared at his mother.

"Stop!" she cried out again. "Don't you put the hay in that barn; put it in the old one."

"Why, he said to put it in here," returned one of the hay-makers, wonderingly. He was a young man, a neighbor's son, whom Adoniram hired by the year to help on the farm.

"Don't you put the hay in the new barn; there's room enough in the old one, ain't there?" said Mrs. Penn.

"Room enough," returned the hired man, in his thick, rustic tones. "Didn't need the new barn, nohow, far as room's concerned. Well, I s'pose he changed his mind." He took hold of the horses' bridles.

Mrs. Penn went back to the house. Soon the kitchen windows were darkened, and a fragrance like warm honey came into the room.

Nanny laid down her work. "I thought father wanted them to put the hay into the new barn?" she said, wonderingly.

"It's all right," replied her mother.

Sammy slid down from the load of hay, and came in to see if dinner was ready.

"I aint' goin' to get a regular dinner to-day, as long as father's gone," said his mother. "I've let the fire go out. You can have some bread an' milk an' pie. I thought we could get along." She set out some bowls of milk, some bread, and a pie on the kitchen table. "You'd better eat your dinner now," said she. "You might jest as well get through with it. I want you to help me afterward."

Nanny and Sammy stared at each other. There was something strange in their mother's manner. Mrs. Penn did not eat anything herself. She went into the pantry, and they heard her moving dishes while they ate. Presently she came out with a pile of plates. She got the clothes-basket out of the shed, and packed them in it. Nanny and Sammy watched. She brought out cups and saucers, and put them in with the plates.

"What you goin' to do, mother?" inquired Nanny, in a timid voice. A sense of something unusual made her tremble, as if it were a ghost. Sammy rolled his eyes over his pie.

"You'll see what I'm goin' to do," replied Mrs. Penn. "If you're through, Nanny, I want you to go up-stairs an' pack up your things; an' I want you, Sammy, to help me take down the bed in the bedroom."

"Oh, mother, what for?" gasped Nanny.

"You'll see."

During the next few hours a feat was performed by this simple, pious New England mother which was equal in its way to Wolfe's storming of the Heights of Abraham. It took no more genius and audacity of bravery for Wolfe to cheer his wondering soldiers up those steep precipices, under the sleeping eyes of the enemy, than for Sarah Penn, at the head of her children, to move all their little household goods into the new barn while her husband was away.

Nanny and Sammy followed their mother's instructions without a murmur; indeed, they were overawed. There is a certain uncanny and superhuman quality about all such purely original undertakings as their mother's was to them. Nanny went back and forth with her light loads, and Sammy tugged with sober energy.

At five o'clock in the afternoon the little house in which the Penns had lived for forty years had emptied itself into the new barn.

Every builder builds somewhat for unknown purposes, and is in a measure a prophet. The architect of Adoniram Penn's barn, while he designed it for the comfort of four-footed animals, had planned better than he knew for the comfort of humans. Sarah Penn saw at a glance its possibilities. Those great box-stalls, with quilts hung before them, would make better bedrooms than the one she had occupied for forty years, and there was a tight carriage-room. The harness-room, with its chimney and shelves, would make a kitchen of her dreams. The great middle space would make a parlor, by-and-by, fit for a palace. Up-stairs there was as much room as down. With partitions and windows, what a house would there be! Sarah looked at the row of stanchions before the allotted space for cows, and reflected that she would have her front entry there.

At six o'clock the stove was up in the harness-room, the kettle was boiling, and the table set for tea. It looked almost as home-like as the abandoned house across the yard had ever done. The young hired man milked, and Sarah directed him calmly to bring the milk to the new barn. He came gaping, dropping little blots of foam from the brimming pails on the grass. Before the next morning he had spread the story of Adoniram Penn's wife moving into the new barn all over the little village. Men assembled in the store and talked it over, women with shawls over their heads scuttled into each other's houses before their work was done. Any deviation from the ordinary course of life in this quiet town was enough to stop all progress in it. Everybody paused to look at the staid, independent figure on the side track. There was a difference of opinion with regard to her. Some held her to be insane; some, of a lawless and rebellious spirit.

Friday the minister went to see her. It was in the forenoon, and she was at the barn door shelling pease for dinner. She looked up and returned his salutation with dignity, then she went on with her work. She did not invite him in. The saintly expression of her face remained fixed, but there was an angry flush over it.

The minister stood awkwardly before her, and talked. She handled the pease as if they were bullets. At last she looked up, and her eyes showed the spirit that her meek front had covered for a lifetime.

"There ain't no use talkin', Mr. Hersey," said she. "I've thought it all over an' over, an' I believe I'm doin' what's right. I've made it the subject of prayer, an' it's betwixt me an' the Lord an' Adoniram. There ain't no call for nobody else to worry about it."

"Well, of course, if you have brought it to the Lord in prayer, and feel satisfied that you are doing right, Mrs. Penn," said the minister, helplessly. His thin gray-bearded face was pathetic. He was a sickly man; his youthful confidence had cooled; he had to scourge himself up to some of his pastoral duties as relentlessly as a Catholic ascetic, and then he was prostrated by the smart.

"I think it's right jest as much as I think it was right for our forefathers to come over from the old country 'cause they didn't have what belonged to 'em," said Mrs. Penn. She arose. The barn threshold might have been Plymouth Rock from her bearing. "I don't doubt you mean well, Mr. Hersey," said she, "but there are things people hadn't ought to interfere with. I've been a member of the church for over forty year. I've got my own mind an' my own feet, an' I'm goin' to think my own thoughts an' go my own ways, an' nobody but the Lord is goin' to dictate to me unless I've a mind to have him. Won't you come in an' set down? How is Mis' Hersey?"

"She is well, I thank you," replied the minister. He added some more perplexed apologetic remarks; then he retreated.

He could expound the intricacies of every character study in the Scriptures, he was competent to grasp the Pilgrim Fathers and all historical innovators, but Sarah Penn was beyond him. He could deal with primal cases, but parallel ones worsted him. But, after all, although it was aside from his province, he wondered more how Adoniram Penn would deal with his wife than how the Lord would. Everybody shared the wonder. When Adoniram's four new cows arrived, Sarah ordered three to be put in the old barn, the other in the house shed where the cooking-stove had stood. That added to the excitement. It was whispered that all four cows were domiciled in the house.

Towards sunset on Saturday, when Adoniram was expected home, there was a knot of men in the road near the new barn. The hired man had milked, but he still hung around the premises. Sarah Penn had supper all ready. There were brown-bread and baked beans and a custard pie; it was the supper that Adoniram loved on a Saturday night. She had on a clean calico, and she bore herself imperturbably. Nanny and Sammy kept close at her heels. Their eyes were large, and Nanny was full of nervous tremors. Still there was to them more pleasant excitement than anything else. An inborn confidence in their mother over their father asserted itself.

Sammy looked out of the harness-room window. "There he is," he announced, in an awed whisper. He and Nanny peeped around the casing. Mrs. Penn kept on about her work. The children watched Adoniram leave the new horse standing in the drive while he went to the house door. It was fastened. Then he went around to the shed. That door was seldom locked, even when the family was away. The thought how her father would be confronted by the cow flashed upon Nanny. There was a hysterical sob in her throat. Adoniram emerged from the shed and stood looking about in a dazed fashion. His lips moved; he was saying something, but they could not hear what it was. The hired man was peeping around a corner of the old barn, but nobody saw him.

Adoniram took the new horse by the bridle and led him across the yard to the new barn. Nanny and Sammy slunk close to their mother. The barn doors rolled back, and there stood Adoniram, with the long mild face of the great Canadian farm horse looking over his shoulder.

Nanny kept behind her mother, but Sammy stepped suddenly forward, and stood in front of her.

Adoniram stared at the group. "What on airth you all down here for?" said he. "What's the matter over to the house?"

"We've come here to live, father," said Sammy. His shrill voice quavered out bravely.

"What"—Adoniram sniffed—"what is it smells like cookin'?" said he. He stepped forward and looked in the open door of the harness-room. Then he turned to his wife. His old bristling face was pale and frightened. "What on airth does this mean, mother?" he gasped.

"You come in here, father," said Sarah. She led the way into the harness-room and shut the door. "Now, father," said she, "you needn't be scared. I ain't crazy. There ain't nothin' to be upset over. But we've come here to live, an' we're goin' to live here. We've got jest as good a right here as new horses an' cows. The house wa'n't fit for us to live in any longer, an' I made up my mind I wa'n't goin' to stay there. I've done my duty by you forty year, an' I'm goin' to do it now; but I'm goin' to live here. You've got to put in some windows and partitions; an' you'll have to buy some furniture."

"Why, mother!" the old man gasped.

"You'd better take your coat off an' get washed—there's the wash-basin—an' then we'll have supper."

"Why, mother!"

Sammy went past the window, leading the new horse to the old barn. The old man saw him, and shook his head speechlessly. He tried to take off his coat, but his arms seemed to lack the power. His wife helped him. She poured some water into the tin basin, and put in a piece of soap. She got the comb and brush, and smoothed his thin gray hair after he had washed. Then she put the beans, hot bread, and tea on the table. Sammy came in, and the family drew up. Adoniram sat looking dazedly at his plate, and they waited.

"Ain't you goin' to ask a blessin', father?" said Sarah.

And the old man bent his head and mumbled.

All through the meal he stopped eating at intervals, and stared furtively at his wife; but he ate well. The home food tasted good to him, and his old frame was too sturdily healthy to be affected by his mind. But after supper he went out, and sat down on the step of the smaller door at the right of the barn, through which he had meant his Jerseys to pass in stately file, but which Sarah designed for her front house door, and he leaned his head on his hands.

After the supper dishes were cleared away and the milk-pans washed, Sarah went out to him. The twilight was deepening. There was a clear green glow in the sky. Before them stretched the smooth level of field; in the distance was a cluster of hay-stacks like the huts of a village; the air was very cool and calm and sweet. The landscape might have been an ideal one of peace.

Sarah bent over and touched her husband on one of his thin, sinewy shoulders. "Father!"

The old man's shoulders heaved: he was weeping.

"Why, don't do so, father," said Sarah.

"I'll—put up the—partitions, an'—everything you—want, mother."

Sarah put her apron up to her face; she was overcome by her own triumph.

Adoniram was like a fortress whose walls had no active resistance, and went down the instant the right besieging tools were used. "Why, mother," he said, hoarsely, "I hadn't no idee you was so set on't as all this comes to."

1891

Unit 3: Reading & Writing About Poetry

CHAPTER 4

Writing about Poetry

*E*xperts generally acknowledge poetry as the oldest form of literature, but the "problem of defining it is the problem of defining its extraordinariness," as one critic observes.

The earliest poetry we know is narrative poetry, which reflected the history, celebrations, beliefs, and mores of ancient peoples in the Egyptian offering lists, utterances, and papyri; in the Greek epics, the Indian Vedas, the Norse sagas, the Hebrew Old Testament, the Babylonian Gilgamesh epic, and elsewhere. Robert Graves called these narratives a "dramatic shorthand record." Cicero believed that the poet performed invaluable service by recording the deeds of national heroes and noblemen. What poetry *is* and what it *does* are questions that have been debated for centuries.

Matthew Arnold said, "There are two offices of poetry—one to add to one's store of thoughts and feelings—another to compose and elevate the mind by sustained tone, numerous allusions, and a grand style." Arnold's is a late definition of poetry which for centuries had been considered a kind of *fiction,* wherein stories were told and a "faigning" (feigning) observable. Sir Philip Sidney thought poetry was "distinctive" because it joined philosophy and history, a theory that John Donne also believed. William Wordsworth in his Preface saw the debate about what poetry is as one concerned with the differences between "matter of fact and science." He was joined in this opinion by Samuel Taylor Coleridge and Leigh Hunt. There is for all discussion, however, one monumental difference today between poetry and prose, and it is that prose mimics ordinary speech, while poetic language is extraordinary in the selection of words it uses and in its metrical rhythms. A stanza from Donne's sardonic "Song" (Go and Catch a Falling Star) provides an example of unusual language filled with bite and imagery:

> Go and catch a falling star
>   Get with child a mandrake root,
> Tell me where all past years are,
>   Or who cleft the Devil's foot,

> Teach me to hear mermaids singing,
> Or to keep off envy's stinging,
>   And find
>   What wind
> Serves to advance an honest mind.

In this single stanza we find stated divisions between "matter of fact" and science, and myth and personal observation. (Donne, after a rakish youth, became a clergyman.) Prose, it was believed by the leading Romantic writers, was better suited for scientific exposition than poetry. Thomas Mann insisted that it was "a fruitless and futile mania" for critics to keep probing for differences between the works of prose writers and poets. Ezra Pound agreed, saying that "all essays about 'poetry' are usually not only dull but inaccurate" and without value.

Poetry is further distinguished by structure or form and its use of meter, which produces rhythm and rhyme. Conversely, some poetry relies heavily on imagery and very little on rhythm and rhyme. In sum, the now traditional differences between poetry and prose are these: poetry *may* be written in meter, but prose is not; poetry *may* use rhyme, while prose does not; poetry most often uses "a special language," but, for the most part, prose does not. (Joyce, of course, would be one of several exceptions.)

The major characteristic of poetry as it evolved through the ages has become its ability to distill monumental themes down to their essences. (We rarely today see a poem that fills a book, like *The Iliad* or *The Odyssey*.) In a time when Americans are said to be upset by global politics, the following two poems might be considered not only prophetic, but good examples of the distillation of themes that have always concerned us. The first, "America" by Claude McKay, is in traditional, fourteen-line, iambic pentameter, sonnet form. The second, by e. e. cummings, "next to of course god," is in "open" or "free verse" form. Consider not only the topic, but the differences in structure, language, and tone:

> Although she feeds me bread of bitterness,
> And sinks into my throat her tiger's tooth,
> Stealing my breath of life, I will confess
> I love this cultured hell that tests my youth!
> Her vigor flows like tides into my blood,
> Giving me strength against her hate.
> Her bigness sweeps my being like a flood.
> Yet as a rebel fronts a kind in state,
> I stand within her walls with not a shred
> Of terror, malice, not a word of jeer.
> Darkly I gaze into the days ahead,
> And see her might and granite wonders there,
> Beneath the touch of Time's unerring hand,
> Like priceless treasures sinking in the sand.

                                    • • •

> "next to of course god america i
> love you land of the pilgrims; and so forth oh

say can you see by the dawn's early my
country 'tis of centuries come and go
and are no more what of it we should worry
in every language even deafanddumb
thy sons acclaim your glorious name by gorry
by jingo by gee by gosh by gum
why talk of beauty what could be more beautiful
than these heroic happy dead
who rushed like lions to the roaring slaughter
they did not stop to think they died instead
then shall the voice of liberty be mute."

He spoke. And drank rapidly a glass of water.

A single reading of a poem, short or long, is not enough to perceive its meaning, for a poem is somewhat like a mystery to be solved, or a language to be understood. Poetry should be studied line by line. Because of its nature to compress or distill, every word in a poem tends to bear more weight than every word in a story or novel. "Sound out" a poem; read it aloud to detect what silent readings may not offer up. Better still, go to poetry readings remembering that poems were originally *sung* and that there are still places in the world where poets and sometimes musical instruments are called singers.

It is important to know when, approximately, a poem was written; as suggested in the fiction section, it is also helpful to know something about the author and his or her life. A poem's title may also give you a clue as to its theme, and with each reading you'll discover more about the work and find yourself responding to it. That's what the poet wants; that's what any writer wants, because the crucial importance about a poem is that you, the reader, come to feel what the poet wants you to. If this occurs, that means you have penetrated his or her imaginative arena, unlocked the mystery, understood the language.

Poets, being "the athletes of language," according to Robert Boynton, are forever challenging our ability to keep up with them. They are like drummers in the band called Literature: they set the pace, diminish or augment it with new or different chords, "sound," images, signals. If we as players somehow lose the beat, we need only "listen" closely to the drummer to get back to it. Poetry is not confined to books; folk singers, blues singers, rockers, and rappers are "the poets of everyday," their lyrics perhaps more current, but certainly linked to the way many people have thought and felt over time.

Your understanding of and sensitivities about popular music may help you with the study of poetry and strengthen the confidence you have in your ability to understand, enjoy, and write about poetry. Like fiction, poetry tells us stories, but they are stories in miniature. The poet leaves it to you to open the work and see his or her world in which you, too, live.

THE ELEMENTS OF POETRY

When you have come to feel the importance of a poet and the special qualities of his or her work, you have reached the stage where you should be capable of writing critical essays about that work. However, critical writing requires that you deal with the major elements of poetry, which are detailed in the following section.

Types of Poetry

Broadly and structurally speaking there are two basic kinds of poetry. The first and by far the more traditional, is the "closed" form, which follows a pattern that we may find in a sonnet or villanelle, "heroic" or "blank" verse *(verso sciolto)*. Closed poetry abides by rules of form set down long ago and rarely departs from them. These rules determine the length of each line, and where rhyme and accent are placed. Of course, as poetry evolved, various authors experimented with the traditional forms.

The "open" form, often called "free verse" or *vers libre*, is considered to be an American-created form as opposed to the closed forms, which are European. The open form relies heavily not on rhyme and not necessarily on the traditional metric feet that create rhythm, but on a perhaps more subtle rhythm called "cadence," and imagery.

Beneath the headings of closed and open are many types of poetry, easily a dozen or even more, which are variations of three major styles in poetry: narrative (treated earlier in this chapter), dramatic monologue, and lyric. Matthew Arnold characterized the monologue as being "The dialogue of the mind with itself." Believed to be popular only since the Middle Ages, it nevertheless is rooted much deeper in the poetic imagination, back to the epics and sagas and papyri, to the Greek plays, which are written in poetry. Everyone knows the beginning of Hamlet's soliloquy (or monologue)—"To be or not to be," spoken while Hamlet ponders revenge. The critical situations of characters in all literature have always been the ideal times for them to range about within themselves for solutions. In the following example of dramatic monologue, Alfred, Lord Tennyson places "Ulysses" in a very special place located between the allegorical renderings of Dante and the myths related by the Homerian *Iliad* and *Odyssey*. In this section, Ulysses from afar contemplates the virtues and perhaps defects in his son:

> This is my son, mine own Telemachus,
> To whom I leave the sceptre and the isle—
> Well-loved of me, discerning to fulfil
> This labour, by slow prudence to make mild
> A rugged people, and thro' soft degrees
> Subdue them to the useful and the good.
> Most blameless is he, centered in the sphere

Of common duties, decent not to fail
In offices of tenderness, and pay
Meet adoration to my household gods,
When I am gone. He works his work, I mine.

"Ulysses" is in blank verse—metered in iambic pentameter without rhyme. It is a closed poem.

Lyric poetry is distinguished by the personal posture of the poet—how he or she views the world. The language is strong yet plain and striking. We are made aware of the world around us through the personification of the elements of which it is composed. Yet lyric poetry is controlled through its structure which defines it, too, as closed, as we see in Wordsworth's "Composed Upon Westminster Bridge, September 3, 1802":

Earth has not anything to show more fair:
Dull would be he of soul who could pass by
A sight so touching in its majesty:
This city now doth, like a garment, wear
The beauty of the morning; silent, bare,
Ships, towers, domes, theatres, and temples lie
Open unto the fields, and to the sky;
All bright and glittering in the smokeless air.
Never did the sun more beautifully steep
In his first splendour, valley, rock, or hill;
Ne'er saw I, never felt, a calm so deep!
The river glideth at his own sweet will:
Dear God! the very houses seem asleep;
And all that mighty heart is lying still!

William Wordsworth became the standard-bearer of lyric poetry (lyric: "fit to be sung with a lyre or harp"), with his 1798 publication of *Lyrical Ballads* (first edition; there were three). By contrast, in the United States Walt Whitman "said his 'God be with you' to the European poets and then parted company with them irrevocably . . . and with his American colleagues, too. He sang no sweet songs, but long, loosely metered chants," wrote critic Max Herzberg. *Leaves of Grass* was Whitman's mark upon the land and mind of America in 1855, and, shortly after, the world.

An example of Whitman's innovative open poetry is his "Cavalry Crossing a Ford," set during the Civil War:

A line in long array where they wind betwixt green islands,
They take a serpentine course, their arms flash in the sun—hark to the musical
    clank,
Behold the silvery river, in it the splashing horses loitering stop to drink,
Behold the brown-faced men, each group, each person a picture, the negligent rest
    on the saddles,
Some emerge on the opposite bank, others are just entering the ford—while,
Scarlet and blue and snowy white,
The guidon flags flutter gayly in the wind.

"Calvary Crossing a Ford" contains very long lines and some short lines. Basically, the language is not used to yield thundering interior or metric rhythms. Like a serpent ("serpentine course"), the cavalry winds from one bank of the river to the other. The emphasis is on alliteration, the repetition of consonant or vowel sounds at the beginning of words: "A line in long array"; "emerge . . . opposite . . . others . . . entering . . . flags flutter . . . ."; "Scarlet and blue and snowy white" not only is alliterative, but has a subtle rhythm as well. The intent of this open poem is to create a picture through word images, and a single picture usually captures one event in progress, "narrates" one story that opens on a wider world. In this case that world is the Civil War.

Voice and Tone

Tone is the "voice" or attitude we encounter in a poem. Tone tells us the way the poet feels about you, himself or herself, the world. Gwendolyn Brooks' diction in "The Bean Eaters" is designed to make us feel a very particular way:

> They eat beans mostly, this old yellow pair.
> Dinner is a casual affair.
> Plain chipware on a plain and creaking wood,
> Tin flatware.
>
> Two who are Mostly Good.
> Two have lived their day,
> But keep on putting on their clothes
> And putting things away.
>
> And remembering . . .
> Remembering, with twinklings and twinges,
> As they lean over the beans in their rented back room that
>   is full of beads and receipts and dolls and cloths,
> Tobacco crumbs, vases and fringes.

Describe the tone of "The Bean Eaters." Note the several images that highlight the condition of these elderly people, and the empathy Brooks expresses. In some ways there is a similarity between the determination of the couple to "keep on" doing things and Ulysses' pledge "to strive, to seek, to find and not to yield" (in the final stanza). In Brooks' poem, also note the structure with both short and long lines, and rhyme, though it is irregular. Is the poem open, closed, or a combination of both?

Note the differences in tone—attitude—and structure between Brooks' poem and Cyn. Zarco's poem:

> Asparagus
>
> There's a washcloth
> with a picture of asparagus
> in my bathroom.

Did you know
that Filipinos were picked
to grow asparagus in the West
because they were short
and built close to the ground?

I'm 5'3". I don't use
that washcloth anymore.

There is a cleanness and brevity of line in this poem that contains a tone of defiance about the past—and the future. It is an open, lyrical poem, but you have to fill in some of the story.

Sound is frequently associated with voice and tone. But the creation of sound in a poem, that is, making you seem to hear sound, is a process of diction. Poets select certain words that we have come to associate with certain sounds. "Splash," "buzz," and "hiss," for example, are commonly associated with water, flying insects, geese, and serpents. The Greek word *onomatopoeia* simply means naming a thing or action by imitating it vocally. Sound often may be sensed in the way a poem is written, for example in Coleridge's "Kubla Khan," before we are actually aware of the sound. But do remember that most poets think about sound because their work traditionally was heard, not read, although there is much poetry written today primarily to be read. The utilization of rhythm, meter, alliteration, assonance, and dissonance (see the glossary on page 159) are crucial in producing sound in a poem.

Imagery and Symbolism

Poetry would not be poetry without imagery (words and phrases that address the senses) and symbolism (words that evoke additional meanings beyond their literal significance). Homer gives us the "rosy-fingered dawn" and the "wine-dark sea," images that have lingered more than 2,000 years. An image, may be created with one or several related words used to make us feel that we are "living in a poem" through hearing, feeling, tasting, seeing, or smelling.

The Symbolist movement began in France late in the nineteenth century. Its members believed poetry could better express and explore the human psyche by recreating human consciousness through symbols, which often reflect inexpressible emotions. In the United States, the "Imagists" were the American counterparts of the Symbolists.

Sometimes the major image in a poem is indicated by its title, as in Imagist Amy Lowell's "Taxi":

When I go away from you
The world beats dead
Like a slackened drum.
I call out for you against the jutted stars
And shout into the ridges of the wind.
Streets coming fast,
One after the other,

Wedge you away from me.
And the lamps of the city prick my eyes
So that I can no longer see your face.
Why should I leave you,
To wound myself upon the sharp edges of the night?

All the related images employed here define a situation. What is it, what's going on? How does the text of the poem fracture the "I" and "you" found in five of the twelve lines? Is this an open or closed poem?

In poetry (and fiction) the function of symbolism is to stand for a state of mind instead of representing a specific object. For example, in everyday life, we know that the green light tells us that we may walk across the street, while the red one advises us not to. The red, white, and blue flag with thirteen stripes and fifty stars is a symbol having many meanings to Americans. If the flag were green with black stripes and red stars it would have very little meaning for most of us because, as Kenneth Burke wrote, "A symbol is the verbal parallel to a pattern of experience," and our experiences have prepared us not for green, black, and red, but red, white, and blue, the flag that stands for the United States of America.

Some poets take standard symbols and create new ones that have reference to the old, familiar ones. For it is in the nature of poetry to create newer and possibly more accurate symbols for the world we know. The first and final stanzas of Gerald Vizenor's "Haiku" offer us familiar symbols with uncommon meanings:

october sunflowers
like rows of defeated soldiers
leaning in the frost

october wind
garage doors open and close
wings of the moth

Although the term "image" calls up something we have seen, in poetic terms we are considering specific, related words that have to do with sensual (the five senses) experiences.

A symbol, on the other hand, stands for something other than what it is.

Simile and Metaphor

A simile is a figure of speech that compares two things from different categories, using signal words such as "like," "as," and "seems." A metaphor also makes a comparison between unlike things but without these signal words.

"Johnson is as tall as Bird" is *not* a simile, but "Johnson is as tall as a small tree" is, because of the dissimilarity of the references or comparisons. Similes use "like" or "as"—"He ran like the wind." Metaphors also substitute one thing for another, hence "tree" for "Bird." Aristotle believed that the ability to find resemblance in disparate things was "the best gift of the poet."

In Maya Angelou's "To a Husband" we find powerful metaphors in the opening lines:

> Your voice at times a fist
>   Tight in your throat
> Jabs ceaselessly at phantoms
>   In the room,
> Your hand a carved and
>   Skimming boat
> Goes down the Nile
>   To point out Pharaoh's tomb.

Note the absence of "like" in the first and fifth lines of the stanza.

Analogy is often associated with simile and metaphor. It presumes a resemblance between two things. This example is from Francis Bacon: "*Money* is like *muck,* not good unless it's spread." *Allusion,* also to be found in this company, is an indirect reference to some person, place, object, or event within a literary work. Babette Deutsch's poem, "Disasters of War: Goya at the Museum," alludes to a famous painting by Francisco y Lucientes Goya (1746–1828) that hangs in the Prado Museum in Madrid.

Diction and Syntax

Diction is the conscious manipulation of language. It has been described as the clothes words wear. But, since words wear out with use and become cliché, for permanence as well as poetic sensibility, diction should suggest rather than state. And the use of symbolism, metaphor, and simile, which in themselves require linguistic knowledge and dexterity, can only be effective through judicious diction—the selection and use of poetic language.

Syntax is the way words are organized in order to have meaning; words so formed become sentences and phrases, which in turn can become poems, stories, novels, or plays, or today's big newspaper story. The word selection or diction in Octavio Paz's "Engaged" is supported by a syntax that seems deceptively repetitious:

> Stretching out on the grass
> a boy and a girl.
> Sucking their oranges, giving kisses
> like waves exchanging foam.
>
> Stretched out on the beach
> a boy and a girl.
> Sucking their limes, giving their kisses
> like clouds exchanging foam.
>
> Stretched out underground
> a boy and a girl.
> Saying nothing, never kissing,
> giving silence for silence.

The poet has described, with slight differences, places where there are always "stretched out" "a boy and a girl," who are "giving" their kisses until the final stanza. Then the first and last two lines surprise. We want to say at the end, "Wait a minute," and reread the poem to absorb that final difference, not so much in the syntax, which led us there, as much as the *place* that makes the disruption in behavior, tone, and meaning. Note the similes within the syntax.

Meter and Rhythm

In Greek, meter means *metron* or measure. Most consistently used in closed poetry (which need not necessarily be "traditional"), meter is the regular recurrence of a pattern of rhythm or rhythms in lines of poetry; meter is the beat we can relate to just as in music. If you think of the poems you remember best, you might discover that they were rhythmical as well as rhymed. Critic John Middleton Murry wrote: "There is a background of metrical sameness separating us like a curtain from the practical world; there is a richness of rhythmical variation to make the world in which we are, worthy of attention." Rhythm is formed by the stress (or accent or beat) on certain syllables within what are called "feet" in lines of poetry. Some words are naturally stressed, others naturally not, so another function of diction is not only to select the right words to make the point of the poem, but to select the right ones with the right stress or lack thereof. In poetry written in English, the typical metrical feet are *iambic* ($\breve{}\,'$), *trochaic* ($'\,\breve{}$), *anapestic* ($\breve{}\,\breve{}\,'$), and *dactylic* ($'\,\breve{}\,\breve{}$). *Scansion* is the method of analyzing the kind of meter and number of feet used in a poetic line.

   Ben Jonson's "Still to Be Neat," which follows, is an example of a rhythmical (and rhymed) poem containing precisely four feet in each line but with interesting metrical variation. Try "scanning" each line.

> Still to be neat, still to be drest,
> As you were going to a feast;
> Still to be pou'dred, still perfum'd:
> Lady, it is to be presum'd,
> Though arts hid causes are not found
> All is not sweet, all is not sound.
>
> Give me a look, give me a face,
> That makes simplicity a grace;
> Robes loosely flowing, hair as free:
> Such sweet neglect more taketh me,
> Than all th'adulteries of art.
> They strike mine eyes, but not mine heart.

You wonder if Jonson is writing about Art or Woman—or both—here, but it is the striking control of meter that creates the rhythm that in the first place entraps us in the poem long enough to examine its theme.

Theme

As indicated in the section on fiction, theme is the essence of subject, which is more general. In that section, poet Wilfred Owen was contrasted with fiction writers Tolstoy and Hemingway. Here is another poet, perhaps the greatest,

William Shakespeare, who within the constraints of the fourteen-line sonnet (number 116), addresses the durability of true love:

> Let me not to the marriage of true minds
> Admit impediments. Love is not love
> Which alters when it alteration finds,
> Or bends with the remover to remove:
> O, no; it is an ever-fixèd mark,
> That looks on tempests and is never shaken:
> It is the star to every wandering bark,
> Whose worth's unknown, although his height be taken.
> Love's not Time's fool, though rosy lips and cheeks
> Within his bending sickle's compass come;
> Love alters not with his brief hours and weeks,
> But bears it out even to the edge of doom.
>   If this be error and upon me proved,
>   I never writ, nor no man ever loved.

Themes in literature provide us with the tools we require for understanding a work. But theme is never stated; we arrive at it through action and insight when we have worked our way inside a story, novel, or poem.

INTERPRETING POETRY

When we say "work our way inside," we mean *knowing* a work of literature as well as we can. Reading and rereading a poem, aloud as well as silently, is one step to interpreting poetry. Another, as in fiction, is to know under what circumstances a poem was written. This, of course, additionally means knowing something about the author, and the more the better since, obviously, poems do not write themselves. Exercising your knowledge of the elements of poetry is a crucial factor in interpretation.

While there can be several interpretations of a work, there are always common elements that writers consider. Decide what kind of poetry is under discussion, dramatic monologue, lyric, or narrative (or a combination of them). Are you writing about closed poetry with its traditional rules, or open poetry which tends to make its own rules? Unlike a story, remember, a poem will render a great theme down to its essences, its most important aspects. Critical analysis requires that, early on in your paper, you state clearly what the theme is. Once you know that, you can then find the elements in the poem to support your opinion that the theme is what you think it is. If you are right, discuss the clues that led you to this conclusion, the words, the images, the lines and their formations.

Should your assignment be to compare two poems, the process is essentially the same. For example, given Shelley's "Ozymandias" and Coleridge's "Kubla Khan," you might arrive at somewhat similar themes that suggest, in sinister fashion, a warning to humankind. Both are set in unworldly locations; both possess an ominous, sometimes eerie tone, yet both are by lyrical poets who use meter, rhythm, and rhyme to convey meaning. The most obvious point of *contrast,* on the other hand, is in the length of the two poems, the brevity of Shelley's, and the length and growth of power in Coleridge's.

Although Coleridge was born twenty years before Shelley, who drowned at 30, both were influenced by Wordsworthian ideals and the philosophies of the Age of Reason, which are other comparisons you can make. Coleridge died at 62, but the lines in his "Kubla Khan" remain, as Rudyard Kipling said, "the most magical in the English language."

EVALUATING POETRY

If your instinct for liking what is good has served you well, trust it now. That is the starting place for evaluating a poem. A good poem should have meaning for you; it should make you think or wonder—and then think and wonder again about its content.

Not all poetry, however, is good, even if it has been published, but it still may be worthy of your consideration. If you examine rhythm or cadence in a closed or open poem, you should be critical of the poet's ability to maintain the beat; if it has broken down without any plausible reason, perhaps the poet tired of maintaining it, or forgot to. This failure might be one that caused you not to like the poem, though you may not have known the reason why.

If a poem has relied heavily on images you do not understand, or offers no hope whatsoever of being made clear, your evaluation will of course be negative, and rightly so. (Some poets work hard not to be understood.) Other poets, while seemingly accessible, are more subtle with the elements they employ, and you may find their work seductive. A poem with an abundance of metaphors or similes is one with too many images. On the other hand, a poem stingy with these and other elements that poetry requires may offer too little to engage you. Imprecise diction may echo like a wrong note played on a musical instrument, but recall that it was the precision of most of the diction that called your attention to the imprecision in the first place. Look for what bounces best off your own sensibilities, taking note of the advice suggested above. It may be worth knowing that for many poets, a poem remains an unfinished work; he or she will often go back to even an already published work in some cases and change something in it, which he or she believes will make it better. For most of us, good poetry makes us feel a way we cannot always explain other than to say, "good."

Go Down, Moses[1]

American Folksong

When Israel was in Egypt's land:
   Let my people go,
Oppress'd so hard they could not stand,
   Let my people go.
     Go down, Moses,   5
       Way down in Egypt land,
     Tell ole Pharaoh,
       Let my people go.

Thus saith the Lord, bold Moses said,
   Let my people go;   10
If not I'll smite your first-born dead,
   Let my people go.
     Go down, Moses, &c.

No more shall they in bondage toil,
   Let my people go;   15
Let them come out with Egypt's spoil,
   Let my people go.
     Go down, Moses, &c.

When Israel out of Egypt came,
   Let my people go;   20
And left the proud oppressive land,
   Let my people go.
     Go down, Moses, &c.

O, 'twas a dark and dismal night,
   Let my people go;   25
When Moses led the Israelites,
   Let my people go.
     Go down, Moses, &c.

'Twas good old Moses and Aaron, too,
   Let my people go;   30
'Twas they that led the armies through,

---

[1] "Go Down, Moses" was taken from J. B. T. Marsh, *The Story of the Jubilee Singers,* revised edition, 1881. By the 1880s, the Fisk University Jubilee Singers were a leading concert attraction, singing spirituals which had been little noticed in the years prior to the Civil War. Hampton Institute, Tuskegee Institute, and other schools soon followed with their own fund-raising groups.

Let my people go.
    Go down, Moses, &c.

The Lord told Moses what to do,
    Let my people go;   35
To lead the children of Israel through,
    Let my people go.
    Go down, Moses, &c.

O come along, Moses, you'll not get lost,
    Let my people go;   40
Stretch out your rod and come across,
    Let my people go.
    Go down, Moses, &c.

As Israel stood by the water side,
    Let my people go;   45
At the command of God it did divide,
    Let my people go.
    Go down, Moses, &c.

When they had reached the other shore,
    Let my people go;   50
They sang a song of triumph o'er,
    Let my people go.
    Go down, Moses, &c.

Pharaoh said he would go across,
    Let my people go;   55
But Pharaoh and his host were lost,
    Let my people go.
    Go down, Moses, &c.

O, Moses, the cloud shall cleave the way,
    Let my people go;   60
A fire by night, a shade by day,
    Let my people go.
    Go down, Moses, &c.

You'll not get lost in the wilderness,
    Let my people go;   65
With a lighted candle in your breast,
    Let my people go.
    Go down, Moses, &c.

Jordan shall stand up like a wall,
    Let my people go;   70
And the walls of Jericho shall fall,
    Let my people go;
        Go down, Moses, &c.

Your foes shall not before you stand,
    Let my people go;   75
And you'll possess fair Canaan's land,
    Let my people go.
        Go down, Moses, &c.

'Twas just about in harvest time,
    Let my people go;   80
When Joshua led his host divine,
    Let my people go.
        Go down, Moses, &c.

O let us all from bondage flee,
    Let my people go;   85
And let us all in Christ be free,
    Let my people go.
        Go down, Moses, &c.

We need not always weep and moan,
    Let my people go;   90
And wear these slavery chains forlorn,
    Let my people go.
        Go down, Moses, &c.

This world's a wilderness of woe,
    Let my people go;   95
O, let us on to Canaan go,
    Let my people go.
        Go down, Moses, &c.

What a beautiful morning that will be,
    Let my people go;   100
When time breaks up in eternity,
    Let my people go.
        Go down, Moses, &c.

O bretheren, bretheren, you'd better be engaged,
    Let my people go;   105
For the devil he's out on a big rampage,

Let my people go.
  Go down, Moses, &c.

The Devil he thought he had me fast,
  Let my people go;   110
But I thought I'd break his chains at last,
  Let my people go.
  Go down, Moses, &c.

O take yer shoes from off yer feet,
  Let my people go;   115
And walk into the golden street,
  Let my people go.
  Go down, Moses, &c.

I'll tell you what I likes de best,
  Let my people go;   120
It is the shouting Methodist,
  Let my people go.
  Go down, Moses, &c.

I do believe without a doubt,
  Let my people go;   125
That a Christian has the right to shout,
  Let my people go.
  Go down, Moses, &c.

ROBERT BLY

Driving to Town Late to Mail a Letter

It is a cold and snowy night. The main street is deserted.
The only things moving are swirls of snow.
As I lift the mailbox door, I feel its cold iron.
There is a privacy I love in this snowy night.
Driving around, I will waste more time.   5

1962

Reprinted from *Silence in the Snowy Fields* by Robert Bly, Wesleyan University Press, 1962, by permission of Robert Bly.

Anne Bradstreet (1612?–1672) was schooled by her father, who was the steward of the Earl of Lincoln, in the Earl's extensive library; thus, for her day, she was better schooled than most women. In 1628 she married Simon Bradstreet, who was her father's assistant. Being Puritans, Anne and Simon, together with her parents, emigrated to the Massachusetts colony in 1630, enduring the hardships of the first years of the Pilgrims in the New World. Despite the difficult living conditions and having eight children, Bradstreet wrote poetry. Her themes were the typical Puritan themes of sin and redemption, but she also wrote on domestic topics, such as her fear of dying in childbirth, and the love for her children and husband. In 1650 she published *The Tenth Muse Lately Sprung Up in America*, a collection of her poetry. This was revised and enlarged in 1678 as *Several Poems Compiled with Great Variety of Wit and Learning, Full of Delight*.

To My Dear and Loving Husband

Anne Bradstreet

If ever two were one, then surely we.
If ever man were loved by wife, then thee;
If ever wife was happy in a man,
Compare with me, ye women, if you can.
I prize thy love more than whole mines of gold,   5
Or all the riches that the East doth hold.
My love is such that rivers cannot quench,
Nor ought[1] but love from thee, give recompense.
Thy love is such I can no way repay,
The heavens reward thee manifold, I pray.   10
Then while we live, in love let's so persevere[2]
That when we live no more we may live ever.

1641–1643?   1678

---

[1]Anything.
[2]Pronounced "per séver" in the seventeenth century.

Questions for Discussion

1. Do you think Bradstreet's love for her husband is realistic, or overstated? What words and phrases support your interpretation?
2. What is the meaning of line 8?
3. What is the meaning of the last two lines? How do they relate to the rest of the poem?
4. How might this poem reflect a Puritan world view?
5. What are the images with which Bradstreet compares her love for her husband?
6. What word does Bradstreet repeat? What is the effect of repeating this word?
7. Bradstreet uses apostrophe, the poetic technique of directly addressing the subject of the poem. How effective is this technique for this poem?

Questions for Reflection and Writing

1. Compare this poem to one or more love poems by other women poets. How are the poems similar? How do they differ?
2. Find one or two images that you like in this poem and explain why they appeal to you.
3. Do some research into the life and times of Anne Bradstreet. What are some of the Puritan themes that appear in her poetry? How did she balance her full domestic life with her writing?

BOB DYLAN

•A Hard Rain's A-Gonna Fall[1]

Oh, where have you been, my blue-eyed son?
Oh, where have you been, my darling young one?
I've stumbled on the side of twelve misty mountains
I've walked and I've crawled on six crooked highways
I've stepped in the middle of seven sad forests   5
I've been out in front of a dozen dead oceans
I've been ten thousand miles in the mouth of a graveyard
And it's a hard, and it's a hard, it's a hard, and it's a hard
And it's a hard rain's a-gonna fall

Oh, what did you see, my blue-eyed son?   10
Oh, what did you see, my darling young one?
I saw a newborn baby with wild wolves all around it
I saw a highway of diamonds with nobody on it
I saw a black branch with blood that kept drippin'
I saw a room full of men with their hammers a-bleedin'   15
I saw a white ladder all covered with water
I saw ten thousand talkers whose tongues were all broken
I saw guns and sharp swords in the hands of young children
And it's a hard, and it's a hard, it's a hard, it's a hard
And it's a hard rain's a-gonna fall   20

And what did you hear, my blue-eyed son?
And what did you hear, my darling young one?
I heard the sound of a thunder, it roared out a warnin'
Heard the roar of a wave that could drown the whole world
Heard one hundred drummers whose hands were a-blazin'   25
Heard ten thousand whisperin' and nobody listenin'
Heard one person starve, I heard many people laughin'
Heard the song of a poet who died in the gutter
Heard the sound of a clown who cried in the alley
And it's a hard, and it's a hard, it's a hard, it's a hard   30
And it's a hard rain's a-gonna fall

Oh, who did you meet, my blue-eyed son?
Who did you meet, my darling young one?
I met a young child beside a dead pony
I met a white man who walked a black dog   35

---

1. This song is from *The Freewheelin' Bob Dylan* (1962).

I met a young woman whose body was burning
I met a young girl, she gave me a rainbow
I met one man who was wounded in love
I met another man who was wounded with hatred
And it's a hard, it's a hard, it's a hard, it's a hard   40
It's a hard rain's a-gonna fall

Oh, what'll you do now, my blue-eyed son?
Oh, what'll you do now, my darling young one?
I'm a-goin' back out 'fore the rain starts a-fallin'
I'll walk to the depths of the deepest black forest   45
Where the people are many and their hands are all empty
Where the pellets of poison are flooding their waters
Where the home in the valley meets the damp dirty prison
Where the executioner's face is always well hidden
Where hunger is ugly, where souls are forgotten   50
Where black is the color, where none is the number
And I'll tell it and think it and speak it and breathe it
And reflect it from the mountain so all souls can see it
Then I'll stand on the ocean until I start sinkin'
But I'll know my song well before I start singin'   55
And it's a hard, it's a hard, it's a hard, it's a hard
It's a hard rain's a-gonna fall

1962

◦═◄ BOB DYLAN ►═◦

The Times They Are A-Changin'[1]

Come gather 'round people
Wherever you roam
And admit that the waters
Around you have grown
And accept it that soon   5
You'll be drenched to the bone
If your time to you is worth savin'
Then you better start swimmin' or you'll sink like a stone
For the times they are a-changin'

Come writers and critics   10
Who prophesize with your pen
And keep your eyes wide
The chance won't come again
And don't speak too soon
For the wheel's still in spin   15
And there's no tellin' who that it's namin'
For the loser now will be later to win
For the times they are a-changin'

Come senators, congressmen
Please heed the call   20
Don't stand in the doorway
Don't block up the hall
For he that gets hurt
Will be he who has stalled
There's a battle outside and it is ragin'   25
It'll soon shake your windows and rattle your walls
For the times they are a-changin'

Come mothers and fathers
Throughout the land
And don't criticize   30
What you can't understand
Your sons and your daughters
Are beyond your command
Your old road is rapidly agin'

---

1. This song is from *The Freewheelin' Bob Dylan* (1962).

Please get out of the new one if you can't lend your hand   35
For the times they are a-changin'

The line it is drawn
The curse it is cast
The slow one now
Will later be fast   40
As the present now
Will later be past
The order is rapidly fadin'
And the first one now will later be last
For the times they are a-changin'   45

                                                                    1963

◄ ROBERT FROST ►

Mending Wall

Something there is that doesn't love a wall,
That sends the frozen-ground-swell under it
And spills the upper boulders in the sun,
And makes gaps even two can pass abreast.
The work of hunters is another thing: 5
I have come after them and made repair
Where they have left not one stone on a stone,
But they would have the rabbit out of hiding,
To please the yelping dogs. The gaps I mean,
No one has seen them made or heard them made,   10
But at spring mending-time we find them there.
I let my neighbor know beyond the hill;
And on a day we meet to walk the line
And set the wall between us once again.
We keep the wall between us as we go.   15
To each the boulders that have fallen to each.
And some are loaves and some so nearly balls
We have to use a spell to make them balance:
"Stay where you are until our backs are turned!"
We wear our fingers rough with handling them.   20
Oh, just another kind of outdoor game,
One on a side. It comes to little more:
There where it is we do not need the wall:
He is all pine and I am apple orchard.
My apple trees will never get across   25
And eat the cones under his pines, I tell him.
He only says, "Good fences make good neighbors."
Spring is the mischief in me, and I wonder
If I could put a notion in his head:
"*Why* do they make good neighbors? Isn't it   30
Where there are cows? But here there are no cows.
Before I built a wall I'd ask to know
What I was walling in or walling out,
And to whom I was like to give offense.
Something there is that doesn't love a wall,   35
That wants it down." I could say "Elves" to him,
But it's not elves exactly, and I'd rather
He said it for himself. I see him there,
Bringing a stone grasped firmly by the top
In each hand, like an old-stone savage armed.   40

He moves in darkness as it seems to me,
Not of woods only and the shade of trees.
He will not go behind his father's saying,
And he likes having thought of it so well
He says again, "Good fences make good neighbors."   45

1914

ROBERT FROST

The Road Not Taken

Two roads diverged in a yellow wood,
And sorry I could not travel both
And be one traveler, long I stood
And looked down one as far as I could
To where it bent in the undergrowth;   5

Then took the other, as just as fair,
And having perhaps the better claim,
Because it was grassy and wanted wear;
Though as for that, the passing there
Had worn them really about the same,   10

And both that morning equally lay
In leaves no step had trodden black.
Oh, I kept the first for another day!
Yet knowing how way leads on to way,
I doubted if I should ever come back.   15

I shall be telling this with a sigh
Somewhere ages and ages hence:
Two roads diverged in a wood, and I—
I took the one less traveled by,
And that has made all the difference.   20

1915, 1916

◄ WOODY GUTHRIE ►

Plane Wreck at Los Gatos[1]
(Deportee)

The crops are all in and the peaches are rott'ning,
The oranges piled in their creosote dumps;
You're flying 'em back to the Mexican border,
To pay all their money to wade back again.

Goodbye to my Juan, goodbye, Rosalita,[2]   5
Adios mis amigos, Jesus y Maria;
You won't have your names when you ride the big airplane,
All they will call you will be "deportees."

My father's own father, he waded that river,
They took all the money he made in his life;   10
My brothers and sisters come working the fruit trees,
And they rode the truck till they took down and died.

Some of us are illegal, and some are not wanted,
Our work contract's out and we have to move on;
Six hundred miles to that Mexican border,   15
They chase us like outlaws, like rustlers, like thieves.

We died in your hills, we died in your deserts,
We died in your valleys and died on your plains,
We died 'neath your trees and we died in your bushes,
Both sides of the river, we died just the same.   20

The sky plane caught fire over Los Gatos Canyon,
A fireball of lightning, and shook all our hills,
Who are all these friends, all scattered like dry leaves?
The radio says they are just deportees.

Is this the best way we can grow our big orchards?   25
Is this the best way we can grow our good fruit?
To fall like dry leaves to rot on my topsoil
And be called by no name except deportees?

1948

---

1. On January 28, 1948, a chartered plane "carrying 28 Mexican farm workers from Oakland to the El Centro, CA, Deportation Center" (*New York Times*) crashed, killing all twenty-eight.
2. The second stanza is a refrain, usually repeated after each succeeding stanza. The song remained a poem until a decade later, when Martin Hoffman put it to music and Pete Seeger began singing it.

WOODY GUTHRIE

This Land Is Your Land

This land is your land, This land is my land,
From California to the New York island;
From the red wood forest to the Gulf Stream waters
This land was made for you and me.

As I was walking that ribbon of highway,   5
I saw above me that endless skyway;
I saw below me that golden valley;
This land was made for you and me.

I've roamed and rambled and I followed my footsteps
To the sparkling sands of her diamond deserts;   10
And all around me a voice was sounding:
This land was made for you and me.

When the sun came shining, and I was strolling,
And the wheat fields waving and the dust clouds rolling,
As the fog was lifting a voice was chanting: 15
This land was made for you and me.

As I went walking, I saw a sign there,
And on the sign it said "No Trespassing,"
But on the other side it didn't say nothing,
That side was made for you and me.   20

In the shadow of the steeple I saw my people,
By the relief office I seen my people;
As they stood there hungry, I stood there asking
Is this land made for you and me?

Nobody living can ever stop me,   25
As I go walking that freedom highway;
Nobody living can ever make me turn back,
This land was made for you and me.

1940

LANGSTON HUGHES

Harlem

What happens to a dream deferred?

    Does it dry up
    like a raisin in the sun?
    Or fester like a sore—
    And then run?   5
    Does it stink like rotten meat?
    Or crust and sugar over—
    like a syrupy sweet?

    Maybe it just sags
    like a heavy load.   10

    Or does it explode?

                                  1951

Langston Hughes (1902–1967) was born in Joplin, Missouri, and lived in Kansas, Illinois, and Ohio before studying at Columbia University and earning an A.B. from Lincoln University in 1929. Hughes was a prolific writer of poetry, plays, songs, fiction, and nonfiction. Much of Hughes's writing offers a transcription of urban life through a portrayal of the speech, habits, attitudes, and feelings of an oppressed people. His work does more, however, than reveal the pain of poverty—it also illustrates racial pride and dignity. Hughes's many books include the poetry collection *Montage of a Dream Deferred* (1951), the novel *Tambourines to Glory* (1958), the short-story collection *The Ways of White Folks* (1934), and the nonfiction work *Black Misery* (1969). Among his many awards and honors, Hughes won a Guggenheim Fellowship and an Anisfeld-Wolfe Award. "The Negro Speaks of Rivers" was first published in 1921 in the NAACP journal *The Crisis* and reprinted in Hughes's first collection of poetry, *The Weary Blues* (1926).

The Negro Speaks of Rivers

Langston Hughes

I've known rivers:
I've known rivers ancient as the world and older than the
    flow of human blood in human veins.

My soul has grown deep like the rivers.

I bathed in the Euphrates when dawns were young.   5
I built my hut near the Congo and it lulled me to sleep.
I looked upon the Nile and raised the pyramids above it.
I heard the singing of the Mississippi when Abe Lincoln
    went down to New Orleans, and I've seen its muddy
    bosom turn all golden in the sunset.   10

I've known rivers:
Ancient, dusky rivers.

My soul has grown deep like the rivers.

Questions for Discussion

1. You know where the Mississippi River is, right? If you don't know the locations of the Euphrates, Congo, or the Nile consult an almanac, atlas, or map. How does knowledge of this geography help inform you regarding this poem?
2. Discuss the implications of the lines: "I've known rivers ancient as the world and older than the/flow of human blood in human veins" in the context of the poem.

3. Note the instances of repetition in the poem. How can this repetition be seen to contribute to the meaning of the poem?

4. What was Abe Lincoln doing in New Orleans? If you don't know, guess, then look it up. When you know (or if you already knew), how does this bit of historical information fit in with the rest of the poem? If you guessed, how close were you?

5. Hughes's work is often described in conjunction with music. In what ways can this poem be said to be musical?

Questions for Reflection and Writing

1. This page <http://www.poets.org/poems/poems.cfm?45442B7C000C07030C71> has a link that will let you download "The Negro Speaks of Rivers" read by Hughes. Read the poem along with him. How does your reading differ from his? What's similar about your readings?

2. Hughes uses rivers as a device to tell a story of a people. What people? What device or image would you use to tell the story of your own people? How do you define "your own people"?

3. Think of the rivers you have seen in person. Which ones have you seen? How old were you? What were you doing, generally, at the time? What is it about rivers, do you think, that makes them such widely used objects and images in art?

4. Interested in putting Hughes into a historical context? This page <http://www.writingproject.org/Resources/hughes.htm> from the National Writing Project will be a great help in getting your research started. Click over and you'll find links to critical writings, biographies, and even some information about a stamp featuring Hughes.

Christopher Marlowe (1564–1593) led a brief life filled with controversy. At Corpus Christi College, Cambridge, college authorities hesitated to grant him his degree, apparently dubious about his frequent absences and suspicious of his political loyalties. A letter from the Privy Council implied that his absences were spent in service to Queen Elizabeth, and the degree was granted. In 1589, he and fellow poet Thomas Watson were jailed on charges of murder for their part in a street fight in which a young man was killed, but both were later released. In May 1593, playwright Thomas Kyd testified before a government council that Marlowe was an atheist, a charge later repeated by a government informant; Marlowe was questioned and released. Twelve days later, in the company of notorious spy Robert Poley, Marlowe was killed in a tavern, supposedly over a dispute concerning the bill. Many have speculated that he was, rather, murdered for political reasons. After Shakespeare, Marlowe was the greatest dramatic writer in English during the sixteenth century. His masterpieces are *Tamburlaine* and *Doctor Faustus*, and his major poetic work is *Hero and Leander*, an original treatment of the mythical story of two drowned lovers. In "The Passionate Shepherd to His Love," one of his most famous lyrics, Marlowe adopts the conventions of pastoral poetry (a conventional mode that celebrates the innocent life of shepherds and shepherdesses).

The Passionate Shepherd to His Love

Christopher Marlowe

Come live with me and be my love,
And we will all the pleasures prove
That valleys, groves, hills, and fields,
Woods, or steepy mountain yields.

And we will sit upon the rocks,   5
Seeing the shepherds feed their flocks
By shallow rivers, to whose falls
Melodious birds sing madrigals.

And I will make thee beds of roses
And a thousand fragrant posies,   10
A cap of flowers and a kirtle°
Embroidered all with leaves of myrtle;

A gown made of the finest wool
Which from our pretty lambs we pull;
Fair-linèd slippers for the cold,   15
With buckles of the purest gold;

A belt of straw and ivy buds,
With coral clasps and amber studs.

---

11 kirtle *skirt*

And if these pleasures may thee move,
Come live with me and be my love.   20

The shepherds' swains shall dance and sing
For thy delight each May morning.
If these delights thy mind may move,
Then live with me and be my love.

Questions for Discussion, Reflection, and Writing

1. What kind of argument does the shepherd construct to persuade the nymph? What kinds of support does he use?
2. What kind of life will the two lead, if she accepts his proposal?
3. Giving him the benefit of the doubt for a moment, what does the "shepherd" actually offer here? How would he expect the "nymph" to understand his offerings?
§. Connect the readings: Compare the pleas of the "shepherd" here to the response of the "nymph" in Raleigh's "The Nymph's Reply." Whose argument do you find more convincing?

Andrew Marvell (1621–1678) was educated at Trinity College, Cambridge. He was sympathetic to the Crown until his appointment as tutor to Mary Fairfax, daughter of one of Cromwell's generals, at which time he switched his loyalty to the Puritan cause. Marvell later served under Cromwell as Assistant Latin Secretary, and he soon became a close friend of Milton. After Cromwell's death, Marvell entered Parliament, where he served for almost twenty years. During the Restoration, he wrote bitter satires in prose and verse that, while not read much today, brought him some fame in his time. Today, we remember him for his lyric poetry. "To His Coy Mistress" (1681) is an example of *carpe diem* lyric—poetry exhorting listeners to "seize the day, for tomorrow we die"—noteworthy especially for its wit and playful irony.

To His Coy Mistress

Andrew Marvell

   Had we but world enough, and time,
This coyness, lady, were no crime.
We would sit down, and think which way
To walk, and pass our long love's day.
Thou by the Indian Ganges' side   5
Shouldst rubies find; I by the tide
Of Humber° would complain. I would
Love you ten years before the flood,
And you should, if you please, refuse
Till the conversion of the Jews.°   10
My vegetable° love should grow
Vaster than empires, and more slow;
An hundred years should go to praise
Thine eyes, and on thy forehead gaze;
Two hundred to adore each breast,   15
But thirty thousand to the rest;
An age at least to every part,
And the last age should show your heart.
For, lady, you deserve this state,°
Nor would I love at lower rate.   20
   But at my back I always hear
Time's wingèd chariot hurrying near;
And yonder all before us lie
Deserts of vast eternity.

Humber an English river
conversion of the Jews at the end of time
vegetable flourishing
state stateliness; pomp

Thy beauty shall no more be found;   25
Nor, in thy marble vault, shall sound
My echoing song; then worms shall try
That long-preserved virginity,
And your quaint honor turn to dust,
And into ashes all my lust: 30
The grave's a fine and private place,
But none, I think, do there embrace.
    Now therefore, while the youthful hue
Sits on thy skin like morning glow,
And while thy willing soul transpires   35
At every pore with instant fires,
Now let us sport us while we may,
And now, like amorous birds of prey,
Rather at once our time devour
Than languish in his slow-chapped° power.   40
Let us roll all our strength and all
Our sweetness up into one ball,
And tear our pleasures with rough strife
Thorough the iron gates of life:

Thus, though we cannot make our sun   45
Stand still, yet we will make him run.

---

chapped jawed

Sir Walter Raleigh (ca. 1552–1618) represented to his contemporaries the Elizabethan Renaissance ideal of the complete individual. Raleigh was a poet, historian, courtier, explorer, colonist, seaman, soldier, and diplomat. The fact that he more often than not failed at his many pursuits did not interfere with his symbolic stature. Found guilty of conspiring against the newly installed King James I, Raleigh was sentenced to death in 1603 and spent fifteen years imprisoned in the Tower of London before his execution in 1618. His poetry is informed with a keen awareness of the transitory nature of existence.

The Nymph's Reply

Sir Walter Raleigh

If all the world and love were young,
And truth in every shepherd's tongue,
These pretty pleasures might me move
To live with thee and be thy love.

Time drives the flocks from field to fold,   5
When rivers rage and rocks grow cold,
And Philomel° becometh dumb;
The rest complains of cares to come.

The flowers do fade, and wanton fields
To wayward winter reckoning yields;   10
A honey tongue, a heart of gall,
Is fancy's spring, but sorrow's fall.

Thy gowns, thy shoes, thy beds of roses,
Thy cap, thy kirtle,° and thy posies
Soon break, soon wither, soon forgotten,—   15
In folly ripe, in reason rotten.

Thy belt of straw and ivy buds,
The coral clasps and amber studs,
All these in me no means can move
To come to thee and be thy love.   20

But could youth last and love still breed,
Had joys no date nor age no need,
Then these delights my mind might move
To live with thee and be thy love.

---

7 Philomel the nightingale
14 kirtle skirt

Questions for Discussion, Reflection, and Writing

1. What is the gist of the "nymph's" argument here? How do you think the "shepherd" might respond?

2. How does the poet weave the imagery of the passing seasons into the argument against the shepherd?

3. What is it, exactly, that the nymph prefers in line 17 to a "belt of straw and ivy buds"?

§. Connect the readings: Raleigh's poem is an explicit reply to Marlowe's "The Passionate Shepherd to His Love." Find and read this poem. Who, in your opinion, makes the better argument? Why?

§. Connect the readings: To what end is the image of fading flowers used in this poem? Find other examples of this image—for example, in Robert Herrick's "To the Virgins"—and discuss the differences in the way it is used.

THEODORE ROETHKE

My Papa's Waltz

The whiskey on your breath
Could make a small boy dizzy;
But I hung on like death:
Such waltzing was not easy.

We romped until the pans   5
Slid from the kitchen shelf;
My mother's countenance
Could not unfrown itself.

The hand that held my wrist
Was battered on one knuckle;   10
At every step you missed
My right ear scraped a buckle.

You beat time on my head
With a palm caked hard by dirt,
Then waltzed me off to bed   15
Still clinging to your shirt.

                                              1948

Christina Rossetti's (1830–1894) father was an Italian political refugee, and her brother was the poet Dante Gabriel Rossetti. Christina was a devout High Anglican who dedicated her life to caring for relatives and doing good works for the church and charity. She broke off two engagements because, by her standards, neither man proved sufficiently devout. The apparent simplicity of many of her poems often masks complex emotional underpinnings. Many of her poems deal with painful breakups. "Uphill" (1862), a religious allegory, is one of her most famous poems..

Uphill

Christina Rossetti

Does the road wind uphill all the way?
    Yes, to the very end.
Will the day's journey take the whole long day?
    From morn to night, my friend.

But is there for the night a resting-place?   5
    A roof for when the slow dark hours begin.

May not the darkness hide it from my face?
    You cannot miss that inn.

Shall I meet other wayfarers at night?
    Those who have gone before.   10
Then must I knock, or call when just in sight?
    They will not keep you standing at that door.

Shall I find comfort, travel-sore and weak?
    Of labor you shall find the sum.
Will there be beds for me and all who seek?   15
    Yea, beds for all who come.

Questions for Discussion, Reflection, and Writing

1. This poem a devotional allegory. Given this, what do you think the road stands for? The day? The inn? The beds?
2. What do you think of the tone of the poem? Point to specific lines that support your interpretation.
3. Connect the readings: Compare this poem to Donne's "Death Be Not Proud" or Keats's "When I Have Fears" in terms of the way it attempts to grapple with a common human fear.

Percy Bysshe Shelley (1792–1822) was a well-born, thoughtful, serious boy who was often bullied at school. He was interested in many fields and studied medicine, philosophy, science, and literature. His studies, his experiences, and perhaps even his being bullied, resulted in radical political ideas that championed the causes of the working class and urged social and religious reform. At Oxford he became close friends with another student, Thomas Jefferson Hogg, and the two of them wrote *The Necessity of Atheism*, a pamplet defending atheism. For this they were expelled. Shelley had also written a gothic novel, *Zastrozzi*, a gothic poem, "St. Irvyne," and with Hogg a collection of erotic poetry, *Posthumous Fragments of Margaret Nicholson*, which they published as the writings of a madwoman. None of these works reflects Shelley's mature style. From 1810 to 1812, Shelley and Hogg, expelled, spent their time together. During this time Shelley met and fell in love with sixteen-year-old Harriet Westbrook, and in 1811 they eloped. But in 1814 Shelley also fell in love with Mary Godwin, the sixteen-year-old daughter of the philosopher William Godwin, whom he had met two years previously. He and Mary eloped to Europe, although Shelley continued to provide for Harriet and their two children. In 1816 Harriet killed herself, and Shelley and Mary married, spending the summer in Switzerland where Shelley met and became close friends with Byron. In 1818, after a brief time back in England, Shelley and Mary moved permanently to Italy, where Shelley had his most productive years. There he wrote his masterpiece verse drama *Prometheus Unbound* (1819) and *Adonais: An Elegy on the Death of John Keats* (1821). In 1822 Shelley and a friend drowned when their sailboat capsized during a storm. Much of Shelley's work reflects his political beliefs about social reform, atheism, free love, and equality of the classes and sexes. A recurring theme is nature as a life force evoking imagination and love.

Ozymandias

Percy Bysshe Shelley

I met a traveller from an antique land
Who said: Two vast and trunkless legs of stone
Stand in the desert . . . Near them, on the sand,
Half sunk, ash attered visage lies, whose frown,
And wrinkled lip, and sneer of cold command,   5
Tell that its sculptor well those passions read
Which yet survive, stamped on these lifeless things,
The hand that mocked them, and the heart that fed:
And on the pedestal these words appear:
'My name is Ozymandias, king of kings: 10
Look on my works, ye Mighty, and despair!'
Nothing beside remains. Round the decay
Of that colossal wreck, boundless and bare
The lone and level sands stretch far away.

Dylan Thomas (1914–1953) was born in the Welsh seaport of Swansea, where his formal education began and ended at Swansea Grammar School. With the publication of *Eighteen Poems* in 1934, Thomas achieved widespread and immediate fame. His lyrical poetry features vivid metaphors, Christian and Freudian imagery, puns, and intricate patterns of sound, yet it tends to be more immediately accessible and emotional than many of the moderns' works. His colorful personality and melodious speaking voice made his reading tours the most successful of any poet in this century. While on his third American reading tour, Thomas died in New York City after a reckless drinking binge. "Do Not Go Gentle" was first published in 1952.

Do Not Go Gentle into That Good Night

Dylan Thomas

Do not go gentle into that good night,
Old age should burn and rave at close of day;
Rage, rage against the dying of the light.

Though wise men at their end know dark is right,
Because their words had forked no lightning they   5
Do not go gentle into that good night.

Good men, the last wave by, crying how bright
Their frail deeds might have danced in a green bay,
Rage, rage against the dying of the light.

Wild men who caught and sang the sun in flight,   10
And learn, too late, they grieved it on its way,
Do not go gentle into that good night.

Grave men, near death, who see with blinding sight
Blind eyes could blaze like meteors and be gay,
Rage, rage against the dying of the light.   15

And you, my father, there on the sad height,
Curse, bless, me now with your fierce tears, I pray.
Do not go gentle into that good night.
Rage, rage against the dying of the light.

Questions for Discussion, Reflection, and Writing

1. To whom is the poem addressed? How did you arrive at your conclusion?

2. What is the tone of the poem?

3. What *is* "that good night"? In what way(s) is the thing described like the night?

4. In what way is the "night" *good?* Is there any contradiction in the warning not to yield to it?

5. Why do the different kinds of men the poet identifies all "rage against the dying of the light"? Why should they?

§ **Connect the readings:** Compare this poem to another poem that addresses mortality, such as Milton's "When I Consider How My Light Is Spent," Keats's "When I Have Fears That I May Cease to Be," and Donne's "Death Be Not Proud."

Phillis Wheatley (1754?–1784) was taken from her home in Senegal, West Africa, and sold into slavery. She was just seven years old. She was on a ship bound for the West Indies, but because of her youth and apparent frailty, she was not sold there but brought to Boston with others who had not been sold. There, the slave ship's captain thinking she was dying, Wheatley was sold to Susanna Wheatley. The Wheatleys soon discovered her literary talent and so taught her to read and write along with their own children. She read the classics, history, astronomy, and religious writing, and was soon writing poetry. Wheatley's first published poem, at the age of thirteen, told the story of a rescue at sea and was published locally. A year later, however, her *Elegiac Poem* was published and gained her national and then international fame. By the time she was eighteen, she had published 28 poems, first published in London as *Poems on Various Subjects*. In 1771 she went to London accompanied by Nathanial, the Wheatley family's son. Her notoriety brought many people to see her, including abolitionists, who made her their *cause célèbre*. Back in the colonies, Wheatley was once again the family's slave, and the Wheatleys did not free her until 1774, after which she stayed on as a paid servant and continued to write poetry. By 1778, however, the Wheatleys had all died, leaving Phillis in a difficult situation. Although she married John Peters that year, she did not get any financial security. Peters was a skilled businessman, but as a black man he could not get his business ventures accepted by the white business community. As a result, Wheatley, never very strong, slowly exhausted her energy working as a cleaning woman and raising three children. Although she continued to write poems, she could not interest the local publishers to print them. Scholars estimate that she wrote perhaps 145 poems, but most have been lost. In December of 1784, with her three children having all died young, and her husband in debtor's jail, Wheatley died alone.

Liberty and Peace

Phillis Wheatley

LO! Freedom comes. Th' prescient Muse foretold,
All Eyes th' accomplish'd Prophecy behold:
Her Port describ'd, "She moves divinely fair,
"Olive and Laurel bind her golden Hair."
She, the bright Progeny of Heaven, descends,   5
And every Grace her sovereign Step attends;
For now kind Heaven, indulgent to our Prayer,
In smiling Peace resolves the Din of War.
Fix'd in Columbia her illustrious Line,
And bids in thee her future Councils shine.   10
To every Realm her Portals open'd wide,
Receives from each the full commercial Tide.
Each Art and Science now with rising Charms
Th' expanding Heart with Emulation warms.
E'en great Britannia sees with dread Surprize,   15
And from the dazzling Splendors turns her Eyes!

Britain, whose Navies swept th' Atlantic o'er,
And Thunder sent to every distant Shore;
E'en thou, in Manners cruel as thou art,
The Sword resign'd, resume the friendly Part!   20
For Galia's Power espous'd Columbia's Cause,
And new-born Rome shall give Britannia Law,
Nor unremember'd in the grateful Strain,
Shall princely Louis' friendly Deeds remain;
The generous Prince th' impending Vengeance eye's,   25
Sees the fierce Wrong, and to the rescue flies.
Perish that Thirst of boundless Power, that drew
On Albion's Head the Curse to Tyrants due.
But thou appeas'd submit to Heaven's decree,
That bids this Realm of Freedom rival thee!   30
Now sheathe the Sword that bade the Brave attone
With guiltless Blood for Madness not their own.
Sent from th' Enjoyment of their native Shore
Ill-fated-never to behold her more!
From every Kingdom on Europa's Coast   35
Throng'd various Troops, their Glory, Strength and Boast.
With heart-felt pity fair Hibernia saw
Columbia menac'd by the Tyrant's Law:
On hostile Fields fraternal Arms engage,
And mutual Deaths, all dealt with mutual Rage: 40
The Muse's Ear hears mother Earth deplore
Her ample Surface smoake with kindred Gore:
The hostile Field destroys the social Ties,
And every-lasting Slumber seals their Eyes.
Columbia mourns, the haughty Foes deride,   45
Her Treasures plunder'd, and her Towns destroy'd:
Witness how Charlestown's curling Smoaks arise,
In sable Columns to the clouded Skies!
The ample Dome, high-wrought with curious Toil,
In one sad Hour the savage Troops despoil.   50
Descending Peace and Power of War confounds;
From every Tongue celestial Peace resounds:
As for the East th' illustrious King of Day,
With rising Radiance drives the Shades away,
So Freedom comes array'd with Charms divine,   55
And in her Train Commerce and Plenty shine.
Britannia owns her Independent Reign,
Hibernia, Scotia, and the Realms of Spain;

And great Germania's ample Coast admires
The generous Spirit that Columbia fires.   60
Auspicious Heaven shall fill with fav'ring Gales,
Where e'er Columbia spreads her swelling Sails:
To every Realm shall Peace her Charms display,
And Heavenly Freedom spread her golden Ray.

Questions for Discussion

1. What does Wheatley think of Liberty and Peace? What kind of liberty and peace does she espouse?
2. What is the relationship between Liberty and Peace?
3. What must happen before liberty and peace can be attained?
4. Who or what are the following: Britannia, Galia, Columbia, Albion, Europa, Hibernia, Scotia, and Germania? What is each one's function in helping to bring about liberty and peace?
5. Why might Wheatley have used the elaborate imagery of this poem?
6. In what places is the reader positioned to view the scenes? What can the reader see from each position that is significant?
7. Where does Wheatley use personification and allegory? What might have been her purposes for using these literary techniques?

Questions for Reflection and Writing

1. Describe Freedom as Wheatley describes "her." Paraphrase the poem, providing a line-by-line restatement of Wheatley's words.
2. After you have paraphrased the poem, write a brief interpretation of it.
3. Paraphrase the poem, as above, and write an interpretation of it in the context of historical events at the time of its writing.

PHILLIS WHEATLEY

On Being Brought from Africa to America

'Twas mercy brought me from my *Pagan* land,
Taught my benighted soul to understand
That there's a God, that there's a *Saviour* too:
Once I redemption neither sought nor knew.
Some view our sable race with scornful eye,   5
"Their colour is a diabolic die."[1]
Remember, *Christians, Negroes,* black as *Cain,*
May be refin'd, and join th' angelic train.

1768   1773

1. Dye.

━━━━━━━━━━━ WALT WHITMAN ━━━━━━━━━━━

From SEA-DRIFT

Out of the Cradle Endlessly Rocking[1]

Out of the cradle endlessly rocking,
Out of the mocking-bird's throat, the musical shuttle,
Out of the Ninth-month[2] midnight,
Over the sterile sands and the fields beyond, where the child leaving his bed
    wander'd alone, bareheaded, barefoot,
Down from the shower'd halo,   5
Up from the mystic play of shadows twining and twisting as if they were alive,
Out from the patches of briers and blackberries,
From the memories of the bird that chanted to me,
From your memories sad brother, from the fitful risings and fallings I heard,
From under that yellow half-moon late-risen and swollen as if with tears,   10
From those beginning notes of yearning and love there in the mist,
From the thousand responses of my heart never to cease,
From the myriad thence-arous'd words,
From the word stronger and more delicious than any,
From such as now they start the scene revisiting,   15
As a flock, twittering, rising, or overhead passing,
Borne hither, ere all eludes me, hurriedly,
A man, yet by these tears a little boy again,
Throwing myself on the sand, confronting the waves,
I, chanter of pains and joys, uniter of here and hereafter,   20
Taking all hints to use them, but swiftly leaping beyond them,
A reminiscence sing.

Once Paumanok,[3]
When the lilac-scent was in the air and Fifth-month grass was growing,
Up this seashore in some briers,   25
Two feather'd guests from Alabama, two together,
And their nest, and four light-green eggs spotted with brown,
And every day the he-bird to and fro near at hand,
And every day the she-bird crouch'd on her nest, silent, with bright eyes,
And every day I, a curious boy, never too close, never disturbing them,   30
Cautiously peering, absorbing, translating.

---

1. "Out of the Cradle Endlessly Rocking" became the first poem in a section titled "Sea-Drift" in the 1881 edition of *Leaves of Grass*. In the 1871 edition this section was titled "Sea-Shore Memories." The sea provided inspiration for Whitman, who in these poems hints at some of the major crises of his life.
2. The Quaker designation for September may here also suggest the human cycle of fertility and birth, in contrast with "sterile sands" in the next line.
3. Whitman liked the Indian name for Long Island ("a fish" or "fish shaped"). This poem, like "Starting from Paumanok," deals with the genesis of his life.

Shine! shine! shine!
Pour down your warmth, great sun!
While we bask, we two together.

Two together!   35
Winds blow south, or winds blow north,
Day come white, or night come black,
Home, or rivers and mountains from home,
Singing all time, minding no time,
While we two keep together.[4]   40

Till of a sudden,
May-be kill'd, unknown to her mate,
One forenoon the she-bird crouch'd not on the nest,
Nor return'd that afternoon, nor the next,
Nor ever appear'd again.   45

And thenceforward all summer in the sound of the sea,
And at night under the full of the moon in calmer weather,
Over the hoarse surging of the sea,
Or flitting from brier to brier by day,
I saw, I heard at intervals the remaining one, the he-bird,   50
The solitary guest from Alabama.

Blow! blow! blow!
Blow up sea-winds along Paumanok's shore;
I wait and I wait till you blow my mate to me.

Yes, when the stars glisten'd,   55
All night long on the prong of a moss-scallop'd stake,
Down almost amid the slapping waves,
Sat the lone singer wonderful causing tears.

He call'd on his mate,
He pour'd forth the meaning which I of all men know.   60

Yes my brother I know,
The rest might not, but I have treasur'd every note,
For more than once dimly down to the beach gliding,
Silent, avoiding the moonbeams, blending myself with the shadows,
Recalling now the obscure shapes, the echoes, the sounds and sights after their
     sorts,   65
The white arms out in the breakers tirelessly tossing,
I, with bare feet, a child, the wind wafting my hair,
Listen'd long and long.

---

4. The mockingbird songs were altered for rhythmic verisimilitude in several editions subsequent to the magazine publication of 1859. Whitman, himself an ornithologist, had also the advice of his friend John Burroughs, the talented naturalist. Note the characteristic reiteration and the staccato twittering (*e.g.*, ll. 80, 91–92, 111).

Listen'd to keep, to sing, now translating the notes,
Following you my brother.   70

Soothe! soothe! soothe!
Close on its wave soothes the wave behind,
And again another behind embracing and lapping, every one close,
But my love soothes not me, not me.

Low hangs the moon, it rose late,   75
It is lagging—O I think it is heavy with love, with love.

O madly the sea pushes upon the land,
With love, with love.

O night! do I not see my love fluttering out among the breakers?
What is that little black thing I see there in the white?   80

Loud! loud! loud!
Loud I call to you, my love!

High and clear I shoot my voice over the waves,
Surely you must know who is here, is here,
You must know who I am, my love.   85

Low-hanging moon!
What is that dusky spot in your brown yellow?
O it is the shape, the shape of my mate!
O moon do not keep her from me any longer.

Land! land! O land!   90
Whichever way I turn, O I think you could give me my mate back again if you
*   only would,*
For I am almost sure I see her dimly whichever way I look.

O rising stars!
Perhaps the one I want so much will rise, will rise with some of you.

O throat! O trembling throat!   95
Sound clearer through the atmosphere!
Pierce the woods, the earth,
Somewhere listening to catch you must be the one I want.

Shake out carols!
Solitary here, the night's carols!   100
Carols of lonesome love! death's carols!

Carols under that lagging, yellow, waning moon!
O under that moon where she droops almost down into the sea!
O reckless despairing carols.

But soft! sink low!   105
Soft! let me just murmur,
And do you wait a moment you husky-nois'd sea,
For somewhere I believe I heard my mate responding to me,

So faint, I must be still, be still to listen,
But not altogether still, for then she might not come immediately to me.   110

Hither my love!
Here I am! here!
With this just-sustain'd note I announce myself to you,
This gentle call is for you my love, for you.

Do not be decoy'd elsewhere,   115
That is the whistle of the wind, it is not my voice,
That is the fluttering, the fluttering of the spray,
Those are the shadows of leaves.

O darkness! O in vain!
O I am very sick and sorrowful.   120

O brown halo in the sky near the moon, drooping upon the sea!
O troubled reflection in the sea!
O throat! O throbbing heart!
And I singing uselessly, uselessly all the night.

O past! O happy life! O songs of joy!   125
In the air, in the woods, over fields,
Loved! loved! loved! loved! loved!
But my mate no more, no more with me!
We two together no more.

The aria sinking,[5]   130
All else continuing, the stars shining,
The winds blowing, the notes of the bird continuous echoing,
With angry moans the fierce old mother incessantly moaning,
On the sands of Paumanok's shore gray and rustling,
The yellow half-moon enlarged, sagging down, drooping, the face of the sea
    almost touching,   135
The boy ecstatic, with his bare feet the waves, with his hair the atmosphere
    dallying,
The love in the heart long pent, now loose, now at last tumultuously bursting,
The aria's meaning, the ears, the soul, swiftly depositing,
The strange tears down the cheeks coursing,
The colloquy there, the trio, each uttering,   140
The undertone, the savage old mother incessantly crying,
To the boy's soul's questions sullenly timing, some drown'd secret hissing,
To the outsetting bard.

Demon or bird! (said the boy's soul,)
Is it indeed toward your mate you sing? or is it really to me?   145

---

5. Robert D. Faner, in *Whitman and the Opera*, 1951, shows Whitman's indebtedness to the aria and other operatic forms of lyric.

For I, that was a child, my tongue's use sleeping, now I have heard you,
Now in a moment I know what I am for, I awake,
And already a thousand singers, a thousand songs, clearer, louder and more
       sorrowful than yours,
A thousand warbling echoes have started to life within me, never to die.
O you singer solitary, singing by yourself, projecting me,   150
O solitary me listening, never more shall I cease perpetuating you,
Never more shall I escape, never more the reverberations,
Never more the cries of unsatisfied love be absent from me,
Never again leave me to be the peaceful child I was before what there in the
       night,
By the sea under the yellow and sagging moon,   155
The messenger there arous'd, the fire, the sweet hell within,
The unknown want, the destiny of me.

O give me the clew! (it lurks in the night here somewhere,)
O if I am to have so much, let me have more!

A word then, (for I will conquer it,)   160
The word final, superior to all,
Subtle, sent up—what is it?—I listen;
Are you whispering it, and have been all the time, you sea-waves?
Is that it from your liquid rims and wet sands?

Whereto answering, the sea,   165
Delaying not, hurrying not,
Whisper'd me through the night, and very plainly before daybreak,
Lisp'd to me the low and delicious word death,
And again death, death, death, death,
Hissing melodious, neither like the bird nor like my arous'd child's heart,   170
But edging near as privately for me rustling at my feet,
Creeping thence steadily up to my ears and laving me softly all over,
Death, death, death, death, death.

Which I do not forget,
But fuse the song of my dusky demon and brother,   175
That he sang to me in the moonlight on Paumanok's gray beach,
With the thousand responsive songs at random,
My own songs awaked from that hour,
And with them the key, the word up from the waves,
The word of the sweetest song and all songs,   180
That strong and delicious word which, creeping to my feet,
(Or like some old crone rocking the cradle, swathed in sweet garments, bending
       aside,)
The sea whisper'd me.

                                 1859, 1881–1882

William **Butler Yeats** (1865–1939) was born in Dublin to moderately prosperous Protestant parents. His father was a lawyer turned artist. As a youth, Yeats spent his time between London, Dublin, and his mother's native county of Sligo. He eventually became the central figure in the Irish Literary Revival of the 1890s. He drew on Irish materials to build a foundation for his own work and to instill national pride in his fellow citizens. With Lady Gregory, he founded the Dublin Abbey Theatre, which he hoped would be the voice of modern Irish culture. While he was an accomplished writer of fiction, drama, literary criticism, essays, and autobiography, he was foremost a poet. He wrote poetry throughout his long life, but it is the work of his last twenty years that makes him one of the most important poets of the twentieth century. His poems are celebrated for their use of symbols and strong rhythms and the remarkable clarity of their imagery. Yeats won the Nobel Prize for Literature in 1923. "The Lake Isle of Innisfree" was published in 1892.

The Lake Isle of Innisfree

William Butler Yeats

I will arise and go now, and go to Innisfree,
And a small cabin build there, of clay and wattles made:
Nine bean-rows will I have there, a hive for the honey-bee,
And live alone in the bee-loud glade.

And I shall have some peace there, for peace comes dropping slow,   5
Dropping from the veils of the morning to where the cricket sings;
There midnight's all a glimmer, and noon a purple glow,
And evening full of the linnet's wings.

I will arise and go now, for always night and day
I hear lake water lapping with low sounds by the shore;   10
While I stand on the roadway, or on the pavements gray,
I hear it in the deep heart's core.

Questions for Discussion, Reflection, and Writing
1. Do you think "Innisfree" exists? In what sense?
2. What does Innisfree signify to the poet? To the reader?
§. Connect the readings: Compare Innisfree as a "refuge" to the imagined refuge presented in Wylie's "Wild Peaches."

Unit 4: Reading & Writing About Drama

CHAPTER 5

Writing about Drama

" *A*ll the world's a stage," wrote Shakespeare, and on that stage we witness the joys and sorrows, the tragedy and comedy, the reality and romance of life. While one traditional purpose of drama is to "suspend your sense of disbelief" so that you can respond emotionally to what you experience, thinking about and describing drama gives you a far deeper understanding of it. Learning about tragedy, comedy, tragicomedy, melodrama, and other types of plays will help you understand the conventions of dramatic literature and playwriting, and through this process, help you to not only experience the world of the play, but aid you in understanding *why* you experience it the way you do.

THE ELEMENTS OF DRAMA

Tragedy and comedy are the best-known categories of dramatic writing perhaps because they were the first to be defined, and have a long, if somewhat erratic, tradition. Aristotle, in his *Poetics*, describes and defines the nature of tragedy, albeit his view was limited because he based it upon tragedy written during the "golden age" of Greek drama, and obviously could not foretell the evolution of the drama through the millennia to follow. But the prolific writings of Aeschylus, Sophocles, and Euripides—the three Greek tragedians whose plays remain extant—provided Aristotle with enough samples to devise a theory of tragic form. For Aristotle, tragedy focused on a hero (male or female) of noble birth, who, through a misdeed or *hamartia*, underwent a decline in stature that led to tragic consequences whether in the realm of material prosperity, physical well-being, or moral rectitude, or a combination of these, as in the case of *Oedipus Rex*. Even the titles of many Greek tragedies are the royal personages upon which the plays focus, such as *Antigone*, *Electra*, and *Agamemnon*.

The development and subsequent action of true tragedy usually derives from one or more of three possible modes of conflict: an internal conflict that the protagonist, or main character, must resolve within himself or herself; a

Chapter 5   Writing about Drama **61**

conflict between a protagonist and an outside antagonist; or one between the protagonist and the society-at-large. Although the play *A Raisin in the Sun* by Lorraine Hansberry might not be classified as a classic tragedy, it embodies all those conflicts that make tragedy possible. Walter Younger is confronted by several simultaneous conflicts. He is at odds with his family who have different ideas concerning how to spend his father's life insurance benefits. He is in conflict with society-at-large in the guise of Mr. Linder, who offers to buy back the home in a white neighborhood that the Younger family has just purchased, rather than allow the African-American family to move in. Finally, he must do battle with his own sense of righteousness and justice, whether to accept the offer that will leave him with enough money to open his liquor store, and tacitly accept the racist motivation behind it; or keep the newly purchased house, and struggle to make a decent life for his family. Most drama that has been acknowledged through history as the finest examples of the playwright's art (such plays as *A Doll's House, Oedipus,* and *Death of a Salesman,* as well as most of the works of Shakespeare) interweave these three elements of conflict.

On the stage today, we rarely see a contemporary tragedy that rigidly conforms to the genre as it was first defined by Aristotle. First of all, few of us truly would be shocked by flaws in so-called great personages, as we have come to consider even the loftiest world leaders as human and subject to the same weaknesses as the rest of us. Tabloids are filled with sordid tales of great men and women and we have grown to take them for granted. Second, playwrights, beginning in the nineteenth century, have broadened their perspective to focus attention on the conflicts and actions of the lower and middle classes, not just the mighty and powerful. One might call this the democratization of tragedy, and this inclination has followed the same trends that have occurred in other art forms, for example, painting, poetry, architecture, and so on. Take for example the very name of the main protagonist in Arthur Miller's *Death of a Salesman*—where "Low-man" suggests his humble status.

Coinciding with the reduction in the stature of characters in tragedy has come a hybrid form that has come to be known as tragicomedy, that is, works of drama that combine the tragic and comic together. *A Raisin in the Sun* combines elements of both tragic and comic form as do David Hwang's *Family Devotions* and Susan Glaspell's *Suppressed Desires*. While these plays address issues such as intergenerational and intercultural conflict, rancor, jealousy, even murder, the playwrights have managed to inject moments of humor that add dimension to human experience.

We do not have a comprehensive theory of comedy from Aristotle (although he planned to write one), but we do have many early extant Greek comedies by the playwright Aristophanes who poked fun at Greek mores, politics, and society. Perhaps his most famous play is *Lysistrata*, which satirizes the absurdity of war as well as the "war between the sexes." Today, political satire is alive and well in film and television, and as you probably know, is a major subject for contemporary stand-up comedians.

The two Roman comic writers whose works are extant are Terence and Plautus. They helped to initiate the type of theater we know as comedy. Influenced by the Greeks, Plautus' plays satirized Roman life, using such devices as bungling behavior, reversals of expectations, and mistaken identity to keep his audience laughing. His most famous play, *The Menaechmi Twins,* was the inspiration for Shakespeare's first play, *The Comedy of Errors.* And today we still see the influence of Roman comedy in such forms as farce and slapstick in the theater and situation comedies on TV. Terence's comedies, on the other hand, did not go for the broad laugh, and just as is true among today's audiences, his more subtle comedies and humanistic themes were not as popular as Plautus', whose work inspired more belly laughs.

Melodrama is a type of drama which, although derived from tragedy, stands apart from it because the conflicts that the characters must confront are contrived or merely clever and the characters are usually less fleshed out than three-dimensional dramatic characters, and they seem to resolve their conflicts in interesting, yet concocted ways. While melodrama is not found as much on the stage today as it was in the nineteenth century, the form is alive and well in many contemporary action-adventure movies like the *Indiana Jones* films and *Romancing the Stone,* where men and women are saved from disaster in the nick of time, much as they are in the old cliché of the damsel in distress who is tied to a railroad track as a speeding train approaches, only to be whisked away at the last moment by a valiant hero.

With the proliferation of drama portraying the common person, many audience members have become accustomed to associating plays with realistic portraits of life and with rather conventional ways of depicting such portraits, as though the theater were a place to see a mirror or reproduction of real life. This couldn't be further from the truth, however. Many so-called schools and movements of drama have depicted life in unrealistic manners. Playwrights such as Eugene Ionesco and Samuel Beckett portray a world that is quite unlike the one with which we are familiar. Plays representing life with an unreal quality include depictions of life as romantic as in Lady Gregory's *The Rising of the Moon;* or absurd as in Samuel Beckett's *Krapp's Last Tape;* or magical as in Langston Hughes' *Soul Gone Home.* Even the contemporary classic *Death of a Salesman* has many scenes of unreality, when, for example, Willie's brother seems to magically appear on stage much in the same way as the ghost appears in *Hamlet.*

Plot

As in fiction, plot is essential to nearly all drama, in fact, possibly more so than to other forms of literature. Plot is a skeleton of the action in a play. It is what happens to characters under the circumstances the playwright has devised. One reason plot is so important in drama is that since plays are meant to be performed and seen, an audience will have little tolerance for pauses in the action. In fiction, on the other hand, action may be interwoven with physical description or characters' thoughts. In drama, what you see is what you get, so to speak. And it is the playwright, in his or her division of acts and scenes, who will determine the pauses in the action, whereas a reader is free to stop and start reading where he or she pleases.

To keep the plot of a drama interesting to its audience, most playwrights try to maintain a heightened level of action through the development of conflicts and obstacles that occur far more readily and densely than they do in real life. It is through such conflict that the plot moves forward. And the greater the stakes involved in these conflicts, the more riveting the play will be and the more you will care about how the conflict is resolved. Take for example an early scene in *A Doll's House* by Henrik Ibsen. Nora, the protagonist, is having a discussion with Krogstad, a man from whom she borrowed money to keep her family intact during a stressful and tenuous period. Krogstad, a bank clerk, fearing that he will be passed by for a promotion by his superior, Helmer (Nora's husband), threatens to blackmail Nora by revealing that she borrowed money from him without her husband's knowledge.

KROGSTAD: . . . My sons are growing up; for their sake, I must try to regain what respectability I can. This job in the bank was the first step on the ladder. And now your husband wants to kick me off that ladder into the dirt.
NORA: But my dear Mr. Krogstad, it simply isn't in my power to help you.
KROGSTAD: You say that because you don't want to help me. But I have the means to make you.
NORA: You don't mean you'd tell my husband that I owe you money?
KROGSTAD: And if I did?
NORA: That' be a filthy trick!

Nora counters that her husband will merely pay back the money that is owed, which would at first glance seem to defuse Krogstad's threat. But Krogstad retaliates and increases the stakes and the conflict by dangling a damaging secret about Nora's loan before her. Several lines later, the following exchange occurs:

KROGSTAD: I promised to get you the money in exchange for an I.O.U., which I drew up.
NORA: Yes, and which I signed.
KROGSTAD: Exactly. But then I added a few lines naming your father as security for the debt. This paragraph was to be signed by your father.
NORA: Was to be? He did sign it.

• • •

KROGSTAD: Tell me, Mrs. Helmer, do you by any chance remember the date of your father's death? The day of the month, I mean.
NORA: Papa died on the twenty-ninth of September.
KROGSTAD: Quite correct; I took the trouble to confirm it. And that leaves me with a curious little problem—[*Takes a paper.*] which I simply cannot solve.
NORA: Problem? I don't see—
KROGSTAD: The problem, Mrs. Helmer, is that your father signed this paper three days after his death.

This building and relaxing and building again of tension is what moves the action of the play forward, giving shape to the plot.

64   Part 2   The Elements of Literature

While the building up of tension in this example is fairly clear, what seems to be mere conversation in a play often contains the seeds of conflict that will have an impact on the later action. This is particularly true of more contemporary plays that portray human action in subtler terms. Take for example one of the many conflicts that beset the Younger family in *A Raisin in the Sun*—the conflict between Walter's ambitions and the caution of his wife, Ruth. It is evident even in this bit of morning banter from Act I:

WALTER: You know what I was thinking 'bout in the bathroom this morning?
RUTH: No!
WALTER: How come you always try to be so pleasant?
RUTH: What is there to be pleasant 'bout?
WALTER: You want to know what I was thinking 'bout in the bathroom or not?
RUTH: I know what you thinking 'bout.
WALTER: 'Bout what me and Willy Harris was talking about last night.
RUTH: Willy Harris is a good-for-nothing loudmouth.

We eventually learn that Willy Harris is involving Walter in a scheme to open up a liquor store, and this has a dramatic impact on Walter's actions during the play, initiating a complex series of conflicts between himself and other members of his family.

While plays rely on rising action that is a result of tensions that in turn are caused by a conflict or a series of conflicts, this conflict must somehow be resolved or at least relieved in the end. It is unlikely that you would feel satisfied with a plot that left a major conflict unresolved. As in most plays, the climax to the rising action in *A Raisin in the Sun* occurs near its end. In this poignant scene, Walter's internal and external conflicts are resolved in a showdown with Mr. Linder when the latter pays his final visit to purchase back a house the Younger family has bought in a white neighborhood:

WALTER: Yeah, Well—what I mean is that we come from people who had a lot of *pride.* I mean—we are very proud people. And that's my sister over there and she's going to be a doctor—and we are very proud—
LINDER: Well—I am sure that is very nice, but—
WALTER: What I am telling you is that we called you over here to tell you that we are very proud and that this—Travis, come here. This is my son, and he makes the sixth generation our family in this country. And we have all thought about your offer—
LINDER: Well, good . . . good—
WALTER: And we have decided to move into our house because my father— my father—he earned it for us brick by brick. We don't want to make no trouble for nobody or fight no causes, and we will try to be good neighbors. And that's *all* we got to say about that. We don't want your money.

The Younger family's conflict now resolved, the play ends with them bantering happily about their move, their spirits uplifted. As you read a play, keep in mind the importance of plot and make notes on how the plot develops. To learn more about plot, you may also want to predict how the plot unfolds, and compare your idea with that of the author's.

Character

Aristotle suggested and playwrights in general follow the rule of thumb that "character is action." Another way of thinking about character is to envision him or her as determined by the choices he or she makes. Take the character of Iago from *Othello*. In the character list he is described as "IAGO, Othello's ensign, a villain." This does not tell us very much. However, in the first scene of *Othello*, we soon find out what kind of person he is. Othello, it appears, has passed over Iago for promotion to lieutenant. Iago is enraged, for—as far as he is concerned—he has the greater experience in matters of war than the candidate Othello has demonstrated. He states his feelings to Roderigo this way:

> Preferment goes by letter and affection,
> And not by old graduation, where each second
> Stood heir to th' first. Now, sir, be judge yourself,
> Whether I in any just term am affined
> To love the Moor.

During the course of the play, Iago's character is revealed as he methodically torments Othello until the latter thinks Desdemona, his wife, has been unfaithful, resulting in the demise of both Othello and his wife. While most of us would like to take revenge upon a seemingly unfair boss, few of us would act upon it as Iago does. Understanding the traits that make character interesting is what allowed Shakespeare to appeal to an audience that was made up of all social classes. So, despite the fact that Shakespeare is renowned for the quality of his language, it is his talent for developing character that makes him a good playwright.

This focus on the relationship between action and character should not give you the impression that a three-dimensional character is fully developed through his or her actions alone or that it is easy to develop a dramatic character. For a character to behave plausibly throughout a play, the playwright must have a strong sense of who that character is, how the character looks, sounds, dresses, thinks, reacts, and so on. Henrik Ibsen, one of the fathers of modern drama (perhaps because of his ability to create such well-motivated characters) said this about the people who inhabited his plays:

> Before I write down one word, I have to have the character in mind through and through, and I must penetrate into the last part of his soul—the individual comes before anything else—the stage set, etc. . . . .

The most interesting characters in drama tend to be complex ones, and their actions although seemingly truthful may not necessarily be anticipated ones. Who would think that the Sergeant in Lady Gregory's *The Rising of the Moon* would let the fugitive go or that Othello would kill his wife or that Willy Loman, despite his pathetic nature, would kill himself so his family could be sustained by his insurance money, or that Oedipus would blind himself? All these actions are credible, but unexpected. In writing about character, ask yourself questions. Most likely they are the same sorts of questions the playwright asked as he or she planned to write. Who is this character? What are the given circumstances of time, place, social class, and situation that he or she must respond to? How does he or she respond?

Not all characters in plays are so fully developed that you will feel you know all about them. Many plays are populated by characters who enter the stage for a small portion of the play. These are often called "secondary characters." But a talented playwright will have even secondary characters. For example, Sylvester, Ma Rainey's nephew in August Wilson's *Ma Rainey's Black Bottom,* is fleshed out, interesting, and a contributing factor in the action of the play, having been endowed with a puerile personality and a noticeable stutter.

Setting

Unlike the movies, where you may be transported from New York to California to Tokyo in the blink of an eye, the settings in plays remain rather static throughout the action, changing perhaps between acts, if at all. And also unlike movies, which can actually show us all the minutiae of life by directly filming it, settings in drama often only suggest the places they depict, or, if it is in the playwright's vision, even distort them. Still other playwrights may not consider setting important at all, and their plays are often devoid of any description as to how the stage should be depicted, leaving it up to you, the reader or playgoer, to fill in the gaps with your imagination.

Besides revealing time and place through props (furniture, everyday objects, and costuming), setting can also exploit stage lighting and special effects such as rear-projected film and sound effects to enhance the mood of a play. Dim lighting might suggest a depressing atmosphere; bright lights, an upbeat one. Advances in theatrical technology have expanded the possibilities of establishing setting, as they have our expectations of how setting is depicted. The Greeks relied upon the simplest of means to suggest time and place—for example, a vertical rectangular box that was painted with a tree on one side, an architectural column on the other (which would be turned according to whether the scene was set in the city or the countryside). Contemporary playwrights, on the other hand, have often called for fairly elaborate staging so that the audience actually sees a fair representation of the place it is meant to depict. In the end, however, the complexity or lack thereof of a setting is usually up to the vision of the playwright. Notice, for example, the opening setting from the contemporary playwright David Hwang's *Family Devotions.*

> The sunroom and backyard of a home in Bel Air. Everywhere is glass—glass roof, glass walls. Upstage of the lanai/sunroom is a patio with a barbecue and a tennis court. The tennis court leads offstage. As the curtain rises, we see a single spotlight on an old Chinese face and hear Chinese music or chanting. Suddenly, the music becomes modern-day funk or rock 'n' roll, and the lights

come up to reveal the set. The face is that of DI-GOU, an older Chinese man wearing a blue suit and carrying an old suitcase. He is peering into the sunroom from the tennis court, through the glass walls. Behind him, a stream of black smoke is coming from the barbecue.

Another function of setting that may perform an important role in the life of a play is its ability to suggest the mood of the environment and/or reveal aspects of the character's or characters' interior emotions. Note Lorraine Hansberry's use of personification in her description of the Younger household at the start of *A Raisin in the Sun*, a description that provides you with an insight into the emotional tenor of the occupants.

> Its furnishings are typical and undistinguished and their primary feature now is that they have clearly had to accommodate the living of too many people for too many years—and they are tired. . . . Now the once loved pattern of the couch upholstery has *to fight to show itself* from under acres of crocheted doilies and couch covers . . . but the *carpet has fought back by showing its weariness*, with depressing uniformity, elsewhere on its surface.

Thus, the setting mirrors the Younger family's life circumstances and their interior lives as well, and at the same time provides an introduction to the play that may rivet your attention and make you want to read more.

The description of setting that introduces Arthur Miller's *Death of a Salesman* produces a similar effect in providing an analogy between Willy's home and its environs and Willy's state of mind in relationship to *his* environment. It is interesting to note that Miller's original title for the play was "The Inside of His Head."

> We are aware of towering, angular shapes behind it, surrounding it on all sides. Only the blue light of the sky falls upon the house and forestage; the surrounding area shows an angry glow of orange. As more light appears, we see a solid vault of apartment houses around the small, fragile-seeming home. An air of the dream clings to the place, a dream rising out of reality.

Staging

Plays are meant to be performed and for audiences to view the performances. If you've ever read a play and then gone to see it performed, you probably became aware of the difference between the two experiences. Seeing a performance of a play is what makes it complete. While you can ascertain certain things from reading plays that you would be hard pressed to do from a performance, for example, arcane references in the dialogue, subtleties of style, camouflaged symbols and the like, being present at a performance of a play adds a dimension to your understanding and appreciation of drama that is impossible from reading.

In staging a play, the theater artist has to consider such elements as casting, makeup, costume, the arrangement and movement of the actors on the stage (referred to as blocking), physical and vocal pacing, vocal qualities—in fact, nearly anything that contributes to communicating the world of the play to the mind of the audience member. While nothing can substitute for seeing a live performance, one way to envision what a play would be like performed when you read it is to imagine how you would see it at a performance. For example, how do you imagine Nora to look in *A Doll's House?* How does Othello or Oedipus carry himself? Is the former tall, short; does he possess a serious demeanor? How is the latter dressed? Oedipus is supposed to have a misshapen foot. How do you imagine him to walk? What sorts of facial and body expressions do the musicians carry in *Ma Rainey's Black Bottom?* Do they appear angry, resigned, frustrated, etc.? It is important for you to consider that while a play in manuscript form is made up of words on a page, the stage is a physical and visual space that must be filled and kept interesting through props, costume, movement, activity, vocal character, lighting, and sound.

Dialogue

When you read a play, particularly a contemporary one like *A Raisin in the Sun* or *Ma Rainey's Black Bottom,* chances are you find the dialogue similar to everyday speech, which is casual, colloquial, and conversational. If so, the playwright is doing a good job at giving you the *illusion* that dialogue is like the daily conversations each of us has. Actually, good dialogue is distilled speech and is structured so that it consistently contributes to the creation or resolution of conflict, moving the action of the play forward, or enlightening us about character. What might appear to you as mere transposition of speech from a tape recorder to the page is actually a craft that requires a keen sense of language and its rhythms. A playwright may very well write and rewrite a play many times until he or she gets it right. One playwright, in a humorous mood, once offered a $10,000 reward for anyone who could show him a tape recorder that recorded dramatic dialogue from real life.

Read the following dialogue from *The Rising of the Moon* by Lady Gregory, and consider how it contributes to the drama:

POLICEMAN B: I think this would be a good place to put up a notice. [*He points to barrel.*]

POLICEMAN X: Better ask him. [*Calls to* SERGEANT.] Will this be a good place for a placard?

[*No answer.*]

POLICEMAN B: Will we put up a notice here on the barrel?

[*No answer.*]

SERGEANT: There's a flight of steps here that leads to the water. This is a place that should be minded well. If he got down there, his friends might have a boat to meet him; they might send it in here from outside.

POLICEMAN B: Would the barrel be a good place to put a notice up?

SERGEANT: It might; you can put it there.

[*They pass the notice up.*]

SERGEANT: [*Reading it.*] Dark hair—dark eyes, smooth face, height five feet five—there's not much to take hold of in that—It's a pity I had no chance of seeing him before he broke out of gaol. They say he's a wonder, that it's he makes all the plans for the whole organization. There isn't another man in Ireland would have broken gaol the way he did. He must have some friends among the gaolers.

POLICEMAN B: A hundred pounds is little enough for the Government to offer for him. You may be sure any man in the force that takes him will get promotion.

SERGEANT: I'll mind this place myself. I wouldn't wonder at all if he came this way.

In only a few sentences, this dialogue establishes a number of important dramatic issues. It establishes the locale. It provides us an understanding of the characters' motivations for their actions. It sets up the mood since the police reveal through their observations that they are in a strange part of the city, making their actions tentative. Their subordinate relationship to the sergeant, their supervisor, is established. Note too that there are pauses in the dialogue when the two police call and the sergeant does not respond. What do you think is implied by the fact that the sergeant does not respond? How do the pauses contribute to the mood? Anton Chekhov, the great Russian playwright, used pauses in the dialogue to great psychological effect, as did the modern playwright Samuel Beckett, notably in *Krapp's Last Tape.*

Another function of a play's dialogue is exposition, which refers to the explanation or description of action, events, or people that are not revealed to us directly. So, for example, without even directly showing the fugitive the police are seeking in *The Rising of the Moon,* Lady Gregory, the playwright, informs us what he looks like when the sergeant reads the "wanted" poster. We also learn—without seeing—the fact that the water is close, providing a likely means for escape. What other things does exposition in the dialogue tell you? Unlike short stories and novels, where the narrator can describe events that have happened in the past or make you privy to the thoughts of a character, plays have only dialogue to serve these functions. A good playwright will interweave exposition into what is being said without your being aware of it. One exercise you might try to gain a better sense of the playwright's art is to study the way he or she employs exposition.

As stated before, dialogue is not merely recorded speech, yet critics often speak of a playwright as "having an ear" for dialogue. This usually means that the author seems to have a talent for imitating the tone, the rhythms of speech, and the regional and/or class dialects of the people he is portraying. Thus, while Cutler, Toledo, Slow Drag, and Levee are characters in a play, August Wilson's talent for rendering regional accents, dialect, and slang allows skilled actors to take what these characters say on the page and make it come alive, giving you the impression of real people.

Theme

Theme is as slippery a topic in talking about drama as it is for any genre of literature. For it asks the questions, "What does the play mean?" or "What is the author trying to say?" Understanding the theme or themes of a play seen on a stage may be even more difficult than deciphering the meaning of other forms of literature, since often you will be emotionally carried along by the action, whereas in a novel or short story, you can always pause and consider the significance of what you have read. Although there is no hard and fast rule, it is perhaps in understanding theme that *reading* a play may have an advantage over *seeing* a play.

Sometimes the title of a play can offer a clue to its theme, as do the titles *A Doll's House, A Raisin in the Sun,* and *The Rising of the Moon.* (Note too that the latter two titles have images that have been traditionally used as symbols.) The phrase "a raisin in the sun" is from a poem by Langston Hughes that deplores the betrayal of the promise to provide African Americans with equal rights; the phrase "rising of the moon" suggests an awakening of what is often repressed or suppressed from consciousness, the moon being a symbol in many cultures of the hidden aspect of human nature.

In Hansberry's play, you will find enacted among the characters the fight to achieve racial justice and the outcome of this fight for one family. In Lady Gregory's play, you find the Sergeant's attitude transform from one of an officious civil servant to a humane individual who gets in touch with his early roots and values. Thus *The Rising of the Moon* can be taken to be a statement about the suppression of the Irish independence movement as symbolized through the encounter between the Sergeant and the Ragged Man. The term "doll" as used in doll's house has meanings that go beyond the literal meaning of a child's plaything. In Ibsen's play, Nora seems to be treated as a doll by her husband, and her rebellion at the end is her escape from this unflattering and demeaning role.

Titles aside, themes in plays can be inferred through the study of other images, actions, and statements, particularly when they recur. When you read a play, be aware of such repetitions, and see if there seems to be a common thread that stitches them together. By this method you may be able to interpret motifs in what you read or see to more general or universal pronouncements about the human condition. Critics have noted the importance of Lena Younger's (Mama) plants in *A Raisin in the Sun* and interpret them as symbols for the determined survival of the Younger family. Other critics make much of the tape recorder in *Krapp's Last Tape,* suggesting that it represents the human experience, which is merely a playing out of what has already been recorded by consciousness, providing the dim view that humans have little say in determining their destinies.

To appreciate the full dimension of what you read, and to find hooks that can provide topics for discussion or writing, look for recurring motifs and character transformations in plays. These will more than likely lead you to discovering a play's theme.

INTERPRETING DRAMA

Interpreting plays, like interpreting other works of literature, is an elusive task. You, like your classmates, and readers in general, come to the specific work with your own background, prejudices, viewpoints, and attitudes. In addition, the time you live in, the place you live in, your cultural heritage: all have an impact on the meaning you extract from literature. To give just one superficial example, a salesman, after seeing a performance of Arthur Miller's play *Death of a Salesman,* is reported to have said to his wife, "I always said the Northeast was a lousy sales territory." Whether his pragmatic response to the play was of the sort Miller wanted audience members to have is doubtful; yet, there are *many* possible valid interpretations of a play, not *the* one true interpretation.

Dramatic literature, perhaps more than other forms of literature, should make this indeterminate aspect of interpretation evident, since most plays are meant to be performed. Thus, even the performance of a play will alter the play's import, being influenced by the director's and actors' visions. Another aspect of plays which makes interpretation problematic is the fact that most plays that have lasting appeal are complex works of art, just as is the case with other forms of literature. Therefore, to tease out the meaning from what you read is not as simple as finding the right answer on a multiple choice test. It is rather like deciphering a secret code or putting together the pieces of a puzzle.

Since it is probably impossible to actually *prove* that your interpretation is the right one, it is better to think of interpretation as an argument, that is, as a statement that you will try to back up with evidence from what you have read or seen. And since plays that stand the test of time tend to be complex, it is perhaps better to develop an argument that addresses one aspect of a play rather than the entire play itself. Another reason for limiting your interpretation of a play is that if you select too broad an interpretation, it may be difficult to include all that you need to support your interpretation in a college-length paper. For example, consider the following interpretation of Miller's *Death of a Salesman:* "*Death of a Salesman* shows the tragic consequences of taking at face value the traditional concepts of 'the American dream' without questioning or considering their merits." While this interpretation is valid, it would be nearly impossible to discuss all the pertinent evidence that exists in the play that supports this theme, since the play is replete with images, dialogue, description, and relationships that advance it.

In reading a play carefully, try to find particular speeches, images, symbols, or statements that present a means of interpreting a particular aspect of the play. For example, character is one aspect of a play that deserves special attention, and to which interpretation can bring fruitful results. You may wish to select a character that interests you, intrigues you, or seems to possess a special quality that may be overlooked by a superficial reading of the play. Take for example one student who read August Wilson's play *Ma Rainey's Black Bottom.* Intrigued by the character of Toledo, he reread the text focusing on Toledo's relationships with the other band members, his philosophical statements and observations, and his action during the course of the play. He was particularly intrigued by a speech of his early in Act I:

TOLEDO: See, now . . . I'll tell you something. As long as the colored man look to white folks to put the crown on what he say . . . as long as he looks to white folks for approval . . . then he ain't never gonna find out who he is and what he's about. He's just gonna be about what white folks want him to be about. That's one sure thing.

Reviewing the play, the student then highlighted Toledo's dialogue and found a pattern that seemed to bear out the idea that Toledo was revealing certain truths about the African American's dilemma in America, and that in a sense he becomes a martyr whose truth cannot be accepted by the other members of the band, and thus is killed in the end for his beliefs.

EVALUATING DRAMA

You may interpret the meaning of a play, the significance of a character, the function of setting, and the like, without ever engaging in probably the most common form of writing about drama: evaluating. Theater critics, whether writing for newspapers like *The New York Times,* magazines like *Newsweek,* television news shows, or radio primarily engage in evaluation. That is, while they may describe and summarize a play, their ultimate purpose is to relate to their audiences the quality of the play, whether it is a masterpiece, a terrible travesty of dramatic art, or something in between.

When you evaluate a play, you may not reach a large audience, but you will, at the least, help hone your own critical abilities, and develop for yourself a sense of what makes or does not make for good dramatic literature. Ultimately, evaluation is a subjective affair, but there are certain guidelines that can help you appreciate the quality of a play, whether or not you agree with its message.

The first thing you might do is ask yourself a series of questions that can guide you into understanding why you like or dislike a play. If it moves you emotionally, why? If you identify with the characters, which ones, and why? Even if the world of the play is foreign to you, that is, takes place at another time, in another culture, or among a class of people you are unfamiliar with, ask yourself whether you find any similarities between the world of the characters and the world you yourself have experienced or could imaginatively experience.

Once you've established your own relationship to the play, you have a base from which you may use more abstract criteria in your evaluation. Earlier in this chapter, continuous *action* was described as being an essential part of most drama. Does the action in the play you have read seem coherent and unified? Most students of literature find coherence and unity important characteristics in determining the quality of a work of literature. If a character acts in a way that seems foreign or implausible to his or her nature, the chances are that the playwright has not fleshed out his conception of just who the character is.

Since plays are nearly all dialogue, one important aspect of evaluating a play is the extent to which the dialogue sounds true. Do the characters speak as if they were real people? Can you distinguish their class, culture, age, and personality from the way they speak? Does the dialogue seem to imitate the rhythms of speech? If the answers to these questions are in the negative, they may have a bearing on the quality of the play.

Universality of appeal is another criterion upon which to evaluate a play. Why is it that plays written over 2,000 years ago—for example, *Oedipus Rex* or *Lysistrata*—are still read and performed today? More than likely it is because the issues that these plays raise are still of concern to contemporary audiences. Or take for example plays that seem to cross cultures successfully. *Death of a Salesman* was translated into Chinese and successfully performed in China, a country that does not even have the profession of salesman. Still, audiences found the play pertinent to their lives. Other issues to consider are whether the play presents its world in an interesting, complex, and original fashion. Most people would agree that the world is a complex place with multidimensional challenges. If a play reflects this world, it could hardly do so by being simplistic. Thus, in evaluating a play, another issue to consider is whether the world it depicts addresses the complexity of life. If it lacks this dimension, chances are the play will fade quickly away in your mind, whereas a play replete with ideas will be one you can turn to again and again, only to discover more intriguing issues about its characters, meaning, and significance.

Nonetheless, two individuals using all these criteria can come to radically different evaluations about a play, as the following excerpts from reviews of two well-known drama critics reveal. Both were responses to a Lorraine Hansberry (author of *A Raisin in the Sun*) play entitled *Les Blancs*. The first is by John Simon writing in *New York Magazine:*

> . . . The result is unmitigated disaster. *Les Blancs* (the very French title in what is clearly a British African colony testifies to the utter confusion) is not only the worst new play on Broadway, of an amateurishness and crudity unrelieved by its sophomoric stabs at wit, it is also, more detestably, a play finished—or finished off—by white liberals that does its utmost to justify the slaughter of whites by blacks. . . . It is a malodorous, unenlightening mess.

The second is by Walter Kerr, writing for *The New York Times:*

> I urge you to see Lorraine Hansberry's . . . ranging, quick-witted, ruefully savage examination of the state of the African mind today. . . . Virtually all of *Les Blancs* is there on the stage, vivid, stinging, intellectually alive, and what is there is mature work, ready to stand without apology alongside the completed work of our best craftsmen. The language in particular is so unmistakably stage language that . . . it achieves an internal pressure, a demand that you listen to it, that is quite rare on our stages today.

If professional critics can differ so radically in their evaluation of a play, you should rely on your own taste, informed by your growing knowledge of fiction, poetry, and drama, when judging any work of literature.

Ishmael Reed (b. 1938) writes essays, criticism, poetry, songs, and novels, in addition to plays. His latest book, *Blues City: A Walk in Oakland* (2003), is a collection of essays. Reed is also the editor of two magazines, *Konch* and *Vines*; the latter is written by college students. Among many other awards and honors, Reed has won a MacArthur ("genius") Fellowship. Reed has taught at Harvard and Yale, and has been a fixture in UC Berkeley's English Department since 1968. *The C Above C Above High C* premiered at the Nuyorican Poets Café in lower Manhattan in April 1997 and was first published in *The Antioch Review* in the summer of 1999.

The C Above C Above High C

Ishmael Reed

ACT ONE

Scene 1

Dressing room of Louis Armstrong. Photos of Armstrong on the mirror. A table with bottles of mineral water, etc. Off-stage, we hear the final strains of Louis Armstrong singing, playing a **high C** *tune followed by applause. Shortly Armstrong enters. He is dressed in a tuxedo and carries his trumpet covered by a handkerchief. He is sweating, grinning fiercely, but then changes to a serious look. Removes his tuxedo jacket and drapes it over a chair, facing the mirror. Sits down. Looks into the mirror. He begins to slowly dab cream on his face and doesn't stop until his face is white.*

ARMSTRONG: It's gettin' harder and harder to get control of this grin.   1

Makes several types of grins.

One day it's going to leave and take off to the next gig. One day I won't be able to turn it off and turn it on so easily.

Removes his black tie, shirt. Wears an undershirt and puts on his stocking cap. Studies his face in the mirror. Rubs his jaw, etc. Turns grin on and off.

My face doesn't belong to me anymore. The public sees one face. The record companies see another. My Lucille doesn't even see me, and my agent only sees money.

Joe Glaser's assistant enters—Gloria, a black woman of about forty, smartly dressed and groomed.

GLORIA: We did it tonight, Pops. The place was packed. People could hardly   2
get in.

Counting money.

Wait till Mr. Glaser sees all of this green. He will be so pleased.
ARMSTRONG: (*Down*) Good.   3
GLORIA: What's wrong? You don't seem all that excited.   4

Armstrong continues to apply cream to his face.

ARMSTRONG: These little school children in Little Rock are gettin' bricks thrown   5
at them. Just for trying to go to school. That little girl, Elizabeth, was attacked by that
mob of hyenas. (*Slide*) These kids are being spat upon. And the only thing on my
mind is whether I can hit a higher **C** on my trumpet than before.

Gloria approaches him and places her hands on his shoulders. Massages them.

GLORIA: You're doing your part, Pops. You're loved by millions of people. Both   6
the white and the coloreds buy your music.

ARMSTRONG: But the Beboppers are calling me an Uncle Tom.   7

*They freeze. Bebopper in spotlight. Has a goatee, wears a beret, dark glasses. A fast, scratchy
Fats Navarro piece is on the soundtrack. The bopper begins to move his feet around in a bop
dance. Music stops.*

BOPPER: (*Arrogant, jive*) That old Uncle Tom shit that Louis Armstrong plays   8
is embarrassing. The man has no velocity. He doesn't know about chord changes. He
can't give you the theory upon which his music is based. All the dude is doing is playing blackface orphan home march music. That's where that hokey tuba sound comes
from. And the banjo. An anachronism. A quaint remnant of plantation life. Only
squares listen to Pops now. We're all listening to Prez, Bird, and Monk. He can't stand
it. He can't challenge us so he calls us names. Like in that whippoorwill song. He
greets the world with a watermelon grin.

Mocks Armstrong's grin. He goes dark.

ARMSTRONG: Maybe they're right.   9

GLORIA: Don't listen to them, Pops. They don't get half the audiences or the   10
money that you get. A lot of them are crazy too, or, at least idiosyncratic. What's that
one they call Thelonious Monk? One strange Negro. Act like he on something. And
that evil little black one named Dewey Davis. He turns his back on the audience and
goes around beating up people.

ARMSTRONG: (*Grinning*) I'm not that kind of person. I see my mission as bring-   11
ing people together. The black and white. The yellows and the browns. When I go
abroad, warring factions drop their weapons. They come to where I'm playing and
party together. This wonderful music that the Lord has given us—I want to spread it
around. People break into smiles when they hear my music. It washes out all of that
hate from their heart. You know, a lot of my fans are doctors. One of them said that
there are killer cells that attack the ones that are viral. He said that the music I
play kicks in the killer cells and these killer cells start fightin' them evil ones.
Something like that. He said that my music builds up the (*hesitantly*) immunity. He
said that I was a healer. Now take that Bebop. Ever go to a Bebop club? The first thing
you notice is that the people are unhappy. Nobody smiles. The musicians look scruffy,
bumified. They wear shiny pants and sometimes they don't even wear a tie. We all
keep our shoes shined and our creases starched. (*Slide*) A tradition that goes back
to old Jelly Roll. Well, anyway, the doctor says that the killer cells get confused when

they hear that music. They can't go to war against the enemy. That's why the fans and the musicians of Bebop look sickly. That's why they die young.

GLORIA: Lucille called while you were onstage. 12

ARMSTRONG: I'll call her. She must feel lonely stuck out in that house in Queens. 13
Do you think that I will have a chance to at least spend a weekend with her?

GLORIA: Exactly one weekend next month to spend with Lucille. After that you 14
take off for England. The Royal Family is asking for a command performance. Here
are the new contracts that just came in from Capitol Records. Mr. Glaser wants
you to sign in all of the places that I've checked off.

Armstrong sighs, then begins to sign.

ARMSTRONG: Why don't Glaser come down himself anymore? 15

Silence. Armstrong pauses, then speaks angrily. Answer me. Don't you hear me talking
to you, woman?

GLORIA: Louis. Something's happening to him. He says that he won't come within 16
ten feet of you.

ARMSTRONG: Why? 17

GLORIA: Says that white people who come near you turn black. Says he's seen 18
it happen.

ARMSTRONG: That Joe Glaser is losing his grip. That's the most ridiculous thing 19
I've heard. But then again, who knows. I often wonder why God made me so black
and blue. All of my life. Maybe being that makes me special. Maybe there is a mission for those whose skin is the color of the cosmos. Whose colors contain all colors.
Who better to unite the world? I read somewhere that most of the universe is composed of dark matter, yet they're always calling us a minority.

GLORIA: Louis, what are you talking about? Louis, have you been smokin' that 20
weed again?

ARMSTRONG: Smoking reefer helps me to get through another day in the United 21
States of America.

GLORIA: (*Sighs*) Look, I have to go. You and the group should meet me in the 22
morning at the airport. I have the tickets. (*She exits*)

ARMSTRONG: (*Takes a drag*) Reefer is mellow. It was a recreational drug for artists 23
in the 20s and 30s. But then, after the war, they brought that heroin. The gangsters
would give the best of the singers and musicians spots. We could have a gig, jam. But
then those heroin people came on the scene, people with no class and no taste took
over the clubs. There was heroin before, but then it was the Jews who sold it. Only
the rich could afford it. But then the Italians took over. They're the ones who introduced needles. They brought a cheaper variety into Harlem. It went over big with
these young Bebop musicians. Guys waking up in the alley with vomit all over their
clothes. Robbing their relatives and their best friends. Shitting blood. These Bop
musicians—if they ain't on the bandstand they're in the emergency room. And
that one they call Bird. He's a bad example for these youngsters. People think that
just because a person's a genius they should be given license to do whatever they
desire. What about that wicked genius, Hitler. These white critics are calling him

the Alto saxophone great. He should be called an Overdose Great. The Pied Piper of Death. New York Jazz is a big mistake. The players have left the melody. Have left the dance. What was that word the scholar who's writing about me said. Nihilism. New York Jazz is nihilistic.

Scene 2

*Bedroom of the Shoreham Hotel in downtown Washington. A king-sized bed. **Above** it hangs a portrait of George Washington. Dwight Eisenhower wakes up screaming. Sits up. He is wearing longjohns. The woman lying in bed is Kay Summersby. She is a middle-aged red-head and very handsome. She is wearing a fancy slip.*

SUMMERSBY: (*Irish brogue*) Ike, what's wrong? 24

EISENHOWER: I had a dream that it was the year 2000. That China had the world's 25 largest economy and that Africa was moving up. Maybe Douglas MacArthur was right. Maybe we should have nuked China.

She begins to hug Eisenhower's back.

SUMMERSBY: Ike, it was just a dream. Ike, last night was so lovely. I was always 26 amazed that a warrior like you could be so gentle in bed.

Ike kisses her hands. He gets out of bed and begins to change into a golf outfit. Golf bag is leaning against the wall.

And then toward the climax, the way you—you stormed my Normandy Beach riding the crests of my waves.

EISENHOWER: Would you like more champagne? 27

She holds out her glass. He pours. Then pours himself one. They toast.

To our love. May it always be as scintillating as champagne.

They drink. They stare into each other's eyes longingly, put down their glasses and kiss passionately.

SUMMERSBY: Remember the champagne we had after the German surrender? The 28 best champagne in Reims.

EISENHOWER: Afterwards we had that buffet supper at the Dorchester Hotel. 29 Then the theatre.

SUMMERSBY: That was the first time you'd eaten in a restaurant in three years. 30 You were mobbed. All of those well-wishers.

EISENHOWER: Yeah. The response of the people. It made all of the hell I had to go 31 through worth it. The quarrels with Montgomery and Patton. (*Slides*) The setbacks. And all of those youngsters killed.

He lights up a cigarette.

That's what always depressed me. Every time I had an opportunity, I'd visit the cemeteries. Pay my respects. You know. I was known as a general who was not only after victories but the welfare of my soldiers. That was always uppermost in my mind.

Video news report about American POWs abandoned by Eisenhower administration.

SUMMERSBY: It had to be done, Ike. Just think how the world would be under   32
Hitler, that—that racist. The presidency must be boring next to being the Allies'
Supreme Commander.

EISENHOWER: I ran because I thought I could do some good. It's not as demand-   33
ing as leading the Allies. I have a good staff. Things are run smoothly. Except

SUMMERSBY: Except what, Ike?   34

EISENHOWER: The Negroes. They want to go to school with white kids. The   35
southerners are good people. (*Slide*) They don't want their children going to school
with some big overgrown Negroes.

She recoils. Black woman appears. Could be the same one who plays Gloria.

WOMAN: When I was a little girl, my mother and I saw a lynch mob dragging the   36
body of a Negro man through the streets of Little Rock, Arkansas. We were told to
get off the streets. We ran. And by cutting through side streets and alleys, we managed to make it to the home of a friend. But we were close enough to hear the screams
of the mob, close enough to smell the sickening odor of burning flesh. That was 1927.
Little Rock.

SUMMERSBY: Ike, what are you saying? That it's okay for blacks to fight against   37
bigotry in Europe, but it's wrong for them to do it here?

EISENHOWER: It just won't work, Kay. It'll not only handicap the black kids,   38
but the poor whites as well. Why I talked to this man Arthur Krock. A big man at
the New York Times. He told me in private that he didn't want to send his kids to
school with Negroes either, and he's a big liberal.

SUMMERSBY: I don't believe you, Ike. I thought that we fought to rid the world   39
of racial hatred and anti-Semitism.

EISENHOWER: Oh, Kay—that's your Irish talking. We treat the Negroes well.   40
They're a helluva lot better off here than in Africa, Kay. I even have one of them
working for me. Look, I have to go.

Silence

SUMMERSBY: Ike. (*Hesitant*) How's Mamie doing?   41

EISENHOWER: She's in a bad way. There's no peace at home. She hasn't been   42
the same since she saw that picture of you and me in that theatre box seat. She takes
a drink in the morning and doesn't stop until she's dead drunk. She has to go to these
Midwest spas to dry out. I think that she hates me. We haven't had sex since the . . .
since she had that . . . that, er, female operation. She still thinks that I was responsible for our son, John, becoming a soldier. She thinks that all soldiers are sluts.

During the war she wrote me a letter about the loose morals of the American
army in Europe. She thinks men start wars as an excuse to establish traveling whore-
houses and to engage in exotic sex.

SUMMERSBY: We didn't mean to hurt her. It's just this love between us is so mighty,   43
so powerful, we couldn't help ourselves, Ike. (*Long kiss*)

EISENHOWER: Goodbye, Kay.   44

She stretches out her arms.

SUMMERSBY: Ike.   45

He approaches her. They begin to dance to Glenn Miller's "Starlight." Spotlight on Mamie Eisenhower while they're dancing. She glares at them, her arms folded. Speaks to audience.

MAMIE: She checked in here under an assumed name. The Shoreham Hotel.   46
Hotels are where these men do all of their dirty work. Meeting their whores. He kept
me locked up in a hotel for two years while he was away in Europe with this woman.
I used to be so attractive. (*Slide*) I sacrificed myself for this man. He couldn't afford
me. He's always broke. They wanted to pay him some good money to do his biography. The fool turned it down. I could have had any man in Texas. My date book
was filled. I had my own maid and a generous allowance. I gave it up to become an
army wife. Went from pheasant under glass to chicken livers and rice. I could have
had a career. Instead, Ike became my career. We married in 1916. Moved thirty-nine
times. We didn't have a home we could call our own until 1952. He was nothing but
a rube when I met him. Farm boy. Didn't even know what a soup spoon was and
thought that a bidet was a bird's bath. I had to teach him the social graces.

Ike and Kay are talking, but we don't hear them. He puts his cap on and kisses Kay on the cheek.

Had to polish his English. West Point couldn't take Kansas out of this hayseed.

Kay puts on a W.A.C. uniform and begins to apply make-up in front of the hotel's mirror. Lil Armstrong enters. Tall, smartly dressed, intellectual type. Victorian-blouse, hip velvet suit, granny shoes.

LIL ARMSTRONG: I know what you're going through, Mamie.   47
MAMIE: Who are you, the hotel maid?   48

Kay embraces herself and begins to whirl about in happiness. Lil glares at Mamie.

LIL : Hotel maid! You white women are all alike. Think that all a sister can do   49
for you is your laundry and your floors.
MAMIE: Just asking.   50
LIL: I was married to Louis Armstrong.   51
MAMIE: Oh, yes. I have some of his records. Can't play them while Ike is home.   52
Know what his favorite songs are?
LIL: What are they?   53
MAMIE: "God Bless America" and "You'll Never Walk Alone."   54

Lil laughs. Mamie keeps her glum expression throughout.

LIL: Well, Louis had better taste, but he and Ike had one thing in common.   55
MAMIE: What's that—I didn't get your name.   56
LIL: Lil. Lil Hardin.   57

Kay puts on a coat and leaves the hotel room.

And who may she be?

MAMIE: My husband's whore. Kay Summersby. 58

LIL: Spindly little thing. 59

MAMIE: You think so? 60

LIL: Flat as roadkill. 61

MAMIE: Well, these men and their wars. Gives them an excuse to stay on the 62
road. They meet women and pour out their souls to these tramps.

LIL: You're not telling me anything. I practically created Louis. When he came 63
to Joe Oliver's band, he didn't even know how to wear a hat.

J. Edgar Hoover enters the room and begins to take photos of the bed, etc.

Wore his hair in that odious New Orleans style. Those ugly bangs.

Sees Mamie's bangs.

I'm sorry, I

MAMIE: (*Relaxes*) Forget about it. I was thinking of getting a different style. 64

LIL: Well, I had to teach Louis, the way you had to teach Ike. When he came up 65
from New Orleans he was just a sack of remains with a trumpet.

MAMIE: That bad? What happened? 66

LIL: Got turned out by one of these green-eyed creole vampires. Everybody told 67
him not to marry this crazy bitch. When they were courting she'd do evil things
like make love to him while knowing full well that her boyfriend would walk in at
any moment. Louis barely escaped one encounter. She was a real wildcat. Liked to
fight men. She'd even fight the police. They were together four years, going back and
forth between the bedroom and attempted murder. Kind of woman who carried a
razor. Her name was Daisy, but it should have been Venus. As in Venus's-flytrap. Louis
was the fly who got stuck.

MAMIE: How did she get rid of him? 68

LIL: Well, Louis never knew his father, and the only thing his mother taught him 69
was how to hold his liquor. Doesn't it tell you something about his relationship with
her that his most vivid memory is of him and his mother carousing the bars and falling
down drunk in the streets? So he adopted Joe Oliver as his father. Joe got Louis to
leave New Orleans for Chicago. He worshipped Joe. But I found out that Joe was
stealing money from Louis and the other band members. I hipped Louis to that and
he still wanted to stay with Joe. Louis didn't know how good he was. When he first
started hitting those **high Cs** he didn't know what he was doing. I had to play it on
the piano to show him what he was doing. It was because of me that he left Joe
Oliver's band and went to New York to work with Fletcher Henderson. We broke up.

MAMIE: Why? 70

LIL: I was always independent. I played in bands when I was a teenager. Could 71
write music and I could play piano as well any man. I was playing in these bands with
men who were my inferiors. They'd never let me play solo. All they wanted was to
get into my pants. Louis wanted a mother. If he could, he'd have married Mayaan.

MAMIE: Who was Mayaan? 72

LIL: His mother. Then he married another woman purely for sex. She was a pros- 73
titute like his mother. Her name was Daisy.

MAMIE: You sound like a woman of good upbringing. Why did you marry him? 74

LIL: I've asked myself that. Here I was, educated at Fisk. I thought that it may   75
have been a rebellion against my mother. We fought all the time. She hated jazz. If
it were only that simple. What about you and Ike?

MAMIE: Our grandmothers and mothers told us that we should be helpmates. I   76
never thought anything different. The biggest compliment Ike made to his mother,
Ida, was that she was a wonderful helpmate.

LIL: What's that man doing?   77

Hoover, in drag, is still creeping around the hotel room, emptying drawers, etc.

MAMIE: Oh, that's J. Edgar Hoover. He's blackmailed everybody in Washington.   78
He was the first to know that Kay was registering in the hotel under an assumed name.

LIL: I didn't know that he was black.   79

MAMIE: Oh, everybody knows it. He's never been accepted as a white man. He   80
says it's a tan, but we all know better. Nobody talks about it. They're scared. He's
ruined people. You'd be surprised the people he's spied on.

LIL: Who, who?   81

MAMIE: You know that pompous ass, Douglas MacArthur.   82

LIL: Who hasn't heard of General MacArthur. (*Mockingly*) "I Shall Return."   83

MAMIE: "Old Soldiers Never Die."   84

LIL: "They just live to testify."   85

They both laugh.

MAMIE: (*Whispers to Lil*) MacArthur was screwing this Chinese teenager into bad   86
health. Edgar knew and so did Drew Pearson.

LIL: Douglas MacArthur!   87

MAMIE: The same.   88

*She sees the champagne that Kay and Ike have left behind in a bucket next to the bed. Mamie
walks over, lifts the bottle.*

What you say we finish this off?

LIL: Why not?   89

*She walks over to where Mamie is standing. Mamie pours herself a glass of champagne, then
pours Lil one. They sit on the bed and quietly begin to sip. We hear Lil Armstrong on piano
in the background.*

MAMIE: Lil, how does that expression go? Behind every great man is a woman.   90

LIL: Should be, Behind every great man there's a chump.   91

Scene 3

*Three people wearing ski masks hold signs that say Basta Auslander, Invasione Africaine,
Keep Central **High** White, Nigerians Out of Zimbabwe. Dark on them. Slide of Central
High School. A Governor Faubus speech could be used here.*

NEWSCASTER: The crisis at Little Rock' Central **High** School continues. Governor   92
Faubus (*slide*) continues to defy a court order that Negro students be admitted to
classes. A mob is building up and sporadic outbreaks of violence are being reported.

Famed trumpeter Louis Armstrong has said that President Eisenhower should show some guts, go to Little Rock and escort the children into the school. (*Incredulous*) Louis Armstrong?

Three whites reappear on stage wearing ski masks and carrying signs bearing racial epithets.

ACT TWO

Scene 1

Dressing room. Joe Glaser and Armstrong. Joe Glaser is a middle-aged Jewish man. Wears a modest suit. Has an easy-going manner.

GLASER: (*Keeping his distance*) Are you out of your mind, Louis? Since when have   93
you been so political?

ARMSTRONG: It just came out. Before I could do anything, I had said it. It just   94
came out. (*Mumbles*)

Well, it accomplished one thing. It got you down here.

GLASER: Look at all of these cancellations. (*Waves papers*)   95

ARMSTRONG: There comes a time when all of us have to take a stand.   96

GLASER: What's come over you, Louis, where is the grinning, lovable, clown-   97
ing Louis that the world has begun to demand? (*Seeing that he has hurt him*) Look, I'm sorry, I apologize.

ARMSTRONG: You needn't. That's what people expect. But this is different. When   98
I saw that Faubus prevent those children from entering that school in Little Rock, and the children being threatened by that mob of ignorant crackers, something came over me. I had to say something. And that cat Eisenhower. Let that joker Faubus defy him.

Glaser has a concerned look.

Is there anything wrong?

GLASER: I didn't want to bring this up, but ever since you blurted out that remark,   99
three goyische have been following us. They were on the plane down here to Washington and I noticed them in the hotel.

ARMSTRONG: Who could they be?   100

GLASER: I think it's the feds. Look, I tried to get you an interview with   101
Eisenhower, but his staff has nixed the idea. They said you could see Nixon when you're in Washington next week. That's better than nothing. Maybe that will take some of the heat off. People are criticizing you. Sammy Davis, that young colored dancer, criticized you. Look, I got to go.

ARMSTRONG: One minute.   102

GLASER: What is it, Louis?   103

ARMSTRONG: Why are you standing way over there?   104

GLASER: I—I   105

ARMSTRONG: Afraid that you will turn black?   106

GLASER: I'm sorry, Louis, but I've seen it happen. Take that Teagarden fellow.   107
(*Slide*) You got him talking and acting like a black man. I'm already a Jew. To be that and a black, too. I'm sorry Louis, but I ain't takin' no chances.

Glaser exits. Pause.

ARMSTRONG: Sammy Davis, Jr., criticizing me, huh. Feds on my ass. That son-   108
of-a-bitch Hoover—I know all about it. My mob contacts tell me that they have a
photo of him making love to another man. He hangs out with Frank Costello and
dresses like a gangster. He put his hands on me and there will be riots all over the
world. They say they want me to go to the Soviet Union. Put my black face out there
to show how liberal we are. Well, I ain't going nowhere. They can cancel the trip.
They can send that no-playin' Benny Goodman in my place.

Scene 2

*Map room of the White House. A large map of the Pacific with notes scribbled on it indi-
cate World War II zones of combat. Ike is waiting for J. Edgar Hoover to arrive. Ike is
dressed in his golf outfit and is practicing some putts. Nathaniel, a black man, is pouring
him a cup of coffee. Nathaniel then returns to his position against the wall. J. Edgar Hoover
enters. He is a dark-skinned, short, rotund black man wearing womens' clothes.*

HOOVER: I didn't want to show you this material in the Oval Office, Mr.   109
President. Who knows, the phone might be tapped.
EISENHOWER: Of course, J. Edgar, I understand. What's on your mind?   110
HOOVER: This Louis Armstrong. He's leading the blacks in some kind of revolt.   111
EISENHOWER: You don't say?   112

Eisenhower is swinging his golf club.

HOOVER: I've been watching him closely, Mr. President; he's a clever one, all   113
right. Take that song "Dinah," for example.

Eisenhower stops swinging. Scratches his head. Gives Hoover a curious look.

Listen to this, Mr. President.

Puts the record on and plays a couple of choruses of Armstrong singing.

EISENHOWER: I rather like that version.   114
HOOVER: You don't get it, General. He's not singing it the way it goes.   115

Sings: "Dinah, the sweetest in Carolina."   116

No, he's singing it a different way. He's singing in some kind of code. He's send-
ing a message to the Negroes. Telling them to rise up and kill white people.
EISENHOWER: You don't say.   117
HOOVER: General, will you put down that golf club and listen?   118

Eisenhower glares at him.

Ah—Mr. President, I need your permission to wiretap his phone. We already
have a couple of men tailing him. You heard what he said. Said that you ought to
take those black children into the school down there, personally take them by the
hand.
EISENHOWER: He said that, J. Edgar?   119

HOOVER: That's not all he said, Mr. Eisenhower. One of our men overheard   120
one of his sidemen call your mother a Negro and said that you were passing for white.
A lot of Negroes believe that.

EISENHOWER: (*Laughs*) That's a new one. I've been called a Jew by the Taft peo-   121
ple, a communist by McCarthy's people, and now a Negro.

HOOVER: He said that you lacked guts.   122

EISENHOWER: (*Angry*) What?   123

HOOVER: After we finish with him, he won't have such a smart dippermouth.   124

EISENHOWER: Dippermouth?   125

HOOVER: That's his nickname.   126

(*Aide enters*)

AIDE: Mr. President, may I speak to you in private?   127

They go to the side of the stage and begin animated conversation which we don't hear. Phone rings. Hoover answers.

HOOVER: Yeah—he stepped out of the room. . . . I think that we'll get our tap on   128
Louis. I'm prepared to tell him about the letter. The one he wrote to Marshall requesting that he divorce Mamie and marry Kay Summersby—that'll get him to play ball.

Hoover and Nat begin a staring contest as the conversation between the aide and Eisenhower is heard.

AIDE: But Mr. President, the situation is deteriorating. Every Klansman in Dixie   129
is headed for Little Rock. The governor has abandoned his duties and become the
mob leader. (*Slide*) We can't assure the safety to those kids. Suppose one of them is
killed. How would that look to the Russians and the Chinese?

EISENHOWER: (*Angrily*) I will never use soldiers against American citizens and   130
that's that. Now I have to get back to my meeting.

Aide exits with frustrated look.

You have my permission to monitor Armstrong's phone, Edgar. If he is posing
a threat to national security, then he has to be monitored.

HOOVER: (*Smiling*) Thanks, General. (*Looks at watch*) Well, I've got to get to the   131
track. Don't worry, Mr. President. We'll take care of this Armstrong. By the way, how
were the arrangements at the Shoreham? (*Winks*)

EISENHOWER: Er—um, fine. Fine, J. Edgar.   132

HOOVER: Good.   133

Hoover exits.

EISENHOWER: How did he know about that, Nat? Did you tell him?   134

NAT: I've been working here for thirty years, Mr. President, and I've never   135
betrayed the confidence of a president. That Hoover is a wicked man. He knows
about everybody in town and is a loathsome blackmailer. And the man's own private
life is degenerate. The man should be fired.

EISENHOWER: But how can I? He knows about me and Kay.   136

NAT: Unfortunately, that's how he remains in power. Getting under peoples' bed   137
sheets. Like a piece of lice. And now he's trying to destroy Louis Armstrong, one of
the most beloved figures in the world of music.

EISENHOWER: But what about his calling me gutless?   138

NAT: Mr. President. Louis has done more for the image of the United States than   139
John Foster Dulles, a man whose very name inspires hate and contempt around the
world. This nutty thing he has about massive retaliation. If somebody attacks us with
A-bombs and we retaliate, it will blow up the world. Louis, on the other hand, is a
gentle person. He's our ambassador of goodwill. (*Slide*)

EISENHOWER: J. Edgar seems to think otherwise.   140

NAT: You should hear what Louis says.   141

EISENHOWER: What Louis says. How can I find that out?   142

Nat goes out and brings Louis in.

What's the meaning of this?

NAT: I brought him here, sir. He was down the hall meeting with Vice-President   143
Nixon. He wanted to see you, but your staff wouldn't hear of it. I'm sure that this misunderstanding can be worked out. You two should talk. Get acquainted. You've only
spent a total of forty-five minutes talking to black leaders since you took office.

Awkward silence.

EISENHOWER: Don't we have a black member of the administration?   144

NAT: Fred Morrow. The man resigned from his good job at CBS when you invited   145
him to join the administration, and now he's living on his savings. People here won't
even answer his calls. And that Alabaman Wilton B. Persons threatened a boycott
if a Negro came to the White House in a capacity other than that of a butler.

EISENHOWER: (*Embarrassed*) I didn't know. Maybe I'll invite him to sit in my box   146
at the baseball game. Well, Armstrong, what do you have to say for yourself?

ARMSTRONG: Mr. President, I'm sorry if I embarrassed you. But those little   147
children—it just made my blood boil when I saw them treated this way. The white
man spitting on that child as she tried to enter the school. It made me mad. And
then you allow this man to defy you. You have him call up the National Guard to
stop those kids from entering school. Ike, are you going to let this moonshine-guzzling,
barefoot redneck do this to you?

EISENHOWER: I can understand. But you know, Louis. I have to think of how his-   148
tory is going to treat me. I've already reached the pinnacle. Why should I get into a
pissing contest with some stupid southern governor? This fool Supreme Court and
that Earl Warren—that liberal—they've just caused a lot of trouble for the good people of the South.

ARMSTRONG: They may be good to you, Mr. President, but my people have caught   149
hell from these good people of the South. We can't get booked in good hotels, and
when my men have to go to the bathroom, they have to sneak and go do it in the
bushes.

EISENHOWER: Is that so?   150

ARMSTRONG: That ain't all. They still have those nightriders. Roaming the coun- 151
tryside. Foaming at the mouth. Terrorizing Negroes. A few months ago, some hill-
billy exploded a bomb outside one of my concerts.

EISENHOWER: It takes time, Louis. You must have patience. Your people should 152
go slow. The good decent people of the South will come around. Your people should
use moral persuasion.

ARMSTRONG: We've tried all of that. Some use oratory. I use my trumpet. But my 153
trumpet can do only so much. Sometimes, it takes the sword, General. Sometimes it
takes more than moral persuasion.

EISENHOWER: I'd never use the bayonet against Americans. 154

ARMSTRONG: Mr. President, I'm a musician and you're a general. Both of us are 155
leaders of men. Both of us had mentors; yours was General Marshall, and mine was
King Oliver. Both of us have to use tactics and strategies to accomplish our goals. We
both try to accomplish what people in our fields never before reached. Every time I
hit those higher registers on my trumpet, I believe that I'm going someplace where
nobody's ever been. That's what you must do, Ike. Hit the **high** note of your career.

EISENHOWER: I've hit the highest of notes. I was the Supreme Commander of an 156
army that scored one of the great victories of history. The presidency is a step down
for me.

ARMSTRONG: That's not what they say in Europe. They say that General 157
Montgomery was—was

EISENHOWER: Go on. 158

ARMSTRONG: They say that Montgomery could have won the war a year earlier 159
if it hadn't been for your blunders. They say that you lost Berlin to the Russians.

EISENHOWER: Goddamnit, who told you that? 160

ARMSTRONG: (*Grins*) Don't get excited, Ike. You know that I travel. People will 161
talk. The royal families of Europe have receptions for me which are attended by
the **high** army brass of different countries. They gossip about the soldiers in Korea.
The ones you left behind?

Sounds of combat. Eisenhower looks stunned, shaken.

EISENHOWER: How did you know about that? 162

ARMSTRONG: Not much you can keep from Pops, General. My band performed 163
at a party for one of the higher-ups in your administration. The cat had a few cups
and started shooting off at the mouth. He said that the North Koreans didn't hand
over all of the soldiers during the prisoner exchange at the end of the war. Said
that they kept some behind, and that these men were sent to Russia and were experimented upon. He said that you knew about it, but kept quiet.

EISENHOWER: (*Nervous, agitated*) We had to do it. We had to sacrifice those men. 164
We wanted to get the war over. It was the best that we could do. (*Defensive*) I told
those clowns that we shouldn't have gotten ourselves in a land war in Asia. You can't
beat those people on the ground. They came at us in human waves in Korea. Those
Asians. They don't give a rat's ass about human lives. If we'd remained, there would
have been more casualties.

ARMSTRONG: People will talk, Ike. I've taken my lumps. Ever since I was a kid 165
they talked about me. Said that I was a hoodlum.

EISENHOWER: Why would they call you that? 166

ARMSTRONG: It was New Year's Eve, January 1, 1913. I never will forget. I fired 167
some shots into the air. I was arrested and put in the Colored Waifs' Home.

EISENHOWER: That's too bad. Your parents must have taken it real hard. 168

ARMSTRONG: I got into trouble a lot when I was a kid, but I straightened up. 169
Playing the bugle. Got myself together. Had some real mentors in the home who
taught me how to play.

EISENHOWER: Is that so? 170

ARMSTRONG: I've been around the block, Ike. While you were living your apple 171
pie life in Abilene, I was gettin' arrested for stealing newspapers.

EISENHOWER: Apple pie, is it? Well, I'll have you know that we lived from meal 172
to meal. My father, a good man, was constantly in debt. He was swindled. He spent
the rest of his life paying off his bills. And my mother. She held the family together
through the hard times. She taught me and my brothers discipline. Perseverance. We
all have her smile.

ARMSTRONG: My mother stood by me, too. Mother always said to me, God bless 173
her, "treat people nice and they will treat you nice." You express that attitude nowadays and you're accused of groveling. Of kissing the behinds of the white public.

EISENHOWER: I've heard that said about you. I thought that you were reasonable, 174
not like that hothead, Roy Wilkens.

ARMSTRONG: Yes, well, they may call me a tom, but I didn't treat my people 175
the way you did yours.

EISENHOWER: I don't follow. 176

ARMSTRONG: Your family came from Germany, from around the Rhine. Yet after 177
the war you starved hundreds of thousands of German prisoners even though you and
they were of the same blood line. The way I look at it, you had internalized your self-
hatred. You also made a deal with the French Nazis in Tunisia.

EISENHOWER: War is a dirty business. Sometimes you have to bargain with the 178
devil.

ARMSTRONG: You're a big hero now, but sooner or later history will catch up with 179
you and she'll not be kind. You have to stand by the kids down in Little Rock. Mr.
President, why are you letting this Orville Faubus do to you what Mussolini and Hitler
couldn't do? Defeat you.

EISENHOWER: It'll work out. 180

ARMSTRONG: Ike, you're a good man, but you're getting the wrong advice. You're 181
surrounded by evil. You know that Hoover likes black entertainment. Some of my
buddies say that he sometimes comes to after-hours joints. Dressed up like a woman.
Goes by the name of Mary. And that ain't all. His black servants call him a soul
brother and he's always giving them the **high**-five.

EISENHOWER: Look, Louis. If you're going to spread scurrilous rumors about people 182
in my administration we can end this interview right now.

ARMSTRONG: Suit yourself, Ike. But eventually, I will get my **high C**. But will you 183
get yours? History smiles upon you right now, but history is a fickle lover. It will

turn on you. The people will eventually discover the real role that you played in the war. How you lost Berlin to the Russians. Your blunders. Your abandonment of the Korean P.O.W.s. The atrocities you inflicted upon unarmed German prisoners. All of it will come out, Ike. It's not too late, Ike. It's not too late to get your **C *above* C *above* high** C. One last deed that will seal your place in history as a great man. (*Begins to exit*)

EISENHOWER: Look, Louis. Before you leave, would you play something on your 184 trumpet?

Armstrong plays "God Bless America," one of Eisenhower's favorite songs. At the conclusion the two men stare at each other. Armstrong's is more of a glare.

ARMSTRONG: (*Dramatic pause*) Do the right thing, Daddy. (*He exits.*)   185

Scene 3

Armstrong is alone on stage.

ARMSTRONG: That Eisenhower isn't such a bad joe. Just a sad melancholy man. 186 Couldn't have the woman that he wanted. It's like a knife in his soul. Took me a long time to find mine. Daisy. I almost ended up in the cemetery with that one. Lil. Man don't like a woman talking back to him and second-guessing him. She was wearing the pants in the family. I liked them headstrong and **high** strung. But Lucille. Washes my clothes, feeds me, gives me sympathy when I'm having a bad day.

BEBOPPER: Hey, Louis. Play something for me on that corny trumpet of yours, 187 you square little black motherfucker.

Louis knocks him down, then helps him up.

ARMSTRONG: You okay, son? (*Brushes him off*) You know, you young boppers have 188 wandered so far off that sometimes it becomes necessary for you to come in contact with the cold fist of reality. Let me share with you a proverb I learned in Africa last year. "The calves follow their mothers. The young plant grows up near the parent stem. The young antelope leaps where its mother has leaped." The melody is the mother, son. That's what you young musicians forget. Don't ever go so far out in deep water that you can't get back. And respect continuity, son. These critics have divided us. Interrupting a chain of tradition that reaches back to the rain forests of Africa. I teach you something. You pass it on to your generation. They pass it on to a future generation. I know that you boys think you're doing something new, but if it wasn't for me, and Joe Oliver, and Bunk Johnson, and Jelly Roll, and a whole bunch of other cats, you wouldn't have your precious Bebop. Understand?

BEBOPPER: Yessir, Mr. Armstrong.   189

ARMSTRONG: Now go and get yourself cleaned up and then get back to practic- 190 ing your scales.

BEBOPPER: Yessir, Mr. Armstrong.   191

Dark. Spotlight on newscaster.

NEWSCASTER: Fifty-two planeloads of **C**123s and **C**130s have brought 1200 battle-   192
equipped paratroopers to Little Rock to see that integration is carried out at Central
High School without further violence. Planeloads of the men of the 101st Airborne
Division stationed at Fort Campbell, Kentucky, started landing at Little Rock Air
Force Base at 3:30 p.m. this afternoon, at half-hour intervals. The troop convoy is
entering Little Rock to take up positions at Central **High** School.

*Spotlight on Lucille Armstrong. Middle-aged. Wears apron. Domestic outfit. On the monitor
we see a Cotton Club routine. Lucille imitates the dance that they are performing on the
screen.*

LUCILLE: I still can do my kicks. Lonely. Maybe I should rent a studio. Get my   193
routines in shape. No time for that. When you marry a public man you are placing
yourself in a prison. Oh, the prison is nice. Furnished well. All of the amenities.
But it's still a prison. You can watch television to while away the time. You can sew
or talk to neighbors. But ultimately you have a rival. This rival gives him more pleasure than what a woman can give. It's easy to compete with those whores who are
always throwing their arms around Louis. It's much harder to compete with a thing.
A trumpet. I know what his other wives knew, Daisy and Lil. That there's no woman
who is going to come between him and that horn. These black musician men. They
are so full of sex that they can eroticize a piece of metal. Louis's other wives couldn't
accept it. I can. Do I have regrets? Sometimes, I wonder whether I would have succeeded. How far I could have gone with my dancing. Whether I would have become
another Katherine Dunham. Or a Pearl Primus, or Eartha Kitt. Sometimes I wonder whether I sacrificed my career for Louis. Should I hover in the shadow of a great
man, just to spend some time in his company? Just to love him. Have his clothes
ready. Cook his meals. Run his household. And no matter where he goes or with
whom he does his one-night stands, he always comes back to Queens. And when
he does, the neighbors turn out as though he were a conquering hero. Dogs barking. Children running after him. People honking their horns. It's like a holiday when
Louis comes home. Those are the days that make it all worthwhile. When my man
is here eating his greens and chitterlings and sweet potato pie. Recovering from
the road, making love to me. Maybe one day people will look back and say that
Mamie and I were wrong. That she gave it all up for a man who went to his grave
loving another woman. Or maybe I will be seen as someone who abandoned a career
just to become a great man's caretaker. Maybe they will dismiss us as victims, shut up
in the 1950s, our opportunities stunted, condemned to carry on the tradition of our
mothers, nurturing children and their husbands. But right now I look forward to those
golden moments and those moments with Louis make it all worthwhile.

*She puts a domestic dress over her Cotton Club outfit. Somebody provides her with a
birthday cake. Stage center lights up and we see Louis sitting in his dressing room applying
white cream to his face. Lucille, Joe Glaser, and Gloria enter. Lucille is carrying a birthday
cake. Louis looks up.*

LUCILLE AND JOE: Happy birthday, Louis.   194

ARMSTRONG: (*Grins*) You guys are full of surprises. Really sweet of you to remem- 195
ber my birthday.

He embraces them. Nathaniel enters.

NAT: Happy birthday, Louis.   196
ARMSTRONG: Nat, what brings you here?   197

Armstrong introduces him all around.

NAT: General Eisenhower wanted me to deliver this telegram to you, personally.   198
ARMSTRONG: It's been eight years since Little Rock. How is Ike doing?   199
NAT: He and Mamie are enjoying the Gettysburg farm. They both seem at peace.   200
GLASER: People still are puzzled about why he sent the troops into Little Rock.   201
So unlike him.

Nat and Louis exchange knowing glances.

Strange, complicated man. A product of the military, yet when he left office, he
warned about the military-industrial complex.

NAT: I hear that Faubus is working as a teller in a blank.   202
ARMSTRONG: Read the telegram.   203
NAT: Mrs. Eisenhower and I are happy to be among those wishing you a happy   204
birthday. The date of your birth, a national holiday, would seem to insure a gala
celebration. May you have many more years of good health and happiness. Signed
Dwight Eisenhower.

LUCILLE: He's got his nerve, Louis. After what that old queen J. Edgar Hoover   205
did to you.

ARMSTRONG: Ike made mistakes. But finally, he got that **C *above C above high**   206
C. Oh yeeeaaaaahhhhhhhhh.

GLASER: What do you mean by that, Louis?   207
ARMSTRONG: Just a secret between Ike and me. Nothing important.   ·208
LUCILLE: Louis, ain't you goin' to cut the cake?   209

*Louis rises and begins to cut the cake as the three begin to sing "Happy Birthday." Freeze:
Spotlight on Eisenhower in suit. In the background of his speech is Armstrong's "Snake Rag"
upon which he does some **high-C** riffs.*

EISENHOWER: For a few minutes this evening, I should like to speak to you about   210
the serious situation that has arisen in Little Rock. To make this talk, I have come
to the President's Office in the White House. I could have spoken from Rhode Island
where I have been staying recently. But I felt that in speaking from the house of
Lincoln, of Jackson, and of Wilson, my words would better convey both the sadness I feel in the action I was compelled today to take, and the firmness with which
I intend to pursue this course until the orders of the Federal Court at Little Rock can
be executed without unlawful interference.

In that city, under the leadership of demagogic extremists, disorderly mobs have
deliberately prevented the carrying out of proper orders from a federal court. Local
authorities have not eliminated that violent opposition. And under the law I yesterday issued a proclamation calling upon the mob to disperse. This morning the mob

again gathered in front of the Central **High** School of Little Rock, obviously for the purpose of again preventing the carrying-out of the court's order relating to the admission of Negro children to that school.

Whenever normal agencies prove inadequate to the task it becomes necessary for the Executive Branch of the Federal Government to use its power and authority to aid in the execution of federal law at Little Rock, Arkansas. This became necessary when my proclamation of yesterday was not observed and the obstruction of justice still continues. It is important that the reasons for my action be understood by all our citizens. As you know, the Supreme Court of the United States has decided that separate public educational facilities for the races are inherently unequal and therefore compulsory school segregation laws are unconstitutional.

Dark.

Questions for Discussion

1. Explain what the Louis Armstrong character means by the statement, "My face doesn't belong to me anymore." How do his actions just before and just after this line reinforce this statement?
2. Who is Elizabeth? How does Armstrong characterize her?
3. How does the J. Edgar Hoover character retain and wield power in the play? What characteristics does the playwright ascribe to Hoover?
4. Describe the Dwight Eisenhower character's dream. How does it relate to other ideas about nationalism presented in the play? How close are the things he sees in the dream to present-day geopolitical reality?
5. Explain the title of the play. What importance does Armstrong place upon "high C's"? How does he relate this feeling to the cause of civil rights?

Questions for Reflection and Writing

1. What distinctions does the play make between the "old jazz" of Louis Armstrong and Jelly Roll and the "bebop," or new jazz, of Charlie Parker and Thelonious Monk? Where do Glenn Miller and Benny Goodman fit in?
2. What is the nature of relationships between men and women in this play? Between men and men? What picture of human sexuality emerges?
3. Isolate two different kinds of war Reed writes about in this play. How are they different? *Are* they different?
4. Study the use of black-and-white imagery throughout the play. What do you think Reed might be suggesting in his use of such imagery?
5. Go online and do a bit of research about the desegregation attempts in Little Rock in the 1950s. (If you're having trouble getting started, check out this hyperlinked bibliography,
   <http://www.eisenhower.utexas.edu/dl/LittleRock/littlerockdocuments.html>
   which provides a great deal of information on the subject.) Using what you have learned, consider: what, if anything, does having more information on the history of the era contribute to your understanding of the play?

William Shakespeare

The Merchant of Venice

1597

Dramatis Personae

THE DUKE OF VENICE
THE PRINCE OF MOROCCO, suitor to Portia
THE PRINCE OF ARRAGON, *Ditto*
ANTONIO, a merchant of Venice
BASSANIO, his friend, suitor to Portia
SOLANIO, friend to Antonio and Bassanio
SALERIO, *Ditto*
GRATIANO, *Ditto*
LORENZO, in love with Jessica
SHYLOCK, a rich Jew
TUBAL, a Jew, his friend
LAUNCELOT GOBBO, a clown, servant to Shylock

OLD GOBBO, father to Launcelot
LEONARDO, servant to Bassanio
BALTHASAR, servant to Portia
STEPHANO, *Ditto*

PORTIA, a rich heiress
NERISSA, her waiting-maid
JESSICA, daughter to Shylock
Magnificoes of Venice, Officers of the Court of Justice,
    Gaoler, Servants, and other Attendants

SCENE: Venice, and PORTIA'S house at Belmont

William Shakespeare

The Merchant of Venice

1597

Act I.

Scene I.

Venice. A street

Enter ANTONIO, SALERIO, and SOLANIO

ANTONIO. In sooth, I know not why I am so sad.
  It wearies me; you say it wearies you;
  But how I caught it, found it, or came by it,
  What stuff 'tis made of, whereof it is born,
  I am to learn;
  And such a want-wit sadness makes of me
  That I have much ado to know myself.
SALERIO. Your mind is tossing on the ocean;
  There where your argosies, with portly sail—
  Like signiors and rich burghers on the flood,
  Or as it were the pageants of the sea—
  Do overpeer the petty traffickers,
  That curtsy to them, do them reverence,
  As they fly by them with their woven wings.
SOLANIO. Believe me, sir, had I such venture forth,
  The better part of my affections would
  Be with my hopes abroad. I should be still
  Plucking the grass to know where sits the wind,
  Peering in maps for ports, and piers, and roads;
  And every object that might make me fear
  Misfortune to my ventures, out of doubt,
  Would make me sad.
SALERIO. My wind, cooling my broth,
  Would blow me to an ague when I thought
  What harm a wind too great might do at sea.
  I should not see the sandy hour-glass run
  But I should think of shallows and of flats,

And see my wealthy Andrew dock'd in sand,
Vailing her high top lower than her ribs
To kiss her burial. Should I go to church
And see the holy edifice of stone,
And not bethink me straight of dangerous rocks,
Which, touching but my gentle vessel's side,
Would scatter all her spices on the stream,
Enrobe the roaring waters with my silks,
And, in a word, but even now worth this,
And now worth nothing? Shall I have the thought
To think on this, and shall I lack the thought
That such a thing bechanc'd would make me sad?
But tell not me; I know Antonio
Is sad to think upon his merchandise.
ANTONIO. Believe me, no; I thank my fortune for it,
  My ventures are not in one bottom trusted,
  Nor to one place; nor is my whole estate
  Upon the fortune of this present year;
  Therefore my merchandise makes me not sad.
SOLANIO. Why then you are in love.
ANTONIO. Fie, fie!
SOLANIO. Not in love neither? Then let us say you are sad
  Because you are not merry; and 'twere as easy
  For you to laugh and leap and say you are merry,
  Because you are not sad. Now, by two-headed Janus,
  Nature hath fram'd strange fellows in her time:
  Some that will evermore peep through their eyes,
  And laugh like parrots at a bag-piper;
  And other of such vinegar aspect
  That they'll not show their teeth in way of smile
  Though Nestor swear the jest be laughable.
    Enter BASSANIO, LORENZO, and GRATIANO

Here comes Bassanio, your most noble kinsman,
Gratiano and Lorenzo. Fare ye well;
We leave you now with better company.
SALERIO. I would have stay'd till I had made you merry,
If worthier friends had not prevented me.
ANTONIO. Your worth is very dear in my regard.
I take it your own business calls on you,
And you embrace th' occasion to depart.
SALERIO. Good morrow, my good lords.
BASSANIO. Good signiors both, when shall we laugh? Say when.
You grow exceeding strange; must it be so?
SALERIO. We'll make our leisures to attend on yours.
                    Exeunt SALERIO and SOLANIO
LORENZO. My Lord Bassanio, since you have found Antonio,
We two will leave you; but at dinner-time,
I pray you, have in mind where we must meet.
BASSANIO. I will not fail you.
GRATIANO. You look not well, Signior Antonio;
You have too much respect upon the world;
They lose it that do buy it with much care.
Believe me, you are marvellously chang'd.
ANTONIO. I hold the world but as the world, Gratiano—
A stage, where every man must play a part,
And mine a sad one.
GRATIANO. Let me play the fool.
With mirth and laughter let old wrinkles come;
And let my liver rather heat with wine
Than my heart cool with mortifying groans.
Why should a man whose blood is warm within
Sit like his grandsire cut in alabaster,
Sleep when he wakes, and creep into the jaundice
By being peevish? I tell thee what, Antonio—
I love thee, and 'tis my love that speaks—
There are a sort of men whose visages
Do cream and mantle like a standing pond,
And do a wilful stillness entertain,
With purpose to be dress'd in an opinion
Of wisdom, gravity, profound conceit;
As who should say 'I am Sir Oracle,
And when I ope my lips let no dog bark.'
O my Antonio, I do know of these
That therefore only are reputed wise
For saying nothing; when, I am very sure,
If they should speak, would almost damn those ears
Which, hearing them, would call their brothers fools.
I'll tell thee more of this another time.
But fish not with this melancholy bait
For this fool gudgeon, this opinion.
Come, good Lorenzo. Fare ye well awhile;
I'll end my exhortation after dinner.
LORENZO. Well, we will leave you then till dinner-time.
I must be one of these same dumb wise men,
For Gratiano never lets me speak.
GRATIANO. Well, keep me company but two years moe,

Thou shalt not know the sound of thine own tongue.
ANTONIO. Fare you well; I'll grow a talker for this gear.
GRATIANO. Thanks, i' faith, for silence is only commendable
In a neat's tongue dried, and a maid not vendible.
                    Exeunt GRATIANO and LORENZO
ANTONIO. Is that anything now?
BASSANIO. Gratiano speaks an infinite deal of nothing, more than any man in all Venice. His reasons are as two grains of wheat hid in, two bushels of chaff: you shall seek all day ere you find them, and when you have them they are not worth the search.
ANTONIO. Well; tell me now what lady is the same To whom you swore a secret pilgrimage,
That you to-day promis'd to tell me of?
BASSANIO. 'Tis not unknown to you, Antonio,
How much I have disabled mine estate
By something showing a more swelling port
Than my faint means would grant continuance;
Nor do I now make moan to be abridg'd
From such a noble rate; but my chief care
Is to come fairly off from the great debts
Wherein my time, something too prodigal,
Hath left me gag'd. To you, Antonio,
I owe the most, in money and in love;
And from your love I have a warranty
To unburden all my plots and purposes
How to get clear of all the debts I owe.
ANTONIO. I pray you, good Bassanio, let me know it;
And if it stand, as you yourself still do,
Within the eye of honour, be assur'd
My purse, my person, my extremest means,
Lie all unlock'd to your occasions.
BASSANIO. In my school-days, when I had lost one shaft,
I shot his fellow of the self-same flight
The self-same way, with more advised watch,
To find the other forth; and by adventuring both
I oft found both. I urge this childhood proof,
Because what follows is pure innocence.
I owe you much; and, like a wilful youth,
That which I owe is lost; but if you please
To shoot another arrow that self way
Which you did shoot the first, I do not doubt,
As I will watch the aim, or to find both,
Or bring your latter hazard back again
And thankfully rest debtor for the first.
ANTONIO. You know me well, and herein spend but time
To wind about my love with circumstance;
And out of doubt you do me now more wrong
In making question of my uttermost
Than if you had made waste of all I have.
Then do but say to me what I should do
That in your knowledge may by me be done,
And I am prest unto it; therefore, speak.
BASSANIO. In Belmont is a lady richly left,
And she is fair and, fairer than that word,

Of wondrous virtues. Sometimes from her eyes
I did receive fair speechless messages.
Her name is Portia—nothing undervalu'd
To Cato's daughter, Brutus' Portia.
Nor is the wide world ignorant of her worth;
For the four winds blow in from every coast
Renowned suitors, and her sunny locks
Hang on her temples like a golden fleece,
Which makes her seat of Belmont Colchos' strond,
And many Jasons come in quest of her.
O my Antonio, had I but the means
To hold a rival place with one of them,
I have a mind presages me such thrift
That I should questionless be fortunate.
ANTONIO. Thou know'st that all my fortunes are at sea;
Neither have I money nor commodity
To raise a present sum; therefore go forth,
Try what my credit can in Venice do;
That shall be rack'd, even to the uttermost,
To furnish thee to Belmont to fair Portia.
Go presently inquire, and so will I,
Where money is; and I no question make
To have it of my trust or for my sake.   Exeunt

Scene II.

Belmont. PORTIA'S house

Enter PORTIA with her waiting-woman, NERISSA

PORTIA. By my troth, Nerissa, my little body is aweary of this
   great world.
NERISSA. You would be, sweet madam, if your miseries were
   in the same abundance as your good fortunes are; and
   yet, for aught I see, they are as sick that surfeit with too
   much as they that starve with nothing. It is no mean
   happiness, therefore, to be seated in the mean:
   superfluity come sooner by white hairs, but competency
   lives longer.
PORTIA. Good sentences, and well pronounc'd.
NERISSA. They would be better, if well followed.
PORTIA. If to do were as easy as to know what were good to
   do, chapels had been churches, and poor men's cottages
   princes' palaces. It is a good divine that follows his own
   instructions; I can easier teach twenty what were good to
   be done than to be one of the twenty to follow mine own
   teaching. The brain may devise laws for the blood, but a
   hot temper leaps o'er a cold decree; such a hare is
   madness the youth, to skip o'er the meshes of good
   counsel the cripple. But this reasoning is not in the
   fashion to choose me a husband. O me, the word
   'choose'! I may neither choose who I would nor refuse
   who I dislike; so is the will of a living daughter curb'd by
   the will of a dead father. Is it not hard, Nerissa, that I
   cannot choose one, nor refuse none?

NERISSA. Your father was ever virtuous, and holy men at
   their death have good inspirations; therefore the lott'ry
   that he hath devised in these three chests, of gold, silver,
   and lead—whereof who chooses his meaning chooses
   you—will no doubt never be chosen by any rightly but
   one who you shall rightly love. But what warmth is there
   in your affection towards any of these princely suitors
   that are already come?
PORTIA. I pray thee over-name them; and as thou namest
   them, I will describe them; and according to my
   description, level at my affection.
NERISSA. First, there is the Neapolitan prince.
PORTIA. Ay, that's a colt indeed, for he doth nothing but
   talk of his horse; and he makes it a great appropriation
   to his own good parts that he can shoe him himself; I am
   much afear'd my lady his mother play'd false with a
   smith.
NERISSA. Then is there the County Palatine.
PORTIA. He doth nothing but frown, as who should say 'An
   you will not have me, choose.' He hears merry tales and
   smiles not. I fear he will prove the weeping philosopher
   when he grows old, being so full of unmannerly sadness
   in his youth. I had rather be married to a death's-head
   with a bone in his mouth than to either of these. God
   defend me from these two!
NERISSA. How say you by the French lord, Monsieur Le
   Bon?
PORTIA. God made him, and therefore let him pass for a
   man. In truth, I know it is a sin to be a mocker, but
   he—why, he hath a horse better than the Neapolitan's, a
   better bad habit of frowning than the Count Palatine; he
   is every man in no man. If a throstle sing he falls straight
   a-cap'ring; he will fence with his own shadow; if I should
   marry him, I should marry twenty husbands. If he would
   despise me, I would forgive him; for if he love me to
   madness, I shall never requite him.
NERISSA. What say you then to Falconbridge, the young
   baron of England?
PORTIA. You know I say nothing to him, for he understands
   not me, nor I him: he hath neither Latin, French, nor
   Italian, and you will come into the court and swear that I
   have a poor pennyworth in the English. He is a proper
   man's picture; but alas, who can converse with a
   dumb-show? How oddly he is suited! I think he bought
   his doublet in Italy, his round hose in France, his bonnet
   in Germany, and his behaviour everywhere.
NERISSA. What think you of the Scottish lord, his
   neighbour?
PORTIA. That he hath a neighbourly charity in him, for he
   borrowed a box of the ear of the Englishman, and swore
   he would pay him again when he was able; I think the
   Frenchman became his surety, and seal'd under for
   another.
NERISSA. How like you the young German, the Duke of
   Saxony's nephew?

PORTIA. Very vilely in the morning when he is sober; and most vilely in the afternoon when he is drunk. When he is best, he is a little worse than a man, and when he is worst, he is little better than a beast. An the worst fall that ever fell, I hope I shall make shift to go without him.

NERISSA. If he should offer to choose, and choose the right casket, you should refuse to perform your father's will, if you should refuse to accept him.

PORTIA. Therefore, for fear of the worst, I pray thee set a deep glass of Rhenish wine on the contrary casket; for if the devil be within and that temptation without, I know he will choose it. I will do anything, Nerissa, ere I will be married to a sponge.

NERISSA. You need not fear, lady, the having any of these lords; they have acquainted me with their determinations, which is indeed to return to their home, and to trouble you with no more suit, unless you may be won by some other sort than your father's imposition, depending on the caskets.

PORTIA. If I live to be as old as Sibylla, I will die as chaste as Diana, unless I be obtained by the manner of my father's will. I am glad this parcel of wooers are so reasonable; for there is not one among them but I dote on his very absence, and I pray God grant them a fair departure.

NERISSA. Do you not remember, lady, in your father's time, a Venetian, a scholar and a soldier, that came hither in company of the Marquis of Montferrat?

PORTIA. Yes, yes, it was Bassanio; as I think, so was he call'd.

NERISSA. True, madam; he, of all the men that ever my foolish eyes look'd upon, was the best deserving a fair lady.

PORTIA. I remember him well, and I remember him worthy of thy praise.

Enter a SERVINGMAN

How now! what news?

SERVINGMAN. The four strangers seek for you, madam, to take their leave; and there is a forerunner come from a fifth, the Prince of Morocco, who brings word the Prince his master will be here to-night.

PORTIA. If I could bid the fifth welcome with so good heart as I can bid the other four farewell, I should be glad of his approach; if he have the condition of a saint and the complexion of a devil, I had rather he should shrive me than wive me.

Come, Nerissa. Sirrah, go before.

Whiles we shut the gate upon one wooer, another knocks at the door.

Exeunt

Scene III.

Venice. A public place

Enter BASSANIO With SHYLOCK the Jew

SHYLOCK. Three thousand ducats—well.

BASSANIO. Ay, sir, for three months.

SHYLOCK. For three months—well.

BASSANIO. For the which, as I told you, Antonio shall be bound.

SHYLOCK. Antonio shall become bound—well.

BASSANIO. May you stead me? Will you pleasure me? Shall I know your answer?

SHYLOCK. Three thousand ducats for three months, and Antonio bound.

BASSANIO. Your answer to that.

SHYLOCK. Antonio is a good man.

BASSANIO. Have you heard any imputation to the contrary?

SHYLOCK. Ho, no, no, no, no; my meaning in saying he is a good man is to have you understand me that he is sufficient; yet his means are in supposition: he hath an argosy bound to Tripolis, another to the Indies; I understand, moreover, upon the Rialto, he hath a third at Mexico, a fourth for England—and other ventures he hath, squand'red abroad. But ships are but boards, sailors but men; there be land-rats and water-rats, water-thieves and land-thieves—I mean pirates; and then there is the peril of waters, winds, and rocks. The man is, notwithstanding, sufficient. Three thousand ducats—I think I may take his bond.

BASSANIO. Be assur'd you may.

SHYLOCK. I will be assur'd I may; and, that I may be assured, I will bethink me. May I speak with Antonio?

BASSANIO. If it please you to dine with us.

SHYLOCK. Yes, to smell pork, to eat of the habitation which your prophet, the Nazarite, conjured the devil into! I will buy with you, sell with you, talk with you, walk with you, and so following; but I will not eat with you, drink with you, nor pray with you. What news on the Rialto? Who is he comes here?

Enter ANTONIO

BASSANIO. This is Signior Antonio.

SHYLOCK. [Aside] How like a fawning publican he looks!
I hate him for he is a Christian;
But more for that in low simplicity
He lends out money gratis, and brings down
The rate of usance here with us in Venice.
If I can catch him once upon the hip,
I will feed fat the ancient grudge I bear him.
He hates our sacred nation; and he rails,
Even there where merchants most do congregate,
On me, my bargains, and my well-won thrift,
Which he calls interest. Cursed be my tribe
If I forgive him!

BASSANIO. Shylock, do you hear?

SHYLOCK. I am debating of my present store,
And, by the near guess of my memory,

I cannot instantly raise up the gross
Of full three thousand ducats. What of that?
Tubal, a wealthy Hebrew of my tribe,
Will furnish me. But soft! how many months
Do you desire? [To ANTONIO] Rest you fair, good
    signior;
Your worship was the last man in our mouths.

ANTONIO. Shylock, albeit I neither lend nor borrow
By taking nor by giving of excess,
Yet, to supply the ripe wants of my friend,
I'll break a custom. [To BASSANIO] Is he yet possess'd
How much ye would?

SHYLOCK. Ay, ay, three thousand ducats.

ANTONIO. And for three months.

SHYLOCK. I had forgot—three months; you told me so.
Well then, your bond; and, let me see—but hear you,
Methoughts you said you neither lend nor borrow
Upon advantage.

ANTONIO. I do never use it.

SHYLOCK. When Jacob graz'd his uncle Laban's sheep—
This Jacob from our holy Abram was,
As his wise mother wrought in his behalf,
The third possessor; ay, he was the third—

ANTONIO. And what of him? Did he take interest?

SHYLOCK. No, not take interest; not, as you would say,
Directly int'rest; mark what Jacob did:
When Laban and himself were compromis'd
That all the eanlings which were streak'd and pied
Should fall as Jacob's hire, the ewes, being rank,
In end of autumn turned to the rams;
And when the work of generation was
Between these woolly breeders in the act,
The skilful shepherd pill'd me certain wands,
And, in the doing of the deed of kind,
He stuck them up before the fulsome ewes,
Who, then conceiving, did in eaning time
Fall parti-colour'd lambs, and those were Jacob's.
This was a way to thrive, and he was blest;
And thrift is blessing, if men steal it not.

ANTONIO. This was a venture, sir, that Jacob serv'd for;
A thing not in his power to bring to pass,
But sway'd and fashion'd by the hand of heaven.
Was this inserted to make interest good?
Or is your gold and silver ewes and rams?

SHYLOCK. I cannot tell; I make it breed as fast.
But note me, signior.

ANTONIO. [Aside] Mark you this, Bassanio,
The devil can cite Scripture for his purpose.
An evil soul producing holy witness
Is like a villain with a smiling cheek,
A goodly apple rotten at the heart.
O, what a goodly outside falsehood hath!

SHYLOCK. Three thousand ducats—'tis a good round sum.
Three months from twelve; then let me see, the rate—

ANTONIO. Well, Shylock, shall we be beholding to you?

SHYLOCK. Signior Antonio, many a time and oft

In the Rialto you have rated me
About my moneys and my usances;
Still have I borne it with a patient shrug,
For suff'rance is the badge of all our tribe;
You call me misbeliever, cut-throat dog,
And spit upon my Jewish gaberdine,
And all for use of that which is mine own.
Well then, it now appears you need my help;
Go to, then; you come to me, and you say
'Shylock, we would have moneys.' You say so—
You that did void your rheum upon my beard
And foot me as you spurn a stranger cur
Over your threshold; moneys is your suit.
What should I say to you? Should I not say
'Hath a dog money? Is it possible
A cur can lend three thousand ducats?' Or
Shall I bend low and, in a bondman's key,
With bated breath and whisp'ring humbleness,
Say this:
'Fair sir, you spit on me on Wednesday last,
You spurn'd me such a day; another time
You call'd me dog; and for these courtesies
I'll lend you thus much moneys'?

ANTONIO. I am as like to call thee so again,
To spit on thee again, to spurn thee too.
If thou wilt lend this money, lend it not
As to thy friends—for when did friendship take
A breed for barren metal of his friend?—
But lend it rather to thine enemy,
Who if he break thou mayst with better face
Exact the penalty.

SHYLOCK. Why, look you, how you storm!
I would be friends with you, and have your love,
Forget the shames that you have stain'd me with,
Supply your present wants, and take no doit
Of usance for my moneys, and you'll not hear me.
This is kind I offer.

BASSANIO. This were kindness.

SHYLOCK. This kindness will I show.
Go with me to a notary, seal me there
Your single bond, and, in a merry sport,
If you repay me not on such a day,
In such a place, such sum or sums as are
Express'd in the condition, let the forfeit
Be nominated for an equal pound
Of your fair flesh, to be cut off and taken
In what part of your body pleaseth me.

ANTONIO. Content, in faith; I'll seal to such a bond,
And say there is much kindness in the Jew.

BASSANIO. You shall not seal to such a bond for me;
I'll rather dwell in my necessity.

ANTONIO. Why, fear not, man; I will not forfeit it;
Within these two months—that's a month before
This bond expires—I do expect return
Of thrice three times the value of this bond.

SHYLOCK. O father Abram, what these Christians are,

Whose own hard dealings teaches them suspect
The thoughts of others! Pray you, tell me this:
If he should break his day, what should I gain
By the exaction of the forfeiture?
A pound of man's flesh taken from a man
Is not so estimable, profitable neither,
As flesh of muttons, beefs, or goats. I say,
To buy his favour, I extend this friendship;
If he will take it, so; if not, adieu;
And, for my love, I pray you wrong me not.
ANTONIO. Yes, Shylock, I will seal unto this bond.
SHYLOCK. Then meet me forthwith at the notary's;

Give him direction for this merry bond,
And I will go and purse the ducats straight,
See to my house, left in the fearful guard
Of an unthrifty knave, and presently
I'll be with you.
ANTONIO. Hie thee, gentle Jew.   Exit SHYLOCK
The Hebrew will turn Christian: he grows kind.
BASSANIO. I like not fair terms and a villain's mind.
ANTONIO. Come on; in this there can be no dismay;
My ships come home a month before the day.
    Exeunt

William Shakespeare

The Merchant of Venice

1597

Act II.

Scene I.

> Belmont. PORTIA'S house

> Flourish of cornets. Enter the PRINCE of MOROCCO,
> a tawny Moor all in white, and three or four
> FOLLOWERS
>   accordingly, with PORTIA, NERISSA, and train

PRINCE OF Morocco. Mislike me not for my complexion,
  The shadowed livery of the burnish'd sun,
  To whom I am a neighbour, and near bred.
  Bring me the fairest creature northward born,
  Where Phoebus' fire scarce thaws the icicles,
  And let us make incision for your love
  To prove whose blood is reddest, his or mine.
  I tell thee, lady, this aspect of mine
  Hath fear'd the valiant; by my love, I swear
  The best-regarded virgins of our clime
  Have lov'd it too. I would not change this hue,
  Except to steal your thoughts, my gentle queen.
PORTIA. In terms of choice I am not solely led
  By nice direction of a maiden's eyes;
  Besides, the lott'ry of my destiny
  Bars me the right of voluntary choosing.
  But, if my father had not scanted me,
  And hedg'd me by his wit to yield myself
  His wife who wins me by that means I told you,
  Yourself, renowned Prince, then stood as fair
  As any comer I have look'd on yet
  For my affection.
PRINCE OF MOROCCO. Even for that I thank you.
  Therefore, I pray you, lead me to the caskets
To try my fortune. By this scimitar,
That slew the Sophy and a Persian prince,
That won three fields of Sultan Solyman,
I would o'erstare the sternest eyes that look,
Outbrave the heart most daring on the earth,
Pluck the young sucking cubs from the she-bear,
Yea, mock the lion when 'a roars for prey,
To win thee, lady. But, alas the while!
If Hercules and Lichas play at dice
Which is the better man, the greater throw
May turn by fortune from the weaker band.
So is Alcides beaten by his page;
And so may I, blind Fortune leading me,
Miss that which one unworthier may attain,
And die with grieving.
PORTIA. You must take your chance,
  And either not attempt to choose at all,
  Or swear before you choose, if you choose wrong,
  Never to speak to lady afterward
  In way of marriage; therefore be advis'd.
PRINCE OF MOROCCO. Nor will not; come, bring me unto
    my chance.
PORTIA. First, forward to the temple. After dinner
  Your hazard shall be made.
PRINCE OF MOROCCO. Good fortune then,
  To make me blest or cursed'st among men!
                    [Cornets, and exeunt]

Scene II.

> Venice. A street

Enter LAUNCELOT GOBBO

LAUNCELOT. Certainly my conscience will serve me to run from this Jew my master. The fiend is at mine elbow and tempts me, saying to me 'Gobbo, Launcelot Gobbo, good Launcelot' or 'good Gobbo' or 'good Launcelot Gobbo, use your legs, take the start, run away.' My conscience says 'No; take heed, honest Launcelot, take heed, honest Gobbo' or, as aforesaid, 'honest Launcelot Gobbo, do not run; scorn running with thy heels.' Well, the most courageous fiend bids me pack. 'Via!' says the fiend; 'away!' says the fiend. 'For the heavens, rouse up a brave mind' says the fiend 'and run.' Well, my conscience, hanging about the neck of my heart, says very wisely to me 'My honest friend Launcelot, being an honest man's son' or rather 'an honest woman's son'; for indeed my father did something smack, something grow to, he had a kind of taste—well, my conscience says 'Launcelot, budge not.' 'Budge,' says the fiend. 'Budge not,' says my conscience. 'Conscience,' say I, (you counsel well.' 'Fiend,' say I, 'you counsel well.' To be rul'd by my conscience, I should stay with the Jew my master, who—God bless the mark!—is a kind of devil; and, to run away from the Jew, I should be ruled by the fiend, who—saving your reverence!—is the devil himself. Certainly the Jew is the very devil incarnation; and, in my conscience, my conscience is but a kind of hard conscience to offer to counsel me to stay with the Jew. The fiend gives the more friendly counsel. I will run, fiend; my heels are at your commandment; I will run.

Enter OLD GOBBO, with a basket

GOBBO. Master young man, you, I pray you, which is the way to master Jew's?

LAUNCELOT. [Aside] O heavens! This is my true-begotten father, who, being more than sand-blind, high-gravel blind, knows me not. I will try confusions with him.

GOBBO. Master young gentleman, I pray you, which is the way to master Jew's?

LAUNCELOT. Turn up on your right hand at the next turning, but, at the next turning of all, on your left; marry, at the very next turning, turn of no hand, but turn down indirectly to the Jew's house.

GOBBO. Be God's sonties, 'twill be a hard way to hit! Can you tell me whether one Launcelot, that dwells with him, dwell with him or no?

LAUNCELOT. Talk you of young Master Launcelot? [Aside] Mark me now; now will I raise the waters.—Talk you of young Master Launcelot?

GOBBO. No master, sir, but a poor man's son; his father, though I say't, is an honest exceeding poor man, and, God be thanked, well to live.

LAUNCELOT. Well, let his father be what 'a will, we talk of young Master Launcelot.

GOBBO. Your worship's friend, and Launcelot, sir.

LAUNCELOT. But I pray you, ergo, old man, ergo, I beseech you, talk you of young Master Launcelot?

GOBBO. Of Launcelot, an't please your mastership.

LAUNCELOT. Ergo, Master Launcelot. Talk not of Master Launcelot, father; for the young gentleman, according to Fates and Destinies and such odd sayings, the Sisters Three and such branches of learning, is indeed deceased; or, as you would say in plain terms, gone to heaven.

GOBBO. Marry, God forbid! The boy was the very staff of my age, my very prop.

LAUNCELOT. Do I look like a cudgel or a hovel-post, a staff or a prop? Do you know me, father?

GOBBO. Alack the day, I know you not, young gentleman; but I pray you tell me, is my boy—God rest his soul!—alive or dead?

LAUNCELOT. Do you not know me, father?

GOBBO. Alack, sir, I am sand-blind; I know you not.

LAUNCELOT. Nay, indeed, if you had your eyes, you might fail of the knowing me: it is a wise father that knows his own child. Well, old man, I will tell you news of your son. Give me your blessing; truth will come to light; murder cannot be hid long; a man's son may, but in the end truth will out.

GOBBO. Pray you, sir, stand up; I am sure you are not Launcelot my boy.

LAUNCELOT. Pray you, let's have no more fooling about it, but give me your blessing; I am Launcelot, your boy that was, your son that is, your child that shall be.

GOBBO. I cannot think you are my son.

LAUNCELOT. I know not what I shall think of that; but I am Launcelot, the Jew's man, and I am sure Margery your wife is my mother.

GOBBO. Her name is Margery, indeed. I'll be sworn, if thou be Launcelot, thou art mine own flesh and blood. Lord worshipp'd might he be, what a beard hast thou got! Thou hast got more hair on thy chin than Dobbin my fill-horse has on his tail.

LAUNCELOT. It should seem, then, that Dobbin's tail grows backward; I am sure he had more hair of his tail than I have of my face when I last saw him.

GOBBO. Lord, how art thou chang'd! How dost thou and thy master agree? I have brought him a present. How 'gree you now?

LAUNCELOT. Well, well; but, for mine own part, as I have set up my rest to run away, so I will not rest till I have run some ground. My master's a very Jew. Give him a present! Give him a halter. I am famish'd in his service; you may tell every finger I have with my ribs. Father, I am glad you are come; give me your present to one Master Bassanio, who indeed gives rare new liveries; if I serve not him, I will run as far as God has any ground. O rare fortune! Here comes the man. To him, father, for I am a Jew, if I serve the Jew any longer.

Enter BASSANIO, with LEONARDO, with a FOLLOWER or two

BASSANIO. You may do so; but let it be so hasted that
  supper be ready at the farthest by five of the clock. See
  these letters delivered, put the liveries to making, and
  desire Gratiano to come anon to my lodging.
    Exit a SERVANT
LAUNCELOT. To him, father.
GOBBO. God bless your worship!
BASSANIO. Gramercy; wouldst thou aught with me?
GOBBO. Here's my son, sir, a poor boy—
LAUNCELOT. Not a poor boy, sir, but the rich Jew's man,
  that would, sir, as my father shall specify—
GOBBO. He hath a great infection, sir, as one would say, to
  serve—
LAUNCELOT. Indeed the short and the long is, I serve the
  Jew, and have a desire, as my father shall specify—
GOBBO. His master and he, saving your worship's
  reverence, are scarce cater-cousins—
LAUNCELOT. To be brief, the very truth is that the Jew,
  having done me wrong, doth cause me, as my father,
  being I hope an old man, shall frutify unto you—
GOBBO. I have here a dish of doves that I would bestow
  upon your worship; and my suit is—
LAUNCELOT. In very brief, the suit is impertinent to myself,
  as your worship shall know by this honest old man; and,
  though I say it, though old man, yet poor man, my
  father.
BASSANIO. One speak for both. What would you?
LAUNCELOT. Serve you, sir.
GOBBO. That is the very defect of the matter, sir.
BASSANIO. I know thee well; thou hast obtain'd thy suit.
  Shylock thy master spoke with me this day,
  And hath preferr'd thee, if it be preferment
  To leave a rich Jew's service to become
  The follower of so poor a gentleman.
LAUNCELOT. The old proverb is very well parted between
  my master Shylock and you, sir: you have the grace of
  God, sir, and he hath enough.
BASSANIO. Thou speak'st it well. Go, father, with thy son.
  Take leave of thy old master, and inquire
  My lodging out. [To a SERVANT] Give him a livery
  More guarded than his fellows'; see it done.
LAUNCELOT. Father, in. I cannot get a service, no! I have
  ne'er a tongue in my head! [Looking on his palm]
  Well; if any man in Italy have a fairer table which doth
  offer to swear upon a book—I shall have good fortune.
  Go to, here's a simple line of life; here's a small trifle of
  wives; alas, fifteen wives is nothing; a'leven widows and
  nine maids is a simple coming-in for one man. And then
  to scape drowning thrice, and to be in peril of my life
  with the edge of a feather-bed-here are simple scapes.
  Well, if Fortune be a woman, she's a good wench for this
  gear. Father, come; I'll take my leave of the Jew in the
  twinkling.

Exeunt LAUNCELOT and OLD GOBBO

BASSANIO. I pray thee, good Leonardo, think on this.
  These things being bought and orderly bestowed,
  Return in haste, for I do feast to-night
  My best esteem'd acquaintance; hie thee, go.
LEONARDO. My best endeavours shall be done herein.

Enter GRATIANO

GRATIANO. Where's your master?
LEONARDO. Yonder, sir, he walks.   Exit
GRATIANO. Signior Bassanio!
BASSANIO. Gratiano!
GRATIANO. I have suit to you.
BASSANIO. You have obtain'd it.
GRATIANO. You must not deny me: I must go with you to
  Belmont.
BASSANIO. Why, then you must. But hear thee, Gratiano:
  Thou art too wild, too rude, and bold of voice—
  Parts that become thee happily enough,
  And in such eyes as ours appear not faults;
  But where thou art not known, why there they show
  Something too liberal. Pray thee, take pain
  To allay with some cold drops of modesty
  Thy skipping spirit; lest through thy wild behaviour
  I be misconst'red in the place I go to
  And lose my hopes.
GRATIANO. Signior Bassanio, hear me:
  If I do not put on a sober habit,
  Talk with respect, and swear but now and then,
  Wear prayer-books in my pocket, look demurely,
  Nay more, while grace is saying hood mine eyes
  Thus with my hat, and sigh, and say amen,
  Use all the observance of civility
  Like one well studied in a sad ostent
  To please his grandam, never trust me more.
BASSANIO. Well, we shall see your bearing.
GRATIANO. Nay, but I bar to-night; you shall not gauge me
  By what we do to-night.
BASSANIO. No, that were pity;
  I would entreat you rather to put on
  Your boldest suit of mirth, for we have friends
  That purpose merriment. But fare you well;
  I have some business.
GRATIANO. And I must to Lorenzo and the rest;
  But we will visit you at supper-time.   Exeunt

Scene III.

Venice. SHYLOCK'S house

Enter JESSICA and LAUNCELOT

JESSICA. I am sorry thou wilt leave my father so.
  Our house is hell; and thou, a merry devil,
  Didst rob it of some taste of tediousness.

But fare thee well; there is a ducat for thee;
And, Launcelot, soon at supper shalt thou see
Lorenzo, who is thy new master's guest.
Give him this letter; do it secretly.
And so farewell. I would not have my father
See me in talk with thee.
LAUNCELOT. Adieu! tears exhibit my tongue. Most
beautiful pagan, most sweet Jew! If a Christian do not
play the knave and get thee, I am much deceived. But,
adieu! these foolish drops do something drown my
manly spirit; adieu!
JESSICA. Farewell, good Launcelot.   Exit LAUNCELOT
Alack, what heinous sin is it in me
To be asham'd to be my father's child!
But though I am a daughter to his blood,
I am not to his manners. O Lorenzo,
If thou keep promise, I shall end this strife,
Become a Christian and thy loving wife.   Exit

Scene IV.

Venice. A street

Enter GRATIANO, LORENZO, SALERIO, and
SOLANIO

LORENZO. Nay, we will slink away in suppertime,
Disguise us at my lodging, and return
All in an hour.
GRATIANO. We have not made good preparation.
SALERIO. We have not spoke us yet of torch-bearers.
SOLANIO. 'Tis vile, unless it may be quaintly ordered;
And better in my mind not undertook.
LORENZO. 'Tis now but four o'clock; we have two hours
To furnish us.

Enter LAUNCELOT, With a letter

Friend Launcelot, what's the news?
LAUNCELOT. An it shall please you to break up this, it shall
seem to signify.
LORENZO. I know the hand; in faith, 'tis a fair hand,
And whiter than the paper it writ on
Is the fair hand that writ.
GRATIANO. Love-news, in faith!
LAUNCELOT. By your leave, sir.
LORENZO. Whither goest thou?
LAUNCELOT. Marry, sir, to bid my old master, the Jew, to
sup to-night with my new master, the Christian.
LORENZO. Hold, here, take this. Tell gentle Jessica I will
not fail her; speak it privately.
Go, gentlemen,   Exit LAUNCELOT
Will you prepare you for this masque to-night?
I am provided of a torch-bearer.
SALERIO. Ay, marry, I'll be gone about it straight.
SOLANIO. And so will I.

LORENZO. Meet me and Gratiano
At Gratiano's lodging some hour hence.
SALERIO. 'Tis good we do so.   Exeunt SALERIO and
SOLANIO
GRATIANO. Was not that letter from fair Jessica?
LORENZO. I must needs tell thee all. She hath directed
How I shall take her from her father's house;
What gold and jewels she is furnish'd with;
What page's suit she hath in readiness.
If e'er the Jew her father come to heaven,
It will be for his gentle daughter's sake;
And never dare misfortune cross her foot,
Unless she do it under this excuse,
That she is issue to a faithless Jew.
Come, go with me, peruse this as thou goest;
Fair Jessica shall be my torch-bearer.   Exeunt

Scene V.

Venice. Before SHYLOCK'S house

Enter SHYLOCK and LAUNCELOT

SHYLOCK. Well, thou shalt see; thy eyes shall be thy judge,
The difference of old Shylock and Bassanio.—
What, Jessica!—Thou shalt not gormandize
As thou hast done with me—What, Jessica!—
And sleep and snore, and rend apparel out—
Why, Jessica, I say!
LAUNCELOT. Why, Jessica!
SHYLOCK. Who bids thee call? I do not bid thee call.
LAUNCELOT. Your worship was wont to tell me I could do
nothing without bidding.

Enter JESSICA

JESSICA. Call you? What is your will?
SHYLOCK. I am bid forth to supper, Jessica;
There are my keys. But wherefore should I go?
I am not bid for love; they flatter me;
But yet I'll go in hate, to feed upon
The prodigal Christian. Jessica, my girl,
Look to my house. I am right loath to go;
There is some ill a-brewing towards my rest,
For I did dream of money-bags to-night.
LAUNCELOT. I beseech you, sir, go; my young master doth
expect your reproach.
SHYLOCK. So do I his.
LAUNCELOT. And they have conspired together; I will not
say you shall see a masque, but if you do, then it was not
for nothing that my nose fell a-bleeding on Black
Monday last at six o'clock i' th' morning, falling out that
year on Ash Wednesday was four year, in th' afternoon.
SHYLOCK. What, are there masques? Hear you me, Jessica:
Lock up my doors, and when you hear the drum,
And the vile squealing of the wry-neck'd fife,

Clamber not you up to the casements then,
Nor thrust your head into the public street
To gaze on Christian fools with varnish'd faces;
But stop my house's ears—I mean my casements;
Let not the sound of shallow fopp'ry enter
My sober house. By Jacob's staff, I swear
I have no mind of feasting forth to-night;
But I will go. Go you before me, sirrah;
Say I will come.
LAUNCELOT. I will go before, sir. Mistress, look out at
    window for all this.
        There will come a Christian by
        Will be worth a Jewess' eye.   Exit
SHYLOCK. What says that fool of Hagar's offspring, ha?
JESSICA. His words were 'Farewell, mistress'; nothing else.
SHYLOCK. The patch is kind enough, but a huge feeder,
    Snail-slow in profit, and he sleeps by day
    More than the wild-cat; drones hive not with me,
    Therefore I part with him; and part with him
    To one that I would have him help to waste
    His borrowed purse. Well, Jessica, go in;
    Perhaps I will return immediately.
    Do as I bid you, shut doors after you.
    Fast bind, fast find—
    A proverb never stale in thrifty mind.   Exit
JESSICA. Farewell; and if my fortune be not crost,
    I have a father, you a daughter, lost.   Exit

Scene VI.

Venice. Before SHYLOCK'S house

Enter the maskers, GRATIANO and SALERIO

GRATIANO. This is the pent-house under which Lorenzo
    Desired us to make stand.
SALERIO. His hour is almost past.
GRATIANO. And it is marvel he out-dwells his hour,
    For lovers ever run before the clock.
SALERIO. O, ten times faster Venus' pigeons fly
    To seal love's bonds new made than they are wont
    To keep obliged faith unforfeited!
GRATIANO. That ever holds: who riseth from a feast
    With that keen appetite that he sits down?
    Where is the horse that doth untread again
    His tedious measures with the unbated fire
    That he did pace them first? All things that are
    Are with more spirit chased than enjoyed.
    How like a younker or a prodigal
    The scarfed bark puts from her native bay,
    Hugg'd and embraced by the strumpet wind;
    How like the prodigal doth she return,
    With over-weather'd ribs and ragged sails,
    Lean, rent, and beggar'd by the strumpet wind!

Enter LORENZO

SALERIO. Here comes Lorenzo; more of this hereafter.
LORENZO. Sweet friends, your patience for my long abode!
    Not I, but my affairs, have made you wait.
    When you shall please to play the thieves for wives,
    I'll watch as long for you then. Approach;
    Here dwells my father Jew. Ho! who's within?

Enter JESSICA, above, in boy's clothes

JESSICA. Who are you? Tell me, for more certainty,
    Albeit I'll swear that I do know your tongue.
LORENZO. Lorenzo, and thy love.
JESSICA. Lorenzo, certain; and my love indeed;
    For who love I so much? And now who knows
    But you, Lorenzo, whether I am yours?
LORENZO. Heaven and thy thoughts are witness that thou
    art.
JESSICA. Here, catch this casket; it is worth the pains.
    I am glad 'tis night, you do not look on me,
    For I am much asham'd of my exchange;
    But love is blind, and lovers cannot see
    The pretty follies that themselves commit,
    For, if they could, Cupid himself would blush
    To see me thus transformed to a boy.
LORENZO. Descend, for you must be my torch-bearer.
JESSICA. What! must I hold a candle to my shames?
    They in themselves, good sooth, are too too light.
    Why, 'tis an office of discovery, love,
    And I should be obscur'd.
LORENZO. So are you, sweet,
    Even in the lovely garnish of a boy.
    But come at once,
    For the close night doth play the runaway,
    And we are stay'd for at Bassanio's feast.
JESSICA. I will make fast the doors, and gild myself
    With some moe ducats, and be with you straight.
                            Exit above

GRATIANO. Now, by my hood, a gentle, and no Jew.
LORENZO. Beshrew me, but I love her heartily,
    For she is wise, if I can judge of her,
    And fair she is, if that mine eyes be true,
    And true she is, as she hath prov'd herself;
    And therefore, like herself, wise, fair, and true,
    Shall she be placed in my constant soul.

Enter JESSICA, below

What, art thou come? On, gentlemen, away;
Our masquing mates by this time for us stay.
                Exit with JESSICA and SALERIO

Enter ANTONIO

ANTONIO. Who's there?

GRATIANO. Signior Antonio?

ANTONIO. Fie, fie, Gratiano, where are all the rest?
 'Tis nine o'clock; our friends all stay for you;
 No masque to-night; the wind is come about;
 Bassanio presently will go aboard;
 I have sent twenty out to seek for you.

GRATIANO. I am glad on't; I desire no more delight
 Than to be under sail and gone to-night.   Exeunt

Scene VII.

Belmont. PORTIA's house

Flourish of cornets. Enter PORTIA, with the PRINCE OF
MOROCCO, and their trains

PORTIA. Go draw aside the curtains and discover
 The several caskets to this noble Prince.
 Now make your choice.

PRINCE OF MOROCCO. The first, of gold, who this
    inscription bears:
 'Who chooseth me shall gain what many men desire.'
 The second, silver, which this promise carries:
 'Who chooseth me shall get as much as he deserves.'
 This third, dull lead, with warning all as blunt:
 'Who chooseth me must give and hazard all he hath.'
 How shall I know if I do choose the right?

PORTIA. The one of them contains my picture, Prince;
 If you choose that, then I am yours withal.

PRINCE OF MOROCCO. Some god direct my judgment! Let
    me see;
 I will survey th' inscriptions back again.
 What says this leaden casket?
 'Who chooseth me must give and hazard all he hath.'
 Must give—for what? For lead? Hazard for lead!
 This casket threatens; men that hazard all
 Do it in hope of fair advantages.
 A golden mind stoops not to shows of dross;
 I'll then nor give nor hazard aught for lead.
 What says the silver with her virgin hue?
 'Who chooseth me shall get as much as he deserves.'
 As much as he deserves! Pause there, Morocco,
 And weigh thy value with an even hand.
 If thou beest rated by thy estimation,
 Thou dost deserve enough, and yet enough
 May not extend so far as to the lady;
 And yet to be afeard of my deserving
 Were but a weak disabling of myself.
 As much as I deserve? Why, that's the lady!
 I do in birth deserve her, and in fortunes,
 In graces, and in qualities of breeding;
 But more than these, in love I do deserve.
 What if I stray'd no farther, but chose here?
 Let's see once more this saying grav'd in gold:
 'Who chooseth me shall gain what many men desire.'

Why, that's the lady! All the world desires her;
 From the four corners of the earth they come
 To kiss this shrine, this mortal-breathing saint.
 The Hyrcanian deserts and the vasty wilds
 Of wide Arabia are as throughfares now
 For princes to come view fair Portia.
 The watery kingdom, whose ambitious head
 Spits in the face of heaven, is no bar
 To stop the foreign spirits, but they come
 As o'er a brook to see fair Portia.
 One of these three contains her heavenly picture.
 Is't like that lead contains her? 'Twere damnation
 To think so base a thought; it were too gross
 To rib her cerecloth in the obscure grave.
 Or shall I think in silver she's immur'd,
 Being ten times undervalued to tried gold?
 O sinful thought! Never so rich a gem
 Was set in worse than gold. They have in England
 A coin that bears the figure of an angel
 Stamp'd in gold; but that's insculp'd upon.
 But here an angel in a golden bed
 Lies all within. Deliver me the key;
 Here do I choose, and thrive I as I may!

PORTIA. There, take it, Prince, and if my form lie there,
 Then I am yours.   [He opens the golden casket]

PRINCE OF MOROCCO. O hell! what have we here?
 A carrion Death, within whose empty eye
 There is a written scroll! I'll read the writing.
    'All that glisters is not gold,
    Often have you heard that told;
    Many a man his life hath sold
    But my outside to behold.
    Gilded tombs do worms infold.
    Had you been as wise as bold,
    Young in limbs, in judgment old,
    Your answer had not been inscroll'd.
    Fare you well, your suit is cold.'
   Cold indeed, and labour lost,
   Then farewell, heat, and welcome, frost.
 Portia, adieu! I have too griev'd a heart
 To take a tedious leave; thus losers part.
               Exit with his train. Flourish of cornets

PORTIA. A gentle riddance. Draw the curtains, go.
 Let all of his complexion choose me so.   Exeunt

Scene VIII.

Venice. A street

Enter SALERIO and SOLANIO

SALERIO. Why, man, I saw Bassanio under sail;
 With him is Gratiano gone along;
 And in their ship I am sure Lorenzo is not.

SOLANIO. The villain Jew with outcries rais'd the Duke,
 Who went with him to search Bassanio's ship.

SALERIO. He came too late, the ship was under sail;
  But there the Duke was given to understand
  That in a gondola were seen together
  Lorenzo and his amorous Jessica;
  Besides, Antonio certified the Duke
  They were not with Bassanio in his ship.
SOLANIO. I never heard a passion so confus'd,
  So strange, outrageous, and so variable,
  As the dog Jew did utter in the streets.
  'My daughter! O my ducats! O my daughter!
  Fled with a Christian! O my Christian ducats!
  Justice! the law! My ducats and my daughter!
  A sealed bag, two sealed bags of ducats,
  Of double ducats, stol'n from me by my daughter!
  And jewels—two stones, two rich and precious stones,
  Stol'n by my daughter! Justice! Find the girl;
  She hath the stones upon her and the ducats.'
SALERIO. Why, all the boys in Venice follow him,
  Crying, his stones, his daughter, and his ducats.
SOLANIO. Let good Antonio look he keep his day,
  Or he shall pay for this.
SALERIO. Marry, well rememb'red;
  I reason'd with a Frenchman yesterday,
  Who told me, in the narrow seas that part
  The French and English, there miscarried
  A vessel of our country richly fraught.
  I thought upon Antonio when he told me,
  And wish'd in silence that it were not his.
SOLANIO. You were best to tell Antonio what you hear;
  Yet do not suddenly, for it may grieve him.
SALERIO. A kinder gentleman treads not the earth.
  I saw Bassanio and Antonio part.
  Bassanio told him he would make some speed
  Of his return. He answered 'Do not so;
  Slubber not business for my sake, Bassanio,
  But stay the very riping of the time;
  And for the Jew's bond which he hath of me,
  Let it not enter in your mind of love;
  Be merry, and employ your chiefest thoughts
  To courtship, and such fair ostents of love
  As shall conveniently become you there.'
  And even there, his eye being big with tears,
  Turning his face, he put his hand behind him,
  And with affection wondrous sensible
  He wrung Bassanio's hand; and so they parted.
SOLANIO. I think he only loves the world for him.
  I pray thee, let us go and find him out,
  And quicken his embraced heaviness
  With some delight or other.
SALERIO. Do we so.   *Exeunt*

Scene IX.

Belmont. PORTIA'S house

Enter NERISSA, *and a* SERVITOR

NERISSA. Quick, quick, I pray thee, draw the curtain
  straight;
  The Prince of Arragon hath ta'en his oath,
  And comes to his election presently.

Flourish of cornets. Enter the PRINCE OF ARRAGON,
PORTIA, *and their trains*

PORTIA. Behold, there stand the caskets, noble Prince.
  If you choose that wherein I am contain'd,
  Straight shall our nuptial rites be solemniz'd;
  But if you fail, without more speech, my lord,
  You must be gone from hence immediately.
ARRAGON. I am enjoin'd by oath to observe three things:
  First, never to unfold to any one
  Which casket 'twas I chose; next, if I fail
  Of the right casket, never in my life
  To woo a maid in way of marriage;
  Lastly,
  If I do fail in fortune of my choice,
  Immediately to leave you and be gone.
PORTIA. To these injunctions every one doth swear
  That comes to hazard for my worthless self.
ARRAGON. And so have I address'd me. Fortune now
  To my heart's hope! Gold, silver, and base lead.
  'Who chooseth me must give and hazard all he hath.'
  You shall look fairer ere I give or hazard.
  What says the golden chest? Ha! let me see:
  'Who chooseth me shall gain what many men desire.'
  What many men desire—that 'many' may be meant
  By the fool multitude, that choose by show,
  Not learning more than the fond eye doth teach;
  Which pries not to th' interior, but, like the martlet,
  Builds in the weather on the outward wall,
  Even in the force and road of casualty.
  I will not choose what many men desire,
  Because I will not jump with common spirits
  And rank me with the barbarous multitudes.
  Why, then to thee, thou silver treasure-house!
  Tell me once more what title thou dost bear.
  'Who chooseth me shall get as much as he deserves.'
  And well said too; for who shall go about
  To cozen fortune, and be honourable
  Without the stamp of merit? Let none presume
  To wear an undeserved dignity.
  O that estates, degrees, and offices,
  Were not deriv'd corruptly, and that clear honour
  Were purchas'd by the merit of the wearer!
  How many then should cover that stand bare!
  How many be commanded that command!
  How much low peasantry would then be gleaned
  From the true seed of honour! and how much honour
  Pick'd from the chaff and ruin of the times,
  To be new varnish'd! Well, but to my choice.

'Who chooseth me shall get as much as he deserves.'
I will assume desert. Give me a key for this,
And instantly unlock my fortunes here.
                    [He opens the silver casket]
PORTIA. [Aside] Too long a pause for that which you find
    there.
ARRAGON. What's here? The portrait of a blinking idiot
    Presenting me a schedule! I will read it.
    How much unlike art thou to Portia!
    How much unlike my hopes and my deservings!
    'Who chooseth me shall have as much as he deserves.'
    Did I deserve no more than a fool's head?
    Is that my prize? Are my deserts no better?
PORTIA. To offend and judge are distinct offices
    And of opposed natures.
ARRAGON. What is here? [Reads]

        'The fire seven times tried this;
        Seven times tried that judgment is
        That did never choose amiss.
        Some there be that shadows kiss,
        Such have but a shadow's bliss.
        There be fools alive iwis
        Silver'd o'er, and so was this.
        Take what wife you will to bed,
        I will ever be your head.
        So be gone; you are sped.'

        Still more fool I shall appear
        By the time I linger here.
        With one fool's head I came to woo,

        But I go away with two.
        Sweet, adieu! I'll keep my oath,
        Patiently to bear my wroth.   Exit with his train

PORTIA. Thus hath the candle sing'd the moth.
    O, these deliberate fools! When they do choose,
    They have the wisdom by their wit to lose.
NERISSA. The ancient saying is no heresy:
    Hanging and wiving goes by destiny.
PORTIA. Come, draw the curtain, Nerissa.

                Enter a SERVANT

SERVANT. Where is my lady?
PORTIA. Here; what would my lord?
SERVANT. Madam, there is alighted at your gate
    A young Venetian, one that comes before
    To signify th' approaching of his lord,
    From whom he bringeth sensible regreets;
    To wit, besides commends and courteous breath,
    Gifts of rich value. Yet I have not seen
    So likely an ambassador of love.
    A day in April never came so sweet
    To show how costly summer was at hand
    As this fore-spurrer comes before his lord.
PORTIA. No more, I pray thee; I am half afeard
    Thou wilt say anon he is some kin to thee,
    Thou spend'st such high-day wit in praising him.
    Come, come, Nerissa, for I long to see
    Quick Cupid's post that comes so mannerly.
NERISSA. Bassanio, Lord Love, if thy will it be!   Exeunt

William Shakespeare

The Merchant of Venice

1597

Act III.

Scene I.

Venice. A street

Enter SOLANIO and SALERIO

SOLANIO. Now, what news on the Rialto?

SALERIO. Why, yet it lives there uncheck'd that Antonio hath a ship of rich lading wreck'd on the narrow seas; the Goodwins I think they call the place, a very dangerous flat and fatal, where the carcases of many a tall ship lie buried, as they say, if my gossip Report be an honest woman of her word.

SOLANIO. I would she were as lying a gossip in that as ever knapp'd ginger or made her neighbours believe she wept for the death of a third husband. But it is true, without any slips of prolixity or crossing the plain highway of talk, that the good Antonio, the honest Antonio—O that I had a title good enough to keep his name company!—

SALERIO. Come, the full stop.

SOLANIO. Ha! What sayest thou? Why, the end is, he hath lost a ship.

SALERIO. I would it might prove the end of his losses.

SOLANIO. Let me say amen betimes, lest the devil cross my prayer, for here he comes in the likeness of a Jew.

Enter SHYLOCK

How now, Shylock? What news among the merchants?

SHYLOCK. You knew, none so well, none so well as you, of my daughter's flight.

SALERIO. That's certain; I, for my part, knew the tailor that made the wings she flew withal.

SOLANIO. And Shylock, for his own part, knew the bird was fledge; and then it is the complexion of them all to leave the dam.

SHYLOCK. She is damn'd for it.

SALERIO. That's certain, if the devil may be her judge.

SHYLOCK. My own flesh and blood to rebel!

SOLANIO. Out upon it, old carrion! Rebels it at these years?

SHYLOCK. I say my daughter is my flesh and my blood.

SALERIO. There is more difference between thy flesh and hers than between jet and ivory; more between your bloods than there is between red wine and Rhenish. But tell us, do you hear whether Antonio have had any loss at sea or no?

SHYLOCK. There I have another bad match: a bankrupt, a prodigal, who dare scarce show his head on the Rialto; a beggar, that was us'd to come so smug upon the mart. Let him look to his bond. He was wont to call me usurer; let him look to his bond. He was wont to lend money for a Christian courtesy; let him look to his bond.

SALERIO. Why, I am sure, if he forfeit, thou wilt not take his flesh. What's that good for?

SHYLOCK. To bait fish withal. If it will feed nothing else, it will feed my revenge. He hath disgrac'd me and hind'red me half a million; laugh'd at my losses, mock'd at my gains, scorned my nation, thwarted my bargains, cooled my friends, heated mine enemies. And what's his reason? I am a Jew. Hath not a Jew eyes? Hath not a Jew hands, organs, dimensions, senses, affections, passions, fed with the same food, hurt with the same weapons, subject to the same diseases, healed by the same means, warmed and cooled by the same winter and summer, as a Christian is? If you prick us, do we not bleed? If you tickle us, do we not laugh? If you poison us, do we not die? And if you wrong us, shall we not revenge? If we are like you in the rest, we will resemble you in that. If a Jew wrong a Christian, what is his humility? Revenge. If a Christian wrong a Jew, what should his sufferance be by Christian example? Why, revenge. The villainy you teach me I will execute; and itshall go hard but I will better the instruction.

Enter a MAN from ANTONIO

MAN. Gentlemen, my master Antonio is at his house, and desires to speak with you both.
SALERIO. We have been up and down to seek him.

Enter TUBAL

SOLANIO. Here comes another of the tribe; a third cannot be match'd, unless the devil himself turn Jew.
                Exeunt SOLANIO, SALERIO, and MAN
SHYLOCK. How now, Tubal, what news from Genoa? Hast thou found my daughter?
TUBAL. I often came where I did hear of her, but cannot find her.
SHYLOCK. Why there, there, there, there! A diamond gone, cost me two thousand ducats in Frankfort! The curse never fell upon our nation till now; I never felt it till now. Two thousand ducats in that, and other precious, precious jewels. I would my daughter were dead at my foot, and the jewels in her ear; would she were hears'd at my foot, and the ducats in her coffin! No news of them? Why, so—and I know not what's spent in the search. Why, thou—loss upon loss! The thief gone with so much, and so much to find the thief; and no satisfaction, no revenge; nor no ill luck stirring but what lights o' my shoulders; no sighs but o' my breathing; no tears but o' my shedding!
TUBAL. Yes, other men have ill luck too: Antonio, as I heard in Genoa—
SHYLOCK. What, what, what? Ill luck, ill luck?
TUBAL. Hath an argosy cast away coming from Tripolis.
SHYLOCK. I thank God, I thank God. Is it true, is it true?
TUBAL. I spoke with some of the sailors that escaped the wreck.
SHYLOCK. I thank thee, good Tubal. Good news, good news—ha, ha!—heard in Genoa.
TUBAL. Your daughter spent in Genoa, as I heard, one night, fourscore ducats.
SHYLOCK. Thou stick'st a dagger in me—I shall never see my gold again. Fourscore ducats at a sitting! Fourscore ducats!
TUBAL. There came divers of Antonio's creditors in my company to Venice that swear he cannot choose but break.

SHYLOCK. I am very glad of it; I'll plague him, I'll torture him; I am glad of it.
TUBAL. One of them showed me a ring that he had of your daughter for a monkey.
SHYLOCK. Out upon her! Thou torturest me, Tubal. It was my turquoise; I had it of Leah when I was a bachelor; I would not have given it for a wilderness of monkeys.
TUBAL. But Antonio is certainly undone.
SHYLOCK. Nay, that's true; that's very true. Go, Tubal, fee me an officer; bespeak him a fortnight before. I will have the heart of him, if he forfeit; for, were he out of Venice, I can make what merchandise I will. Go, Tubal, and meet me at our synagogue; go, good Tubal; at our synagogue, Tubal.   *Exeunt*

Scene II.

Belmont. PORTIA'S house

Enter BASSANIO, PORTIA, GRATIANO, NERISSA, and all
                their trains

PORTIA. I pray you tarry; pause a day or two
  Before you hazard; for, in choosing wrong,
  I lose your company; therefore forbear a while.
  There's something tells me—but it is not love—
  I would not lose you; and you know yourself
  Hate counsels not in such a quality.
  But lest you should not understand me well—
  And yet a maiden hath no tongue but thought—
  I would detain you here some month or two
  Before you venture for me. I could teach you
  How to choose right, but then I am forsworn;
  So will I never be; so may you miss me;
  But if you do, you'll make me wish a sin,
  That I had been forsworn. Beshrew your eyes!
  They have o'erlook'd me and divided me;
  One half of me is yours, the other half yours—
  Mine own, I would say; but if mine, then yours,
  And so all yours. O! these naughty times
  Puts bars between the owners and their rights;
  And so, though yours, not yours. Prove it so,
  Let fortune go to hell for it, not I.
  I speak too long, but 'tis to peize the time,
  To eke it, and to draw it out in length,
  To stay you from election.
BASSANIO. Let me choose;
  For as I am, I live upon the rack.
PORTIA. Upon the rack, Bassanio? Then confess
  What treason there is mingled with your love.
BASSANIO. None but that ugly treason of mistrust
  Which makes me fear th' enjoying of my love;
  There may as well be amity and life
  'Tween snow and fire as treason and my love.
PORTIA. Ay, but I fear you speak upon the rack,

Where men enforced do speak anything.
BASSANIO. Promise me life, and I'll confess the truth.
PORTIA. Well then, confess and live.
BASSANIO. 'Confess' and 'love'
  Had been the very sum of my confession.
  O happy torment, when my torturer
  Doth teach me answers for deliverance!
  But let me to my fortune and the caskets.
PORTIA. Away, then; I am lock'd in one of them.
  If you do love me, you will find me out.
  Nerissa and the rest, stand all aloof;
  Let music sound while he doth make his choice;
  Then, if he lose, he makes a swan-like end,
  Fading in music. That the comparison
  May stand more proper, my eye shall be the stream
  And wat'ry death-bed for him. He may win;
  And what is music then? Then music is
  Even as the flourish when true subjects bow
  To a new-crowned monarch; such it is
  As are those dulcet sounds in break of day
  That creep into the dreaming bridegroom's ear
  And summon him to marriage. Now he goes,
  With no less presence, but with much more love,
  Than young Alcides when he did redeem
  The virgin tribute paid by howling Troy
  To the sea-monster. I stand for sacrifice;
  The rest aloof are the Dardanian wives,
  With bleared visages come forth to view
  The issue of th' exploit. Go, Hercules!
  Live thou, I live. With much much more dismay
  I view the fight than thou that mak'st the fray.

A SONG

the whilst BASSANIO comments on the caskets to himself

      Tell me where is fancy bred,
      Or in the heart or in the head,
      How begot, how nourished?
        Reply, reply.
      It is engend'red in the eyes,
      With gazing fed; and fancy dies
      In the cradle where it lies.
        Let us all ring fancy's knell:
        I'll begin it—Ding, dong, bell.
ALL.   Ding, dong, bell.

BASSANIO. So may the outward shows be least themselves;
  The world is still deceiv'd with ornament.
  In law, what plea so tainted and corrupt
  But, being season'd with a gracious voice,
  Obscures the show of evil? In religion,
  What damned error but some sober brow
  Will bless it, and approve it with a text,
  Hiding the grossness with fair ornament?
  There is no vice so simple but assumes

Some mark of virtue on his outward parts.
  How many cowards, whose hearts are all as false
  As stairs of sand, wear yet upon their chins
  The beards of Hercules and frowning Mars;
  Who, inward search'd, have livers white as milk!
  And these assume but valour's excrement
  To render them redoubted. Look on beauty
  And you shall see 'tis purchas'd by the weight,
  Which therein works a miracle in nature,
  Making them lightest that wear most of it;
  So are those crisped snaky golden locks
  Which make such wanton gambols with the wind
  Upon supposed fairness often known
  To be the dowry of a second head—
  The skull that bred them in the sepulchre.
  Thus ornament is but the guiled shore
  To a most dangerous sea; the beauteous scarf
  Veiling an Indian beauty; in a word,
  The seeming truth which cunning times put on
  To entrap the wisest. Therefore, thou gaudy gold,
  Hard food for Midas, I will none of thee;
  Nor none of thee, thou pale and common drudge
  'Tween man and man; but thou, thou meagre lead,
  Which rather threaten'st than dost promise aught,
  Thy plainness moves me more than eloquence,
  And here choose I. Joy be the consequence!
PORTIA. [Aside] How all the other passions fleet to air,
  As doubtful thoughts, and rash-embrac'd despair,
  And shudd'ring fear, and green-ey'd jealousy!
  O love, be moderate, allay thy ecstasy,
  In measure rain thy joy, scant this excess!
  I feel too much thy blessing. Make it less,
  For fear I surfeit.
BASSANIO. [Opening the leaden casket] What find I here?
  Fair Portia's counterfeit! What demi-god
  Hath come so near creation? Move these eyes?
  Or whether riding on the balls of mine
  Seem they in motion? Here are sever'd lips,
  Parted with sugar breath; so sweet a bar
  Should sunder such sweet friends. Here in her hairs
  The painter plays the spider, and hath woven
  A golden mesh t' entrap the hearts of men
  Faster than gnats in cobwebs. But her eyes—
  How could he see to do them? Having made one,
  Methinks it should have power to steal both his,
  And leave itself unfurnish'd. Yet look how far
  The substance of my praise doth wrong this shadow
  In underprizing it, so far this shadow
  Doth limp behind the substance. Here's the scroll,
  The continent and summary of my fortune.
    'You that choose not by the view,
    Chance as fair and choose as true!
    Since this fortune falls to you,
    Be content and seek no new.
    If you be well pleas'd with this,
    And hold your fortune for your bliss,

Turn to where your lady is
  And claim her with a loving kiss.'
A gentle scroll. Fair lady, by your leave;
I come by note, to give and to receive.
Like one of two contending in a prize,
That thinks he hath done well in people's eyes,
Hearing applause and universal shout,
Giddy in spirit, still gazing in a doubt
Whether those peals of praise be his or no;
So, thrice-fair lady, stand I even so,
As doubtful whether what I see be true,
Until confirm'd, sign'd, ratified by you.
PORTIA. You see me, Lord Bassanio, where I stand,
  Such as I am. Though for myself alone
  I would not be ambitious in my wish
  To wish myself much better, yet for you
  I would be trebled twenty times myself,
  A thousand times more fair, ten thousand times more rich,
  That only to stand high in your account
  I might in virtues, beauties, livings, friends,
  Exceed account. But the full sum of me
  Is sum of something which, to term in gross,
  Is an unlesson'd girl, unschool'd, unpractis'd;
  Happy in this, she is not yet so old
  But she may learn; happier than this,
  She is not bred so dull but she can learn;
  Happiest of all is that her gentle spirit
  Commits itself to yours to be directed,
  As from her lord, her governor, her king.
  Myself and what is mine to you and yours
  Is now converted. But now I was the lord
  Of this fair mansion, master of my servants,
  Queen o'er myself; and even now, but now,
  This house, these servants, and this same myself,
  Are yours—my lord's. I give them with this ring,
  Which when you part from, lose, or give away,
  Let it presage the ruin of your love,
  And be my vantage to exclaim on you.
BASSANIO. Madam, you have bereft me of all words;
  Only my blood speaks to you in my veins;
  And there is such confusion in my powers
  As, after some oration fairly spoke
  By a beloved prince, there doth appear
  Among the buzzing pleased multitude,
  Where every something, being blent together,
  Turns to a wild of nothing, save of joy
  Express'd and not express'd. But when this ring
  Parts from this finger, then parts life from hence;
  O, then be bold to say Bassanio's dead!
NERISSA. My lord and lady, it is now our time
  That have stood by and seen our wishes prosper
  To cry 'Good joy.' Good joy, my lord and lady!
GRATIANO. My Lord Bassanio, and my gentle lady,
  I wish you all the joy that you can wish,
  For I am sure you can wish none from me;
  And, when your honours mean to solemnize

The bargain of your faith, I do beseech you
  Even at that time I may be married too.
BASSANIO. With all my heart, so thou canst get a wife.
GRATIANO. I thank your lordship, you have got me one.
  My eyes, my lord, can look as swift as yours:
  You saw the mistress, I beheld the maid;
  You lov'd, I lov'd; for intermission
  No more pertains to me, my lord, than you.
  Your fortune stood upon the caskets there,
  And so did mine too, as the matter falls;
  For wooing here until I sweat again,
  And swearing till my very roof was dry
  With oaths of love, at last—if promise last—
  I got a promise of this fair one here
  To have her love, provided that your fortune
  Achiev'd her mistress.
PORTIA. Is this true, Nerissa?
NERISSA. Madam, it is, so you stand pleas'd withal.
BASSANIO. And do you, Gratiano, mean good faith?
GRATIANO. Yes, faith, my lord.
BASSANIO. Our feast shall be much honoured in your
  marriage.
GRATIANO. We'll play with them: the first boy for a
  thousand ducats.
NERISSA. What, and stake down?
GRATIANO. No; we shall ne'er win at that sport, and stake
  down—
  But who comes here? Lorenzo and his infidel?
  What, and my old Venetian friend, Salerio!

  Enter LORENZO, JESSICA, and SALERIO, a
  messenger
    from Venice

BASSANIO. Lorenzo and Salerio, welcome hither,
  If that the youth of my new int'rest here
  Have power to bid you welcome. By your leave,
  I bid my very friends and countrymen,
  Sweet Portia, welcome.
PORTIA. So do I, my lord;
  They are entirely welcome.
LORENZO. I thank your honour. For my part, my lord,
  My purpose was not to have seen you here;
  But meeting with Salerio by the way,
  He did entreat me, past all saying nay,
  To come with him along.
SALERIO. I did, my lord,
  And I have reason for it. Signior Antonio
  Commends him to you.   [Gives BASSANIO a
    letter]
BASSANIO. Ere I ope his letter,
  I pray you tell me how my good friend doth.
SALERIO. Not sick, my lord, unless it be in mind;
  Nor well, unless in mind; his letter there
  Will show you his estate.   [BASSANIO opens the letter]
GRATIANO. Nerissa, cheer yond stranger; bid her welcome.

Your hand, Salerio. What's the news from Venice?
How doth that royal merchant, good Antonio?
I know he will be glad of our success:
We are the Jasons, we have won the fleece.
SALERIO. I would you had won the fleece that he hath lost.
PORTIA. There are some shrewd contents in yond same
     paper
That steals the colour from Bassanio's cheek:
Some dear friend dead, else nothing in the world
Could turn so much the constitution
Of any constant man. What, worse and worse!
With leave, Bassanio: I am half yourself,
And I must freely have the half of anything
That this same paper brings you.
BASSANIO. O sweet Portia,
Here are a few of the unpleasant'st words
That ever blotted paper! Gentle lady,
When I did first impart my love to you,
I freely told you all the wealth I had
Ran in my veins—I was a gentleman;
And then I told you true. And yet, dear lady,
Rating myself at nothing, you shall see
How much I was a braggart. When I told you
My state was nothing, I should then have told you
That I was worse than nothing; for indeed
I have engag'd myself to a dear friend,
Engag'd my friend to his mere enemy,
To feed my means. Here is a letter, lady,
The paper as the body of my friend,
And every word in it a gaping wound
Issuing life-blood. But is it true, Salerio?
Hath all his ventures fail'd? What, not one hit?
From Tripolis, from Mexico, and England,
From Lisbon, Barbary, and India,
And not one vessel scape the dreadful touch
Of merchant-marring rocks?
SALERIO. Not one, my lord.
Besides, it should appear that, if he had
The present money to discharge the Jew,
He would not take it. Never did I know
A creature that did bear the shape of man
So keen and greedy to confound a man.
He plies the Duke at morning and at night,
And doth impeach the freedom of the state,
If they deny him justice. Twenty merchants,
The Duke himself, and the magnificoes
Of greatest port, have all persuaded with him;
But none can drive him from the envious plea
Of forfeiture, of justice, and his bond.
JESSICA. When I was with him, I have heard him swear
To Tubal and to Chus, his countrymen,
That he would rather have Antonio's flesh
Than twenty times the value of the sum
That he did owe him; and I know, my lord,
If law, authority, and power, deny not,
It will go hard with poor Antonio.

PORTIA. Is it your dear friend that is thus in trouble?
BASSANIO. The dearest friend to me, the kindest man,
The best condition'd and unwearied spirit
In doing courtesies; and one in whom
The ancient Roman honour more appears
Than any that draws breath in Italy.
PORTIA. What sum owes he the Jew?
BASSANIO. For me, three thousand ducats.
PORTIA. What! no more?
Pay him six thousand, and deface the bond;
Double six thousand, and then treble that,
Before a friend of this description
Shall lose a hair through Bassanio's fault.
First go with me to church and call me wife,
And then away to Venice to your friend;
For never shall you lie by Portia's side
With an unquiet soul. You shall have gold
To pay the petty debt twenty times over.
When it is paid, bring your true friend along.
My maid Nerissa and myself meantime
Will live as maids and widows. Come, away;
For you shall hence upon your wedding day.
Bid your friends welcome, show a merry cheer;
Since you are dear bought, I will love you dear.
But let me hear the letter of your friend.
BASSANIO. [Reads] 'Sweet Bassanio, my ships have all
     miscarried, my creditors grow cruel, my estate is very
     low, my bond to the Jew is forfeit; and since, in paying it,
     it is impossible I should live, all debts are clear'd
     between you and I, if I might but see you at my death.
     Notwithstanding, use your pleasure; if your love do not
     persuade you to come, let not my letter.'
PORTIA. O love, dispatch all business and be gone!
BASSANIO. Since I have your good leave to go away,
I will make haste; but, till I come again,
No bed shall e'er be guilty of my stay,
Nor rest be interposer 'twixt us twain.   Exeunt

Scene III.

Venice. A street

Enter SHYLOCK, SOLANIO, ANTONIO, and
GAOLER

SHYLOCK. Gaoler, look to him. Tell not me of mercy—
This is the fool that lent out money gratis.
Gaoler, look to him.
ANTONIO. Hear me yet, good Shylock.
SHYLOCK. I'll have my bond; speak not against my bond.
I have sworn an oath that I will have my bond.
Thou call'dst me dog before thou hadst a cause,
But, since I am a dog, beware my fangs;
The Duke shall grant me justice. I do wonder,
Thou naughty gaoler, that thou art so fond
To come abroad with him at his request.

ANTONIO. I pray thee hear me speak.

SHYLOCK. I'll have my bond. I will not hear thee speak;
  I'll have my bond; and therefore speak no more.
  I'll not be made a soft and dull-ey'd fool,
  To shake the head, relent, and sigh, and yield,
  To Christian intercessors. Follow not;
  I'll have no speaking; I will have my bond.   Exit

SOLANIO. It is the most impenetrable cur
  That ever kept with men.

ANTONIO. Let him alone;
  I'll follow him no more with bootless prayers.
  He seeks my life; his reason well I know:
  I oft deliver'd from his forfeitures
  Many that have at times made moan to me;
  Therefore he hates me.

SOLANIO. I am sure the Duke
  Will never grant this forfeiture to hold.

ANTONIO. The Duke cannot deny the course of law;
  For the commodity that strangers have
  With us in Venice, if it be denied,
  Will much impeach the justice of the state,
  Since that the trade and profit of the city
  Consisteth of all nations. Therefore, go;
  These griefs and losses have so bated me
  That I shall hardly spare a pound of flesh
  To-morrow to my bloody creditor.
  Well, gaoler, on; pray God Bassanio come
  To see me pay his debt, and then I care not.   Exeunt

Scene IV.

Belmont. PORTIA'S house

Enter PORTIA, NERISSA, LORENZO, JESSICA, and
BALTHASAR

LORENZO. Madam, although I speak it in your presence,
  You have a noble and a true conceit
  Of godlike amity, which appears most strongly
  In bearing thus the absence of your lord.
  But if you knew to whom you show this honour,
  How true a gentleman you send relief,
  How dear a lover of my lord your husband,
  I know you would be prouder of the work
  Than customary bounty can enforce you.

PORTIA. I never did repent for doing good,
  Nor shall not now; for in companions
  That do converse and waste the time together,
  Whose souls do bear an equal yoke of love,
  There must be needs a like proportion
  Of lineaments, of manners, and of spirit,
  Which makes me think that this Antonio,
  Being the bosom lover of my lord,
  Must needs be like my lord. If it be so,
  How little is the cost I have bestowed
  In purchasing the semblance of my soul

From out the state of hellish cruelty!
This comes too near the praising of myself;
Therefore, no more of it; hear other things.
Lorenzo, I commit into your hands
The husbandry and manage of my house
Until my lord's return; for mine own part,
I have toward heaven breath'd a secret vow
To live in prayer and contemplation,
Only attended by Nerissa here,
Until her husband and my lord's return.
There is a monastery two miles off,
And there we will abide. I do desire you
Not to deny this imposition,
The which my love and some necessity
Now lays upon you.

LORENZO. Madam, with all my heart
  I shall obey you in an fair commands.

PORTIA. My people do already know my mind,
  And will acknowledge you and Jessica
  In place of Lord Bassanio and myself.
  So fare you well till we shall meet again.

LORENZO. Fair thoughts and happy hours attend on you!

JESSICA. I wish your ladyship all heart's content.

PORTIA. I thank you for your wish, and am well pleas'd
  To wish it back on you. Fare you well, Jessica.
              Exeunt JESSICA and LORENZO

Now, Balthasar,
As I have ever found thee honest-true,
So let me find thee still. Take this same letter,
And use thou all th' endeavour of a man
In speed to Padua; see thou render this
Into my cousin's hands, Doctor Bellario;
And look what notes and garments he doth give thee,
Bring them, I pray thee, with imagin'd speed
Unto the traject, to the common ferry
Which trades to Venice. Waste no time in words,
But get thee gone; I shall be there before thee.

BALTHASAR. Madam, I go with all convenient speed.
  Exit

PORTIA. Come on, Nerissa, I have work in hand
  That you yet know not of; we'll see our husbands
  Before they think of us.

NERISSA. Shall they see us?

PORTIA. They shall, Nerissa; but in such a habit
  That they shall think we are accomplished
  With that we lack. I'll hold thee any wager,
  When we are both accoutred like young men,
  I'll prove the prettier fellow of the two,
  And wear my dagger with the braver grace,
  And speak between the change of man and boy
  With a reed voice; and turn two mincing steps
  Into a manly stride; and speak of frays
  Like a fine bragging youth; and tell quaint lies,
  How honourable ladies sought my love,
  Which I denying, they fell sick and died—
  I could not do withal. Then I'll repent,

And wish for all that, that I had not kill'd them.
And twenty of these puny lies I'll tell,
That men shall swear I have discontinued school
About a twelvemonth. I have within my mind
A thousand raw tricks of these bragging Jacks,
Which I will practise.
NERISSA. Why, shall we turn to men?
PORTIA. Fie, what a question's that,
If thou wert near a lewd interpreter!
But come, I'll tell thee all my whole device
When I am in my coach, which stays for us
At the park gate; and therefore haste away,
For we must measure twenty miles to-day.   Exeunt

Scene V.

Belmont. The garden

Enter LAUNCELOT and JESSICA

LAUNCELOT. Yes, truly; for, look you, the sins of the father
are to be laid upon the children; therefore, I promise
you, I fear you. I was always plain with you, and so now I
speak my agitation of the matter; therefore be o' good
cheer, for truly I think you are damn'd. There is but one
hope in it that can do you any good, and that is but a
kind of bastard hope, neither.
JESSICA. And what hope is that, I pray thee?
LAUNCELOT. Marry, you may partly hope that your father
got you not—that you are not the Jew's daughter.
JESSICA. That were a kind of bastard hope indeed; so the
sins of my mother should be visited upon me.
LAUNCELOT. Truly then I fear you are damn'd both by
father and mother; thus when I shun Scylla, your father,
I fall into Charybdis, your mother; well, you are gone
both ways.
JESSICA. I shall be sav'd by my husband; he hath made me a
Christian.
LAUNCELOT. Truly, the more to blame he; we were
Christians enow before, e'en as many as could well live
one by another. This making of Christians will raise the
price of hogs; if we grow all to be pork-eaters, we shall
not shortly have a rasher on the coals for money.

Enter LORENZO

JESSICA. I'll tell my husband, Launcelot, what you say; here
he comes.
LORENZO. I shall grow jealous of you shortly, Launcelot, if
you thus get my wife into corners.
JESSICA. Nay, you need nor fear us, Lorenzo; Launcelot and
I are out; he tells me flatly there's no mercy for me in
heaven, because I am a Jew's daughter; and he says you
are no good member of the commonwealth, for in
converting Jews to Christians you raise the price of pork.

LORENZO. I shall answer that better to the commonwealth
than you can the getting up of the negro's belly; the
Moor is with child by you, Launcelot.
LAUNCELOT. It is much that the Moor should be more than
reason; but if she be less than an honest woman, she is
indeed more than I took her for.
LORENZO. How every fool can play upon the word! I think
the best grace of wit will shortly turn into silence, and
discourse grow commendable in none only but parrots.
Go in, sirrah; bid them prepare for dinner.
LAUNCELOT. That is done, sir; they have all stomachs.
LORENZO. Goodly Lord, what a wit-snapper are you! Then
bid them prepare dinner.
LAUNCELOT. That is done too, sir, only 'cover' is the word.
LORENZO. Will you cover, then, sir?
LAUNCELOT. Not so, sir, neither; I know my duty.
LORENZO. Yet more quarrelling with occasion! Wilt thou
show the whole wealth of thy wit in an instant? I pray
thee understand a plain man in his plain meaning: go to
thy fellows, bid them cover the table, serve in the meat,
and we will come in to dinner.
LAUNCELOT. For the table, sir, it shall be serv'd in; for the
meat, sir, it shall be cover'd; for your coming in to
dinner, sir, why, let it be as humours and conceits shall
govern.
                                        Exit
LORENZO. O dear discretion, how his words are suited!
The fool hath planted in his memory
An army of good words; and I do know
A many fools that stand in better place,
Garnish'd like him, that for a tricksy word
Defy the matter. How cheer'st thou, Jessica?
And now, good sweet, say thy opinion,
How dost thou like the Lord Bassanio's wife?
JESSICA. Past all expressing. It is very meet
The Lord Bassanio live an upright life,
For, having such a blessing in his lady,
He finds the joys of heaven here on earth;
And if on earth he do not merit it,
In reason he should never come to heaven.
Why, if two gods should play some heavenly match,
And on the wager lay two earthly women,
And Portia one, there must be something else
Pawn'd with the other; for the poor rude world
Hath not her fellow.
LORENZO. Even such a husband
Hast thou of me as she is for a wife.
JESSICA. Nay, but ask my opinion too of that.
LORENZO. I will anon; first let us go to dinner.
JESSICA. Nay, let me praise you while I have a stomach.
LORENZO. No, pray thee, let it serve for table-talk;
Then howsome'er thou speak'st, 'mong other things
I shall digest it.
JESSICA. Well, I'll set you forth.   Exeunt

William Shakespeare

The Merchant of Venice

1597

Act IV.

Scene I.

Venice. The court of justice

Enter the DUKE, the MAGNIFICOES, ANTONIO, BASSANIO,
GRATIANO, SALERIO, and OTHERS

DUKE OF VENICE. What, is Antonio here?
ANTONIO. Ready, so please your Grace.
DUKE OF VENICE. I am sorry for thee; thou art come to answer
 A stony adversary, an inhuman wretch,
 Uncapable of pity, void and empty
 From any dram of mercy.
ANTONIO. I have heard
 Your Grace hath ta'en great pains to qualify
 His rigorous course; but since he stands obdurate,
 And that no lawful means can carry me
 Out of his envy's reach, I do oppose
 My patience to his fury, and am arm'd
 To suffer with a quietness of spirit
 The very tyranny and rage of his.
DUKE OF VENICE. Go one, and call the Jew into the court.
SALERIO. He is ready at the door; he comes, my lord.

Enter SHYLOCK

DUKE OF VENICE. Make room, and let him stand before our face.
 Shylock, the world thinks, and I think so too,
 That thou but leadest this fashion of thy malice
 To the last hour of act; and then, 'tis thought,

Thou'lt show thy mercy and remorse, more strange
Than is thy strange apparent cruelty;
And where thou now exacts the penalty,
Which is a pound of this poor merchant's flesh,
Thou wilt not only loose the forfeiture,
But, touch'd with human gentleness and love,
Forgive a moiety of the principal,
Glancing an eye of pity on his losses,
That have of late so huddled on his back—
Enow to press a royal merchant down,
And pluck commiseration of his state
From brassy bosoms and rough hearts of flint,
From stubborn Turks and Tartars, never train'd
To offices of tender courtesy.
We all expect a gentle answer, Jew.
SHYLOCK. I have possess'd your Grace of what I purpose,
And by our holy Sabbath have I sworn
To have the due and forfeit of my bond.
If you deny it, let the danger light
Upon your charter and your city's freedom.
You'll ask me why I rather choose to have
A weight of carrion flesh than to receive
Three thousand ducats. I'll not answer that,
But say it is my humour—is it answer'd?
What if my house be troubled with a rat,
And I be pleas'd to give ten thousand ducats
To have it ban'd? What, are you answer'd yet?
Some men there are love not a gaping pig;
Some that are mad if they behold a cat;
And others, when the bagpipe sings i' th' nose,
Cannot contain their urine; for affection,
Mistress of passion, sways it to the mood
Of what it likes or loathes. Now, for your answer:

As there is no firm reason to be rend'red
Why he cannot abide a gaping pig;
Why he, a harmless necessary cat;
Why he, a woollen bagpipe, but of force
Must yield to such inevitable shame
As to offend, himself being offended;
So can I give no reason, nor I will not,
More than a lodg'd hate and a certain loathing
I bear Antonio, that I follow thus
A losing suit against him. Are you answered?
BASSANIO. This is no answer, thou unfeeling man,
  To excuse the current of thy cruelty.
SHYLOCK. I am not bound to please thee with my answers.
BASSANIO. Do all men kill the things they do not love?
SHYLOCK. Hates any man the thing he would not kill?
BASSANIO. Every offence is not a hate at first.
SHYLOCK. What, wouldst thou have a serpent sting thee
    twice?
ANTONIO. I pray you, think you question with the Jew.
  You may as well go stand upon the beach
  And bid the main flood bate his usual height;
  You may as well use question with the wolf,
  Why he hath made the ewe bleat for the lamb;
  You may as well forbid the mountain pines
  To wag their high tops and to make no noise
  When they are fretten with the gusts of heaven;
  You may as well do anything most hard
  As seek to soften that—than which what's harder?—
  His jewish heart. Therefore, I do beseech you,
  Make no moe offers, use no farther means,
  But with all brief and plain conveniency
  Let me have judgment, and the Jew his will.
BASSANIO. For thy three thousand ducats here is six.
SHYLOCK. If every ducat in six thousand ducats
  Were in six parts, and every part a ducat,
  I would not draw them; I would have my bond.
DUKE OF VENICE. How shalt thou hope for mercy,
    rend'ring none?
SHYLOCK. What judgment shall I dread, doing no wrong?
  You have among you many a purchas'd slave,
  Which, fike your asses and your dogs and mules,
  You use in abject and in slavish parts,
  Because you bought them; shall I say to you
  'Let them be free, marry them to your heirs—
  Why sweat they under burdens?—let their beds
  Be made as soft as yours, and let their palates
  Be season'd with such viands'? You will answer
  'The slaves are ours.' So do I answer you:
  The pound of flesh which I demand of him
  Is dearly bought, 'tis mine, and I will have it.
  If you deny me, fie upon your law!
  There is no force in the decrees of Venice.
  I stand for judgment; answer; shall I have it?
DUKE OF VENICE. Upon my power I may dismiss this court,
  Unless Bellario, a learned doctor,
  Whom I have sent for to determine this,

Come here to-day.
SALERIO. My lord, here stays without
  A messenger with letters from the doctor,
  New come from Padua.
DUKE OF VENICE. Bring us the letters; call the messenger.
BASSANIO. Good cheer, Antonio! What, man, courage yet!
  The Jew shall have my flesh, blood, bones, and all,
  Ere thou shalt lose for me one drop of blood.
ANTONIO. I am a tainted wether of the flock,
  Meetest for death; the weakest kind of fruit
  Drops earliest to the ground, and so let me.
  You cannot better be employ'd, Bassanio,
  Than to live still, and write mine epitaph.

Enter NERISSA dressed like a lawyer's clerk

DUKE OF VENICE. Came you from Padua, from Bellario?
NERISSA. From both, my lord. Bellario greets your Grace.
                              [Presents a letter]
BASSANIO. Why dost thou whet thy knife so earnestly?
SHYLOCK. To cut the forfeiture from that bankrupt there.
GRATIANO. Not on thy sole, but on thy soul, harsh Jew,
  Thou mak'st thy knife keen; but no metal can,
  No, not the hangman's axe, bear half the keenness
  Of thy sharp envy. Can no prayers pierce thee?
SHYLOCK. No, none that thou hast wit enough to make.
GRATIANO. O, be thou damn'd, inexecrable dog!
  And for thy life let justice be accus'd.
  Thou almost mak'st me waver in my faith,
  To hold opinion with Pythagoras
  That souls of animals infuse themselves
  Into the trunks of men. Thy currish spirit
  Govern'd a wolf who, hang'd for human slaughter,
  Even from the gallows did his fell soul fleet,
  And, whilst thou layest in thy unhallowed dam,
  Infus'd itself in thee; for thy desires
  Are wolfish, bloody, starv'd and ravenous.
SHYLOCK. Till thou canst rail the seal from off my bond,
  Thou but offend'st thy lungs to speak so loud;
  Repair thy wit, good youth, or it will fall
  To cureless ruin. I stand here for law.
DUKE OF VENICE. This letter from Bellario doth commend
  A young and learned doctor to our court.
  Where is he?
NERISSA. He attendeth here hard by
  To know your answer, whether you'll admit him.
DUKE OF VENICE. With all my heart. Some three or four of
    you
  Go give him courteous conduct to this place.
  Meantime, the court shall hear Bellario's letter.
CLERK. [Reads] 'Your Grace shall understand that at the
    receipt of your letter I am very sick; but in the instant
    that your messenger came, in loving visitation was with
    me a young doctor of Rome—his name is Balthazar. I
    acquainted him with the cause in controversy between
    the Jew and Antonio the merchant; we turn'd o'er many

books together; he is furnished with my opinion which, bettered with his own learning-the greatness whereof I cannot enough commend—comes with him at my importunity to fill up your Grace's request in my stead. I beseech you let his lack of years be no impediment to let him lack a reverend estimation, for I never knew so young a body with so old a head. I leave him to your gracious acceptance, whose trial shall better publish his commendation.'

Enter PORTIA for BALTHAZAR, dressed like a Doctor of Laws

DUKE OF VENICE. YOU hear the learn'd Bellario, what he writes;
And here, I take it, is the doctor come.
Give me your hand; come you from old Bellario?
PORTIA. I did, my lord.
DUKE OF VENICE. You are welcome; take your place.
Are you acquainted with the difference
That holds this present question in the court?
PORTIA. I am informed throughly of the cause.
Which is the merchant here, and which the Jew?
DUKE OF VENICE. Antonio and old Shylock, both stand forth.
PORTIA. Is your name Shylock?
SHYLOCK. Shylock is my name.
PORTIA. Of a strange nature is the suit you follow;
Yet in such rule that the Venetian law
Cannot impugn you as you do proceed.
You stand within his danger, do you not?
ANTONIO. Ay, so he says.
PORTIA. Do you confess the bond?
ANTONIO. I do.
PORTIA. Then must the Jew be merciful.
SHYLOCK. On what compulsion must I? Tell me that.
PORTIA. The quality of mercy is not strain'd;
It droppeth as the gentle rain from heaven
Upon the place beneath. It is twice blest:
It blesseth him that gives and him that takes.
'Tis mightiest in the mightiest; it becomes
The throned monarch better than his crown;
His sceptre shows the force of temporal power,
The attribute to awe and majesty,
Wherein doth sit the dread and fear of kings;
But mercy is above this sceptred sway,
It is enthroned in the hearts of kings,
It is an attribute to God himself;
And earthly power doth then show likest God's
When mercy seasons justice. Therefore, Jew,
Though justice be thy plea, consider this—
That in the course of justice none of us
Should see salvation; we do pray for mercy,
And that same prayer doth teach us all to render
The deeds of mercy. I have spoke thus much
To mitigate the justice of thy plea,

Which if thou follow, this strict court of Venice
Must needs give sentence 'gainst the merchant there.
SHYLOCK. My deeds upon my head! I crave the law,
The penalty and forfeit of my bond.
BASSANIO. Yes; here I tender it for him in the court;
Yea, twice the sum; if that will not suffice,
I will be bound to pay it ten times o'er
On forfeit of my hands, my head, my heart;
If this will not suffice, it must appear
That malice bears down truth. And, I beseech you,
Wrest once the law to your authority;
To do a great right do a little wrong,
And curb this cruel devil of his will.
PORTIA. It must not be; there is no power in Venice
Can alter a decree established;
'Twill be recorded for a precedent,
And many an error, by the same example,
Will rush into the state; it cannot be.
SHYLOCK. A Daniel come to judgment! Yea, a Daniel!
O wise young judge, how I do honour thee!
PORTIA. I pray you, let me look upon the bond.
SHYLOCK. Here 'tis, most reverend Doctor; here it is.
PORTIA. Shylock, there's thrice thy money off'red thee.
SHYLOCK. An oath, an oath! I have an oath in heaven.
Shall I lay perjury upon my soul?
No, not for Venice.
PORTIA. Why, this bond is forfeit;
And lawfully by this the Jew may claim
A pound of flesh, to be by him cut off
Nearest the merchant's heart. Be merciful.
Take thrice thy money; bid me tear the bond.
SHYLOCK. When it is paid according to the tenour.
It doth appear you are a worthy judge;
You know the law; your exposition
Hath been most sound; I charge you by the law,
Whereof you are a well-deserving pillar,
Proceed to judgment. By my soul I swear
There is no power in the tongue of man
To alter me. I stay here on my bond.
ANTONIO. Most heartily I do beseech the court
To give the judgment.
PORTIA. Why then, thus it is:
You must prepare your bosom for his knife.
SHYLOCK. O noble judge! O excellent young man!
PORTIA. For the intent and purpose of the law
Hath full relation to the penalty,
Which here appeareth due upon the bond.
SHYLOCK. 'Tis very true. O wise and upright judge,
How much more elder art thou than thy looks!
PORTIA. Therefore, lay bare your bosom.
SHYLOCK. Ay, his breast—
So says the bond; doth it not, noble judge?
'Nearest his heart,' those are the very words.
PORTIA. It is so. Are there balance here to weigh
The flesh?
SHYLOCK. I have them ready.

PORTIA. Have by some surgeon, Shylock, on your charge,
To stop his wounds, lest he do bleed to death.
SHYLOCK. Is it so nominated in the bond?
PORTIA. It is not so express'd, but what of that?
'Twere good you do so much for charity.
SHYLOCK. I cannot find it; 'tis not in the bond.
PORTIA. You, merchant, have you anything to say?
ANTONIO. But little: I am arm'd and well prepar'd.
Give me your hand, Bassanio; fare you well.
Grieve not that I am fall'n to this for you,
For herein Fortune shows herself more kind
Than is her custom. It is still her use
To let the wretched man outlive his wealth,
To view with hollow eye and wrinkled brow
An age of poverty; from which ling'ring penance
Of such misery doth she cut me off.
Commend me to your honourable wife;
Tell her the process of Antonio's end;
Say how I lov'd you; speak me fair in death;
And, when the tale is told, bid her be judge
Whether Bassanio had not once a love.
Repent but you that you shall lose your friend,
And he repents not that he pays your debt;
For if the Jew do cut but deep enough,
I'll pay it instantly with all my heart.
BASSANIO. Antonio, I am married to a wife
Which is as dear to me as life itself;
But life itself, my wife, and all the world,
Are not with me esteem'd above thy life;
I would lose all, ay, sacrifice them all
Here to this devil, to deliver you.
PORTIA. Your wife would give you little thanks for that,
If she were by to hear you make the offer.
GRATIANO. I have a wife who I protest I love;
I would she were in heaven, so she could
Entreat some power to change this currish Jew.
NERISSA. 'Tis well you offer it behind her back;
The wish would make else an unquiet house.
SHYLOCK. [Aside] These be the Christian husbands! I
have a daughter—
Would any of the stock of Barrabas
Had been her husband, rather than a Christian!—
We trifle time; I pray thee pursue sentence.
PORTIA. A pound of that same merchant's flesh is thine.
The court awards it and the law doth give it.
SHYLOCK. Most rightful judge!
PORTIA. And you must cut this flesh from off his breast.
The law allows it and the court awards it.
SHYLOCK. Most learned judge! A sentence! Come, prepare.
PORTIA. Tarry a little; there is something else.
This bond doth give thee here no jot of blood:
The words expressly are 'a pound of flesh.'
Take then thy bond, take thou thy pound of flesh;
But, in the cutting it, if thou dost shed
One drop of Christian blood, thy lands and goods
Are, by the laws of Venice, confiscate

Unto the state of Venice.
GRATIANO. O upright judge! Mark, Jew. O learned judge!
SHYLOCK. Is that the law?
PORTIA. Thyself shalt see the act;
For, as thou urgest justice, be assur'd
Thou shalt have justice, more than thou desir'st.
GRATIANO. O learned judge! Mark, Jew. A learned judge!
SHYLOCK. I take this offer then: pay the bond thrice,
And let the Christian go.
BASSANIO. Here is the money.
PORTIA. Soft!
The Jew shall have all justice. Soft! No haste.
He shall have nothing but the penalty.
GRATIANO. O Jew! an upright judge, a learned judge!
PORTIA. Therefore, prepare thee to cut off the flesh.
Shed thou no blood, nor cut thou less nor more
But just a pound of flesh; if thou tak'st more
Or less than a just pound—be it but so much
As makes it light or heavy in the substance,
Or the division of the twentieth part
Of one poor scruple; nay, if the scale do turn
But in the estimation of a hair—
Thou diest, and all thy goods are confiscate.
GRATIANO. A second Daniel, a Daniel, Jew!
Now, infidel, I have you on the hip.
PORTIA. Why doth the Jew pause? Take thy forfeiture.
SHYLOCK. Give me my principal, and let me go.
BASSANIO. I have it ready for thee; here it is.
PORTIA. He hath refus'd it in the open court;
He shall have merely justice, and his bond.
GRATIANO. A Daniel still say I, a second Daniel!
I thank thee, Jew, for teaching me that word.
SHYLOCK. Shall I not have barely my principal?
PORTIA. Thou shalt have nothing but the forfeiture
To be so taken at thy peril, Jew.
SHYLOCK. Why, then the devil give him good of it!
I'll stay no longer question.
PORTIA. Tarry, Jew.
The law hath yet another hold on you.
It is enacted in the laws of Venice,
If it be proved against an alien
That by direct or indirect attempts
He seek the life of any citizen,
The party 'gainst the which he doth contrive
Shall seize one half his goods; the other half
Comes to the privy coffer of the state;
And the offender's life lies in the mercy
Of the Duke only, 'gainst all other voice.
In which predicament, I say, thou stand'st;
For it appears by manifest proceeding
That indirectly, and directly too,
Thou hast contrived against the very life
Of the defendant; and thou hast incurr'd
The danger formerly by me rehears'd.
Down, therefore, and beg mercy of the Duke.
GRATIANO. Beg that thou mayst have leave to hang thyself;

And yet, thy wealth being forfeit to the state,
Thou hast not left the value of a cord;
Therefore thou must be hang'd at the state's charge.
DUKE OF VENICE. That thou shalt see the difference of our
   spirit,
I pardon thee thy life before thou ask it.
For half thy wealth, it is Antonio's;
The other half comes to the general state,
Which humbleness may drive unto a fine.
PORTIA. Ay, for the state; not for Antonio.
SHYLOCK. Nay, take my life and all, pardon not that.
   You take my house when you do take the prop
   That doth sustain my house; you take my life
   When you do take the means whereby I live.
PORTIA. What mercy can you render him, Antonio?
GRATIANO. A halter gratis; nothing else, for God's sake!
ANTONIO. So please my lord the Duke and all the court
   To quit the fine for one half of his goods;
   I am content, so he will let me have
   The other half in use, to render it
   Upon his death unto the gentleman
   That lately stole his daughter—
   Two things provided more; that, for this favour,
   He presently become a Christian;
   The other, that he do record a gift,
   Here in the court, of all he dies possess'd
   Unto his son Lorenzo and his daughter.
DUKE OF VENICE. He shall do this, or else I do recant
   The pardon that I late pronounced here.
PORTIA. Art thou contented, Jew? What dost thou say?
SHYLOCK. I am content.
PORTIA. Clerk, draw a deed of gift.
SHYLOCK. I pray you, give me leave to go from hence;
   I am not well; send the deed after me
   And I will sign it.
DUKE OF VENICE. Get thee gone, but do it.
GRATIANO. In christ'ning shalt thou have two god-fathers;
   Had I been judge, thou shouldst have had ten more,
   To bring thee to the gallows, not to the font.
                    Exit SHYLOCK
DUKE OF VENICE. Sir, I entreat you home with me to
   dinner.
PORTIA. I humbly do desire your Grace of pardon;
   I must away this night toward Padua,
   And it is meet I presently set forth.
DUKE OF VENICE. I am sorry that your leisure serves you not.
   Antonio, gratify this gentleman,
   For in my mind you are much bound to him.
            Exeunt DUKE, MAGNIFICOES, and train
BASSANIO. Most worthy gentleman, I and my friend
   Have by your wisdom been this day acquitted
   Of grievous penalties; in lieu whereof
   Three thousand ducats, due unto the Jew,
   We freely cope your courteous pains withal.
ANTONIO. And stand indebted, over and above,
   In love and service to you evermore.

PORTIA. He is well paid that is well satisfied,
   And I, delivering you, am satisfied,
   And therein do account myself well paid.
   My mind was never yet more mercenary.
   I pray you, know me when we meet again;
   I wish you well, and so I take my leave.
BASSANIO. Dear sir, of force I must attempt you further;
   Take some remembrance of us, as a tribute,
   Not as fee. Grant me two things, I pray you,
   Not to deny me, and to pardon me.
PORTIA. You press me far, and therefore I will yield.
   [To ANTONIO] Give me your gloves, I'll wear them for
      your sake.
   [To BASSANIO] And, for your love, I'll take this ring
      from you.
   Do not draw back your hand; I'll take no more,
   And you in love shall not deny me this.
BASSANIO. This ring, good sir—alas, it is a trifle;
   I will not shame myself to give you this.
PORTIA. I will have nothing else but only this;
   And now, methinks, I have a mind to it.
BASSANIO.. There's more depends on this than on the
      value.
   The dearest ring in Venice will I give you,
   And find it out by proclamation;
   Only for this, I pray you, pardon me.
PORTIA. I see, sir, you are liberal in offers;
   You taught me first to beg, and now, methinks,
   You teach me how a beggar should be answer'd.
BASSANIO. Good sir, this ring was given me by my wife;
   And, when she put it on, she made me vow
   That I should neither sell, nor give, nor lose it.
PORTIA. That 'scuse serves many men to save their gifts.
   And if your wife be not a mad woman,
   And know how well I have deserv'd this ring,
   She would not hold out enemy for ever
   For giving it to me. Well, peace be with you!
                 Exeunt PORTIA and NERISSA
ANTONIO. My Lord Bassanio, let him have the ring.
   Let his deservings, and my love withal,
   Be valued 'gainst your wife's commandment.
BASSANIO. Go, Gratiano, run and overtake him;
   Give him the ring, and bring him, if thou canst,
   Unto Antonio's house. Away, make haste.   Exit
      GRATIANO
   Come, you and I will thither presently;
   And in the morning early will we both
   Fly toward Belmont. Come, Antonio.   Exeunt

Scene II.

               Venice. A street

          Enter PORTIA and NERISSA

PORTIA. Inquire the Jew's house out, give him this deed,

And let him sign it; we'll away tonight,
And be a day before our husbands home.
This deed will be well welcome to Lorenzo.

Enter GRATIANO

GRATIANO. Fair sir, you are well o'erta'en.
  My Lord Bassanio, upon more advice,
  Hath sent you here this ring, and doth entreat
  Your company at dinner.
PORTIA. That cannot be.
  His ring I do accept most thankfully,
  And so, I pray you, tell him. Furthermore,

I pray you show my youth old Shylock's house.
GRATIANO. That will I do.
NERISSA. Sir, I would speak with you.
  [Aside to PORTIA] I'll See if I can get my husband's ring,
  Which I did make him swear to keep for ever.
PORTIA. [To NERISSA] Thou Mayst, I warrant. We shall
    have old swearing
  That they did give the rings away to men;
  But we'll outface them, and outswear them too.
  [Aloud] Away, make haste, thou know'st where I will tarry.
NERISSA. Come, good sir, will you show me to this house?
                    Exeunt

William Shakespeare

The Merchant of Venice

1597

Act V.

Scene I.

Belmont. The garden before PORTIA'S house

Enter LORENZO and JESSICA

LORENZO. The moon shines bright. In such a night as this,
  When the sweet wind did gently kiss the trees,
  And they did make no noise—in such a night,
  Troilus methinks mounted the Troyan walls,
  And sigh'd his soul toward the Grecian tents,
  Where Cressid lay that night.
JESSICA. In such a night
  Did Thisby fearfully o'ertrip the dew,
  And saw the lion's shadow ere himself,
  And ran dismayed away.
LORENZO. In such a night
  Stood Dido with a willow in her hand
  Upon the wild sea-banks, and waft her love
  To come again to Carthage.
JESSICA. In such a night
  Medea gathered the enchanted herbs
  That did renew old AEson.
 LORENZO. In such a night
  Did Jessica steal from the wealthy Jew,
  And with an unthrift love did run from Venice
  As far as Belmont.
JESSICA. In such a night
  Did young Lorenzo swear he lov'd her well,
  Stealing her soul with many vows of faith,
  And ne'er a true one.
LORENZO. In such a night
  Did pretty Jessica, like a little shrew,
  Slander her love, and he forgave it her.
JESSICA. I would out-night you, did no body come;
  But, hark, I hear the footing of a man.

Enter STEPHANO

LORENZO. Who comes so fast in silence of the night?
STEPHANO. A friend.
LORENZO. A friend! What friend? Your name, I pray you,
  friend?
STEPHANO. Stephano is my name, and I bring word
  My mistress will before the break of day
  Be here at Belmont; she doth stray about
  By holy crosses, where she kneels and prays
  For happy wedlock hours.
LORENZO. Who comes with her?
STEPHANO. None but a holy hermit and her maid.
  I pray you, is my master yet return'd?
LORENZO. He is not, nor we have not heard from him.
  But go we in, I pray thee, Jessica,
  And ceremoniously let us prepare
Some welcome for the mistress of the house.

Enter LAUNCELOT

LAUNCELOT. Sola, sola! wo ha, ho! sola, sola!
LORENZO. Who calls?
LAUNCELOT. Sola! Did you see Master Lorenzo? Master
  Lorenzo! Sola, sola!
LORENZO. Leave holloaing, man. Here!
LAUNCELOT. Sola! Where, where?
LORENZO. Here!

LAUNCELOT. Tell him there's a post come from my master
  with his horn full of good news; my master will be here
  ere morning.
                              Exit
LORENZO. Sweet soul, let's in, and there expect their
  coming.
  And yet no matter—why should we go in?
  My friend Stephano, signify, I pray you,
  Within the house, your mistress is at hand;
  And bring your music forth into the air.   Exit
    STEPHANO
  How sweet the moonlight sleeps upon this bank!
  Here will we sit and let the sounds of music
  Creep in our ears; soft stillness and the night
  Become the touches of sweet harmony.
  Sit, Jessica. Look how the floor of heaven
  Is thick inlaid with patines of bright gold;
  There's not the smallest orb which thou behold'st
  But in his motion like an angel sings,
  Still quiring to the young-ey'd cherubins;
  Such harmony is in immortal souls,
  But whilst this muddy vesture of decay
  Doth grossly close it in, we cannot hear it.

    Enter MUSICIANS

  Come, ho, and wake Diana with a hymn;
  With sweetest touches pierce your mistress' ear.
  And draw her home with music.   [Music]
JESSICA. I am never merry when I hear sweet music.
LORENZO. The reason is your spirits are attentive;
  For do but note a wild and wanton herd,
  Or race of youthful and unhandled colts,
  Fetching mad bounds, bellowing and neighing loud,
  Which is the hot condition of their blood—
  If they but hear perchance a trumpet sound,
  Or any air of music touch their ears,
  You shall perceive them make a mutual stand,
  Their savage eyes turn'd to a modest gaze
  By the sweet power of music. Therefore the poet
  Did feign that Orpheus drew trees, stones, and floods;
  Since nought so stockish, hard, and full of rage,
  But music for the time doth change his nature.
  The man that hath no music in himself,
  Nor is not mov'd with concord of sweet sounds,
  Is fit for treasons, stratagems, and spoils;
  The motions of his spirit are dull as night,
  And his affections dark as Erebus.
  Let no such man be trusted. Mark the music.

    Enter PORTIA and NERISSA

PORTIA. That light we see is burning in my hall.
  How far that little candle throws his beams!
  So shines a good deed in a naughty world.
NERISSA. When the moon shone, we did not see the candle.

PORTIA. So doth the greater glory dim the less:
  A substitute shines brightly as a king
  Until a king be by, and then his state
  Empties itself, as doth an inland brook
  Into the main of waters. Music! hark!
NERISSA. It is your music, madam, of the house.
PORTIA. Nothing is good, I see, without respect;
  Methinks it sounds much sweeter than by day.
NERISSA. Silence bestows that virtue on it, madam.
PORTIA. The crow doth sing as sweetly as the lark
  When neither is attended; and I think
  ne nightingale, if she should sing by day,
  When every goose is cackling, would be thought
  No better a musician than the wren.
  How many things by season season'd are
  To their right praise and true perfection!
  Peace, ho! The moon sleeps with Endymion,
  And would not be awak'd.   [Music ceases]
LORENZO. That is the voice,
  Or I am much deceiv'd, of Portia.
PORTIA. He knows me as the blind man knows the cuckoo,
  By the bad voice.
LORENZO. Dear lady, welcome home.
PORTIA. We have been praying for our husbands' welfare,
  Which speed, we hope, the better for our words.
  Are they return'd?
LORENZO. Madam, they are not yet;
  But there is come a messenger before,
  To signify their coming.
PORTIA.. Go in, Nerissa;
  Give order to my servants that they take
  No note at all of our being absent hence;
  Nor you, Lorenzo; Jessica, nor you.   [A tucket sounds]
LORENZO. Your husband is at hand; I hear his trumpet.
  We are no tell-tales, madam, fear you not.
PORTIA. This night methinks is but the daylight sick;
  It looks a little paler; 'tis a day
  Such as the day is when the sun is hid.

    Enter BASSANIO, ANTONIO, GRATIANO, and their
    followers

BASSANIO. We should hold day with the Antipodes,
  If you would walk in absence of the sun.
PORTIA. Let me give light, but let me not be light,
  For a light wife doth make a heavy husband,
  And never be Bassanio so for me;
  But God sort all! You are welcome home, my lord.
BASSANIO. I thank you, madam; give welcome to my friend.
  This is the man, this is Antonio,
  To whom I am so infinitely bound.
PORTIA. You should in all sense be much bound to him,
  For, as I hear, he was much bound for you.
ANTONIO. No more than I am well acquitted of.
PORTIA. Sir, you are very welcome to our house.
  It must appear in other ways than words,

Therefore I scant this breathing courtesy.
GRATIANO. [To NERISSA] By yonder moon I swear you
  do me wrong;
In faith, I gave it to the judge's clerk.
Would he were gelt that had it, for my part,
Since you do take it, love, so much at heart.
PORTIA. A quarrel, ho, already! What's the matter?
GRATIANO. About a hoop of gold, a paltry ring
That she did give me, whose posy was
For all the world like cutler's poetry
Upon a knife, 'Love me, and leave me not.'
NERISSA. What talk you of the posy or the value?
You swore to me, when I did give it you,
That you would wear it till your hour of death,
And that it should lie with you in your grave;
Though not for me, yet for your vehement oaths,
You should have been respective and have kept it.
Gave it a judge's clerk! No, God's my judge,
The clerk will ne'er wear hair on's face that had it.
GRATIANO. He will, an if he live to be a man.
NERISSA. Ay, if a woman live to be a man.
GRATIANO. Now by this hand I gave it to a youth,
A kind of boy, a little scrubbed boy
No higher than thyself, the judge's clerk;
A prating boy that begg'd it as a fee;
I could not for my heart deny it him.
PORTIA. You were to blame, I must be plain with you,
To part so slightly with your wife's first gift,
A thing stuck on with oaths upon your finger
And so riveted with faith unto your flesh.
I gave my love a ring, and made him swear
Never to part with it, and here he stands;
I dare be sworn for him he would not leave it
Nor pluck it from his finger for the wealth
That the world masters. Now, in faith, Gratiano,
You give your wife too unkind a cause of grief;
An 'twere to me, I should be mad at it.
BASSANIO. [Aside] Why, I were best to cut my left hand off,
And swear I lost the ring defending it.
GRATIANO. My Lord Bassanio gave his ring away
Unto the judge that begg'd it, and indeed
Deserv'd it too; and then the boy, his clerk,
That took some pains in writing, he begg'd mine;
And neither man nor master would take aught
But the two rings.
PORTIA. What ring gave you, my lord?
Not that, I hope, which you receiv'd of me.
BASSANIO. If I could add a lie unto a fault,
I would deny it; but you see my finger
Hath not the ring upon it; it is gone.
PORTIA. Even so void is your false heart of truth;
By heaven, I will ne'er come in your bed
Until I see the ring.
NERISSA. Nor I in yours
Till I again see mine.
BASSANIO. Sweet Portia,

If you did know to whom I gave the ring,
If you did know for whom I gave the ring,
And would conceive for what I gave the ring,
And how unwillingly I left the ring,
When nought would be accepted but the ring,
You would abate the strength of your displeasure.
PORTIA. If you had known the virtue of the ring,
Or half her worthiness that gave the ring,
Or your own honour to contain the ring,
You would not then have parted with the ring.
What man is there so much unreasonable,
If you had pleas'd to have defended it
With any terms of zeal, wanted the modesty
To urge the thing held as a ceremony?
Nerissa teaches me what to believe:
I'll die for't but some woman had the ring.
BASSANIO. No, by my honour, madam, by my soul,
No woman had it, but a civil doctor,
Which did refuse three thousand ducats of me,
And begg'd the ring; the which I did deny him,
And suffer'd him to go displeas'd away—
Even he that had held up the very life
Of my dear friend. What should I say, sweet lady?
I was enforc'd to send it after him;
I was beset with shame and courtesy;
My honour would not let ingratitude
So much besmear it. Pardon me, good lady;
For by these blessed candles of the night,
Had you been there, I think you would have begg'd
The ring of me to give the worthy doctor.
PORTIA. Let not that doctor e'er come near my house;
Since he hath got the jewel that I loved,
And that which you did swear to keep for me,
I will become as liberal as you;
I'll not deny him anything I have,
No, not my body, nor my husband's bed.
Know him I shall, I am well sure of it.
Lie not a night from home; watch me like Argus;
If you do not, if I be left alone,
Now, by mine honour which is yet mine own,
I'll have that doctor for mine bedfellow.
NERISSA. And I his clerk; therefore be well advis'd
How you do leave me to mine own protection.
GRATIANO. Well, do you so, let not me take him then;
For, if I do, I'll mar the young clerk's pen.
ANTONIO. I am th' unhappy subject of these quarrels.
PORTIA. Sir, grieve not you; you are welcome not
  withstanding.
BASSANIO. Portia, forgive me this enforced wrong;
And in the hearing of these many friends
I swear to thee, even by thine own fair eyes,
Wherein I see myself—
PORTIA. Mark you but that!
In both my eyes he doubly sees himself,
In each eye one; swear by your double self,
And there's an oath of credit.

BASSANIO. Nay, but hear me.
  Pardon this fault, and by my soul I swear
  I never more will break an oath with thee.
ANTONIO. I once did lend my body for his wealth,
  Which, but for him that had your husband's ring,
  Had quite miscarried; I dare be bound again,
  My soul upon the forfeit, that your lord
  Will never more break faith advisedly.
PORTIA. Then you shall be his surety. Give him this,
  And bid him keep it better than the other.
ANTONIO. Here, Lord Bassanio, swear to keep this ring.
BASSANIO. By heaven, it is the same I gave the doctor!
PORTIA. I had it of him. Pardon me, Bassanio,
  For, by this ring, the doctor lay with me.
NERISSA. And pardon me, my gentle Gratiano,
  For that same scrubbed boy, the doctor's clerk,
  In lieu of this, last night did lie with me.
GRATIANO. Why, this is like the mending of highways
  In summer, where the ways are fair enough.
  What, are we cuckolds ere we have deserv'd it?
PORTIA. Speak not so grossly. You are all amaz'd.
  Here is a letter; read it at your leisure;
  It comes from Padua, from Bellario;
  There you shall find that Portia was the doctor,
  Nerissa there her clerk. Lorenzo here
  Shall witness I set forth as soon as you,
  And even but now return'd; I have not yet
  Enter'd my house. Antonio, you are welcome;
  And I have better news in store for you
  Than you expect. Unseal this letter soon;
  There you shall find three of your argosies
  Are richly come to harbour suddenly.
  You shall not know by what strange accident
  I chanced on this letter.
ANTONIO. I am dumb.
BASSANIO. Were you the doctor, and I knew you not?
GRATIANO. Were you the clerk that is to make me cuckold?
NERISSA. Ay, but the clerk that never means to do it,
  Unless he live until he be a man.
BASSANIO. Sweet doctor, you shall be my bedfellow;
  When I am absent, then lie with my wife.
ANTONIO. Sweet lady, you have given me life and living;
  For here I read for certain that my ships
  Are safely come to road.
PORTIA. How now, Lorenzo!
  My clerk hath some good comforts too for you.
NERISSA. Ay, and I'll give them him without a fee.
  There do I give to you and Jessica,
  From the rich Jew, a special deed of gift,
  After his death, of all he dies possess'd of.
LORENZO. Fair ladies, you drop manna in the way
  Of starved people.
PORTIA. It is almost morning,
  And yet I am sure you are not satisfied
  Of these events at full. Let us go in,
  And charge us there upon inter'gatories,
  And we will answer all things faithfully.
GRATIANO. Let it be so. The first inter'gatory
  That my Nerissa shall be sworn on is,
  Whether till the next night she had rather stay,
  Or go to bed now, being two hours to day.
  But were the day come, I should wish it dark,
  Till I were couching with the doctor's clerk.
  Well, while I live, I'll fear no other thing
  So sore as keeping safe Nerissa's ring.   Exeunt

THE END

Oscar Wilde (1854–1900) was born in Dublin, his father a leading surgeon and his mother a well-known writer (under the pen name "Speranza"), feminist, and Irish nationalist. A brilliant student, Wilde won prizes for his linguistic talents even as early as boarding school. He received scholarships to Trinity College in Dublin and Magdalen College, Oxford University, where he studied classics and from which he received a B.A. in 1878. At Oxford, he studied under Walter Pater and John Ruskin, and formed his "art for art's sake" philosophy. He traveled through Europe, writing poetry; his long poem *Ravenna* won a prize from Oxford University. In 1879 he moved to London, was a neighbor of the American artist, James McNeill Whistler, and thus began their long-standing intellectual feud. (Whistler accused Wilde of plagiarism and Wilde thought Whistler was a bad artist.) A first play, *Vera; or the Nihilists* (1883), did not have much success, partly because it was considered offensive to the royal families of England and Russia. Wilde turned to writing poetry and critical essays. His *Poems* (1881) received a mixed response. Meanwhile, his dandyism and posturing made him well known in the fashionable circles but also a subject of caricature by *Punch* and other magazines. Wilde did not mind, as it added to his celebrity. In 1882 he went on a lecture tour to the United States and Canada, giving 125 lectures on art and poetry. *The Happy Prince and Other Tales* (1888) finally secured him the critical response he wanted, as did the novel *The Picture of Dorian Gray* (1890, revised 1891) and the collection of critical essays *Intentions* (1891), in which his famous essays on art, "The Critic as Artist" and "The Decay of Lying" appear. Further collections of stories and poetry appeared, but the plays were what people came to see. *Lady Windermere's Fan* (1892), *A Woman of No Importance* (1893), and *The Ideal Husband* (1895) played to full houses and great reviews. Even his one-act play, *Salomé*, considered shocking and decadent, was generally accepted by the public. Shortly after *The Importance of Being Earnest* opened in 1895, Wilde was accused of homosexuality by the father of Wilde's lover. When he said he was innocent, the father was arrested for libel; in the ensuing trial, Wilde dropped his suit when the evidence began to go against him but was, in turn, put on trial for homosexuality. Convicted, he served two years in prison, during which time he wrote the letters *De Profundis* (1905) and the long poem *Ballad of Reading Gaol* (1898), exposing the horrid conditions of prison life. After being released from prison, Wilde moved to France, never to return to England.

The Importance of Being Earnest

Oscar Wilde

THE PERSONS OF THE PLAY

JOHN WORTHING, J.P.

ALGERNON MONCRIEFF

REV. CANON CHASUBLE, D.D.

MERRIMAN, BUTLER

LANE, MANSERVANT

LADY BRACKNELL

HON. GWENDOLEN FAIRFAX

CECILY CARDEW

MISS PRISM, GOVERNESS

THE SCENES OF THE PLAY

Act I, ALGERNON MONCRIEFF's *Flat in Half-Moon Street, W.*
Act II, *The Garden at the Manor House, Woolton.*
Act III, *Morning-room at the Manor House, Woolton.*

Time, The Present.

FIRST ACT

SCENE—*Morning-room in* ALGERNON'S *flat in Half-Moon Street. The room is luxuri-*   1
ously and artistically furnished. The sound of a piano is heard in the adjoining room.

    [LANE *is arranging afternoon tea on the table, and after the music has ceased,*   2
ALGERNON *enters.*]

    Alg. Did you hear what I was playing, Lane?   3

    Lane. I didn't think it polite to listen, sir.   4

    Alg. I'm sorry for that, for your sake. I don't play accurately—anyone can play   5
accurately—but I play with wonderful expression. As far as the piano is concerned,
sentiment is my forte. I keep science for Life.

    Lane. Yes, sir.   6

    Alg. And, speaking of the science of Life, have you got the cucumber sandwiches   7
cut for Lady Bracknell?

    Lane. Yes, sir. [*Hands them on a salver.*]   8

    Alg. [*Inspects them, takes two, and sits down on the sofa.*] Oh!. . . by the way, Lane,   9
I see from your book that on Thursday night, when Lord Shoreman and Mr. Worthing
were dining with me, eight bottles of champagne are entered as having been
consumed.

    Lane. Yes, sir; eight bottles and a pint.   10

    Alg. Why is it that at a bachelor's establishment the servants invariably drink   11
the champagne? I ask merely for information.

    Lane. I attribute it to the superior quality of the wine, sir. I have often observed   12
that in married households the champagne is rarely of a first-rate brand.

    Alg. Good Heavens! Is marriage so demoralising as that?   13

    Lane. I believe it is a very pleasant state, sir. I have had very little experience   14
of it myself up to the present. I have only been married once. That was in consequence of a misunderstanding between myself and a young person.

    Alg. [*Languidly.*] I don't know that I am much interested in your family life, Lane.   15

    Lane. No, sir; it is not a very interesting subject. I never think of it myself.   16

    Alg. Very natural, I am sure. That will do, Lane, thank you.   17

    Lane. Thank you, sir. [LANE *goes out.*]   18

    Alg. Lane's views on marriage seem somewhat lax. Really, if the lower orders   19
don't set us a good example, what on earth is the use of them? They seem, as a class,
to have absolutely no sense of moral responsibility.

    [*Enter* LANE.]   20

    Lane. Mr. Ernest Worthing.   21

[*Enter* JACK.] [LANE *goes out.*]   22

Alg. How are you, my dear Ernest? What brings you up to town?   23

Jack. Oh, pleasure, pleasure! What else should bring one anywhere? Eating as   24
usual, I see, Algy!

Alg. [*Stiffly.*] I believe it is customary in good society to take some slight refresh-   25
ment at five o'clock. Where have you been since last Thursday?

Jack. [*Sitting down on the sofa.*] In the country.   26

Alg. What on earth do you do there?   27

Jack. [*Pulling off his gloves.*] When one is in town one amuses oneself. When one   28
is in the country one amuses other people. It is excessively boring.

Alg. And who are the people you amuse?   29

Jack. [*Airily.*] Oh, neighbours, neighbours.   30

Alg. Got nice neighbours in your part of Shropshire?   31

Jack. Perfectly horrid! Never speak to one of them.   32

Alg. How immensely you must amuse them! [*Goes over and takes sandwich.*] By   33
the way, Shropshire is your county, is it not?

Jack. Eh? Shropshire? Yes, of course. Hallo! Why all these cups? Why cucum-   34
ber sandwiches? Why such reckless extravagance in one so young? Who is coming
to tea?

Alg. Oh! merely Aunt Augusta and Gwendolen.   35

Jack. How perfectly delightful!   36

Alg. Yes, that is all very well; but I am afraid Aunt Augusta won't quite approve   37
of your being here.

Jack. May I ask why?   38

Alg. My dear fellow, the way you flirt with Gwendolen is perfectly disgraceful.   39
It is almost as bad as the way Gwendolen flirts with you.

Jack. I am in love with Gwendolen. I have come up to town expressly to propose   40
to her.

Alg. I thought you had come up for pleasure? . . . I call that business.   41

Jack. How utterly unromantic you are!   42

Alg. I really don't see anything romantic in proposing. It is very romantic to be   43
in love. But there is nothing romantic about a definite proposal. Why, one may be
accepted. One usually is, I believe. Then the excitement is all over. The very essence
of romance is uncertainty. If ever I get married, I'll certainly try to forget the fact.

Jack. I have no doubt about that, dear Algy. The Divorce Court was specially   44
invented for people whose memories are so curiously constituted.

Alg. Oh! there is no use speculating on that subject. Divorces are made in   45
Heaven—[JACK *puts out his hand to take a sandwich.* ALGERNON *at once interferes.*] Please
don't touch the cucumber sandwiches. They are ordered specially for Aunt Augusta.
[*Takes one and eats it.*]

Jack. Well, you have been eating them all the time.   46

Alg. That is quite a different matter. She is my aunt. [*Takes plate from below.*]   47
Have some bread and butter. The bread and butter is for Gwendolen. Gwendolen
is devoted to bread and butter.

Jack. [*Advancing to table and helping himself*.] And very good bread and butter it   48
is too.

Alg. Well, my dear fellow, you need not eat as if you were going to eat it all.   49
You behave as if you were married to her already. You are not married to her already,
and I don't think you ever will be.

Jack. Why, on earth do you say that?   50

Alg. Well, in the first place girls never marry the men they flirt with. Girls don't   51
think it right.

Jack. Oh, that is nonsense!   52

Alg. It isn't. It is a great truth. It accounts for the extraordinary number of bach-   53
elors that one sees all over the place. In the second place, I don't give my consent.

Jack. Your consent!   54

Alg. My dear fellow, Gwendolen is my first cousin. And before I allow you to   55
marry her, you will have to clear up the whole question of Cecily. [*Rings bell*.]

Jack. Cecily! What on earth do you mean? What do you mean, Algy, by Cecily?   56
I don't know anyone of the name of Cecily.

[*Enter* LANE.]   57

Alg. Bring me that cigarette case Mr. Worthing left in the smoking-room the   58
last time he dined here.

Lane. Yes, sir. [LANE *goes out*.]   59

Jack. Do you mean to say you have had my cigarette case all this time? I wish   60
to goodness you had let me know. I have been writing frantic letters to Scotland Yard
about it. I was very nearly offering a large reward.

Alg. Well, I wish you would offer one. I happen to be more than usually hard up.   61

Jack. There is no good offering a large reward now that the thing is found.   62

[*Enter* LANE *with the cigarette case on a salver.* ALGERNON *takes it at once.* LANE *goes*   63
out.]

Alg. I think that is rather mean of you, Ernest, I must say. [*Opens case and exam-*   64
ines it.] However, it makes no matter, for, now that I look at the inscription inside, I
find that the thing isn't yours after all.

Jack. Of course it's mine. [*Moving to him*.] You have seen me with it a hundred   65
times, and you have no right whatsoever to read what is written inside. It is a very
ungentlemanly thing to read a private cigarette case.

Alg. Oh! it is absurd to have a hard-and-fast rule about what one should read   66
and what one shouldn't. More than half of modern culture depends on what one
shouldn't read.

Jack. I am quite aware of the fact, and I don't propose to discuss modern culture.   67
It isn't the sort of thing one should talk of in private. I simply want my cigarette case
back.

Alg. Yes; but this isn't your cigarette case. This cigarette case is a present from   68
someone of the name of Cecily, and you said you didn't know anyone of that name.

Jack. Well, if you want to know, Cecily happens to be my aunt.   69

Alg. Your aunt!   70

Jack. Yes. Charming old lady she is, too. Lives at Tunbridge Wells. Just give it 71
back to me, Algy.

Alg. [*Retreating to back of sofa.*] But why does she call herself Cecily if she is 72
your aunt and lives at Tunbridge Wells? [*Reading.*] "From little Cecily with her fondest love."

Jack. [*Moving to sofa and kneeling upon it.*] My dear fellow, what on earth is there 73
in that? Some aunts are tall, some aunts are not tall. That is a matter that surely an
aunt may be allowed to decide for herself. You seem to think that every aunt should
be exactly like your aunt! That is absurd! For Heaven's sake give me back my cigarette case. [*Follows* ALGY *round the room.*]

Alg. Yes. But why does your aunt call you her uncle? "From little Cecily, with 74
her fondest love to her dear Uncle Jack." There is no objection, I admit, to an aunt
being a small aunt, but why an aunt, no matter what her size may be, should call
her own nephew her uncle, I can't quite make out. Besides, your name isn't Jack at
all; it is Ernest.

Jack. It isn't Ernest; it's Jack. 75

Alg. You have always told me it was Ernest. I have introduced you to everyone 76
as Ernest. You answer to the name of Ernest. You look as if your name was Ernest.
You are the most earnest looking person I ever saw in my life. It is perfectly absurd
your saying that your name isn't Ernest. It's on your cards. Here is one of them. [*Taking
it from case.*] "Mr. Ernest Worthing, B. 4, The Albany." I'll keep this as a proof that
your name is Ernest if ever you attempt to deny, it to me, or to Gwendolen, or to anyone else. [*Puts the card in his pocket.*]

Jack. Well, my name is Ernest in town and Jack in the country, and the cigarette 77
case was given to me in the country.

Alg. Yes, but that does not account for the fact that your small Aunt Cecily, who 78
lives at Tunbridge Wells, calls you her dear uncle. Come, old boy, you had much better have the thing out at once.

Jack. My dear Algy, you talk exactly as if you were a dentist. It is very vulgar to 79
talk like a dentist when one isn't a dentist. It produces a false impression.

Alg. Well, that is exactly what dentists always do. Now, go on! Tell me the whole 80
thing. I may mention that I have always suspected you of being a confirmed and secret
Bunburyist; and I am quite sure of it now.

Jack. Bunburyist! What on earth do you mean by a Bunburyist? 81

Alg. I'll reveal to you the meaning of that incomparable expression as soon as you 82
are kind enough to inform me why you are Ernest in town and Jack in the country.

Jack. Well, produce my cigarette case first. 83

Alg. Here it is. [*Hands cigarette case.*] Now produce your explanation, and pray 84
make it improbable. [*Sits on sofa.*]

Jack. My dear fellow, there is nothing improbable about my explanation at all. 85
In fact it's perfectly ordinary. Old Mr. Thomas Cardew, who adopted me when I
was a little boy, made me in his will guardian to his granddaughter, Miss Cecily
Cardew. Cecily, who addresses me as her uncle from motives of respect that you could
not possibly appreciate, lives at my place in the country under the charge of her
admirable governess, Miss Prism.

Alg. Where is that place in the country, by the way?   86

Jack. That is nothing to you, dear boy. You are not going to be invited. I may tell   87
you candidly that the place is not in Shropshire.

Alg. I suspected that, my dear fellow! I have Bunburyed all over Shropshire on two   88
separate occasions. Now go on. Why are you Ernest in town and Jack in the country?

Jack. My dear Algy, I don't know whether you will be able to understand my real   89
motives. You are hardly serious enough. When one is placed in the position of
guardian, one has to adopt a very high moral tone on all subjects. It's one's duty to do
so. And as a high moral tone can hardly be said to conduce very much to either one's
health or one's happiness, in order to get up to town I have always pretended to have
a younger brother of the name of Ernest, who lives in the Albany, and gets into the
most dreadful scrapes. That, my dear Algy, is the whole truth pure and simple.

Alg. The truth is rarely pure and never simple. Modern life would be very tedious   90
if it were either, and modern literature a complete impossibility!

Jack. That wouldn't be at all a bad thing.   91

Alg. Literary criticism is, not your forte, my dear fellow. Don't try it. You should   92
leave that to people who haven't been at a University. They do it so well in the daily
papers. What you really are is a Bunburyist. I was quite right in saying you were a
Bunburyist. You are one of the most advanced Bunburyists I know.

Jack. What on earth do you mean?   93

Alg. You have invented a very useful young brother called Ernest, in order that   94
you may be able to come up to town as often as you like. I have invented an invaluable permanent invalid called Bunbury, in order that I may be able to go down into
the country whenever I choose. Bunbury is perfectly invaluable. If it wasn't for
Bunbury's extraordinary bad health, for instance, I wouldn't be able to dine with you
at Willis's to-night, for I have been really engaged to Aunt Augusta for more than
a week.

Jack. I haven't asked you to dine with me anywhere to-night.   95

Alg. I know. You are absurdly careless about sending out invitations. It is very   96
foolish of you. Nothing annoys people so much as not receiving invitations.

Jack. You had much better dine with your Aunt Augusta.   97

Alg. I haven't the smallest intention of doing anything of the kind. To begin   98
with, I dined there on Monday, and once a week is quite enough to dine with one's
own relations. In the second place, whenever I do dine there I am always treated as
a member of the family, and sent down with either no woman at all, or two. In the
third place, I know perfectly well whom she will place me next to, to-night. She will
place me next to Mary Farquhar, who always flirts with her own husband across the
dinner-table. That is not very pleasant. Indeed, it is not even decent . . . and that sort
of thing is enormously on the increase. The amount of women in London who flirt
with their own husbands is perfectly scandalous. It looks so bad. It is simply washing one's clean linen in public. Besides, now that I know you to be a confirmed
Bunburyist, I naturally want to talk to you about Bunburying. I want to tell you the
rules.

Jack. I'm not a Bunburyist at all. If Gwendolen accepts me, I am going to kill my   99
brother, indeed I think I'll kill him in any case. Cecily is a little too much

interested in him. It is rather a bore. So I am going to get rid of Ernest. And I strongly advise you to do the same with Mr. . . . with your invalid friend who has the absurd name.

Alg. Nothing will induce me to part with Bunbury, and if you ever get married, 100 which seems to me extremely problematic, you will be very glad to know Bunbury. A man who marries without knowing Bunbury has a very tedious time of it.

Jack. That is nonsense. If I marry a charming girl like Gwendolen, and she is the 101 only girl I ever saw in my life that I would marry, I certainly won't want to know Bunbury.

Alg. Then your wife will. You don't seem to realize, that in married life three is 102 company and two is none.

Jack. [*Sententiously.*] That, my dear young friend, is the theory that the corrupt 103 French Drama has been propounding for the last fifty years.

Alg. Yes; and that the happy English home has proved in half the time. 104

Jack. For Heaven's sake, don't try to be cynical. It's perfectly easy to be cynical. 105

Alg. My dear fellow, it isn't easy to be anything now-a-days. There's such a lot 106 of beastly competition about. [*The sound of an electric bell is heard.*] Ah! that must be Aunt Augusta. Only relatives, or creditors, ever ring in that Wagnerian manner. Now, if I get her out of the way for ten minutes, so that you can have an opportunity for proposing to Gwendolen, may I dine with you to-night at Willis's?

Jack. I suppose so, if you want to. 107

Alg. Yes, but you must be serious about it. I hate people who are not serious about 108 meals. It is so shallow of them.

[*Enter* LANE.] 109

Lane. Lady Bracknell and Miss Fairfax. 110

[ALGERNON *goes forward to meet them. Enter* LADY BRACKNELL *and* GWENDOLEN.] 111

Lady Bra. Good afternoon, dear Algernon. I hope you are behaving very well. 112

Alg. I'm feeling very well, Aunt Augusta. 113

Lady Bra. That's not quite the same thing. In fact the two things rarely go 114 together. [*Sees* JACK *and bows to him with icy coldness.*]

Alg. [*To* GWENDOLEN.] Dear me, you are smart! 115

Gwen. I am always smart! Aren't I, Mr. Worthing? 116

Jack. You are quite perfect, Miss Fairfax. 117

Gwen. Oh! I hope I am not that. It would leave no room for developments, 118 and I intend to develop in many directions.

[GWENDOLEN *and* JACK *sit down together in the corner.*] 119

Lady Bra. I'm sorry if we are a little late, Algernon, but I was obliged to call on 120 dear Lady Harbury. I hadn't been there since her poor husband's death. I never saw a woman so altered; she looks quite twenty years younger. And now I'll have a cup of tea, and one of those nice cucumber sandwiches you promised me.

Alg. Certainly, Aunt Augusta. [*Goes over to tea-table.*] 121

Lady Bra. Won't you come and sit here, Gwendolen? 122

Gwen. Thanks, mamma, I'm quite comfortable where I am. 123

Alg. [*Picking up empty plate in horror.*] Good Heavens! Lane! Why, are there no 124 cucumber sandwiches? I ordered them specially.

Lane. [*Gravely.*] There were no cucumbers in the market this morning, sir, I went 125 down twice.

Alg. No cucumbers! 126

Lane. No, sir. Not even for ready money. 127

Alg. That will do, Lane, thank you. 128

Lane. Thank you, sir. 129

Alg. I am greatly distressed, Aunt Augusta, about there being no cucumbers, not 130 even for ready money.

Lady Bra. It really makes no matter, Algernon. I had some crumpets with Lady 131 Harbury, who seems to me to be living entirely for pleasure now.

Alg. I hear her hair has turned quite gold from grief. 132

Lady Bra. It certainly has changed its color. From what cause I, of course, can- 133 not say. [ALGERNON *crosses and hands tea.*] Thank you. I've quite a treat for you to-night, Algernon. I am going to send you down with Mary Farquhar. She is such a nice woman, and so attentive to her husband. It's delightful to watch them.

Alg. I am afraid, Aunt Augusta, I shall have to give up the pleasure of dining 134 with you to-night after all.

Lady Bra. [*Frowning.*] I hope not, Algernon. It would put my table completely 135 out. Your uncle would have to dine upstairs. Fortunately he is accustomed to that.

Alg. It's a great bore, and, I need hardly say, a terrible disappointment to me, but 136 the fact is I have just had a telegram to say that my poor friend Bunbury is very ill again. [*Exchanges glances with* JACK.] They seem to think I should be with him.

Lady Bra. It is very strange. This Mr. Bunbury seems to suffer from curiously bad 137 health.

Alg. Yes; poor Bunbury is a dreadful invalid. 138

Lady Bra. Well, I must say, Algernon, that I think it is high time that Mr. 139 Bunbury made up his mind whether he was going to live or to die. This shilly-shallying with the question is absurd. Nor do I in any way approve of the modern sympathy with invalids. I consider it morbid. Illness of any kind is hardly a thing to be encouraged in others. Health is the primary duty of life. I am always telling that to your poor uncle, but he never seems to take much notice . . . as far as any improvement in his ailments goes. I should be obliged if you would ask Mr. Bunbury, from me, to be kind enough not to have a relapse on Saturday, for I rely on you to arrange my music for me. It is my last reception, and one wants something that will encourage conversation, particularly at the end of the season when everyone has practically said whatever they had to say, which, in most cases, was probably not much.

Alg. I'll speak to Bunbury, Aunt Augusta, if he is still conscious, and I think I 140 can promise you he'll be all right by Saturday. Of course the music is a great difficulty. You see, if one plays good music, people don't listen, and if one plays bad music, people don't talk. But I'll run over the programme I've drawn out, if you will kindly come into the next room for a moment.

Lady Bra. Thank you, Algernon. It is very thoughtful of you. [*Rising, and following* 141
ALGERNON.] I'm sure the programme will be delightful, after a few expurgations.
French songs I cannot possibly allow. People always seem to think that they are
improper, and either look shocked, which is vulgar, or laugh, which is worse. But
German sounds a thoroughly respectable language, and indeed, I believe is so.
Gwendolen, you will accompany me.

Gwen. Certainly, mamma. 142

[LADY BRACKNELL *and* ALGERNON *go into the music-room,* GWENDOLEN *remains* 143
behind.]

Jack. Charming day it has been, Miss Fairfax. 144

Gwen. Pray don't talk to me about the weather, Mr. Worthing. Whenever peo- 145
ple talk to me about the weather, I always feel quite certain that they mean something else. And that makes me so nervous.

Jack. I do mean something else. 146

Gwen. I thought so. In fact, I am never wrong. 147

Jack. And I would like to be allowed to take advantage of Lady Bracknell's tem- 148
porary absence . . .

Gwen. I would certainly advise you to do so. Mamma has a way of coming back 149
suddenly into a room that I have often had to speak to her about.

Jack. [*Nervously.*] Miss Fairfax, ever since I met you I have admired you more 150
than any girl . . . I have ever met since . . . I met you.

Gwen. Yes, I am quite aware of the fact. And I often wish that in public, at 151
any rate, you had been more demonstrative. For me you have always had an irresistible fascination. Even before I met you I was far from indifferent to you. [JACK *looks
at her in amazement.*] We live, as I hope you know, Mr. Worthing, in an age of ideals.
The fact is constantly mentioned in the more expensive monthly magazines, and has
reached the provincial pulpits I am told: and my ideal has always been to love some
one of the name of Ernest. There is something in that name that inspires absolute
confidence. The moment Algernon first mentioned to me that he had a friend called
Ernest, I knew I was destined to love you.

Jack. You really love me, Gwendolen? 152

Gwen. Passionately! 153

Jack. Darling! You don't know how happy you've made me. 154

Gwen. My own Ernest! 155

Jack. But you don't really mean to say that you couldn't love me if my name 156
wasn't Ernest?

Gwen. But your name is Ernest. 157

Jack. Yes, I know it is. But supposing it was something else? Do you mean to 158
say you couldn't love me then?

Gwen. [*Glibly.*] Ah! that is clearly a metaphysical speculation, and like most 159
metaphysical speculations has very little reference at all to the actual facts of real life,
as we know them.

Jack. Personally, darling, to speak quite candidly, I don't much care about the 160
name of Ernest . . . I don't think the name suits me at all.

Gwen. It suits you perfectly. It is a divine name. It has a music of its own. It 161
produces vibrations.

Jack. Well, really, Gwendolen, I must say that I think there are lots of other much 162
nicer names. I think Jack, for instance, a charming name.

Gwen. Jack? . . . No, there is very little music in the name Jack, if any at all, 163
indeed. It does not thrill. It produces absolutely no vibrations. . . . I have known several Jacks, and they all, without exception, were more than usually plain. Besides,
Jack is a notorious domesticity for John! And I pity any woman who is married to a
man called John. She would probably never be allowed to know the entrancing pleasure of a single moment's solitude. The only really safe name is Ernest.

Jack. Gwendolen, I must get christened at once—I mean we must get married 164
at once. There is no time to be lost.

Gwen. Married, Mr. Worthing? 165

Jack. [*Astounded.*] Well . . . surely. You know that I love you, and you led me to 166
believe, Miss Fairfax, that you were not absolutely indifferent to me.

Gwen. I adore you. But you haven't proposed to me yet. Nothing has been said 167
at all about marriage. The subject has not even been touched on.

Jack. Well . . . may I propose to you now? 168

Gwen. I think it would be an admirable opportunity. And to spare you any pos- 169
sible disappointment, Mr. Worthing, I think it only fair to tell you quite frankly
beforehand that I am fully determined to accept you.

Jack. Gwendolen! 170

Gwen. Yes, Mr. Worthing, what have you got to say to me? 171

Jack. You know what I have got to say to you. 172

Gwen. Yes, but you don't say it. 173

Jack. Gwendolen, will you marry me? [*Goes on his knees.*] 174

Gwen. Of course I will, darling. How long you have been about it! I am afraid 175
you have had very little experience in how to propose.

Jack. My own one, I have never loved anyone in the world but you. 176

Gwen. Yes, but men often propose for practice. I know my brother Gerald does. 177
All my girl-friends tell me so. What wonderfully blue eyes you have, Ernest! They
are quite, quite blue. I hope you will always look at me just like that, especially when
there are other people present.

[*Enter* LADY BRACKNELL.] 178

Lady Bra. Mr. Worthing! Rise, sir, from this semi-recumbent posture. It is most 179
indecorous.

Gwen. Mamma! [*He tries to rise; she restrains him.*] I must beg you to retire. This 180
is no place for you. Besides, Mr. Worthing has not quite finished yet.

Lady Bra. Finished what, may I ask? 181

Gwen. I am engaged to Mr. Worthing, mamma. [*They rise together.*] 182

Lady Bra. Pardon me, you are not engaged to anyone. When you do become 183
engaged to some one, I, or your father, should his health permit him, will inform you
of the fact. An engagement should come on a young girl as a surprise, pleasant or
unpleasant, as the case may be. It is hardly a matter that she could be allowed to arrange

for herself. . . . And now I have a few questions to put to you, Mr. Worthing. While I am making these inquiries, you, Gwendolen, will wait for me below in the carriage.

Gwen. [*Reproachfully.*] Mamma!   184

Lady Bra. In the carriage, Gwendolen! [GWENDOLEN *goes to the door. She and* JACK   185 *blow kisses to each other behind* LADY BRACKNELL'S *back.* LADY BRACKNELL *looks vaguely about as if she could not understand what the noise was. Finally turns round.*] Gwendolen, the carriage!

Gwen. Yes, mamma. [*Goes out, looking back at* JACK.]   186

Lady Bra. [*Sitting down.*] You can take a seat, Mr. Worthing.   187

[*Looks in her pocket for note-book and pencil.*]   188

Jack. Thank you, Lady Bracknell, I prefer standing.   189

Lady Bra. [*Pencil and note-book in hand.*] I feel bound to tell you that you are   190 not down on my list of eligible young men, although I have the same list as the dear Duchess of Bolton has. We work together, in fact. However, I am quite ready to enter your name, should your answers be what a really affectionate mother requires. Do you smoke?

Jack. Well, yes, I must admit I smoke.   191

Lady Bra. I am glad to hear it. A man should always have an occupation of some   192 kind. There are far too many idle men in London as it is. How old are you?

Jack. Twenty-nine.   193

Lady Bra. A very good age to be married at. I have always been of opinion that   194 a man who desires to get married should know either everything or nothing. Which do you know?

Jack. [*After some hesitation.*] I know nothing, Lady Bracknell.   195

Lady Bra. I am pleased to hear it. I do not approve of anything that tampers with   196 natural ignorance. Ignorance is like a delicate exotic fruit; touch it and the bloom is gone. The whole theory of modern education is radically unsound. Fortunately in England, at any rate, education produces no effect whatsoever. If it did, it would prove a serious danger to the upper classes, and probably lead to acts of violence in Grosvenor Square. What is your income?

Jack. Between seven and eight thousand a year.   197

Lady Bra. [*Makes a note in her book.*] In land, or in investments?   198

Jack. In investments, chiefly.   199

Lady Bra. That is satisfactory. What between the duties expected of one dur-   200 ing one's lifetime, and the duties exacted from one after one's death, land has ceased to be either a profit or a pleasure. It gives one position, and prevents one from keeping it up. That's all that can be said about land.

Jack. I have a country house with some land, of course, attached to it, about   201 fifteen hundred acres, I believe; but I don't depend on that for my real income. In fact, as far as I can make out, the poachers are the only people who make anything out of it.

Lady Bra. A country house! How many bedrooms? Well, that point can be   202 cleared up afterwards. You have a town house, I hope? A girl with a simple, unspoiled nature, like Gwendolen, could hardly be expected to reside in the country.

Jack. Well, I own a house in Belgrave Square, but it is let by the year to Lady 203
Bloxham. Of course, I can get it back whenever I like, at six months' notice.

Lady Bra. Lady Bloxham? I don't know her. 204

Jack. Oh, she goes about very little. She is a lady considerably advanced in years. 205

Lady Bra. Ah, now-a-days that is no guarantee of respectability of character. 206
What number in Belgrave Square?

Jack. 149. 207

Lady Bra. [*Shaking her head.*] The unfashionable side. I thought there was some- 208
thing. However, that could easily be altered.

Jack. Do you mean the fashion, or the side? 209

Lady Bra. [*Sternly.*] Both, if necessary, I presume. What are your politics? 210

Jack. Well, I am afraid I really have none. I am a Liberal Unionist. 211

Lady Bra. Oh, they count as Tories. They dine with us. Or come in the evening, 212
at any rate. Now to minor matters. Are your parents living?

Jack. I have lost both my parents. 213

Lady Bra. Both? . . . That seems like carelessness. Who was your father? He 214
was evidently a man of some wealth. Was he born in what the Radical papers call the
purple of commerce, or did he rise from the ranks of aristocracy?

Jack. I am afraid I really don't know. The fact is, Lady Bracknell, I said I had lost 215
my parents. It would be nearer the truth to say that my parents seem to have lost
me. . . . I don't actually know who I am by birth. I was well, I was found.

Lady Bra. Found! 216

Jack. The late Mr. Thomas Cardew, an old gentleman of a very charitable and 217
kindly disposition, found me, and gave me the name of Worthing, because he happened to have a first-class ticket for Worthing in his pocket at the time. Worthing
is a place in Sussex. It is a seaside resort.

Lady Bra. Where did the charitable gentleman who had a first-class ticket for 218
this seaside resort find you?

Jack. [*Gravely.*] In a hand-bag. 219

Lady Bra. A hand-bag? 220

Jack. [*Very seriously.*] Yes, Lady Bracknell. I was in a hand-bag—a somewhat large, 221
black leather hand-bag, with handles to it—an ordinary hand-bag, in fact.

Lady Bra. In what locality did this Mr. James, or Thomas, Cardew come across 222
this ordinary hand-bag?

Jack. In the cloak-room at Victoria Station. It was given to him in mistake for 223
his own.

Lady Bra. The cloak-room at Victoria Station? 224

Jack. Yes. The Brighton line. 225

Lady Bra. The line is immaterial. Mr. Worthing, I confess I feel somewhat bewil- 226
dered by what you have just told me. To be born, or at any rate, bred in a hand-
bag, whether it had handles or not, seems to me to display a contempt for the ordinary
decencies of family life that remind one of the worst excesses of the French
Revolution. And I presume you know what that unfortunate movement led to? As
for the particular locality in which the hand-bag was found, a cloak-room at a railway station might serve to conceal a social indiscretion—has probably, indeed, been

used for that purpose before now—but it could hardly be regarded as an assured basis for a recognized position in good society.

Jack. May I ask you then what you would advise me to do? I need hardly say I would do anything in the world to ensure Gwendolen's happiness. 227

Lady Bra. I would strongly advise you, Mr. Worthing, to try and acquire some relations as soon as possible, and to make a definite effort to produce at any rate one parent, of either sex, before the season is quite over. 228

Jack. I don't see how I could possibly manage to do that. I can produce the hand-bag at any moment. It is in my dressing-room at home. I really think that should satisfy you, Lady Bracknell. 229

Lady Bra. Me, sir! What has it to do with me? You can hardly imagine that I and Lord Bracknell would dream of allowing our only daughter—a girl brought up with the utmost care—to marry into a cloak-room, and form an alliance with a parcel? Good morning, Mr. Worthing! 230

[LADY BRACKNELL *sweeps out in majestic indignation.*] 231

Jack. Good morning! [ALGERNON, *from the other room, strikes up the Wedding March.* JACK *looks perfectly furious, and goes to the door.*] For goodness' sake don't play that ghastly tune, Algy! How idiotic you are! 232

[*The music stops, and* ALGERNON *enters cheerily.*] 233

Alg. Didn't it go off all right, old boy? You don't mean to say Gwendolen refused you, I know it is a way she has. She is always refusing people. I think it is most ill-natured of her. 234

Jack. Oh, Gwendolen is as right as a trivet. As far as she is concerned, we are engaged. Her mother is perfectly unbearable. Never met such a Gorgon . . . I don't really know what a Gorgon is like, but I am quite sure that Lady Bracknell is one. In any case, she is a monster, without being a myth, which is rather unfair . . . I beg your pardon, Algy, I suppose I shouldn't talk about your own aunt in that way before you. 235

Alg. My dear boy, I love hearing my relations abused. It is the only thing that makes me put up with them at all. Relations are simply a tedious pack of people who haven't got the remotest knowledge of how to live, nor the smallest instinct about when to die. 236

Jack. Oh, that is nonsense! 237

Alg. It isn't! 238

Jack. Well, I won't argue about the matter. You always want to argue about things. 239

Alg. That is exactly what things were originally made for. 240

Jack. Upon my word, if I thought that, I'd shoot myself. . . [*A pause.*] You don't think there is any chance of Gwendolen becoming like her mother in about a hundred and fifty years, do you, Algy? 241

Alg. All women become like their mothers. That is their tragedy. No man does. That's his. 242

Jack. Is that clever? 243

Alg. It is perfectly phrased! and quite as true as any observation in civilized life should be. 244

Jack. I am sick to death of cleverness. Everybody is clever now-a-days. You can't   245
go anywhere without meeting clever people. The thing has become an absolute public nuisance. I wish to goodness we had a few fools left.

Alg. We have.   246

Jack. I should extremely like to meet them. What do they talk about?   247

Alg. The fools? Oh! about the clever people, of course.   248

Jack. What fools!   249

Alg. By the way, did you tell Gwendolen the truth about your being Ernest in   250
town, and Jack in the country?

Jack. [*In a very patronising manner*.] My dear fellow, the truth isn't quite the sort   251
of thing one tells to a nice sweet refined girl. What extraordinary ideas you have
about the way to behave to a woman!

Alg. The only way to behave to a woman is to make love to her, if she is pretty,   252
and to someone else if she is plain.

Jack. Oh, that is nonsense.   253

Alg. What about your brother? What about the profligate Ernest?   254

Jack. Oh, before the end of the week I shall have got rid of him. I'll say he died   255
in Paris of apoplexy. Lots of people die of apoplexy, quite suddenly, don't they?

Alg. Yes, but it's hereditary, my dear fellow. It's a sort of thing that runs in fam-   256
ilies. You had much better say a severe chill.

Jack. You are sure a severe chill isn't hereditary, or anything of that kind?   257

Alg. Of course it isn't!   258

Jack. Very well, then. My poor brother Ernest is carried off suddenly in Paris,   259
by a severe chill. That gets rid of him.

Alg. But I thought you said that . . . Miss Cardew was a little too much inter-   260
ested in your poor brother, Ernest? Won't she feel his loss a good deal?

Jack. Oh, that is all right. Cecily is not a silly romantic girl, I am glad to say. She   261
has got a capital appetite, goes for long walks, and pays no attention at all to her
lessons.

Alg. I would rather like to see Cecily.   262

Jack. I will take very good care you never do. She is excessively pretty, and she   263
is only just eighteen.

Alg. Have you told Gwendolen yet that you have an excessively pretty ward who   264
is only just eighteen?

Jack. Oh! one doesn't blurt these things out to people. Cecily, and Gwendolen   265
are perfectly certain to be extremely great friends. I'll bet you anything you like
that half an hour after they have met, they will be calling each other sister.

Alg. Women only do that when they have called each other a lot of other things   266
first. Now, my dear boy, if we want to get a good table at Willis's, we really must go
and dress. Do you know it is nearly seven?

Jack. [*Irritably*.] Oh! it always is nearly seven.   267

Alg. Well, I'm hungry.   268

Jack. I never knew you when you weren't. . . .   269

Alg. What shall we do after dinner? Go to the theatre?   270

Jack. Oh no! I loathe listening.   271

Alg. Well, let us go to the club? 272

Jack. Oh no! I hate talking. 273

Alg. Well, we might trot round to the Empire at ten? 274

Jack. Oh no! I can't bear looking at things. It is so silly. 275

Alg. Well, what shall we do? 276

Jack. Nothing! 277

Alg. It is awfully hard work doing nothing. However, I don't mind hard work 278
where there is no definite object of any kind.

[*Enter* LANE.] 279

Lane. Miss Fairfax. 280

[*Enter* GWENDOLEN. LANE *goes out.*] 281

Alg. Gwendolen, upon my word! 282

Gwen. Algy, kindly turn your back. I have something very particular to say to 283
Mr. Worthing.

Alg. Really, Gwendolen, I don't think I can allow this at all. 284

Gwen. Algy, you always adopt a strictly immoral attitude towards life. You are 285
not quite old enough to do that. [ALGERNON *retires to the fireplace.*]

Jack. My own darling! 286

Gwen. Ernest, we may never be married. From the expression on mamma's face 287
I fear we never shall. Few parents now-a-days pay any regard to what their children
say to them. The old-fashioned respect for the young is fast dying out. Whatever
influence I ever had over mamma, I lost at the age of three. But although she may
prevent us from becoming man and wife, and I may marry someone else, and marry
often, nothing that she can possibly do can alter my eternal devotion to you.

Jack. Dear Gwendolen! 288

Gwen. The story of your romantic origin, as related to me by mamma, with 289
unpleasing comments, has naturally stirred the deeper fibres of my nature. Your
Christian name has an irresistible fascination. The simplicity of your character makes
you exquisitely incomprehensible to me. Your town address at the Albany I have.
What is your address in the country?

Jack. The Manor House, Woolton, Hertfordshire. 290

[ALGERNON, *who has been carefully listening, smiles to himself, and writes the address* 291
on his shirt-cuff. Then picks up the Railway Guide.]

Gwen. There is a good postal service, I suppose? It may be necessary to do some- 292
thing desperate. That of course will require serious consideration. I will communicate with you daily.

Jack. My own one! 293

Gwen. How long do you remain in town? 294

Jack. Till Monday. 295

Gwen. Good! Algy, you may turn round now. 296

Alg. Thanks, I've turned round already. 297

Gwen. You may also ring the bell. 298

Jack. You will let me see you to your carriage, my own darling?   299

Gwen. Certainly.   300

Jack. [*To* LANE, *who now enters.*] I will see Miss Fairfax out.   301

Lane. Yes. sir. [JACK *and* GWENDOLEN *go off.*]   302

[LANE *presents several letters on a salver to* ALGERNON. *It is to be surmised that they*   303
are bills, as ALGERNON, *after looking at the envelopes, tears them up.*]

Alg. A glass of sherry, Lane.   304

Lane. Yes, sir.   305

Alg. To-morrow, Lane, I'm going Bunburying.   306

Lane. Yes, sir.   307

Alg. I shall probably not be back till Monday. You can put up my dress clothes,   308
my smoking Jacket, and all the Bunbury suits. . . .

Lane. Yes, sir. [*Handing sherry.*]   309

Alg. I hope to-morrow will be a fine day, Lane.   310

Lane. It never is, sir.   311

Alg. Lane, you're a perfect pessimist.   312

Lane. I do my best to give satisfaction, sir.   313

[*Enter* JACK. LANE *goes off.*]   314

Jack. There's a sensible, intellectual girl! the only girl I ever cared for in my   315
life. [ALGERNON *is laughing immoderately.*] What on earth are you so amused at?

Alg. Oh, I'm a little anxious about poor Bunbury, that is all.   316

Jack. If you don't take care, your friend Bunbury will get you into a serious scrape   317
some day.

Alg. I love scrapes. They are the only things that are never serious.   318

Jack. Oh, that's nonsense, Algy. You never talk anything but nonsense.   319

Alg. Nobody ever does.   320

[JACK *looks indignantly at him, leaves the room.* ALGERNON *lights a cigarette, reads his*   321
shirt-cuff, and smiles.]

SECOND ACT

SCENE—*Garden at the Manor House. A flight of gray stone steps leads up to the house.*   322
The garden, an old-fashioned one, full of roses. Time of year, July. Basket chairs, and a
table covered with books, are set under a large yew tree.

[MISS PRISM *discovered seated at the table.* CECILY *is at the back watering flowers.*]   323

Miss Pri. [*Calling.*] Cecily, Cecily! Surely such a utilitarian occupation as the   324
watering of flowers is rather Moulton's duty than yours? Especially at a moment when
intellectual pleasures await you. Your German grammar is on the table. Pray open
it at page fifteen. We will repeat yesterday's lesson.

Cec. [*Coming over very slowly.*] But I don't like German. It isn't at all a becom-   325
ing language. I know perfectly well that I look quite plain after my German lesson.

Miss Pri. Child, you know how anxious your guardian is that you should improve 326
yourself in every way. He laid particular stress on your German, as he was leaving for
town yesterday. Indeed, he always lays stress on your German when he is leaving
for town.

Cec. Dear Uncle Jack is so very serious! Sometimes he is so serious that I think 327
he cannot be quite well.

Miss Pri. [*Drawing herself up.*] Your guardian enjoys the best of health, and his 328
gravity of demeanour is especially to be commended in one so comparatively young
as he is. I know no one who has a higher sense of duty and responsibility.

Cec. I suppose that is why he often looks a little bored when we three are 329
together.

Miss Pri. Cecily! I am surprised at you. Mr. Worthing has many troubles in his 330
life. Idle merriment and triviality would be out of place in his conversation. You must
remember his constant anxiety about that unfortunate young man his brother.

Cec. I wish Uncle Jack would allow that unfortunate young man, his brother, to 331
come down here sometimes. We might have a good influence over him, Miss Prism.
I am sure you certainly would. You know German, and geology, and things of that
kind influence a man very much. [CECILY *begins to write in her diary.*]

Miss Pri. [*Shaking her head.*] I do not think that even I could produce any effect 332
on a character that according to his own brother's admission is irretrievably weak and
vacillating. Indeed I am not sure that I would desire to reclaim him. I am not in favour
of this modern mania for turning bad people into good people at a moment's notice.
As a man sows so let him reap. You must put away your diary, Cecily. I really don't
see why you should keep a diary at all.

Cec. I keep a diary in order to enter the wonderful secrets of my life. If I didn't 333
write them down I should probably forget all about them.

Miss Pri. Memory, my dear Cecily, is the diary that we all carry about with us. 334

Cec. Yes, but it usually chronicles the things that have never happened, and 335
couldn't possibly have happened. I believe that Memory is responsible for nearly
all the three-volume novels that Mudie sends us.

Miss Pri. Do not speak slightingly of the three-volume novel, Cecily. I wrote one 336
myself in earlier days.

Cec. Did you really, Miss Prism? How wonderfully clever you are! I hope it did 337
not end happily? I don't like novels that end happily. They depress me so much.

Miss Pri. The good ended happily, and the bad unhappily. That is what Fiction 338
means.

Cec. I suppose so. But it seems very unfair. And was your novel ever published? 339

Miss Pri. Alas! no. The manuscript unfortunately was abandoned. I use the word 340
in the sense of lost or mislaid. To your work, child, these speculations are profitless.

Cec. [*Smiling.*] But I see dear Dr. Chasuble coming up through the garden. 341

Miss Pri. [*Rising and advancing.*] Dr. Chasuble! This is indeed a pleasure. 342

[*Enter* CANON CHASUBLE.] 343

Chas. And how are we this morning? Miss Prism, you are, I trust, well? 344

Cec. Miss Prism has just been complaining of a slight headache. I think it would   345
do her so much good to have a short stroll with you in the Park, Dr. Chasuble.

Miss Pri. Cecily, I have not mentioned anything about a headache.   346

Cec. No, dear Miss Prism, I know that, but I felt instinctively that you had a   347
headache. Indeed I was thinking about that, and not about my German lesson, when
the Rector came in.

Chas. I hope Cecily, you are not inattentive.   348

Cec. Oh, I am afraid I am.   349

Chas. That is strange. Were I fortunate enough to be Miss Prism's pupil, I would   350
hang upon her lips. [MISS PRISM *glares.*] I spoke metaphorically. My metaphor was
drawn from bees. Ahem! Mr. Worthing, I suppose, has not returned from town yet?

Miss Pri. We do not expect him till Monday afternoon.   351

Chas. Ah yes, he usually likes to spend his Sunday in London. He is not one of   352
those whose sole aim is enjoyment, as, by all accounts, that unfortunate young man
his brother seems to be. But I must not disturb Egeria and her pupil any longer.

Miss Pri. Egeria? My name is Laetitia, Doctor.   353

Chas. [*Bowing.*] A classical allusion merely, drawn from the Pagan authors. I shall   354
see you both no doubt at Evensong?

Miss Pri. I think, dear Doctor, I will have a stroll with you. I find I have a   355
headache after all, and a walk might do it good.

Chas. With pleasure, Miss Prism, with pleasure. We might go as far as the schools   356
and back.

Miss Pri. That would be delightful. Cecily, you will read your Political Economy   357
in my absence. The chapter on the Fall of the Rupee you may omit. It is somewhat
too sensational. Even these metallic problems have their melodramatic side.

[*Goes down the garden with* DR. CHASUBLE.]   358

Cec. [*Picks up books and throws them back on table.*] Horrid Political Economy!   359
Horrid Geography! Horrid, horrid German!

[*Enter* MERRIMAN *with a card on a salver.*]   360

Merr. Mr. Ernest Worthing has just driven over from the station. He has brought   361
his luggage with him.

Cec. [*Takes the card and reads it.*] "Mr. Ernest Worthing, B. 4 The Albany, W."   362
Uncle Jack's brother! Did you tell him Mr. Worthing was in town?

Merr. Yes, Miss. He seemed very much disappointed. I mentioned that you and   363
Miss Prism were in the garden. He said he was anxious to speak to you privately for
a moment.

Cec. Ask Mr. Ernest Worthing to come here. I suppose you had better talk to   364
the housekeeper about a room for him.

Merr. Yes, Miss. [MERRIMAN *goes off.*]   365

Cec. I have never met any really wicked person before. I feel rather frightened.   366
I am so afraid he will look just like everyone else.

[*Enter* ALGERNON, *very gay and debonnair.*]   367

He does! 368

Alg. [*Raising his hat.*] You are my little cousin Cecily, I'm sure. 369

Cec. You are under some strange mistake. I am not little. In fact, I believe I am 370 more than usually tall for my age. [ALGERNON *is rather taken aback.*) But I am your cousin Cecily. You, I see from your card, are Uncle Jack's brother, my cousin Ernest, my wicked cousin Ernest.

Alg. Oh! I am not really wicked at all, Cousin Cecily. You mustn't think that I 371 am wicked.

Cec. If you are not, then you have certainly been deceiving us all in a very inex- 372 cusable manner. I hope you have not been leading a double life, pretending to be wicked and being really good all the time. That would be hypocrisy.

Alg. [*Looks at her in amazement.*] Oh! Of course I have been rather reckless. 373

Cec. I am glad to hear it. 374

Alg. In fact, now you mention the subject, I have been very bad in my own small 375 way.

Cec. I don't think you should be so proud of that, though I am sure it must 376 have been very pleasant.

Alg. It is much pleasanter being here with you. 377

Cec. I can't understand how you are here at all. Uncle Jack won't be back till 378 Monday afternoon.

Alg. That is a great disappointment. I am obliged to go up by the first train on 379 Monday morning. I have a business appointment that I am anxious . . . to miss.

Cec. Couldn't you miss it anywhere but in London? 380

Alg. No: the appointment is in London. 381

Cec. Well, I know, of course, how important it is not to keep a business engage- 382 ment, if one wants to retain any sense of the beauty of life, but still I think you had better wait till Uncle Jack arrives. I know he wants to speak to you about your emi- grating.

Alg. About my what? 383

Cec. Your emigrating. He has gone up to buy your outfit. 384

Alg. I certainly wouldn't let Jack buy my outfit. He has no taste in neckties at 385 all.

Cec. I don't think you will require neckties. Uncle Jack is sending you to 386 Australia.

Alg. Australia? I'd sooner die. 387

Cec. Well, he said at dinner on Wednesday night, that you would have to choose 388 between this world, the next world, and Australia.

Alg. Oh, well! The accounts I have received of Australia and the next world are 389 not particularly encouraging. This world is good enough for me, Cousin Cecily.

Cec. Yes, but are you good enough for it? 390

Alg. I'm afraid I'm not that. That is why I want you to reform me. You might 391 make that your mission, if you don't mind, Cousin Cecily.

Cec. I'm afraid I've no time, this afternoon. 392

Alg. Well, would you mind my reforming myself this afternoon? 393

Cec. It is rather Quixotic of you. But I think you should try. 394

Alg. I will. I feel better already.   395

Cec. You are looking a little worse.   396

Alg. That is because I am hungry.   397

Cec. How thoughtless of me. I should have remembered that when one is going 398
to lead an entirely new life, one requires regular and wholesome meals. Won't you
come in?

Alg. Thank you. Might I have a buttonhole first? I never have any appetite unless 399
I have a buttonhole first.

Cec. A Marechale Niel? [*Picks up scissors.*]   400

Alg. No, I'd sooner have a pink rose.   401

Cec. Why? [*Cuts a flower.*]   402

Alg. Because you are like a pink rose, Cousin Cecily.   403

Cec. I don't think it can be right for you to talk to me like that. Miss Prism never 404
says such things to me.

Alg. Then Miss Prism is a shortsighted old lady. [CECILY *puts the rose in his but-* 405
tonhole.] You are the prettiest girl I ever saw.

Cec. Miss Prism says that all good looks are a snare.   406

Alg. They are a snare that every sensible man would like to be caught in.   407

Cec. Oh! I don't think I would care to catch a sensible man. I shouldn't know 408
what to talk to him about.

[*They pass into the house.* MISS PRISM *and* DR. CHASUBLE *return.*]   409

Miss Pri. You are too much alone, dear Dr. Chasuble. You should get married. A 410
misanthrope I can understand—a womanthrope, never!

Chas. [*With a scholar's shudder.*] Believe me, I do not deserve so neologistic a 411
phrase. The precept as well as the practice of the Primitive Church was distinctly
against matrimony.

Miss Pri. [*Sententiously.*] That is obviously the reason why the Primitive Church 412
has not lasted up to the present day. And you do not seem to realize, dear Doctor,
that by persistently remaining single, a man converts himself into a permanent
public temptation. Men should be more careful; this very celibacy leads weaker
vessels astray.

Chas. But is a man not equally attractive when married?   413

Miss Pri. No married man is ever attractive except to his wife.   414

Chas. And often, I've been told, not even to her.   415

Miss Pri. That depends on the intellectual sympathies of the woman. Maturity 416
can always be depended on. Ripeness can be trusted. Young women are green.
[DR. CHASUBLE *starts.*] I spoke horticulturally. My metaphor was drawn from fruits.
But where is Cecily?

Chas. Perhaps she followed us to the schools.   417

[*Enter* JACK *slowly from the back of the garden. He is dressed in the deepest mourning,* 418
with crape hatband and black gloves.]

Miss Pri. Mr. Worthing!   419

Chas. Mr. Worthing!   420

Miss Pri. This is indeed a surprise. We did not look for you till Monday afternoon. 421

Jack. [*Shakes* MISS PRISM's *hand in a tragic manner.*] I have returned sooner than 422
I expected. Dr. Chasuble, I hope you are well?

Chas. Dear Mr. Worthing, I trust this garb of woe does not betoken some terri- 423
ble calamity?

Jack. My brother. 424

Miss Pri. More shameful debts and extravagance? 425

Chas. Still leading his life of pleasure? 426

Jack. [*Shaking his head.*] Dead! 427

Chas. Your brother Ernest dead? 428

Jack. Quite dead. 429

Miss Pri. What a lesson for him! I trust he will profit by it. 430

Chas. Mr. Worthing, I offer you my sincere condolence. You have at least the 431
consolation of knowing that you were always the most generous and forgiving of
brothers.

Jack. Poor Ernest! He had many faults, but it is a sad, sad blow. 432

Chas. Very sad indeed. Were you with him at the end? 433

Jack. No. He died abroad; in Paris, in fact. I had a telegram last night from the 434
manager of the Grand Hotel.

Chas. Was the cause of death mentioned? 435

Jack. A severe chill, it seems. 436

Miss Pri. As a man sows, so shall he reap. 437

Chas. [*Raising his hand.*] Charity, dear Miss Prism, charity! None of us are per- 438
fect. I myself am peculiarly susceptible to draughts. Will the interment take place
here?

Jack. No. He seemed to have expressed a desire to be buried in Paris. 439

Chas. In Paris! [*Shakes his head.*] I fear that hardly points to any very serious state 440
of mind at the last. You would no doubt wish me to make some slight allusion to this
tragic domestic affliction next Sunday. [JACK *presses his hand convulsively.*] My sermon
on the meaning of the manna in the wilderness can be adapted to almost any occasion, joyful, or, as in the present case, distressing. [*All sigh.*] I have preached it at
harvest celebrations, christenings, confirmations, on days of humiliation and festal
days. The last time I delivered it was in the Cathedral, as a charity sermon on behalf
of the Society for the Prevention of Discontent among the Upper Orders. The Bishop,
who was present, was much struck by some of the analogies I drew.

Jack. Ah! that reminds me, you mentioned christenings, I think, Dr. Chasuble? 441
I suppose you know how to christen all right? [DR. CHASUBLE *looks astounded.*] I mean,
of course, you are continually christening, aren't you?

Miss Pri. It is, I regret to say, one of the Rector's most constant duties in this 442
parish. I have often spoken to the poorer classes on the subject. But they don't seem
to know what thrift is.

Chas. But is there any particular infant in whom you are interested, 443
Mr. Worthing? Your brother was, I believe, unmarried, was he not?

Jack. Oh yes. 444

Miss Pri. [*Bitterly.*] People who live entirely for pleasure usually are.   445

Jack. But it is not for any child, dear Doctor. I am very fond of children. No! the   446
fact is, I would like to be christened myself, this afternoon, if you have nothing better to do.

 Chas. But surely, Mr. Worthing, you have been christened already?   447

 Jack. I don't remember anything about it.   448

 Chas. But have you any grave doubts on the subject?   449

 Jack. I certainly intend to have. Of course I don't know if the thing would bother   450
you in any way, or if you think I am a little too old now.

 Chas. Not at all. The sprinkling, and, indeed, the immersion of adults is a per-   451
fectly canonical practice.

 Jack. Immersion!   452

 Chas. You need have no apprehensions. Sprinkling is all that is necessary, or   453
indeed I think advisable. Our weather is so changeable. At what hour would you wish
the ceremony performed?

 Jack. Oh, I might trot round about five if that would suit you.   454

 Chas. Perfectly, perfectly! In fact I have two similar ceremonies to perform at   455
that time. A case of twins that occurred recently in one of the outlying cottages on
your own estate. Poor Jenkins the carter, a most hard-working man.

 Jack. Oh! I don't see much fun in being christened along with other babies. It   456
would be childish. Would half-past five do?

 Chas. Admirably! Admirably! [*Takes out watch.*] And now, dear Mr. Worthing,   457
I will not intrude any longer into a house of sorrow. I would merely beg you not to be
too much bowed down by grief. What seem to us bitter trials are often blessings in
disguise.

 Miss Pri. This seems to me a blessing of an extremely obvious kind.   458

[*Enter* CECILY *from the house.*]   459

 Cec. Uncle Jack! Oh, I am pleased to see you back. But what horrid clothes   460
you have got on! Do go and change them.

 Miss Pri. Cecily!   461

 Chas. My child! my child! [CECILY *goes towards* JACK; *he kisses her brow in a melan-*   462
choly manner.]

 Cec. What is the matter, Uncle Jack? Do look happy! You look as if you had a   463
toothache, and I have got such a surprise for you. Who do you think is in the dining-
room? Your brother!

 Jack. Who?   464

 Cec. Your brother Ernest. He arrived about half an hour ago.   465

 Jack. What nonsense! I haven't got a brother!   466

 Cec. Oh, don't say that. However badly he may have behaved to you in the past   467
he is still your brother. You couldn't be so heartless as to disown him. I'll tell him to
come out. And you will shake hands with him, won't you, Uncle Jack? [*Runs back
into the house.*]

 Chas. These are very joyful tidings.   468

Miss Pri. After we had all been resigned to his loss, his sudden return seems to 469
me peculiarly distressing.

Jack. My brother is in the dining-room? I don't know what it all means. I think 470
it is perfectly absurd.

[*Enter* ALGERNON *and* CECILY *hand in hand. They come slowly up to* JACK.] 471

Jack. Good Heavens! [*Motions* ALGERNON *away.*] 472

Alg. Brother John, I have come down from town to tell you that I am very sorry 473
for all the trouble I have given you, and that I intend to lead a better life in the future.
[JACK *glares at him and does not take his hand.*]

Cec. Uncle Jack, you are not going to refuse your own brother's hand? 474

Jack. Nothing will induce me to take his hand. I think his coming down here 475
disgraceful. He knows perfectly well why.

Cec. Uncle Jack, do be nice. There is some good in one everyone. Ernest has 476
been telling me about his poor invalid friend Mr. Bunbury whom he goes to visit so
often. And surely there must be much good in one who is kind to an invalid, and
leaves the pleasures of London to sit by a bed of pain.

Jack. Oh! he has been talking about Bunbury, has he? 477

Cec. Yes, he has told me all about poor Mr. Bunbury, and his terrible state of 478
health.

Jack. Bunbury! Well, I won't have him talk to you about Bunbury or about any- 479
thing else. It is enough to drive one perfectly frantic.

Alg. Of course I admit that the faults were all on my side. But I must say that I 480
think Brother John's coldness to me is peculiarly painful. I expected a more enthu-
siastic welcome, especially considering it is the first time I have come here.

Cec. Uncle Jack, if you don't shake hands with Ernest, I will never forgive you. 481

Jack. Never forgive me? 482

Cec. Never, never, never! 483

Jack. Well, this is the last time I shall ever do it. 484

[*Shakes hands with* ALGERNON *and glares.*] 485

Chas. It is pleasant, is it not, to see so perfect a reconciliation? I think we might 486
leave the two brothers together.

Miss Pri. Cecily, you will come with us. 487

Cec. Certainly, Miss Prism. My little task of reconciliation is over. 488

Chas. You have done a beautiful action to-day, dear child. 489

Miss Pri. We must not be premature in our judgments. 490

Cec. I feel very happy. [*They all go off.*] 491

Jack. You young scoundrel, Algy, you must get out of this place as soon as pos- 492
sible. I don't allow any Bunburying here.

[*Enter* MERRIMAN.] 493

Merr. I have put Mr. Ernest's things in the room next to yours, sir. I suppose that 494
is all right?

Jack. What? 495

Merr. Mr. Ernest's luggage, sir. I have unpacked it and put it in the room next to   496
your own.

Jack. His luggage?   497

Merr. Yes, sir. Three portmanteaus, a dressing-case, two hat boxes, and a large   498
luncheon-basket.

Alg. I am afraid I can't stay more than a week this time.   499

Jack. Merriman, order the dog-cart at once. Mr. Ernest has been suddenly called   500
back to town.

Merr. Yes, sir. [*Goes back into the house.*]   501

Alg. What a fearful liar you are, Jack. I have not been called back to town at all.   502

Jack. Yes, you have.   503

Alg. I haven't heard anyone call me.   504

Jack. Your duty as a gentleman calls you back.   505

Alg. My duty as a gentleman has never interfered with my pleasures in the small-   506
est degree.

Jack. I can quite understand that.   507

Alg. Well, Cecily is a darling.   508

Jack. You are not to talk of Miss Cardew like that. I don't like it.   509

Alg. Well, I don't like your clothes. You look perfectly ridiculous in them. Why   510
on earth don't you go up and change? It is perfectly childish to be in deep mourning for a man who is actually staying for a whole week with you in your house as a
guest. I call it grotesque.

Jack. You are certainly not staying with me for a whole week as a guest or any-   511
thing else. You have got to leave . . . by the four-five train.

Alg. I certainly won't leave you so long as you are in mourning. It would be most   512
unfriendly. If I were in mourning you would stay with me, I suppose. I should think
it very unkind if you didn't.

Jack. Well, will you go if I change my clothes?   513

Alg. Yes, if you are not too long. I never saw anybody take so long to dress, and   514
with such little result.

Jack. Well, at any rate, that is better than being always over-dressed as you are.   515

Alg. If I am occasionally a little over-dressed, I make up for it by being always   516
immensely over-educated.

Jack. Your vanity is ridiculous, your conduct an outrage, and your presence in   517
my garden utterly absurd. However, you have got to catch the four-five, and I hope
you will have a pleasant journey back to town. This Bunburying, as you call it, has
not been a great success for you. [*Goes into the house.*]

Alg. I think it has been a great success. I'm in love with Cecily, and that is   518
everything.

[*Enter* CECILY *at the back of the garden. She picks up the can and begins to water the*   519
flowers.]

But I must see her before I go, and make arrangements for another Bunbury. Ah,   520
there she is.

Cec. Oh, I merely came back to water the roses. I thought you were with Uncle 521
Jack.

    Alg. He's gone to order the dog-cart for me. 522

    Cec. Oh, is he going to take you for a nice drive? 523

    Alg. He's going to send me away. 524

    Cec. Then have we got to part? 525

    Alg. I am afraid so. It's very painful parting. 526

    Cec. It is always painful to part from people whom one has known for a very brief 527
space of time. The absence of old friends one can endure with equanimity. But even
a momentary separation from anyone to whom one has just been introduced is almost
unbearable.

    Alg. Thank you. 528

[*Enter* MERRIMAN.] 529

    Merr. The dog-cart is at the door, sir. [ALGERNON *looks appealingly at* CECILY.] 530

    Cec. It can wait, Merriman . . . for . . . five minutes. 531

    Merr. Yes, Miss. [*Exit* MERRIMAN.] 532

    Alg. I hope, Cecily, I shall not offend you if I state quite frankly and openly 533
that you seem to me to be in every way the visible personification of absolute
perfection.

    Cec. I think your frankness does you great credit, Ernest. If you will allow me I 534
will copy your remarks into my diary. [*Goes over to table and begins writing in diary.*]

    Alg. Do you really keep a diary? I'd give anything to look at it. May I? 535

    Cec. Oh no. [*Puts her hand over it.*] You see, it is simply a very young girl's record 536
of her own thoughts and impressions, and consequently meant for publication. When
it appears in volume form I hope you will order a copy. But pray, Ernest, don't stop.
I delight in taking down from dictation. I have reached "absolute perfection." You
can go on. I am quite ready for more.

    Alg. [*Somewhat taken aback.*] Ahem! Ahem! 537

    Cec. Oh, don't cough, Ernest. When one is dictating one should speak fluently 538
and not cough. Besides, I don't know how to spell a cough. [*Writes as* ALGERNON
speaks.]

    Alg. [*Speaking very rapidly.*] Cecily, ever since I first looked upon your wonder- 539
ful and incomparable beauty, I have dared to love you wildly, passionately, devotedly,
hopelessly.

    Cec. I don't think that you should tell me that you love me wildly, passion- 540
ately, devotedly, hopelessly. Hopelessly doesn't seem to make much sense, does it?

    Alg. Cecily! 541

[*Enter* MERRIMAN.] 542

    Merr. The dog-cart is waiting, sir. 543

    Alg. Tell it to come round next week, at the same hour. 544

    Merr. [*Looks at* CECILY, *who makes no sign.*] Yes, sir. 545

[MERRIMAN *retires.*] 546

Cec. Uncle Jack would be very much annoyed if he knew you were staying on 547
till next week, at the same hour.

Alg. Oh, I don't care about Jack. I don't care for anybody in the whole world but 548
you. I love you, Cecily. You will marry me, won't you?

Cec. You silly boy! Of course. Why, we have been engaged for the last three 549
months.

Alg. For the last three months? 550

Cec. Yes, it will be exactly, three months on Thursday. 551

Alg. But how did we become engaged? 552

Cec. Well, ever since dear Uncle Jack first confessed to us that he had a younger 553
brother who was very wicked and bad, you of course have formed the chief topic of
conversation between myself and Miss Prism. And of course a man who is much
talked about is always very attractive. One feels there must be something in him after
all. I daresay it was foolish of me, but I fell in love with you, Ernest.

Alg. Darling! And when was the engagement actually settled? 554

Cec. On the 14th of February last. Worn out by your entire ignorance of my exis- 555
tence, I determined to end the matter one way or the other, and after a long struggle
with myself I accepted you under this dear told tree here. The next day I bought
this little ring in your name, and this is the little bangle with the true lovers' knot I
promised you always to wear.

Alg. Did I give you this? It's very pretty, isn't it? 556

Cec. Yes, you've wonderfully good taste, Ernest. It's the excuse I've always given 557
for your leading such a bad life. And this is the box in which I keep all your dear
letters. [*Kneels at table, opens box, and produces letters tied up with blue ribbon.*]

Alg. My letters! But my own sweet Cecily, I have never written you any letters. 558

Cec. You need hardly remind me of that, Ernest. I remember only too well that 559
I was forced to write your letters for you. I always wrote three times a week, and sometimes oftener.

Alg. Oh, do let me read them, Cecily? 560

Cec. Oh, I couldn't possibly. They would make you far too conceited. [*Replaces* 561
box.] The three you wrote me after I had broken off the engagement are so beautiful,
and so badly spelled, that even now I can hardly read them without crying a little.

Alg. But was our engagement ever broken off? 562

Cec. Of course it was. On the 22nd of last March. You can see the entry if you 563
like. [*Shows diary.*] "To-day I broke off my engagement with Ernest. I feel it is better
to do so. The weather still continues charming."

Alg. But why on earth did you break it off? What had I done? I had done noth- 564
ing at all. Cecily, I am very much hurt indeed to hear you broke it off. Particularly
when the weather was so charming.

Cec. It would hardly have been a really serious engagement if it hadn't been bro- 565
ken off at least once. But I forgave you before the week was out.

Alg. [*Crossing to her, and kneeling.*] What a perfect angel you are, Cecily. 566

Cec. You dear romantic boy. [*He kisses her, she puts her fingers through his hair.*] I 567
hope your hair curls naturally, does it?

Alg. Yes, darling, with a little help from others. 568

Cec. I am so glad. 569

Alg. You'll never break off our engagement again, Cecily? 570

Cec. I don't think I could break it off now that I have actually met you. Besides, 571
of course, there is the question of your name.

Alg. Yes, of course. [*Nervously.*] 572

Cec. You must not laugh at me, darling, but it had always been a girlish dream 573
of mine to love some one whose name was Ernest. [ALGERNON *rises,* CECILY *also.*] There
is something in that name that seems to inspire absolute confidence. I pity any poor-
married woman whose husband is not called Ernest.

Alg. But, my dear child, do you mean to say you could not love me if I had some 574
other name?

Cec. But what name? 575

Alg. Oh, any name you like—Algernon—for instance . . . 576

Cec. But I don't like the name of Algernon. 577

Alg. Well, my own dear, sweet, loving little darling, I really can't see why you 578
should object to the name of Algernon. It is not at all a bad name. In fact, it is rather
an aristocratic name. Half of the chaps who get into the Bankruptcy Court are called
Algernon. But seriously, Cecily . . . [*Moving to her.*] . . . if my name was Algy, couldn't
you love me?

Cec. [*Rising.*] I might respect you, Ernest, I might admire your character, but I 579
fear that I should not be able to give you my undivided attention.

Alg. Ahem! Cecily! [*Picking up hat.*] Your Rector here is, I suppose, thoroughly 580
experienced in the practice of all the rites and ceremonials of the Church?

Cec. Oh, yes. Dr. Chasuble is a most learned man. He has never written a sin- 581
gle book, so you can imagine how much he knows.

Alg. I must see him at once on a most important christening—I mean on most 582
important business.

Cec. Oh! 583

Alg. I sha'n't be away more than half an hour. 584

Cec. Considering that we have been engaged since February the 14th, and that 585
I only met you to-day for the first time, I think it is rather hard that you should leave
me for so long a period as half an hour. Couldn't you make it twenty minutes?

Alg. I'll be back in no time. 586

[*Kisses her and rushes down the garden.*] 587

Cec. What an impetuous boy he is! I like his hair so much. I must enter his 588
proposal in my diary.

[*Enter* MERRIMAN.] 589

Merr. A Miss Fairfax has just called to see Mr. Worthing. On very important 590
business Miss Fairfax states.

Cec. Isn't Mr. Worthing in his library? 591

Merr. Mr. Worthing went over in the direction of the Rectory some time ago. 592

Cec. Pray ask the lady to come out here; Mr. Worthing is sure to be back soon. 593
And you can bring tea.

Merr. Yes, Miss. [*Goes out.*]   594

Cec. Miss Fairfax! I suppose one of the many good elderly women who are asso- 595
ciated with Uncle Jack in some of his philanthropic work in London. I don't quite
like women who are interested in philanthropic work. I think it is so forward of
them.

[*Enter* MERRIMAN.]   596

Merr. Miss Fairfax.   597

[*Enter* GWENDOLEN.] [*Exit* MERRIMAN.]   598

Cec. [*Advancing to meet her.*] Pray let me introduce myself to you. My name is 599
Cecily Cardew.

Gwen. Cecily Cardew? [*Moving to her and shaking hands.*] What a very sweet 600
name! Something tells me that we are going to be great friends. I like you already
more than I can say. My first impressions of people are never wrong.

Cec. How nice of you to like me so much after we have known each other such 601
a comparatively short time. Pray sit down.

Gwen. [*Still standing up.*] I may call you Cecily, may I not?   602
Cec. With pleasure!   603
Gwen. And you will always call me Gwendolen, won't you?   604
Cec. If you wish.   605
Gwen. Then that is all quite settled, is it not?   606
Cec. I hope so. [*A pause. They both sit down together.*]   607
Gwen. Perhaps this might be a favourable opportunity for my mentioning who 608
I am. My father is Lord Bracknell. You have never heard of papa, I suppose?
Cec. I don't think so.   609
Gwen. Outside the family circle, papa, I am glad to say, is entirely unknown. I 610
think that is quite as it should be. The home seems to me to be the proper sphere
for the man. And certainly once a man begins to neglect his domestic duties he
becomes painfully effeminate, does he not? And I don't like that. It makes men so
very attractive. Cecily, mamma, whose views on education are remarkably strict, has
brought me up to be extremely short-sighted; it is part of her system; so do you mind
my looking at you through my glasses?
Cec. Oh! not at all, Gwendolen. I am very fond of being looked at.   611
Gwen. [*After examining* CECILY *carefully through a lorgnette.*] You are here on a 612
short visit, I suppose.
Cec. Oh no! I live here.   613
Gwen. [*Severely.*] Really? Your mother, no doubt, or some female relative of 614
advanced years, resides here also?
Cec. Oh no! I have no mother, nor, in fact, any relations.   615
Gwen. Indeed?   616
Cec. My dear guardian, with the assistance of Miss Prism, has the arduous task 617
of looking after me.
Gwen. Your guardian?   618
Cec. Yes, I am Mr. Worthing's ward.   619

Gwen. Oh! It is strange he never mentioned to me that he had a ward. How   620
secretive of him! He grows more interesting hourly. I am not sure, however, that
the news inspires me with feelings of unmixed delight. [*Rising and going to her.*] I am
very fond of you, Cecily; I have liked you ever since I met you! But I am bound to
state that now that I know that you are Mr. Worthing's ward, I cannot help expressing a wish you were—well just a little older than you seem to be—and not quite so
very alluring in appearance. In fact, if I may speak candidly—

Cec. Pray do! I think that whenever one has anything unpleasant to say, one   621
should always be quite candid.

Gwen. Well, to speak with perfect candour, Cecily, I wish that you were fully   622
forty-two, and more than usually plain for your age. Ernest has a strong, upright
nature. He is the very soul of truth and honour. Disloyalty would be as impossible
to him as deception. But even men of the noblest possible moral character are
extremely susceptible to the influence of the physical charms of others. Modern,
no less than Ancient History, supplies us with many most painful examples of what
I refer to. If it were not so, indeed, History would be quite unreadable.

Cec. I beg your pardon, Gwendolen, did you say Ernest?   623
Gwen. Yes.   624
Cec. Oh, but it is not Mr. Ernest Worthing who is my guardian. It is his brother—   625
his elder brother.

Gwen. [*Sitting down again.*] Ernest never mentioned to me that he had a brother.   626
Cec. I am sorry to say they have not been on good terms for a long time.   627
Gwen. Ah! that accounts for it. And now that I think of it I have never heard   628
any man mention his brother. The subject seems distasteful to most men. Cecily, you
have lifted a load from my mind. I was growing almost anxious. It would have been
terrible if any cloud had come across a friendship like ours, would it not? Of course
you are quite, quite sure that it is not Mr. Ernest Worthing who is your guardian?

Cec. Quite sure. [*A pause.*] In fact, I am going to be his.   629
Gwen. [*Enquiringly.*] I beg your pardon?   630
Cec. [*Rather shy and confidingly.*] Dearest Gwendolen, there is no reason why I   631
should make a secret of it to you. Our little county newspaper is sure to chronicle the
fact next week. Mr. Ernest Worthing and I are engaged to be married.

Gwen. [*Quite politely, rising.*] My darling Cecily, I think there must be some slight   632
error. Mr. Ernest Worthing is engaged to me. The announcement will appear in "The
Morning Post" on Saturday at the latest.

Cec. [*Very politely, rising.*] I am afraid you must be under some misconception.   633
Ernest proposed to me exactly ten minutes ago. [*Shows diary.*]

Gwen. [*Examines diary through her lorgnette carefully.*] It is certainly very curious,   634
for he asked me to be his wife yesterday afternoon at 5:30. If you would care to verify
the incident, pray do so. [*Produces diary of her own.*] I never travel without my diary.
One should always have something sensational to read in the train. I am so sorry, dear
Cecily, if it is any disappointment to you, but I am afraid *I* have the prior claim.

Cec. It would distress me more than I can tell you, dear Gwendolen, if it caused   635
you any mental or physical anguish, but I feel bound to point out that since Ernest
proposed to you he clearly has changed his mind.

Gwen. [*Meditatively.*] If the poor fellow has been entrapped into any foolish prom-   636
ise I shall consider it my duty to rescue him at once, and with a firm hand.

Cec. [*Thoughtfully and sadly.*] Whatever unfortunate entanglement my dear   637
boy may have got into, I will never reproach him with it after we are married.

Gwen. Do you allude to me, Miss Cardew, as an entanglement? You are pre-   638
sumptuous. On an occasion of this kind it becomes more than a moral duty to speak
one's mind. It becomes a pleasure.

Cec. Do you suggest, Miss Fairfax, that I entrapped Ernest into an engagement?   639
How dare you? This is no time for wearing the shallow mask of manners. When I see
a spade I call it a spade.

Gwen. [*Satirically.*] I am glad to say that I have never seen a spade. It is obvious   640
that our social spheres have been widely different.

[*Enter* MERRIMAN, *followed by the footman. He carries a salver, table cloth, and plate*   641
stand. CECILY *is about to retort. The presence of the servants exercises a restraining influ-*
ence, under which both girls chafe.]

Merr. Shall I lay tea here as usual, Miss?   642

Cec. [STERNLY, *in a calm voice.*] Yes, as usual. [MERRIMAN *begins to clear table and*   643
lay cloth. A long pause. CECILY *and* GWENDOLEN *glare at each other.*]

Gwen. Are there many interesting walks in the vicinity, Miss Cardew?   644

Cec. Oh! yes! a great many. From the top of one of the hills quite close one   645
can see five counties.

Gwen. Five counties! I don't think I should like that. I hate crowds.   646

Cec. [*Sweetly.*] I suppose that is why you live in town? [GWENDOLEN *bites her*   647
lip, and beats her foot nervously with her parasol.]

Gwen. [*Looking round.*] Quite a well-kept garden this is, Miss Cardew.   648

Cec. So glad you like it, Miss Fairfax.   649

Gwen. I had no idea there were any flowers in the country.   650

Cec. Oh, flowers are as common here, Miss Fairfax, as people are in London.   651

Gwen. Personally I cannot understand how anybody manages to exist in the   652
country, if anybody who is anybody does. The country always bores me to death.

Cec. Ah! This is what the newspapers call agricultural depression, is it not? I   653
believe the aristocracy are suffering very much from it just at present. It is almost
an epidemic amongst them, I have been told. May I offer you some tea, Miss Fairfax?

Gwen. [*With elaborate politeness.*] Thank you. [*Aside.*] Detestable girl! But I require   654
tea!

Cec. [*Sweetly.*] Sugar?   655

Gwen. [*Superciliously.*] No, thank you. Sugar is not fashionable any more. [CECILY   656
looks angrily at her, takes up the tongs and puts four lumps of sugar into the cup.]

Cec. [*Sweetly.*] Cake or bread and butter?   657

Gwen. [*In a bored manner.*] Bread and butter, please. Cake is rarely seen at the   658
best houses nowadays.

Cec. [*Cuts a very large slice of cake, and puts it on the tray.*] Hand that to Miss   659
Fairfax.

[MERRIMAN *does so, and goes out with footman.* GWENDOLEN *drinks the tea and makes* 660
a grimace. Puts down cup at once, reaches out hand to the bread and butter, looks at it, and
finds it is cake. Rises in indignation.]

Gwen. You have filled my tea with lumps of sugar, and though I asked most 661
distinctly for bread and butter, you have given me cake. I am known for the gentleness of my disposition, and the extraordinary sweetness of my nature, but I warn you,
Miss Cardew, you may go too far.

Cec. [*Rising.*] To save my poor, innocent, trusting boy from the machinations 662
of any other girl there are no lengths to which I would not go.

Gwen. From the moment I saw you I distrusted you. I felt that you were false and 663
deceitful. I am never deceived in such matters. My first impressions of people are
invariably right.

Cec. It seems to me, Miss Fairfax, that I am trespassing on your valuable time. 664
No doubt you have many other calls of a similar character to make in the neigh-
bourhood.

[*Enter* JACK.] 665

Gwen. [*Catching sight of him.*] Ernest! My own Ernest! 666

Jack. Gwendolen! Darling! [*Offers to kiss her.*] 667

Gwen. [*Drawing back.*] A moment! May I ask if you are engaged to be married 668
to this young lady? [*Points to* CECILY.]

Jack. [*Laughing.*] To dear little Cecily! Of course not! What could have put such 669
an idea into your pretty little head?

Gwen. Thank you. You may! [*Offers her cheek.*] 670

Cec. [*Very sweetly.*] I knew there must be some misunderstanding, Miss Fairfax. 671
The gentleman whose arm is at present round your waist is my dear guardian, Mr. John
Worthing.

Gwen. I beg your pardon? 672

Cec. This is Uncle Jack. 673

Gwen. [*Receding.*] Jack! Oh! 674

[*Enter* ALGERNON.] 675

Cec. Here is Ernest. 676

Alg. [*Goes straight over to* CECILY *without noticing anyone else.*] My own love! [*Offers* 677
to kiss her.]

Cec. [*Drawing back.*] A moment, Ernest! May I ask you—are you engaged to 678
be married to this young lady?

Alg. [*Looking round.*] To what young lady? Good Heavens! Gwendolen! 679

Cec. Yes! to good Heavens, Gwendolen, I mean to Gwendolen. 680

Alg. [*Laughing.*] Of course not! What could have put such an idea into your pretty 681
little head?

Cec. Thank you. [*Presenting her cheek to be kissed.*] You may. [*Algernon kisses* 682
her.]

Gwen. I felt there was some slight error, Miss Cardew. The gentleman who is 683
now embracing you is my cousin, Mr. Algernon Moncrieff.

Cec. [*Breaking away from* ALGERNON.] Algernon Moncrieff! Oh! [*The two girls* 684 *move towards each other and put their arms round each other's waists as if for protection.*]

Cec. Are you called Algernon? 685

Alg. I cannot deny it. 686

Cec. Oh! 687

Gwen. Is your name really John? 688

Jack. [*Standing rather proudly.*] I could deny it if I liked. I could deny anything if 689 I liked. But my name certainly is John. It has been John for years.

Cec. [*To* GWENDOLEN.] A gross deception has been practiced on both of us. 690

Gwen. My poor wounded Cecily! 691

Cec. My sweet wronged Gwendolen! 692

Gwen. [*Slowly and seriously.*] You will call me sister, will you not? [*They embrace.* 693 JACK *and* ALGERNON *groan and walk up and down.*]

Cec. [*Rather brightly.*] There is just one question I would like to be allowed to ask 694 my guardian.

Gwen. An admirable idea! Mr. Worthing, there is just one question I would like 695 to be permitted to put to you. Where is your brother Ernest? We are both engaged to be married to your brother Ernest, so it is a matter of some importance to us to know where your brother Ernest is at present.

Jack. [*Slowly and hesitatingly.*] Gwendolen—Cecily—it is very painful for me to 696 be forced to speak the truth. It is the first time in my life that I have ever been reduced to such a painful position, and I am really quite inexperienced in doing anything of the kind. However I will tell you quite frankly that I have no brother Ernest. I have no brother at all. I never had a brother in my life, and I certainly have not the smallest intention of ever having one in the future.

Cec. [*Surprised.*] No brother at all? 697

Jack. [*Cheerily.*] None! 698

Gwen. [*Severely.*] Had you never a brother of any kind? 699

Jack. [*Pleasantly.*] Never. Not even of any kind. 700

Gwen. I am afraid it is quite clear, Cecily, that neither of us is engaged to be 701 married to anyone.

Cec. It is not a very pleasant position for a young girl suddenly to find herself in. 702 Is it?

Gwen. Let us go into the house. They will hardly venture to come after us there. 703

Cec. No, men are so cowardly, aren't they? 704

[*They retire into the house with scornful looks.*] 705

Jack. This ghastly state of things is what you call Bunburying, I suppose? 706

Alg. Yes, and a perfectly wonderful Bunbury it is. The most wonderful Bunbury 707 I have ever had in my life.

Jack. Well, you've no right whatsoever to Bunbury here. 708

Alg. That is absurd. One has a right to Bunbury anywhere one chooses. Every 709 serious Bunburyist knows that.

Jack. Serious Bunburyist! Good Heavens! 710

Alg. Well, one must be serious about something, if one wants to have any amuse- 711
ment in life. I happen to be serious about Bunburying. What on earth you are serious about I haven't got the remotest idea. About everything, I should fancy. You have
such an absolutely trivial nature.

Jack. Well, the only small satisfaction I have in the whole of this wretched busi- 712
ness is that your friend Bunbury is quite exploded. You won't be able to run down
to the country quite so often as you used to do, dear Algy. And a very good thing too.

Alg. Your brother is a little off colour, isn't he, dear Jack? You won't be able to 713
disappear to London quite so frequently as your wicked custom was. And not a bad
thing either.

Jack. As for your conduct towards Miss Cardew, I must say that your taking in 714
a sweet, simple, innocent girl like that was quite inexcusable. To say nothing of the
fact that she is my ward.

Alg. I can see no possible defence at all for your deceiving a brilliant, clever, thor- 715
oughly experienced young lady like Miss Fairfax. To say nothing of the fact that
she is my cousin.

Jack. I wanted to be engaged to Gwendolen, that is all. I love her.   716

Alg. Well, I simply wanted to be engaged to Cecily. I adore her.   717

Jack. There is certainly no chance of your marrying Miss Cardew.   718

Alg. I don't think there is much likelihood, Jack, of you and Miss Fairfax being 719
united.

Jack. Well, that is no business of yours.   720

Alg. If it was my business, I wouldn't talk about it. [*Begins to eat muffins.*] It is very 721
vulgar to talk about one's business. Only people like stockbrokers do that, and then
merely at dinner-parties.

Jack. How you can sit there, calmly eating muffins when we are in this horri- 722
ble trouble, I can't make out. You seem to me to be perfectly heartless.

Alg. Well, I can't eat muffins in an agitated manner. The butter would proba- 723
bly get on my cuffs. One should always eat muffins quite calmly. It is the only way
to eat them.

Jack. I say it's perfectly heartless your eating muffins at all, under the circum- 724
stances.

Alg. When I am in trouble, eating is the only thing that consoles me. Indeed, 725
when I am in really great trouble, as anyone who knows me intimately will tell you,
I refuse everything except food and drink. At the present moment I am eating muffins
because I am unhappy. Besides, I am particularly fond of muffins. [*Rising.*]

Jack. [*Rising.*] Well, that is no reason why you should eat them all in that greedy 726
way. [*Takes muffins from* ALGERNON.]

Alg. [*Offering tea-cake.*] I wish you would have tea-cake instead. I don't like 727
tea-cake.

Jack. Good Heavens! I suppose a man may eat his own muffins in his own garden. 728

Alg. But you have just said it was perfectly heartless to eat muffins.   729

Jack. I said it was perfectly heartless of you, under the circumstances. That is a 730
very different thing.

Alg. That may be. But the muffins are the same. [*He seizes the muffin-dish from* 731
JACK.]

Jack. Algy, I wish to goodness you would go. 732

Alg. You can't possibly ask me to go without having some dinner. It's absurd. I 733
never go without my dinner. No one ever does, except vegetarians and people like
that. Besides I have just made arrangements with Dr. Chasuble, to be christened at
a quarter to six under the name of Ernest.

Jack. My dear fellow, the sooner you give up that nonsense the better. I made 734
arrangements this morning with Dr. Chasuble to be christened myself at 5:30, and
I naturally will take the name of Ernest. Gwendolen would wish it. We can't both be
christened Ernest. It's absurd. Besides, I have a perfect right to be christened if I like.
There is no evidence at all that I ever have been christened by anybody. I should
think it extremely probable I never was, and so does Dr. Chasuble. It is entirely different in your case. You have been christened already.

Alg. Yes, but I have not been christened for years. 735

Jack. Yes, but you have been christened. That is the important thing. 736

Alg. Quite so. So I know my constitution can stand it. If you are not quite sure 737
about your ever having been christened, I must say I think it rather dangerous your
venturing on it now. It might make you very unwell. You can hardly have forgotten
that someone very closely connected with you was very nearly carried off this week
in Paris by a severe chill.

Jack. Yes, but you said yourself that a severe chill was not hereditary. 738

Alg. It usen't to be, I know—but I daresay it is now. Science is always making 739
wonderful improvements in things.

Jack. [*Picking up the muffin-dish.*] Oh, that is nonsense; you are always talking 740
nonsense.

Alg. Jack, you are at the muffins again. I wish you wouldn't. There are only 741
two left. [*Takes them.*] I told you I was particularly fond of muffins.

Jack. But I hate tea-cake. 742

Alg. Why on earth then do you allow tea-cake to be served up for your guests? 743
What ideas you have of hospitality!

Jack. Algernon! I have already told you to go. I don't want you here. Why don't 744
you go?

Alg. I haven't quite finished my tea yet! and there is still one muffin left. [JACK 745
groans, and sinks into a chair. ALGERNON *still continues eating.*]

THIRD ACT

SCENE—*Morning-room at the Manor House.* 746

[GWENDOLEN *and* CECILY *are at the window, looking out into the garden.*] 747

Gwen. The fact that they did not follow us at once into the house, as anyone 748
else would have done, seems to me to show that they have some sense of shame
left.

Cec. They have been eating muffins. That looks like repentance. 749

Gwen. [*After a pause.*] They don't seem to notice us at all. Couldn't you cough? 750

Cec. But I haven't got a cough. 751

Gwen. They're looking at us. What effrontery! 752

Cec. They're approaching. That's very forward of them. 753

Gwen. Let us preserve a dignified silence. 754

Cec. Certainly. It's the only thing to do now. 755

[*Enter* JACK *followed by* ALGERNON. *They whistle some dreadful popular air from a* 756
British Opera.]

Gwen. This dignified silence seems to produce an unpleasant effect. 757

Cec. A most distasteful one. 758

Gwen. But we will not be the first to speak. 759

Cec. Certainly not. 760

Gwen. Mr. Worthing, I have something very particular to ask you. Much depends 761
on your reply.

Cec. Gwendolen, your common sense is invaluable. Mr. Moncrieff, kindly answer 762
me the following question. Why did you pretend to be my guardian's brother?

Alg. In order that I might have an opportunity of meeting you. 763

Cec. [*To* GWENDOLEN.] That certainly seems a satisfactory explanation, does it 764
not?

Gwen. Yes, dear, if you can believe him. 765

Cec. I don't. But that does not affect the wonderful beauty of his answer. 766

Gwen. True. In matters of grave importance, style, not sincerity is the vital thing. 767
Mr. Worthing, what explanation can you offer to me for pretending to have a brother?
Was it in order that you might have an opportunity of coming up to town to see
me as often as possible?

Jack. Can you doubt it, Miss Fairfax? 768

Gwen. I have the gravest doubts upon the subject. But I intend to crush them. 769
This is not the moment for German scepticism. [*Moving to* CECILY.] Their explanations appear to be quite satisfactory, especially Mr. Worthing's. That seems to me
to have the stamp of truth upon it.

Cec. I am more than content with what Mr. Moncrieff said. His voice alone 770
inspires one with absolute credulity.

Gwen. Then you think we should forgive them? 771

Cec. Yes. I mean no. 772

Gwen. True! I had forgotten. There are principles at stake that one cannot sur- 773
render. Which of us should tell them? The task is not a pleasant one.

Cec. Could we not both speak at the same time? 774

Gwen. An excellent idea! I nearly always speak at the same time as other peo- 775
ple. Will you take the time from me?

Cec. Certainly. [GWENDOLEN *beats time with uplifted finger.*] 776

Gwen and Cec. [*Speaking together.*] Your Christian names are still an insupera- 777
ble barrier. That is all!

Jack and Alg. [*Speaking together.*] Our Christian names! Is that all? But we are 778
going to be christened this afternoon.

Gwen. [*To* JACK.] For my sake you are prepared to do this terrible thing? 779

Jack. I am.   780

Cec. [*To* ALGERNON.] To please me you are ready to face this fearful ordeal?   781

Alg. I am!   782

Gwen. How absurd to talk of the equality of the sexes! Where questions of self-   783
sacrifice are concerned, men are infinitely beyond us.

Jack. We are. [*Clasps hands with* ALGERNON.]   784

Cec. They have moments of physical courage of which we women know   785
absolutely nothing.

Gwen. [*To* JACK.] Darling!   786

Alg. [*To* CECILY.] Darling! [*They fall into each other's arms.*]   787

[*Enter* MERRIMAN. *When he enters he coughs loudly, seeing the situation.*]   788

Merr. Ahem! Ahem! Lady Bracknell!   789

Jack. Good Heavens!   790

[*Enter* LADY BRACKNELL. *The couples separate in alarm. Exit* MERRIMAN.]   791

Lady Bra. Gwendolen! What does this mean?   792

Gwen. Merely that I am engaged to be married to Mr. Worthing, mamma.   793

Lady Bra. Come here. Sit down. Sit down immediately. Hesitation of any kind   794
is a sign of mental decay in the young, of physical weakness in the old. [*Turns to* JACK.]
Apprised, sir, of my daughter's sudden flight by her trusty maid, whose confidence I
purchased by means of a small coin, I followed her at once by a luggage train. Her
unhappy father is, I am glad to say, under the impression that she is attending a more
than usually lengthy lecture by the University Extension Scheme on the Influence
of a permanent income on Thought. I do not propose to undeceive him. Indeed I
have never undeceived him on any question. I would consider it wrong. But of course,
you will clearly understand that all communication between yourself and my daughter must cease immediately from this moment. On this point, as indeed on all points,
I am firm.

Jack. I am engaged to be married to Gwendolen, Lady Bracknell!   795

Lady Bra. You are nothing of the kind, so. And now, as regards Algernon! . . .   796
Algernon!

Alg. Yes, Aunt Augusta.   797

Lady Bra. May I ask if it is in this house that your invalid friend Mr. Bunbury   798
resides?

Alg. [*Stammering.*] Oh! No! Bunbury doesn't live here. Bunbury is somewhere   799
else at present. In fact, Bunbury is dead.

Lady Bra. Dead! When did Mr. Bunbury die? His death must have been   800
extremely sudden.

Alg. [*Airily.*] Oh! I killed Bunbury this afternoon. I mean poor Bunbury died this   801
afternoon.

Lady Bra. What did he die of?   802

Alg. Bunbury? Oh, he was quite exploded.   803

Lady Bra. Exploded! Was he the victim of a revolutionary outrage? I was not   804
aware that Mr. Bunbury was interested in social legislation. If so, he is well punished
for his morbidity.

Alg. My dear Aunt Augusta, I mean he was found out! The doctors found out 805
that Bunbury could not live, that is what I mean—so Bunbury died.

Lady Bra. He seems to have had great confidence in the opinion of his physi- 806
cians. I am glad, however, that he made up his mind at the last to some definite course
of action, and acted under proper medical advice. And now that we have finally
got rid of this Mr. Bunbury, may I ask, Mr. Worthing, who is that young person whose
hand my nephew Algernon is now holding in what seems to me a peculiarly unnecessary manner?

Jack. That lady is Miss Cecily Cardew, my ward. [LADY BRACKNELL *bows coldly to* 807
CECILY.]

Alg. I am engaged to be married to Cecily, Aunt Augusta. 808

Lady Bra. I beg your pardon? 809

Cec. Mr. Moncrieff and I are engaged to be married, Lady Bracknell. 810

Lady Bra. [*With a shiver, crossing to the sofa and sitting down.*] I do not know 811
whether there is anything peculiarly exciting in the air of this particular part of
Hertfordshire, but the number of engagements that go on seems to me considerably above the proper average that statistics have laid down for our guidance. I think
some preliminary enquiry on my part would not be out of place. Mr. Worthing, is
Miss Cardew at all connected with any of the larger railway stations in London? I
merely desire information. Until yesterday I had no idea that there were any families or persons whose origin was a Terminus. [JACK *looks perfectly furious, but restrains
himself.*]

Jack. [*In a clear, cold voice.*] Miss Cardew is the granddaughter of the late 812
Mr. Thomas Cardew of 149, Belgrave Square, S.W.; Gervase Park, Dorking, Surrey;
and the Sporran, Fifeshire, N.B.

Lady Bra. That sounds not unsatisfactory. Three addresses always inspire con- 813
fidence, even in tradesmen. But what proof have I of their authenticity?

Jack. I have carefully preserved the Court Guides of the period. They are open 814
to your inspection, Lady Bracknell.

Lady Bra. [*Grimly.*] I have known strange errors in that publication. 815

Jack. Miss Cardew's family solicitors are Messrs. Markby, Markby, and Markby. 816

Lady Bra. Markby, Markby, and Markby? A firm of the very highest position in 817
their profession. Indeed I am told that one of the Mr. Markbys is occasionally to be
seen at dinner parties. So far I am satisfied.

Jack. [*Very irritably.*] How extremely kind of you, Lady Bracknell! I have also 818
in my possession, you will be pleased to hear, certificates of Miss Cardew's birth, baptism, whooping cough, registration, vaccination, confirmation, and the measles; both
the German and the English variety.

Lady Bra. Ah! A life crowded with incident, I see; though perhaps somewhat 819
too exciting for a young girl. I am not myself in favour of premature experiences.
[*Rises, looks at her watch.*] Gwendolen! the time approaches for our departure. We
have not a moment to lose. As a matter of form, Mr. Worthing, I had better ask
you if Miss Cardew has any little fortune.

Jack. Oh! about a hundred and thirty thousand pounds in the Funds. That is all. 820
Good-bye, Lady Bracknell. So pleased to have seen you.

Lady Bra. [*Sitting down again.*] A moment, Mr. Worthing. A hundred and thirty   821
thousand pounds! And in the Funds! Miss Cardew seems to me a most attractive
young lady, now that I look at her. Few girls of the present day have any really solid
qualities, any of the qualities that last, and improve with time. We live, I regret to
say, in an age of surfaces. [*To* CECILY.] Come over here, dear. [CECILY *goes across.*] Pretty
child! your dress is sadly simple, and your hair seems almost as Nature might have
left it. But we can soon alter all that. A thoroughly experienced French maid produces a really marvellous result in a very brief space of time. I remember recom-
mending one to young Lady Lancing, and after three months her own husband did
not know her.

Jack. [*Aside.*] And after six months nobody knew her.   822

Lady Bra. [*Glares at* JACK *for a few moments. Then bends, with a practised smile,*   823
to CECILY.] Kindly turn round, sweet child. [CECILY *turns completely round.*] No, the
side view is what I want. [CECILY *presents her profile.*] Yes, quite as I expected. There
are distinct social possibilities in your profile. The two weak points in our age are
its want of principle and its want of profile. The chin a little higher, dear. Style largely
depends on the way the chin is worn. They are worn very high, just at present.
Algernon!

Alg. Yes, Aunt Augusta!   824

Lady Bra. There are distinct social possibilities in Miss Cardew's profile.   825

Alg. Cecily is the sweetest, dearest, prettiest girl in the whole world. And I don't   826
care twopence about social possibilities.

Lady Bra. Never speak disrespectfully of Society, Algernon. Only people who   827
can't get into it do that. [*To* CECILY.] Dear child, of course you know that Algernon
has nothing but his debts to depend upon. But I do not approve of mercenary mar-
riages. When I married Lord Bracknell I had no fortune of any kind. But I never
dreamed for a moment of allowing that to stand in my way. Well, I suppose I must
give my consent.

Alg. Thank you, Aunt Augusta.   828

Lady Bra. Cecily, you may kiss me!   829

Cec. [*Kisses her.*] Thank you, Lady Bracknell.   830

Lady Bra. You may also address me as Aunt Augusta for the future.   831

Cec. Thank you, Aunt Augusta.   832

Lady Bra. The marriage, I think, had better take place quite soon.   833

Alg. Thank you, Aunt Augusta.   834

Cec. Thank you, Aunt Augusta.   835

Lady Bra. To speak frankly, I am not in favour of long engagements. They give   836
people the opportunity of finding out each other's character before marriage, which
I think is never advisable.

Jack. I beg your pardon for interrupting you, Lady Bracknell, but this engage-   837
ment is quite out of the question. I am Miss Cardew's guardian, and she cannot marry
without my consent until she comes of age. That consent I absolutely decline to give.

Lady Bra. Upon what grounds, may I ask? Algernon is an extremely, I may almost   838
say an ostentatiously, eligible young man. He has nothing, but he looks everything.
What more can one desire?

Jack. It pains me very much to have to speak frankly to you, Lady Bracknell, 839
about your nephew, but the fact is that I do not approve at all of his moral character. I suspect him of being untruthful. [ALGERNON *and* CECILY *look at him in indignant
amazement.*]

Lady Bra. Untruthful! My nephew Algernon? Impossible! He is an Oxonian. 840

Jack. I fear there can be no possible doubt about the matter. This afternoon, dur- 841
ing my temporary absence in London on an important question of romance, he
obtained admission to my house by means of the false pretense of being my brother.
Under an assumed name he drank, I've just been informed by my butler, an entire
pint bottle of my Perrier-Jouet, Brut, '89; a wine I was specially reserving for myself.
Continuing his disgraceful deception, he succeeded in the course of the afternoon in
alienating the affections of my only ward. He subsequently stayed to tea, and devoured
every single muffin. And what makes his conduct all the more heartless is, that he
was perfectly well aware from the first that I have no brother, that I never had a
brother, and that I don't intend to have a brother, not even of any kind. I distinctly
told him so myself yesterday afternoon.

Lady Bra. Ahem! Mr. Worthing, after careful consideration I have decided 842
entirely to overlook my nephew's conduct to you.

Jack. That is very generous of you, Lady Bracknell. My own decision, however, 843
is unalterable. I decline to give my consent.

Lady Bra. [*To* CECILY.] Come here, sweet child. [CECILY *goes over.*] How old are 844
you, dear?

Cec. Well, I am really only eighteen, but I always admit to twenty when I go 845
to evening parties.

Lady Bra. You are perfectly right in making some slight alteration. Indeed, no 846
woman should ever be quite accurate about her age. It looks so calculating. . . . [*In
a meditative manner.*] Eighteen, but admitting to twenty at evening parties. Well, it
will not be very long before you are of age and free from the restraints of tutelage. So
I don't think your guardian's consent is, after all, a matter of any importance.

Jack. Pray excuse me, Lady Bracknell, for interrupting you again, but it is only 847
fair to tell you that according to the terms of her grandfather's will Miss Cardew does
not come legally of age till she is thirty-five.

Lady Bra. That does not seem to me to be a grave objection. Thirty-five is a very 848
attractive age. London society is full of women of the very highest birth who have,
of their own free choice, remained thirty-five for years. Lady Dumbleton is an instance
in point. To my own knowledge she has been thirty-five ever since she arrived at the
age of forty, which was many years ago now, I see no reason why our dear Cecily
should not be even still more attractive at the age you mention than she is at present. There will be a large accumulation of property.

Cec. Algy, could you wait for me till I was thirty-five? 849

Alg. Of course I could, Cecily. You know I could. 850

Cec. Yes, I felt it instinctively, but I couldn't wait all that time. I hate waiting 851
even five minutes for anybody. It always makes me rather cross. I am not punctual
myself, I know, but I do like punctuality in others, and waiting, even to be married,
is quite out of the question.

Alg. Then what is to be done, Cecily?   852

Cec. I don't know, Mr. Moncrieff.   853

Lady Bra. My dear Mr. Worthing, as Miss Cardew states positively that she can- 854
not wait till she is thirty-five—a remark which I am bound to say seems to me to show
a somewhat impatient nature—I would beg of you to reconsider your decision.

Jack. But, my dear Lady Bracknell, the matter is entirely in your own hands. The 855
moment you consent to my marriage with Gwendolen, I will most gladly allow your
nephew to form an alliance with my ward.

Lady Bra. [*Rising and drawing herself up.*] You must be quite aware that what 856
you propose is out of the question.

Jack. Then a passionate celibacy is all that any of us can look forward to.   857

Lady Bra. That is not the destiny I propose for Gwendolen. Algernon, of course, 858
can choose for himself. [*Pulls out her watch.*] Come, dear; [GWENDOLEN *rises.*] we have
already missed five, if not six, trains. To miss any more might expose us to comment on the platform.

[*Enter* DR. CHASUBLE.]   859

Chas. Everything is quite ready for the christenings.   860

Lady Bra. The christenings, sir! Is not that somewhat premature?   861

Chas. [*Looking rather puzzled, and pointing to* JACK *and* ALGERNON.] Both these 862
gentlemen have expressed a desire for immediate baptism.

Lady Bra. At their age? The idea is grotesque and irreligious! Algernon, I for- 863
bid you to be baptised. I will not hear of such excesses. Lord Bracknell would be highly
displeased if he learned that that was the way in which you wasted your time and
money.

Chas. Am I to understand then that there are to be no christenings at all this 864
afternoon?

Jack. I don't think that, as things are now, it would be of much practical value 865
to either of us, Dr. Chasuble.

Chas. I am grieved to hear such sentiments from you, Mr. Worthing. They savour 866
of the heretical views of the Anabaptists, views that I have completely refuted in four
of my unpublished sermons. However, as your present mood seems to be one peculiarly secular, I will return to the church at once. Indeed, I have just been informed
by the pew-opener that for the last hour and a half Miss Prism has been waiting for
me in the vestry.

Lady Bra. [*Starting.*] Miss Prism! Did I hear you mention a Miss Prism?   867

Chas. Yes, Lady Bracknell. I am on my way to join her.   868

Lady Bra. Pray, allow me to detain you for a moment. This matter may prove 869
to be one of vital importance to Lord Bracknell and myself. Is this Miss Prism a female
of repellent aspect, remotely connected with education?

Chas. [*Somewhat indignantly.*] She is the most cultivated of ladies, and the very 870
picture of respectability.

Lady Bra. It is obviously the same person. May I ask what position she holds in 871
your household?

Chas. [*Severely.*] I am a celibate, madam.   872

Jack. [*Interposing.*] Miss Prism, Lady Bracknell, has been for the last three years   873
Miss Cardew's esteemed governess and valued companion.

Lady Bra. In spite of what I hear of her, I must see her at once. Let her be sent   874
for.

Chas. [*Looking off.*] She approaches; she is nigh.   875

[*Enter* MISS PRISM *hurriedly.*]   876

Miss Pri. I was told you expected me in the vestry, dear Canon. I have been wait-   877
ing for you there for an hour and three quarters. [*Catches sight of* LADY BRACKNELL *who
has fixed her with a stony glare.* MISS PRISM *grows pale and quails. She looks anxiously round
as if desirous to escape.*]

Lady Bra. [*In a severe, judicial voice.*] Prism! [MISS PRISM *bows her head in shame.*]   878
Come here, Prism! [MISS PRISM *approaches in a humble manner.*] Prism! Where is that
baby? [*General consternation. The* CANON *starts back in horror.* ALGERNON *and* JACK *pretend to be anxious to shield* CECILY *and* GWENDOLEN *from hearing the details of a terrible
public scandal.*] Twenty-eight years ago, Prism, you left Lord Bracknell's house, Number
104, Upper Grosvenor Street, in charge of a perambulator that contained a baby,
of the male sex. You never returned. A few weeks later, through the elaborate investigations of the Metropolitan police, the perambulator was discovered at midnight,
standing by itself in a remote corner of Bayswater. It contained the manuscript of a
three-volume novel of more than usually revolting sentimentality. [MISS PRISM *starts
in involuntary indignation.*] But the baby was not there! [*Everyone looks at* MISS PRISM.]
Prism! Where is that baby? [*A pause.*]

Miss Pri. Lady Bracknell, I admit with shame that I do not know. I only wish I   879
did. The plain facts of the case are these. On the morning of the day you mention,
a day that is forever branded on my memory, I prepared as usual to take the baby
out in its perambulator. I had also with me a somewhat old, but capacious hand-
bag, in which I had intended to place the manuscript of a work of fiction that I had
written during my few unoccupied hours. In a moment of mental abstraction, for
which I can never forgive myself, I deposited the manuscript in the bassinette, and
placed the baby in the hand-bag.

Jack. [*Who has been listening attentively.*] But where did you deposit the hand-bag?   880

Miss Pri. Do not ask me, Mr. Worthing.   881

Jack. Miss Prism, this is a matter of no small importance to me. I insist on know-   882
ing where you deposited the hand-bag that contained that infant.

Miss Pri. I left it in the cloak room of one of the larger railway stations in London.   883

Jack. What railway station?   884

Miss Pri. [*Quite crushed.*] Victoria. The Brighton line. [*Sinks into a chair.*]   885

Jack. I must retire to my room for a moment. Gwendolen, wait for me here.   886

Gwen. If you are not too long, I will wait here for you all my life.   887

[*Exit* JACK *in great excitement.*]   888

Chas. What do you think this means, Lady Bracknell?   889

Lady Bra. I dare not even suspect, Dr. Chasuble. I need hardly tell you that in 890 families of high position strange coincidences are not supposed to occur. They are hardly considered the thing.

[*Noises heard overhead as if someone was throwing trunks about. Everyone looks up.*] 891

Cec. Uncle Jack seems strangely agitated. 892

Chas. Your guardian has a very emotional nature. 893

Lady Bra. This noise is extremely unpleasant. It sounds as if he was having an argu- 894 ment. I dislike arguments of any kind. They are always vulgar, and often convincing.

Chas. [*Looking up.*] It has stopped now. [*The noise is redoubled.*]

Lady Bra. I wish he would arrive at some conclusion. 895

Gwen. This suspense is terrible. I hope it will last. 896

[*Enter* JACK *with a hand-bag of black leather in his hand.*] 897

Jack. [*Rushing over to* MISS PRISM.] Is this the hand-bag, Miss Prism? Examine it 898 carefully before you speak. The happiness of more than one life depends on your 899 answer.

Miss Pri. [*Calmly.*] It seems to be mine. Yes, here is the injury it received through 900 the upsetting of a Gower Street omnibus in younger and happier days. Here is the stain on the lining caused by the explosion of a temperance beverage, an incident that occurred at Leamington. And here, on the lock, are my initials. I had forgotten that in an extravagant mood I had had them placed there. The bag is undoubtedly mine. I am delighted to have it so unexpectedly restored to me. It has been a great inconvenience being without it all these years.

Jack. [*In a pathetic voice.*] Miss Prism, more is restored to you than this hand-bag. 901 I was the baby you placed in it.

Miss Pri. [*Amazed.*] You? 902

Jack. [*Embracing her.*] Yes . . . Mother! 903

Miss Pri. [*Recoiling in indignant astonishment.*] Mr. Worthing! I am unmarried! 904

Jack. Unmarried! I do not deny that is a serious blow. But after all, who has a 905 right to cast a stone against one who has suffered? Cannot repentance wipe out an act of folly? Why should there be one law for men, and another for women? Mother, I forgive you. [*Tries to embrace her again.*]

Miss Pri. [*Still more indignant.*] Mr. Worthing, there is some error. [*Pointing to* LADY 906 BRACKNELL.] There is the lady who can tell you who you really are.

Jack. [*After a pause.*] Lady Bracknell, I hate to seem inquisitive, but would you 907 kindly inform me who I am?

Lady Bra. I am afraid that the news I have to give you will not altogether please 908 you. You are the son of my poor sister, Mrs. Moncrieff, and consequently Algernon's elder brother.

Jack. Algy's elder brother! Then I have a brother after all. I knew I had a brother! 909 I always said I had a brother! Cecily, how could you have ever doubted that I had a brother? [*Seizes hold of* ALGERNON.] Dr. Chasuble, my unfortunate brother. Miss Prism, my unfortunate brother. Gwendolen, my unfortunate brother. Algy, you young scoundrel, you will have to treat me with more respect in the future. You have never behaved to me like a brother in all your life.

Alg. Well, not till today, old boy, I admit. I did my best, however, though I was out of practise. [*Shakes hands.*] 910

Gwen. [*To* JACK.] My own! But what own are you? What is your Christian name, now that you have become someone else? 911

Jack. Good Heavens!. . . I had quite forgotten that point. Your decision on the subject of my name is irrevocable, I suppose? 912

Gwen. I never change, except in my affections. 913

Cec. What a noble nature you have, Gwendolen! 914

Jack. Then the question had better be cleared up at once. Aunt Augusta, a moment. At the time when Miss Prism left me in the hand-bag, had I been christened already? 915

Lady Bra. Every luxury that money could buy, including christening, had been lavished on you by your fond and doting parents. 916

Jack. Then I was christened! That is settled. Now, what name was I given? Let me know the worst. 917

Lady Bra. Being the eldest son you were naturally christened after your father. 918

Jack. [*Irritably.*] Yes, but what was my father's Christian name? 919

Lady Bra. [*Meditatively.*] I cannot at the present moment recall what the General's Christian name was. But I have no doubt he had one. He was eccentric, I admit. But only in later years. And that was the result of the Indian climate, and marriage, and indigestion, and other things of that kind. 920

Jack. Algy! Can't you recollect what our father's Christian name was? 921

Alg. My dear boy, we were never even on speaking terms. He died before I was a year old. 922

Jack. His name would appear in the Army Lists of the period, I suppose, Aunt Augusta? 923

Lady Bra. The General was essentially a man of peace, except in his domestic life. But I have no doubt his name would appear in any military directory. 924

Jack. The Army Lists of the last forty years are here. These delightful records should have been my constant study. [*Rushes to bookcase and tears the books out.*] M. Generals . . . Mallam, Maxbohm, Magley, what ghastly names they have—Markby, Migsby, Mobbs, Moncrieff, Lieutenant 1840, Captain, Lieutenant-Colonel, Colonel, General 1869, Christian names, Ernest, John. [*Puts book very quietly down and speaks quite calmly.*] I always told you, Gwendolen, my name was Ernest, didn't I? Well, it is Ernest after all. I mean it naturally is Ernest. 925

Lady Bra. Yes, I remember now that the General was called Ernest. I knew I had some particular reason for disliking the name. 926

Gwen. Ernest! My own Ernest! I felt from the first that you could have no other name! 927

Jack. Gwendolen, it is a terrible thing for a man to find out suddenly that all his life he has been speaking nothing but the truth. Can you forgive me? 928

Gwen. I can. For I feel that you are sure to change. 929

Jack. My own one! 930

Chas. [*To* MISS PRISM.] Laetitia! [*Embraces her.*]   931

Miss Pri. [*Enthusiastically.*] Frederick! At last!   932

Alg. Cecily! [*Embraces her.*] At last!   933

Jack. Gwendolen! [*Embraces her.*] At last!   934

Lady Bra. My nephew, you seem to be displaying signs of triviality.   935

Jack. On the contrary, Aunt Augusta, I've now realized for the first time in my   936
life the vital Importance of Being Ernest.

Questions for Discussion

1. Why is it important to be earnest? Is being earnest the same thing as being truthful?

2. What point does Wilde make about truth and falsehood? Is it acceptable for these characters to deceive one another?

3. As a satire, what does this play satirize? What ills in society does the play isolate and criticize?

4. In your opinion, is this play still relevant? In what way is it relevant, and in what way is it not?

5. Why is Lady Bracknell necessary for the play to work? What would the play be like without her?

6. One way the humor works in this play is that the characters often say the opposite of what is expected. Find examples of this use of humor—why is this humor effective?

7. What are some of the puns with which Wilde peppers the play? What do they mean?

Questions for Reflection and Writing

1. Read an act or part of an act aloud with friends. Write about the experience. How should this play be read to be most effective?

2. Look up "comedy of manners" in a dictionary of literary terms. How is this play a comedy of manners?

3. See a performance, live or taped. Write a review of the play. To extend this assignment, read about how this play was received when it was first performed in 1895 and compare your review with critical or public response at the time.

Unit 5: Reading & Writing About Essays

Sara **Corbett** (b. 1969) is a contributing writer for *The New York Times Magazine*. She received an MFA from the University of Iowa and was a Jay C. and Ruth Halls Fiction Fellow at the University of Wisconsin—Madison in 1992–1993. She is a co-founder of The Telling Room, an organization that conducts writing workshops for children based in Portland, Maine, where she currently lives. She has written several children's books for the series "A World of Difference": *Hats Off to Hats* (1995); *Shake, Rattle and Strum* (1995); *Animals and Us* (1996); *Hold Everything!* (1996); and *What a Doll!* (1996), as well as co-writing a screenplay based on her 2000 *New York Times* article "On the Run with Wolf B36." She is particularly interested in environmental health, and participated in the Environmental Working Group's Human Toxome Project in 2007, which analyzed her blood and urine for traces of toxic chemicals, and which may be the basis for a forthcoming article. She has also written articles for Inside magazine, *Travel and Leisure, Mother Jones,* and *Esquire,* as well as a nonfiction book, *Venus to the Hoop: A Gold Medal Year in Women's Basketball* (1998).

The Lost Boys

Sara Corbett

One evening in late January, Peter Dut, 21, leads his two teenage brothers through the brightly lit corridors of the Minneapolis airport, trying to mask his confusion. Two days earlier, the brothers, refugees from Africa, had encountered their first light switch and their first set of stairs. An aid worker in Nairobi had demonstrated the flush toilet to them—also the seat belt, the shoelace, the fork. And now they find themselves alone in Minneapolis, three bone-thin African boys confronted by a swirling river of white faces and rolling suitcases.   1

Finally, a traveling businessman recognizes their uncertainty. "Where are you flying to?" he asks kindly, and the eldest brother tells him in halting, bookish English. A few days earlier, they left a small mud hut in a blistering-hot Kenyan refugee camp, where they had lived as orphans for nine years after walking for hundreds of miles across Sudan. They are now headed to a new home in the U.S.A. "Where?" the man asks in disbelief when Peter Dut says the city's name. "Fargo? North Dakota? You gotta be kidding me. It's too cold there. You'll never survive it!"   2

And then he laughs. Peter Dut has no idea why.   3

In the meantime, the temperature in Fargo has dropped to 15 below. The boys tell me that, until now, all they have known about cold is what they felt grasping a bottle of frozen water. An aid worker handed it to them one day during a "cultural orientation" session at the Kakuma Refugee Camp, a place where the temperature hovers around 100 degrees.   4

Peter Dut and his two brothers belong to an unusual group of refugees referred to by aid organizations as the Lost Boys of Sudan, a group of roughly 10,000 boys who arrived in Kenya in 1992 seeking refuge from their country's   5 fractious civil war. The fighting pits a northern Islamic government against rebels in the south who practice Christianity and tribal religions.

The Lost Boys were named after Peter Pan's posse of orphans. According to U.S.   6
State Department estimates, some 17,000 boys were separated from their families and fled southern Sudan in an exodus of biblical proportions after fighting intensified in 1987. They arrived in throngs, homeless and parentless, having trekked about 1,000 miles, from Sudan to Ethiopia, back to Sudan, and finally to Kenya. The majority of the boys belonged to the Dinka or Nuer tribes, and most were then between the ages of 8 and 18. (Most of the boys don't know for sure how old they are; aid workers assigned them approximate ages after they arrived in 1992.)

Along the way, the boys endured attacks from the northern army and   7
marauding bandits, as well as lions who preyed on the slowest and weakest among them. Many died from starvation or thirst. Others drowned or were eaten by crocodiles as they tried to cross a swollen Ethiopian river. By the time the Lost Boys reached the Kakuma Refugee Camp, their numbers had been cut nearly in half.

Now, after nine years of subsisting on rationed corn mush and lentils and living largely ungoverned by adults, the Lost Boys of Sudan are coming to America.   8
In 1999, the United Nations High Commissioner for Refugees, which handles refugee cases around the world, and the U.S. government agreed to send 3,600 of the boys to the U.S.—since going back to Sudan was out of the question. About 500 of the Lost Boys still under the age of 18 will be living in apartments or foster homes across the U.S. by the end of this year. The boys will start school at a grade level normal for their age, thanks to a tough English-language program at their refugee camp. The remaining 3,100 Lost Boys will be resettled as adults. After five years, each boy will be eligible for citizenship, provided he has turned 21.

NIGHTTIME IN AMERICA?

On the night that I stand waiting for Peter Dut and his brothers to land in Fargo,   9
tendrils of snow are snaking across the tarmac. The three boys file through the gate without money or coats or luggage beyond their small backpacks. The younger brothers, Maduk, 17, and Riak, 15, appear petrified. As a social worker passes out coats, Peter Dut studies the black night through the airport window. "Excuse me," he says, worriedly. "Can you tell me, please, is it now night or day?"

This is a stove burner. This is a can opener. This is a brush for your teeth. The   10
new things come in a tumble. The brothers' home is a sparsely furnished, two-bedroom apartment in a complex on Fargo's south side. Rent is $445 a month. It has been stocked with donations from area churches and businesses: toothpaste, bread, beans, bananas.

A caseworker empties a garbage bag full of donated clothing, which looks to   11
have come straight from the closet of an elderly man. I know how lucky the boys are: The State Department estimates that war, famine, and disease in southern Sudan have killed more than 2 million people and displaced another 4 million. Still I cringe to think of the boys showing up for school in these clothes.

The next day, when I return to the apartment at noon, the boys have been up   12
since 5 and are terribly hungry. "What about your food?" I ask, gesturing to the bread and bananas and the box of cereal sitting on the counter.

Peter grins sheepishly. I suddenly realize that the boys, in a lifetime of cook- 13
ing maize and beans over a fire pit, have never opened a box. I am placed in the
role of teacher. And so begins an opening spree. We open potato chips. We open
a can of beans. We untwist the tie on the bagged loaf of bread. Soon, the boys are
seated and eating a hot meal.

LIVING ON LEAVES AND BERRIES

The three brothers have come a long way since they fled their village in Sudan 14
with their parents and three sisters—all of whom were later killed by Sudanese
Army soldiers. The Lost Boys first survived a 6- to 10-week walk to Ethiopia, often
subsisting on leaves and berries and the occasional boon of a warthog carcass.
Some boys staved off dehydration by drinking their own urine. Many fell behind;
some were devoured by lions or trampled by buffalo.

The Lost Boys lived for three years in Ethiopia, in UN-supported camps, 15
before they were forced back into Sudan by a new Ethiopian government no
longer sympathetic to their plight. Somehow, more than 10,000 of the boys miraculously trailed into Kenya's UN camps in the summer of 1992—as Sudanese government planes bombed the rear of their procession.

For the Lost Boys, then, a new life in America might easily seem to be the 16
answer to every dream. But the real world has been more complicated than that.
Within weeks of arriving, Riak is placed in a local junior high; Maduk starts high
school classes; and Peter begins adult-education classes.

REFUGEE BLUES

Five weeks later, Riak listens quietly through a lesson on Elizabethan history at 17
school, all but ignored by white students around him.

Nearby at Fargo South High School, Maduk is frequently alone as well, copy- 18
ing passages from his geography textbook, trying not to look at the short skirts
worn by many of the girls.

Peter Dut worries about money. The three brothers say they receive just $107 19
in food stamps each month and spend most of their $510 monthly cash assistance
on rent and utilities.

Resettlement workers say the brothers are just undergoing the normal transi- 20
tion. Scott Burtsfield, who coordinates resettlement efforts in Fargo through
Lutheran Social Services, says: "The first three months are always the toughest. It
really does get better."

The Lost Boys can only hope so; they have few other options. A return to 21
southern Sudan could be fatal. "There is nothing left for the Lost Boys to go home
to—it's a war zone," says Mary Anne Fitzgerald, a Nairobi-based relief consultant.

Some Sudanese elders have criticized sending boys to the U.S. They worry 22
their children will lose their African identity. One afternoon, an 18-year-old Lost
Boy translated a part of a tape an elder had sent along with many boys: "He is
saying: 'Don't drink. Don't smoke. Don't kill. Go to school every day, and remember, America is not your home.'"

But if adjustment is hard, the boys also experience consoling moments. 23

One of these comes on a quiet Friday night last winter. As the boys make a 24 dinner of rice and lentils, Peter changes into an African outfit, a finely woven green tunic, with a skullcap to match, bought with precious food rations at Kakuma.

Just then, the doorbell rings unexpectedly. And out of the cold tumble four 25 Sudanese boys—all of whom have resettled as refugees over the last several years. I watch one, an 18-year-old named Sunday, wrap his arms encouragingly, around Peter Dut.

"It's a hard life here, Sunday whispers to the older boy, "but it's a free life, too." 26

Questions for Discussion

1. What is the significance of the label "Lost Boys"? What is ironic about the label?

2. Why were the boys wandering? What did governments do that kept them moving? Have they found a home or are they still wandering?

3. What did Fargo look like to Peter Dut and his brothers when they first arrived? What knowledge did they bring with them about the place?

4. What do the Dut brothers understand about the world that their North Dakota classmates do not know? How might the brothers' experiences help them adjust to their new home?

5. What strategies did the brothers use to survive in Sudan and Ethiopia? How will they probably adapt those strategies to survive in the United States?

6. What makes this subject an appropriate one for the *New York Times Magazine*?

7. What about Corbett's style, organization, and techniques makes her essay a typical piece of feature writing?

Questions for Reflection and Writing

1. What might be done on a local level to alleviate a local problem? Write a proposal that would solve the problem.

2. How has the United States media reported on the Lost Boys? What were the follow-up stories or correspondence to this article? Discuss what influence Corbett's article has had on policy or public opinion.

3. What has happened to the girls and parents of Sudan? Research the current situation in Sudan and report on what has happened to the various groups of people there. Is the situation improving or disintegrating? Extend this assignment by proposing a solution to at least one part of the situation.

Edwidge Danticat (pronounced Ed-*weedj* Dan-ti-*cah*) was born in 1969 in Port-au-Prince, Haiti. Her parents emigrated to the United States when she was a toddler, leaving Danticat to be raised by her aunt. She followed her parents to New York when she was twelve, already writing stories. She attended Barnard College to study French literature and there continued to write short stories, some of which are included in her collection *Krik? Krak!* (1995). While at Brown University, where she earned an MFA, she wrote her second book, a novel, *Breath, Eyes, Memory* (1994). Subsequent novels include *The Farming of Bones* (1998) and *The Dew Breaker* (2004), both about Haitian events, as well as the young adult novel *Behind the Mountains* (2002). Another young adult book tells the true story of the *Anacaona* described in "We Are Ugly," *Anacaona, Golden Flower, Haiti*, 1490, part of Scholastic's Royal Diary series. In a travelogue and memoir, *After the Dance: A Walk through Carnival in Jacmel, Haiti* (2002), Danticat recounts a trip to her home country, and a recent memoir, *Brother, I'm Dying* (2007), tells the story of her uncle's death in 2004 while in the custody of the Department of Homeland Security. Danticat has also written plays, has collaborated with Jonathan Demme on a documentary about Haiti, and is the editor of collections such as *The Butterfly's Way: Voices from the Haitian Dyaspora in the United States* (2001). Danticat currently lives in Brooklyn.

We Are Ugly, But We Are Here

Edwidge Danticat

One of the first people murdered on our land was a queen. Her name was Anacaona and she was an Arawak Indian. She was a poet, dancer, and even a painter. She ruled over the western part of an island so lush and green that the Arawaks called it Ayiti—land of high. When the Spaniards came from across the sea to look for gold, Anacaona was one of their first victims. She was raped and killed and her village pillaged in a tradition of ongoing cruelty and atrocity. Anacaona's land is now the poorest country in the Western hemisphere, a place of continuous political unrest. Thus, for some, it is easy to forget that this land was the first Black Republic, home to the first people of African descent to uproot slavery and create an independent nation in 1804.

I was born under Haiti's dictatorial Duvalier regime. When I was four, my parents left Haiti to seek a better life in the United States. I must admit that their motives were more economic than political. But as anyone who knows Haiti will tell you, economics and politics are very intrinsically related in Haiti. Who is in power determines to a great extent whether or not people will eat.

I am twenty-six years old now and have spent more than half of my life in the United States. My most vivid memories of Haiti involve incidents that represent the general situation there. In Haiti, there are a lot of "blackouts," sudden power failures. At those times, you can't read or study or watch TV, so you sit

1

2

3

Edwidge Danticat, "We Are Ugly, But We Are Here." First published in *The Caribbean Writer*, Vol. 10 (1996) and reprinted by permission of Edwidge Danticat and Aragi Inc.

around a candle and listen to stories from the elders in the house. My grandmother was an old country woman who always felt displaced in the city of Port-au-Prince—where we lived—and had nothing but her patched-up quilts and her stories to console her. She was the one who told me about Anacaona. I used to share a room with her. I was in the room when she died. She was over a hundred years old. She died with her eyes wide open and I was the one who closed her eyes. I still miss the countless mystical stories that she told us. However, I accepted her death very easily because in Haiti death was always around us.

As a little girl, I attended more than my share of funerals. My uncle and legal guardian was a Baptist minister and his family was expected to attend every funeral he presided over. I went to all the funerals he presided over. I went to all the funerals in the same white lace dress. Perhaps it was because I attended so many funerals that I have such a strong feeling that death is not the end, that the people we bury are going off to live somewhere else. But at the same time, they will always be hovering around to watch over us and guide us through our journeys.

When I was eight, my uncle's brother-in-law went on a long journey to cut cane in the Dominican Republic. He came back, deathly ill. I remember his wife twirling feathers inside his nostrils and rubbing black pepper on his upper lip to make him sneeze. She strongly believed that if he sneezed, he would live. At night, it was my job to watch the sky above the house for signs of falling stars. In Haitian folklore, when a star falls out of the sky, it means someone will die. A star did fall out of the sky and he did die.

I have memories of Jean Claude "Baby Doc" Duvalier and his wife, racing by in their Mercedes Benz and throwing money out of the window to the very poor children in our neighborhood. The children nearly killed each other trying to catch a coin or a glimpse of Baby Doc. One Christmas, they announced on the radio that the first lady, Baby Doc's wife, was giving away free toys at the Palace. My cousins and I went and were nearly killed in the mob of children who flooded the palace lawns.

All of this now brings many questions buzzing to my head. Where was really my place in all of this? What was my grandmother's place? What is the legacy of the daughters of Anacaona? What do we all have left to remember, the daughters of Haiti?

Watching the news reports, it is often hard to tell whether there are real living and breathing women in conflict-stricken places like Haiti. The evening news broadcasts only allow us a brief glimpse of presidential coups, rejected boat people, and sabotaged elections. The women's stories never manage to make the front page. However they do exist.

I know women who, when the soldiers came to their homes in Haiti, would tell their daughters to lie still and play dead. I once met a woman whose sister was shot in her pregnant stomach because she was wearing a t-shirt with an "anti-military image." I know a mother who was arrested and beaten for working with a pro-democracy group. Her body remains laced with scars where the soldiers put out their cigarettes on her flesh. At night, this woman still smells the ashes of the cigarette butts that were stuffed lit inside her nostrils. In the same jail cell, she watched as paramilitary "attach's" raped her fourteen-year-old daughter at gun point. When mother and daughter took a tiny boat to the United States, the mother had no idea that her daughter was pregnant. Nor did she know that the child had gotten the HIV virus from one of the paramilitary men who had raped her. The grandchild—the offspring of the rape—was named Anacaona, after the queen, because that family of women is from the same region where Anacaona was murdered. The infant Anacaona has a face which no longer shows any trace of indigenous blood; however, her story echoes back to the first flow of blood on a land that has seen much more than its share.

There is a Haitian saying which might upset the aesthetic images of most   10
women. *Nou led, Nou la,* it says. We are ugly, but we are here. Like the modesty that is somewhat common in Haitian culture, this saying makes a deeper claim for poor Haitian women than maintaining beauty, be it skin deep or otherwise. For most of us, what is worth celebrating is the fact that we are here, that we—against all the odds—exist. To the women who might greet each other with this saying when they meet along the countryside, the very essence of life lies in survival. It is always worth reminding our sisters that we have lived yet another day to answer the roll call of an often painful and very difficult life. It is in this spirit that to this day a woman remembers to name her child Anacaona, a name which resonates both the splendor and agony of a past that haunts so many women.

When they were enslaved, our foremothers believed that when they died their   11
spirits would return to Africa, most specifically to a peaceful land we call *Guinin,* where gods and goddesses live. The women who came before me were women who spoke half of one language and half another. They spoke the French and Spanish of their captors mixed in with their own African language. These women seemed to be speaking in tongue when they prayed to their old gods, the ancient African spirits. Even though they were afraid that their old deities would no longer under-stand them, they invented a new language—our Creole patois—with which to describe their new surroundings, a language from which colorful phrases blos-somed to fit the desperate circumstances. When these women greeted each other, they found themselves speaking in codes.

How are we today, Sister?   12
I am ugly, but I am here.

These days, many of my sisters are greeting each other away from the home-   13
lands where they first learned to speak in tongues. Many have made it to other shores, after traveling endless miles on the high seas, on rickety boats that almost took their lives. Two years ago, a mother jumped into the sea when she discovered that her baby daughter had died in her arms on a journey which they had hoped would take them to a brighter future. Mother and child, they sank to the bottom of an ocean which already holds millions of souls from the middle passage—the holocaust of the slave trade—that is our legacy. That woman's sacrifice moved

then-deposed Haitian President Jean Bertrand Aristide to the brink of tears. However, like the rest of us, he took comfort in the past sacrifices that were made for all of us, so that we could be here.

The past is full of examples when our foremothers and forefathers showed   14
such deep trust in the sea that they would jump off slave ships and let the waves embrace them. They too believed that the sea was the beginning and the end of all things, the road to freedom and their entrance to *Guinin*. These women have been part of the very construction of my being ever since I was a little girl. Women like my grandmother who had taught me the story of Anacaona, the queen.

My grandmother believed that if a life is lost, then another one springs up   15
replanted somewhere else, the next life even stronger than the last. She believed that no one really dies as long as someone remembers, someone who will acknowledge that this person had—in spite of everything—been here. We are part of an endless circle, the daughters of Anacaona. We have stumbled, but have not fallen. We are ill-favored, but we still endure. Every once in a while, we must scream this as far as the wind can carry our voices: We are ugly, but we are here! And here to stay.

Frederick Douglass (1817–1895) was famous for the autobiographies that chronicled his life as a slave in Maryland and as a 20-year-old escapee in Massachusetts. He eventually became a popular antislavery lecturer and political appointee. Although he was born into slavery, Douglass secretly became literate on his own. Best known for his *Narrative of the Life of Frederick Douglass, an American Slave* (1845, rev. 1892), Douglass spent several years abroad in England and Ireland to avoid capture as a fugitive slave, although he later returned to purchase his own freedom.

Believing in the need for a self-sustaining black abolitionist movement, Douglass soon founded *North Star,* an abolitionist newspaper, in Rochester, New York, as the culmination of a split with William Lloyd Garrison, who led the white abolitionist movement. During the Civil War, Douglass entreated the Lincoln administration to adopt the cause of emancipation of the slaves as the aim of the war and to enlist blacks in the Union's struggle. Following the Civil War, Douglass accepted several appointments from 1871 to 1891. Throughout Reconstruction Douglass campaigned for black rights and actively defended women's rights. His other autobiographies include *My Bondage and My Freedom* (1855) and *The Life and Times of Frederick Douglass* (1892). Although autobiography has only recently been recognized as literature, Douglass's *Narrative* has been noted for its literary elements, such as the contrast between the voice of the writer in the present and the voice of the writer's past, the book's use of metaphors, and its account of personal transformation and maturation.

What to the Slave Is the Fourth of July?

Frederick Douglass

An address delivered in Rochester, New York, on July 5, 1852

Mr. President, Friends and Fellow Citizens: He who could address this audience without a quailing sensation, has stronger nerves than I have. I do not remember ever to have appeared as a speaker before any assembly more shrinkingly, nor with greater distrust of my ability, than I do this day. A feeling has crept over me, quite unfavorable to the exercise of my limited powers of speech. The task before me is one which requires much previous thought and study for its proper performance. I know that apologies of this sort are generally considered flat and unmeaning. I trust, however, that mine will not be so considered. Should I seem at ease, my appearance would much misrepresent me. The little experience I have had in addressing public meetings, in country school houses, avails me nothing on the present occasion.

The papers and placards say, that I am to deliver a 4th [of] July oration. This certainly sounds large, and out of the common way, for me. It is true that I have often had the privilege to speak in this beautiful Hall, and to address many who now honor me with their presence. But neither their familiar faces, nor the perfect gauge I think I have of Corinthian Hall, seems to free me from embarrassment.

The fact is, ladies and gentlemen, the distance between this platform and the slave plantation, from which I escaped, is considerable—and the difficulties to be overcome in getting from the latter to the former, are by no means slight. That I am here to-day is, to me, a matter of astonishment as well as of gratitude. You will not, therefore, be surprised, if in what I have got to say, I evince no elaborate preparation, nor grace my speech with any high sounding exordium. With little experience and with less learning, I have been able to throw my thoughts hastily and imperfectly together; and trusting to your patient and generous indulgence, I will proceed to lay them before you.

This, for the purpose of this celebration, is the 4th of July. It is the birthday of   4
your National Independence, and of your political freedom. This, to you, is what the Passover was to the emancipated people of God. It carries your minds back to the day, and to the act of your great deliverance; and to the signs, and to the wonders, associated with that act, and that day. This celebration also marks the beginning of another year of your national life; and reminds you that the Republic of America is now 76 years old. I am glad, fellow-citizens, that your nation is so young. Seventy-six years, though a good old age for a man, is but a mere speck in the life of a nation. Three score and ten is the allotted time for individual men; but nations number their years by thousands. According to this fact, you are, even now, only in the beginning of your national career, still lingering in the period of childhood. I repeat, I am glad this is so. There is hope in the thought, and hope is much needed, under the dark clouds which lower above the horizon. The eye of the reformer is met with angry flashes, portending disastrous times; but his heart may well beat lighter at the thought that America is young, and that she is still in the impressible stage of her existence. May he not hope that high lessons of wisdom, of justice and of truth, will yet give direction to her destiny? Were the nation older, the patriot's heart might be sadder, and the reformer's brow heavier. Its future might be shrouded in gloom, and the hope of its prophets go out in sorrow. There is consolation in the thought that America is young. Great streams are not easily turned from channels, worn deep in the course of ages. They may sometimes rise in quiet and stately majesty, and inundate the land, refreshing and fertilizing the earth with their mysterious properties. They may also rise in wrath and fury, and bear away, on their angry waves, the accumulated wealth of years of toil and hardship. They, however, gradually flow back to the same old channel, and flow on as serenely as ever. But, while the river may not be turned aside, it may dry up, and leave nothing behind but the withered branch, and the unsightly rock, to howl in the abyss-sweeping wind, the sad tale of departed glory. As with rivers so with nations.

Fellow-citizens, I shall not presume to dwell at length on the associations that   5
cluster about this day. The simple story of it is that, 76 years ago, the people of this country were British subjects. The style and title of your "sovereign people" (in which you now glory) was not then born. You were under the British Crown. Your fathers esteemed the English Government as the home government; and England as the fatherland. This home government, you know, although a considerable distance from your home, did, in the exercise of its parental prerogatives, impose upon its colonial children, such restraints, burdens and limitations, as in its mature judgement, it deemed wise, right and proper.

But, your fathers, who had not adopted the fashionable idea of this day, of the   6
infallibility of government, and the absolute character of its acts, presumed to differ from the home government in respect to the wisdom and the justice of some of

those burdens and restraints. They went so far in their excitement as to pronounce the measures of government unjust, unreasonable, and oppressive, and altogether such as ought not to be quietly submitted to. I scarcely need say, fellow-citizens, that my opinion of those measures fully accords with that of your fathers. Such a declaration of agreement on my part would not be worth much to anybody. It would, certainly, prove nothing, as to what part I might have taken, had I lived during the great controversy of 1776. To say *now* that America was right, and England wrong, is exceedingly easy. Everybody can say it; the dastard, not less than the noble brave, can flippantly descant on the tyranny of England towards the American Colonies. It is fashionable to do so; but there was a time when to pronounce against England, and in favor of the cause of the colonies, tried men's souls. They who did so were accounted in their day, plotters of mischief, agitators and rebels, dangerous men. To side with the right, against the wrong, with the weak against the strong, and with the oppressed against the oppressor! *here* lies the merit, and the one which, of all others, seems unfashionable in our day. The cause of liberty may be stabbed by the men who glory in the deeds of your fathers. But, to proceed.

Feeling themselves harshly and unjustly treated by the home government, your fathers, like men of honesty, and men of spirit, earnestly sought redress. They petitioned and remonstrated; they did so in a decorous, respectful, and loyal manner. Their conduct was wholly unexceptionable. This, however, did not answer the purpose. They saw themselves treated with sovereign indifference, coldness and scorn. Yet they persevered. They were not the men to look back. 7

As the sheet anchor takes a firmer hold, when the ship is tossed by the storm, so did the cause of your fathers grow stronger, as it breasted the chilling blasts of kingly displeasure. The greatest and best of British statesmen admitted its justice, and the loftiest eloquence of the British Senate came to its support. But, with that blindness which seems to be the unvarying characteristic of tyrants, since Pharaoh and his hosts were drowned in the Red Sea, the British Government persisted in the exactions complained of. 8

The madness of this course, we believe, is admitted now, even by England; but we fear the lesson is wholly lost on our present rulers. 9

Oppression makes a wise man mad. Your fathers were wise men, and if they did not go mad, they became restive under this treatment. They felt themselves the victims of grievous wrongs, wholly incurable in their colonial capacity. With brave men there is always a remedy for oppression. Just here, the idea of a total separation of the colonies from the crown was born! It was a startling idea, much more so, than we, at this distance of time, regard it. The timid and the prudent (as has been intimated) of that day, were, of course, shocked and alarmed by it. 10

Such people lived then, had lived before, and will, probably, ever have a place on this planet; and their course, in respect to any great change (no matter how great the good to be attained, or the wrong to be redressed by it), may be calculated with as much precision as can be the course of the stars. They hate all changes, but silver, gold and copper change! Of this sort of change they are always strongly in favor. 11

These people were called tories in the days of your fathers; and the appellation, probably, conveyed the same idea that is meant by a more modern, though a 12 some what less euphonious term, which we often find in our papers, applied to some of our old politicians.

Their opposition to the then dangerous thought was earnest and powerful; but, amid all their terror and affrighted vociferations against it, the alarming and revolutionary idea moved on, and the country with it.   13

On the 2d of July, 1776, the old Continental Congress, to the dismay of the lovers of ease, and the worshippers of property, clothed that dreadful idea with all the authority of national sanction. They did so in the form of a resolution; and as we seldom hit upon resolutions, drawn up in our day, whose transparency is at all equal to this, it may refresh your minds and help my story if I read it.   14

> Resolved, That these united colonies *are*, and of right, ought to be free and Independent States; that they are absolved from all allegiance to the British Crown; and that all political connection between them and the State of Great Britain *is*, and ought to be, dissolved.   15

Citizens, your fathers made good that resolution. They succeeded; and today you reap the fruits of their success. The freedom gained is yours; and you, therefore, may properly celebrate this anniversary. The 4th of July is the first great fact in your nation's history—the very ring-bolt in the chain of your yet undeveloped destiny.   16

Pride and patriotism, not less than gratitude, prompt you to celebrate and to hold it in perpetual remembrance. I have said that the Declaration of Independence is the RING-BOLT to the chain of your nation's destiny; so, indeed, I regard it. The principles contained in that instrument are saving principles. Stand by those principles, be true to them on all occasions, in all places, against all foes, and at whatever cost.   17

From the round top of your ship of state, dark and threatening clouds may be seen. Heavy billows, like mountains in the distance, disclose to the leeward huge forms of flinty rocks! That *bolt* drawn, that *chain* broken, and all is lost. *Cling to this day—cling to it*, and to its principles, with the grasp of a storm-tossed mariner to a spar at midnight.   18

The coming into being of a nation, in any circumstances, is an interesting event. But, besides general considerations, there were peculiar circumstances which make the advent of this republic an event of special attractiveness.   19

The whole scene, as I look back to it, was simple, dignified and sublime.   20

The population of the country, at the time, stood at the insignificant number of three millions. The country was poor in the munitions of war. The population was weak and scattered, and the country a wilderness unsubdued. There were then no means of concert and combination, such as exist now. Neither steam nor lightning had then been reduced to order and discipline. From the Potomac to the Delaware was a journey of many days. Under these, and unnumerable other disadvantages, your fathers declared for liberty and independence and triumphed.   21

Fellow Citizens, I am not wanting in respect for the fathers of this republic. The signers of the Declaration of Independence were brave men. They were great men too—great enough to give fame to a great age. It does not often happen to a nation to raise, at one time, such a number of truly great men. The point from which I am compelled to view them is not, certainly, the most favorable; and yet I cannot   22 contemplate their great deeds with less than admiration. They were statesmen, patriots and heroes, and for the good they did, and the principles they contended for, I will unite with you to honor their memory.

They loved their country better than their own private interests; and, though   23
this is not the highest form of human excellence, all will concede that it is a rare virtue, and that when it is exhibited, it ought to command respect. He who will, intelligently, lay down his life for his country, is a man whom it is not in human nature to despise. Your fathers staked their lives, their fortunes, and their sacred honor, on the cause of their country. In their admiration of liberty, they lost sight of all other interests.

They were peace men; but they preferred revolution to peaceful submission to   24
bondage. They were quiet men; but they did not shrink from agitating against oppression. They showed forbearance; but that they knew its limits. They believed in order; but not in the order of tyranny. With them, nothing was "*settled*" that was not right. With them, justice, liberty and humanity were "*final*"; not slavery and oppression. You may well cherish the memory of such men. They were great in their day and generation. Their solid manhood stands out the more as we contrast it with these degenerate times.

How circumspect, exact and proportionate were all their movements! How unlike   25
the politicians of an hour! Their statesmanship looked beyond the passing moment, and stretched away in strength into the distant future. They seized upon eternal principles, and set a glorious example in their defence. Mark them! . . .

The Narrative of the Life of Frederick Douglass

CHAPTER I

Frederick Douglass

I was born in Tuckahoe, near Hillsborough, and about twelve miles from Easton, in   1
Talbot county, Maryland. I have no accurate knowledge of my age, never having seen
any authentic record containing it. By far the larger part of the slaves know as little
of their ages as horses know of theirs, and it is the wish of most masters within my
knowledge to keep their slaves thus ignorant. I do not remember to have ever met
a slave who could tell of his birthday. They seldom come nearer to it than planting-
time, harvest-time, cherry-time, spring-time, or fall-time. A want of information concerning my own was a source of unhappiness to me even during childhood. The white
children could tell their ages. I could not tell why I ought to be deprived of the
same privilege. I was not allowed to make any inquiries of my master concerning it.
He deemed all such inquiries on the part of a slave improper and impertinent, and
evidence of a restless spirit. The nearest estimate I can give makes me now between
twenty-seven and twenty-eight years of age. I come to this, from hearing my master
say, some time during 1835, I was about seventeen years old.

My mother was named Harriet Bailey. She was the daughter of Isaac and Betsey   2
Bailey, both colored, and quite dark. My mother was of a darker complexion than
either my grandmother or grandfather.

My father was a white man. He was admitted to be such by all I ever heard speak   3
of my parentage. The opinion was also whispered that my master was my father;
but of the correctness of this opinion, I know nothing; the means of knowing was
withheld from me. My mother and I were separated when I was but an infant—before
I knew her as my mother. It is a common custom, in the part of Maryland from which
I ran away, to part children from their mothers at a very early age. Frequently, before
the child has reached its twelfth month, its mother is taken from it, and hired out on
some farm a considerable distance off, and the child is placed under the care of an
old woman, too old for field labor. For what this separation is done, I do not know,
unless it be to hinder the development of the child's affection toward its mother, and
to blunt and destroy the natural affection of the mother for the child. This is the
inevitable result.

I never saw my mother, to know her as such, more than four or five times in   4
my life; and each of these times was very short in duration, and at night. She was
hired by a Mr. Stewart, who lived about twelve miles from my home. She made her
journeys to see me in the night, travelling the whole distance on foot, after the
performance of her day's work. She was a field hand, and a whipping is the penalty
of not being in the field at sunrise, unless a slave has special permission from his or
her master to the contrary—a permission which they seldom get, and one that gives
to him that gives it the proud name of being a kind master. I do not recollect of
ever seeing my mother by the light of day. She was with me in the night. She would
lie down with me, and get me to sleep, but long before I waked she was gone. Very

little communication ever took place between us. Death soon ended what little we could have while she lived, and with it her hardships and suffering. She died when I was about seven years old, on one of my master's farms, near Lee's Mill. I was not allowed to be present during her illness, at her death, or burial. She was gone long before I knew any thing about it. Never having enjoyed, to any considerable extent, her soothing presence, her tender and watchful care, I received the tidings of her death with much the same emotions I should have probably felt at the death of a stranger.

Called thus suddenly away, she left me without the slightest intimation of who my father was. The whisper that my master was my father, may or may not be true; and, true or false, it is of but little consequence to my purpose whilst the fact remains, in all its glaring odiousness, that slaveholders have ordained, and by law established, that the children of slave women shall in all cases follow the condition of their mothers; and this is done too obviously to administer to their own lusts, and make a gratification of their wicked desires profitable as well as pleasurable; for by this cunning arrangement, the slaveholder, in cases not a few, sustains to his slaves the double relation of master and father.

I know of such cases; and it is worthy of remark that such slaves invariably suffer greater hardships, and have more to contend with, than others. They are, in the first place, a constant offence to their mistress. She is ever disposed to find fault with them; they can seldom do any thing to please her; she is never better pleased than when she sees them under the lash, especially when she suspects her husband of showing to his mulatto children favors which he withholds from his black slaves. The master is frequently compelled to sell this class of his slaves, out of deference to the feelings of his white wife; and, cruel as the deed may strike any one to be, for a man to sell his own children to human flesh-mongers, it is often the dictate of humanity for him to do so; for, unless he does this, he must not only whip them himself, but must stand by and see one white son tie up his brother, of but few shades darker complexion than himself, and ply the gory lash to his naked back; and if he lisp one word of disapproval, it is set down to his parental partiality, and only makes a bad matter worse, both for himself and the slave whom he would protect and defend.

Every year brings with it multitudes of this class of slaves. It was doubtless in consequence of a knowledge of this fact, that one great statesman of the south predicted the downfall of slavery by the inevitable laws of population. Whether this prophecy is ever fulfilled or not, it is nevertheless plain that a very different-looking class of people are springing up at the south, and are now held in slavery, from those originally brought to this country from Africa; and if their increase do no other good, it will do away the force of the argument, that God cursed Ham, and therefore American slavery is right. If the lineal descendants of Ham are alone to be scripturally enslaved, it is certain that slavery at the south must soon become unscriptural; for thousands are ushered into the world, annually, who, like myself, owe their existence to white fathers, and those fathers most frequently their own masters.

I have had two masters. My first master's name was Anthony. I do not remember his first name. He was generally called Captain Anthony—a title which, I presume, he acquired by sailing a craft on the Chesapeake Bay. He was not considered

5

6

7

8

a rich slaveholder. He owned two or three farms, and about thirty slaves. His farms and slaves were under the care of an overseer. The overseer's name was Plummer. Mr. Plummer was a miserable drunkard, a profane swearer, and a savage monster. He always went armed with a cowskin and a heavy cudgel. I have known him to cut and slash the women's heads so horribly, that even master would be enraged at his cruelty, and would threaten to whip him if he did not mind himself. Master, however, was not a humane slaveholder. It required extraordinary barbarity on the part of an overseer to affect him. He was a cruel man, hardened by a long life of slaveholding. He would at times seem to take great pleasure in whipping a slave. I have often been awakened at the dawn of day by the most heart-rending shrieks of an own aunt of mine, whom he used to tie up to a joist, and whip upon her naked back till she was literally covered with blood. No words, no tears, no prayers, from his gory victim, seemed to move his iron heart from its bloody purpose. The louder she screamed, the harder he whipped; and where the blood ran fastest, there he whipped longest. He would whip her to make her scream, and whip her to make her hush; and not until overcome by fatigue, would he cease to swing the blood-clotted cowskin. I remember the first time I ever witnessed this horrible exhibition. I was quite a child, but I well remember it. I never shall forget it whilst I remember any thing. It was the first of a long series of such outrages, of which I was doomed to be a witness and a participant. It struck me with awful force. It was the blood-stained gate, the entrance to the hell of slavery, through which I was about to pass. It was a most terrible spectacle. I wish I could commit to paper the feelings with which I beheld it.

This occurrence took place very soon after I went to live with my old master,   9
and under the following circumstances. Aunt Hester went out one night,—where or for what I do not know,—and happened to be absent when my master desired her presence. He had ordered her not to go out evenings, and warned her that she must never let him catch her in company with a young man, who was paying attention to her belonging to Colonel Lloyd. The young man's name was Ned Roberts, generally called Lloyd's Ned. Why master was so careful of her, may be safely left to conjecture. She was a woman of noble form, and of graceful proportions, having very few equals, and fewer superiors, in personal appearance, among the colored or white women of our neighborhood.

Aunt Hester had not only disobeyed his orders in going out, but had been found   10
in company with Lloyd's Ned; which circumstance, I found, from what he said while whipping her, was the chief offence. Had he been a man of pure morals himself, he might have been thought interested in protecting the innocence of my aunt; but those who knew him will not suspect him of any such virtue. Before he commenced whipping Aunt Hester, he took her into the kitchen, and stripped her from neck to waist, leaving her neck, shoulders, and back, entirely naked. He then told her to cross her hands, calling her at the same time a d—d b—h. After crossing her hands, he tied them with a strong rope, and led her to a stool under a large hook in the joist, put in for the purpose. He made her get upon the stool, and tied her hands to the hook. She now stood fair for his infernal purpose. Her arms were stretched up at their full length, so that she stood upon the ends of her toes. He then said to her, "Now, you d—d b—h, I'll learn you how to disobey my orders!" and after rolling up his

sleeves, he commenced to lay on the heavy cowskin, and soon the warm, red blood (amid heart-rending shrieks from her, and horrid oaths from him) came dripping to the floor. I was so terrified and horror-stricken at the sight, that I hid myself in a closet, and dared not venture out till long after the bloody transaction was over. I expected it would be my turn next. It was all new to me. I had never seen any thing like it before. I had always lived with my grandmother on the outskirts of the plantation, where she was put to raise the children of the younger women. I had therefore been, until now, out of the way of the bloody scenes that often occurred on the plantation.

Barbara Ehrenreich (1941–   ) received a Ph.D. in Biology from Rockefeller University in 1968. Born in Butte, Montana, Ehrenreich has worked as college professor, editor, and columnist for such magazines as *Mother Jones* and *Time*. Her journalistic writing earned her the Sydney Hillman Award for Journalism and a shared Magazine Award for Excellence in Reporting. Her books include *The Hearts of Men: American Dreams and the Flight from Commitment* (1983), *Blood Rites: Origins and History of the Passions of War* (1997), and *Nickel and Dimed: On (Not) Getting by in America* (2001). The following piece "Class Struggle 101" was first published in the November 2003 issue of *The Progressive* and consequently in her collection of essays entitled *This Land Is Their Land: Reports from a Divided Nation* (2008).

Class Struggle 101

Barbara Ehrenreich

On the evening of August 24, I had dinner with Randy Marcum, who works in   1
the boiler room at Miami University of Ohio. Joining us were about ten other campus workers, plus some of their student supporters. It was a hefty meal—the best the Holiday Inn had to offer—complete with wine and dessert. Which was a good thing, because three weeks later, Marcum was on a hunger strike to dramatize the poverty of Miami University's food service and maintenance workers.

Welcome to higher education, twenty-first-century style, where the most   2
important course offered is not listed in the college catalog. It's called Class Struggle, and it pits the men in suits—administrators and trustees—against the men and women who keep the school running: maintenance workers, groundspeople, clerical and technical workers, housekeepers, food service workers. Yale has gotten all the national attention, with its tumultuous three-week-long strike that just ended in a stunning victory for the university's clerical and maintenance workers. But similar clashes are going on in less illustrious places, like the University of North Carolina at Chapel Hill, where housekeepers, who have been trying to win union recognition for years, led a lively rally and teach-in on September 23.

As for Miami University, 460 maintenance workers are now out on strike, as   3
I write at the end of September. Randy has ended his fast in order to build up energy for the picket line. The students have erected a tent city in front of the administration building. And faculty members are planning their own night in the tent city. Union picketers humiliated the university by turning away the union camera crews who had come to televise a Miami RedHawks vs. Cincinnati Bearcats game.

College presidents, deans, provosts, chancellors—along with their deputies,   4
assistants, and other members of the ever-proliferating educational administrative workforce—insist that their labor problems are a sorry distraction from their

Reprinted by permission from *The Progressive*, 409 East Main Street, Madison, WI, 53703. *www.progressive.org.*

institutions' noble purpose of enlightening young minds. But administrators like to cloak themselves in the moral authority of Western Civilization, such as it is, which means that labor issues are hardly peripheral to the university's educational mission. On an increasing number of campuses, incoming students are greeted at a formal fall convocation in which the top administrators—suited up in full medieval mortarboard-and-gown attire—deliver platitudinous speeches about Character, Integrity, and Truth. The message is that these weirdly costumed folks are not mere executives of a corporation but the guardians of an ancient and sacred tradition. So when these same dignitaries turn out to be grossly underpaying their employees and harassing the "troublemakers" among them, they do so with the apparent blessing of Aristotle, Plato, and Shakespeare.

If the university has so much to teach about social inequality, why shouldn't 5 the students get credit for learning it? The covert lessons from the administration should be formalized as course offerings. Here's the curriculum.

Elementary Class Structure of the United States: The University as 6 Microcosm. In this four-credit course, we will examine the pay gradient from housekeeper (approximately $19,000/year) to president (more than $270,000 for Miami University's James C. Garland and about $500,000 for Yale's Richard Levin). In the final exam, students will be asked to discuss the rationale for this pay gap in terms of the payees' contributions to the university, ongoing housing and wardrobe expenses, and intrinsic human worth.

Presidential Architecture: A three-credit seminar course featuring field trips 7 through university-provided presidential dwellings, including "great rooms," wet bars, saunas, guest suites, and exercise rooms, with a side trip, if time permits, to the trailer parks favored by the housekeeping and maintenance staff.

Race, Gender, and Occupational Preference: In this advanced sociology 8 seminar, we will analyze the way campus workers sort themselves into various occupations on the basis of race and gender, and we will explore various theories attempting to explain this phenomenon—for example, the Innate Athleticism theory of why African Americans so often prefer manual labor, and the Nimble Fingers theory of why females can usually be found doing the clerical work.

Topics in University Financing: A four-credit business course tracing the 9 development of the current two-pronged approach to financing institutions of higher learning—tuition increases for the students plus pay decreases for the staff. Alternative approaches to financing, featuring militant campaigns for adequate public funding for higher education, will be thoroughly critiqued.

A cynic might say that the true purpose of college is to teach exactly such 10 lessons. After all, college graduates are a relative elite, comprising only 25 percent of the adult population, and they are expected to fill the kind of administrative and managerial jobs that make it a positive advantage to be able to starve workers, impose layoffs, and bust unions without losing a minute of sleep. Some students catch on with lightning-like speed, such as Yale's precocious Scott Wexler, eighteen, who confided to *The New York Times*, "I kind of like walking through the picket lines." This young man will make a fine assistant regional manager at Wal-Mart—or possibly a college president.

Fortunately, not all students are buying the administrations' lesson plan. At 11 Harvard in the spring of 2001, students occupied an administration building for twenty-one days to persuade the administration to bargain with campus janitors, many of whom were paid only $6.50 an hour. Last spring, Stanford students went on their own hunger strike in support of campus blue collar workers. And it's not just the super-elite schools that have been generating vigorous student-labor alliances. At mainstream public universities like those of Maryland and Virginia, there are plenty of students who would agree with Miami University's Justin Katko, when he writes that he got involved in the campus workers' struggle because "I could not allow such extreme disparities as are found on college campuses . . . to exist without being ashamed of myself for apathy."

It's hard to concentrate in classrooms that were cleaned during the night by 12 people who can barely make rent. You tend to choke on your chicken fingers when the cafeteria is staffed by men and women who have to work a second job in order to feed their own children.

Questions for Discussion

1. Why does Ehrenreich choose to describe the "hefty meal" she ate at the Holiday Inn with campus workers and student supporters with such detail (paragraph 1)? What drives her choice to provide specific information about this meal to readers?

2. Explain what Ehrenreich means by what she calls "Class Struggle" and its relationship to higher education.

3. Examine the courses and seminars that Ehrenreich advocates as part of a new curriculum based on uncovering "social inequality." What does Ehrenreich mean to accomplish by including specific details of these courses and seminars? How do the details she supplies about these classes contribute to the overall argument in her essay?

4. Why does Ehrenreich feel that "college graduates are a relative elite"?

5. What are specific examples of students that are not "buying the administrations' lesson plan"? Why does Ehrenreich include these examples in her piece?

6. Examine the last paragraph which consists of two sentences. Why does Ehrenreich choose to end her piece so succinctly and what type of emotion does it generate for readers?

Questions for Reflection and Writing

1. What do you think of Ehrenreich's argument about making "the covert lessons from the administration . . . formalized as course offerings" (paragraph 5)? Would classes that focus on "social inequality" be beneficial for college students (paragraph 5)? Why or why not? Paying specific attention to the courses and seminars Ehrenreich describes as part of a curricular shift in higher education, write a short essay where you choose to promote or argue against Ehrenreich's proposed change. Feel free to use examples from your own educational experiences both inside and outside the classroom in writing your response.

2. At the opening of her piece, Ehrenreich writes about "Randy Marcum, who works in the boiler room at Miami University of Ohio" (paragraph 1). Do you know any campus workers at your college/university who may be struggling financially like Randy? Take note of campus workers you see at your school in the span of a week and record what activities they perform on a sheet of paper and reflect on these. Next, do some research on the amount of pay these campus workers receive per hour. In a reflective essay, consider how this observation and research you have conducted may have changed or strengthened certain reactions you had during your first reading of Ehrenreich's writing.

3. Imagine you are asked to interview Scott Wexler for a follow-up story on students that do not support campus workers' strikes (paragraph 10). Based on his response to *The New York Times* that Ehrenreich quotes (paragraph 10), what questions do you ask him and why? Write your interview questions for Scott and explain your rationale behind them in a short response. Next, imagine actually conducting this interview. What emotions would you feel when asking your particular questions? Do you feel tense, nervous, defensive, etc.? Where do you think these emotions come from? After each interview question in your written response, record a few notes on the emotions you could potentially experience and the possible reasons for them.

Barbara Jordan (1936–1996) was born in Houston, Texas. She earned her B.A. from Texas Southern University in 1956 and her law degree from Boston University School of Law in 1959. Jordan was the first African American to be elected to the Texas Senate since Reconstruction, where she served for five years (1967–1972). She then became the first African American woman from a Southern state to be elected to the United States House of Representatives. In 1974, Jordan was appointed to the House Judiciary Committee where she enthralled the nation with her speech calling for the impeachment of President Nixon. Jordan left the Senate in 1979 but remained politically active. Until the early 1990s, Jordan taught at the Lyndon B. Johnson School of Public Affairs at the University of Texas. The recipient of numerous awards, including the Presidential Medal of Honor in 1994, perhaps the most prestigious award was given to Jordan posthumously. Following her death on January 17, 1996, Jordan's body lay in state in the LBJ Library on the campus of the University of Texas at Austin. She is buried in the Texas State Cemetery, the first black woman to be interred on its grounds.

Statement on the Articles of Impeachment

Barbara Jordan

Thank you, Mr. Chairman.

Mr. Chairman, I join my colleague Mr. Rangel in thanking you for giving the junior members of this committee the glorious opportunity of sharing the pain of this inquiry. Mr. Chairman, you are a strong man, and it has not been easy but we have tried as best we can to give you as much assistance as possible.

Earlier today, we heard the beginning of the Preamble to the Constitution of the United States: "We, the people." It's a very eloquent beginning. But when that document was completed on the seventeenth of September in 1787, I was not included in that "We, the people." I felt somehow for many years that George Washington and Alexander Hamilton just left me out by mistake. But through the process of amendment, interpretation, and court decision, I have finally been included in "We, the people."

Today I am an inquisitor. An hyperbole would not be fictional and would not overstate the solemnness that I feel right now. My faith in the Constitution is whole; it is complete; it is total. And I am not going to sit here and be an idle spectator to the diminution, the subversion, the destruction, of the Constitution.

"Who can so properly be the inquisitors for the nation as the representatives of the nation themselves?" "The subjects of its jurisdiction are those offenses which proceed from the misconduct of public men." And that's what we're talking about. In other words, [the jurisdiction comes] from the abuse or violation of some public trust.

It is wrong, I suggest, it is a misreading of the Constitution for any member here to assert that for a member to vote for an article of impeachment means that

Barbara Charline Jordan, "Statement on the Articles of Impeachment," delivered July 25, 1974, House Judiciary Committee.

that member must be convinced that the President should be removed from office. The Constitution doesn't say that. The powers relating to impeachment are an essential check in the hands of the body of the legislature against and upon the encroachments of the executive. The division between the two branches of the legislature, the House and the Senate, assigning to the one the right to accuse and to the other the right to judge, the framers of this Constitution were very astute. They did not make the accusers and the judgers—and the judges the same person.

We know the nature of impeachment. We've been talking about it awhile now. It is chiefly designed for the President and his high ministers to somehow be called into account. It is designed to "bridle" the executive if he engages in excesses. "It is designed as a method of national inquest into the conduct of public men." The framers confided in the Congress the power if need be, to remove the President in order to strike a delicate balance between a President swollen with power and grown tyrannical, and preservation of the independence of the executive.

The nature of impeachment: a narrowly channeled exception to the separation-of-powers maxim. The Federal Convention of 1787 said that. It limited impeachment to high crimes and misdemeanors and discounted and opposed the term "maladministration." "It is to be used only for great misdemeanors," so it was said in the North Carolina ratification convention. And in the Virginia ratification convention: "We do not trust our liberty to a particular branch. We need one branch to check the other."

"No one need be afraid"—the North Carolina ratification convention—"No one need be afraid that officers who commit oppression will pass with immunity." "Prosecutions of impeachments will seldom fail to agitate the passions of the whole community," said Hamilton in the Federalist Papers, number 65. "We divide into parties more or less friendly or inimical to the accused." I do not mean political parties in that sense.

The drawing of political lines goes to the motivation behind impeachment; but impeachment must proceed within the confines of the constitutional term "high crime[s] and misdemeanors." Of the impeachment process, it was Woodrow Wilson who said that "Nothing short of the grossest offenses against the plain law of the land will suffice to give them speed and effectiveness. Indignation so great as to overgrow party interest may secure a conviction; but nothing else can."

Common sense would be revolted if we engaged upon this process for petty reasons. Congress has a lot to do: Appropriations, Tax Reform, Health Insurance, Campaign Finance Reform, Housing, Environmental Protection, Energy Sufficiency, Mass Transportation. Pettiness cannot be allowed to stand in the face of such overwhelming problems. So today we are not being petty. We are trying to be big, because the task we have before us is a big one.

This morning, in a discussion of the evidence, we were told that the evidence which purports to support the allegations of misuse of the CIA by the President is thin. We're told that that evidence is insufficient. What that recital of the evidence this morning did not include is what the President did know on June the 23rd, 1972.

The President did know that it was Republican money, that it was money from 13
the Committee for the Re-Election of the President, which was found in the possession of one of the burglars arrested on June the 17th. What the President did know
on the 23rd of June was the prior activities of E. Howard Hunt, which included his
participation in the break-in of Daniel Ellsberg's psychiatrist, which included
Howard Hunt's participation in the Dita Beard ITT affair, which included Howard
Hunt's fabrication of cables designed to discredit the Kennedy Administration.

We were further cautioned today that perhaps these proceedings ought to be 14
delayed because certainly there would be new evidence forthcoming from the
President of the United States. There has not even been an obfuscated indication
that this committee would receive any additional materials from the President.
The committee subpoena is outstanding, and if the President wants to supply that
material, the committee sits here. The fact is that on yesterday, the American people waited with great anxiety for eight hours, not knowing whether their President
would obey an order of the Supreme Court of the United States.

At this point, I would like to juxtapose a few of the impeachment criteria with 15
some of the actions the President has engaged in. Impeachment criteria: James
Madison, from the Virginia ratification convention. "If the President be connected in any suspicious manner with any person and there be grounds to believe
that he will shelter him, he may be impeached."

We have heard time and time again that the evidence reflects the payment to 16
defendants money. The President had knowledge that these funds were being paid
and these were funds collected for the 1972 presidential campaign. We know that
the President met with Mr. Henry Petersen 27 times to discuss matters related to
Watergate, and immediately thereafter met with the very persons who were implicated in the information Mr. Petersen was receiving. The words are: "If the
President is connected in any suspicious manner with any person and there be
grounds to believe that he will shelter that person, he may be impeached."

Justice Story: "Impeachment" is attended—"is intended for occasional and 17
extraordinary cases where a superior power acting for the whole people is put into
operation to protect their rights and rescue their liberties from violations." We
know about the Huston plan. We know about the break-in of the psychiatrist's
office. We know that there was absolute complete direction on September 3rd
when the President indicated that a surreptitious entry had been made in
Dr. Fielding's office, after having met with Mr. Ehrlichman and Mr. Young.
"Protect their rights." "Rescue their liberties from violation."

The Carolina ratification convention impeachment criteria: those are 18
impeachable "who behave amiss or betray their public trust." Beginning shortly
after the Watergate break-in and continuing to the present time, the President has
engaged in a series of public statements and actions designed to thwart the lawful
investigation by government prosecutors. Moreover, the President has made public announcements and assertions bearing on the Watergate case, which the evidence will show he knew to be false. These assertions, false assertions,
impeachable, those who misbehave. Those who "behave amiss or betray the public trust."

James Madison again at the Constitutional Convention: "A President is   19
impeachable if he attempts to subvert the Constitution." The Constitution
charges the President with the task of taking care that the laws be faithfully executed, and yet the President has counseled his aides to commit perjury, willfully
disregard the secrecy of grand jury proceedings, conceal surreptitious entry,
attempt to compromise a federal judge, while publicly displaying his cooperation
with the processes of criminal justice. "A President is impeachable if he attempts
to subvert the Constitution."

If the impeachment provision in the Constitution of the United States will   20
not reach the offenses charged here, then perhaps that 18th-century Constitution
should be abandoned to a 20th-century paper shredder.

Has the President committed offenses, and planned, and directed, and acqui-   21
esced in a course of conduct which the Constitution will not tolerate? That's the
question. We know that. We know the question. We should now forthwith proceed to answer the question. It is reason, and not passion, which must guide our
deliberations, guide our debate, and guide our decision.

I yield back the balance of my time, Mr. Chairman.   22

Perri Klass (1958–   ) was born in Tuna-puna, Trinidad, and earned an M.D. from Harvard in 1986. She has been a pediatrician at the Children's Hospital Boston since 1986. She writes nonfiction and novels as well as short stories and has won the O. Henry Award five times for the latter. Her books include *A Not Entirely Benign Procedure: Four Years as a Medical Student* (1987) and the collection of stories *Love and Modern Medicine* (2001). Her work also appears in periodicals such as *Massachusetts Medicine*, *Vogue*, and *Esquire*, and she has a monthly column called "Vital Signs" in *Discover* magazine. "Macho" is taken from *A Not Entirely Benign Procedure*.

Macho

Perri Klass

Purely by coincidence, our team has four women and one man. The two interns and the two medical students are female, and the resident, who leads the team, is male. We are clattering up the stairs one morning in approved hospital fashion, conveying by our purposeful demeanor: out of the way, doctors coming, decisions to make, lives to save. (In fact, what we are actually trying to do is to rush through morning rounds in time to get to breakfast before the cafeteria stops serving hot food, but never mind that now.) We barrel through the door into the intensive care unit, and some other resident, standing by, announces, "Here comes The A-Team." Immediately our resident swings around to respond to some undertone he has detected: 1

"Are you saying my team is weak? Huh? You saying my team is weak?"   2

We continue on our rounds, the resident occasionally prompting one of the interns, "You should be pushing me out of the way, you know. Go on, push me out of the way." He means that since she is on call that day, she should be first through every door, first to lay hands on every patient.   3

My fellow medical student and I trail along in the rear, a position that accurately reflects our place in the hierarchy and also my energy level (this is, after all, 7:00 A.M.). She whispers to me, "Straighten your back! Suck in your stomach! This is war!" And as we start to clatter down the stairs to breakfast, our morning mission successfully accomplished, she and I are both singing under our breaths, "Macho macho doc, I wanna be a macho doc. . . ."   4

Macho in medicine can mean a number of things. Everyone knows it's out there as a style, either an ideal or an object of ridicule. You hear echoes of it in the highest praise one can receive in the hospital, "Strong work," which may be said to an intern who got a very sick patient through the night or to a medical student who successfully fielded some obscure questions on rounds. And the all-purpose term of disparagement is "Weak." They're being really weak down in the emergency room tonight, admitting people who could just as well be sent home. Dr. So-and-so is being weak with that patient—why doesn't he just tell him he *has* to have the surgery? You   5 were pretty weak this morning when they were asking you about rheumatic heart disease—better read up on it.

Macho can refer to your willingness to get tough with your patients, to keep them from pushing you around. It can refer to your eagerness to do invasive procedures— "The hell with radiology, I wanna go for the biopsy." Talk like that and they'll call you a cowboy, and generally mean it as a compliment. Macho can mean territoriality: certain doctors resent calling in expert consultations and, when they finally have to, await the recommendations with truculent eagerness to disregard them. "These are *our* patients and *we* make all the decisions," I heard over and over from one resident I worked under. The essence of macho, any kind of macho, after all, is that life is a perpetual contest. You must not let others intrude on your stomping grounds. You must not let anyone tell you what to do. And of course, the most basic macho fear is the fear of being laughed at; whatever you do, you must not let anyone mock you— or your team.

A medical student once said to me when I teased him about not being able to work the Addressograph machine after six weeks in the hospital, "That's secretarial work. I can draw a blood gas blindfolded, from thirty feet away!"

Life in the hospital is full of opportunities to prove yourself, if you want to look at it that way. "I want you guys to be able to get blood from a stone," announced our new resident on his first day as our leader. The "guys," the other female medical student and I, must have looked a little dubious, because he continued, "Okay, it may mean the patient gets stuck a few extra times, but I don't want you giving up just because of that." And sure enough, when I came to tell him that I had stuck one particular woman six times without success, and could he please come show me where he thought a decent vein might be, he sent me back in to try her ankles. "Blood from a stone!" he called after me, and when I finally got a tube of this unfortunate woman's blood, he patted me on the back and said, "Strong work."

If we are at war, then who is the enemy? Rightly the enemy is disease, and even if that is not your favorite metaphor, it is a rather common way to think of medicine: we are combating these deadly processes for the bodies of our patients. They become battlefields, lying there passively in bed while the evil armies of pathology and the resplendent forces of modern medicine fight it out. Still, there are very good doctors who seem to think that way, who take disease as a personal enemy and battle it with fury and dedication. The real problem arises because all too often the patient comes to personify the disease, and somehow the patient becomes the enemy.

We don't say, or think, "Mrs. Hawthorne's cancer is making her sicker." We say, "Mrs. Hawthorne's crumping on me," and Mrs. Hawthorne represents the challenge we cannot meet, the disease we cannot cure. And instead of hating her cancer, it's not hard to start hating Mrs. Hawthorne—especially if she has an irritating personality, and most especially of all if she somehow seems to be blaming us. That is, if every day the doctor sees the challenge again in the patient's eye, hears it in the patient's voice: "You can't do anything for me, can you, despite all the tests and all the medicines?"

The patient may want the doctor to continue fighting, may even take renewed hope as new therapies are instituted, but the doctor, knowing them to be essentially futile, may become angrier and angrier. When the disease has essentially won and the patient continues to present the challenge, the macho doctor is left with no appropriate response. He cannot sidestep the challenge by offering comfort rather than combat, because comfort is not in his repertoire. And unable to do battle against the disease to any real effect, he may feel almost ready to battle the patient.

I have been talking as if macho medicine is a male preserve, and to a large extent   12
that's true. Certainly there are some female doctors who end up being fairly macho and, much more important, many men who are not macho at all. Some of the gentlest, most reasonable doctors I worked with were male, good teachers and superb healers. But there are also many macho docs, and certainly it is pervasive as a style in the hospital. I don't believe that would be the case if the majority of doctors up to now had been female, and perhaps it will change over time as more women become doctors. The tradition of medical training is partly a tradition of hazing, boot camp, basic training. New buzzwords are now being muttered, like "nurturing" or "supportive," but there are many doctors riding the range out there to whom you wouldn't dare mutter any such words.

"Sup-por-tive," you can almost hear The Duke drawl as the doctor looks down   13
at the newest sissy in town. At which point you tuck your hypodermic needle back into its holster and march, on the double, back into that pesky varmint's room to let him know who's boss in this here hospital.

Questions for Discussion

1. What's the tone of the opening vignette presented in this excerpt? How does Klass create this tone? What does the scene resemble?
2. According to the author, what is the highest praise one can receive in a hospital? Why is this significant?
3. What meanings does the word *macho* take on throughout this essay?
4. In paragraph 9, Klass uses a metaphor to identify the way many in the medical profession imagine their role at work. What are the consequences of this self-perception?
5. Klass refers to legendary movie star John Wayne ("The Duke") in the last paragraph of this excerpt. What effect does the reference have?

Questions for Reflection and Writing

1. Have you encountered the attitude Klass describes? What's your response to this "insider's view" of the medical profession? Write an essay describing your experience of the medical profession, from the other end of the stethoscope.
2. Choose a blue-collar profession (e.g., truck driving, firefighting, lumberjacking) traditionally associated with machismo and compare it to Klass's presentation of macho medical practice. Alternatively, choose a traditionally "feminine" profession—nursing, secretarial work, or teaching, for example—and write a corollary piece entitled "Femme" (or something similar).

3. Klass points to signs of change in the medical profession toward the end of her excerpt: specifically, she mentions the impact of more women in the profession and changes made to the medical school curriculum. Do you agree that these changes should radically alter the way doctors view the world? *Have* things changed much in the medical profession since this essay was written in 1987? Do some research to find out. (One interesting place to start is the homepage of the American Medical Student Association, at www.amsa.org.)

━━━━━ ◄ ABRAHAM LINCOLN ►━ ━━━━━

• First Inaugural Address[1]

FELLOW CITIZENS OF THE UNITED STATES:

In compliance with a custom as old as the government itself, I appear before you to address you briefly, and to take in your presence the oath prescribed by the Constitution of the United States to be taken by the President "before he enters on the execution of his office."

I do not consider it necessary at present for me to discuss those matters of administration about which there is no special anxiety or excitement.

Apprehension seems to exist among the people of the Southern states that by the accession of a Republican administration their property and their peace and personal security are to be endangered.[2] There has never been any reasonable cause for such apprehension. Indeed, the most ample evidence to the contrary has all the while existed and been open to their inspection. It is found in nearly all the published speeches of him who now addresses you. I do but quote from one of those speeches when I declare that "I have no purpose, directly or indirectly, to interfere with the institution of slavery in the states where it exists. I believe I have no lawful right to do so, and I have no inclination to do so."[3] Those who nominated and elected me did so with full knowledge that I had made this and many similar declarations, and had never recanted them. And, more than this, they placed in the platform for my acceptance, and as a law to themselves and to me, the clear and emphatic resolution which I now read:

"*Resolved,* That the maintenance inviolate of the rights of the states, and especially the right of each state to order and control its own domestic institutions according to its own judgment exclusively, is essential to that balance of power on which the perfection and endurance of our political fabric depend; and we denounce the lawless invasion by armed force of the soil of any state or territory, no matter under what pretext, as among the gravest of crimes."

1. Lincoln's inauguration on March 4, 1861, coincided with a national crisis, reflected in his passionate appeal for friendship and unity between the North and the South. Since his election on November 6, 1860, South Carolina had seceded from the Union (December 20), calling for the withdrawal of federal garrisons from Forts Moultrie and Sumter in Charleston Harbor. Similar ordinances had been swiftly passed by Mississippi, Florida, Alabama, Georgia, Louisiana, and Texas, in spite of the passing of an emergency amendment (never ratified) affirming the constitutionality of slavery in the slave states. Yet Lincoln's speech "was as indulgent as he could make it without renouncing constitutional duties" (Thomas, *Abraham Lincoln,* p. 247). The last paragraph, emphasizing this spirit of conciliation, was based on an idea submitted by Seward as an addition to the original draft. Lincoln "transformed the Secretary's graceless sentences into a moving and exalted plea" (Thomas, *Abraham Lincoln,* p. 248). The president spoke from a platform outside the uncompleted Capitol building—the huge bronze statue of Freedom, destined for the dome, still symbolically recumbent on the ground nearby.
2. Lincoln's "house divided" speech at the Illinois state Republican convention of June 16, 1858, had been widely quoted; he realized that he must now offset the effect of his earlier dictum that "this government cannot endure permanently half slave and half free."
3. Referring to the amendment, just passed by Congress, reaffirming the constitutional guarantee of slavery in states where it already existed.

I now reiterate these sentiments; and, in doing so, I only press upon the public attention the most conclusive evidence of which the case is susceptible, that the property, peace, and security of no section are to be in any wise endangered by the now incoming administration. I add, too, that all the protection which, consistently with the Constitution and the laws, can be given, will be cheerfully given to all the states when lawfully demanded for whatever cause—as cheerfully to one section as to another.

There is much controversy about the delivering up of fugitives from service or labor. The clause I now read is as plainly written in the Constitution as any other of its provisions:

"No person held to service or labor in one state, under the laws thereof, escaping into another, shall in consequence of any law or regulation therein be discharged from such service or labor, but shall be delivered up on claim of the party to whom such service or labor may be due."

It is scarcely questioned that this provision was intended by those who made it for the reclaiming of what we call fugitive slaves; and the intention of the lawgiver is the law. All members of Congress swear their support to the whole Constitution—to this provision as much as to any other. To the proposition, then, that slaves whose cases come within the terms of this clause "shall be delivered up," their oaths are unanimous. Now, if they would make the effort in good temper, could they not with nearly equal unanimity frame and pass a law by means of which to keep good that unanimous oath?

There is some difference of opinion whether this clause should be enforced by national or by state authority; but surely that difference is not a very material one. If the slave is to be surrendered, it can be of but little consequence to him or to others by which authority it is done. And should anyone in any case be content that his oath shall go unkept on a merely unsubstantial controversy as to how it shall be kept?

Again, in any law upon this subject, ought not all the safeguards of liberty known in civilized and humane jurisprudence to be introduced, so that a free man be not, in any case, surrendered as a slave? And might it not be well at the same time to provide by law for the enforcement of that clause in the Constitution which guarantees that "the citizens of each state shall be entitled to all privileges and immunities of citizens in the several states"?

I take the official oath today with no mental reservations, and with no purpose to construe the Constitution or laws by any hypercritical rules. And while I do not choose now to specify particular acts of Congress as proper to be enforced, I do suggest that it will be much safer for all, both in official and private stations, to conform to and abide by all those acts which stand unrepealed, than to violate any of them, trusting to find immunity in having them held to be unconstitutional.

It is seventy-two years since the first inauguration of a president under our national Constitution. During that period fifteen different and greatly distinguished citizens have, in succession, administered the executive branch of the government. They have conducted it through many perils, and generally with great success. Yet, with all this scope of precedent, I now enter upon the same task for the brief constitutional term of four years under great and peculiar difficulty. A disruption of the federal Union, heretofore only menaced, is now formidably attempted.[4]

I hold that, in contemplation of universal law and of the Constitution, the union of these states is perpetual.[5] Perpetuity is implied, if not expressed, in the fundamental law of all national governments. It is safe to assert that no government proper ever had a provision in its organic law for its own termination. Continue to execute all the express provisions of our national Constitution, and the Union will endure forever—it being impossible to destroy it except by some action not provided for in the instrument itself.

Again, if the United States be not a government proper, but an association of states in the nature of contract merely, can it, as a contract, be peaceably unmade by less than all the parties who made it? One party to a contract may violate it—break it, so to speak; but does it not require all to lawfully rescind it?

Descending from these general principles, we find the proposition that in legal contemplation the Union is perpetual confirmed by the history of the Union itself. The Union is much older than the Constitution. It was formed, in fact, by the Articles of Association in 1774. It was matured and continued by the Declaration of Independence in 1776. It was further matured, and the faith of all the then thirteen states expressly plighted and engaged that it should be perpetual, by the Articles of Confederation in 1778. And, finally, in 1787 one of the declared objects for ordaining and establishing the Constitution was "to form a more perfect Union."

But if the destruction of the Union by one or by a part only of the states be lawfully possible, the Union is less perfect than before the Constitution, having lost the vital element of perpetuity.

It follows from these views that no state upon its own mere motion can lawfully get out of the Union; that resolves and ordinances to that effect are legally void; and that acts of violence, within any state or states, against the authority of the United States, are insurrectionary or revolutionary, according to circumstances.

I therefore consider that, in view of the Constitution and the laws, the Union is unbroken; and to the extent of my ability I shall take care, as the Constitution itself expressly enjoins upon me, that the laws of the Union be faithfully executed in all the states.[6] Doing this I deem to be only a simple duty on my part; and I shall perform it so far as practicable, unless my rightful masters, the American people, shall withhold the requisite means, or in some authoritative manner direct the contrary. I trust this will not be regarded as a menace, but only as the declared purpose of the Union that it will constitutionally defend and maintain itself.

In doing this there needs to be no bloodshed or violence; and there shall be none, unless it be forced upon the national authority. The power confided to me will be used to hold, occupy, and possess the property and places belonging to the

---

4. The secession of seven states.
5. It was Lincoln's strategy to regard the secession ordinances as unconstitutional and hence of no effect. The seceded states could reconsider, or the federal authorities could deal with the southern uprising as a civil disorder within the Union.
6. Hence even the seceded states, while subject to the police power of the national government, were still assured of all the guarantees of the Constitution.

government, and to collect the duties and imposts; but beyond what may be necessary for these objects, there will be no invasion, no using of force against or among the people anywhere. Where hostility to the United States, in any interior locality, shall be so great and universal as to prevent competent resident citizens from holding the federal offices, there will be no attempt to force obnoxious strangers among the people for that object. While the strict legal right may exist in the government to enforce the exercise of these offices, the attempt to do so would be so irritating, and so nearly impracticable withal, that I deem it better to forego for the time the uses of such offices.

The mails, unless repelled, will continue to be furnished in all parts of the Union. So far as possible, the people everywhere shall have that sense of perfect security which is most favorable to calm thought and reflection. The course here indicated will be followed unless current events and experience shall show a modification or change to be proper; and in every case and exigency my best discretion will be exercised according to circumstances actually existing, and with a view and a hope of a peaceful solution of the national troubles, and the restoration of fraternal sympathies and affections.

That there are persons in one section or another who seek to destroy the Union at all events, and are glad of any pretext to do it, I will neither affirm nor deny; but if there be such, I need address no word to them. To those, however, who really love the Union may I not speak?

Before entering upon so grave a matter as the destruction of our national fabric, with all its benefits, its memories, and its hopes, would it not be wise to ascertain precisely why we do it? Will you hazard so desperate a step while there is any possibility that any portion of the ills you fly from have no real existence? Will you, while the certain ills you fly to are greater than all the real ones you fly from— will you risk the commission of so fearful a mistake?

All profess to be content in the Union if all constitutional rights can be maintained. Is it true, then, that any right, plainly written in the Constitution, has been denied? I think not. Happily the human mind is so constituted that no party can reach to the audacity of doing this. Think, if you can, of a single instance in which a plainly written provision of the Constitution has ever been denied. If by the mere force of numbers a majority should deprive a minority of any clearly written constitutional right, it might, in a moral point of view, justify revolution—certainly would if such a right were a vital one. But such is not our case. All the vital rights of minorities and of individuals are so plainly assured to them by affirmations and negations, guaranties and prohibitions, in the Constitution, that controversies never arise concerning them. But no organic law can ever be framed with a provision specifically applicable to every question which may occur in practical administration. No foresight can anticipate, nor any document of reasonable length contain, express provisions for all possible questions. Shall fugitives from labor be surrendered by national or by state authority? The Constitution does not expressly say. *May* Congress prohibit slavery in the territories? The Constitution does not expressly say. *Must* Congress protect slavery in the territories? The Constitution does not expressly say.

From questions of this class spring all our constitutional controversies, and we divide upon them into majorities and minorities. If the minority will not acquiesce, the majority must, or the government must cease. There is no other alternative; for continuing the government is acquiescence on one side or the other.

If a minority in such case will secede rather than acquiesce, they make a precedent which in turn will divide and ruin them; for a minority of their own will secede from them whenever a majority refuses to be controlled by such minority. For instance, why may not any portion of a new confederacy a year or two hence arbitrarily secede again, precisely as portions of the present Union now claim to secede from it? All who cherish disunion sentiments are now being educated to the exact temper of doing this.

Is there such perfect identity of interests among the states to compose a new Union, as to produce harmony only, and prevent renewed secession?

Plainly, the central idea of secession is the essence of anarchy. A majority held in restraint by constitutional checks and limitations, and always changing easily with deliberate changes of popular opinions and sentiments, is the only true sovereign of a free people. Whoever rejects it does, of necessity, fly to anarchy or to despotism. Unanimity is impossible; the rule of a minority, as a permanent arrangement, is wholly inadmissible; so that, rejecting the majority principle, anarchy or despotism in some form is all that is left.

I do not forget the position, assumed by some, that constitutional questions are to be decided by the Supreme Court; nor do I deny that such decisions must be binding, in any case, upon the parties to a suit, as to the object of that suit, while they are also entitled to very high respect and consideration in all parallel cases by all other departments of the government. And while it is obviously possible that such decision may be erroneous in any given case, still the evil effect following it, being limited to that particular case, with the chance that it may be overruled and never become a precedent for other cases, can better be borne than could the evils of a different practice. At the same time, the candid citizen must confess that if the policy of the government, upon vital questions affecting the whole people, is to be irrevocably fixed by decisions of the Supreme Court, the instant they are made, in ordinary litigation between parties in personal actions, the people will have ceased to be their own rulers, having to that extent practically resigned their government into the hands of that eminent tribunal. Nor is there in this view any assault upon the court or the judges. It is a duty from which they may not shrink to decide cases properly brought before them, and it is no fault of theirs if others seek to turn their decisions to political purposes.

One section of our country believes slavery is right, and ought to be extended, while the other believes it is wrong, and ought not to be extended. This is the only substantial dispute. The fugitive-slave clause of the Constitution, and the law for the suppression of the foreign slave-trade, are each as well enforced, perhaps, as any law can ever be in a community where the moral sense of the people imperfectly supports the law itself. The great body of the people abide by the dry legal obligation in both cases, and a few break over in each. This, I think, cannot be perfectly cured; and it would be worse in both cases after the separation of the sections than before. The foreign slave-trade, now imperfectly suppressed, would be ultimately revived, without restriction, in one section, while fugitive slaves, now only partially surrendered, would not be surrendered at all by the other.

Physically speaking, we cannot separate. We cannot remove our respective sections from each other, nor build an impassable wall between them. A husband

and wife may be divorced, and go out of the presence and beyond the reach of each other; but the different parts of our country cannot do this. They cannot but remain face to face; and intercourse, either amicable or hostile, must continue between them. Is it possible, then, to make that intercourse more advantageous or more satisfactory after separation than before? Can aliens make treaties easier than friends can make laws? Can treaties be more faithfully enforced between aliens than laws can among friends? Suppose you go to war, you cannot fight always; and when, after much loss on both sides, and no gain on either, you cease fighting, the identical old questions as to terms of intercourse are again upon you.

This country, with its institutions, belongs to the people who inhabit it. Whenever they shall grow weary of the existing government, they can exercise their constitutional right of amending it, or their revolutionary right to dismember or overthrow it. I cannot be ignorant of the fact that many worthy and patriotic citizens are desirous of having the national Constitution amended. While I make no recommendation of amendments, I fully recognize the rightful authority of the people over the whole subject, to be exercised in either of the modes prescribed in the instrument itself; and I should, under existing circumstances, favor rather than oppose a fair opportunity being afforded the people to act upon it. I will venture to add that to me the convention mode seems preferable, in that it allows amendments to originate with the people themselves, instead of only permitting them to take or reject propositions originated by others not especially chosen for the purpose, and which might not be precisely such as they would wish to either accept or refuse. I understand a proposed amendment to the Constitution—which amendment, however, I have not seen—has passed Congress, to the effect that the federal government shall never interfere with the domestic institutions of the states, including that of persons held to service. To avoid misconstruction of what I have said, I depart from my purpose not to speak of particular amendments so far as to say that, holding such a provision to now be implied constitutional law, I have no objection to its being made express and irrevocable.[7]

The chief magistrate derives all his authority from the people, and they have conferred none upon him to fix terms for the separation of the states. The people themselves can do this also if they choose; but the Executive, as such, has nothing to do with it. His duty is to administer the present government, as it came to his hands, and to transmit it, unimpaired by him, to his successor.

Why should there not be a patient confidence in the ultimate justice of the people? Is there any better or equal hope in the world? In our present differences is either party without faith of being in the right? If the Almighty Ruler of Nations, with His eternal truth and justice, be on your side of the North, or on yours of the South, that truth and that justice will surely prevail by the judgment of this great tribunal of the American people.

By the frame of the government under which we live, this same people have wisely given their public servants but little power for mischief; and have, with equal wisdom, provided for the return of that little to their own hands at very

---

7. A second reference to his recognition of the emergency amendment. This sentence was a last-minute interpolation, made to emphasize this conciliatory attitude toward the South.

short intervals. While the people retain their virtue and vigilance, no administration, by any extreme of wickedness or folly, can very seriously injure the government in the short space of four years.

My countrymen, one and all, think calmly and well upon this whole subject. Nothing valuable can be lost by taking time. If there be an object to hurry any of you in hot haste to a step which you would never take deliberately, that object will be frustrated by taking time; but no good object can be frustrated by it. Such of you as are now dissatisfied, still have the old Constitution unimpaired, and, on the sensitive point, the laws of your own framing under it; while the new administration will have no immediate power, if it would, to change either. If it were admitted that you who are dissatisfied hold the right side in the dispute, there still is no single good reason for precipitate action. Intelligence, patriotism, Christianity, and a firm reliance on Him who has never yet forsaken this favored land, are still competent to adjust in the best way all our present difficulty.

In your hands, my dissatisfied fellow countrymen, and not in mine, is the momentous issue of civil war. The government will not assail you. You can have no conflict without being yourselves the aggressors. You have no oath registered in heaven to destroy the government, while I shall have the most solemn one to "preserve, protect, and defend it."[8]

I am loath to close. We are not enemies, but friends. We must not be enemies. Though passion may have strained, it must not break our bonds of affection. The mystic chords of memory, stretching from every battlefield and patriot grave to every living heart and hearthstone all over this broad land, will yet swell the chorus of the Union when again touched, as surely they will be, by the better angels of our nature.

1861

8. Lincoln's original draft ended here.

Thomas Paine (1737–1809) was born in Thetford, England. Paine was a sailor, a tax clerk, a soldier, and an inventor, and later in life became a writer with the help of Benjamin Franklin. A political philosopher who promoted change through revolution rather than reform, Paine is most renowned for his role in the American Revolution. His most influential works are *Common Sense* (1776), from which "Origin and Design of Government in General" is taken, *The Rights of Man* (1791), and *The Age of Reason* (1794). Paine's perceived atheistic views threw him out of public favor late in his life, and he died isolated and nearly friendless.

Common Sense

Thomas Paine

1776

INTRODUCTION

Perhaps the sentiments contained in the following pages, are not yet sufficiently fash- 1
ionable to procure them general favor; a long habit of not thinking a thing wrong,
gives it a superficial appearance of being right, and raises at first a formidable out-
cry in defence of custom. But tumult soon subsides. Time makes more converts than
reason.

As a long and violent abuse of power is generally the means of calling the right 2
of it in question, (and in matters too which might never have been thought of, had
not the sufferers been aggravated into the inquiry,) and as the king of England hath
undertaken in his own right, to support the parliament in what he calls theirs, and
as the good people of this country are grievously oppressed by the combination, they
have an undoubted privilege to inquire into the pretensions of both, and equally to
reject the usurpations of either.

In the following sheets, the author hath studiously avoided every thing which 3
is personal among ourselves. Compliments as well as censure to individuals make no
part thereof. The wise and the worthy need not the triumph of a pamphlet; and those
whose sentiments are injudicious or unfriendly, will cease of themselves, unless too
much pains is bestowed upon their conversion.

The cause of America is, in a great measure, the cause of all mankind. Many cir- 4
cumstances have, and will arise, which are not local, but universal, and through which
the principles of all lovers of mankind are affected, and in the event of which, their
affections are interested. The laying a country desolate with fire and sword, declar-
ing war against the natural rights of all mankind, and extirpating the defenders thereof
from the face of the earth, is the concern of every man to whom nature hath given
the power of feeling; of which class, regardless of party censure, is

THE AUTHOR.
Philadelphia, Feb. 14, 1776.

CHAPTER 1

Of the Origin and Design of Government in General. With Concise Remarks on the English Constitution

Some writers have so confounded society with government, as to leave little or no   5
distinction between them; whereas they are not only different, but have different origins. Society is produced by our wants, and government by our wickedness; the former promotes our happiness positively by uniting our affections, the latter negatively by restraining our vices. The one encourages intercourse, the other creates distinctions. The first is a patron, the last a punisher.

Society in every state is a blessing, but government even in its best state is but   6
a necessary evil in its worst state an intolerable one; for when we suffer, or are exposed to the same miseries by a government, which we might expect in a country without government, our calamities is heightened by reflecting that we furnish the means by which we suffer! Government, like dress, is the badge of lost innocence; the palaces of kings are built on the ruins of the bowers of paradise. For were the impulses of conscience clear, uniform, and irresistibly obeyed, man would need no other lawgiver; but that not being the case, he finds it necessary to surrender up a part of his property to furnish means for the protection of the rest; and this he is induced to do by the same prudence which in every other case advises him out of two evils to choose the least. Wherefore, security being the true design and end of government, it unanswerably follows that whatever form thereof appears most likely to ensure it to us, with the least expense and greatest benefit, is preferable to all others.

In order to gain a clear and just idea of the design and end of government, let us   7
suppose a small number of persons settled in some sequestered part of the earth, unconnected with the rest, they will then represent the first peopling of any country, or of the world. In this state of natural liberty, society will be their first thought. A thousand motives will excite them thereto, the strength of one man is so unequal to his wants, and his mind so unfitted for perpetual solitude, that he is soon obliged to seek assistance and relief of another, who in his turn requires the same. Four or five united would be able to raise a tolerable dwelling in the midst of a wilderness, but one man might labor out the common period of life without accomplishing any thing; when he had felled his timber he could not remove it, nor erect it after it was removed; hunger in the mean time would urge him from his work, and every different want call him a different way. Disease, nay even misfortune would be death, for though neither might be mortal, yet either would disable him from living, and reduce him to a state in which he might rather be said to perish than to die.

Thus necessity, like a gravitating power, would soon form our newly arrived emi-   8
grants into society, the reciprocal blessings of which, would supersede, and render the obligations of law and government unnecessary while they remained perfectly just to each other; but as nothing but heaven is impregnable to vice, it will unavoidably happen, that in proportion as they surmount the first difficulties of emigration, which bound them together in a common cause, they will begin to relax in their duty and attachment to each other; and this remissness, will point out the necessity, of establishing some form of government to supply the defect of moral virtue.

Some convenient tree will afford them a State-House, under the branches of   9
which, the whole colony may assemble to deliberate on public matters. It is more
than probable that their first laws will have the title only of Regulations, and be
enforced by no other penalty than public disesteem. In this first parliament every
man, by natural right will have a seat.

But as the colony increases, the public concerns will increase likewise, and the   10
distance at which the members may be separated, will render it too inconvenient for
all of them to meet on every occasion as at first, when their number was small, their
habitations near, and the public concerns few and trifling. This will point out the
convenience of their consenting to leave the legislative part to be managed by a select
number chosen from the whole body, who are supposed to have the same concerns
at stake which those have who appointed them, and who will act in the same manner as the whole body would act were they present. If the colony continue increasing, it will become necessary to augment the number of the representatives, and that
the interest of every part of the colony may be attended to, it will be found best to
divide the whole into convenient parts, each part sending its proper number; and
that the elected might never form to themselves an interest separate from the elec-
tors, prudence will point out the propriety of having elections often; because as the
elected might by that means return and mix again with the general body of the elec-
tors in a few months, their fidelity to the public will be secured by the prudent reflection of not making a rod for themselves. And as this frequent interchange will
establish a common interest with every part of the community, they will mutually
and naturally support each other, and on this (not on the unmeaning name of king)
depends the strength of government, and the happiness of the governed.

Here then is the origin and rise of government; namely, a mode rendered nec-   11
essary by the inability of moral virtue to govern the world; here too is the design and
end of government, viz., freedom and security. And however our eyes may be dazzled
with snow, or our ears deceived by sound; however prejudice may warp our wills, or
interest darken our understanding, the simple voice of nature and of reason will
say, it is right.

I draw my idea of the form of government from a principle in nature, which   12
no art can overturn, viz., that the more simple any thing is, the less liable it is to be
disordered, and the easier repaired when disordered; and with this maxim in view, I
offer a few remarks on the so much boasted constitution of England. That it was noble
for the dark and slavish times in which it was erected is granted. When the world was
overrun with tyranny the least therefrom was a glorious rescue. But that it is imperfect, subject to convulsions, and incapable of producing what it seems to promise,
is easily demonstrated.

Absolute governments (though the disgrace of human nature) have this advan-   13
tage with them, that they are simple; if the people suffer, they know the head from
which their suffering springs, know likewise the remedy, and are not bewildered by
a variety of causes and cures. But the constitution of England is so exceedingly complex, that the nation may suffer for years together without being able to discover in
which part the fault lies, some will say in one and some in another, and every political physician will advise a different medicine.

I know it is difficult to get over local or long standing prejudices, yet if we will   14
suffer ourselves to examine the component parts of the English constitution, we shall
find them to be the base remains of two ancient tyrannies, compounded with some
new republican materials.

First.—The remains of monarchical tyranny in the person of the king.   15

Secondly.—The remains of aristocratical tyranny in the persons of the peers.   16

Thirdly.—The new republican materials, in the persons of the commons, on   17
whose virtue depends the freedom of England.

The two first, by being hereditary, are independent of the people; wherefore in   18
a constitutional sense they contribute nothing towards the freedom of the state.

To say that the constitution of England is a union of three powers reciprocally   19
checking each other, is farcical, either the words have no meaning, or they are flat
contradictions.

To say that the commons is a check upon the king, presupposes two things.   20

First.—That the king is not to be trusted without being looked after, or in other   21
words, that a thirst for absolute power is the natural disease of monarchy.

Secondly.—That the commons, by being appointed for that purpose, are either   22
wiser or more worthy of confidence than the crown.

But as the same constitution which gives the commons a power to check the king   23
by withholding the supplies, gives afterwards the king a power to check the commons,
by empowering him to reject their other bills; it again supposes that the king is wiser
than those whom it has already supposed to be wiser than him. A mere absurdity!

There is something exceedingly ridiculous in the composition of monarchy; it   24
first excludes a man from the means of information, yet empowers him to act in cases
where the highest judgment is required. The state of a king shuts him from the world,
yet the business of a king requires him to know it thoroughly; wherefore the different parts, unnaturally opposing and destroying each other, prove the whole character to be absurd and useless.

Some writers have explained the English constitution thus; the king, say they, is   25
one, the people another; the peers are an house in behalf of the king; the commons in
behalf of the people; but this hath all the distinctions of an house divided against itself;
and though the expressions be pleasantly arranged, yet when examined they appear
idle and ambiguous; and it will always happen, that the nicest construction that words
are capable of, when applied to the description of something which either cannot exist,
or is too incomprehensible to be within the compass of description, will be words of
sound only, and though they may amuse the ear, they cannot inform the mind, for
this explanation includes a previous question, viz. How came the king by a power which
the people are afraid to trust, and always obliged to check? Such a power could not be
the gift of a wise people, neither can any power, which needs checking, be from God;
yet the provision, which the constitution makes, supposes such a power to exist.

But the provision is unequal to the task; the means either cannot or will not   26
accomplish the end, and the whole affair is a felo de se; for as the greater weight
will always carry up the less, and as all the wheels of a machine are put in motion
by one, it only remains to know which power in the constitution has the most weight,
for that will govern; and though the others, or a part of them, may clog, or, as the

phrase is, check the rapidity of its motion, yet so long as they cannot stop it, their endeavors will be ineffectual; the first moving power will at last have its way, and what it wants in speed is supplied by time.

That the crown is this overbearing part in the English constitution needs not be   27 mentioned, and that it derives its whole consequence merely from being the giver of places pensions is self evident, wherefore, though we have and wise enough to shut and lock a door against absolute monarchy, we at the same time have been foolish enough to put the crown in possession of the key.

The prejudice of Englishmen, in favor of their own government by king, lords,   28 and commons, arises as much or more from national pride than reason. Individuals are undoubtedly safer in England than in some other countries, but the will of the king is as much the law of the land in Britain as in France, with this difference, that instead of proceeding directly from his mouth, it is handed to the people under the most formidable shape of an act of parliament. For the fate of Charles the First, hath only made kings more subtle not—more just.

Wherefore, laying aside all national pride and prejudice in favor of modes and   29 forms, the plain truth is, that it is wholly owing to the constitution of the people, and not to the constitution of the government that the crown is not as oppressive in England as in Turkey.

An inquiry into the constitutional errors in the English form of government is   30 at this time highly necessary; for as we are never in a proper condition of doing justice to others, while we continue under the influence of some leading partiality, so neither are we capable of doing it to ourselves while we remain fettered by any obstinate prejudice. And as a man, who is attached to a prostitute, is unfitted to choose or judge of a wife, so any prepossession in favor of a rotten constitution of government will disable us from discerning a good one.

Amanda Ripley, a writer-reporter for *Time* Magazine in New York, has also worked at *Washington City Paper*, *Congressional Quarterly*, and *American Lawyer*. In addition, Ripley has published freelance articles, primarily on legal, social, and political issues, in *The New York Times Magazine* and *The Washington Monthly*. "What Is a Life Worth?" first appeared in *Time* on February 3, 2002.

What Is a Life Worth?

Amanda Ripley

A train barreled over Joseph Hewins' body on a wintry evening in 1845 in the   1
Massachusetts Berkshires. Hewins had spent the workday shoveling snow off the tracks, only to be killed on his trip back to town when a switchman got distracted. Hewins left behind a wife and three children, who were poor even before his death. His widow sued but lost at every level. Had the train merely chopped off Hewins' leg, the railroad would have paid. But in the perverse logic of that time, when a man died, he took his legal claims with him. And so the thinking went for most of the century, until something unheard of began to happen. The courts started to put a dollar value on a life—after death.

The concept of assigning a price tag to a life has always made people intensely   2
squeamish. After all, isn't it degrading to presume that money can make a family whole again? And what of the disparities? Is a poor man's life worth less than a rich man's? Over the past 100 years, U.S. courts have crafted their answers to these questions. Forensic economists testify on the value of a life every day. They can even tell you the average valuation of an injured knee (about $200,000). But until now, the public at large has not had to reckon with the process and its imperfections. Until the terrorist attacks of Sept. 11 created a small city's worth of grieving families and the government established an unprecedented fund to compensate them, the mathematics of loss was a little-known science. Now the process is on garish display, and it is tempting to avert the eyes.

On the morning of Jan. 18, about 70 family members file into the rows of crim-   3
son seats at the Norwalk, Conn., city hall auditorium. They listen quietly to special master Kenneth Feinberg, whom the government has entrusted with dispersing its money to those most affected by the Sept. 11 tragedy. His first job is to persuade them to join the federal Victim Compensation Fund, the country's largest experiment in paying mass victims and their families without placing blame. The effort is being closely watched for the precedents it will set.

Much has been made of the enormous charity funds raised after the attacks.   4
Donations to those groups do funnel thousands of dollars to the victims' families— in particular, the families of fire fighters and police officers. But overall, the nearly $2 billion in charity money is chump change compared with the cash that will flow out of government coffers. There is no limit to the federal fund, but the tab is likely

to be triple the size of the charity pot. And while charity funds are doled out to a vast pool of people, including businesses hurt by the attacks, the government money will go exclusively to the injured and to families of the deceased.

HOW THE FUND WORKS

Unlimited	**2**
Total amount of money in the fund	Number of years family have to file claims
$250,000	**246**
Flat payment to families for pain and suffering	Number of claims files as of Jan. 31
$50,000	**120**
Additional pain-and-suffering payment for spouse and for each child	Number of days the special master has to decide each claim
0	**0**
Federal taxes owed on any award	Chances to appeal the decision

---

Feinberg, in a black-and-white polka-dot tie, speaks in short, punchy sentences and a loud voice. He has already given the speech 32 times up and down the East Coast. The main thrust: The government, for the first time ever, has agreed to write large checks to victims' families without any litigation. The checks will arrive within four months after a claim is filed—no legal fees, no agonizing 10-year lawsuit. But every award will be based on a cold calculus, much the way courts handle wrongful-death claims.

That means different sums for different families. In a TIME/CNN poll taken last month, 86% said all families should receive the same amount. But that's not how it's going to work.

The calculus has several steps, Feinberg explains. First, the government will estimate how much a victim would have earned over his or her lifetime had the planes never crashed. That means a broker's family will qualify for a vastly higher award than a window washer's family. To estimate this amount, each family was handed an easy-to-read chart on the way into the meeting: Find your loved one's age and income and follow your finger to the magic number. Note that the lifetime earnings have been boosted by a flat $250,000 for "pain and suffering"—noneconomic losses, they are called. Tack on an extra $50,000 in pain and suffering for a spouse and for each child. The charts, while functional, are brutal, crystallizing how readily the legal system commodifies life.

Then—and this is crucial—don't get too excited. That first number may be quite 8
high—in the millions for many. But you must, according to the rules of the fund, sub-
tract all the money you are getting from other sources except charities. A court
settlement would not be diminished this way, but this is not a court, Feinberg repeatedly points out. Deduct life insurance, pension, Social Security death benefits, and
workers' compensation. Now you have the total award the government is offering
you for your loss.

The deductions have the effect of equalizing the differences in the awards. Critics 9
have called this Feinberg's "Robin Hood strategy." For many people in the room, the
number is now at or close to zero. Feinberg says he will make sure no one gets zero.
"Leave it to me," he says. But nowhere will that be written into the rules when they
are finalized in mid-February. Likewise, many fiancés and gay partners will be at
the mercy of Feinberg's discretion in seeking awards. Before finding out exactly what
they will get—and the rules are complex—families will have to agree never to sue
anyone for the attacks. "Normally, that would be a difficult call," says Feinberg. "Not
here. The right to sue in this case is simply not a reasonable alternative."

That's because Congress has capped the liability of the airlines, the airport own- 10
ers, the aircraft manufacturers, the towers' landlord and the city of New York. In
the name of the economy, the government severely restricted the victims' rights to
sue—whether they join the fund or not. It is this lack of a viable option, even if they
would not take it, that galls many families.

Congress created the fund as a safety net for the victims' families, to ensure that 11
they maintain something resembling their current standard of living—whether they
get assistance from private insurance or government money. The families see it as
so much more. For the traumatized, the charts are like a Rorschach test. Some view
the money as a halfhearted apology for the breakdown in security and intelligence
that made the attacks possible. Others can't help seeing the award as a callous measure of their loved one's value. Many regard it as a substitute for the millions they think
they may have got in court, had the liability not been capped. When the total comes
out to be underwhelming, these families take it personally. There's a fundamental
clash between the way they interpret the purpose of the fund and the way the government sees it.

After Feinberg speaks, he stands back and braces himself for an artillery of angry 12
rhetorical questions. Gerry Sweeney, whose brother died in Tower 2, Floor 105, points
at Feinberg and explains why $250,000 is not enough for pain and suffering in the
case of her now fatherless nephew. "Have you ever seen a 12-year-old have a nervous breakdown?" she asks. Another woman concocts an analogy to illustrate for
Feinberg what it was like to talk to loved ones as they came to accept their immi-
nent, violent deaths and to watch the towers collapse on live TV. "If your wife was
brutally raped and murdered and you had to watch and listen to it happen, what
would you think the right amount would be?" Finally, Maureen Halvorson, who
lost her husband and her brother, speaks up from the front row in a quiet, bewildered
voice. "I just can't accept the fact that the Federal Government is saying my husband
and my brother are worth nothing." Feinberg is silent.

The more than 3,000 victims of the Sept. 11 attacks are frozen in snapshots,   13
wide-smiling men and women in crisp suits and uniforms who liked to build bird-
houses on weekends and play practical jokes. In the literature of grief, they have
become hardworking innocents, heroes and saints. But those they left behind are
decidedly human. Some compete with others for most bereaved status; others demand
an apology even when no one is listening. Some are popping pills, and others cannot leave the house. Most days, they are inconsolable. And as the rest of the country begins to ease back into normalcy, these families stand, indignant, in the way.

Already, some Americans have lost patience with them. "My tax money should   14
not be given to someone with a $750,000 mortgage to pay who needs a set of fresh,
matching towels in her bathroom every season," one person wrote anonymously to
the Department of Justice's Web page on victim compensation. "I'm shocked and
appalled and very disappointed," wrote a Florida resident, "that some individuals are
living in such a rare and well-gilded ivory tower that they feel $250,000 is not suf-
ficient compensation. Most of us, the working people of America, make $20,000 to
$40,000 per year. Where do these wealthy, spoiled, greedy folks in New York get
off, pretending that what happened to them was so uniquely horrible? I'm over it.
Yeah, it was unique. Yeah, it was horrible. Yeah, I sent money to help. And after reading about them suing for more money, I begin to regret it."

It's true that some families' behavior has been less than dignified. The divorced   15
parents of a woman killed in the Pentagon, who are eligible for money because
their daughter left no dependents, have filed competing claims. Lawyers are now
involved. Says her father: "I guarantee she loved her daddy as much as she loved
her mom. I feel that I'm entitled to something."

And it's also a fact that these families will get more money from charities and   16
the government combined than anyone has so far received after the Oklahoma City
bombing or the 1998 bombing of the Nairobi embassy. For that matter, if these victims
had been killed in a drive-by shooting, they probably would not have received more
than a few thousand dollars from state victim-compensation funds.

That fact is not lost on the public, particularly people whose relatives have died   17
in everyday tragedies. At the *Wichita Eagle* in Kansas, editorial-page director Phil
Brownlee has received calls and letters from locals disgusted by the families' com-
plaints, and he agrees. "It's just frustrating that the goodwill demonstrated by the government seems to be deteriorating," he says. "Now you've got families who are upset
with what most Americans deem to be generous contributions. It's the loss of the
spirit of Sept. 11, the souring of that sense of solidarity."

But it may not be fair to compare Sept. 11 with a street crime or even Oklahoma   18
City. After all, these recent attacks involved an orchestrated, simultaneous security
breach on four airplanes, carried out by 19 men who had been living and training on our
soil. A better comparison might be past international terrorist attacks and plane
crashes. Those that have been resolved—and that's a major distinction—do show
higher payouts than the average amount likely to come out of the Sept. 11 federal fund.

In 25 major aviation accidents between 1970 and 1984, the average compen-   19
sation for victims who went to trial was $1 million in current dollars, according to
a Rand Corp. analysis. Average compensation for cases settled without a lawsuit was

$415,000. The biggest aviation payout in history followed the crash of Pan Am Flight 103 over Lockerbie, Scotland, in 1988. Settlements ranged all over the spectrum, with a couple dozen exceeding $10 million, according to Manhattan attorney Lee Kreindler, who acted as lead counsel. Dividing the total $500 million payout over the 270 victims yields an average award of $1.85 million. However, the families had to hand about a third of their awards to their lawyers, and they waited seven to eight years to see any money. And the families of the six people killed in the 1993 World Trade Center bombing are still waiting for their day in civil court.

In the end, most families will probably choose the fund over litigation. The   20
Lockerbie millions are simply not a realistic possibility. It is always extremely difficult to sue the government. And the liability for the Sept. 11 attacks was capped by Congress at about $1.5 billion per plane. So while the families of those killed in the Pennsylvania and Pentagon crashes may have enough to go around, there are far too many victims in New York. "The court model works perfectly when you don't have $50 billion in damages or 3,000 deaths," says Leo Boyle, a Boston lawyer and president of the Association of Trial Lawyers of America, which supports the fund option and has lined up more than 2,000 attorneys to offer free help navigating its rules. Even without the caps, Boyle insists, victims could not have extracted more money by putting United and American Airlines through bankruptcy. So far, only a handful of suits have been filed.

In any event, there was no talking Congress out of the liability caps when it   21
drafted the airline-bailout package 10 days after the attacks. The airlines could not fly without insurance, and their coverage was far short of what it would take to pay the damages. Federal Reserve Chairman Alan Greenspan privately told congressional leaders that getting the planes up again was the single biggest "multiplier" that could revive the economy on every level. So the Democrats, who usually balk at limiting the ability to sue, accepted the idea of an airline bailout—as long as it came with a mechanism to compensate victims. Oklahoma Senator Don Nickles, the No. 2 Republican in the Senate and a longtime proponent of tort reform, pushed hard to limit how much the victims' families could claim, but he did not prevail.

But once the interim rules were drawn up by Feinberg's office—in conjunction   22
with the Department of Justice and the Office of Management and Budget—there were some surprises. In particular, the figures for pain and suffering astonished some who had backed the fund. "The numbers are low by any measure," says Boyle. Feinberg says he chose the $250,000 figure because that's how much beneficiaries receive from the Federal Government when fire fighters and police die on the job. The additional $50,000 for the spouse and each child is, he admits, "just some rough approximation of what I thought was fair." He calls the fund "rough justice."

The American Tort Reform Association, backed mostly by Republicans, has   23
been lobbying since 1986 to limit noneconomic damages in some suits to $250,000. John Ashcroft, head of the Justice Department, pushed for such a cap on punitive damages when he was a Senator. But Feinberg, a Democrat, insists he was not pressured by the Administration to keep the numbers low.

No matter how many times tearful widows accuse him of protecting the airlines,   24
Feinberg does not blush. A lawyer with decades of experience in the messy art of

compromise (Feinberg was special master for the $180 million distributed to veterans exposed to Agent Orange), he is accustomed to rage. "On Tuesday I get whacked for this or that in New Jersey. The next day it's New York. It goes with the job." But he rejects the theory that greed is a factor. "People have had a loved one wrenched from them suddenly, without warning, and we are only five months beyond that disaster. It was nearly yesterday. And they are desperately seeking, from what I've seen, to place as much of a value on that lost loved one as they can. So here is where they seek to amplify the value of that memory. They do it by saying we want more, as a validation of the loss. That's not greed. That's human nature."

Susan and Harvey Blomberg of Fairfield County, Conn., have been to three meetings on the victim-compensation fund, even though, as parents of a victim who has left a wife and kids behind, they are not in line for compensation. The rules give preference to the victim's spouse and children. But the Blombergs come to these meetings to be part of something, to be counted. And they linger after everyone else has left. "My daughter-in-law was upset when we went to the meetings," Susan says. "She said, 'It's not really about you. It's about the widows and children.' And I said, 'I want more information.' You can't compare grief, because nobody can get inside you. But I feel like an orphan. When they did this formula, why didn't they consider the parents? My daughter-in-law was married for five years. We had Jonathan for 33 years." 25

"It's a horrible thing that this is where our energies need to be pulled," says Cheri Sparacio, 37, the widow of Thomas Sparacio, a currency trader at Euro Brokers who died in Tower 2. In their modest house in Staten Island, littered with the toys of her twin two-year-olds, she explains why she sees the estimated $138,000 she would 26

HOW THREE FAMILIES COULD FARE

To estimate these families' awards, TIME asked Gary Albrecht, head of the society of Litigation Economists, to run some numbers based on the fund's draft rules:

THE INSURANCE EXECUTIVE

Risk Calculus: Halvorson's job took him to distant lands, so he bought extra insurance.

Families with large insurance policies, like this one, will get much smaller awards under the rules

- **Victim:** James Halvorson, 56, earned $500,000 a year at Marsh & McLennan. Married with one adult son. Caretaker for mother.
- **Gross Award:** $1.4 million
- **Deductions:** $2.6 million for multiple Insurance policies
- **Final award:** $0

THE CURRENCY TRADER

Father Figure: Sporacio with twins Jonathan and Eric. A third son is due in March.

Traditional death benefits like Social Security will shrink the award

- **Victim:** Thomas Sporacio, 35 earned $60,000 at Euro Brokers. Married with twins, age 2, and a baby on the way
- **Gross Award:** $1.6 million
- **Deductions:** $491,842 Social Security, $379,084 workers' compensation; $543,890 life insurance and pension
- **Final Award:** $137,842

THE SECURITY GUARD

Quiet Hero: Fields, with his four children, died helping others escape from the towers

This family starts out with the smallest award, but ends up with the largest

- **Victim:** Samuel Fields, 36, worked for Summit Security, earning $22,000 a year. Married with four kids and one on the way
- **Gross Award:** $1 million
- **Deductions:** $215,864 Social Security, $263,757 workers' compensation, $90,236 life insurance
- **Final Award:** $444,010

---

get from the fund as a cheap bribe. "The government is not taking any responsibility for what it's done. This was just one screw-up after another." She is also worried about her financial stability; in less than a month, she will have their third child. Thomas was the primary wage earner, although Cheri worked as a part-time school psychologist until Sept. 11. She doesn't see how she can go back to work with an infant and two toddlers unless she hires full-time help. "Please, come step into my shoes for a minute," she says, her eyes flat and unblinking. "I am not looking to go to Tahiti."

But uptown in the apartment where Samuel Fields once lived, the fund acts like 27 a quiet equalizer, a way for the government to guarantee that victims with less insurance emerge with basic support. Fields was a security guard for six years in Tower 1.

He made $22,000 a year and lived with his family in a housing project in Harlem. On Sept. 11, he helped people evacuate the building and then went back inside to help some more. Fields never came home. Next month his widow Angela will give birth to their fifth child. Because Fields made a small salary, his family's preliminary award is less than Sparacio's. But his family's deductions are also smaller. In the end, Angela's estimated $444,010 award will probably be three times the size of Cheri's.

28   In valuing different lives differently—the first part of the equation—the fund follows common legal practice. Courts always grant money on the basis of a person's earning power in life. That's because the courts are not attempting to replace "souls," says Philip Bobbitt, a law professor at the University of Texas who has written about the allocation of scarce resources in times of tragedy. "We're not trying to make you psychologically whole. Where we can calculate the loss is in economic loss." The Feinberg plan differs from legal norms in deducting the value of life insurance and pensions. Also, it allows no flexibility in determining noneconomic damages. In court, pain and suffering would be weighed individually.

29   Money aside, a lawsuit can be an investigative device like no other, forcing answers about what led to a death. Some Sept. 11 families say they might file suit for that reason alone, even if they never get a dime. And for other families, there is enormous value in no lawsuits at all. David Gordenstein lost his wife, Lisa Fenn Gordenstein, on American Flight 11. "Am I sad? I've had my heart torn out," he says. But he would rather devote his life to raising his two young daughters than pursuing a lawsuit. He will probably file a claim with the federal fund, which he acknowledges is not perfect. "I am proud of what my country tried to do. I think the intention is noble."

30   The night before Lisa died, she slipped a clipping under the door of David's home office, something she often did. It was a saying from theologian Charles Swindoll that read, "Attitude, to me, is more important than facts. It is more important than the past, than education, than money, than circumstances, than failures, than successes, than what other people think or say or do . . . It will make or break a company, a church, a home." David read it at her memorial. And while he jokes that it's kind of clichéd—"typical Lisa"—he says he thinks its message might help carry his family through this.

Richard Rodriguez (1944–   ), the son of Mexican immigrants, grew up in Sacramento, California, and received a B.A. from Stanford University and an M.A. from Columbia University. He completed graduate study at the University of California, Berkeley, and at the Warburg Institute in London on a Fulbright Fellowship. In 1982, he published *Hunger of Memory: The Education of Richard Rodriguez,* a collection of autobiographical essays describing the challenges of growing up in an immigrant household and of enduring the process of assimilation into the American mainstream. His *Days of Obligation* (1992) was a Pulitzer Prize finalist, and he won a Foster Peabody Award in 1997 for his essays on *The News Hour with Jim Lehrer,* the PBS news program on which he is a social commentator. He is currently a contributing editor at New American Media in San Francisco and is writing a book on monotheism and desert ecology.

The Fear of Losing a Culture

Richard Rodriguez

What is culture, after all? The immigrant shrugs. Latin Americans initially come   1
to the U.S. with only the things they need in mind—not abstractions like culture. They need dollars. They need food. Maybe they need to get out of the way of bullets. Most of us who concern ourselves with Hispanic-American culture, as painters, musicians, writers—or as sons and daughters—are the children of immigrants. We have grown up on this side of the border, in the land of Elvis Presley and Thomas Edison. Our lives are prescribed by the mall, by the 7-Eleven, by the Internal Revenue Service. Our imaginations vacillate between an Edenic Latin America, which nevertheless betrayed our parents, and the repellent plate-glass doors of a real American city, which has been good to us.

Hispanic-American culture stands where the past meets the future. The cul-   2
tural meeting represents not just a Hispanic milestone, not simply a celebration at the crossroads. America transforms into pleasure what it cannot avoid. Hispanic-American culture of the sort that is now in evidence (the teen movie, the rock song) may exist in an hourglass, may in fact be irrelevant. The U.S. Border Patrol works through the night to arrest the flow of illegal immigrants over the border, even as Americans stand patiently in line for *La Bamba.* While Americans vote to declare, once and for all, that English shall be the official language of the U.S., Madonna starts recording in Spanish.

Before a national TV audience, Rita Moreno tells Geraldo Rivera that her   3
dream as an actress is to play a character rather like herself: "I speak English perfectly well . . . I'm not dying from poverty . . . I want to play that kind of Hispanic woman, which is to say, an American citizen." This is an actress talking; these are show-biz pieties. But Moreno expresses as well a general Hispanic-American predicament. Hispanics want to belong to America without betraying the past.

Yet we fear losing ground in any negotiation with America. Our fear, most of all, is of losing our culture.

We come from an expansive, an intimate, culture that has long been judged 4 second-rate by the U.S. Out of pride as much as affection, we are reluctant to give up our past. Our notoriety in the U.S. has been our resistance to assimilation. The guarded symbol of Hispanic-American culture has been the tongue of flame: Spanish. But the remarkable legacy Hispanics carry from Latin America is not language—an inflatable skin—but breath itself, capacity of soul, an inclination to live. The genius of Latin America is the habit of synthesis. We assimilate.

What Latin America knows is that people create one another when they 5 meet. In the music of Latin America you will hear the litany of bloodlines: the African drum, the German accordion, the cry from the minaret. The U.S. stands as the opposing New World experiment. In North America the Indian and the European stood separate. Whereas Latin America was formed by a Catholic dream of one world, of meltdown conversion, the U.S. was shaped by Protestant individualism. America has believed its national strength derives from separateness, from diversity. The glamour of the U.S. is the Easter promise: you can be born again in your lifetime. You can separate yourself from your past. You can get a divorce, lose weight, touch up your roots.

Immigrants still come for that promise, but the U.S. has wavered in its faith. 6 America is no longer sure that economic strength derives from individualism. And America is no longer sure that there is space enough, sky enough, to sustain the cabin on the prairie. Now, as we near the end of the American Century, two alternative cultures beckon the American imagination: the Asian and the Latin American. Both are highly communal cultures, in contrast to the literalness of American culture. Americans devour what they might otherwise fear to become. Sushi will make them lean, subtle corporate warriors. Combination Plate No. 3, smothered in mestizo gravy, will burn a hole in their hearts.

Latin America offers passion. Latin America has a life—big clouds, unam- 7 biguous themes, tragedy, epic—that the U.S., for all its quality of life, yearns to have. Latin America offers an undistressed leisure, a crowded kitchen table, even a full sorrow. Such is the urgency of America's need that it reaches right past a fledgling, homegrown Hispanic-American culture for the darker bottle of Mexican beer, for the denser novel of a Latin American master.

For a long time, Hispanics in the U.S. felt hostility. Perhaps because we were 8 preoccupied by nostalgia, we withheld our Latin American gift. We denied the value of assimilation. But as our presence is judged less foreign in America, we will produce a more generous art, less timid, less parochial. Hispanic Americans do not have a pure Latin American art to offer. Expect bastard themes. Expect winking ironies, comic conclusions. For Hispanics live on this side of the border, where Kraft manufactures Mexican-style Velveeta, and where Jack in the Box serves Fajita Pita. Expect marriage. We will change America even as we will be changed. We will disappear with you into a new miscegenation.

Along and across the border there remain real conflicts, real fears. But the 9 ancient tear separating Europe from itself—the Catholic Mediterranean from the

Protestant north—may yet heal itself in the New World. For generations, Latin America has been the place, the bed, of a confluence of so many races and cultures that Protestant North America shuddered to imagine it.

The time has come to imagine it. 10

Questions for Discussion

1. Why do you think Rodriguez begins with a direct question about culture? What is more present in the minds of immigrants than culture? What's paradoxical in his description of how immigrants' children imagine the places representing their cultural geography?

2. What does Rodriguez mean by the Hispanic-American culture standing "where the past meets the future"?

3. How does Rita Moreno's comment to Geraldo Rivera communicate what Hispanics want?

4. How do you react to the writer's claim that the United States sees his culture as "second-rate"? To his description of Americans' resentment of Spanish speakers? Offer support from your personal experience or popular culture for support.

5. How do Asian and Latin American cultures appeal to the American imagination? What do you think Rodriguez means by the terms "communal" cultures as opposed to the "literalness" of Americans?

6. What does America envy about Latin American culture? What should it expect from its art in the future?

7. How does Rodriguez's portrayal of American attitudes toward Hispanic Americans relate to Judith Ortiz Cofer's description in "The Myth of the Latin Woman" of her treatment as a Puerto Rican American?

Questions for Reflection and Writing

1. Compare this essay's main points to those of Peter Marin in "Toward Something American" and the dilemma he sees immigrants as facing. How do both essays treat the subject of cultural assimilation and alienation? How do the essays compare in their portraits of "mainstream" America's response to Hispanic-Americans?

2. Explain Rodriguez's point that Latin America's and North America's histories represent opposing attitudes toward assimilation. Are the examples he cites effective? How do you interpret Rodriguez's remark that "people create one another when they meet"? Is this merely poetic, or is it accurate? How desirable is this creation or re-creation, in your opinion?

3. In a brief essay, analyze the writer's culinary metaphor involving Americans' reactions to sushi and the mestizo gravy-covered combination plate. What does Rodriguez mean by saying Americans "devour what they might otherwise fear to become"? Do you agree? Look up the origin of the word mestizo: how are its meaning and the reference to "combination plate" significant, given the writer's focus on Americans' feelings toward assimilation?

Elizabeth Cady Stanton (1815–1902) was born in Johnstown, New York, and attended Emma Willard's Troy Female Seminary. She was a pioneering women's rights leader and a writer. Stanton was also the editor of the national feminist newspaper *Revolution*, a contemporary of Susan B. Anthony, and president of the National Women's Suffrage Association from 1869 to 1890. She and Anthony can reasonably be said to have started the women's movement in the United States. In this reminiscence, Stanton recalls two life-changing events from her youth. "You Should Have Been a Boy!" is taken from her autobiography, *Eighty Years and More (1815–1897): Reminiscences of Elizabeth Cady Stanton* (1898).

You Should Have Been a Boy!

Elizabeth Cady Stanton

When I was eleven years old, two events occurred which changed considerably the current of my life. My only brother, who had just graduated from Union College, came home to die. A young man of great talent and promise, he was the pride of my father's heart. We early felt that this son filled a larger place in our father's affections and future plans than the five daughters together. Well do I remember how tenderly he watched my brother in his last illness, the sighs and tears he gave vent to as he slowly walked up and down the hall, and, when the last sad moment came, and we were all assembled to say farewell in the silent chamber of death, how broken were his utterances as he knelt and prayed for comfort and support. I still recall, too, going into the large darkened parlor to see my brother, and finding the casket, mirrors, and pictures all draped in white, and my father seated by his side, pale and immovable. As he took no notice of me, after standing a long while, I climbed upon his knee, when he mechanically put his arm about me and, with my head resting against his beating heart, we both sat in silence, he thinking of the wreck of all his hopes in the loss of a dear son, and I wondering what could be said or done to fill the void in his breast. At length he heaved a deep sigh and said: "Oh, my daughter, I wish you were a boy!" Throwing my arms about his neck, I replied: "I will try to be all my brother was."

Then and there I resolved that I would not give so much time as heretofore to play, but would study and strive to be at the head of all my classes and thus delight my father's heart. All that day and far into the night I pondered the problem of boyhood. I thought that the chief thing to be done in order to equal boys was to be learned and courageous. So I decided to study Greek and learn to manage a horse. Having formed this conclusion I fell asleep. My resolutions, unlike many such made at night, did not vanish with the coming light. I arose early and hastened to put them into execution. They were resolutions never to be forgotten—destined to mold my character anew. As soon as I was dressed I hastened to our good pastor, Rev. Simon Hosack, who was always early at work in his garden.

"Doctor," said I, "which do you like best, boys or girls?"

"Why, girls, to be sure; I would not give you for all the boys in Christendom." 4

"My father," I replied, "prefers boys; he wishes I was one, and I intend to be as 5
near like one as possible. I am going to ride on horseback and study Greek. Will
you give me a Greek lesson now, doctor? I want to begin at once."

"Yes, child," said he, throwing down his hoe, "come into my library and we 6
will begin without delay."

He entered fully into the feeling of suffering and sorrow which took possession 7
of me when I discovered that a girl weighed less in the scale of being than a boy,
and he praised my determination to prove the contrary. The old grammar which
he had studied in the University of Glasgow was soon in my hands, and the Greek
article was learned before breakfast.

Then came the sad pageantry of death, the weeping of friends, the dark rooms, 8
the ghostly stillness, the exhortation to the living to prepare for death, the solemn
prayer, the mournful chant, the funeral cortege, the solemn, tolling bell, the burial.
How I suffered during those sad days! What strange undefined fears of the unknown
took possession of me! For months afterward, at the twilight hour, I went with my
father to the new-made grave. Near it stood two tall poplar trees, against one of which
I leaned, while my father threw himself on the grave, with outstretched arms, as if to
embrace his child. At last the frosts and storms of November came and threw a chilling barrier between the living and the dead, and we went there no more.

During all this time I kept up my lessons at the parsonage and made rapid 9
progress. I surprised even my teacher, who thought me capable of doing anything. I
learned to drive, and to leap a fence and ditch on horseback. I taxed every power,
hoping some day to hear my father say: "Well, a girl is as good as a boy, after all." But
he never said it. When the doctor came over to spend the evening with us, I would
whisper in his ear: "Tell my father how fast I get on," and he would tell him, and
was lavish in his praises. But my father only paced the room, sighed, and showed that
he wished I were a boy; and I, not knowing why he felt thus, would hide my tears
of vexation on the doctor's shoulder.

Soon after this I began to study Latin, Greek, and mathematics with a class of 10
boys in the Academy, many of whom were much older than I. For three years one
boy kept his place at the head of the class, and I always stood next. Two prizes were
offered in Greek. I strove for one and took the second. How well I remember my
joy in receiving that prize. There was no sentiment of ambition, rivalry, or triumph
over my companions, nor feeling of satisfaction in receiving this honor in the presence of those assembled on the day of the exhibition. One thought alone filled my
mind. "Now," said I, "my father will be satisfied with me." So, as soon as we were dis-
missed, I ran down the hill, rushed breathless into his office, laid the new Greek
Testament, which was my prize, on his table and exclaimed: "There, I got it!" He
took up the book, asked me some questions about the class, the teachers, the spec-
tators, and evidently pleased, handed it back to me. Then, while I stood looking and
waiting for him to say something which would show that he recognized the equality of the daughter with the son, he kissed me on the forehead and exclaimed, with
a sigh, "Ah, you should have been a boy!"

Sojourner Truth (1797–1883) was born a slave in Hurley, New York, under the name Isabella Baumfree. She became a free woman in 1827 when New York State abolished slavery, and changed her name to Sojourner Truth in 1843 to express her religious convictions. Although unable to read or write, Truth made a name for herself as an electrifying speaker. She toured the nation with black leaders like Frederick Douglass, speaking out for equality, both racial and sexual. Truth met with Abraham Lincoln in 1864, advising him about the problems the newly freed slaves faced. She gave her "Ain't I a Woman" speech in 1851 at the Women's Rights Convention in Akron, Ohio. This speech was faithfully recorded in the June 21, 1851, issue of the *Anti-Slavery Bugle*, edited by Marcus Robinson (with whom Truth worked). In 1863, Truth's speech was rewritten by Frances Dana Gage, the organizer of the 1851 Akron convention, and published in the April 23, 1863, issue of the New York *Independent*. Though well-meaning, Gage's version perpetuated inaccuracies about Truth and her speech, most notably in characterizing the northern-born Truth as speaking in Southern dialect. Robinson's text and Gage's version are both reproduced below.

Ain't I a Woman?

Sojourner Truth

MARCUS ROBINSON, FROM *THE ANTI-SLAVERY BUGLE*, JUNE 21, 1851

One of the most unique and interesting speeches of the convention was made by Sojourner Truth, an emancipated slave. It is impossible to transfer it to paper, or convey any adequate idea of the effect it produced upon the audience. Those only can appreciate it who saw her powerful form, her whole-souled, earnest gesture, and listened to her strong and truthful tones. She came forward to the platform and addressing the President said with great simplicity: "May I say a few words?" Receiving an affirmative answer, she proceeded: 1

> I want to say a few words about this matter. I am a woman's rights. I have as much muscle as any man, and can do as much work as any man. I have plowed and reaped and husked and chopped and mowed, and can any man do more than that? I have heard much about the sexes being equal. I can carry as much as any man, and can eat as much too, if I can get it. I am as strong as any man that is now. As for intellect, all I can say is, if a woman have a pint, and a man a quart—why can't she have her little pint full? You need not be afraid to give us our rights for fear we will take too much— for we can't take more than our pint'll hold. The poor men seems to be all in confusion, and don't know what to do. Why children, if you have woman's rights, give it to her and you will feel better. You will have your own rights, and they won't be so much trouble. I can't read, but I can hear. I have heard the bible and have learned that Eve caused man to sin. Well, if woman upset the world, do give her a chance to set it right side up again. The Lady has spoken about Jesus, how he never spurned woman from him, and she was right. When Lazarus died, Mary and Martha came to him with faith and love and besought him to raise their brother. And Jesus wept and Lazarus came forth. And how came Jesus into the world? Through God who created him and the woman who bore him. Man, where was your part? But the women are coming up blessed be God and a few of the men are coming up with them. But man is in a tight place, the poor slave is on him, woman is coming on him, he is surely between a hawk and a buzzard.

FRANCES DANA GAGE, FROM *THE NEW YORK INDEPENDENT*,
APRIL 23, 1863

The leaders of the movement trembled upon seeing a tall, gaunt black woman in a
gray dress and white turban, surmounted with an uncouth sunbonnet, march deliberately into the church, walk with the air of a queen up the aisle, and take her seat
upon the pulpit steps. A buzz of disapprobation was heard all over the house, and
there fell on the listening ear, "An abolition affair!" "Woman's rights and niggers!"
"I told you so!" "Go it, darkey!"

  I chanced on that occasion to wear my first laurels in public life as president of
the meeting. At my request order was restored and the business of the Convention
went on. Morning, afternoon, and evening exercises came and went. . . . Again
and again, timorous and trembling ones came to me and said, with earnestness, "Don't
let her speak, Mrs. Gage, it will ruin us. Every newspaper in the land will have our
cause mixed up with abolition and niggers and we shall be utterly denounced." My
only answer was, "We shall see when the time comes."

  The second day the work waxed warm. Methodist, Baptist, Episcopal,
Presbyterian, and Universalist ministers came in to hear and discuss the resolutions
presented. One claimed superior rights and privileges for man, on the grounds of
"superior intellect"; another, because of the "manhood of Christ; if God had desired
the equality of woman, He would have given some token of His will through the
birth, life and death of the Saviour." Another gave us a theological view of the "sin
of the first mother."

  There were very few women in those days who dared to "speak in meeting"
and the august teachers of the people were seemingly getting the best of us, while the
boys in the galleries, and the sneerers among the pews, were hugely enjoying the dis-
comfiture, as they supposed of the "strong-minded." . . . When, slowly from her seat
in the corner rose Sojourner Truth, who till now had scarcely lifted her head. "Don't
let her speak!" gasped half a dozen in my ear. She moved slowly and solemnly to
the front, laid her old bonnet at her feet, and turned her great speaking eyes to me.
There was a hissing sound of disapprobation above and below. I rose and announced
"Sojourner Truth," and begged the audience to keep silence for a few moments.

  The tumult subsided at once, and every eye was fixed on this almost Amazon
form, which stood nearly six feet high, head erect, and eyes piercing the upper air
like one in a dream. At her first word there was a profound hush. She spoke in deep
tones, which, though not loud, reached every ear in the house, and away through the
throng at the doors and windows.

  "Wall, chilern, whar dar is so much racket dar must be somethin' out o' kilter.
I tink dat 'twixt de nigger of de Souf and de womin at de Norf, all talkin' 'bout rights,
de white men will be in a fix pretty soon. But what's all dis here talkin' 'bout?

  "Dat man ober dar say dat womin needs to be helped into carriages, and lifted
ober ditches, and to hab de best place everywhar. Nobody eber halps me into carriages, or ober mudpuddles, or gibs me any best place!"

  And raising herself to her full height, and her voice to a pitch like rolling thunder, she asked, "And ar'n't I a woman? Look at me! Look at my arm! [And here she

2

3

4

5

6

7

8

9

bared her right arm to the shoulder, showing her tremendous muscular power] " I have ploughed, and planted, and gathered into barns, and no man could head me! And ar'n't I a woman? I could work as much and eat as much as a man—when I could get it—and bear de lash as well! And ar'n't' I a woman? I have borne thirteen chilern, and seen 'em mos' all sold off the slavery, and when I cried out with my mother's grief, none but Jesus heard me! And ar'n't I a woman?

"Den dey talks 'bout dis ting in de head; what dis dey call it?" "Intellect," whispered someone near. "Dat's it, honey. What's dat got to do wid womin's rights or nigger's rights? If my cup won't hold but a pint, and yourn holds a quart, wouldn't ye be mean not to let me have my little half-measure full?" And she pointed her significant finger, and sent a keen glance at the minister who had made the argument. The cheering was long and loud.   10

"Den dat little man in black dar, he say women can't have as much rights as men, 'cause Christ wan't a woman! Whar did your Christ come from?" Rolling thunder couldn't have stilled that crowd, as did those deep, wonderful tones, as she stood there with outstretched arms and eyes of fire. Raising her voice still louder, she repeated, "Whar did your Christ come from? From God and a woman! Man had nothin' to do wid Him." Oh, what a rebuke that was to the little man.   11

Turning again to another objector, she took up the defense of Mother Eve, I cannot follow her through it all. It was pointed and witty, and solemn; eliciting at almost every sentence deafening applause; and she ended by asserting, "If de fust woman God ever made was strong enough to turn de world upside down all alone, dese women togedder [and she glanced her eye over the platform] ought to be able to turn it back, and get it right side up again! And now dey is asking to do it, de men better let 'em." Long continued cheering greeted this. "Bleeged to ye for hearin' on me, and now ole Sojourner han't got nothin' more to say."   12

Amid roars of applause, she returned to her corner, leaving more than one of us with streaming eyes, and hearts beating with gratitude. She had taken us up in her strong arms and carried us safely over the slough of difficulty, turning the whole tide in our favor. I have never in my life seen anything like the magical influence that subdued the mobbish spirit of the day, and turned the sneers and jeers of an excited crowd into notes of respect and admiration. Hundreds rushed up to shake hands with her, and congratulate the glorious old mother, and bid her God-speed on her mission of "testifyin' agin concerning the wickedness of this 'ere people."   13

Kurt Vonnegut (1922–2007) received an M.A. in 1971 from the University of Chicago, which he originally left in 1947 due to lack of money after drafting three theses. A testament to his esteemed publishing career, University of Chicago accepted his novel *Cat's Cradle* (1963) in place of a thesis in awarding his degree. Born in 1922 in Indianapolis, Indiana, Vonnegut studied from 1940–1942 at Cornell University before enlisting in the U.S. Army. While serving, Vonnegut fought in the Battle of the Bulge and was taken prisoner of war, wounded, and received the Purple Heart. War is a common theme throughout many of his published writings which include fifteen novels, five collections of short stories, eight plays, and various essays published in collections and in periodicals such as *Cosmopolitan*, the *Ladies' Home Journal*, and the *Saturday Evening Post*. His work is known for combining science fiction, philosophy, and humor, and for its pessimism about the possibility of a meaningful life, with human kindness as perhaps the only saving grace. Some of Vonnegut's best-known works include *Slaughterhouse Five* (1969), *Breakfast of Champions* (1973), and *Jailbird* (1979). This short piece entitled "How to write with style" was originally published in 1980 by the International Paper Company.

How To Write With Style

Kurt Vonnegut

Newspaper reporters and technical writers are trained to reveal almost nothing about themselves in their writings. This makes them freaks in the world of writers, since almost all of the other ink-stained wretches in that world reveal a lot about themselves to readers. We call these revelations, accidental and intentional, elements of style. 1

These revelations tell us as readers what sort of person it is with whom we are spending time. Does the writer sound ignorant or informed, stupid or bright, crooked or honest, humorless or playful—? And on and on. 2

Why should you examine your writing style with the idea of improving it? Do so as a mark of respect for your readers, whatever you're writing. If you scribble your thoughts any which way, your readers will surely feel that you care nothing about them. They will mark you down as an egomaniac or a chowderhead—or worse, they will stop reading you. 3

The most damning revelation you can make about yourself is that you do not know what is interesting and what is not. Don't you yourself like or dislike writers mainly for what they choose to show you or make you think about? Did you ever admire an empty-headed writer for his or her mastery of the language? No. 4

So your own winning style must begin with ideas in your head. 5

FIND A SUBJECT YOU CARE ABOUT

Find a subject you care about and which you in your heart feel others should care about. It is this genuine caring, and not your games with language, which will be the most compelling and seductive element in your style. 6

I am not urging you to write a novel, by the way—although I would not be   7
sorry if you wrote one, provided you genuinely cared about something. A petition
to the mayor about a pothole in front of your house or a love letter to the girl next
door will do.

DO NOT RAMBLE, THOUGH

I won't ramble on about that.   8

KEEP IT SIMPLE

As for your use of language: Remember that two great masters of language,   9
William Shakespeare and James Joyce, wrote sentences which were almost child-
like when their subjects were most profound. "To be or not to be?" asks
Shakespeare's Hamlet. The longest word is three letters long. Joyce, when he was
frisky, could put together a sentence as intricate as a necklace for Cleopatra, but
my favorite sentence in his short story "Eveline" is this one: "She was tired." At
that point in the story, no other words could break the heart of a reader as those
three words do.

Simplicity of language is not only reputable, but perhaps even sacred. The   10
Bible opens with a sentence well within the writing skills of a lively fourteen-year-
old: "In the beginning God created the heaven and the earth."

HAVE THE GUTS TO CUT

It may be that you, too, are capable of making necklaces for Cleopatra, so to speak.   11
But your eloquence should be the servant of the ideas in your head. Your rule
might be this: If a sentence, no matter how excellent, does not illuminate your
subject in some new and useful way, scratch it out.

SOUND LIKE YOURSELF

The writing style which is most natural to you is bound to echo the speech you   12
heard when a child. English was the novelist Joseph Conrad's third language, and
much that seems piquant in his use of English was no doubt colored by his first language, which was Polish. And lucky indeed is the writer who has grown up in
Ireland, for the English spoken there is so amusing and musical. I myself grew up
in Indianapolis, where common speech sounds like a band saw cutting galvanized
tin, and employs a vocabulary as unornamental as a monkey wrench.

In some of the more remote hollows of Appalachia, children still grow up   13
hearing songs and locutions of Elizabethan times. Yes, and many Americans grow
up hearing a language other than English, or an English dialect a majority of
Americans cannot understand.

All these varieties of speech are beautiful, just as the varieties of butterflies are   14
beautiful. No matter what your first language, you should treasure it all your life.
If it happens not to be standard English, and if it shows itself when you write standard English, the result is usually delightful, like a very pretty girl with one eye that
is green and one that is blue.

I myself find that I trust my own writing most, and others seem to trust it most,   15
too, when I sound most like a person from Indianapolis, which is what I am. What
alternatives do I have? The one most vehemently recommended by teachers has
no doubt been pressed on you, as well: to write like cultivated Englishmen of a
century or more ago.

SAY WHAT YOU MEAN TO SAY

I used to be exasperated by such teachers, but I am no more. I understand now   16
that all those antique essays and stories with which I was to compare my own
work were not magnificent for their datedness or foreignness, but for saying precisely what their authors meant them to say. My teachers wished me to write
accurately, always selecting the most effective words, and relating the words to
one another unambiguously, rigidly, like parts of a machine. The teachers did not
want to turn me into an Englishman after all. They hoped that I would become
understandable—and therefore understood. And there went my dream of doing
with words what Pablo Picasso did with paint or what any number of jazz idols did
with music. If I broke all the rules of punctuation, had words mean whatever I
wanted them to mean, and strung them together higgledy-piggledy, I would simply not be understood. So you, too, had better avoid Picasso-style or jazz-style writing, if you have something worth saying and wish to be understood.

Readers want our pages to look very much like pages they have seen before.   17
Why? This is because they themselves have a tough job to do, and they need all
the help they can get from us.

PITY THE READERS

They have to identify thousands of little marks on paper, and make sense of them   18
immediately. They have to *read,* an art so difficult that most people don't really
master it even after having studied it all through grade school and high school—
twelve long years.

So this discussion must finally acknowledge that our stylistic options as writ-   19
ers are neither numerous nor glamorous, since our readers are bound to be such
imperfect artists. Our audience requires us to be sympathetic and patient teachers,
ever willing to simplify and clarify—whereas we would rather soar high above the
crowd, singing like nightingales.

That is the bad news. The good news is that we Americans are governed   20
under a unique Constitution, which allows us to write whatever we please without
fear of punishment. So the most meaningful aspect of our styles, which is what we
choose to write about, is utterly unlimited.

FOR REALLY DETAILED ADVICE

For a discussion of literary style in a narrower sense, in a more technical sense, I   21
commend to your attention *The Elements of Style,* by William Strunk, Jr. and E.B.
White (Macmillan, 1979). E.B. White is, of course, one of the most admirable literary stylists this country has so far produced.

You should realize, too, that no one would care how well or how badly   22
Mr. White expressed himself, if he did not have perfectly enchanting things to say.

Questions for Discussion

1. According to Vonnegut, what makes newspaper reporters and technical writers "freaks in the world of writers" (paragraph 1)? Why does Vonnegut include this information in the opening of his piece?

2. What three examples does Vonnegut give readers of well-known written texts that use simple language? Do you find these three examples convincing in terms of "simplicity of language" being important in your own writing? Why or why not?

3. Examine the metaphor that Vonnegut uses in his piece that compares a descriptive sentence to "a necklace for Cleopatra." How does this metaphor illustrate the point Vonnegut is making about wordy sentences? Is this metaphor effective for promoting the use of simple language? Why or why not?

4. How does Vonnegut feel about "varieties of speech" and their use in writing? Why?

5. Vonnegut writes about his "dream of doing with words what Pablo Picasso did with paint or what any number of jazz idols did with music." What are his reasons for giving up this dream and what does he suggest instead? Do you agree or disagree with Vonnegut's advice to distance writing in terms of expression from art forms such as painting and music?

6. Look closely at the last sentence of Vonnegut's piece. How would you describe the author's tone? How does Vonnegut's tone in his closing paragraph ultimately reinforce the advice he is giving? Why?

Questions for Reflection and Writing

1. Vonnegut writes "that he used to be exasperated by such teachers" who wanted to have him compare his writing to other authors. Think of your own experiences with writing teachers. Was there anything similarly "exasperating" for you as a writer with a teacher? Or was there something equally illuminating or productive you learned from a writing teacher? Reflect on a time in your own writing education where a teacher had a strong effect on you as a student and write a short response about it. Now, compare what you wrote with a fellow student's response and note the differences and similarities.

2. Do you feel your writing "echo[s] the speech you heard as a child" (paragraph 12)? Why or why not? Does your writing represent your own "variety of speech"? If so, what "variety of speech" does it represent? In a short essay, try to identify what your writing sounds like and if it is an authentic representation of the way you speak.

3. Are there any particular sections of Vonnegut's piece where he seems to have a very specific audience in mind? If so, what would this audience consist of? Are there any suggestions you might want to make to Vonnegut in order to make his piece reach a broader audience? If so, what would these be?

Unit 6: Research Essay

2 CHAPTER

Conducting Traditional Academic Research

You're sitting in class, and your teacher asks you to write a paper on the history of television. No problem. You love TV, watch it all the time, and have plenty to say about it. She explains the details of the paper, and as you watch the clock, hoping you'll get out a few minutes early, you hear her say a few dreaded words: "I want eight outside sources on this paper." Your heart sinks. You've written very few research papers in your life, and you've never used the library where you're going to school right now. You even start to wonder if it's too late to drop the class, but because this course is a requirement for your major, you really have no choice. You're going to have to do some research. The last time you wrote a paper, you hit Google and found a lot of great articles; you quoted them and listed them correctly in parenthetical citations and on the works-cited page. However, your teacher marked you down because your sources weren't good enough. You're really not sure how to find the right sources, or even what makes one source scholarly and another one unacceptable, and you're starting to freak out just a little.

Don't panic. This reaction is typical when it comes to writing papers. In fact, one of the most fundamental steps to mastering information competency is to understand what sources you should and shouldn't trust. When writing an academic paper, you'll want to present top-notch sources so that your audience will respect your arguments. The trouble is, trustworthy sources are often hard to find, and many are not online yet. To do proper research, you'll probably have to go to an academic library and hit the stacks of books yourself.

Many instructors will insist that your paper draw exclusively on scholarly sources—work written by and for scholars. This chapter focuses on how to find such sources and use them in your paper. (Other professors will allow sources that are less traditionally academic in nature; for tips on using those sources, see Chapter 3.) To gain competency over academic information, you must work toward a couple of goals. First, you must understand the tricks to navigating an academic library, and second, you must understand the basics of the modern academic search engine.

Research Tip: Librarians

Never forget to talk to your reference librarians. They are specialists in research and search engines. If they can't find the information you are looking for, it probably doesn't exist. Most librarians also know the different instructors on your campus, and they understand their expectations. They may even be able to suggest people you could interview to learn more about your subject. Finally, most libraries offer tours to groups and individuals as well as workshops and classes dedicated to research skills. Talk to your local librarians and your instructor to see if such options exist and are right for you.

NAVIGATING THE LIBRARY

Systems of Classification

The first step in understanding how a library works is to understand the basic system it uses to classify and catalog its sources. Without a basic knowledge of this, you'll never find the book you want, even if it's sitting on a shelf waiting for you to find it.

There are two primary systems used to organize a library's holdings in the United States: the Library of Congress Classification system (LCC) and the Dewey Decimal Classification system (DDC). Both of these systems generate specific numbers and letters to identify particular books. No matter what library you visit, the identifying information assigned to a book within each system will be the same.

To locate a book within a library, you need only match up the call number you've discovered when you searched the library's catalog with the number pasted on the spine of the book on the shelves (also known as "the stacks"). A library will use one of these two systems (your school's library will probably use the Library of Congress system, and your public library will probably use the Dewey Decimal system), so being familiar with both will help you tremendously when you use different libraries. There are also classification systems used commercially, the ISBN and ISSN systems, that ensure that every book published has a unique number for cataloging and ordering purposes.

An immediate goal of doing research is simply to find the books you're interested in. You will need to log on to a library catalog search engine, which in most libraries has replaced the outdated card catalog system, and identify pertinent books and find their call numbers. However, understanding the two classification systems will help you understand the numbers the search engine gives you. (For more information on how to use the search engines, see the Library Catalog Searches section on p. 22.)

LIBRARY OF CONGRESS CLASSIFICATION

If you're researching in an American academic library at the college or university level, there's a good chance your library will use the Library of Congress Classification system. The Library of Congress is the largest library in the world, containing more than 130 million items on approximately 530 miles of bookshelves. With so many books

Century

to organize, librarians developed a system of classification that makes organization easier and more uniform. When you look up a book using this system, you'll get a call number, such as the following: **PR2894.W43 2003.** Although this may look like a stream of random numbers, the system has its own logic: it divides all fields of study into twenty-one categories, each assigned a letter based on the following list.

A: General Works

B: Philosophy, Psychology, Religion

C: Auxiliary Sciences of History

D: World History and History of Europe, Asia, Africa, Australia, New Zealand, etc.

E: History of the Americas

F: History of the Americas

G: Geography, Anthropology, Recreation

H: Social Sciences

J: Political Science

K: Law

L: Education

M: Music and Books on Music

N: Fine Arts

P: Language and Literature

Q: Science

R: Medicine

S: Agriculture

T: Technology

U: Military Science

V: Naval Science

Z: Bibliography, Library Science, Information Resources (General)

Note: For a more comprehensive look at this list and the subdivisions, visit the Library of Congress website at http://www.loc.gov/catdir/cpso/lcco/lcco.html.

These twenty-one categories are also broken down into subcategories. For example, category P is language and literature, but if you see PS, you're dealing with American Literature, and PR is the prefix for English Literature. To get even more specific, the system then gives books a series of between one and four numbers, called a "caption." Each specific area of study is assigned a caption of numbers. For example, the call number **PR2894.W43 2003** is for a book on William Shakespeare called *Shakespeare: For All Time,* written by Stanley Wells in the year 2003. A similar call number, **PR2894. D88 1989,** is for a book that is also on the topic of Shakespeare: *William Shakespeare: A Literary Life,* by Richard Dutton, published in 1989.

Notice that both call numbers start with PR for English Literature and both have the caption number 2894, which is a number for the study of Shakespeare. Thus, any book that starts with PR2894 will be on the topic of Shakespeare, no matter what library the book is found in. As you explore your major field of study more and write more research papers, you'll find yourself slowly getting familiar with the call numbers in your particular area of interest.

Research Tip: Search the Stacks

Because Library of Congress call numbers follow this logical pattern, it is a great idea to get one or two good call numbers and then head back to the shelves where the books are located. After you find one book, its neighbors are sure to be on similar topics. Pick up the books on either side of the one you found through the search engine and scan through their tables of contents and indexes. You can find some great resources by browsing through these pages.

DEWEY DECIMAL CLASSIFICATION

If you're researching at a local public library or high school library, you're likely to find the Dewey Decimal Classification system in use instead of the LCC. The Dewey Decimal system is similar to the Library of Congress system in that it assigns a code for a general category and then gets more specific by adding a decimal followed by more numbers and letters to that initial number.

The Dewey Decimal system divides all knowledge into ten major categories, each with a basic three-digit number:

000   Generalities
100   Philosophy and Psychology
200   Religion
300   Social Sciences
400   Language
500   Natural Science and Mathematics
600   Technology (Applied Sciences)
700   The Arts
800   Literature and Rhetoric
900   Geography and History

Looking at literature again, we find that any book in the 800s deals with literature or rhetoric. More specifically, any book in the 820s will be about English Literature. The book *Shakespeare: For All Time,* mentioned earlier, has a Dewey Decimal number of **822.33 W4629s.** If you looked for more books on Shakespeare using the Dewey Decimal system, you'd soon learn that the number 822.33 will always be assigned to books about Shakespeare, so finding this one book will lead to many others on the same topic.

ISBN AND ISSN SYSTEMS

Similar to the call numbers generated by the Library of Congress and the Dewey Decimal systems, there is a number known as the International Standard Book Number, or ISBN. The ISBN is ten digits long (sometimes the letter X appears with the numbers to indicate the number 10 in a single digit), and it is always separated into four hyphenated sections. This number is not generated to help organize libraries; instead, it is primarily used in international marketing to ensure that every book has a unique number for cataloging and ordering purposes. The ISBN probably won't be used in your typical academic library, but it is a great way to identify books at bookstores. If you are using a web resource such as Amazon.com or Barnesandnoble.com to find out more about a book, the ISBN can ensure that you have the proper text.

Research Tip: Professors

Always remember that the instructors on your campus are experts in various fields of study. Professors who are teaching courses you are taking now or who taught courses you took in the past usually encourage inquisitive students to visit them in their offices. Take them up on this. Even professors whose courses you haven't taken yet may be willing to be interviewed on a subject or to give advice about research. You should be ready with some good questions and preliminary research to prove to them that you are seriously interested in their areas of study.

Also, many professors keep books and resources on reserve in your library. Ask them or the library staff what materials your professors may have on reserve—these could turn out to be some of the best sources on your subject.

LIBRARY CATALOG SEARCHES

Most libraries now use a computerized search engine as a way to navigate their book and journal holdings. Although search engines differ, some basic principles apply to all your searches. Many college libraries have a separate search engine for their book holdings and then subscribe to a few database services that will help you find periodical articles. On the next page is a look at Bakersfield College's Grace Van Dyke Bird Library's book catalog page. Most library catalogs will be fairly similar to this one.

The search scrollbar shows several types of searches you can execute. You must choose the best type of search for your particular needs, or you'll leave the library frustrated, unable to find sources that are sitting on the shelves, waiting to be discovered. The screen shown is for a basic search. The tabs at the top of the page, however, show several options that allow you to conduct more advanced searches, including

"Advanced" and "Power" searches. If you're unable to find a useful source or limit your search adequately using the basic search screen, go to an advanced search in your own library's book catalog for more options. Here is a sample of this library's "Power Search."

Note how many more options have come up to assist you in this Power Search. Now you can search by subject, title, author's name, keyword that is likely to be found, and any number of other options. These advanced searches may be intimidating, but play around with them and get to know their features. You can't break a search engine. (For tips on finding and narrowing a topic to research, see Chapter 1.)

Research Tip: Using Books in Research

When you have a book in hand, you are holding not only a potential source but also, figuratively, another kind of search engine. Inside a book that addresses your topic, you may find dozens of other sources you can use. Look at the source's works-cited list, footnotes, or endnotes. If you are examining a scholarly book, the author will have cited every single fact, idea, and statistic he or she has taken from other sources (unless the information is considered "common knowledge"). You can track down these sources using your library catalog.

You should also look at the table of contents and the index. A quick look at the table of contents will let you know if this book is really on the same topic as your paper. The index in the back of the book will identify pages mentioning key people, facts, concepts, and terminology that you should be looking for. If a key term related to your topic isn't listed in the index, the book may not be as helpful to you as you thought at first, and you may need to keep digging.

Types of Searches

You can perform several types of searches in most library catalogs, including searches by title, keyword, subject, author, and call number. You'll likely need each type of search eventually in your research career. Always keep in mind the type of search you're attempting. If you try to do a Title Search but provide the name of the author instead, you won't get any hits. This seemingly little mistake can cost you hours and send you packing up for home without any sources. The goal of every search is to end up with a call number so that you can find where the books are cataloged.

For each type of search described next, follow the example of the type of research done for the title search. In other words, after you find one book, let it lead you to more subjects, more titles, and more authors. You need to mine every source for as much information and as many leads to other sources as you can find.

TITLE SEARCH

If you already know the title of a book you are searching for, a **title search** is the easiest way to find its call number in your library. However, this type of search is also useful for searching for new sources. Use your imagination (and maybe a thesaurus). If you're researching a book on the subject of the history of television, for example, you can assume that books with useful information would include the words "history" and "television" in their titles. Thus, in the search box, you would enter "history television" and begin the title search. If your library has any books with these words in the title, you'll find them. This is often a great way to begin your research because authors typically include the most important concepts in the titles or subtitles of their books.

Following is an example of a title search using the words "history" and "television."

As you can see, eighteen titles in the Bakersfield College library match this search. This page typically shows you the call number (for this library, it is Library of Congress Classification), as well as whether the book is checked in. If you attend a larger university with multiple libraries, this search will also tell you at which library the book is housed. A quick look at the titles can probably rule out some of these sources right away. For example, source number one is an electronic book, source number two is a DVD, and book number three on the list is a traditional printbook called *Prime-time Television: A Concise History*. After you find a source that looks good, you can select it and look for more details about the book.

Several interesting options come up when you explore this book's entry (see page 26). Notice, for example, the list on the left side of the screen titled "Subjects." The subjects listed include "Television broadcasting—United States—History." In many search engines, these results will be hyperlinks, so if you click them, you'll be guided to all the other books written on this subject within the library. Similarly, the author's name is a hyperlink (in this case, there are three: Barbara Moore, Marvin R. Bensman, and Jim Van Dyke). You can click the name, and it will link to a list of all books in the library written by the author. Toward the bottom, you'll find which library the book is located in as well as the collection, whether it's on the shelf or checked out, when it's due back, and ultimately, the LCC call number: PN1992.3.U5 M623 2006.

Even though you started with a title search, after you get one hit, you can mine it for more and more information: subjects, authors, call numbers, and so on. This process is the same no matter which type of search you start with.

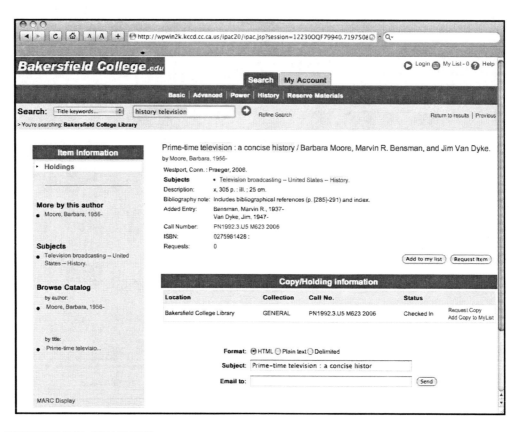

KEYWORD SEARCH

A second type of search is a **keyword search.** It may be called a "subject keyword" or some other slight variation in your particular library's database, but the function is the same. This type of search is a very broad search; it takes the word(s) you are interested in and searches for them in multiple areas—the author, title, etc. If the word(s) you identify are included anywhere in the database's entry, the book will show up in this search.

The keyword search has powerful strengths and some weaknesses. It is strong because it typically yields a great many results because it has very few parameters limiting it. This same thing, however, can be its weakness because sometimes you will get far too many results, and many of them may not be on the topic you had in mind. It is a fabulous place to start your searches, though, because it will very likely give you some books to start with.

AUTHOR SEARCH

Another type of search is the **author search,** which provides records on a specific author. Most authors become experts in one specific field of study, so if you have found one who has written a really good book on your subject, check to see if he or she has written a few more. When you conduct an author search, you'll need to consider how your college's catalog works. Some require you to list the author's last name and then the first name, whereas others allow you to use an author keyword search and will look for any author with that name.

Researchers can sometimes get confused when they look for books written about famous authors. If you are looking for books that discuss William Shakespeare or Plato, you should *not* do an author search because it will only find works written *by* these authors, not works *about* these authors. To find books about Plato, for example, you would need to do a subject or title search using "Plato" as your research parameter.

SUBJECT SEARCH

You can also conduct a **subject search,** a more advanced type of search than a title or author search. Many libraries use the Library of Congress's own system of subject headings, which have been in use since 1898 and are very well established. These headings, although very thorough, can be confusing and counterintuitive. You must be careful to specify the exact term when using these subject headings. For example, if you did a subject search using the search term "TV history" instead of "Television—History," which is the Library of Congress's term, you would find no books on your subject.

To find the proper subject terms, you need to consult the *Library of Congress Subject Headings Guides.* These are a series of large red books that are probably located very near the computers in your college's library (ask a librarian to direct you). If you look up the specific subject you're interested in, the guide will give you the headings used by the Library of Congress. They are often not what you would think they would be. For example, if you are researching the subject of date rape, you need to look under the subject heading "acquaintance rape." The *Library of Congress Subject Headings Guides* would cross-reference the term for you and point you in the right direction; however, if you jumped straight into a subject search without consulting the *Guides,* you may have missed several sources on your topic.

Following is a sample entry from the *Library of Congress Subject Heading Guides* (also called the "big red books" because they're big and red). If you looked up the term "television" in the guide, here is a brief portion of what you'd find (the entry for "television" takes up several pages in the *Guides*).

Television
- UF   Radio Vision
       TV
- BT   Artificial satellites in telecommunication
       Electronic systems
       Optoelectronic devices
       Telecommunications
- RT   Astronautics—Optical communication systems
- NT   African American women on television
       African Americans on television
       Aggressiveness on television

The abbreviations in this entry give you information about the other terms you could start searching under. UF means "used for." Any terms listed under UF (in this case "Radio Vision" and "TV") will be somewhat interchangeable with the term "television" in your searches. BT means "broader term" and indicates headings that you could use if you wanted to research subjects on a more general level than your initial search term.

For example, "Electronic systems" include dozens of technologies, of which television is only one. RT means "related term" and gives you terms for searches on topics that are similar to television.

NT means "narrower term." These terms will be more specific and give you a more focused search. In this example, "African Americans on television" comes up as just one of dozens of subfields you could explore. In this way, the *Guides* can help you to find a more narrow focus for an overly broad research topic.

Finally, the category SA, not shown in the example, means "see also." It indicates other terms you could use in your search. By learning how to navigate the entries in the *Library of Congress Subject Headings Guides,* you will have an easier time narrowing or broadening your focus, and you will be able to discover several alternative terms you can search with. Although you can find several subject headings on your own by searching your library's online catalog, you will not get as many variations as you will if you consult the big red books first.

CALL NUMBER/ISBN/ISSN SEARCH

After you find a call number using one of the search methods previously discussed, you can use a **call number** or **ISBN/ISSN search** to locate promising books on your subject. For a call number search, you would enter the call number you've found by copying and pasting the number and selecting "Call Number" in the scrollbar options. When you apply the search, the catalog should bring up a list of books by call number. As discussed earlier, the closer a book is to your initial call number, the closer it will be to your subject matter. A call number search is a great way to get a quick overview of how many holdings your particular library has on any given topic. If you use ISBN or ISSN numbers, you can search for them in the same manner.

Research Tip: Online Bookstores

To find information on a book quickly, go to an online bookstore and do a search on an author, a title, or even an ISBN you've found using any of the search methods mentioned in this chapter. This search will give you general information and perhaps an excerpt from a professional book-reviewing periodical, such as Library Journal, Kirkus Reviews, or *Publishers Weekly,* or from other reputable periodicals. This can be a handy way to quickly find information about a book or an author. Sometimes reviewers will compare and contrast the book you are looking at with others on the same subject, and you may learn about an even better book in this way. If a book you want isn't available in your local libraries or as an interlibrary loan, you may want to buy a book online at one of these sites or a site that specializes in used books. Pay attention to the ISBN, not just the title and the author, to make sure that you are getting the latest version in case there have been revisions.

Don't take too seriously the amateur reviews by people posting personal commentaries; they range from the useful (if you are lucky) to the seriously misleading. Some people give ratings to books they didn't understand—some will even rate books that they never actually read.

Boolean Logic

In the nineteenth century, a mathematician and logician named George Boole developed a system that we still use today in computer searches. This system is called **Boolean Logic.** In Boolean Logic, you use terms (and symbols) called **Boolean operators** to get more specific results when you search. Following is a list of Boolean operators. Try them in your Web and scholarly searches.

AND

If you use the AND operator, you are telling the search engine to only find results that contain both of two terms. For example, you could search for *television* AND *history*. Now your hits will include only results containing both terms; if a site mentions only one term, it will be ignored. Note: You can also use the + symbol for this operator.

NOT

If you use the NOT operator, you are specifying that you don't want a certain term in your search results. For example, if you are looking up television and keep getting hits that include an author named Shelly Stockton, whom you are trying to avoid, you can limit the search to keep her out. To do so, you would search the following: *television* NOT *Stockton*. This would eliminate any hits that contain the writer's name. Note: You can also use the − symbol for this operator.

OR

If you are trying to expand your search, you can use the OR operator. For example, if you want any results on television, but you're also interested in cable, you can search *television* AND *cable*. You'll find any source containing the word "television" as well as any source that contains the word "cable." Note: If you don't use any punctuation between the search terms, it is the same as the OR operator.

" "

If you surround your search term with quotation marks, you will do something similar to the AND operator. If you did a search for *"Television History"* it would be the same as a search for *Television* AND *History* (or *Television + History*). However, you can get more sophisticated searches by using both the quotation marks and the AND operator. You could expand your search and use the following term: *"Television History"* + *"Situation Comedies."* Now, your search will find only results that contain both sets of phrases together. This is great technique to use if you are getting thousands of hits and don't want to sift through all of them for relevant information.

*

Although not technically a Boolean term, many search engines allow for "wild card" characters, also known as truncation or stemming characters, such as the asterisk (*). If you are searching for anything about the terms *sociology, sociologist*

30   CHAPTER 2   Conducting Traditional Academic Research

(singular), *sociologists* (plural), or *social,* you can add the asterisk wild card character to the end of the term like this: *soci*.* This will tell the search engine to find any variation of the word, no matter what the suffix is. You should realize, however, that many engines use different wild card symbols, so look for the one specific to your database or ask your librarians for clarification.

Database or Platform	Internal Wild Card Character	End-of-Word Wild Card Character
EBSCOhost Databases	? (represents one character)	* (represents unlimited characters) Examples: *film** filmed filmgoer filmgoers films etc.
LexisNexis	* (represents one character)	! (represents unlimited characters) Examples: Film! Filmgoer Filmgoers etc. * (represents one character) Examples: Film* Films
ProQuest Databases	? (represents one character)	* (represents unlimited characters) ? (represents one character)
Gale/Cengage Databases	? (cannot use this character if default sorting is by relevance)	* (represents unlimited characters)
OVID Databases	? (represents unlimited characters) # (represents one character) $ (represents unlimited characters) $x (up to *x* number of characters)	? (represents unlimited characters) # (represents one character) $ (represents unlimited characters) $x (up to *x* number of characters)
JSTOR		+ (simple plurals; *s* or *es* only)

ONLINE PERIODICAL DATABASES

When you look for sources in periodicals, you will usually need to consult a different search engine than your library's catalog. Generally, your library home page will differentiate between the library book catalog and the periodical search engines. There are many popular search engines for periodicals, such as EBSCOhost, Gale/Cengage, and LexisNexis. These are subscriber services, which means that your campus library pays each service a fee to give students access to its databases of periodicals.

All the functions previously described in the discussion of library catalogs are likely to apply to the periodical databases available at your library. You can search by author, subject, or title to get your search results. The main difference between searching for books and periodical articles, however, is the method of retrieving the actual information. A search for books generates a list of authors, titles, publication information, and call numbers; a search for periodical articles also generates a list of authors and titles, along with dates and the issue and volume numbers for the periodicals. For many articles, especially older ones, you will need to find the physical copy of the article you've just found by locating the hard copy of the journal in the stacks of your library. You may want to make photocopies of the articles. For more recent articles, though, you'll often be able to download an electronic copy.

Here is a sample search screen from a periodical search engine, in this case the Gale/Cengage service's *Expanded Academic ASAP* database (previously known as InfoTrac).

32   CHAPTER 2   Conducting Traditional Academic Research

Limiting and Refining Your Searches

As in the preceding sample, most databases will allow you to limit your searches to suit your needs as a researcher. You can use the advanced search options to make sure that you get only articles that are published within a certain time frame, are full text, are refereed, or are currently held by your library. With journal databases containing thousands of articles from hundreds of journals, you'll regularly get results with thousands of hits. This is simply too much material to sift through. If this happens, you'll need to limit and refine your search to get a more manageable number. Here are five ways to limit your searches and refine your results.

ADDING TERMS

The easiest way to limit your search is to add some terms. By adding a few more details to your search, you'll find that many irrelevant results will disappear. For example, instead of just searching for *television history,* include extra terms like *cable, satellite, minorities, violence, advertising,* or other terms that may lead to more specific articles. This will eliminate many articles that don't pertain to your specific topic.

FULL TEXT

In the preceding sample page, you'll notice that you can limit the results "to documents with full text." This means that the only results you'll get are articles that include the full copy of the text in an electronic format. You can then email them to yourself, print them, or save them to your hard drive for later reference. However, if you fall into the trap of wanting all your research to be electronic, you may be missing some valuable resources. Although you will find plenty of full-text journals, you will find many more that are not full text. Your responsibility as a researcher is to track down the best materials, not the easiest, get the physical journals off the shelves, and make photocopies of the articles for your own use. Most articles published before the mid 1990s are not stored in electronic formats yet. To properly research your subject, you should not limit yourself to electronic materials. You also need to know your instructor's preferences. The requirements for your class may dictate a specific number of sources from different categories, and exclude some types of sources entirely.

PEER REVIEWED OR REFEREED

The sample search engine page also allows you to limit the results "to peer-reviewed publications." Such articles are scholarly and typically found in academic journals. This kind of limitation is a very good idea for information you plan to use in your paper. By limiting your search in this way, you'll be sure you get only academic articles that have been reviewed by a panel of experts in the field before being accepted for publication.

LIBRARY HOLDINGS

Another way to limit your search is by library holdings. This means that the search will list only those periodicals that your library subscribes to. Even if there isn't a full-text version of this article available in the database, you'll be able to find it in your library and make a copy of it for later use. If you don't select this box, the database will list every single article it contains, even though many of them may not be available in your library.

BY PUBLICATION DATE

Many periodical search engines also allow you to search by date. This option can be very useful when you need to find information about a very recent event and want to limit your search to the past few months. It is also helpful when you are searching for specific newspaper articles and you know when the story initially broke.

Research Tip: Book Reviews

When you search using a periodical database, many of the articles you will turn up are reviews of scholarly books that have just been released. These are brief reviews published in scholarly journals that are important to read when you're trying to determine whether a new book might be a good source, but you shouldn't rely on the content of these reviews for your paper. Instead of using a review as a source for your paper, locate the book the reviewer is writing about and use it. Why rely on someone's opinion of an author's research or argument when you can cite the actual work?

After you enter your search parameters, you'll get a page like the one shown next. It will show you all the sources within this database on the subject you've chosen to research. Again, we've entered the search term *television history*.

Century

Some of these articles will seem more pertinent than others, and you'll select ones you're interested in exploring further. After you do, the engine generates specific details about the article or gives the whole article itself if the full text is available, as in the example shown in the next screen.

Notice, however, that the previous example still shows 1,733 hits just on the academic journals. This is still too large a number to try to sift through with any efficiency. Instead, you should still narrow the field.

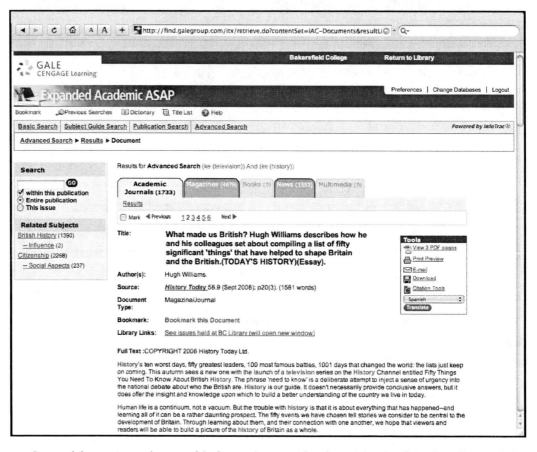

Several important pieces of information can be found in the first few lines of the journal results. Look at some of the details from the result in the preceding screen example:

- The title and author: "What made us british? Hugh Williams describes how he and his colleagues set about compiling a list of fifty significant 'things' that have helped to shape Britain and the British," written by Hugh Williams (note that the title is not capitalized according to MLA guidelines, as it must be when you create your list of works cited)

- The name of the journal itself: *History Today*.

- The volume and issue number: volume 58, issue number 9, the date (Sept. 2008), and the page number it starts on (page 20), and the number of pages (3).

All the information listed here is vital, giving you what you would need to locate this article if the database did not contain a full-text version. Just under the abstract, however, the database indicates that the full text is available and gives copyright information, so you can email this article to yourself if you decide that the information it contains is useful.

GOVERNMENT PUBLICATIONS

The government catalogs data on many facets of our lives, and much of this data is presented in documents, publications, reports, and websites that are open to the public.

Local: The local government will have many interesting facts about your hometown and county. You can view reports from the Hall of Records, the Hall of Justice, city surveyors, often even reports by the sheriff's and police departments. If you are looking for information on taxes, land holdings, environmental impact reports, or even a local radio station's FCC license, they are all public record that you can track down. You can also check your hometown's website for reports and names and numbers of people you could contact to get this information.

State/Federal: States and the federal government spend billions of dollars. These expenditures leave long paper trails, and much of this material may be helpful in your research. Federal agencies, such as the Federal Communications Commission (FCC) and the Food and Drug Administration (FDA), have detailed websites with many published findings. There are also storehouses of public documents, such as those maintained by the Government Printing Office, found at http://www.access.gpo.gov.

THE INTERNET

The Internet is a vast ocean of information, but most of this information is far too informal and untrustworthy to include in your research papers. However, at times you will need to access the Net as part of your academic searches.

First, you should be aware that there is a major difference between the online periodical databases discussed earlier and the Internet as a whole. When you access a periodical database, such as EBSCOhost, you are technically doing research on the Internet, but you're in a scholarly database doing valid academic research. When you use a generic search engine such as Yahoo or Google, however, your search is no longer limited to scholarly sources. Many instructors will insist that you not use sources from the Internet in your papers. However, they probably mean that you should limit your use of electronic sources to the periodical databases, such as EBSCOhost and Expanded Academic ASAP, or government publications found online. A scholarly journal article is still a reputable, high-quality source even if you use the digital version, not the paper one.

You can find some scholarly information on the Net, however. Sites such as Google's scholarly database, found at http://scholar.google.com/, or Genamic's Journal Seek, at http://www.journalseek.net/, offer access to some scholarly articles. These sites are usually portals to scholarly work that was originally published elsewhere. Many such sites exist, though several of them charge a fee for you to access the material, like Questia, an online digital library of books and articles in the humanities and social sciences. Again, it will be your job as a researcher to verify the quality and authorship of the sources you find here. (For more information on how to use Internet search engines and when it is appropriate to do so, see Chapter 3.)

INTERVIEWS, SURVEYS, AND FIELD RESEARCH

All research need not be done in a library. In fact, many writers, researchers, and professors use successful research out in the field to help generate data and produce evidence. Personal research such as this can involve interviewing experts on your subject, gathering your own statistics through surveys and studies, and conducting observations and experiments. Even if you end up not being able to use any information you get from interviews in your papers, these interviews make you a much more informed researcher and can help guide you and generate questions as you continue your scholarly research.

Personal Interviews

In your community are thousands of experts in various fields who may be happy to share their expertise with you as you research. If you contact these people and set up a formal interview, you can tap their knowledge. Some people you could interview are your local sheriff or police chief, a city politician (such as the mayor or a city council member), doctors, administrators of a local veteran's hospital, or college and university professors. Contact these people and tell them you're a student, and they may be pleased at the chance to share their knowledge and opinions.

When you decide to interview someone, aim for the top. Don't just interview a cousin of yours who is in the police academy—try to get the police chief or a homicide detective. For example, if you are writing a paper on the history of television, don't just interview your boyfriend or girlfriend who just finished a class on media theory. See if you can get an interview or email response from the producer of a local news show, an editor at your local newspaper, a radio station manager, or a professor who studies the media.

Following is a list of things to consider while conducting an interview.

SCHEDULING

When you decide whom you want to interview, you should contact them first and ask permission to schedule an interview at a later date. Don't expect busy people to take time out of their day for a random and lengthy interview. Call, write, or email them to get permission and to set an appointment. They will want to know the topics that you plan to cover. It isn't a bad idea to give them a list of possible questions in advance. In fact, give them every courtesy you can think of while setting up the interview. If they are kind enough to volunteer to share their expertise and valuable time with you, you should be very gracious at every stage.

GENERATING QUESTIONS

Before your interview date arrives, you should thoroughly prepare yourself. You need to generate a written list of questions to ask. Otherwise, you could have a penetrating sequence of questions in mind, but get nervous or side-tracked and forget some of the best questions you thought of. If you have a typed list of questions, you'll stay on track, and the people you interview will understand that you've done your homework and are taking their time seriously. Think of open-ended questions that require explanations instead of simple yes/no questions. This way, you are likely to gather detailed information, and you may even learn about some issues you hadn't even thought about before the interview.

Of course, if other questions come up during the interview, jot them down and ask them before you leave, but don't go in expecting to wing it.

BEING PROFESSIONAL

Treat the people you are interviewing as the professionals they are; this means that you need to behave equally professionally. Avoid slang and swear words, and dress as if you're going on a job interview. Even if you interview a person who is not in a profession, the right attitude on your part will help elicit thoughtful, careful responses. Finally, remember to thank your subjects afterward for their time. You may not need them anymore, but they could decide to never again take the time to help a student if you don't acknowledge the time and effort they put into answering your questions. Besides, you may still need them—as you type up your notes or write the first draft of your paper, you may realize that you need to clarify one or more points. If you haven't acted in a courteous and professional manner, they will feel like dealing with you again is a waste of their time.

TAKING NOTES

Typically, people speak faster than we can write, so if you are interviewing someone in person or over the telephone, it is a good idea to both take written notes and record the session. Your notes will keep your major thoughts on paper, but the recorded interview will be an infallible source to refer back to later. Many college and university libraries have recorders you can check out as a student in case you don't have one. You can also attach microphones to many iPods and laptops. Be sure to ask for permission to take notes and record the interview in advance.

STAYING ON TOPIC

Interviews don't always go as you expect them to go. The experts you talk to may be busy, impatient, or distracted. They may want to avoid some of the issues you bring up or seem interested in only one aspect of your topic. At all times, remember that this is their time. Don't push them; just adapt. Try to steer the interview back to where you want it to go, but if you find too much resistance, don't go too far and risk upsetting them.

CLARIFYING IMPORTANT INFORMATION

Don't forget to get accurate background information from your subjects. How long have they been in this field of work? What makes them experts? Where degrees do they

38   CHAPTER 2   Conducting Traditional Academic Research

have, and where did they obtain them? Also, be sure you get titles and names spelled correctly and dates authenticated. You can politely interrupt and get clarification as the interview progresses, or you can jot some reminders to yourself about points that need clarification at the end. Be sure that you keep aware of the time.

Telephone and Email Interviews

You can also conduct interviews through phone or email. For example, some well-known experts are also college and university professors, and they can easily be tracked down using their institutions' websites. You can find office phone numbers, email addresses, and even office hours. You may be able to interview renowned experts on your topic. Most of the preceding guidelines are applicable to phone or email interviews. Always email or call first and ask to set up a time to call back for a phone interview or to ask for permission to send a list of questions via email. If you are doing your interviews by phone, you must make your subjects aware in advance that you would like to record them. Comply with their wishes—it isn't ethical to record subjects without their permission.

For many students, an email interview is preferable to a phone interview. Very few people have the devices needed to record a phone conversation. If you send email questions, however, you have your subject's verbatim responses.

Sample Interview Questions

Following is a list of some sample questions you could generate before conducting an interview. These questions were prepared by a student writing a paper on the subject of television news and its role in democracy. Her subjects were news anchors working at each of the three local television stations. Notice that the questions are fairly specific, so that she would be more likely to get stronger responses. Also note that for questions 6, 7, and 9, she prepared some follow-up questions in case she got a "yes" response to any of them and needed more elaboration. In practice, most interview subjects are likely to give fairly detailed answers to questions instead of simple yes or no answers, but follow-up questions are important in case a subject needs prompting—or in case a subject is very willing to talk but goes off on tangents. These questions also helped to keep her consistent with each of the three individuals she interviewed.

Date: _____

Place: _____

Interviewee: _____

Question 1: How long have you been a reporter?

Question 2: How has television news changed since you started?

Question 3: How do you think television news compares to news from other sources, like newspapers, news magazines, the Internet, and radio?

Question 4: What do you think are the strengths of television news?

Question 5: What do you think are the weaknesses of television news?

Question 6: Have you ever had pressure to not air a story?

    Follow-Up Question 1: Who tried to get the story stopped, and why?

    Follow-Up Question 2: Can you elaborate? Did the story end up getting aired?

Question 7: Have you known anyone else who had pressure to not air a story?

    Follow-Up Question 1: Who tried to get the story stopped, and why?

    Follow-Up Question 2: Did the story end up getting aired?

Question 8: Do you think television news programs in general do a good job presenting the news?

Question 9: Do you think television news is important to American democracy?
Follow-Up Question: In what ways?

Question 10: Do you think the current corporate ownership of most news outlets has hurt journalism in any way?

Question 11: What do you see as the future of television news?

Surveys and Statistical Studies

You may want to conduct your own research and get statistics about an issue. To do so, you will need to design a survey that asks questions that will help you in your research. After you give this to participants, you'll be able to come up with your own statistical information. (Don't forget to save the completed surveys; your professor may want to see your research.)

One of the most important questions to ask before you begin a survey is, "What sample size is required for a survey?" There is no definitive answer to this question; large samples with rigorous selection will give you more accurate results, but, as a student, you are limited in what you can do. Your target sample size for a survey depends on the resources available to you, the purpose of your study, and the statistical quality needed. It is best to discuss this with your professor before proceeding—you don't want to take the time and the trouble to do field research and find that days of work were lost because your professor deems your sample size too small or unrepresentative. After you decide on a sample size, don't back off. If you find yourself with only eighty percent of the number of subjects you had hoped for, keep going, even if it's taking longer than you anticipated. Trust your original assessment.

Depending on the nature of your research, there will be several places you can go to distribute the surveys. If you intend to interview only college students or faculty members, obviously your campus (or any nearby campuses) will be the best place to go. Some of your professors may even be willing to take some class time to let students voluntarily fill out questionnaires if they aren't too long. If you want a broader sampling of participants, you should go to a popular spot, such as a coffee house or shopping

40 CHAPTER 2 Conducting Traditional Academic Research

center. Be sure to ask permission of managers first. You can also have a simple survey that can be given over the telephone and make some cold calls to people—be sure you call at an appropriate time, though (not too early or too late, and not during dinner). Be prepared to be hung up on by people who have no interest in being questioned by you.

Following are some ideas on how to generate a successful field survey.

DON'T TRY TO DO TOO MUCH

Don't get overly ambitious and try to generate a lot of data. Design your survey with a clear idea of exactly what beliefs and attitudes you are trying to measure, and be practical. Limit the scope. You will need to be pretty specific to make sure that the results that you generate mean something, but if you try to ask too many questions, potential subjects may not want to take the time. You should be able to say, "This will only take a minute or two of your time" and really mean it. It's a good idea to rehearse your survey with a few friends—this will give you a realistic idea of how much time the survey will take, and they may even catch problems with your questions that you didn't see.

KEEP QUESTIONS CLEAR

You need to create questions that will not confuse the participants. Make sure that the language is clear and unambiguous and that you avoid technical language or jargon. Don't try to impress people with your vocabulary. If your question is worded poorly, the participants may interpret it incorrectly and skew your statistics. Use multiple choice, yes/no, and true/false questions. You'll have much more luck snagging potential participants if your survey won't take a lot of time. Few people will want to write short essays for you, but many people will fill in a couple of bubbles while they're on the go. This differs from generating interview questions, because interviews often aim for more complex, longer reactions.

AVOID BIAS AND OVERSIMPLIFICATION

Make sure your questions are straightforward, unemotional, and free from any hint of bias. It is very easy to load a question with language that makes it hard for someone not to agree with you. People tend to want to be liked, even by strangers, and sometimes they will give the answers they think that interviewers want to hear or that the people reading written survey questions want to read. If you wanted to know about subjects' feelings about abortion laws, for example, questions like "Do you feel it is ever moral to take an innocent unborn life?" or "Do you support a woman's right to control her own body?" are going to elicit very skewed results.

Also, if you are dealing with complex, nuanced issues, you should avoid questions that are too simplistic. "Are you in favor of gun control?" may seem like a straightforward, unbiased question, but it would mean very different things to different people, and your subjects will bring their own habits of thought to the question. A member of the National Rifle Association might automatically answer "No," but this same person might believe that it is perfectly reasonable not to allow people convicted of terrorist acts or people who are demonstrably psychotic to own guns. A member of the Brady Campaign to Prevent Gun Violence would answer "Yes" because this organization lobbies for gun control laws, but you still wouldn't know exactly how this person feels about the issue of individuals owning guns—some members may want private gun ownership banned altogether, but many others don't. You would get the most accurate results if you generated very specific questions, such as "Under which of the following situations should individuals be banned from owning guns?" followed by clear scenarios.

DON'T GET PERSONAL

Don't ask for any information that isn't needed for your study. You should avoid questions about race, sexual orientation, religion, political leanings, or age unless they directly pertain to the study. If any of these traits are relevant to the study, tell people in advance. Also, don't ask for data such as a phone number, social security number, student ID number, or an address; you have no business gathering that information in the first place, and your potential subjects may think you're trying to scam them. Don't even ask for names.

INCLUDE A SUMMARY

At the top of the survey, it is a good idea to summarize its purpose. Let the participants know what it is you are researching and why these questions will help you. This is especially important if you're asking for information that may seem personal (see the preceding section). It's a good idea to orally tell the participants what your survey is about before they start, but putting a summary on the survey itself will be helpful in case you are dealing with several people and don't get a chance to talk to everyone.

BE PROFESSIONAL

Always remain professional and welcoming. You are asking people to take time out of their day to help you out, so do it with a smile. Never get upset at someone for not agreeing to complete your survey (they may feel that you are "spamming" them, so if they walk away, don't hold it against them). Dress well and have clean forms, clipboards, and writing implements. If your surveys are handwritten, or if you have to ask potential subjects if they have a pencil or pen, they are likely to refuse to participate.

SAMPLE SURVEY

Following is a sample survey on the topic of television history. It is designed to assess current viewing patterns that can help prove a point about modern television. It is intended to be distributed on campus to other students.

42 CHAPTER 2 Conducting Traditional Academic Research

Summary: This survey is about television viewing patterns, and the answers it generates will be used in a research paper on the history of television. It should only take a minute or two to complete this survey, and I appreciate the help you are giving me.

Your Information

Age: _____ Gender: _____

Year in School: _____

Major: _____

Questions—Circle the Most Accurate Letter:

1. How often do you watch television each day?
    A. 0 Hours

    B. 1–3 Hours

    C. 4–7 Hours

    D. 8+ Hours

2. How many televisions are in your home?
    A. None

    B. 1

    C. 2–3

    D. 4+

3. How many people live in your home?
    A. Just me.

    B. 2

    C. 3–4

    D. 5+

4. Do you have cable/satellite TV?
    A. Yes

    B. No

5. Do you have a hard disk recorder/service (like TiVo, ReplayTV, etc.)?
    A. Yes

    B. No

6. Do you ever rent episodes of television shows through services like Netflix or check them out from a library?
    A. Yes

    B. No

7. Do you own any television shows on commercially produced DVDs?

   A. Yes

   B. No

8. Please rank the following types of programming by preference, with "1" as the highest rating. Leave blank any types of programming that you do not watch.

News	_____
Reality shows	_____
Comedies	_____
Dramas	_____
Crime dramas	_____
Science fiction/fantasy	_____

9. Please rank the following modes of relaxation by preference, with "1" as the highest rating. Leave blank any activities you do not use for relaxation.

Television viewing	_____
Playing a sport/exercising	_____
Going to a movie in a theater	_____
Reading (books and/or periodicals)	_____
Going to a club or bar	_____
Playing a video or Internet game	_____
Pursuing a hobby	_____

10. Do you have an all-time favorite TV show?

   A. Yes

   B. No

   If "yes," what is it? _____

Research Tip: Online Surveys

If you are part of an active online community, you may feel comfortable administering a survey through the Internet. You could post it on a blog you participate in, on a website or MySpace account you maintain, or even a chat room. There are also some websites, such as Survey Monkey (http://surveymonkey.com), which let you conduct online surveys.

You may be able to get many more people to participate in a survey conducted via the Web, and you may be able to draw people in from a much broader geographic location. Follow all the suggestions for conducting a face-to-face survey here, and you should be fine. Just be very careful about the conclusions that you attempt to draw from such surveys—you may have a broader geographical area, but in every other respect, you have a sample that is unrepresentative of the population at large because you will be reaching only people who were initially attracted to specific sites, blogs, or chat rooms.

Century

Field Research

You may need to go into the field to conduct an observation or an experiment, especially for classes that focus on science and empirical data. Professional observations occur all the time, and they affect our daily lives. If you are on a sports team, your coach will observe tapes of your performance, looking for patterns to help improve your game. If you are in a school play, the director will observe your movements and try to correct errors in your blocking and offer suggestions on your delivery. When marketing firms and advertising agencies need to know shopping patterns, they may conduct an observation at your local mall—if customers tend to shop at the same two stores, they may develop a cross-promotion between them to lure in future shoppers. The same type of observations can be done by you when you are doing research for a paper.

Typically, experiments and observations begin with a hypothesis you plan to test. The resulting findings are included in your paper. For example, if you decided to see how popular television shows released on DVD are, you could station yourself near the counter of a DVD/video-renting store (be sure to ask permission and to not block traffic) some Friday evening from 5:30 to 6:30 to test this hypothesis: "A significant percentage of DVD rentals are for popular television shows." All you would need is a checklist with two columns: "television shows" and "movies." Of course, you would have to decide what you consider a "significant percentage" and be prepared to explain and defend this in your paper. You might also refine the observation somewhat and have three columns: "current television shows," "vintage television shows," and "movies." Other breakdowns are conceivable, but you wouldn't want too many columns or you wouldn't be able to keep up if business was brisk. With field research, you want to think your assumptions and research design through carefully before you begin.

CHAPTER 3

Conducting Other Types of Research

You've enrolled in a film class, and your professor has just finished discussing movies that depict historic battles. In class, you've watched *Black Hawk Down, Band of Brothers,* and Frank Miller's *300,* all films based on historical wars and real people. Your instructor has assigned a paper about these films and how war is depicted in them. She wants you to cover the impression of war these films leave with the viewer, but she doesn't require research as a mandatory element. You don't know much about these wars or what actually occurred, however, so you've decided to look into the historical events behind these films to see how the fictional accounts compare to historical accounts.

Because the paper doesn't require scholarly sources, you decide to skip the library and look elsewhere. After all, you're researching for your own sake, not necessarily for academic sources to quote in your paper. There are plenty of options. You could start, of course, by searching the Web. It is a vast and endless source of information, and surely you'll find hundreds of sites on these battles. You also have other options. You could look to the print media. If you go back to the time when the films were originally released, you'd find newspaper reviews and magazine articles discussing these movies (and in the case of all three of these particular films, you can track down the books they were originally based on); in the case of *Black Hawk Down* and *Band of Brothers,* you could even find articles on the battles themselves in the times they were fought. Even the airwaves can be of help. Cable channels sometimes do research into the backgrounds of popular films like these and produce television documentaries comparing the fictionalizations to the historians' accounts and even providing interviews if there are survivors.

There are thousands of avenues that never require a person to set foot in a library to track down information. We turn to these sources on a regular basis. This type of research is perhaps the most common research ever done, and most of us consider it such a part of daily life that it doesn't "feel" like research at all. It's not something that is academic in scope, just something to ease a curiosity or inform us about the world at large.

This type of daily research is a key tool in becoming more competent at finding and evaluating information. You need to learn the skills of searching through mundane systems, such as the general Internet, print media, and television and radio. Although

Century

much of the research discussed in this chapter is nonscholarly and should not be used directly in a truly academic paper, it still has a place in college life. These sources provide starting points to begin the research process and help generate ideas. By understanding some basics of navigating the mediated world in which we live, we can come much closer to true information competency.

RESEARCH INTO POP CULTURE: NET DOMAINS

A fast way to learn something about a website is to look at its domain. The domain is the final part of the URL (short for Universal Resource Locator, the web address), and it is commonly a three-letter title that is preceded by a period (typically called a "dot"). The typical website ends in a .com domain, usually referred to as a "dotcom." This is the most common website in existence, and it's typically not scholarly, so many professors suggest that you avoid using these public websites in your papers. However, other types of websites (such as educational websites hosted by universities and professional academic organizations) are great for research. Following is a list of different types of web domains and some thoughts on when you should use them.

.com

> **Who publishes them:** Typically, individuals and corporations. These are the most populous sites on the Internet and exist for countless reasons: some to inform, some to make money—and some to misinform, so be careful.

> **When to use them:** They are great places to go for some prewriting and topic generation, but most .coms are sources you should be wary of when looking for material to use in your paper.

.gov

> **Who publishes them:** Government organizations (such as the FDA, FCC, White House, etc.)

> **When to use them:** Often such organizations publish statistics and yearly reports full of useful information. Usually, these sites contain information that is published with citations and verification of where the information came from.

.org

> **Who publishes them:** Nonprofit organizations (such as FactCheck.org, Amnesty International, Greenpeace, Doctors Without Borders, Reporters Without Borders, and various charities).

When to use them: These are useful sources for topic generation and getting some initial ideas. These sites can sometimes be used in papers because they often have their facts verified and typically provide citations showing where the information on the site is from, so you can track it down yourself. The only downside is that sometimes these sites can be one-sided on a given issue and may slight opposing viewpoints.

.edu

Who publishes them: Educational institutions such as colleges, universities, and high schools.

When to use them: These can be good sites for you to use in a paper. Many are published by the world's leading institutions of higher learning, and they often contain information that comes from scholarly sources and studies. Sometimes, however, these sites will be written by students and published as part of assignments, so you should check up on the author(s) before trusting them enough to use in a paper.

Other domain types

There are several other types of Net domains you may run into. They include .net, .tv, .biz, .info., which are often connected to businesses of various types, and various abbreviations for different countries (such as .eu for Europe and .uk for the United Kingdom).

THE WORLD WIDE WEB

The Internet is a global network of millions of computers, and the part you are probably most familiar with is called the World Wide Web. The Web is a system of hyperlinked files that we access through a **Web browser** (such as Mozilla's Firefox, Apple's Safari, or Microsoft's Internet Explorer). The Web is an endless series of sites and resources; becoming skilled in its use—which frequently means recognizing what to ignore—is a vital part of modern-day information competency.

Search Engines

After you open your Web browser and secure a connection to the Internet, you need a **search engine.** Search engines are Web resources that enable you to search the Internet for whatever information you are looking for. When you sign on to the Internet, a search engine is often part of your start-up page. You are undoubtedly familiar with at least one search engine and may even have one bookmarked or set as your home page. Google.com and Yahoo.com are probably the two biggest, but other engines such as the America Online keyword search system are also very popular.

Century

48   CHAPTER 3   Conducting Other Types of Research

Search engines are indiscriminate resource tools that can take you as easily to biased sites, pornography, and shady money-making schemes as they can take you to respectable information. Information and disinformation will come to you in waves, unfiltered and without reliable ranking. It is up to you, the savvy Net user, to determine what's worth reading and what is pure garbage.

Following are some images of a typical search engine. The first shows Google, the most widely used search engine on the Net. You can customize your own version of Google to contain specific elements that attract you (headlines, weather, entertainment, etc.), but the basic Google web page is a no-frills affair consisting of little more than a box to type in search terms.

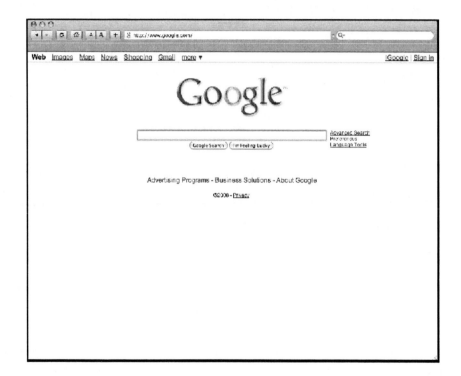

After you enter your search term, you click the Google Search button to initiate your search. You will be directed to a list of all the sites that the software matched to your search query; these results are often called **hits.** An example of a search for "Television History" appears on the next page. This is a list of all the sites that Google's software found to match these two search terms. The list is a series of hyperlinks with brief descriptions next to them. You should be able to quickly scroll through the hits to find what interests you and ignore the rest.

Note that toward the top, it says the results displayed are one through ten of about 20,400,000. This means that there are over 20 million "hits" for this search term. If this were your search, you'd want to reduce this number to something more manageable. If you add a term to expand your original query from "Television History" to "Cable Television History," the results drop to 23 million, and if you change it to "Cable Television Advertising History," the results drop to 1.3 million. More than a million hits are still far too many to reliably read, though, so refining your search even more will be necessary for such a broad topic. (For more ideas, see the section on Boolean Logic in Chapter 2.)

One of the unique features of Google is its I'm Feeling Lucky button. This button changes the results of your search. Instead of getting a list of all the sites you could go to, the software takes you to the first site on the list. This severely limits your results, but at times, it can be handy if you want to know the most popular site for a given search term. Note their terminology here: "I'm Feeling Lucky." This implies that you'll have to be very lucky to get what you are after on the first attempt. Web searches take time if you want to find quality material on your subject, and Google acknowledges this by suggesting that getting what you were after on the first site you find is a matter of dumb luck.

Another feature of Google and many other search engines is the Advanced Search option (see page 50). This allows you to refine your search in many ways. The next image shows that you can limit your search by a specific language, a particular type of file format, a date of publication, even domains (so you could search only in YouTube, for example). This type of refined search helps you to filter out the millions of sites that could clog your results page, and it helps you find just the information that will be useful.

Another popular search engine is Yahoo.com. Yahoo is a source for news updates, free email accounts, and searching the Web. Many people come to sites like Yahoo for their daily news and information, and many use Yahoo's search engine for every trip

50   CHAPTER 3   Conducting Other Types of Research

around the Web. You'll notice below that everything from shopping to weather and from news to music is all found here on Yahoo's home page. As with all search engines, you enter the term(s) you want to scour the Web for, and click the appropriate button (for Yahoo, it's the Web Search button) to get your results.

Search Types

With both the Yahoo and the basic Google images shown earlier, note that atop the search bar, you find several tabs that allow you to perform specific searches. Each type of search yields wildly different results. Explore these different types of searches and see what is most appropriate for the types of results you're hoping to find. Following is a list of some of the major types of searches you can perform.

WEB

This type of search is the most common and will scour the entire Internet for any websites containing the search terms you've used. Search engines all generate their results using different means, so you may want to scroll through the hits instead of merely clicking the first one. You may also want to search using multiple search engines or meta search engines (see pp. 52–53) to fully explore your topic.

IMAGES

If you are looking for an image of a particular historical figure, landmark, or even a celebrity, you can select to search only for images. This option typically finds the picture and loads it on your screen without actually taking you to the site it was originally found on.

VIDEO

Similar to the Image search, this search type yields only videos to view with your computer. Most videos are free to view, but many will take you to "mature" websites you may prefer to avoid.

NEWS

This is a very helpful research tool for academic work. This search option looks through only journalistic news pieces posted on the Web—all other websites are ignored. Normally, the hits will link you to the stories themselves. Some of the sites require you to be a subscriber to the original newspaper or magazine, but many will let you access the story for free or by merely registering for a free account.

MAPS

You can limit your search to maps and directions. This may have a limited place in your more formal research, but it is very handy in daily life. Popular sites include MapQuest, Google Maps, and Yahoo! Maps.

LOCAL

This search is similar to a web search, a news search, or even a map search, but it provides results for an area that you specify (typically by ZIP code). This is very handy for staying up on local events or doing academic research on issues in your hometown.

Ways to Confirm Information

Searching on the Net can yield good results, but it is not short on pitfalls. Much of the information you'll find will be woefully biased or even outright dishonest. Whether

52   CHAPTER 3   Conducting Other Types of Research

your search is for academic research or for personal information, you should get in the habit of verifying any information you come upon. For more information on how to evaluate and qualify your sources, see Chapter 4. Following, however, are a few tips for verifying information found on the Web.

■ **Look for the .edu domain.** This means that a school, college, or university is responsible for publishing this on the Web. You can usually find the original author as well as contact information for the author on educational sites, and the information tends to be much more reliable because people's scholarly reputations are on the line when they publish such a site.

■ **Search using multiple search engines.** Every search engine uses different parameters to determine what sites it finds and lists for you, and you'd be wise to search on a variety of engines. If you use different engines, you may be exposed to different websites. The most popular sites will all be near the top of each engine's list of hits, but you will nonetheless see a surprising amount of variety as you read further down the lists.

Meta Search Engines (Metacrawlers)

Several search engines bill themselves as "meta search engines." These engines don't actually search the Web themselves; they search the resources of multiple search engines

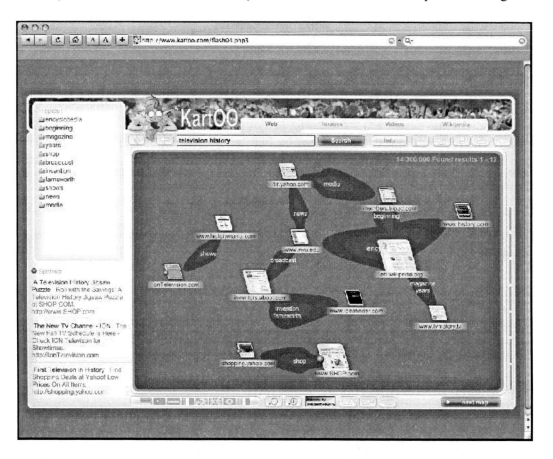

by sending a query to several search engines at once and combining the results. Your results will be more varied and come from more databases, so these are good resources when you are searching for something that's hard to find on the Web. The downside is that you may get far too many hits to be useful, or you may find that the filters used by the meta search engine are cutting out sites you'd have liked to be informed of.

Some of the more popular meta search engines are Dogpile, Excite, Vivisimo, Metacrawler, Kartoo, and Mamma. Many of the metacrawlers come up with innovative graphic organization to manage the many hits they get. On page 52 is a picture of the results for a search on "Television History" from Kartoo. Kartoo innovated a way to organize search results as a "map," and when you scroll over one particular file, the links it makes to other files all appear. Also, on the left side, a bar appears full of topics similar to your search parameter, so you can see other relevant subjects that you may not have thought of.

Research Tip: Vocabulary Check

When studying research writing, one word that comes up quite a lot is "cite." So, too, does the word "site." This can get confusing for many students. What's the difference?

Cite is the word used to describe how you give credit to any information you get from an outside source. Example: *Be sure you cite all your quotes, or you are plagiarizing.*

Site is the word used to describe a place or location, such as a website or a job site. Example: *One of my favorite sites on the Net is theonion.com.*

Sight is the word used to describe vision. Example: *She has extremely good eye sight.*

Miscellaneous Sites of Interest

Following is a list of some sites that may be of interest to you as a researcher and everyday viewer of the Web.

Allmusic (http://www.allmusic.com/). As the name implies, Allmusic is a database of music. It contains detailed listings of musicians and their music, with detailed biographies of the artists, full discographies, and references to other artists they influenced or were influenced by. Two other parts of this database are called Allgames and Allmovies. Allgames is a list of summaries of video games and their histories, and Allmovies gives detailed synopses of movies and biographies of actors; however, unlike IMDb, it lacks thorough lists of everyone involved in these projects. Sidebars tells several facts about the films, including original box office receipts and keywords and themes associated with them.

Bartleby.com: Great Books Online (http://www.bartleby.com/). Named after Herman Melville's title character in "Bartleby, the Scrivener," the site describes itself as "the most comprehensive reference publisher on the web, meeting the needs of students, educators, and the intellectually curious." Bartleby.com is known for its fully downloadable books and resources, and it lists categories under four broad subject headings: Reference, Verse, Fiction, and Nonfiction.

CIA World Factbook (https://www.cia.gov/cia/publications/factbook/). The World Fact Book is a database published online by America's Central Intelligence Agency (CIA). This database contains important information about every country on Earth, from the biggest to the smallest. It allows users to select a nation and find up-to-date census information on statistical data on issues such as capital cities, total population, ethnic percentages, major imports and exports, diseases, type of governance, and even finances, such as the Gross Domestic Product. Although this website is not written by scholars, it is funded by one of America's largest intelligence-gathering agencies, and the data presented here is thought to make up one of the most accurate such databases released to the public.

Encyclopedia of Life (http://www.eol.org). The EOL is an online encyclopedia whose lofty goal is to catalog detailed pages for each of the 1.8 million known species on Earth. Though still in its infancy, this site promises to be useful to scientists and the general public alike, stating that "It can be a handy field guide that people take with them on hikes on a personal digital assistant. It can tell you all the plants that might be found in your neighborhood" and serve "as a catalog, database, and learning tool about every organism that has ever lived on the planet. In the same way that dictionaries help literacy, the Encyclopedia can help biodiversity literacy." This site will be monitored, edited, and written by scholars, but eventually there will be a place for everyone to update the entries, like a peer-critiqued wiki. EOL's creators hope that the full encyclopedia will be completed by 2018.

FactCheck.org: Annenberg Political Fact Check (http://factcheck.org/). FactCheck is a nonprofit, nonpartisan organization whose purpose is to reduce the inaccuracies, confusion, and deliberate deception that confront voters. It monitors statements made by "major U.S. political players" in debates, speeches, interviews, advertisements, and news releases. According to its mission statement, "Our goal is to apply the best practices of both journalism and scholarship, and to increase public knowledge and understanding." FactCheck.org is a project of the Annenberg Public Policy Center of the University of Pennsylvania.

FindLaw Academic Law Reviews and Journals (http://stu.findlaw.com/journals/). This is a law journal search engine, with journals and academic law reviews organized by topic, such as Constitutional law, criminal law, cyberspace law, military law, and tax law. It offers an introduction to legal citation and is designed for law students, but it is useful for anyone writing a paper on a topic concerning law.

History News Network (http://hnn.us/). How can history be "news"? These lines from HNN's mission statement give us some idea: "Among the many duties we assume are these: To expose politicians who misrepresent history. To point out bogus analogies. To deflate beguiling myths. To remind Americans of the irony of history. To put events in context. To remind us all of the complexity of history. Because we believe history is complicated our pages are open to people of all political persuasions. Left, right, center: all are welcome." Its several main departments include a Hot Topics page and a Students Shortcut page. The latter has links to many resources, such as live chats with professionals from the Library of Congress, comprehensive lists of reference sites, primary sources covering U.S. history, an indexed, searchable database of more than 5,000 U.S. and world history sites, guidance on how to "do" history, and a special section on 9/11.

HowStuffWorks (http://www.howstuffworks.com/). HowStuffWorks was founded in 1998 by a professor with the delightfully appropriate name of Marshall Brain. The site promises that "No topic is too big or too small for our expert editorial staff to unmask." The range of topics is huge—go straight to their home page, and you'll see their choices of a couple of dozen topics for the day, with headings like "How the Patriot Act Works," "How Pirates Work," and "How Archeology Works." The range is enormous, with articles on why our stomachs growl, along with articles on electric cars, government watch lists, and serial killers. *Time* magazine has named it one of the "25 Web Sites We Can't Live Without."

IMDb (http://www.imdb.com/). The International Movie Database is a thorough database of the film, television, and video game industry. You can search this database by title, actor, director, and producer; members of a movie's crew, such as editors, camera operators, and gaffers, are also listed here. If a person has been in a movie or voiced a game, there is a very good chance that he or she will be listed and that a brief biography may be included. IMDb even provides lists of the works of authors whose books, plays, or short stories have been adapted for movies, such as William Shakespeare or Jane Austen.

Innocence Project (http://www.innocenceproject.org/). If you want to do research on the criminal justice system, this site will give you some interesting perspectives and information. There are actually several Innocence Projects in the United States, but this site is the national organization. It was founded in 1992 by two law professors to assist prisoners who could be proven innocent through DNA testing. More than 200 people in the United States have been exonerated by DNA testing, including a number who spent years on death row. The site includes a section explaining and giving statistics on the seven most common causes of wrongful convictions, including eyewitness misidentification, unreliable or limited science, and the use of "snitches." There are also profiles of people who have been exonerated.

Library of Congress (http://www.loc.gov/index.html). The Library of
Congress's website is an amazing research resource. The LOC is the world's
largest library, boasting more than 130 million items and over 500 miles
of shelf space. Every year, the LOC scans more and more documents and
posts more and more recordings for full web access. If you are near the
Washington, D.C. area, you should go to this library for one of the finest
research experiences imaginable (but for the rest of us, its website will have
to do).

Luminarium Anthology of English Literature (http://www.luminarium.org/).
Created and maintained by Annina Jokinen, this award-winning site features
works from the Medieval period up through the Restoration, along with
biographies and links to critical essays and information. The site also hosts
the Luminarium Encyclopedia, which has the ambition of becoming the
"Who's Who and What's What in Medieval and Renaissance England."

Nieman Watchdog: Questions the Press Should Ask (http://www.niemanwatchdog.
org/index.cfm). The Nieman Foundation for Journalism at Harvard University was founded in 1938 "to promote and elevate the standards of journalism
in the United States." Its website states, "Great questions are a key to great
journalism. But often, in the press of deadlines, the flood of raw information,
manipulated news, deliberate misinformation and just plain junk, great questions are hard to develop. Reporters and editors need to know what's happening,
why it happened, who's involved, who's affected and what happens next. . . ."
This site suggests penetrating, critical questions a responsible press should ask
about national and international issues and provides commentary, discussions,
interviews, and links to articles.

OpenSecrets.org (http://opensecrets.org/about/index.php). This is the site for
the Center for Responsive Politics, a nonpartisan, independent, nonprofit
research group that tracks money in U.S. politics and studies its effect on
elections, public policy, and citizens' lives. According to its mission statement, it "aims to create a more educated voter, an involved citizenry and a
more responsive government." Its awards and honors include several Webby
Awards, a National Press Club award for "Distinguished Contribution to
Online Journalism," and inclusion on *Time* and *Forbes* best websites lists.

ScienceDirect (http://www.sciencedirect.com). This site promises "more than a
quarter of the world's scientific, medical and technical information online."
It lists categories under four broad subject headings: Physical Sciences
and Engineering, Life Sciences, Health Sciences, and Social Sciences and
Humanities, and it boasts more than 2,000 peer-reviewed journals. You have
to register to use it, but registration is free and allows you various specialized
search capabilities, and you can scan 75 million article abstracts.

Slashdot (http://slashdot.org/). Slashdot is a news website offering "News for
nerds. Stuff that matters." Slashdot is a regularly updated holding of news
stories from around the Web, all dealing with gadgets and technology. If you
need information on games, hardware, software, computers, or networking,

this is the place to go. Slashdot is famous for its active community of regular users who post on every news story. Every story on its site can also be linked here via RSS feed, and the site has an "ask Slashdot" section where users can post tech questions and get answers back quickly. (RSS stands for Really Simple Syndication. An RSS document, usually called a "feed," "web feed," or "channel," can contain a summary of content from an associated site or the full text. RSS feeds are used for frequently updated content such as news headlines.)

Snopes.com (http://www.snopes.com/). Do gang members really drive with their lights out as an initiation rite and then kill motorists who flash their headlights at them? Do iPods and cell phones really make lightning strike injuries to people more severe? Can Internet users really get cash rewards for forwarding an email to test an AOL email-tracking system? ("PLEEEEEEASE READ!!!! It was on the news!") Did Al Gore really claim that he "invented the Internet"? Snopes.com researches widely circulated rumors, urban legends, "strange news stories," gossip, "old wives' tales," and similar items. When someone emails you a claim, an alert, or a political rumor, you should check it out here before believing it or passing it along. (The answers to the four questions are #1, No; #2, Yes; #3, No; and #4, No.)

Space.com (http://space.com/). This site is a storehouse of articles, images, video, and links involving all things outer space. Topics such as science news, NASA, the International Space Station, the Hubble telescope, astronomy, technology, space flights, SETI (the search for extra terrestrial life), and the Mars rovers are all covered here. In 2003, this site was recognized by the Online News Association for its superb coverage of the space shuttle *Columbia* disaster.

SurLaLune Fairy Tale Pages (http://www.surlalunefairytales.com/). Created and maintained by Heidie Anne Heiner, this site describes itself as "A portal to the realm of fairy tale and folklore studies featuring 45 annotated fairy tales, including their histories, similar tales across cultures, and over 1,400 illustrations." This is a wonderful starting site for anyone doing folklore or fairy tale studies, especially if they are interested in cross-cultural variants. It offers more than 1,500 folktales and fairy tales from around the world. FAQ sections on children and fairy tales, women and fairy tales, and Disney and fairy tales list numerous books on these subjects.

The Pew Research Center (http://pewresearch.org/). The Pew Research Center is a nonpartisan organization that conducts public opinion polls and social science research on issues and trends affecting America and the world. The Center's work is carried out by eight projects, each with its own website accessible from the site: The Pew Research Center for the People and the Press; Project for Excellence in Journalism; Stateline.org, a news source that tracks and analyzes policy trends in the fifty states; Pew Internet and American Life Project; Pew Forum on Religion and Public Life; Pew Hispanic Center; Pew Global Attitudes Project; and Social & Demographic Trends.

58   CHAPTER 3   Conducting Other Types of Research

The Victorian Web (http://www.victorianweb.org/). This award-winning site has been put together by scholars from several institutions and countries with an interest in the culture, politics, authors, literature, social history, religions, philosophies, science, and gender issues of the Victorian period. The site offers a wealth of information in more than 28,000 documents. It also includes material on some authors who predate the Victorian period but were influential to it, such as Jane Austen, William Wordsworth, Jonathan Swift, and Alexander Pope.

The Webby Awards (http://www.webbyawards.com). The Webby Award, established in 1996, is the "leading international award honoring excellence on the Internet." The Webbys are presented by the International Academy of Digital Arts and Sciences, a "550-member body of leading Web experts, business figures, luminaries, visionaries and creative celebrities." Browsing through the annual lists of award winners can lead you to some informative, provocative, and fun sites. In 2008, Stephen Colbert won the Webby's 2008 "Person of the Year" award for his innovative use of the web for interaction with his show's fans, "from Google bombing to make him the top search result for 'greatest living American' to challenging the 'truthiness' of Wikipedia."

VoS: Voice of the Shuttle (http://vos.ucsb.edu/). This site is excellent for research in the humanities and social sciences, with deep research links (as of this writing) in twenty-eight categories, including Art, Media Studies, Gender and Sexuality, Cyberculture, Literature, and Politics and Government. There are also links to a variety of resources, such as scholarly journals, "zines" (small press publications and alternative newsletters), conferences, listservs, newsgroups, libraries, and museums. VoS is "woven" by the University of California, Santa Barbara's Alan Liu with the help of graduate students and other contributors.

Wikipedia (http://www.wikipedia.org/). The term "wiki" means quick in Hawaiian, making it an apt name for websites that let anyone add to, edit, modify, and even delete content. Wikipedia is a wildly popular wiki encyclopedia that was started in 2001. As we write this, it boasts more than 9 million articles in more than 250 languages, with 75,000 active volunteer "wikipedians" working on additions and revisions, but it also warns, "Because Wikipedia is an ongoing work to which, in principle, anybody can contribute, it differs from a paper-based reference source in important ways. In particular, older articles tend to be more comprehensive and balanced, while newer articles more frequently contain significant misinformation, unencyclopedic content, or vandalism. Users need to be aware of this to obtain valid information and avoid misinformation that has been recently added and not yet removed." There is no central editor or mechanism of true peer review. Thousands of people comb through entries daily to check for errors, jokes, or bias, but there can still be errors (both massive and minor) in every entry you read. Many professors frown on its use in any academic setting, so understand that the likelihood of encountering mistakes here makes this a shoddy tool for serious research. However, in daily life, this site can be helpful because it has entries on every topic imaginable, and it can point you in the direction of scholarly research through its own citations. Just remember not to take anything here at face value.

News Websites

We've come a long way from town criers, who were the first news delivery systems. They used to walk town streets ringing bells and "crying" out official public announcements. Widespread literacy and the invention of printing presses created newspapers, broadcast technology brought us radio and television news, and now we have the Internet. With more and more people getting their news exclusively from the Net, news websites have become increasingly thorough. They have stories that are updated by the minute; they also have opinion pieces and blogs that help give different perspectives on the news. These sites are increasingly high tech, innovating podcasts and streaming videos, and many traditional newspapers and televised news shows now have their own news sites. Most news sites are free, but some will ask you to register with them to give them accurate records of their users.

Following are some of the biggest and best sources for news on the Web, including the sites of the five highest-circulating newspapers in the United States:

Yahoo News: http://news.yahoo.com/

Google News: http://news.google.com/

BBC News: http://news.bbc.co.uk/

CNN: http://www.cnn.com/

MSNBC: http://www.msnbc.msn.com/

USA Today: http://www.usatoday.com/

The Wall Street Journal: http://online.wsj.com/public/us

The New York Times: http://www.nytimes.com/

The Washington Post: http://www.washingtonpost.com/

The Los Angeles Times: http://www.latimes.com/

PRINT MEDIA AND NEWS

Although you may feel completely natural using the Internet, a vast number of people still get information about the world from print sources. Newspapers, popular magazines, and even newsletters are very common ways to get information. Make sure that in your research and your daily life, you rely on more than one medium of information; in other words, even if the Web is your comfort zone, take a look at what the print media has to offer for some more variety about the information of our world. Typically, journalists who write articles for highly regarded print news sources have strict standards and do research to verify leads before going to print. Thus, in most cases, the traditional press is viewed as more reliable than what is posted exclusively on the

Web—of course, the Web versions of print media contain much of the same information. (For more information on news media, see Chapter 18.)

Local Newspapers

Your city (or a larger city nearby) is sure to print a daily newspaper. This is a great resource for several things: 1) Local News. If there is a hot political issue in your hometown, and you need to research it, your local paper is the most logical place to turn. For your academic work, this may be the only source for local statistics, political races, and even information on crime. 2) Recent and Current Events. If something has happened recently (within the last month or two), and you want to use it in an essay or research paper, the only likely sources are going to be local newspapers (which may have online versions). 3) Entertainment and the Arts. A major reason to get a paper is to see what entertainment is happening in your town. Art shows, movie times, concerts, and many other interesting events can be reliably tracked down in your local paper.

Major Newspapers

Several major newspapers are distributed all across America, not just in their hometowns. *USA Today*, the *Wall Street Journal,* the *New York Times,* the *Washington Post,* and the *Los Angeles Times* are the nation's most widely circulated papers, and they are published from coast to coast. Similarly, you can find regional papers, such as the *San Francisco Chronicle,* which is popular for all of the Pacific Northwest, or the *Chicago Sun-Times,* which you can find throughout the Midwest.

These papers have many more resources than local papers, and they can usually afford more investigative journalists (including high-caliber reporters who win awards, such as the Pulitzer Prize, for their work) and more in-depth reporting. Just as with local papers, if there is a recently broken story, these newspapers are the only place to find information (books and scholarly journals won't be in print for a year or more after a newsworthy event takes place, but the newspaper will go to print the next morning). These national papers often break major stories that concern the entire country, such as the 2007 *Washington Post* series on the terrible conditions veterans endured at Walter Reed Army Medical Center.

The major papers are very powerful sources of news, and to maintain mastery over information competency, you must visit them from time to time. However, don't simply return over and over to news outlets and papers that spin stories in ways that fit your preferred worldview. The key to being truly well-informed is to look at a variety of sources and to see for yourself what information different sources leave out of their articles and editorials.

Popular Magazines

Many popular magazines lack the journalistic seriousness of major newspapers. Whereas a newspaper (in theory) exists primarily to disseminate news, magazines tend to focus more on entertainment and lifestyle issues. However, many serious and informative magazines do exist, including those that feature articles on news and culture alongside literature and the arts, such as the *Atlantic Monthly* and the *New Yorker.*

Wired, Scientific American, National Geographic, and *Rolling Stone* are more specialized magazines that also offer serious reporting on various issues. The *Columbia Journalism Review* and the *American Journalism Review* focus on reporting and editorials about the news media. These magazines are considered to define their respective industries. In scholarly research, your professors may not want you to use these sources because the articles are not generated using scholarly methodology, but for information about the world around us, they can't be beat.

News Magazines

Some magazines exist somewhere between the casual entertainment of the popular magazine and the rigorous journalistic standard of a major newspaper, such as *US World and News Report* and *News Weekly*. Also, the news sections of magazines like *Time, Newsweek,* and *The Economist* are as rigorously reported as those in most major newspapers. They are great sources for real world information, but you may want to verify their findings with some independent research before using them in your papers, the same as you would for stories in newspapers.

TELEVISION, RADIO, AND BROADCAST NEWS

The airwaves are another source for finding information. Though television is a much more passive medium than the options listed previously (you just sit around and watch it instead of actively tracking it down and reading through it), it can still be an effective way to gather information about our world. The obvious choice is to watch the news for facts and information, but don't underestimate the ability of some shows on cable channels or on the radio to inform us. National Public Radio is noteworthy for its in-depth news coverage and even for breaking stories through its own investigative reporters. But remember the Golden Rule of Research: consult as wide a variety of reputable sources as possible. Never rely on information presented in just one broadcast or in just one medium.

Local News

Much like local newspapers, local televised news broadcasts are very helpful when you're trying to find information about your community. Local politicians are regularly interviewed, and roving news cameras are able to capture footage of everything from city council meetings to street crime and traffic jams. If you have any reason to research local events, you should get in the habit of closely monitoring the evening news. Consider recording it and sifting through it later at a higher speed if you're serious about using the local news as an information resource. Try to record all the local news stations for different perspectives and to develop a feel for the types of information each favors or skips and for any tendencies to slant certain types of news stories.

Network and Cable News

The major television networks (ABC, NBC, CBS) produce big-budget news shows that are broadcast nationally. These shows cover events of national importance and have the budgets to send reporters around the world in search of major stories. Similar to these network news broadcasts are programs on the big cable news networks such as CNN and MSNBC. These networks have large budgets and a global reach as well, but they are easier to access because they run twenty-four hours a day and repeat major stories every hour. Again, if you're researching a breaking news story that wouldn't be in print yet, the televised news is one of the best resources for you. A VCR or DVR to record these broadcasts can be your best friend when you're trying to gather information, be it academic or personal. Be warned, though, that many cable news networks are thought by media critics to have strong political biases. (For more on the news media and possible "spin," see Chapter 21.)

Television News Magazines

News magazines are television shows that focus on the news in a longer format. Instead of focusing on breaking news stories and trying to get them to you the moment after they happen, these magazine shows take their time and produce detailed, in-depth news segments with background information and interviews designed to present differing perspectives. A typical television news story will be only a few minutes long, but the news magazine stories will last fifteen minutes to an hour or more. Really hard-hitting journalism can occur in this format. The news magazine format was born with CBS's successful *60 Minutes*. *60 Minutes* and PBS's *Frontline* are widely considered the highest quality news magazines, with the most journalistic integrity and with coverage of important stories that may be neglected by other television news shows (though *60 Minutes* also frequently airs human interest stories and profiles of celebrities, like Stephen Colbert, Bill O'Reilly, and Will Smith). *Dateline* and *20/20* are also popular news magazines. You can visit these programs' websites for videos of some of their stories, links to related information, and, in some cases, podcasts. Apple's iTunes store offers subscriptions to many news shows in podcast format for free.

Educational Television

Many cable networks focus on educational shows that give us accounts of crucial moments in history, in-depth biographies of famous people, and facts about the world in general. Networks such as The Discovery Channel, The History Channel, The Documentary Channel, The Biography Channel, and A&E thrive on this type of programming. Other networks, such as HBO and PBS, are also famous for award-winning educational documentaries. When you are interested in an issue, check the programming guide of these channels, or, better yet, visit their websites. Most will keep detailed archives of their past shows and documentaries. You may have to rent or buy the material you track down, but it can often be worth it if information is your goal. Sometimes important programs are available through video and DVD rental outlets. As with news programs, you can visit these networks' websites for videos, links to related information, and podcasts.

Radio

An old standard in mass media communication is the radio, and there are thousands of radio shows out there that do a good job of passing along information (but just as many that don't). With the tumultuous start of satellite radio, radio is a changing medium. Most radio stations focus on popular music, but they often have news segments; however, these segments are likely to focus on local news and tend to be fairly shallow. For gathering information on the radio, the daily news broadcasts and programs of National Public Radio (NPR) can be particularly helpful. NPR is an internationally acclaimed producer of noncommercial programming. Because it is an independent, nonprofit membership organization, its programming isn't dictated by advertisers and ratings. You can also visit NPR's website for transcripts of some of its stories, links to related information, recorded broadcasts, and podcasts. Apple's iTunes store offers free subscriptions to many of NPR's shows in podcast format.

Another format is "talk radio," typically found on the AM band. Talk radio is very popular with a lot of people, featuring highly opinionated hosts and citizens who call in to discuss various current events. Think of talk radio as, essentially, a collection of oral blogs. As such, these shows have the same potential weaknesses of blogs. Anybody can say anything with no ethical or editorial oversight. The news and information you find in this format is almost always unabashedly biased, usually toward the extremes of right or left, based on the personality of the hosts and the owners of the stations. If you find such shows entertaining, enjoy them—just don't consider them good sources for information or examples of critical thinking. (If you have to do an assignment for a logic class on formal and informal fallacies, they're a gold mine.)

Research Tip

With the exception of the programming produced by nonprofit organizations such as PBS and NPR, all television and radio programs exist only as long as they draw good ratings and attract and maintain advertising revenue. We aren't accusing the majority of television and radio news programs of superficiality or dishonesty, we are just noting that factors related to profits and financial risks determine what stories are reported and how they are framed. You are better off with scholarly, verifiable, peer-edited sources, as discussed in Chapter 4, especially if you plan to use them in your papers. (For a more thorough discussion of the financial issues that guide the media, see Section 3, the Anthology of Readings.)

Documentaries

Documentaries occupy a niche of their own. They sometimes air on television, but they aren't generally made by television networks. Some are made by directors such as Ken Burns and Errol Morris, who devote their careers to in-depth explorations of various subjects; others are made by people who are trying to draw the world's attention to a particular topic of importance to them. They can be good sources of information.

Be careful, though—some documentary makers are more interested in propaganda than in the truth, and with new technologies, documentary filmmaking has grown so cheap that virtually anyone can make one. Even people who are trying to be scrupulously

64   CHAPTER 3   Conducting Other Types of Research

honest cannot show you the "whole" truth; they might shoot hundreds or thousands of hours to create films that are usually less than two hours long. They exercise judgment over what to keep and what to cut, and, in the hands of people whose primary purpose is to shape your perceptions, a film can seem to prove whatever case the filmmaker wants.

You should evaluate documentaries as rigorously as any other vehicle for information. Reading multiple reviews in journals and magazines (avoiding those that are clearly politically slanted) is a good way to find out how worthwhile a documentary is. In fact, reviews can themselves be sources of information when the reviewer has a background in the subject. Documentaries may not be sources that you can use in a paper, but they can give you a feel for a topic and put a human face on issues, as well as suggest areas for research. They can also be riveting. For example, the 2001 Academy-Award-winning *Murder on a Sunday Morning* follows the story of an African American teenager picked up and arrested for the brutal murder of a white tourist in Florida. The director, Jean-Xavier de Lestrade, showed up at a courthouse one day to start work on a film on the American justice system, and he and his crew followed the case from the beginning to the end, not knowing how it would turn out. This film raises penetrating questions about eyewitness testimony, racial issues, and police and prosecutorial tactics and evidence gathering.

The other Oscar-winning documentaries of the decade (through the 2008 awards) are *One Day in September,* about a Palestinian terrorist group's taking of Israeli hostages at the 1972 Olympic games in Munich, directed by Kevin MacDonald (2000); *Bowling for Columbine,* which explores America's unique relationship with guns, directed by Michael Moore (2002); *The Fog of War: Eleven Lessons from the Life of Robert S. McNamara,* featuring interviews with the former Secretary of Defense during the Vietnam War, directed by Errol Morris (2003); *Born into Brothels: Calcutta's Red Light Kids,* about the impoverished children of Indian prostitutes, directed by Ross Kauffman and Zana Briski (2004); *March of the Penguins,* about the annual journey of Emperor penguins as they march in single file to their breeding ground, directed by Luc Jacquet (2005); *An Inconvenient Truth,* about Al Gore's campaign to raise awareness about global warming, directed by Davis Guggenheim (2006); and *Taxi to the Dark Side,* an exploration of U.S. torture practices in Afghanistan, Iraq, and Guantánamo Bay, directed by Alex Gibney (2007). Documentaries such as these offer information, entertainment, and food for thought on issues that are often highly controversial. No matter what side you take on an issue, they are fantastic sources for anyone trying to generate topics for a paper because they likely cover several major arguments on their subject matter.

CHAPTER 4

Evaluating Sources and Reading Critically

After days of talking to colleagues, thumbing through your class texts, and pre-writing, you've found a topic for the research paper that is due in your American history class: you've chosen the civil rights movement. You figure that it is associated with a lot of important figures—Martin Luther King, Jr., Rosa Parks, Malcolm X, and President Kennedy—and it affected everything from politics to urban development and basic finances of the 1960s. There is plenty to research and many areas you could choose as your final focus after you've gathered your research material.

Your instructor has approved this topic, so now you need to start finding good sources for your paper. You get online and conduct a Net search, and hundreds of articles and sites come up. You read some of the online material, and you realize that a lot of it is contradictory. You go to your school library's searchable online catalog, and you see a couple of dozen books that could be relevant. A search of articles shows well over a hundred hits on various aspects of the civil rights movement—far too many to reliably read through. You were a little afraid when you started that you wouldn't be able to find enough information, but now you feel confused and overwhelmed. Ironically, you first felt that the numerous aspects you could think about when researching civil rights would make the paper easy to write, but they have, in fact, made it look harder. Where do you start? How do you narrow down all these lists? How do you know what sources are the best? A key element to becoming competent with information is to be able to evaluate sources and read critically while researching. If you master these skills, you won't be confused by an avalanche of material.

TYPES OF SOURCES

The first step in choosing sources is recognizing what a scholarly source actually is: a well-documented book or article written by one or more experts that is intended to be read by other experts and scholars in the field and by people like you who are trying to develop expertise. You also need to be able to distinguish between primary, secondary, and tertiary sources. We'll explain what primary, secondary, and tertiary sources are before moving into ways to differentiate between scholarly and nonscholarly sources and how to evaluate authors and publications.

66   CHAPTER 4   Evaluating Sources and Reading Critically

Primary Sources

Primary sources provide original research or are original documents, not interpretations or excerpts of other research or documents. Examples include articles that record original observations or documentations, such as scientific studies, historical documents, and works of literature. When you are looking at scientific information, primary sources are especially valuable because of all the detail about the research they provide. Scientists are interested in replicability, which is the degree to which a scientific study can be repeated to see if its findings and outcomes will occur again if the study is reproduced by other investigators. Scientific reports have to provide detailed, accurate information about testing procedures, control groups, experimental groups, and so on, as well as information on possible confounding factors. (A *confounding factor,* also called a *confounding variable,* is a variable that is related to one or more of the variables defined in a study. A confounding factor may falsely demonstrate an apparent association between the study's dependent and independent variables where no true association between them exists.)

Secondary Sources

Secondary sources are one step removed from primary sources; they may take complete or partial data from primary sources and summarize, paraphrase, and interpret information. Examples include the books or articles that present a scholarly analysis of primary source material and books and articles about scientific research, historical events, and current affairs. In a study of literature, the books and articles you find that provide an examination or interpretation of the literature are secondary sources.

Tertiary Sources

Tertiary sources take information from secondary sources, though they may combine it with information taken from primary sources. Examples include various reference works, including online encyclopedias, many articles in popular magazines, and even advertisements.

Distortion of Sources

A common problem with secondary and tertiary sources is that the information they present from primary sources is an interpretation of the original material. Sometimes these interpretations can distort the primary source material, either accidentally or deliberately. Accidental distortions are likely to occur when someone who is not an expert interprets data for a popular audience, or a writer who is expert enough to understand the data inadvertently creates a misleading picture through oversimplification. Scientists are a lot less likely to try to make sweeping claims about the implications of their research than are writers for the popular market.

For example, an article in a scholarly journal reported the results of a study noting a correlation between a lower rate of heart attacks in a group of 100 men between the ages of fifty and sixty who took B-complex supplements for a year. This research became the basis of an article published in a popular magazine. The magazine article was titled "Taking B Vitamins Will Lower Your Chances of Having a Heart Attack." Whereas the original article discussed the smallness of the sample size, the short time frame of the study, the homogeneity of the group (women or younger or older men might respond differently), and the need for further research, the magazine article slighted those issues, and the title certainly didn't reflect the caution of the original researchers. After all, the publishers of the magazine want to sell magazines, and there is a ready market out there of people who want to believe that popping vitamins will protect them until they get around to losing weight, exercising, and breaking their junk food addictions.

Deliberate distortions occur when authors of books or articles or the creators of advertising campaigns have a particular agenda that they want to push, and they take information and quotations out of context to present a different picture than the one you'd find in the original work. Thus, a source may seem to be offering scientific or other types of evidence to bolster a claim, even providing documentation, but it is really just pushing propaganda. For example, in 2006 the Competitive Enterprise Institute (which is partially funded by oil companies) released its "Glaciers" TV ad. "Glaciers" shows the cover of *Science* magazine opening, and an announcer states,

> Greenland's glaciers are growing, not melting; The Antarctic ice sheet is getting thicker, not thinner. Did you see any big headlines about that? Why are they trying to scare us? Global warming alarmists claim the glaciers are melting because of carbon dioxide from the fuels we use. Let's force people to cut back, they say.
>
> But we depend on those fuels to grow our food, move our children, light up our lives. And as for carbon dioxide, it isn't smog or smoke. It's what we breathe out and plants breathe in. Carbon dioxide. They call it pollution. We call it life.

The day after this ad first aired, Brooks Hanson, a deputy editor at *Science,* stated in a news release that "The text of the CEI ad misrepresents the conclusions of the two cited *Science* papers and our current state of knowledge by selective referencing." In the same news release, Professor Curt Davis, the lead author of the study cited by the CEI, said that the CEI was engaging in "a deliberate effort to confuse and mislead the public about the global warming debate. They are selectively using only parts of my previous research to support their claims. They are not telling the entire story to the public."

Secondary and tertiary sources can provide you with good information. However, often their greatest value is to point you toward a primary source. On the other hand, a primary source may be extremely complex and too difficult for most people outside a given field to understand. Also, when dealing with the analysis of a work of literature, the scholars in the field are, by definition, creating secondary sources when they analyze different texts. Thus, research is not as simple as choosing primary sources over secondary and tertiary ones. You still need to know how to evaluate any source you look at, because secondary and tertiary sources can constitute scholarly works.

POPULAR VERSUS SCHOLARLY: HOW TO TELL THE DIFFERENCE

There are many types of sources—both scholarly and nonscholarly. Following is a list of twelve types of sources you are likely to encounter, from books to websites to wiki-pedias. **Periodicals** refer to magazines, newspapers, and scholarly journals because all of these are published periodically (monthly, bimonthly, or on some regular basis). You must consider the strengths and weaknesses of each type of source before using it in your paper.

Though it is hard to say for sure that one type of source is definitely better than another when it comes to researching, the following list is arranged with quality in mind. The types of sources at the beginning of the list are more academically sound, whereas the sources toward the end of the list should probably be avoided for most academic papers. Numbers one and two on the list (Scholarly Books and Scholarly Periodicals), for example, are widely considered the two best types of sources to use in your research, but books are not necessarily better than periodicals. The purpose of your research and your field of study will determine the distinctions you will make and the types of sources you will use.

Scholarly Books

These books are written by professional scholars, who rely on research, statistical data, and supporting evidence to prove their assertions and arguments. This is the type of writing that you should aspire to in your own research papers. Because scholarly books emphasize careful, detailed, thorough research and analysis, they are the most thorough, accurate, and well-documented types of sources you can use in your paper. However, these books are slow to research and write, so for research detailing events from the past year or so, you may want to look at other types of sources, such as articles from scholarly periodicals.

Articles from Scholarly Periodicals

These articles are published not to make money, but to educate and inform and to advance the reputations of the authors. They are particularly good sources because they are usually "refereed"; the article is read by several experts in its field and deemed of high academic quality before it is published. Articles are obviously shorter than scholarly books, but for current research, you can find the most recent work in scholarly journals. Scholarly articles provide a full list of citations just like scholarly books do, and they are the type of writing that you should aspire to in your own papers. Scholarly dissertations and findings from academic conferences are examples of this kind of writing, and you can also find scholarly articles in **anthologies,** books that are filled with selections written by different scholars.

Specialized Encyclopedias and Dictionaries

In the reference section of most libraries, you will find specialized encyclopedias and dictionaries. These reference works are written by experts in the field and vary widely in subject matter. You can find specialized encyclopedias or dictionaries on subjects ranging from American presidents to the Vietnam War. Because they focus on particular topics and disciplines, they are able to be more thorough than general encyclopedias. They typically have citations of outside sources, which can suggest other resources, and are often written by professors and other researchers. They also may indicate terms and keywords that you can use when searching for articles in indexes and databases.

Government Publications

Various government agencies write regular reports or professional publications. These range in purpose from securing future funding for the agencies to educating the public or informing a larger governing body, such as Congress, of their findings. Organizations such as the U.S. Census Bureau use top-notch statistical methodology, and groups like the Federal Communications Commission regularly publish their public hearings and reports. Most government publications are considered solid research material for any paper. However, do some research to find out if there have been any controversies associated with any of the material, such as accusations by government scientists that information not favorable to a given administration's political agenda was suppressed or rewritten. Sadly, this has been known to happen.

Professional Websites

Although it is often a good idea to avoid use of websites in your academic papers, some sites are very well put together and very well documented. Often government groups have websites, as do professional and academic groups. These websites are often as thorough and reliable as government publications and scholarly articles, even though they are found on the Web instead of in print. (For more on websites, see Chapter 3.)

Newspapers

Newspapers are good sources of information, especially for very current issues. If a political scandal erupted only a week ago, newspapers are probably the best place to go to find published information. The only downside to the newspaper, however, is that the daily news is not its only concern. Newspaper publishers need to make money to stay afloat, and many answer to larger corporations that now own them. It is possible that a newspaper may report only part of the story in order to keep readership up or a major sponsor happy. Ideally, quality journalism with integrity will guide the paper you read, but you can't assume this to be so, so read several newspapers to get a well-rounded idea of the news.

Industry Periodicals

Although popular magazines are far outside the realm of true academic scholarship, some periodicals are considered the best in one particular industry. The *Wall Street Journal,* for example, is the standard publication for the financial industry. On a more popular level, *Rolling Stone* is considered the best publication for music news and interviews with musical artists. Though these sources are not officially scholarly, you may find some good, exclusive content in them.

Popular Books

Even though a popular book may be a best seller, if it fails to include scholarly documentation and a professional tone, you should avoid using it as a source. The best-selling guru of the day may be a tempting source, especially if you already have his or her book on your shelf. However, such books are often full of opinion instead of fact, and some diligent time in the library will yield you a book with strong scholarly support written by a true expert in the field.

General Encyclopedias

Encyclopedias, such as *Grolier's,* Microsoft's *Encarta,* or *Encyclopedia Britannica,* are great for learning general information about a topic and generating prewriting ideas, but they are poor sources to include in your papers at the college/university level. Since they deal with an enormous number of topics, the information they provide is relatively brief and shallow.

Popular Magazines

General interest and popular magazines are fun to read and often published in their entirety on the Web (thus, they are very easy to find while researching). Although you may use these magazines to prewrite and generate initial ideas for your paper, you should avoid actually citing them in the body of your paper itself. You should avoid using popular news magazines such as *Time* and *Newsweek* and general interest magazines such as *Wired* and *O, The Oprah Magazine* as sources in a typical scholarly paper.

Popular Websites

The average website, such as those published by individuals on sites like MySpace or by corporations, may contain interesting material, but beware. You may use it, only to find later on that the authors were mistaken, joking, or just plain lying. Information on popular websites is often hearsay or simply copied from another source and pasted into the site. It is your job as a researcher to find the primary source, not rely on random websites, even ones that seem credible and look professional. Your library may also provide workshops on evaluating websites, which can help you if your instructor allows you to use material found on the Web.

Wikis

The wiki (from the Hawaiian "Wiki," meaning "quick") phenomenon exploded with the publication of Wikipedia on the web. Wikis are "open source," which means that the entries are written by anyone who logs in; people can even add or delete information in existing entries. Because of this access, people can publish false information just to get a laugh or simply because they don't realize that it is faulty. Although Wikipedia, the world's largest and most important wiki encyclopedia, claims that "scores of contributors monitor the list of contributions (particularly to important or controversial articles), and will quickly delete nonsense or obviously wrong articles, and undo baseless edits," it also concedes that "there is almost certainly inaccurate information in it, somewhere, which has not yet been discovered to be wrong." Wikis can be great sources for a quick look at a topic, but they should not be regarded as definitive. If you find a provocative piece of information on a wiki, look for the same information in a scholarly source. Quote that scholarly source, not the wiki, in your paper.

As mentioned, this list includes both popular and scholarly sources. This distinction is of vital importance to academic research. In a research paper, you want to rely primarily (perhaps exclusively) on scholarly sources. A scholarly source is usually written by a professional scholar, is well documented, and is intended to educate and inform. A nonscholarly source is usually written by a journalist or a nonacademic author, it often has no documentation, it may rely on eyewitness accounts, and it is published primarily to entertain and appeal to mass audiences, not to educate.

If you are in doubt about whether a source is scholarly or nonscholarly, there are several ways to determine the difference. How can you tell if a book, magazine, journal article, or website can be described as a scholarly source? Here are some basic guidelines:

Distinguishing Between Scholarly and Nonscholarly Sources

Scholarly Sources	Nonscholarly Sources
■ Books or articles written by scholars or experts in the field, with their institutional affiliations provided.	■ Books or articles written by people who are not scholars or experts in the field. They may or may not be professional writers.
■ Always cite their sources of information through such methods as bibliographies, in-text citations, footnotes, and end notes.	■ Rarely offer information (citations or bibliographies) about the sources of information.
■ Include information like research methods and results and specialized vocabulary.	■ Report events or opinions or summarize findings of other sources in simple language.
■ Are aimed at scholarly audiences, such as other researchers and experts.	■ Are generally published for profit and may be vehicles of opinion.
■ Are usually published in scholarly journals or by university presses or other publishing companies with reputations for scholarly works.	■ Are published in popular magazines or by popular publishing houses, sometimes those with an overt agenda (they may publish only right-wing or left-wing books, for example, or books with a particular religious bent).

EVALUATING AN AUTHOR

What are the author's credentials and educational background? Is the book or article in the area of the author's expertise? This may seem obvious, but there is nothing to stop a corporate lawyer from writing a book attacking climate change or a professor of electrical engineering from writing articles claiming that the Holocaust is a myth. Some professional authors synthesize information taken from expert sources, but they aren't experts themselves. A true scholar in the field is more trustworthy than a non-expert writing for the popular market.

What can you find out about the author's affiliations? Is he or she connected to a research institution concerned with developing greater knowledge about an issue? Or is he or she affiliated with an organization with an agenda that might suggest bias? What are its goals? The *Encyclopedia of Associations,* a standard library reference work, can give you information on more than 135,000 organizations worldwide. A database version, *Associations Unlimited,* combines data from the entire *Encyclopedia of Associations,* covering more than 456,000 organizations. Knowing about an association or organization can help you if you cannot find any information on an author. A source may seem unbiased, logical, and informative, but you should know if a sponsoring association has a political or economic agenda. If it does have one, this doesn't mean that your source can't be valuable, but it warns you to look out for a possible slant in the presentation or even the omission of relevant facts. You can also often find information online on a group or institution's own website (though some groups are self-flattering and less than candid with their descriptions of themselves and their goals).

What other works has this author written? Has this author published more than one book in this area? If he or she has published a number of books, that may indicate that he or she is a recognized expert in the field. Library references like *Contemporary Authors* and *Who's Who?* are very helpful for providing information about authors. After you access these references, some questions you should ask yourself include the following: Have you seen the author's name cited in other sources or bibliographies on your research topic?

Have other experts in the field given the book positive reviews? Don't simply trust what the blurb on the back cover says—it's there to sell the book. Information about the author's credentials and institutional affiliations is helpful, but phrases like "brilliant insights" and "leading expert" are not. Biographical information at the beginning or end of articles in periodicals should be approached in the same way. Factual information about education and affiliations is useful; flattering endorsements are suspect (authors often write their own biographies for articles). There is one way in which flattering endorsements can help you, though—look at the names of the people supplying the endorsements, and look them up. Are they verifiable experts? Do they have agendas to push or axes to grind? For in-depth information about a book, the multi-volume reference *Book Review Digest* in your college library is great, as is the *Book Review Index* on the Web. The reviews provide information about the author and the book itself, and may even compare the book to others on the subject, which can help you find other sources. If you can't find a review in one of these reference works, sometimes you can find one or more reviews by typing the author's name and the book's title and the phrase "book review" into a search engine. However, consider the source of the review—is it from a reputable source itself?

What is the author's tone? Is it serious, dignified, and respectful of dissenting opinion? Is it breezy, chatty, and informal? Is it emotional, argumentative, or even derisive? Serious experts, when they disagree, tend to do so maturely, showing professional courtesy.

Can you find any interviews with an author? Authors are often remarkably informal and frank in interviews, and when they are, you can get a feel for how they approach a topic.

HANDY EVALUATION REFERENCES IN THE LIBRARY

American Men & Women of Science
Book Review Digest
Book Review Index
Contemporary Authors
Encyclopedia of Associations
Magazines for Libraries
Who's Who?

EVALUATING A PERIODICAL

If you are using an article as a source, what kind of periodical published it? Is it in a scholarly journal, or is it in a popular magazine? You should be able to distinguish between types of periodicals. This doesn't mean that you should always avoid magazines—some have high standards. However, with a scholarly journal, much of the evaluation of a source has already been done for you. Articles in scholarly journals have been chosen and reviewed by other scholars in the same discipline. (For help in determining the type of periodical, see Distinguishing Between Scholarly Journals and Popular Magazines on the next page.) You can also consult a copy of *Magazines for Libraries*, which provides annotations and expert evaluations of approximately 7,000 periodicals, with more than 100 major subject headings. The annotations also describe the strengths and weaknesses of periodicals in relation to others within the same fields. This is a standard reference work for college libraries. Don't let the title mislead you; it deals with a range of periodical types, including scholarly journals, not simply popular magazines.

Scholarly journals often provide an **abstract** at the beginning of articles. This gives you a complete summary of the article and will help you make a decision about whether the article will be useful to you. Sometimes magazine articles begin with a brief summary or statement of purpose above or below the title. You might also check journal and magazine articles to see if they have summaries at the end. Skim the article for headings, and read the information immediately after each heading.

Century

Distinguishing Between Scholarly Journals and Popular Magazines	
Scholarly Journals	Popular Magazines
■ Are usually published by professional organizations, associations, scholarly groups or universities and colleges.	■ Are published by corporations.
■ Generally publish only articles that are peer reviewed by other experts.	■ Do not have a peer review process.
■ Have covers and pages that tend to be plain in design, with few or no pictures or graphics; the covers tend to use black, white, and one color, and all issues look alike.	■ Use colors and images on covers and the pages. Except for the magazine name and locale, the covers tend to be very different each issue.
■ Rarely feature advertisements; if they do have advertisements, they are likely to be for scholarly books.	■ Are filled with advertisements.
■ Always name authors and provide their credentials.	■ May publish articles without bylines.
■ Often have issues that are successively numbered throughout a year, with each issue after the first beginning with the page number following the last page number of the preceding issue.	■ Usually begin each issue with a page one.
■ Have articles that are often quite lengthy.	■ Have articles in a variety of lengths, including those that are quite short, even less than a page long.
■ Are usually published only a few times a year, typically four times (though some publish as frequently as once a month or as infrequently as twice a year).	■ Are published relatively frequently, typically once a week or once a month.
■ Are usually found in libraries (or a professor's office).	■ Are available at bookstores, magazine stands, convenience stores, and supermarkets.

As noted previously, some popular magazines have high standards. Magazines like the *New Yorker, Atlantic Monthly, The Economist, Scientific Review,* and *Discover* have very good reputations—they sometimes even publish articles by authors who have published in scholarly journals but who have reason to reach a wider audience. Don't automatically abandon a source from a magazine, just be extra careful about evaluating it. However, for some research papers, you will definitely want articles only from scholarly journals. When you search an index such as Expanded Academic ASAP and some others, you can limit your search to "refereed publications." This means they are peer reviewed by scholars in the same field, so you know that all the articles your search turns up are from scholarly journals.

EVALUATING A BOOK

If you are using a book as a source, you can try to find information on the publisher. University presses or other publishing companies with reputations for scholarly works can signal that a work is likely to be scholarly. They are not automatic endorsements, of course, but they indicate a level of seriousness. See what information you can find on a publisher's own website—it can be very illuminating. In some cases, a publisher's site will indicate that it publishes only works that reflect a particular set of political, economic, social, or religious values. Knowing this can alert you to possible biases.

When was the article or book originally published? Some research paper topics are in areas of rapid development, such as the sciences, and books and articles can be out of date in less than a decade. Research in the humanities, on the other hand, has a much longer shelf life. Look for the copyright year. You can usually find this and other information on a page that follows the book's title page and precedes the table of contents. It might be immediately before the table of contents or before a dedication page. Look for a page with small print. You'll see information about the publisher, including the address, followed by information on where and when the book was first published and the date it was copyrighted. A brand new book might be a reissue of a book that is years, even decades, old. You should also look to see what edition it is. This gives you more information than just the date alone. If a book has gone through multiple editions, it might suggest that it has become a standard source. Also, later editions aren't always simply reissued books—sometimes they include added, updated material.

The next set of steps involves examining the contents of a book. Learning how to properly pull information out of different parts of your sources is one more step in your mastery of information competency.

Table of Contents/Introduction

Does the table of contents look helpful? Is an introduction provided? Sometimes a book with a title that sounds perfect turns out not to cover exactly what you thought it would. Keep your research question in mind. The table of contents and the introduction can help you to decide whether you want to keep reading. The introduction can also be helpful in other ways. If it is written by the author, you will get an idea of his or her tone and style. This can give you a hint about whether the author's approach is serious and open-minded or shallow and biased. If the introduction is written by someone else, look that person up. Sometimes, if a leading expert in a field writes an introduction for a book, that in itself serves as a very positive evaluation from a reputable source. Introductions, whether written by the author or someone else, will give you a good idea about where the author is heading with the topic.

Bibliography

The word "bibliography" (from Greek *biblion*, "book," and *graphia*, "writing") originally referred to a list of books, but now it covers all texts used in a source. Does this book provide a bibliography? How extensive is it? Do you see the names of people who are experts in the field? Is there a "Selected Bibliography," which includes sources of interest not used in the book? This can help to indicate the scope of the author's knowledge on the subject. Is there a section of end notes that points to other sources? (Sometimes these can be found at ends of chapters.)

Index

An index is an alphabetical list of terms, names, places, and subjects at the back of a book with the page numbers where they can be found. As you do your research, compile a list of important items to check for in indexes. You're not supposed to judge a book by its cover, but this handy list right before the back cover is a different matter. When you are doing research and faced with hundreds of books on dozens of subjects, the index can help you lock on to the best sources for your topic and weed out weaker ones. If key terms you're finding in your research all get several listings in the index, you've made a great find. If the index has no such terms, the book may not be useful to your research goals.

Body of the Book

Does the body give you an idea of the book's relevance and accessibility? Look for references in the index to information that would be valuable to you, and go to those sections of the book to see how extensively these areas are covered. How well are you able to follow the author's ideas? Is the language clear to you? Pick one or more chapters that look valuable in the table of contents, and go to them, reading their first and last paragraphs. This will tell you a great deal about what the chapter actually covers.

EVALUATING AN ONLINE SOURCE

Many of the preceding strategies for evaluating information are applicable to any type of resource, but the Web provides an array of challenges because anybody— even you—can put anything on the Web. Because evaluating online sources can be especially challenging, we have provided a detailed checklist of questions for you to ask:

1. *Is an author provided?* If so, does the site provide background information and credentials? As with other types of source, you should look at the relevance of an author's credentials. People naturally want to look as impressive as possible, and they will give you a full list of credentials, but they may be in areas not especially relevant to the topic being discussed. Also, see if you can use a search engine to find out more about the author—sometimes people fake credentials. The Internet is a very informal place, and anyone can put up a site saying pretty much anything.

2. *What is the domain name?* The domain tells you where the web page comes from. In the United States, the most common domains are .com (for commercial entities), .edu (for educational institutions), .gov, .mil, and .us

(for government agencies), .net (network related), and .org (for nonprofit and research organizations). Outside the United States, domains indicate countries of origin, such as .uk (for United Kingdom) and .ca (for Canada). The domain gives you some insight as to the credibility of the material, but it doesn't tell you everything. A page with an .edu domain may be an official university web page, but it could also be a page for student work.

3. *What can you find out about the site's sponsor?* Is it an individual, a company, a university, or a group or organization? Does it have an About Us section? (Other names to look for include Philosophy, Who We Are, and Background.) If so, read the information provided, but don't assume that the information is entirely candid and accurate. Use it as a starting point, and investigate other people, groups, or sites that it mentions. With serious research, you can't "one-stop shop"—you may need to get off the Net and go to the library to find out about the organizations and associations that sponsor different sites.

4. *Are there links to other sites?* What do you find when you follow a site's links? Sometimes a site that looks very reasonable is only a couple of links away to an extremist group. Even if the linked sites are not extremist in orientation, they can give you an idea of possible slants. Conversely, you may find that the links take you to reputable, solid groups, institutions, and organizations.

5. *Is there any apparent bias in the site?* (Remember that *bias* means a particular slant or disposition.) The presence of a discernible bias doesn't automatically indicate that a site is publishing false information, but it will affect the information presented and its interpretation. It is especially important to look for bias when a site presents information that corresponds to your own feelings about a subject. (Such information tends to "feel right" to us.) Look to see if the site posts links to original sources of information, or if it presents only summaries, paraphrases, or quotations. In other words, is it asking you to simply trust it, or is it giving you a chance to easily find the original source material?

6. *When was the site last updated?* Information that looks great may have been posted years ago and may no longer be accurate or relevant. If there is no date, that is a bad sign.

7. *When was the article or other material you are reading posted?* Even if the page itself has been updated recently, it doesn't necessarily mean that an article on the site is recent. Look for a date for the article itself.

8. *Does the site reproduce an article or section from another source?* Articles can easily be altered. If it does reproduce an article, does it have permission to reproduce and does it provide copyright information, as well as a link to the original source if it is online?

There are some good online directories that allow you to search by topic areas and that also provide evaluations. They include *Librarians' Internet Index, Academic.Info,* and *Infomine.*

(See Chapter 18, "The Internet," for more information).

HANDY EVALUATION REFERENCES FOR WEBSITES

- Evaluation of Information Sources (http://www.vuw.ac.nz/staff/alastair_smith/evaln/evaln.htm)
- Stanford Web Credibility Project (http://credibility.stanford.edu/)
- The Good, The Bad & The Ugly: or, Why It's a Good Idea to Evaluate Web Sources (http://lib.nmsu.edu/instruction/evalcrit.html)
- Evaluating Internet Information (http://www.library.jhu.edu/researchhelp/general/evaluating/)
- How to Evaluate Medical Information Found on the Internet (http://new.cmanet.org/publicdoc.cfm/60/0/GENER/99)
- Evaluating Foreign and International Legal Databases on the Internet (http://www.llrx.com/features/evaluating.htm)

EVALUATING CONTENT

The evaluation process isn't finished after you decide that a source looks good. You have to engage in an ongoing evaluation process as you read. Make sure you can separate facts from opinions. Facts can be checked and verified. This doesn't mean simply looking to see if your author provides citations. (We can think of at least one popular writer famous for providing citations that don't tend to stand up when traced to their sources.) Some writers are very good at making you think their opinions are facts. Be prepared to check anything that you will present as evidence in your own work. Be especially alert for sweeping generalizations that aren't backed up with statistics, but instead rely on anecdotal evidence (informal accounts of evidence and observations).

You need to carefully evaluate not just the evidence presented, but the quality of an author's argument. You should already have some idea of an author's tone. Emotive tones often go along with shaky argumentation. But a serious tone doesn't guarantee a logical or well-supported set of arguments, and sometimes an author with a questionable tone may offer logically sound arguments and solid evidence. Still, tone can be a signal that you need to be especially cautious. (See Chapter 5 for more information on evaluating arguments.)

ACTIVE READING

Whether you are looking at material you find on your own while doing the research for a paper or reading essays in an assigned textbook, you need to make sure that you are reading effectively. To do that, you need to be an active, not a passive, reader. Passive readers pick up a book or periodical and just start reading. You probably know what it feels like to read an essay or a chapter in a book and then, when you finish, you realize that you don't remember much about what you read at all. You read every single word, but the ideas just didn't stick. You may have highlighted what seemed to be important sections, but this doesn't seem to have helped. That's because you were reading passively. You need to engage with the text.

Think about lectures. Do you just sit there passively, listening to the professor, trusting that later you'll be able to remember everything he or she said? Of course not. Good students take notes, jotting down main points and important details and asking questions to clarify what they are being told. You need to be just as active—or even more so—when you read. Be prepared to take notes, the same as if you were listening to a lecture. Formulate questions as you read and then write them down. If you find that the text itself answers your questions later, add the page numbers with the answers after your questions. If you don't find answers the first time through, the questions will be ready when you reread the material. Active reading helps you to stay focused and involved and to concentrate more successfully. You'll improve your comprehension because you will be monitoring it as you go.

Additionally, be prepared to read books and articles more than once. Your professors have probably read the books they are teaching many times. Much scholarly writing is very dense and difficult to understand in just one reading. Many students think that they should understand what they've read the first time around. Don't be embarrassed or afraid to reread passages or entire works more than once to fully get their meanings.

Previewing Your Reading

Following are some preliminary steps that will help you approach a text thoughtfully:

1. *Essays/Articles/Chapters.* For essays, articles, and chapters in books, think about the title and try to predict content from that. Read the first paragraph and the last paragraph before you read the body. These paragraphs tend to emphasize the main points of the body. The first paragraph provides an overview and may provide a thesis. The conclusion probably sums up main points. If you read both of these in advance of the more fact-filled body, you will know exactly what ideas and arguments to focus on while reading. For both the introduction and conclusion, try paraphrasing the main ideas. One of the best ways to check to see whether you understand an idea is to try putting it into your own words. If you have difficulty, try reading these sections again. Also, scan to see if there are subheadings. You can find lots of clues about main ideas by looking at subheadings; terms in bold font; information in boxes; and pictorial matter, such as graphs, charts, drawings, and photographs.

2. *Whole Books.* If you are working with an entire book, follow the suggestions we just made, but also read the introduction or preface if one is provided, and look at the chapter titles in the table of contents. If the book has a section labeled "Conclusion," read that right after you read the introduction. Read it first if

there isn't an introduction. If you already know what information you need to find in the book, check to see if there is an index, and use that to go straight to what for you are the most important sections to see how thoroughly the book deals with crucial material. For example, if you're researching advertising, check the index in the back of the book. If advertising isn't listed among the major topics back there, this may not be the book for you.

3. *Audience and Purpose.* As part of your previewing process, ask yourself if you can determine the author's purpose—is it to argue, persuade, or just inform? Who is the author's intended audience? The general public? Fellow scholars in the field? People who already agree with the writer's views? People who disagree? If you can figure this out in advance, it may assist you in assessing the major ideas of the source.

FINDING AND NOTING MAIN IDEAS

After you've finished previewing your reading materials, you are ready to start looking for main ideas. Following are some tips to help you do that.

Paragraphs

As you read the body, focus on individual paragraphs, looking for the main ideas. The main idea of a reading is the central thought or message. The topic is the subject matter—the main idea is what is being expressed about the subject matter. Often the main idea of a paragraph is contained in what is called a **topic sentence,** which can be thought of as the thesis statement of the paragraph. This sentence makes an assertion about the subject of the paragraph, much the way a thesis in an essay or paper does. Where the thesis of a whole essay or paper is likely to be argumentative, however, a topic sentence supplies information, makes an evaluation, identifies a problem, adds evidence or examples to back an assertion up, and so on. Topic sentences are often the first sentences in paragraphs, but they can be found elsewhere in the paragraph—one trick is to look for the most general sentence. Sentences that have details provide evidence and discussion of the topic sentence. Ask yourself, "What general point does the author seem to make about the topic?" After you have found the topic sentence, write it down. Next, write down your own paraphrase of that sentence. If you can't, reread the whole paragraph to see if that helps. In some cases, a paragraph won't include a topic sentence at all. As an active reader, you need to decide what main idea is implied by all the sentences in the paragraph. Write that down.

Repetition

As you move through the reading's paragraphs, look for any ideas that are repeated in different ways. Repetition signals importance, and thoughts that are repeated are likely to be main ideas. Write these ideas down in your own words, too—or, if you have already written them down as topic sentences, underline or highlight them to underscore their importance. Look for transition words such as "consequently," "however," "furthermore," and "nevertheless"; these can offer clues about both importance and meaning.

Surprises

Also, you should look for information that surprises you. Do you see anything that challenges ideas that you hold? Does any of the information seem wrong or seem to contradict the notions typically held by other scholars and authors that you've found in your research? Pay careful attention to the evidence the text offers in support of this information. Look for any apparent inconsistencies or contradictions. Note these. When you reread the text, see if they are explained or resolved.

Vocabulary

Identify words you don't understand and look them up in a collegiate dictionary before proceeding. Don't assume that you can guess their meaning from the context. This doesn't always work, and if you just guess, you run the risk of misunderstanding key points. Write these words and definitions down—this will help you learn them. Write down key terms that are emphasized and repeated even if you know their meaning already—they will help you as you think about the passage. If the language is highly specialized and your dictionary doesn't contain these terms, make a note of the terms you don't understand and ask your instructor about them before or during class.

REVIEWING YOUR NOTES

After you have come to the end of an essay, article, or chapter, look at all the main ideas that you have written down in your notes. Try to determine the ones that are the most important. Next, ask yourself what facts, evidence, reasons, statistics, studies, and arguments have been offered in support. If you aren't sure, go back and reread passages until you can answer those questions, writing the answers down. It's a good idea to add page citations if you will be using the reading in an essay or research paper so that you can quickly find the material when you are writing your draft.

OUTLINING MATERIAL

It can also be useful to make an outline or a paragraph-long summary of the essay, article, or chapter. This tests your understanding of the material. If you read the material and can't effectively reproduce the main points, you need to go back and reread some more. You can also freewrite a brief response about the reading. What reactions do you have? What confuses you? What is most interesting to you?

ANNOTATING A TEXT

If you are reading a text that you own, you can annotate it as you go. This means writing your ideas in the margins. If you have a library book, consider making photocopies of the important sections and chapters so that you can annotate these. You could even scan the material into your computer and type comments alongside the original material in a different colored font. In fact, some instructors require that you turn in copies of the sources that you use with your papers, so they can track your annotations. Simply highlighting or underlining sections are passive activities, but annotating is active—it forces you to think as you go. Highlighting and underlining can (and should) be used in concert with annotating, however.

Following is a checklist to help you annotate a reading

- Look for important terms and definitions.
- Note where important information can be found with keywords or symbols.
- Write short summaries at the ends of sections.
- Write main ideas for paragraphs or sections.
- Write questions about crucial ideas next to the sections where the answers are found.
- Write questions the material raises but doesn't answer directly.
- If the author is constructing arguments, write "claim" or "conclusion" or an abbreviation, like "concl.," next to sections where the author draws conclusions about important arguments, and "premise 1," "premise 2," etc., to identify the premises. See Chapter 5 for a discussion of how to evaluate arguments and an explanation of

the Toulmin Method, which can help you to analyze the structure and strength or weakness of many arguments.

- Be alert to the author's techniques of persuasion. Aristotle described three "appeals": *ethos* (the image a speaker or writer projects), *logos* (use of logic and evidence), and *pathos* (stirring up emotions). Write these terms next to sections when pertinent. (Chapter 5 contains a detailed discussion of these appeals.)
- Be aware of the different modes of writing used in the author's rhetoric. For a full list of rhetorical modes, see page 164.
- Write "statistics" or "stats" next to sections that offer statistical evidence or where the author fails to provide statistics needed to back up evidence. (You might add a question mark for sections where statistics are missing.)

Annotated Student Reading

The following is a sample of how you can annotate your own reading as you research and gather evidence for your papers. This piece (Ben Bagdikian's "Grand Theft") can be found in Chapter 20.

The student used two highlighters while scanning this material. She highlighted phrases and words in yellow if she wanted to look into them more later on. She used a blue highlighter for terms that she needed to define.

Annotating a Text **83**

For 25 years, a handful of large corporations that specialize in every mass medium of any consequence has dominated what the majority of people in the United States see about the world beyond their personal experience. These giant media firms, unlike any in the past, thanks to the hands-off attitude of the Federal Communications Commission (FCC) majority, are unhampered by laws and regulation. In the process, they have been major agents of change in the social values and politics of the United States.

They have, in my opinion, damaged our democracy. Given that the majority of Americans say they get their news, commentary and daily entertainment from this handful of conglomerates, the conglomerates fail the needs of democracy every day.

Our modern democracy depends not just on laws and the Constitution, but a vision of the real nature of the United States and its people. It is only humane philosophy that holds together the country's extraordinary diversity of ethnicity, race, vastly varied geography and a wide range of cultures. There are imperfections within every individual and community. But underneath it, we expect the generality of our population to retain a basic sense of decency and kindness in real life.

We also depend on our voters to approach each election with some knowledge of the variety of ideas and proposals at stake. This variety and richness of issues and ideas were once reflected by competing newspapers whose news and editorial principles covered the entire political spectrum. Every city of any size was exposed to the early Hearst and E. W. Scripps newspapers that were the champions of working people and critics of the rich who exploited workers and used their power to evade taxes. There were middle-of-the-road papers, and a sizeable number of pro-business papers (like the old New York Sun). They were, of course, a mixed bag. Not a few tabloids screamed daily headlines of blood and guts.

With all of that, the major papers represented the needs and demands of the mass of ordinary people and kept badgering politicians who ignored them.

Today, there is no such broad political spectrum and little or no competition among media. There is only a handful of exceptions to the rule of one daily paper per city. On radio and television, Americans see limited ideas and the largest media groups spreading ever-more extreme right-wing politics, and nightly use of violence and sex that tell parents and their children that they live in a cruel country. They have made sex a crude commodity as an inexpensive attention getter. They have made sex, of all things, boring.

Instead of newsboys earlier in the nineteenth century hawking a variety of papers to the people leaving their downtown factories and offices for home, we have cars commuting between suburbs with radio turned to news of traffic and crime. At home, TV is the major home appliance. What it displays day and night is controlled by a handful of giant media conglomerates, heavily tilted to the political right. And all of them have substantial control of every medium—newspapers, magazines, books, radio, television and movies.

The giant conglomerates with this kind of control are Time Warner, the largest media company in the world; Rupert Murdoch's News Corporation, which owns the Fox networks, a steady source of conservative commentary; Viacom, the old CBS

I wonder how many there are?

Specifically?

Main Idea

Explain

Look this up.

What are current laws and regulations?

Concl.

Look for actual percentages.

Look for examples.

Pathos (A little vague.)

Pathos

Who? They must be important—I should look them up.

Pathos

Look up.

Premise 1

Premise 2

Premise 3

I always heard that the news media was liberal. Is it mainly left-wing or right-wing? Or neither?

How???

Who are the major companies?

Research these different companies.

Sounds familiar— who is he, exactly?

Aren't they a defense contractor, too?	with similarly heavy holdings in all the other important media; Bertelsmann, the German company with masses of U.S. publications, book houses, and partnerships with the other giant media companies; Disney, which has come a long way from concentrating on Mickey Mouse and now, in the pattern of its fellow giants, owns 164 separate media properties from radio and TV stations to magazines and a multitude of other outlets in print and motion picture companies; and General Electric, owner of NBC and its multiple subsidiaries.
Ethos	
Are there any left-wing talk show commentators on radio?	One radio firm, ClearChannel, the sponsor of Rush Limbaugh and other exclusively right-wing commentators, owns 2,400 stations, dwarfing all other radio outlets in size and audience.
How many radio stations are in the US?	
Ethos	In their control of most of our newspapers, the great majority of our radio and television, of our most widely distributed books, magazines and motion pictures, these conglomerates have cheapened what once was a civilized mix of programming.
Pathos	
Who?	We have large cadres of talented screenwriters who periodically complain that they have exciting and touching material that the networks reject in favor of repetitious junk. These writers do it for the money and could quit, as some of them have. But they once got paid for writing original dramas like those of Paddy Chayevsky and other playwrights whose work was heard in earlier days of television.
Premise 4	
Find some current examples. How do they compare?	Programs appealing to the variety of our national tastes and variations in politics are so rare they approach extinction. The choices for the majority of Americans are the prime-time network shows that range from the relatively harmless petty jokes and dating games typified by "Seinfeld" to the unrelieved sex and violence of Murdoch's Fox network and "reality" shows in which "real people"—that is, nonprofessional amateurs—are willingly subjected to contests in sexual seduction, deceit and violation of friendships. Most TV drama is an avalanche of violence.
Statistics?	
The main idea of this entire section seems to be that letting a few conglomerates own most of our media is hurting democracy by limiting and slanting what Americans know about important issues.	

Here are other techniques to help you read actively and critically.

SASE

SASE stands for "summarize, analyze, synthesize, and evaluate." This method is another effective way to find main ideas and supporting information and to critically evaluate an author's arguments. It can also help you cast the material you are reading into a form that you can use in your paper—if you decide that the material is good enough.

Summarize

Start by taking a chapter, article, or even an extended passage from your source and seeing if you can recognize the main points and state them in your own words. Remember that summarizing means presenting only the author's ideas, not your opinions of them.

Analyze

Next, analyze the material by breaking it into its component parts. How does each part contribute to the whole? If there are assertions, what does the author provide to back up those assertions? Are there facts that can be checked for accuracy? Are there assumptions that are not backed up? How much of an argument depends on the author's assumption of beliefs shared by the potential audience? (When a writer makes an assertion that supports our worldview, we sometimes take it for a fact when it isn't.)

Synthesize

The third step is synthesis. Think about what else you have read about the topic. How does the information presented here compare to what you have read from other sources? (If you are just beginning your research, you may want to reread your earliest sources later on.)

Evaluate

Finally, evaluate the material. How thorough is the information? Is any important information missing? How well do the premises of arguments support their conclusions? Are there any logical fallacies? Some arguments are implicit and not always easy to recognize. Explicit arguments state their premises and conclusions clearly, but implicit arguments are more indirect; they may leave conclusions or even some premises unstated. See if you can find all the arguments in a passage that you read, including those the author just implies. (For more on understanding arguments and logical fallacies, see Chapter 5.)

DOUBLE-COLUMN NOTE TAKING

A note-taking method that encourages active and engaged reading is called *double-column note taking* or the *double-entry journal*. This is a reading journal that you use for taking notes from sources you plan to use for a research paper. You can draw a vertical line down the center of a page, or you can use facing pages in your notebook (which gives you more room to write). One column or page will be used for the notes that you take from your sources. You should be as organized as you would be with paper cards or e-cards (see Chapter 6), making sure that you write down page numbers and information for works-cited entries. The second column will be used for your reactions. As you collect ideas and evidence from your sources, you also ask questions; indicate information that confuses, surprises, or delights you; note what you believe and disbelieve; and so on. It is a lot like annotating the text itself—in fact, any ideas we discussed in the guidelines for text annotations can be employed here. Instead of annotating an entire text, however, you are annotating the notes that you take from the text. You can even simply freewrite. The following example shows some double-column notes on the same text the student annotated. At the top she put the bibliographical entry, and in the left column she put quotations and paraphrases from the source. In the right column (appropriately enough, since it is a right-brain activity), she put her own reactions.

Century

Bagdikian, Ben. "Grand Theft: The Conglomeratization of Media and the Degradation of Culture: Twenty-five Years of Monitoring The Multinationals." Multinational Monitor 26.1-2 (Jan.-Feb. 2005): 35-7. Expanded Academic ASAP. Thomson Gale. Web. 19 Oct. 2008.

"For 25 years, a handful of large corporations that specialize in every mass medium of any consequence has dominated what the majority of people in the United States see about the world beyond their personal experience. These giant media firms, unlike any in the past, thanks to the hands-off attitude of the Federal Communications Commission (FCC) majority, are unhampered by laws and regulation."	What's a "handful"?? I wonder how many there are exactly? I wonder what mass media he excludes from "consequence"? Get more information on the FCC. What are current laws and regulations?
B. says democracy depends on "a vision of the real nature" of the US and people here.	I don't know what he means by our "real nature." This sounds pretty stirring, but it's also pretty vague—at least at this point.
He says TV and radio spread radical right-wing politics.	I always heard that the news media was liberal. Is it mainly left-wing or right-wing? Or neither? I better look for some real studies and statistics.
The "nightly use of violence and sex that tell parents and their children that they live in a cruel country."	I bet I could find studies on the effects of sex and violence on TV, especially effects on kids. Would this be relevant to my topic of media and democracy?
ClearChannel—sponsor of Rush Limbaugh & other right-wing talk show hosts owns 2,400 stations.	Limbaugh is pretty extreme—I wonder how many people actually listen to him? And how many radio stations are there in the US? What proportion is 2,400? Are there any big left-wing talk show hosts? On TV there are people like Bill Maher, Jon Stewart, and Steven Colbert. But they take pot shots at everybody. They seem more liberal than conservative, but they can be pretty merciless to liberals. They pretty much go after anybody who does or says something stupid, no matter what political party. Maybe I should compare the numbers of people who watch these TV shows with the numbers of people who listen to Limbaugh and people like him. And what are the demographics?

THE RHETORICAL PRÉCIS

In 1988, Margaret Woodworth developed a method she called the rhetorical précis, which helped students to significantly improve their reading comprehension, as well as their ability to effectively use source materials in their own writing. The rhetorical précis is very like a summary (*précis* means "concise summary"), but with a crucial difference: you evaluate the content of the work and the methods the writer employs to inform and persuade you. A rhetorical précis requires you to look at a writer's strategies as well as the work's content. Because you must be very specific and concise when you write a rhetorical précis, it is an excellent tool for building your skills at understanding the sources you read. (See Chapter 5 for more information about rhetoric.) The format is very specific:

Précis Sentence 1 includes the name of the writer, the genre and title of the work, the date of the work in parentheses, and a "rhetorically accurate verb" (one that describes what kind of action is performed), such as "asserts," "argues," "implies," "demonstrates," or "traces" followed by a "that clause" containing the work's major assertion (it can be the thesis statement). Information about the writer can be included parenthetically after the name, if you choose.

Précis Sentence 2 is an explanation of how the writer develops and supports the work's major assertion. Generally, you should summarize the author's steps in the order in which they occur in the work.

Précis Sentence 3 states your understanding of the writer's purpose, followed by an "in order" phrase. ("Her purpose is to inform readers of . . . in order to help them understand . . . .")

Précis Sentence 4 describes the intended audience and can include what you perceive to be the relationship the writer establishes with the audience.

Following is an example of a rhetorical précis on the article "Grand Theft: The Conglomeratization of Media and the Degradation of Culture" by Ben Bagdikian. The article can be found in Chapter 20. Note that this follows the requirements for the four sentences mentioned previously, and it helps to illuminate the major argument and intent of this piece:

> Ben Bagdikian, in his journal article "Grand Theft: The Conglomeratization of Media and the Degradation of Culture" (2005), argues that a handful of massive media conglomerates have harmed and undermined American democracy. The author supports his main argument by discussing specific corporations, the need for television ratings, the FCC, and public hearings that prove that American citizens aren't being heard. His purpose is to persuade his audience that corporations have grown so strong, our ability to self govern is now at risk in order to get his readers to take political action to protect and, in some cases, reinstate regulations to keep a few corporate media monopolies from controlling all U.S. news. This piece is intended for an audience of Americans who may be unaware of the condition of the American media; Bagdikian wants them to share his deep concern.

General Reference

CHAPTER 8

Integrating Sources into Writing

If you watch the evening news, you should be familiar with what journalists call "eyewitness accounts." If a storm is moving into a region, a reporter is there "live," in the horrible weather, showing you that there is indeed a storm moving in. If a shooting occurred, a reporter arrives on the scene and interviews those who may have seen the tragic event. Conversely, you may see a news interview that occurs back at the studio, but such interviews typically include a prominent scientist, politician, soldier, or law enforcement agent—in other words, the interview is with a recognized expert in some important field. Without these accounts, the stories would lose a lot of validity. A reporter simply telling you about the incoming storm lacks the impact—the proof—that a reporter in the field provides.

Writing papers is very similar. Unless you provide some proof—an expert testimonial or evidence that you've found (the academic equivalent of an eyewitness account)—your audience will be left unconvinced. However, although journalists need to provide proof and a summary of events that have occurred, they are morally obliged to go no further. Ideally, their job is to report the facts to you and let you decide on their significance. As a writer, you're often asked to go beyond this stage. You don't just report; you interpret and come to conclusions for the audience.

Many times in your college career, your instructors are going to ask for your assessment, conclusion, and opinion in a paper. For such papers, you need to prove you've thought critically about the topic, have paid attention to class readings and lectures, and can provide some unique insights on the topic. Mostly, such papers are all about *you*. However, many more professors are going to require that you write a paper based not on your own ideas, but the ideas of the experts in the field. For this type of project, you need to master the processes of researching and interpreting your findings.

But why do students need to research at all when writing papers? The purpose of research is multifaceted. First, including summaries, quotations, and paraphrases from respected sources on your topic lets readers know that you yourself have become more of an expert. By displaying such research, you establish your own credibility and demonstrate your hard work by showing that you've read and understood some of the best scholars on your topic.

More important, however, is that research helps you to support your own arguments. If you simply state in a paper that global warming is threatening polar bears with extinction, skeptics who think global climate change is exaggerated have no reason to believe you. However, if you can present information that you found in an article published by scientists in a refereed scholarly journal that analyzes twenty years of data showing that polar bears' hunting seasons are growing shorter and shorter, and that, as a consequence, their health is declining from less access to food, your audience now has reason to believe that you may be on to something. In an academic research paper, virtually every point you make should have outside support proving that the ideas presented in your thesis are widely shared and can be supported. There is strength in numbers. You must present the work of other scholars in your paper, people who will "stand with you" and help prove that your conclusions are valid.

If you've done quick or shoddy research, you will showcase your lack of preparation in your paper. Your audience will be able to tell the difference between a half-hour research session or a Web search from your laptop versus deeper research that takes days, weeks, or even months. If all your sources come from the same anthology or you've used a general encyclopedia, it will prove that you haven't fully explored your topic. Moreover, if all your sources are strongly tilted toward one agenda or scholarly camp, it may prove that you were less interested in finding facts than you were in proving your argument. Be sure to let your research change your opinions, and stay open-minded during the entire process. Your audience will dismiss your argument if you don't acknowledge and address opposing viewpoints in your paper.

SUMMARY, SYNTHESIS, AND CRITICAL THOUGHT

In any writing task, there are three levels of thought you could demonstrate: **summary, synthesis,** and **critical thought.** For some brief writing assignments, a professor may simply ask for a summary or synthesis as the goal for a paper. However, if you are asked to complete a successful piece of argumentative research writing, you will need to show the third and most difficult level: critical thought.

Summary

The first level of thought is what the reporters mentioned in the preceding example do. It is simple summary. In a summary, you research, you compile data and evidence, and you report it to your audience exactly as you found it in the first place. Unlike television reporters, however, you're not providing video clips and interviews with people on the street. You're providing well-documented and thorough research—a paper trail that other scholars can follow if they need to find the same data or verify a claim. Your findings will range from statistical facts and historical dates to illuminated ideas and conclusions of some of the best scholars working today. This type of information is crucial to any good research paper; however, it is not the ultimate goal of many writers.

A paper that does nothing but regurgitate facts and data is not very intellectually stimulating. In fact, it can be quite boring. Readers could simply read your works-cited

Summary, Synthesis, and Critical Thought   **171**

page or bibliography and go straight to the sources themselves. If you don't critique or assess your sources, readers will wonder what is the relevance of your paper. Your paper will be a sea of statistics that never supports a thesis or comes to a particular conclusion. To create a meaningful research paper, you need to think critically about your sources.

Synthesis

Synthesis is a more advanced level of writing than summary, and it is an important skill to master. In a summary, you present material to your audience exactly as reported in the first place; in a synthesis, you bring several sources together to make one larger point. After you've provided outside materials, you need to prove to the reader that you've not only understood this information, but you've mastered it. You need to prove that you've read through several sources and have presented the best of the information gathered for your paper.

If you're writing a paper about the history of television, you won't just present every source in a simple summary. Instead, you'll present them in an order (perhaps chronologically for the purposes of your paper) and select only the information that will directly support the theme or thesis of your paper. You'll also present material from multiple sources here, whereas in a summary, you discuss only one source. In a good synthesis, your paper reports important facts to the audience, but includes no grand conclusions or intricate argument. This type of paper is good for a basic history report or an overview of general policies or facts.

For example, for the paper you are writing about television history, you find a source that discusses modern-day advertisers on television. Here is what the source says: "Moreover, to appease advertisers, media firms are increasingly giving them greater identification with and control over the programming. Proctor and Gamble, one of the world's largest advertisers, has signed major production deals with both Sony's Columbia TriStar Television and with Viacom's Paramount to coproduce television programs" (McChesney 41).

While you read this quotation, it reminded you of an article you took some notes from as you researched. You paraphrased the argument in the article, and you include this paraphrase in your paper, as well. The article explained that soap operas are called "soaps" because they were directly sponsored and funded by soap companies. There would be ads in the middle of the show, acted out by the same people on the stage for a soap opera scene. You report this fact next to the quotation, but all you do is report the facts here.

When writing a paper using synthesis as the highest level of thought, all you do is report the facts you've found in these sources. You are including this type of material for many sources, so you're not simply compiling a summary. However, because you never provide an interpretation, argument, or critical exploration of the material, you still aren't at the highest level of cognition—critical thought.

Source: McChesney, Robert. *Rich Media, Poor Democracy: Communications Politics in Dubious Times*. New York: New, 1999. Print.

Century

A **Socratic Dialog** is a dialectical method of inquiry—that is, it involves an exchange of propositions and counter-propositions to reach a correct conclusion. Socrates would ask probing questions to cause people to reveal—and thus be compelled to examine—their methods of reasoning and underlying assumptions in order to test the logic and accuracy of their arguments. The goal of asking such questions was to strip away bias, misinformation, and logical fallacies to ultimately reach the truth.

Critical Thought

Critical thought is the highest level of thought that can occur in academic writing. It is based upon a strong, argumentative thesis, which you support by not only summarizing and synthesizing sources, but by critically examining and scrutinizing the sources, as well. Critical thought tends to be question-based, just like a Socratic Dialog. By asking yourself several important questions (or applying these questions to the sources you're considering for your paper), you start to generate new thoughts and angles to approach in your argument. In fact, your thesis sentence is often an answer to a question you've generated earlier in the writing process.

To perform critical thought in your paper, your thesis may be designed to state a problem, create a solution, or take a stance or position for or against something. These levels of thought are not possible with the basic nature of a summary or the fact-finding synthesis. Instead of simply presenting the facts you've found, you both state them and then critique them. Whereas a synthesis is ultimately about the sources themselves, a paper full of critical thought is a mix of the scholars' ideas and your own.

What the experts say is always crucial in any research endeavor. However, good critical thinking goes beyond paraphrasing the opinions of experts. You must present a mixture of their thoughts and facts and your own conclusions. For example, you won't just provide a quotation and then leave it as it is. Instead, you critically interpret this outside material. You tell the audience how this information ties in to your own thesis. You ask questions of the experts, and you discuss their findings actively and critically.

Critical thought is often question based. In your paper, you should generate answers for several key questions about the source material:

- Is the author of the source a true scholar and worthy of your attention?
- Were the statistics gathered using a true empirical, scientific method, or are they in some way flawed or skewed?
- Could the author's integrity be compromised by his or her sources of funding?
- Do the conclusions line up with what other scholars say about the same topic?
- Are the source's conclusions logically valid, or do they use fallacies and jump to inaccurate conclusions?
- How do these ideas line up with your own arguments and conclusions?
- If experts disagree, can you present both sides and explain whose arguments are strongest, and why?

Mastering critical thought is a difficult process, but it yields the highest quality and most interesting and successful papers.

PRESENTING INFORMATION: SUMMARIES, PARAPHRASES, AND DIRECT QUOTATIONS

There are three ways to present material in your papers: **summarizing, paraphrasing, and directly quoting.** Each of them should be used at different times for different rhetorical purposes, so mastering all three is crucial. (Guidelines for creating parenthetical in-text citations for MLA papers are given in Chapter 12, and guidelines for creating parenthetical in-text citations for APA papers are given in Chapter 14.) Following is a brief description of these ways to present information and some suggestions as to when you should use each one.

Summaries

When you take longer source material and state it briefly in your own words, you are summarizing. The key to summarizing is to provide your readers with only the main points found in the original passage. Often, you may summarize an entire argument or source in just a few sentences for the purposes of supporting your thesis. To summarize, you ignore the original style and length of the piece and present a concise version of it in your own words.

When summarizing, do not use quotation marks—you should not copy the exact language of the source material. Also, specific details and minor arguments are not typically included in a summary, simply the major facts and arguments. Keep in mind that even though you may be summarizing several pages of a source into a few sentences, you still need to provide a citation in the appropriate documentation style (MLA, APA, etc.) and must list the source in your works-cited page.

Following is an example of some original material from Mike Davis's *Ecology of Fear: Los Angeles and the Imagination of Disaster*. Pay attention to key details and then look at the summary of it that follows.

Once or twice each decade, Hawaii sends Los Angeles a big, wet kiss. Sweeping far south of its usual path, the westerly jet stream hijacks warm water-laden air from the Hawaiian archipelago and hurls it toward the Southern California coast. This "Kona" storm system—dubbed the "Pineapple Express" by television weather reporters—often carries several cubic kilometers of water, or the equivalent of half of Los Angeles's annual precipitation. And when the billowing, dark turbulence of the storm front collides with the high mountain wall surrounding the Los Angeles Basin, it sometimes produces rainfall of a ferocity unrivaled anywhere on earth, even in the tropical monsoon belts.

Source: Davis, Mike. *Ecology of Fear: Los Angeles and the Imagination of Disaster*. New York: Vintage, 1999. Print.

174   CHAPTER 8   Integrating Sources into Writing

HERE IS A GOOD SUMMARY OF THIS PASSAGE

A couple of times a decade, a Kona storm system from Hawaii brings half of Los Angeles's annual rain in one single storm system (Davis 1).

Note how many details are left out of this summary—the fact that the storm comes from a different place than most California storms, the fact that the storm is called the Pineapple Express, the fact that this storm produces worse rain than at any other place on Earth. This summary really just tells the reader that there is a storm from Hawaii, it's called a Kona system, and it produces a lot of rain for Los Angeles. Your paper's thesis may not have needed any of this extra information, so you cut it out, paring down the information to just things you need for your own argument. Also, note that the entire tone and language of the passage has changed in your summary. The idiosyncratic style of the original language (wording such as the "big wet kiss" of the storm) is now gone, and, instead, we have one or two simple facts in a much more straightforward, academic tone.

HERE IS A WEAK SUMMARY OF THAT SAME PASSAGE

A few times a decade, a Kona storm system from the Hawaiian jet stream hijacks warm water-laden air and brings half of Los Angeles's annual rain in one single storm system (Davis 1).

Note that the language "jet stream hijacks warm water-laden air" is taken word-for-word from the original material. If you're using any verbatim language like this, you need to skip the summary and go for a direct quotation instead, or your paper could receive an "F" for plagiarizing the passage.

WHEN TO SUMMARIZE

Following are several legitimate reasons to summarize. Never use summarizing as an excuse to take one bit of information out of context to make it seem that a passage supports your thesis if in reality it does not.

1. The original passage is too long. Often, you read a wonderful passage that includes information you deem helpful, but is rather long. A summary is a great way to distill information into manageable size. You may very well be boiling down an entire chapter or source to one sentence in order for it to fit your paper's needs. Often stating things simply and quickly is the best way to convey information.

2. The original language isn't appropriate. Many sources are written to be entertaining instead of educational. If you find such a source, you may still want to use the information, but you want to clean up the tone of the passage. In the previous example, the "wet kiss" language is not particularly scholarly in tone, so avoiding such rhetorical flourishes and stating things in more professional language will have a greater impact in your paper.

3. You need only one piece of information. Sometimes the source material contains many facts and statistics in a section, but you need only one bit of that data. In such cases, summarize only one part of the original material in your paper. There is no need to quote or paraphrase a passage that contains information that does not directly support your thesis statement. Select only information that is relevant and important for inclusion in your writing. Summarizing is often the best way to ensure this.

4. You have too many statistics and data. You may find a great scientific source full of statistics and data, but you don't want your own paper to be flooded with graphs and mathematics. Instead of quoting statistic after statistic, you may just summarize them into shorter units of information that are easier to take in.

Paraphrasing

Sometimes you need to restate source material in your own words, while still including all the points it makes. When you do this, it is called a paraphrase. A paraphrase conveys all the ideas in a passage, unlike a summary, but like a summary, you put all the ideas into your own words. A paraphrase should ideally be the same length as or even slightly longer than the original passage. If you paraphrase a single sentence from a source, your version should be a single sentence. If you are using a full paragraph from the source, your paraphrase should be a full paragraph as well. You will not alter the length of the original material as significantly as you will in a summary.

One danger of paraphrasing is that you may use language that too closely resembles the original. The paraphrase cannot contain direct phrases or wording from the original. If it does, you should quote the source instead or put quotation marks around phrases that you just cannot put into your own words. One of the major reasons to paraphrase is to keep the length and content of source material fairly similar while changing the wording to be consistent with the style of the rest of your paper. If you use the same words as the original, you fail to maintain consistency, and, even worse, you risk plagiarizing the source. Remember that even though you are rewording the original material, you are still using someone else's facts. Thus, you must provide an in-text citation and include the source in your works-cited page. Following is a piece of original source material from T. Colin Campbell and Thomas M. Campbell's *The China Study*.

It was widely thought that much of the childhood malnutrition in the world was caused by a lack of protein, especially from animal-based foods. Universities and governments around the world were working to alleviate a perceived "protein gap" in the developing world. In this project, however, I uncovered a dark secret. Children who ate the highest protein diets were the ones most likely to get liver cancer! They were the children of the wealthiest families.

Source: Campbell, T. Colin, and Thomas M. Campbell II. *The China Study: The Most Comprehensive Study of Nutrition Ever Conducted and the Startling Implications for Diet, Weight Loss and Long-term Health.* Dallas: Benbella, 2005. Print.

HERE IS A STRONG PARAPHRASE OF THE ORIGINAL MATERIAL

Many nutritionists have traditionally held that worldwide childhood malnutrition was caused by a deficiency in protein from animal sources. Research institutions and

Century

government groups worldwide thought there was a "protein gap" between wealthy and developing nations. In a twenty-year study of nutrition and health, however, Dr. T. Colin Campbell discovered something rather shocking. Children from the wealthiest families who ate the most protein were the ones who had the highest percentages of liver cancer (Campbell and Campbell 1).

Notice that the wording in the paraphrase is significantly different from the original (aside from use of the term "protein gap"). The dramatic flair of the italicized sentence with the exclamation point has been replaced by a sentence that doesn't use such emphasis. This rewording is more consistent with the tone of the student's paper. Also notice that this paraphrase needed some rewording in the third sentence. Instead of the use of the original "I," the scientist's name was supplied, acknowledging the source material on which this paragraph is based. Finally, note that the idea of a "dark secret" is supplanted by "something rather shocking."

HERE IS A WEAK PARAPHRASE OF THE ORIGINAL MATERIAL

Many experts in the world thought that global childhood malnutrition was caused by a lack of protein, especially from animal-based foods. Research institution and government groups worldwide thought there was a protein gap between wealth and developing nations. In the study found here, however, I uncovered something shocking. Children from the wealthiest families who ate the most protein were the ones who had the highest percentages of liver cancer (Campbell and Campbell 1).

This paraphrase has a few major problems. First, the opening sentence uses wording too close to the original source. The author should have used a different term than "animal-based foods." Similarly, the phrase "protein gap" is used without use of quotation marks, and you can never use an exact phrase without using quotation marks. Also, the third sentence is confusing because it retains the original use of the word "I." This makes the sentence hard to follow—does "I" refer to the author of the original work or the author of the paraphrase? This should be revised for clarity.

WHEN TO PARAPHRASE

There are three primary circumstances that call for paraphrasing:

1. The original language is not academic in tone. Like the preceding summary example, you may find that the original source material uses slang or is a bit too casual for your tastes. You may want to paraphrase the information, keeping the same length and content, but writing in an academic voice.

2. The original language may be difficult for your audience to understand. Perhaps the original is a scientific paper full of technical jargon and language the average reader will not understand. You may want to reword it to make the content easier for your audience to read. Instead of using a direct quote that may be confusing and hard to digest, a paraphrase will make the content easier to comprehend.

3. The original language sounds outdated. You may have reason to use a source that is decades old or even older. The source may use language that is outdated, even archaic sounding, and just doesn't fit with the rest of your paper. By paraphrasing it, you retain all the original content, but you can update the style and make it easier for your audience to read.

Remember that you must always be honest when you paraphrase. Don't succumb to the temptation to alter or slant information to support your thesis.

Direct Quotations

When you find language in an outside source that is so perfect and informative you need to use it exactly as it is, you use a **direct quotation.** When you use a direct quotation, one of the most important things to remember is that you must—with the exception of the following circumstances—reproduce the exact quotation, using every word and every punctuation mark in the original. If you find yourself unhappy with how the original author worded something, you should paraphrase the source.

You can make minor alterations to the body of a quotation, such as adding information to clarify it or cutting out unnecessary wordiness, by using brackets to distinguish your additions or changes from the original quotation. You should do this only if you are in no way changing the meaning of the original passage. However, if you see an obvious typographical error, you can fix it; for example, change "teh" to "the." (For more information on this and on the technical details of using quotation marks, adherence to MLA or APA style, how to make changes within a quotation, how to include a long quotation, etc., see Chapters 9–14.)

WHEN TO DIRECTLY QUOTE

1. The original wording is compelling. Often, you'll find quotations that say exactly what you're thinking, but they say it far more eloquently and gracefully than you could have put it. In this case, you should quote the material. Many published authors write for a living, so make use of their years of experience at crafting sentences. When you read a passage during research and think, "Wow, I wish I could say it that way," you may want to include it as a direct quotation.

2. The quotation will help establish credibility. Many scholars from the past and present have become famous and have set the standards in their field of study. Use of their thoughts and their exact words will give your paper even more credibility than simply paraphrasing them. Well-known thinkers, such as Martin Luther King, Jr., Albert Einstein, and Noam Chomsky, carry a lot of weight and can impress your audience.

HOW TO INCORPORATE SOURCES INTO YOUR PAPERS

Every time you include material from an outside source (be it a summary, paraphrase, or direct quotation), you need to remember that the audience may be encountering this material for the first time. They have no idea where this material came from; they have no idea who the author is; they don't even understand the connections between this material and your thesis. It is up to you to tell the audience all these things. Information with no introduction or exploration can actually make a paper harder to read. Unless you introduce and then critically examine every quotation, summary, and paraphrase that you provide, the audience won't understand how your source information helps further your thesis. A bit of information used improperly in your paper will weaken its impact and could even result in inadvertent plagiarism. (See Chapter 9 for more advice about recognizing and avoiding plagiarism.)

INTRODUCING YOUR SOURCES

To begin the process of critically exploring your sources, you need to get in the habit of introducing your experts to your audience. You've read several books and articles on your topic by the time you conclude your paper. Ideally, you've become a bit of an expert on the subject—but remember that your audience may not be nearly as informed as you have become. To educate the reader on the quality of the authors you've chosen, you need to provide an introduction to your sources before you use them. (Note that this process of introduction is different from writing the introduction of your entire paper, and it's even different from the topic sentence of your paragraphs.) These introductions typically come after the topic sentence but before use of the source material.

Why Introduce Your Sources?

1. It is important to distinguish between the source and you. One of the biggest reasons to always introduce outside information is to let the audience know where the source starts and you stop. When you paraphrase and summarize, if you fail to provide a brief introduction about where the information came from, your readers will be confused. It is very easy to paraphrase something poorly and have the readers believe that the entire thought was your own, when it was not. By introducing the material before you give it, you clue your readers in; you tell them "This is someone else's information, and I'm just borrowing it."

When you quote, it is going to be more obvious which thoughts are yours and which ones come from outside sources because of your use of quotation marks. However, you'll still need to introduce the information for the following reasons listed.

2. You should establish the credibility of the author. With the rapid spread of information and computer databases full of journal articles, dissertations, and scientific reports, even the most learned scholars will not have read everything on their subject. You may cite a source that even an expert has never heard of. However, a quick introduction lets the reader know something about the author. What do you know about his or her field? Background? Experience? Credentials? Giving your readers additional information about the author of your source lends credibility to the ideas you use. Even if your audience is unfamiliar with the author, this extra information goes a long way to establishing his or her credibility as a scholar and an author.

How to Introduce Your Sources

The trick with introducing your sources is to figure out how to provide a maximum of information about the source and its author in a minimum amount of space. After all, although introducing your sources is important, the bulk of your paper needs to focus on the information you've gathered and your interpretation of it. Typically, you want to provide two elements in these brief introductions: the authors' names and why they are experts worth considering.

Following are some examples of the types of introductions you might use in your paper. Keep in mind that these are not the entire body paragraphs. You would still include a topic sentence before these citations and a thorough discussion of them afterward within your body paragraph (see p. 154).

INTRODUCTION OF A SOURCE WITH ONE AUTHOR

This basic source introduction includes mention of the author's full name and important background information that bolsters his or her credibility in the field. When you introduce the author, specifying degrees held by the author (Ph.D., M.A., M.D., etc.) doesn't really tell your readers much—hundreds of thousands of people have degrees, but that alone doesn't mean that all of them are credible experts.

Example: According to award-winning inventor Ray Kurzweil, the man described in 2005 by Bill Gates as the person best able to predict the future direction of artificial intelligence, "nanotechnology will enable the design of nanobots: robots designed at the molecular level, measured in microns (millionths of a meter) such as respirocytes (mechanical red-blood cells)" (28).

Source: Kurzweil, Ray. *The Singularity Is Near: When Humans Transcend Biology*. New York: Viking, 2005. Print.

This source's introduction quickly lets the reader know the author's full name and that he is well regarded by other experts, and then it proceeds with the quotation itself. Note that the example begins the sentence with "According to," but here are some other variations you may consider. Don't feel limited here; use different language to give the reader some variety.

Example: Artificial intelligence expert Ray Kurzweil, winner of the Lemelson-MIT Prize and the National Medal of Technology, says that "nanotechnology will enable the design of nanobots: robots designed at the molecular level, measured in microns (millionths of a meter) such as respirocytes (mechanical red-blood cells)" (28).

Some other phrases you could use to introduce the quotation include these:

> According to Kurzweil . . .
>
> One argument Kurzweil makes is that . . .
>
> Kurzweil argues . . .
>
> Kurzweil asserts . . .
>
> Kurzweil maintains . . .
>
> Kurzweil contends . . .
>
> Kurzweil suggests . . .

INTRODUCTION OF SOURCE WHEN CITED REPEATEDLY

Often, you will use one source repeatedly within your paper. You may cite a passage and need a paragraph or two to critically discuss its meaning. After you're done, you may have more evidence you need to cite. You should introduce this source thoroughly the first time, but every time thereafter you need not repeat the title or the author's first name.

Example: Kurzweil also says that "nanobots will have myriad roles within the human body, including reversing human aging" (28).

INTRODUCTION OF A SOURCE WRITTEN BY MULTIPLE AUTHORS

Many sources are collaborative efforts, so you need to introduce all authors as well as the source. The first time you introduce them you should use the full first and last name of each author.

Example: Ray Kurzweil, winner of the Lemelson-MIT Prize and the National Medal of Technology, and Terry Grossman, who is the founder and medical director of Frontier Medical Institute, claim that as we "peer even further into the 21st century, nanotechnology will enable us to rebuild and extend our bodies and brains and create virtually any product from mere information, resulting in remarkable gains in prosperity" (5).

Note: Your citation requires no information other than the page number because you have mentioned both authors in your text, and so your readers will look for an entry indicating both Kurzweil and Grossman as authors on your works-cited page, not just the entry indicating the book authored only by Kurzweil.

If you have already introduced both authors, you can simply use their last names.

Example: Kurzweil and Grossman further claim that as we "peer even further into the 21st century, nanotechnology will enable us to rebuild and extend our bodies and brains and create virtually any product from mere information, resulting in remarkable gains in prosperity" (5).

Source: Kurzweil, Ray, and Terry Grossman. *Fantastic Voyage: Live Long Enough to Live Forever.* New York: Rodale, 2004. Print.

INTRODUCTION OF A SOURCE WITH NO AUTHOR INFORMATION

Some source material may have no author listed. In such cases, you still need to introduce the source before you quote it.

Example: One source on nanotechnology, *Nanotech and the Next Big Wave,* asserts that "nanotechnology will make us smarter by increasing the number of neurons that can fire in our brains" (128).

INTRODUCTION OF A PARAPHRASE

Whether you use a direct quotation or a paraphrase, you must still indicate where the information came from. In fact, it's even more important to introduce a paraphrase because the lack of quotation marks makes it difficult for a reader to understand which arguments are yours and which belong to outside sources. Following is an example of a paraphrase without an introduction. It is virtually impossible to tell which ideas are original and which are borrowed from a source. The only clue we have is the parenthetical citation at the end.

Weak example: In the future, nanotechnolgoy will lead to use of nanobots which are robots which are built at the molecular level. Things this small are measured in microns which are one millionth of a meter, and they include artificial red-blood cells known as respirocytes (Kurzweil 28).

Following is the same paraphrase, but notice how the introduction makes it clear that this is not the student writer's ideas and gives credit to the appropriate source.

Strong example: According to Ray Kurzweil, nanotechnology will lead to use of nanobots, which are robots that are built at the molecular level. Machines this small are measured in microns, which are one millionth of a meter, and they include artificial red-blood cells known as respirocytes (28).

INTRODUCTION OF A SUMMARY

Much like the introduction of a paraphrase, summaries need introductions because readers will not be able to tell the difference between a quick summary of a source or your own idea.

Example: According to Ray Kurzweil, in the future, microscopic nanobots will be possible (28).

Do not "emote." When you introduce a source, don't gush about its quality in your introduction. You should avoid saying things like "In this groundbreaking book" or "his insightful research." Let the source material, the qualifications of the original author, and your critical thought of the source prove the quality.

When Not to Introduce a Source

SIMPLE DATES OR STATISTICS

Sometimes you may want to include a simple fact or date without going through all the effort of an introduction. In such cases, this information will be small side notes in your argument, but will help establish some minor facts. You will still provide a full citation for all such information, and you'll include it in your works-cited page; however, for brevity, you'll skip the introduction.

Example: In 1997, children between the age of four and twelve spent $24 billion, and these purchases were directly influenced by advertisements they saw on television (McChesney 45).

AFTER THE MATERIAL

Always introduce the material *before* the quotation, paraphrase, or summary. To properly introduce a source, you have to give the information right away. If you quote or paraphrase and then tell the audience where the information came from later, you will cause confusion.

ANALYZING AND INTERPRETING INFORMATION FROM SOURCES

Although informing the audience where information comes from is an important step in your research project, the true key to good research writing is what you do with the information after you present it. You can provide a brilliant quotation in your paper, but if you fail to examine it and present your own critical interpretation of this quotation, you might as well not present research at all. Only by exploring the importance of information do you begin the highest level of paper writing—prose that demonstrates critical thinking skills.

How to Discuss Information

The following three tasks will help you discuss your outside sources. If you perform at least one of these three tasks after you present information, you've started to incorporate your source material successfully into your paper. Ideally, however, you'll perform more than one.

TASK 1: INFORMATION COMPETENCY

You will probably provide in your paper several statistics or interesting conclusions a scholar has reached. If your audience reads the quick quotation or the paraphrase you've provided, they may very well ask themselves, "so what?" With information so readily available, your readers can find the material you quoted rather easily and read the scholars' works themselves instead of your short "snapshot" of the ideas.

What your paper should do to stand out, though, is provide unique insights and interpretations of this material. What do *you* think about these ideas? How do *you* interpret their statistical data? Your handling of this information is really what information competency is all about. Any of your readers can find what you find if they dig hard enough. What they can't find without reading your paper is what you think about it.

Similarly, your discussion of complex material will let your instructor understand that you fully comprehend the material in question. Often research material is difficult to understand and interpret. By commenting on the information's importance and using and interpreting complex passages to support your own argument, you prove that you're competent in handling even the most difficult information.

TASK 2: CONNECTION OF SOURCE MATERIAL TO YOUR OWN THESIS AND ARGUMENTS

When you insert the information you have found in your research into your paper, it will do nothing to prove your arguments or support your thesis until you make the connections yourself. Do not leave it to the audience to connect the dots, or they may never be able to—they may even try to do so and come up with a different picture than the one you intended because they don't understand the material as well as you now do. When you discuss how the outside information supports your arguments, however, you will make all these connections clear to your audience. If you don't let the reader know *how* specific information supports your thesis, your thesis has not actually been supported at all.

TASK 3: EXPLORATION OF HOW YOUR SOURCE MATERIAL TIES IN TO OTHER IDEAS IN THIS BODY OF SCHOLARSHIP

You should have compiled a great deal of research by the time you print your final paper and submit it. In essence, you've become an expert on your topic while researching. You may have used a combination of scholarly books and articles that nobody else has synthesized in the same way. You need to take advantage of that information—use the unique perspective that is your own individual mind working with the specific sources you've read.

Surely your professor has read many of the sources you've chosen to incorporate into your paper, but probably not all of them. And if she has, she probably hasn't ever joined these specific facts together in the same way that you yourself may have. Not only are you showing off your information competency by explaining and analyzing the information, you're showing off your grasp of at least a portion of the scholarly body of work on this subject.

Century

9 CHAPTER

Understanding and Avoiding Plagiarism

It's Sunday morning, and Sandy's research paper is due Monday. She has been staring at her computer screen for almost an hour. She's checked her email and hit her MySpace page for a while, but she can't think of a way to get started on her paper. Sandy's starting to feel a bit shocked that the last few weeks went by so fast. She has several fantastic library books sitting on her desk, as well as some articles she found in the college library database. She's read parts of most of the articles and scanned sections of the books, but she hasn't had a lot of time—she's taking an overload, she's on the volleyball team, and she has an active social life—and she has to admit to herself that she really hasn't understood most of what she has read during her research. Besides, she finds it pretty boring.

Finally, Sandy turns to the Internet for some ideas just to help her get started. Her topic is Reality TV, and she enters that term into a search engine along with "research" and "paper," and pretty soon she stumbles across an article on a site called GradeSaver posted by "Anonymous" and dated July 3, 2006. It is all about the movie *The Truman Show* and how it satirizes reality TV. She reads the first paragraph and gets excited. It sounds great:

> Peter Weir's *The Truman Show* is a film of great satirical intellect and poignancy. However, beneath the facade, this "comedy" conveys important social messages that provide a warning for the future. It mocks human beings' automatic acceptance of what they are presented with and shows how manipulative and addictive the media can be. On a deeper level, the film also cautions against accepting absolute authority, the interminable hunt for Utopia, and the evils inspired by the desire for wealth. Whether *The Truman Show* is a satire, a comedy, a documentary, a fable, or even a hoax is debatable, but what is impossible to question is the need to consider its themes and digest its principal lessons.

She's saved! Wow, she thinks, the name "GradeSaver" sure applies. The research paper is worth thirty-five percent of the course grade. Her panic vanishes. She'll be able to turn her paper in the next day after all. She doesn't plan on just copying the paper—that would be totally cheating—but she can copy and paste it, go through and paraphrase it, and add some of her own thoughts and sources. Besides, she isn't even an English major; she's majoring in agriculture, and it's not like she's going to have to write research papers when she leaves college. This is just one of those classes she has to take and pass to get her college degree. And her schedule is so busy that she doesn't have time to do everything expected of her. Each professor seems to think that theirs is the only class students are taking.

She pastes the article into her Word document and starts to type. Pretty soon (with the help of a thesaurus) she has her first paragraph:

The Truman Show by Peter Weir is a deeply emotional, moving, satirical, intellectual movie. Nevertheless, beneath the surface, this so-called comedy transmits crucial social messages that give us a warning for the future. It makes fun of people's automatic acceptance of things they are presented with and shows that the media can be manipulative and addictive. The movie also cautions against accepting authority that is absolute, the unending search for Utopia, and the evils caused by wanting wealth. We can debate whether *The Truman Show* is a satire, a comedy, factual, or even a hoax, but we cannot question the need to look at its themes and contemplate its principal lessons.

By the end of the day, she has taken the GradeSaver essay, altered its wording and the order of some of its paragraphs, added information about Reality TV from her books and articles (at least one factoid from each), and, for good measure, thrown in some more paraphrases from other articles she finds on the Net. After she has finished her works-cited page (which does not, of course, mention GradeSaver) and printed the whole thing out, she has a sense of satisfaction—she's finished the assignment, and she even feels like she's really learned something about the subject. Besides, she now has time to study for a test she has in her math class Tuesday.

A week later, Sandy is flabbergasted when her professor gravely hands the research paper back to her with an "F" for plagiarism and a note telling her that she will receive an "F" for the entire course and a mark on her permanent record for violating her college's policy on academic honesty. He has stapled a copy of the GradeSaver paper to the back of her assignment as well, so she abandons all thought of trying to convince him that she didn't cheat. That night—angry, frightened, and humiliated—she cries herself to sleep.

There are lots of reasons students find themselves tempted to cheat. Often, those who do so rationalize that it isn't even wrong—or at least not "seriously" wrong. They have lots of pressures, not a lot of time, and, besides, "everybody does it," including people in the "real world." Also, the Internet has made stealing other people's work much easier than it was in the past. A 2003 study of 18,000 students enrolled in twenty-three colleges in the United States found that nearly forty percent of them admitted to using the Internet to plagiarize. So, you might ask, "Why is it such a big deal?"

The first and most obvious answer is that plagiarism—the unattributed use of other people's ideas or words—is unethical. It is both a form of lying and a form of theft. When you plagiarize, you are lying to your professor about the work you have done (or not done), and you are stealing another person's ideas and benefiting undeservedly from that person's hard work. You might rationalize that you aren't stealing from someone else if the paper has been posted on the Net to use or if you have actually paid money to a friend or a term-paper mill, but it is intellectual theft, nonetheless—and you are undisputedly lying to your professor.

A second answer is that if you plagiarize, you are not only robbing someone else, you are robbing yourself: you are depriving yourself of developing skills that would make you a better scholar while in school and a better critical thinker and intelligent consumer of information after you graduate.

A third answer—and the one that may be the most compelling to students who are seriously tempted to cheat—is that you can get caught and flunk not only the assignment, but an entire class. Depending on your institution, you could even be placed on academic probation or expelled. Sure, lots of students manage to get away with plagiarizing—at least for a while—but lots of students get caught, too. Your professors have been reading in their disciplines a lot longer than you have, and they may recognize works they have read before. They have also been reading students' papers for a long time, and students have their own distinctive writing styles. When a student displays newly sophisticated diction and sentence structure and suddenly drops idiosyncratic writing habits, a professor will see the change in style as a pretty strong clue that the student has copied or only slightly modified all or part of someone else's work. Furthermore, though this seems to come as a surprise to many students, most of your professors are at least as adept at searching the Internet as you are. Think about it—if you can find an article on the Net, so can anyone else. Also, students aren't the only people who lead busy lives, and more and more professors are turning to professional services such as Turnitin, Plagiarism.org, Integriguard, and MyDropBox to quickly and efficiently identify plagiarized papers.

Some types of plagiarism are not as obvious as Sandy's. In fact, some students plagiarize without even realizing that they are doing so, either through misunderstanding how to properly use and document sources or because of other mistakes. This chapter will help you to avoid any kind of plagiarism by discussing common problems and by telling you when to document the sources that you use. (See Chapters 12, 13, and 14 for detailed information on parenthetical in-text citations and works-cited pages in MLA and APA styles).

TYPES OF PLAGIARISM

We can divide plagiarism into five main categories: total plagiarism, substantial plagiarism, incidental/occasional plagiarism, "buddy"/tutor plagiarism, and accidental plagiarism.

Total plagiarism occurs when students turn in other people's work as their own. It is intentional and the most blatant and offensive form of academic dishonesty, and it can meet with very harsh punishments. Total plagiarism might involve an entire paper copied or purchased off the Internet or written by another student, or a "patchwork quilt" of a paper stitched together from a series of other works. Such papers may have language changed and may even have citations from sources the student has found and inserted in order to disguise the paper's true origins.

Substantial plagiarism occurs when students do most of the writing in their own papers but frequently (1) borrow ideas and rephrase them without giving credit to the original source, (2) borrow exact phrases and sentences without enclosing them in quotation marks and without giving credit to the original source, (3) or borrow exact phrases and sentences without enclosing them in quotation marks even though credit is given to the original source. These acts of plagiarism are also deliberate and blatant.

Incidental/occasional plagiarism occurs when students write their own papers, but there are sections that will not withstand strict scrutiny because of one or more passages where exact quotations of sentences and phrases are not enclosed in quotation marks even though they are attributed to their sources, or there are one or more passages where paraphrased ideas are not attributed to their sources. Sometimes examples of plagiarism in this category may be accidental.

"Buddy"/tutor plagiarism occurs when students get too much help from friends or tutors. It is certainly a good idea to have someone else look at your paper, but don't allow or ask them to help you rewrite it. Use another person's input to help you find technical errors or to alert you to areas that aren't clear, but do the rewriting yourself. Remember, tutors are there to show you your mistakes and to teach you how to correct them; they are not supposed to correct your paper and fix all the problems for you.

Accidental plagiarism occurs when students don't realize that using other people's ideas and paraphrasing them is plagiarism if the source is not clearly identified. It can also occur when people haven't been careful while taking notes and forget to put quotation marks around direct quotations, or they polish the paraphrased language of an attributed source and inadvertently rephrase it into the original language of the source without adding quotation marks (for tips on how to avoid these problems while note taking, see Chapter 6). This is perhaps the most common form of plagiarism and can be corrected with proper citations and documentation format.

AVOIDING PLAGIARISM

There are three rules for avoiding plagiarism, the first of which is pretty obvious:

1. Be honest. Don't buy, borrow, or steal anybody else's words or ideas.
2. Cite *all* material that you take from a nonfiction source, whether you quote, paraphrase, or summarize, unless it is common knowledge (we'll discuss that in greater length later). You should also cite any graphical material that you copy, such as charts and illustrations. If you are writing an essay about a single work of literature, the convention is to cite page numbers only for direct quotations from the work of literature, and not when you summarize any sections, but you still must cite all information you take from critical sources concerning the work of literature if you use any outside sources.
3. Use language and sentence structures that are essentially your own—simply changing or rearranging a few words here and there isn't enough to avoid charges of stealing.

ORIGINAL PARAGRAPH WRITTEN BY GEORGE ORWELL IN HIS ESSAY "POLITICS AND THE ENGLISH LANGUAGE"

Most people who bother with the matter at all would admit that the English language is in a bad way, but it is generally assumed that we cannot by conscious action do anything about it. Our civilization is decadent, and our language—so the argument runs—must inevitably share in the general collapse. It follows that any struggle against the abuse of

188   CHAPTER 9   Understanding and Avoiding Plagiarism

language is a sentimental archaism, like preferring candles to electric light or hansom cabs to aeroplanes. Underneath this lies the half-conscious belief that language is a natural growth and not an instrument which we shape for our own purposes.

PLAGIARIZED PARAGRAPH, WITH PLAGIARIZED WORDS AND PHRASES HIGHLIGHTED

Many individuals who bother with the issue would admit that the English language is in terrible shape; however, we generally assumed we cannot alter this by conscious action. Our society is decadent, so our language, it is argued, shares in the problem. Some people might argue that trying to stop the abuse of language is old-fashioned and useless because they half-consciously think language is natural instead of something we shape as we please.

The student who wrote the paragraph above is guilty of plagiarism for three reasons: 1) phrases are copied verbatim from the original but are not enclosed in quotation marks, 2) the original author is not given, and 3) there is no citation indicating the page number the material was taken from. The effect of the plagiarized material is to indicate that all the words and ideas are the student's own.

PLAGIARIZED PARAGRAPH, WITH PLAGIARIZED WORDS AND PHRASES HIGHLIGHTED

Many individuals who bother with the issue would admit that the English language is in terrible shape; however, we generally assumed we cannot alter this by conscious action. Our society is decadent, so our language, it is argued, shares in the problem. Some people might argue that trying to stop the abuse of language is old-fashioned and useless because they half-consciously think language is natural instead of something we shape as we please (Orwell 12).

The paragraph above is still plagiarized because even though the author and page number appear in a parenthetical citation at the end of the sentence, phrases are copied verbatim from the original but are not enclosed in quotation marks. The effect of the plagiarized material is to indicate that although the ideas are Orwell's, all the words are the student's paraphrase of the original passage, which is clearly not the case.

PLAGIARIZED PARAGRAPH

Many individuals who ponder the condition of the English language are likely to conclude that it is in terrible shape, but they probably take for granted that we cannot think of any solutions. Some people might argue that society is in a moral and cultural decline; therefore, it follows that our discourse must also decline and that to try to fight this shows an inability to deal realistically with the times. This attitude suggests an unexamined assumption that language is something that evolves on its own, as opposed to a tool we utilize for our own purposes.

Though the paragraph above is an effective paraphrase (we don't worry about the words "English language" not being enclosed in quotation marks because there is no other logical way to name it), the student has still clearly plagiarized because 1) the author is not given, and 2) there is no citation indicating the page number the material was taken from. The effect of the plagiarized material is to indicate that all the ideas are the student's own.

UNPLAGIARIZED PARAGRAPH

Many individuals who ponder the condition of the English language are likely to conclude that it is in terrible shape, but they probably take for granted that we cannot think of any solutions. This attitude suggests an unexamined assumption that language is something that evolves on its own, as opposed to a tool we utilize for our own purposes. "Our civilization is decadent, and our language—so the argument runs—must inevitably share in the general collapse" (Orwell 12).

This example is *not* plagiarized. Most of the paragraph is put into the student's own words, and the passage ends with both a direct quotation and an MLA-style parenthetical citation.

UNPLAGIARIZED PARAGRAPH

As George Orwell points out about the English of his time—and his observations hold true today—many individuals who ponder the condition of the English language are likely to conclude that it is in terrible shape, but they probably take for granted that we cannot think of any solutions. Some people might argue that society is in a moral and cultural decline; therefore, it follows that our discourse must also decline and that to try to fight this shows an inability to deal realistically with the times. This attitude suggests an unexamined assumption that language is something that evolves on its own, as opposed to a tool we utilize for our own purposes (12).

This paragraph also avoids plagiarizing. It is the same paraphrase from the previous example, but it begins by attributing the ideas to their originator, George Orwell, and there is a parenthetical citation at the end to let the reader know the page number of the original material (the last name is not needed within the parentheses in this case because Orwell is mentioned before the paraphrase).

UNPLAGIARIZED PARAGRAPH

Many individuals who ponder the condition of the English language are likely to conclude that it is in terrible shape, but they probably take for granted that we cannot think of any solutions. Some people might argue that society is in a moral and cultural decline; therefore, it follows that our discourse must also decline and that to try to fight this shows an inability to deal realistically with the times. This attitude suggests an unexamined assumption that language is something that evolves on its own, as opposed to a tool we utilize for our own purposes (Orwell 12).

This example contains no verbatim word use, and it has a proper citation, so this student has also avoided plagiarism.

190   CHAPTER 9   Understanding and Avoiding Plagiarism

COMMON KNOWLEDGE EXCEPTIONS

Common knowledge exceptions refer to generally known facts. Here are examples of different types of common knowledge exceptions:

1. Information known by the average person (for example, President Abraham Lincoln was assassinated by John Wilkes Booth in 1865; U.S. and British forces invaded Iraq in 2003).

2. Information known by the average scholar in a particular discipline (for example, William Shakespeare died in 1616 at the age of 52; Milton Friedman won the Nobel Prize for Economics in 1976).

3. Information that is repeated in many different sources (for example, thalidomide is known to cause birth defects; the Great Fire of London happened in 1666). "Many" is an ambiguous term, and there is no universal agreement on exactly how many sources it takes to make something "common knowledge," but the standard assumption in academia is that facts are common knowledge if you can find the same information reported in at least five different sources (it isn't a bad idea to ask your own professor for guidance).

To be safe, if you aren't sure if an idea is "common knowledge," assume that it isn't, and cite the source of your information. After all, it is a lot less hazardous to have a citation that you don't need than it is to risk a charge of plagiarism.

Frequently, students get nervous and worry that they have "too many" citations. Think about it: you are writing research papers, which means that you are presenting research—you are supposed to have a lot of in-text citations. Citations let your reader know what sources you used, the page numbers of information found in print sources, and where to look for complete publication information on your works-cited page. (For graceful introduction of sources and how to discuss their relevance and show that you have thought critically about their assertions, see Chapter 8.)

WRITING TIP

If you quote someone, don't set up the quotation by saying that person "quoted" something, as in *Neil Postman quoted, "Anyone who has studied the history of technology knows that technological change is always a Faustian bargain."* Neil Postman didn't quote that sentence, he wrote it—you are the person doing the quoting, not him. Instead, you would say, *Neil Postman stated, "Anyone who has studied the history of technology knows that technological change is always a Faustian bargain."*

Century

11 CHAPTER

Formatting the MLA-Style Paper

You've just finished all the stages of the writing process for your research paper. You've done your prewriting and generated a solid thesis. You hit the library and the online databases and found plenty of sources and organized your ideas into notes. You wrote an outline, generated a rough draft, and revised that draft. But you aren't done yet. You need to make sure that your paper is in the proper format. That can lead you to dozens of questions. For example, when you use a quotation, how do you let the reader know where it comes from? Do you use footnotes or put page numbers in parentheses? When do you italicize or underline the titles of works, and when do you put them in quotation marks, instead? Where do your page numbers go? Where do you put your name and the title of your paper? How big should you make the margins?

These questions are all matters of paper formatting, and there are systems developed to help you format papers properly. A properly formatted paper looks professional, and it also reinforces your credibility when you take care to attribute information that is not common knowledge to your sources, a practice that protects you from charges of plagiarism (see Chapter 9 for a discussion on plagiarism).

Modern Language Association (MLA) style is one of the most commonly used styles for college and university papers because it is the standard for courses in liberal arts and the humanities. It provides guidelines for formatting manuscripts and properly referencing sources through in-text parenthetical citations (see Chapter 8 for more on integrating your sources into your papers) and Works Cited and Works Consulted pages, all of which will be described in this chapter. MLA is a very comprehensive system of paper formatting. It covers everything from the general appearance of your paper to the in-text citations within it and the list of sources used at the end. The Modern Language Association does not publish its documentation guidelines on the Web. For an authoritative explanation of MLA style, see the *MLA Handbook for Writers of Research Papers* (for high school and undergraduate college students) and the *MLA Style Manual and Guide to Scholarly Publishing* (for graduate students, scholars, and professional writers). The MLA website at http://www.mla.org also includes a helpful list of frequently asked questions about the style.

This chapter shows you the basic important elements of MLA style and helps prepare you to write properly formatted essays and research papers. (For the format of papers written using American Psychological Association, APA or style, see Chapter 14.) It closes with a sample student paper in correct MLA format.

MLA DOCUMENT GUIDELINES

General Appearance

MLA style requires that the general appearance and basic physical layout of your paper conform to certain guidelines. These guidelines are as follows:

- *Paper Size:* Whether you use a computer or a typewriter, your paper should be printed on one side only of eight-and-a-half-by eleven-inch white paper with one-inch margins on all sides. (The default margin for Microsoft Word is typically 1.25 on the left and right, so you will need to change this.)

- *Alignment:* Justification is the term used to explain how the type is aligned on your paper. If you are using a computer, justify the lines of your paper at the left margin; don't right-justify, center, or full-justify them.

- *Font Size: Font* is the style of typeface you use in your writing. No matter how tempted you may be by the variety of fonts available, choose a simple, legible font such as Times New Roman, 12 point. (If your instructor has given you a page count instead of a word count, don't try to achieve the desired number of pages by using an extra-large font.)

- *Indentations:* Indent the opening lines of paragraphs one-half inch (five spaces) from the left margin. Block quotations (quotations that take up more than four lines in a paper) are indented one inch (ten spaces) from the left margin but not indented on the right. In works cited entries, every line of an entry after the first is indented one-half inch from the left margin.

- *Sentence Spacing:* MLA style recommends using only one space after terminal punctuation marks (periods, question marks, and exclamation points), but your instructor may prefer two spaces, so ask.

- *Line Spacing:* The entire paper (with the exception of content footnotes, if you have them) should be double-spaced, including your heading; indented quotations (any quotations that are longer than four lines should be indented); any endnotes, tables and appendixes; and the works-cited page or any other source lists. Don't add extra spaces above or below titles or in between the works-cited entries.

- *Fastening:* Most instructors prefer that you fasten the pages with a single staple in the upper-left corner. Also, most instructors prefer that you do not use folders and report covers because they must be removed prior to reading when they grade your papers. It may not look as fancy, but a plain paper with a simple staple is typically what your instructor wants.

Many of these format elements will be easier for you to incorporate into your paper if you use a computer. In fact, some instructors will insist that you use a computer for your papers, not only because it is more efficient to do so, but also because computer literacy is a requirement for college and university students. Even if you do not own a computer, your school undoubtedly provides computers for student use.

Here is an image of a typical MLA paper's headers and first page. Use it as a reference for all general formatting details mentioned here.

Century

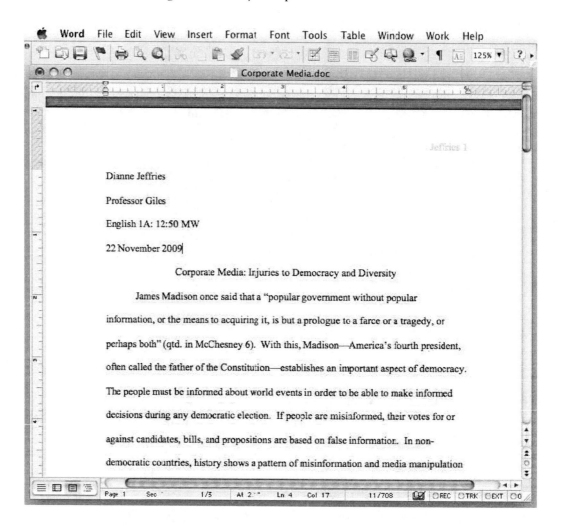

First Page

Title pages are no longer standard for research papers and other essays in MLA style. Instead, you will usually use a simple **personal and class identification heading** on the first page of your paper (see the image above), a **header,** and a **title** above the body of your paper.

Personal and Class Identification Heading

The heading should contain the following information, and, just like the rest of the document, it should be entirely double-spaced.

1. **Your full name.**
2. **Your professor's name.** The title "Professor" should precede his or her last name; don't use a first name.
3. **The name of the course.** Some professors who teach more than one section of the same course also want students to follow the course name with a colon

and the starting time and days abbreviated to the first letters, for example, English 1A: 10:30 MTW.

4. **The date the paper is due.** MLA has a specific format for listing the date. The day should precede the month, which should not be abbreviated.

For example: 8 September 2009

Header

In the upper-right corner of each page of your paper, you should provide a header that consists of your last name, a space, and the page number positioned one-half inch below the top of the page. This upper-right header must appear on every page of your paper. You should not try to create this header by simply typing it in what you judge to be the upper-right corner of each page, because if you add or delete any information, the header will no longer appear in the right place. Instead, you should learn how your particular word processing software handles headers. In virtually every word processor, there is a way to set your last name and auto-number the pages.

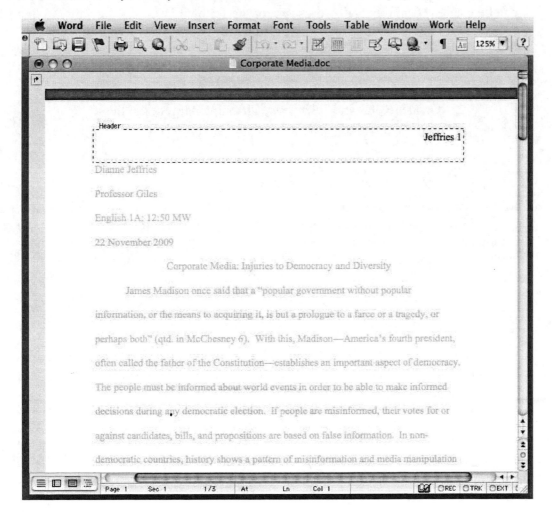

Title

The title of your essay should be carefully thought out and should indicate the topic and scope of your paper. Avoid, for example, titling your paper "Research Paper Number One." Your title should be double-spaced below the heading and centered (remember not to add an extra line—the distance between the last line of your heading and the title should be the same as the distance between each line of the heading and each line of the rest of the paper). Use the Center Alignment icon in your toolbar to properly center the title; do not simply hit the space bar until it looks like the title may be centered. The title should not be followed by a period, but you can end it with a question mark or an exclamation point. Don't italicize or underline your title or put it in bold type or within quotation marks. (However, if you use part of a work's title within your own title, it should be formatted properly.)

In MLA format, titles of books and journals are italicized or underlined, for instance, and titles of essays and poems are enclosed in quotation marks. MLA recommends italics over underlining. (Check with your instructor, though—many don't like students to use italics and would prefer the use of underlining instead because it can be clearer.) Capitalize all words except the following (unless they are the first words of a title or subtitle): articles (*a, an,* and *the*), prepositions, coordinating conjunctions, and the *to* in infinitives (as in "How to Capitalize Titles"). If your title is lengthy enough to go to two or more lines, use an inverted pyramid. Here is an example:

Gender Roles and Television: Changing Attitudes in the

United States, Great Britain, and Germany

Tables, Illustrations, and Appendixes

You may want to include photos, illustrations, tables, or graphs in your research paper. Generally, you should place tables and illustrations as close as possible to the sections of your paper that they augment, unless they are lengthy and would interrupt the flow of the paper. In that case, you can gather them together in one or more appendixes.

TABLES

For the heading of a table, follow the word *Table* with the appropriate Arabic numeral aligned at the left margin above the table, and add an explanatory caption on the next line, also aligned at the left margin, and capitalized the way you would a title (see the preceding section). As with all else in the paper, double-space the headings and the contents of the table. Follow the table with its source and any notes you add. Use dividing lines as necessary for clarity to set the table off from the caption and source information and any headings inside it from the figures that follow. Following is an example of an MLA-style table based on data collected from the sample student survey found in Chapter 2.

TABLE 1 Summary of Television Viewing Patterns Survey [a]	
Question	Response
Hours of TV per day	4–7 Hours
TVs in Home	2–3
Persons in Home	3–4
Cable/Satellite Subscriptions	178
DVR Service Subscriptions	47
TV show DVD Rentals	111
Own TV shows on DVD	52

Source: Summary of Television Viewing Patterns Survey. Personal Survey. 18 October 2009.

[a] This graph represents a 250-person survey conducted over the course of one week on the campus of Bakersfield College. These numbers are the averages for the questions asked.

Fig. 1: "Light Classical" by Al Naso

ILLUSTRATIONS

Illustrations include drawings, maps, photographs, and other visuals and are referred to in your paper as Figures (abbreviated to Fig.). The label Fig. is followed by the appropriate Arabic numeral and an explanatory caption, and it appears below the illustration, as shown above. Source material and notes follow the caption.

APPENDIXES

"To append" means to add something as a supplement, and extra material added after the conclusion of the paper is placed inside *appendixes*. If you have numerous tables, illustrations, or other material, such as samples of questionnaires and their results or lists of interview questions, it is best to include them at the end of the paper. Each appendix should begin on a new page. Label each page with the word *Appendix* centered at the top, followed by the capital letter *A* for the first appendix, *B* for the second appendix, and so on. The appendix title should be treated just like the title of your paper: double-space the title above the appendix, and don't italicize or underline it or put it in bold type or within quotation marks. Don't include extra lines between the heading and the text of the appendix. The appendix itself should be double-spaced, just like the rest of the paper. Your table, illustration, or other material should appear below the heading, formatted just the way it would be if you had placed it within the body of your paper.

Footnotes and Endnotes

Parenthetical citations (see Chapter 7 on integrating sources into your writing) are used to identify the sources that you use in your paper and to direct your readers to the proper entries in your list of works cited, but you can use notes—either footnotes or endnotes—to provide additional information about your topic that you consider important or simply interesting, but that doesn't really fit anywhere in the body of your paper. Although such information may be worthwhile to your readers, it shouldn't interrupt the flow or logical organization of your paper. For example, if you're writing a paper about racial stereotyping in the early years of television, and you quote a source who uses the term "Uncle Tom," you could include a footnote that discusses the origin of the term in *Uncle Tom's Cabin,* an antislavery novel written by Harriet Beecher Stowe and published in book form in 1852. This information may not be directly relevant to your paragraph, but it is still interesting and informative. You can use either endnotes or footnotes to provide supplementary information or observations in MLA style. Ask if your instructor has a preference; if not, go with the endnotes, which are easier to format.

Footnotes and endnotes are numbered consecutively throughout a paper. Add the numbers in superscript. To do this, add the number at the end of the sentence you want to follow with a note, and highlight it. In the Format menu, click Font, and then click the Font tab. Select the Superscript check box. Your footnote or endnote will begin with the same number in superscript preceding it. Endnotes go on a page headed *Notes,* with the heading treated like any other title, and the page double-spaced. Indent each note a half-inch from the left margin, and begin it with the proper number in superscript. This page should follow the body of the paper and precede the works-cited page. Footnotes go at the bottom of pages within the paper, beginning two double spaces (four lines) below the text. They are the only items in your paper that should be single spaced, but if you have more than one footnote on a page, add an extra space between them. In the example that follows, note that the name James Madison in the first line has a raised number 1 next to it; this points to footnote 1 at the bottom of the page.

James Madison[1] once said that a "popular government without popular information, or the means to acquiring it, is but a prologue to a farce or a tragedy, or perhaps both" (qtd. in McChesney 6). With this, Madison—America's fourth president, often called the father of the Constitution—establishes an important aspect of democracy. The people must be informed about world events in order to be able to make informed decisions during any democratic election. If people are misinformed, their votes for or against candidates, bills, and propositions are based on false information. In non-democratic countries, history shows a pattern of misinformation and media manipulation emphasizing propaganda, suppression of the truth, and even mass brain washing. The ideal of American journalism and freedom of speech is supposed to protect us from governmental influence over the mass media, ensuring us reliable news and information.

However, with the recent and steady rise in power of the modern corporation, the media is no longer as free as many would think. Instead of the kinds of governmental intrusions on the news media that non-democratic countries endure, we face a system of corporate ownership, which dominates news media instead. As corporations have grown over the last one hundred years, they slowly acquired more and more aspects of the "mediascape," and now a few corporations own the majority of television stations, movie

[1] James Madison was the fourth president of the United States and major contributor to the Constitution and its Federalist Papers.

Corrections and Insertions

Sometimes you find a mistake in a paper after you have printed it out and typed it—at times, right before you are about to submit it. Ask your professor if brief corrections are allowed—many will say they are not. If so, write the corrections neatly in ink with a blue or black pen directly above the faulty word or words, using a caret (^) to indicate where the correction belongs. In the case of missing punctuation marks, add the mark where it belongs instead of adding it above the line with a caret. Even if your professor says that inserted corrections are acceptable, use them only for infrequent or minor corrections. If you have to make quite a few corrections, or if any of the corrections are large and detailed, retype the pages involved.

ANNOTATED SAMPLE MLA PAPER

We are closing this chapter with an annotated sample paper written by a student utilizing some of the sources that you'll find in this book. This sample paper will show you the correct format for an MLA-style paper, as well as showing how a student supports an argumentative thesis with documentation from credible sources, correctly attributed through in-text citations and a works cited page.

Jeffries   1

Dianne Jeffries

Professor Rupert Giles

English 1A: 12:50 MW

22 November 2009

Corporate Media: Injuries to Democracy and Diversity

James Madison once said that a "popular government

without popular information, or the means to acquiring it, is

but a prologue to a farce or a tragedy, or perhaps both" (qtd. in

McChesney 6). With this, Madison—America's fourth presi-

dent, often called the father of the Constitution—establishes an

important aspect of democracy. The people must be informed

about world events in order to be able to make informed deci-

sions during any democratic election. If people are misinformed,

their votes for or against candidates, bills, and propositions are

based on false information. In non-democratic countries, history

shows a pattern of misinformation and media manipulation

emphasizing propaganda, suppression of the truth, and even

mass brain washing. The ideal of American journalism and

freedom of speech is supposed to protect us from governmental

influences over the mass media, ensuring us reliable news and

information. However, with the recent and steady rise in power

of the modern corporation, the media is no longer as free as

Annotations (in left margin):

The student's last name and page number appear as a header one-half inch from the top in the right corner of every page in the paper. Use the header function in your word processing program.

The paper's top, bottom, and left and right margins should be one inch.

The student's name, the professor's name, class name, and the date of submission appear in the upper-left corner. The day precedes the month in MLA format.

The title is centered and double-spaced. Colons set off subtitles. Do not add extra spaces above or below titles.

Opening the paper with a quotation helps to "hook" the reader and generate interest in the subject matter.

Use "qtd. in" for people quoted by your sources.

Dianne's introduction starts with broad statements that gradually reveal the paper's topic by getting more specific as we near the thesis.

Jeffries   2

many would think. Instead of the kinds of governmental intrusions on the news media that non-democratic countries endure, we face a system of corporate ownership, which dominates news media instead. As corporations have grown over the last one hundred years, they slowly acquired more and more aspects of the "mediascape," and now a few corporations own the majority of television stations, movie studios, publishing houses, and newspaper and magazine printing presses. Over time, the American corporation has transformed from being just a business model to the nation's most powerful force. Today, modern corporations' power over the media has damaged democracy by limiting public exposure to a diverse and comprehensive range of information, perspectives, and analyses, even resulting in lies and misinformation in the news media.

To begin an effective discussion of the corporate damage to American democracy, a look at the evolution of the corporate entity would be logical. Kalle Lasn, filmmaker and creator and editor of the magazine *Adbusters,* a nonprofit anti-consumerism organization, discusses the history of the American corporation. He suggests that all of American history has been filled with oversized corporations, dating all the way back to the Boston Tea Party and the dumping of the

> Dianne's introduction is now getting very specific as the thesis nears.

> The first paragraph ends with the paper's thesis statement, which clearly states the assertation that the paper aims to prove.

> The second paragraph's topic sentence follows a transition sentence.

> Dianne establishes this author's credentials here before paraphrasing him. Because this is the first mention of the author, she uses his whole name.

Century

Jeffries   3

Citations don't need authors' last names if the name is in the sentence.

East India Tea Company's leaves into Boston Harbor (66). The events of the Tea Party made early Americans wary of corporate power, but as time went on, Americans forgot the lessons of the early colonies. Indeed, Lasn later discusses a change in this apprehension that came with the court case *Santa Clara County v. Southern Pacific Railroad* (a legal battle over a railroad route), in which the final outcome was "that a private corporation was a 'natural person' under the U.S. Constitution and therefore entitled to protection under the Bill of Rights" (68). This landmark ruling empowered the corporation, affording them all the legal rights of a human being, and it led to the modern era.

During this modern era of the corporation, these companies gained increasing wealth, power, and influence. Lasn argues that corporations "merged, consolidated, restructured and metamorphosed into ever larger and more complex units of resource extraction, production, distribution and marketing, to the point where many of them became economically more powerful than many countries" (69). Here, Lasn suggests that now corporations not only share the same rights as any American citizen, but the largest and most powerful have greater wealth than many smaller nations. The court

Because Lasn was already fully introduced above, Dianne only needed to use his last name at this point.

Discussion of the quotation helps give the readers a critical context for the material.

Annotated Sample MLA Paper   **259**

Jeffries   4

ruling in *Santa Clara County v. Southern Pacific Railroad*
is what slowly let these once small businesses grow to be
modern-day financial powerhouses. However, the recession
of the 1980s slowed down corporate growth.

Indeed, in the 1980s, the financial recession caused a
slump in production and purchases for the American public.
Naomi Klein, media activist and author of the influential
book on advertising, *No Logo,* suggests that in the 1980s,

> A consensus emerged that corporations were bloated,
>
> oversized; they owned too much, employed too many
>
> people, and were weighted down by *too many things*.
>
> The very process of producing—running one's own
>
> factories, being responsible for tens of thousands
>
> of full-time, permanent employees—began to look
>
> less like the route to success and more like a clunky
>
> liability. (4)

Thus, in order to avoid this "clunky liability," corporations
needed to change how they made money.

Instead of making money by selling a quality product,
corporations started to practice "branding." Branding is
when a corporation makes the identity of a certain brand

Transitional sentences at the end of paragraphs introduce topic sentences in the following paragraphs.

Because this quotation was over four lines long, Dianne followed MLA guidelines by indenting the quotation one inch from the left margin and omitting the quotation marks.

Jeffries   5

name (such as Coke, Nike, or The Gap) become synony-mous with high quality, luxury, or just "being cool." This branding worked better than anyone could have ever hoped and seemed to end the financial woes that the recession brought to corporate America. Klein discusses this corporate success story:

> The astronomical growth in the wealth and cultural influ-ence of multinational corporations over the last fifteen years can arguably be traced back to a single, seemingly innocuous idea developed by management theorists in the mid-1980s: that successful corporations must prima-rily produce brands, as opposed to products. (1)

When corporations focused on enhancing their brands instead of manufacturing products, as Klein suggests, they started making record earnings and grew in power and stature. Making a high-quality burger that tasted good did not sell nearly as well as selling the notion of "cool" or by convincing the audience that they are indeed "loving it," as McDonald's suggests in their highly successful ad campaign. Brand loyalty proved far more successful for the corporation than high-quality products seemed to.

Dianne takes time to discuss her own interpretations of this outside material to help prove her current argument.

Annotated Sample MLA Paper   **261**

Jeffries   6

With cunning marketing that makes citizens loyal to a brand, and with artifical entities having the same rights as a real human being, corporations have grown enough to dominate everything from what we eat to what we watch and read and even think. Several corporations have gotten so large that they've been able to buy an almost endless number of smaller corporations, helping to secure their financial might and cultural influence. Ben Bagdikian, author of several books about the modern media system, discusses many of the major corporations, which he calls media conglomerates. In his 1983 book *The Media Monopoly,* he showed that at the time only fifty corporations controlled a huge majority of all American news media. By 2003 (and his completely revised and updated edition of this book, called *The New Media Monopoly*) just five of these corporations—Time Warner, Disney, Viacom/CBS, News Corp, and Bertelsmann—controlled most of the media in the United States.

Indeed, in 2003, these five corporations were controlled by just five men: Richard Parsons, head of Time Warner; Michael Eisner, head of Disney; Sumner Redstone, head of Viacom; Rupert Murdoch, head of News Corps (and current owner of the *Wall Street Journal*); and Reinhard Mohn, a

> Use colons to introduce sentence elements only if they follow independent clauses.

Jeffries 7

man who had deceived the public about his company's Nazi history (Bagdikian, *New* 27–28). These conglomerates have merged and bought out every type of information technology possible—magazines, newspapers, websites, cable networks, even Internet service providers and the physical infrastructure of satellite systems and phone lines. If there is a way to get information about our world, odds are these conglomerates own it, and that is where free speech—and its corollary, free, accurate, and uncensored information—becomes limited for citizens.

Also, while discussing the media conglomerates, Bagdikian argues that they have dealt a blow to our democracy. He states that since the "majority of Americans say they get their news, commentary and daily entertainment from this handful of conglomerates, the conglomerates fail the needs of democracy every day. Our modern democracy depends not just on laws and the Constitution, but a vision of the real nature of the United States and its people" ("Grand" par. 1–2). Here, Bagdikian shows that a free flow of information is essential to running a true democracy, but the conglomerates don't really want us to have access to a free flow of information because a completely informed population might be less

> This is the format for a citation for two or more works by the same author. The author's last name is followed by a comma and the first important word or words of the title of the work.

> In a citation for a second source by the same author, the first important word of the article title enclosed in quotations is sufficient since the author's name is in the sentence. Numbers indicate the paragraph of an electronic source.

Jeffries   8

likely to buy the same products or sit by in ignorance while corporate lobbyists get politicians to push through laws that benefit corporations but hurt consumers. Most major media are owned by corporations, with the biggest ones absorbing smaller competitors, giving tremendous power to a few companies with holdings in a variety of industries, so conflicts of interest interfere with investigative journalism and accurate, fearless reporting. Clearly, as these conglomerates are allowed to grow, our access to information continually shrinks, but Bagdikian is not the only scholar to think so.

Another scholar of the media is Robert McChesney. McChesney, author of eight books and over 200 articles on media ownership, was perhaps the first to worry about the threat to democracy due to media ownership. McChesney argues that three different areas are crucial to a healthy participatory self-government.

- Lack of extreme gaps between the rich and poor of a nation

- Feeling of kinship on the part of citizens to their communities ·

- Reliable and honest systems of political communication through the mass media (5).

Reminder of thesis statement.

Often bullets, charts, illustrations, or other visual elements help to make information easier to digest.

Jeffries 9

Of these three areas, McChesney seems to argue that the third category—an effective system of political communication—is the most important and most at risk in our culture. Quite simply, without a reliable method of public communication, free speech is severely hampered.

In fact, in his book (appropriately titled *Corporate Media and the Threat to Democracy*), McChesney suggests that

> the commercial basis of U.S. media has negative implications for the exercise of political democracy: it encourages a weak political culture that makes depoliticization, apathy and selfishness rational choices for the citizenry, and it permits the business and commercial interests that actually rule U.S. society to have inordinate influence over media content . . . for those committed to democracy, it is imperative to reform the media system. (7)

In this quotation, McChesney not only shows the negative impact of the media conglomerates, he even posits that someone who is truly dedicated to democracy and free speech must explore ways to change things. One government body is indeed doing some fact finding to try to find a way to change

Dianne continues to discuss her quotations and tie them back in to her own arguments.

Jeffries   10

things in favor of the citizens, and that is the Federal Communications Commission.

The FCC's primary function is to manage and safeguard the American airwaves (and net connections), ensuring that the public airwaves are still owned and run by and for the people and ensuring that free speech is not only possible, but strong and viable. In the fall of 2006, the FCC held a public hearing at the University of Southern California on the topic of regulations in corporate media ownership. They held an open discussion with the public to get feedback on what the people felt about the media conglomerates. In his opening statement at these proceedings, one of the five FCC commissioners, Jonathan Adelstein, claimed that "there should be no disagreement that our media ownership proceeding is, fundamentally, about one thing: *our democracy*" (par. 2). Adelstein also says that "central to our American democracy is the 'uninhibited marketplace of ideas,' where everyone is able to exchange and share music, news, information and entertainment programming over the public airwaves" (par. 2). However, with a few major corporations owning so many media outlets, everyone is not able to participate in the "marketplace of ideas" and share music, news, or information that is important to them.

When electronic sources number the paragraphs, provide the abbreviation for "paragraph" followed by the number.

Jeffries   11

Instead, we are all forced to watch, listen to, and read very few

corporate-generated ideas such as an endless regurgitation of

similar reality shows, rehashes of the same tired situation com-

edies, and shallow or biased news reports. This lack of media

diversity harms McChesney's second key to democracy, an

important connection to community. Many minority voices are

never heard in this corporate media environment, so the sense

of "community" may not be strong enough.

The paragraph ends with a sentence that serves to tie this argument back to the earlier argument about McChesney.

Another FCC commissioner is also concerned with how

the lack of unique voices can break down a community.

In his own opening statements to the 2006 public hearing,

Commissioner Michael J. Copps asks if he and others actu-

ally have access to the public airwaves—can regular citizens

actually get a show or advertisement aired, or will we be

priced out of the market by multi-billion dollar corpora-

tions? (par. 7) After asking this question, Copps emphasized

a very important point—that the airwaves are *public* air-

waves. "They belong to you and me and every other person

in this country, not to any corporation or conglomerate. We

allow broadcasters to use the airwaves—for free—in return

for offering programs that serve the public interest" (par. 7).

Copps indicates here that there is a dichotomy. Though the

Annotated Sample MLA Paper   **267**

Jeffries   12

public airwaves belong to the citizenry, they are entirely dominated by corporate interests bent on gaining advertising revenue, not serving the needs of the people. Thus, the corporations own the capability to communicate and speak to the masses, and our own power of free speech and diversity are severely limited.

In spite of this corporate stranglehold on information, however, there is one way that we can still get important news stories on a variety of issues. We can look at "watchdog groups," which monitor the media. Project Censored is a national research effort begun in 1976 in the Communications Studies Department at Sonoma State University. It compares the news published in independent media with the news covered by the mainstream, corporate-owned media. Every year, Project Censored creates a list of twenty-five significant news stories "that have been overlooked, under-reported or self-censored by the country's major national news media" (*Project Censored*). They publish the stories in a yearbook and on the Internet at their website.

Stories that the project spotlighted as important news ignored by corporate media include "Factories, Cities Across USA Exceed Water Pollution Limits" by Sunny Lewis of the

> Dianne provides a citation for a web page because the site didn't have individual article titles.

Jeffries   13

Environment News Service. This story revealed that between
July 2003 and December 2004, "More than 62 percent of
industrial and municipal facilities across the country discharged more pollution into U.S. waterways than their Clean
Water Act permits, and "The average facility discharged
pollution in excess of its permit limit by more than 275
percent, or almost four times the legal limit" (qtd. in *Project
Censored*). This discrepancy between fact and reported news
shows that the corporations that own the media do not want
the public to get too upset about corporate poisoning of
drinking water.

   A particularly disturbing 2003 story that Project Censored
highlighted and that was perhaps understandably ignored
by mainstream media is one that revealed that a Florida
court ruled that media can legally lie. Two investigators
were hired by Fox News at WTVT in Florida for a story on
bovine growth hormone (BGH), which is manufactured by
Monsanto Corporation. According to Project Censored, the
"couple produced a four-part series revealing that there were
many health risks related to BGH and that Florida supermar-
ket chains did little to avoid selling milk from cows treated
with the hormone, despite assuring customers otherwise"

Though this source was written by Lewis, the citation is
for Project Censored because
Project Censored is the source
found in the works-cited page.

Jeffries   14

(*Project Censored*). Monsanto pressured Fox to revise the
story and include false statements as facts; Fox told the reporters to change the story to fit Monsanto's demands. They
were fired when they refused. When the reporters sued Fox
for being wrongfully fired,

> FOX asserted that there are no written rules against
>
> distorting news in the media. They argued that, under
>
> the First Amendment, broadcasters have the right to lie
>
> or deliberately distort news reports on public airwaves.
>
> Fox attorneys did not dispute Akre's claim that they
>
> pressured her to broadcast a false story, they simply
>
> maintained that it was their right to do so. (*Project
>
> Censored*)

This Florida case shows that major broadcasters are not
only capable of telling lies to the public through their own
airwaves, but they are actually lying. Though a Florida
jury ruled in favor of one of the reporters, an appeals court
overturned the ruling, and Fox won the legal battle. This is
not a story that Fox itself or any other corporate media outlet
showcased; such a story might shake the public's belief that
they are being correctly served by big media.

Dianne connects her example
to her thesis statement.

Jeffries 15

There are other problems with corporations' priorities for the public. Corporate news media is increasingly looking more like entertainment than news. Jake Halpern authored a book called *Fame Junkies,* which is about Americans' supposed obsession with celebrities. In an article in the *Wall Street Journal* (which has since been bought by Rupert Murdoch's News Corporation), Halpern provided statistics that included the fact that in 2004, the three major news networks gave Martha Stewart five times more news coverage than they gave the genocide in Darfur, and that CNN's coverage of Britney Spears when she lost custody of her children was three times greater than its coverage of the war in Iraq (Halpern). Ironically, Halpern was scheduled to appear on CNN that day to discuss his book, but when he arrived, he was told that his interview had been cancelled. When he inquired about what had happened, he was asked, "Didn't you hear, Britney Spears just lost custody of her kids?" (Halpern). An author being bumped for a celebrity may not be very disturbing, but the amount of time the public is being fed stories about Britney Spears, Martha Stewart, Lindsay Lohan, and Paris Hilton is disturbing.

Jeffries   16

One might ask, why is this disturbing if this is what
people want to hear? One answer would be that it takes
time away from genuine news. For every Paris Hilton story,
one can only imagine what stories get cut from the air. The
question this raises is, are we getting a constant stream of
stories about celebrity scandals because it really is what
the American public wants to hear? A 2007 study by the
Pew Research Center for People and the Press says no. This
study looked at 165 separate national surveys and found that
celebrity scandal ranks lowest among all news preferences
("Two Decades"). This statistic helps to prove that the people
are tired of watching the same tired stories about celebrities in trouble, but it dominates the airwaves because it is
cheap, easy, and helps fill the need for twenty-four hours of
information being broadcast on cable networks. However,
when critical news about things as important as genocide get
less air time than a story about Martha Stewart, the corporate control of the media truly fails to serve the needs of the
American public.

Serving the needs of the people should be of paramount
importance to every citizen in our mediated world, however,
not simply the financial bottom line of corporate America.

> Rhetorical questions can serve as effective transition sentences.

Jeffries   17

A conclusion should clearly remind the readers of the paper's thesis statement and the arguments that support it.

Corporations used to be manageable and closely monitored by the people and the government. The current corporate dominance of the airwaves, though, undermines our ability to stay well informed, feel a sense of community, and therefore fully participate in our own democratic government. We cannot let corporations control and limit what we know about our own country and the rest of the world. As President Madison, one of the fathers of this democracy, said, "popular government without popular information, or the means to acquiring it, is but a prologue to a farce or a tragedy, or perhaps both" (qtd. in McChesney 6). If the corporations become the ultimate gatekeepers of the powers of mass communication, our own ability to engage in true free speech and to have complete access to the information we need to make truly informed decisions about everything from our health to the leaders we elect will be only a farce or a tragedy as Madison predicted.

Ending the paper with the same quotation it opened with helps Dianne to provide a stronger sense of closure by coming "full circle."

All entries on the works-cited page are in alphabetical order, and everything is double-spaced.

In each entry, every line after the first line is indented.

Works Cited

Adelstein, Jonathan S. Statement. Broadcast Media Ownership Public Hearing, University of Southern California. 3 Oct. 2006. Print.

Bagdikian, Ben. "Grand Theft: The Conglomeratization of Media and the Degradation of Culture: Twenty-Five Years of Monitoring the Multinationals." *Multinational Monitor* 26. 1–2 (Jan.–Feb. 2005): 35–7. *Expanded Academic ASAP*. Thomson Gale. Web. 19 Oct. 2008.

---. *The New Media Monopoly.* Boston: Beacon, 2004. Print.

Copps, Michael, J. Broadcast Media Ownership Public Hearing, University of Southern California. 3 Oct. 2006. Remarks.

Halpern, Jake. "Britney Spears, 'Breaking News.'" *Wall Street Journal Online.* 4 Oct. 2007. Web. 18 Oct. 2009.

Klein, Naomi. *No Logo: Taking Aim at the Brand Bullies.* New York: Picador, 1999. Print.

Lasn, Kalle. *Culture Jam: The Uncooling of America.* New York: Eagle Brook, 1999. Print.

McChesney, Robert W. *Corporate Media and the Threat to Democracy.* The Open Media Pamphlet Series. New York: Seven Stories, 1997. Print.

Project Censored. Sonoma State University. Web. 2 Nov. 2009.

"Two Decades of American News Preferences." Pew Center Publications. 22 Aug. 2007. Web. 2 Nov. 2009.

Here, Dianne uses three hyphens to indicate that this is the second source written by Bagdikian and used in this paper.

Shorten the names of publishers to the first important word or words, omitting words like *Publishers* and *Press.* (See separate guidelines for university presses.)

When there is no author, alphabetize an entry by the first important word of the title.

Century

12 CHAPTER

Creating MLA-Style Parenthetical Citations

WHEN YOU SHOULD USE PARENTHETICAL CITATIONS

Whether you are writing a paper in MLA or APA format, you need to indicate the sources that you use each time you take information from any of them and, in the case of most print sources, the page numbers the information comes from. MLA- and APA-style papers use **parenthetical in-text citations** rather than footnotes or endnotes for publication information. You must cite all the nonfiction sources used within research papers and other essays, whether paraphrased, summarized, or directly quoted, unless the material cited is considered "common knowledge." In-text citations are also used in MLA-style papers discussing literary works to identify the page numbers for direct quotations from these works of literature. (If you are writing about literature, you need in-text citations only for direct quotations from the work, not for summaries of the plot, character descriptions, and other comments about what takes place in the fictional world.)

In-text citations don't stand alone, of course. The first word in a parenthetical citation, usually the last name of an author or the first important word or words of a work without an author listed, must correspond to the first words that begin the entries on your lists of sources used at the end of the paper. This way, your readers can easily locate the full publication and other relevant information for each source that you used in your paper. MLA-style papers usually call these lists Works Cited if you include citations only for material you used or Works Consulted if you also include citations for material you read for background but didn't actually incorporate into your paper (see Chapter 13). APA papers usually call these lists References (see Chapter 14).

Remember that you must document *all* ideas you take from nonfiction sources and use in your research papers, not just direct quotations. If you fail to do so, you are plagiarizing. (For more information on how to recognize and avoid plagiarism, see Chapter 9.)

PLACEMENT OF PARENTHETICAL CITATIONS

Place a citation as close to the quoted, paraphrased, or summarized material as possible without disrupting the sentence. When material from one source and the same page numbers is used throughout a paragraph, use one citation at the end of the paragraph rather than a citation at the end of each sentence. However, if you have added your own thoughts inside the paragraph, you need multiple citations to distinguish between your source's ideas and your own.

In most cases, a parenthetical citation includes the author's last name and the specific page number for the information cited, or just the page number if the author is clearly identified elsewhere in the sentence, but there are also many instances when you need to include additional information in your citation. The following section gives you the guidelines for MLA in-text citations, including use of authors' names, placement of citations, and treatment of electronic sources. (For APA guidelines on in-text citations, see Chapter 14.)

1. Author's Name Given in Your Sentence

2. Author's Name Not Given in Your Sentence

3. More Than One Work by the Same Author

4. Two Authors with the Same Last Name

5. Two or Three Authors

6. Four or More Authors

7. No Author Provided

8. Sacred Texts and Commonly Studied Literature

9. Sources Quoting Other Works

10. Indented Quotations

11. Quotations Within Quotations

12. Information from More Than One Source

13. Work in an Anthology

14. Online and Other Electronic Sources

15. Other Nonprint Sources

1. AUTHOR'S NAME GIVEN IN YOUR SENTENCE

Often in writing, you will introduce the author before giving the actual quotation, summary, or paraphrase. In such cases, you need include only the page numbers in your parenthetical citation. The reader will be able to find the author's name in your sentence and on the works-cited page because you have given it in your text. In the parentheses, do not use the abbreviation "p" or "page" before the number; simply give the number by itself. In the following examples, the author is citing an author with the last name of Zipes. Because the author is mentioned in the text of this paper, his name does not need to appear in the parentheses with the page numbers. Notice that the sentences' periods follow the citations; they do not directly follow the sentences

276   CHAPTER 12   Creating MLA-Style Parenthetical Citations

themselves. When you are quoting directly, the closing quotation mark should precede the citation. See the following examples.

Paraphrased material:

> Zipes argues that we really cannot absolutely separate the oral, folkloric fairy tale from the literary fairy tale because we cannot trace stories to their origins (222).

Quoted material:

> Zipes states that "This is an impossible task because there are very few if any records with the exception of paintings, drawings, etchings, inscriptions and other cultural artifacts that reveal how tales were told and received thousands of years ago" (222).

You may want to quote the same source more than once in a single paragraph in your paper. As long as you do not include any quotations from other sources in between, you can use one parenthetical citation after the last quotation.

> "Austen's irony is both worldly and unworldly, finding nothing to be surprised at in human immorality, but nothing to be cynically indulged about it either." Her irony is subtle and put to the task of defending the cultural and moral status quo. "One should not be misled by Austen's good-natured irony into imagining that she is, in the modern sense of the word, a liberal" (Eagleton 107, 108).

2. AUTHOR'S NAME NOT GIVEN IN YOUR SENTENCE

If you choose not to provide the name of the author in your own sentence, you will need to provide the name in your parenthetical citation. Without this information, your audience will not be able to identify the correct entry for the source on your works-cited page. In this case, provide the name and a space and then the page number.

Paraphrased material:

> Following the Thomas-Hill hearings, sexual harassment became an issue of greater importance to the American public (Mayer and Abramson 352).

Quoted material:

> "But it may have been inside the Senate itself that the hearings left their most lasting impression" (Mayer and Abramson 352–53).

3. MORE THAN ONE WORK BY THE SAME AUTHOR

If you are citing more than one work by an individual author, include the first important word or words (don't use *a, an,* and *the*) of the title of the work you are citing in addition to the author's name and relevant page number(s). Remember to underline or use quotation marks around the title as appropriate. Separate the author's name—if you need it in the citation—and the title with a comma:

> "The term 'neoliberalism' suggests a system of principles that is both new and based on classical liberal ideas: Adam Smith is revered as the patron saint" (Chomsky, *Profit* 19).

4. TWO AUTHORS WITH THE SAME LAST NAME

If the document uses two sources by authors with the same last name, include each author's first name in the text or the parenthetical citation. In the following example, Martin Amis is talking about his father, novelist Kingsley Amis, whose works are also included in the paper:

> "In retrospect I can see that these questions would have played on my father's deepest fears" (Amis, Martin 3).

5. TWO OR THREE AUTHORS

If the work you are citing has two or three authors, use all their last names, even if two or more of them share a last name. If you are citing three authors, be sure you separate each name with a comma and use *and* before the last name in the list. Always keep the authors in the order in which they are listed in their book.

> "It would be a mistake to underestimate the significance of *Frankenstein*'s title page, with its allusive subtitle" (Gilbert and Gubar 224).

> "Even the most casual assessment of the daily flow of news reveals a complex tapestry of issues and events" (Neuman, Just, and Crigler 39).

6. FOUR OR MORE AUTHORS

If a source has four or more authors, there are two ways you can write the citation. First, you can include the first author's last name followed by *et al.* (an abbreviation of the Latin phrase *et alli,* meaning "and others") either in the text or in the parenthetical citation:

> "And some essayists are not out to change the world at all: some are completely indifferent to immediate circumstances or practical ends" (Scholes et al.3).

> Scholes et al. point out that "some essayists are not out to change the world at all: some are completely indifferent to immediate circumstances or practical ends" (3).

You can also name all the authors:

> "And some essayists are not out to change the world at all: some are completely indifferent to immediate circumstances or practical ends" (Scholes, Klaus, Comley, and Silverman 3).

> Scholes, Klaus, Comley, and Silverman point out that "some essayists are not out to change the world at all: some are completely indifferent to immediate circumstances or practical ends" (3).

7. NO AUTHOR PROVIDED

If a source does not include an author's name, substitute for the author's name the title or a shortened form of the title in the text or a parenthetical citation. You can use the first important word or more; the idea is to give as short a form of the title as you can without risking it being confused with a similar title beginning an entry on your works-cited page. Format the title words the same way they are formatted on the

278   CHAPTER 12   Creating MLA-Style Parenthetical Citations

works-cited page; if the title is in quotation marks on that page, it must be treated the same way in the citation, and so on.

> The term *annus horribilis* means "horrible year," and it was brought into somewhat popular use after Queen Elizabeth II publicly used it to describe the year that her sons' respective marriages foundered and Windsor Castle caught fire (*Latin* 13).

8. SACRED TEXTS AND COMMONLY STUDIED LITERATURE

Commonly studied works of literature and sacred texts are reprinted in many editions, so you can help your readers by providing more information than the page number from your edition. With prose works of literature, such as novels, novellas, and plays, giving a chapter number or an act number will make it possible for your audience to easily find a quotation even if they have a different edition of the work than you do. Start with the author's last name unless it is clearly indicated before the quotation, follow with the page number (with no comma between them), and then add a semicolon and the supplemental information. Use the abbreviations *pt.* for part, *ch.* for chapter, *bk.* for book, *sec.* for section. If your source doesn't have page numbers, this information is especially important.

> Jude and Sue are shocked and horrified when they discover the hanged bodies of their three children. Grief-stricken, they realize that the eldest child killed his siblings and then himself, leaving a note which reads, "Done because we are too menny" (Hardy 331; pt. 6, sec. 2).

Commonly studied poems and verse plays don't need page numbers in citations. Instead, give the numbers of the works' divisions—such as books, parts, cantos, acts, and scenes—followed by the numbers of the lines, separated by a period. If you are using a line number, precede it by *line*. Use arabic numerals unless your instructor requests Roman numerals (some professors prefer Roman numerals for the acts and scenes in plays).

> Hamlet's disgust manifests itself once again when, in a speech to Rosencrantz and Guildenstern, he describes the sky as "A foul and pestilent congregation of vapors" (2.2.311).

> In Eliot's "The Love Song of J. Alfred Prufrock," the narrator exclaims, "No! I am not Prince Hamlet, nor was meant to be" (line 111).

With sacred texts, just as with other works, you need to clearly indicate in your paper how your readers can find the appropriate entry on your works-cited page. Indicate the word that begins the entry on the works-cited list, either in the parenthetical citation or in your paper. This could be the last name of the editor of a critical edition, the first important word of the title of the section you use, or the important first word or words of the entire text.

> "[Amos] is unique in opening with a motto, a short, general thematic statement that is meant to (re)focus how the book should be understood" (Berlin and Brettler 1177).

> "In the beginning / The Universe was the Self, / Pure Consciousness, alone" (Upanishads 211).

9. SOURCES QUOTING OTHER WORKS

If your source quotes someone else, indicate that person's name in your sentence, and put your source's name inside the citation preceded by the abbreviation for "quoted in."

> Janet Smith pointed out that "the Grimms did not refrain from changing stories when it suited their purposes" (qtd. in Tatar 321).

10. LONG QUOTATIONS

When you use a direct quotation in your paper that is four full lines or longer (in your paper, not the original source you're reading), you need to set off the quotation and indent it. The following list gives the proper format for a long quotation.

- Indent the entire quotation one inch or ten spaces, roughly the length of two standard tabs. This will be twice the indentation of your typical paragraphs.
- Double-space the quotation, just like the rest of the paper.
- Do not change fonts or type sizes for a long quotation.
- Do not use quotation marks. The indentation, instead of quotation marks, will indicate that this is a quotation.
- The end punctuation precedes the parenthetical citation instead of following it.

Following is an example. (Note that the sentence that introduces the quotation is the beginning of a new paragraph, so it is already indented one-half inch. The quotation is indented a full inch to indicate it is a long quotation.) As in a shorter quotation, because Jack Zipes is named in the sentence, his name need not appear within the citation. The sentence that introduces the quotation ends with a colon.

> Jack Zipes disputes the approach used by many folklore scholars:
>
> > For the past three hundred years or more scholars and critics have sought to define and classify the oral folk tale and the literary fairy tale, as though they could be clearly distinguished from one another, and as though we could trace their origins to some primeval source. This is an impossible task because there are very few if any records with the exception of paintings, drawings, etchings, inscriptions and other cultural artifacts that reveal how tales were told and received thousands of years ago. (222)

11. QUOTATIONS WITHIN QUOTATIONS

Enclose quoted material (or titles that require quotation marks) that is within other quoted material within single quotation marks (use the apostrophe key) unless the material takes up more than four lines in your paper. Because you omit quotation marks when you indent lengthy quotations, you can use regular double quotation marks for quotations inside longer quotations because they won't cause confusion about where the larger quotation ends.

> According to David Riggs, "During that same summer of 1592, Robert Greene famously attacked Shakespeare as an 'upstart Crow, beautified with our feathers,' much as Nashe had attacked Kyd three years previously" (282).

12. INFORMATION FROM MORE THAN ONE SOURCE

If you have information that comes from different sources, indicate them all.

> Women across the social spectrum shared and modified fairy tales (Smith 172, Warner 316–17).

13. WORK IN AN ANTHOLOGY

For quotations or other information taken from works you get from an anthology (a collection of works, usually by different authors), make sure that you list the last name of the author of the work, not the editor of the anthology. The author's name will come before the editor's name in the works-cited page. For example, an essay by Edwin C. Baker, called "Implications of Rival Visions of Electoral Campaigns," is in a book titled *Mediated Politics: Communication in the Future of Democracy,* which is edited by Lance W. Bennett and Robert M. Entman. If you used information from this essay, you would provide Baker's name in your citation, followed by the page number.

> "Both our electoral process and our media coverage of elections are a disgrace" (Baker 342).

If you used Baker's name in your sentence, all you would need is the page number.

14. ONLINE AND OTHER ELECTRONIC SOURCES

In-text citations for online and other electronic sources, such as email, are treated much as those for print texts are; you need to provide the authors' last names if you have them and the important words of titles if you do not. The only real difference occurs because electronic texts do not usually have page numbers. If you try to assign page numbers for an online article that you print out yourself, you cannot be sure that the page numbers would be the same if someone else printed out the same article from a different browser and using a different printer. In general, you should give page numbers only when you have found an article or other work that is reprinted in PDF format, because the page numbers provided will be the same as the print version of the source.

Sometimes numbered paragraphs appear in an electronic source. In such cases, you may use the paragraph numbers. The paragraph number should appear in your citation. After the author's name, you should include a comma and the abbreviation *par.*

If you give the name of the author in your sentence, you can actually omit an in-text citation when you have no numbers to put in the parentheses; your audience can find all the publication information on the works-cited page by locating the author's name at the beginning of the bibliographic entry.

> "The CIA's Publications Review Board has expressly forbidden Valerie Plame to reveal details of her past at the Agency in her upcoming memoir, saying that she can't even say she worked for them" (Douglas).

> "The CIA's Publications Review Board has expressly forbidden Valerie Plame to reveal details of her past at the Agency in her upcoming memoir, saying that she can't even say she worked for them" (Douglas, par. 6)

Nick Douglas reports that "The CIA's Publications Review Board has expressly forbidden Valerie Plame to reveal details of her past at the Agency in her upcoming memoir, saying that she can't even say she worked for them."

15. OTHER NONPRINT SOURCES

As with online and other electronic sources, use an author's name if one is available or the title of the work if one is not—the point to remember is that you must give the information that your readers need to find the proper entry in the alphabetized list of works cited. If you have used a director's name as the first word in an entry about a film, that name is what you must use in your citation. If you use the title of the film as your first word, that title is what you should use. If you have taken information from a lecture or speech, include the name of the lecturer or speaker.

"Toto, I've got a feeling we're not in Kansas anymore" (Fleming).

"Toto, I've got a feeling we're not in Kansas anymore" (*Wizard*).

L. Frank Baum's *The Wizard of Oz* has been regarded as an American fairy tale, and the 1939 film version, directed by Victor Fleming, has become iconic (Powell).

13 CHAPTER

Preparing the MLA List of Works Cited

A bibliography is a list of sources that you compile while researching a paper. MLA-style papers usually call these lists Works Cited if you include citations only for material you used or Works Consulted if you also include citations for material you read for background but didn't actually incorporate into your paper (see Chapter 13). APA papers usually call these lists References (see Chapter 14). There are also Annotated Bibliographies, which include annotations (brief summaries that may also include evaluations) after each entry on a list of sources. (See the explanation and examples at the end of this chapter.) For simplicity's sake, we will refer to all bibliographical citations as works-cited entries—the format is the same, no matter what you call the list itself. Following is the directory of the different examples of works-cited entries in this chapter.

DIRECTORY OF SAMPLE WORKS-CITED ENTRIES

284   CHAPTER 13   Preparing the MLA List of Works Cited

ARRANGEMENT OF ENTRIES ON THE WORKS-CITED PAGE

MLA guidelines require that you arrange all the entries on your works-cited page alphabetically, no matter what type of source you are using. Begin with the author's name, inverting the first and last names. If a source has more than one author, invert only the name of the first author because that is the only name relevant to alphabetizing the entry. You should treat authors' names exactly as they appear on the title page of the source you're citing; do not use their initials unless that is how their names appear on the title page. Do not include titles and degrees, such as Dr. or PhD, when you name the authors on the works-cited page.

Often you will have to look at more than one example to create a citation. For instance, you may be creating a works-cited page and realize that you not only have two essays by the same author, but both essays also have translators. Also, the essays appeared in periodicals, not books. You aren't going to find a single example with each of those factors here—and you probably wouldn't find it in any other stylebook or text, either. No one can give you every possible combination, so you have to look at instructions in different categories and at more than one example. In the fourth and seventh categories in the section on books, we show you what to do when you have more than one work by an author and when you have a translated work. You would need to take information from both of those categories and also from the section on periodicals to create the correct citations.

WORKS-CITED ENTRIES FOR BOOKS, WORKS IN BOOKS, AND PLAYS

The basic book entry is probably the most common type of entry you will ever include in a works-cited list. Basic entries for published plays look just the same. All the information you need to complete this type of works-cited entry is provided on the title page of the book or on its copyright page, which generally follows the title page (see sample on next page). Typically, the title page provides the title and subtitle of the book, the author(s), and even the city and publishing house. On the copyright page, you'll find the full publication information: the address of the publishing company, ISBN number, Library of Congress Subject Headings, copyright dates, and most recent year of publication. Learn to mine these opening pages for all your works-cited information.

The McGraw-Hill Companies

Higher Education

Published by McGraw-Hill, an imprint of The McGraw-Hill Companies, Inc., 1221 Avenue of the Americas, New York, NY 10020. Copyright © 2009. All rights reserved. No part of this publication may be reproduced or distributed in any form or by any means, or stored in a database or retrieval system, without the prior written consent of The McGraw-Hill Companies, Inc., including, but not limited to, in any network or other electronic storage or transmission, or broadcast for distance learning.

This book is printed on acid-free paper.

1 2 3 4 5 6 7 8 9 0 QPD/QPD 0 9 8

ISBN: 978-0-07-337842-8
MHID: 0-07-337842-9

Editor in Chief: *Michael Ryan*
Publisher: *David Patterson*
Sponsoring Editor: *Allison McNamara*
Marketing Manager: *James Headley*
Developmental Editor: *Emily Pecora*
Production Editor: *Regina Ernst*
Manuscript Editor: *Leslie Ann Weber*
Cover Designer: *Carole Lawson*
Photo Research: *Brian Pecko*
Production Supervisor: *Louis Swaim*
Composition: *10/12 Minion by Aptara, Inc.*
Printing: *45# New Era Matte Plus, Quebecor World, Inc.*

Cover: © IT Stock Free

Photo Credits: CO-1, © SuperStock; CO-2, © prettyfoto/Alamy; CO-3, © Goodshoot/Punch-Stock; CO-4, Brand X Pictures; CO-5, © Digital Vision/Getty Images; CO-6, Brand X Pictures; CO-7, © 2005 image100 Ltd. All Rights Reserved.; CO-8, © Digital Vision/Getty Images; CO-9, © Greatstock Photographic Library/Alamy; CO-10, CO-11, Brand X Pictures; CO-12, © Digital Vision/PunchStock; CO-13, © Ingram Publishing/SuperStock; CO-14, Doug Menuez/Getty Images; CO-15, Brand X Pictures/PunchStock; CO-16, © Digital Vision/Getty Images

Library of Congress Cataloging-in-Publication Data

Bruno, Holly Elissa.
Leading on purpose : emotionally intelligent early childhood administration / Holly Elissa Bruno. — 1st ed.
p. cm.
Includes bibliographical references and index.
ISBN-13: 978-0-07-337842-8 (alk. paper)
ISBN-10: 0-07-337842-9 (alk. paper)
1. Early childhood education—Administration. 2. Educational leadership—Psychological aspects. 3. Emotional intelligence. I. Title.
LB2822.6.B78 2009
372.12—dc22
2008039642

The Internet addresses listed in the text were accurate at the time of publication. The inclusion of a Web site does not indicate an endorsement by the authors or McGraw-Hill, and McGraw-Hill does not guarantee the accuracy of the information presented at these sites.

www.mhhe.com

The following list indicates most possible components for a basic book entry:

1. **Author:** Begin with the author's name (first and last names reversed), followed by a period. If there is a middle name or initial, it should follow the first name. In the case of pseudonyms, you may add an author's real name in brackets in between the pen name and the period (for example, Genêt [Janet Flanner]). You can also follow initials with the full name in brackets for clarification (for example, Eliot, T[homas] S[terns]), but this is generally not considered necessary. If there is more than one author, put *and* before the last author's name, and a comma after the preceding author even if there are only two authors. Only reverse the first and last names of the first author listed.

2. **Title:** Next, you'll give the title, italicized or underlined. If a question mark or exclamation point is part of the title, italicize or underline it with the rest of the title, but do not italicize or underline the period after the title. If there is a subtitle, it should be set off from the title with a colon. End with a period unless a question mark or exclamation point is part of the title.

3. **Translator:** If the book has been translated, use the abbreviation "Trans." after the title, followed by the name of the translator. (If other information is relevant, such as the editor of a critical edition, an introduction by another author, or an illustrator, present the names in the order given on the book's title page).

4. **Edition:** Indicate the edition after the title, abbreviated, but *only* if the book is not a first edition or it is a critical or revised edition.

5. **City of Publication:** Give the city in which the book was published next (the first one listed if more than one city is named on the title page). Do not give the state, province, or country unless the city is not well known or could be confused with another city with the same name (for example, "Paris, TX"). Follow the city's name with a colon.

6. **Publisher:** Provide the name of the publisher, shortened to the most important word if it is not a university press. For example, Alfred A. Knopf, Inc., would be shortened to Knopf; Free Press would be shortened to Free; and Simon and Schuster, Inc., would be shortened to Simon. For university presses, abbreviate university to *U* and Press to *P.* For example, University of South Carolina Press would become U of South Carolina P, and Oxford University Press would become Oxford UP (note that periods do not follow *U* or *P* and the letters *U* and *P* are not separated by spaces when they are together). Follow the publisher's name with a comma to set it off from the year of publication. You do not need a publisher if the book was published before 1900; in such cases, give the city, followed by a comma, followed by the year.

7. **Year:** Look for the most recent year of publication given. If no publication date is provided, use the most recent copyright date. If you cannot find any dates, use *n. d.* End with a period.

   When you have a book that was originally published many years earlier than the edition that you have, the convention is to also include the original year of publication after the book's title, preceded and followed by periods. This way, your readers will have a more accurate idea of the age of the source than they would if you merely provided the date of publication of the edition that you are using.

8. **Medium of Publication:** With the increasing availability of sources, including books, in electronic form, the most current MLA guidelines require the medium of publication following the year of publication, so follow the year of publication with the word *print,* capitalized and followed by a period.

9. **Pertinent Supplementary Information:** Sometimes additional information is helpful to readers who want more information about your sources, such as the complete number of volumes of a multivolume set.

Here is an example of a basic book entry:

Diamond, Jared. *Guns, Germs, and Steel: The Fates of Human Societies.* New

York: Norton, 1999. Print.

To cite a work within a book when you are using only one selection from the book, you need to combine information about the individual work and the publication information about the book itself. (See #18, Multiple Selections from an Anthology, on p. 290, for additional information.)

These basic types of entries are very simple. However, you will soon encounter dozens of variations as you write your college papers. The basics will always remain the same, but you will need to provide extra information if you are using a book with, for example, more than one author, just one part of a book, a book in a series, a multivolume work, a book with a translator, and so on.

Sample MLA Works-Cited Entries

Following is a directory of sample works-cited entries.

1. BOOK OR PLAY BY A SINGLE AUTHOR

Cave, Nick. *And the Ass Saw the Angel.* New York: Penguin, 1990. Print.

Ishay, Micheline R. *The History of Human Rights: From Ancient Times to the Globalization Era.* Berkeley: U of California P, 2004. Print.

Stoppard, Tom. *Rosencrantz and Guildenstern Are Dead.* New York: Grove, 1967. Print.

Set titles off from subtitles with colons. If you are unsure whether a phrase below a title on the cover of a book or in its title page is a subtitle or just a descriptive phrase, check the Library of Congress cataloging-in-publication data, which can be found on the copyright page of the book.

2. BOOK BY TWO OR THREE AUTHORS

Always give the authors' names in the order that they are presented in your source. Note in the following example that only the first author's first and last names are reversed.

Gallagher, Catherine, and Stephen Greenblatt. *Practicing New Historicism.* Chicago: U of Chicago P, 2000. Print.

3. BOOK BY MORE THAN THREE AUTHORS

When you are citing a book with four or more authors or editors, you may use *et al.* (Latin for *et alii,* which means "and others"), followed by a period, in place of the names of the authors after the first one. (You can name all of the authors if you choose to, however. Just be consistent and use either all their last names or et al. after the first author's last name in your in-text citations.)

Bennett, Jeffrey, et al. *The Cosmic Perspective: Media Update.* New York: Addison, 2004. Print.

4. TWO OR MORE WORKS BY THE SAME AUTHOR(S)

Note that the entries are alphabetized according to the first important words of the titles. *9* is treated as *nine.* When you use more than one work by the same author or authors, use their names in the first entry only, and use three hyphens for the works by the same authors that follow. If the individuals named are editors, compilers, or translators, follow

288   CHAPTER 13   Preparing the MLA List of Works Cited

the three hyphens with a comma and the correct abbreviation: *ed., comp.,* or *trans.* Insert an *s* before the period of the abbreviation if more than one individual is listed. If the order of the names of works with multiple authors is changed, do not use the hyphens. Order is important; it indicates the lead author of a work. If an author of a single work that you use is a co-author of other works that you cite in your paper, do not hyphenate his or her name. You should never combine the three hyphens with other authors' names.

Chomsky, Noam. *9-11*. New York: Seven Stories, 2001. Print.

- - -. *Profit over People: Neoliberalism and Global Order*. New York: Seven Stories, 1999. Print.

Herman, Edward S., and Noam Chomsky. *Manufacturing Consent: The Political Economy of the Mass Media*. New York: Pantheon, 1988. Print.

Rampton, Sheldon, and John Stauber. *Trust Us, We're Experts! How Industry Manipulates Science and Gambles with Your Future*. New York: Tarcher, 2002. Print.

Stauber, John, and Sheldon Rampton. *Toxic Sludge Is Good For You: Lies, Damn Lies and the Public Relations Industry*. Monroe, ME: Common Courage, 1995. Print.

Gilbert, Sandra M., and Susan Gubar, eds. *Feminist Literary Theory and Criticism: A Norton Reader*. New York: Norton, 2007. Print.

- - -. *The Madwoman in the Attic: The Woman Writer and the Nineteenth-Century Imagination*. New Haven: Yale UP, 2000. Print.

5. AN ILLUSTRATED BOOK OR GRAPHIC NOVEL

When illustrations are a significant part of a book, begin with the author and the title, as usual, and follow the title with the abbreviation of "illustrated by," *Illus.*, and the illustrator's name. If the illustrator's work is your focus, begin with that name, and follow the title of the book with "By" and the author's name.

Carroll, Lewis. *The Story of Sylvie and Bruno*. Illus. Harry Furniss. 1904. New York: Mayflower, 1980. A facsimile of the 1926 edition. Print.

Gorey, Edward, illus. *Old Possum's Book of Practical Cats*. By T. S. Eliot. New York: Harcourt,1982. Print.

In a graphic novel, the text and illustrations are equally important. If the text's author is also its illustrator, the entry will be the same as with any other novel.

> Gibbons, Dave. *The Originals*. Vertigo, 2006. Print.

When different people collaborate, begin with the person whose contributions you focus on, and include the other contributor or contributors after the title, using the appropriate abbreviations for their functions.

> Gaiman, Neil. *Preludes and Nocturnes*. Illus. Sam Kieth, Mike Dingenberg,
>
>   and Malcolm Jones, III. Introd. Karen Berger. New York: DC Comics,
>
>   1991. Print. Vol. 1 of *The Sandman*. 10 vols. Print.

> Harris, Joe, and Stuart Moore, adapt. *The Nightmare Factory*. By Thomas
>
>   Ligotti. Illus. Colleen Doran and Ben Templesmith. New York: Harper,
>
>   2007. Print.

6. BOOK WITH AN AUTHOR NOT LISTED

When a source does not have a listed author, you should alphabetize by the first important word of the title, ignoring (but not moving) *a, an,* and *the* (these parts of speech are called *articles*).

> *Beowulf*. Trans. Burton Raffel. New York: Signet, 1999. Print.

7. TRANSLATIONS

If the work was written in another language and translated, include the translator's name if provided, preceded by the abbreviation *Trans.*

> Ellul, Jacques. *Propaganda: The Formation of Men's Attitudes*. Trans. Konrad
>
>   Kelle and Jean Lerner. New York: Knopf, 1965. Print.

For books that are much older than their publication date would indicate, the convention is to put the original year of publication after the book's title.

> Machiavelli, Niccolò. *The Prince*. 1513. Trans. and ed. Robert M. Adams.
>
>   2nd ed. A Norton Critical ed. New York: 1991. Print.

8. BOOK THAT IS PART OF A MULTIVOLUME WORK

If the book has more than one volume and you use only one volume, list the volume you have used, followed by number of the volume used if you are using part of a multivolume work.

Casanova, Jacques. *The Memoirs of Jacques Casanova de Seingalt*. Trans.

Arthur Machen. Vol. 2. New York: Putnam, 1945. Print.

You may add the total number of volumes in the work, if you choose, as supplementary information at the end of the entry, but this is not a requirement. If the work appeared in print over a number of years, you may provide the inclusive years, as well.

Casanova, Jacques. *The Memoirs of Jacques Casanova de Seingalt*. Trans.

Arthur Machen. New York: Putnam, 1945. Print. 6 vols.

9. EDITION (OTHER THAN FIRST)

Cirlot, J. E. *A Dictionary of Symbols*. Trans. Jack Sage. 2nd ed. New York:

Barnes, 1995. Print.

Pratkanis, Anthony, and Elliot Aronson. *Age of Propaganda: The Everyday Use and Abuse of Persuasion*. Rev. ed. New York: Freeman, 2001. Print.

10. WORK IN A COLLECTION OF AN AUTHOR'S WORK

Carter, Angela. "The Snow Child." *The Bloody Chamber and Other Stories*.

New York: Penguin, 1979. 91–92. Print.

11. BOOK WITH THE TITLE OF A BOOK OR A PLAY IN ITS TITLE

If a title contains another title that would ordinarily be italicized or underlined, do not italicize or underline it.

Ward, Candace, ed. Everyman *and Other Miracle and Morality Plays*. New

York: Dover, 1995. Print.

12. SACRED TEXT

Sacred texts, unlike other books, are neither underlined nor italicized unless they are unique and distinct in some way from other versions, such as critical editions. With critical editions, which add commentary on the sacred writings, you may begin with the editors of the text. Books not in English often have variant spellings. Use the spelling found on the book. If acronyms are used, retain all the capital letters.

Ali, Maulana Muhammed. *The Holy Qur'an with English Translation and Commentary*. Columbus: Ahmadiyya Anjuman Ishaat, 1991. Print.

Felder, Cain Hope, ed. *The Original African Heritage Study Bible*. Valley Forge:

Judson, 2007. Print.

Holy Bible. King James Version. Philadelphia: National, 1978. Print.

Berlin, Adele, and Marc Zvi Brettler, eds. *The Jewish Study Bible*. Jewish Publication Society TANAKH Translation. Oxford: Oxford UP, 2004. Print.

The Upanishads. Trans. Eknath Easwaran. Tomales, CA: Nilgiri, 2007. Print.

13. ANTHOLOGY

To cite an anthology, provide the name(s) of the editor or compiler of the book if it is
an anthology, followed by the correct abbreviations (*ed.* or *comp.*, with an *s* before the
period if there is more than one individual).

Bennett, W. Lance, and Robert M. Entman, eds. *Mediated Politics: Communication in the Future of Democracy*. New York: Cambridge UP, 2004. Print.

14. ARTICLE, ESSAY, POEM, SHORT STORY, OR OTHER SHORT WORK FROM AN ANTHOLOGY

Use this format when you are using only a single work from an anthology; if you take
more than one work from an anthology, use the cross-referencing method described
on page 290. If you are taking a chapter, essay, article, short story, or other work from
a book or anthology, begin with the author of this work. If you are citing one specific
part of the book, such as a chapter or article, include the title of the part of the book,
enclosed in quotation marks. End with a period within the closing quotation mark unless a question mark or exclamation point is part of the title; if it is, it should also be
within the closing quotation mark.

1. **Author:** Begin with the author's name (first and last names reversed), followed
   by a period. (Follow the same guidelines listed previously if there is more than
   one author.)
2. **Title of the Selection:** The title of the selection will usually be given in quotation marks following the name of the author of the selection. End with a period
   within the closing quotation mark, followed by the title of the book.
3. **Translator:** Provide the name of a translator if there is one, preceded by
   Trans.
4. **Title of the Book:** Next, you'll give the title and subtitle of the book, italicized
   or underlined, followed by a period (unless the title has its own end punctuation
   mark, like a question mark).
5. **Editor's Name:** The name of the editor of the anthology or other type of book
   in which the selection appears follows the title of the book; it is not inverted
   but is preceded by the abbreviation *Ed.* It is followed by the name of the city
   of publication.

292   CHAPTER 13   Preparing the MLA List of Works Cited

6. **Edition:** Indicate the edition after the title if the book is not a first edition or it is a critical or revised edition.

7. **City, Publisher, and Year:** Follow with the city of publication, a colon, the shortened name of the publisher, a comma, the year, and a period, according to the guidelines listed earlier.

8. **Page Numbers:** Follow the publication information with the first and last page numbers of the selection. Give the complete numbers for any numbers between one and ninety-nine, but with higher numbers you should shorten the final page number if it falls within the same range (100–99, 1100–200, 1125–35). End with a period.

9. **Medium of Publication:** Follow publication information with the word *print,* capitalized and followed by a period.

10. **Pertinent Supplementary Information:** Although not a requirement and usually not necessary, you may end with any extra information that may be important for the readers to know.

> Holland, Peter. "Farce." *The Cambridge Companion to English Restoration*
>
> *Theatre.* Ed. Deborah Payne Fisk. Cambridge: Cambridge UP, 2005.
>
> 107–26. Print.

> Lacan, Jacques. "The Symbolic Order." Trans. Alan Sheridan. *Literary*
>
> *Theory: An Anthology.* Ed. Julie Rivkin and Michael Ryan. Rev. ed.
>
> Oxford: Blackwell, 1998. 184–89. Print.

15. ARTICLE, ESSAY, POEM, SHORT STORY, OR OTHER WORK WITHOUT AN AUTHOR

When a selection does not have an author, begin with the title. Remember to alphabetize the entry on your works-cited page by the first important word (not the articles *a, an,* or *the*) of the title.

> "The King of the Cats." *"The King of the Cats" and Other Feline Fairy Tales.*
>
> Ed. John Richard Stephens. Boston: Faber, 1993. 24–25. Print.

16. UNTITLED INTRODUCTION, PREFACE, FOREWORD, OR CONCLUSION

If your source is an untitled introduction, preface, foreword, afterword, or conclusion, provide·the appropriate designation but do not enclose it in quotation marks.

> Ishay, Micheline R. Introduction. *The History of Human Rights: From Ancient*
>
> *Times to the Globalization Era.* Berkeley: U of California P, 2004. 2–14.
>
> Print.

Works-Cited Entries for Books, Works in Books, and Plays   **293**

17. BOOK, PLAY, OR NOVEL IN AN ANTHOLOGY

Books, plays, and novels that are included in anthologies are treated the same way that shorter works, such as articles and essays, are treated; however, you should italicize or underline the titles, not enclose them in quotation marks.

> Kyd, Thomas. *The Spanish Tragedy*. 1592. *Four Revenge Tragedies*. Ed. Katherine
>
> Eisaman Maus. Oxford: Oxford UP, 1995. 1–91. Print.

18. MULTIPLE SELECTIONS FROM AN ANTHOLOGY (CROSS-REFERENCING)

When you need to cite more than one selection from an anthology, it is time consuming and unnecessary to type the publication information for the anthology for every selection you are listing. Instead, MLA allows you to cross-reference multiple works to an anthology by using the editor's last name in front of the work's page numbers. Your readers can find the rest of the publication information in the entry for the anthology, which you provide only once. Each cross-reference should include the following information: (1) author, (2) title of work, (3) editor's last name (note that this information is not followed by a period or comma), and (4) inclusive page numbers for the work. If a work has a translator, the translator's name follows the title of the work.

> Baker, C. Edwin. "Implications of Rival Visions of Electoral Campaigns."
>
> Bennett and Entman 342–61. Print.

In the following example of a list of sources, W. Lance Bennett and Robert M. Entman are the editors of an anthology called *Mediated Politics: Communication in the Future of Democracy*. Note that the entry for the anthology does not contain any information about any of the individual works. Note as well that all entries are arranged alphabetically. Do not begin with an anthology unless its editors' last names would put it at the top of the list. Note that each entry begins flush with the left margin.

Works Cited

> Baker, C. Edwin. "Implications of Rival Visions of Electoral Campaigns."
>
> Bennett and Entman 342–61. Print.
>
> Bennett, W. Lance, and Robert M. Entman, eds. *Mediated Politics: Communica-*
>
> *tion in the Future of Democracy*. New York: Cambridge UP, 2004. Print.
>
> Carpini, Michael X. Delli, and Bruce A. Williams. "Let Us Infotain You." Ben-
>
> nett and Entman 160–81. Print.
>
> Underwood, Doug. "Reporting and the Push for Market-Oriented Journalism:
>
> Media Organizations and Business." Bennett and Entman 99–116. Print.

Sometimes editors of anthologies include their own articles. You must still give their last names after their article's title so that your readers know what anthology the selection is taken from. In the following example, the entry for the article by Bennett and Entman precedes the entry for the anthology because the *C* of the article title comes before the *M* of the anthology title.

Bennett, W. Lance, and Robert M. Entman. "Communication in the Future of

Democracy: A Conclusion." Bennett and Entman 468–80. Print.

- - -, eds. *Mediated Politics: Communication in the Future of Democracy*. New

York: Cambridge UP, 2004. Print.

19. REPRINTED WORK

For a reprinted work, give the original publication information found for the work, followed by the abbreviation for reprinted (*Rpt.*), the word *in,* and the publication information for the anthology. Following are some variations you may encounter.
A work taken from a collection by the author:

Merriam, Eve. "Tryst." *The Nixon Poems*. New York: Atheneum, 1970. Rpt. in

No More Masks: An Anthology of Poems by Women. Ed. Florence Howe

and Ellen Bass. Garden City: Anchor, 1973. Print.

An article from a weekly magazine reprinted in an anthology when the anthology does not provide the page numbers of the article:

Said, Edward R. "The Clash of Ignorance." *The Nation* 3 Oct. 2001. Rpt. in *A

Just Response:* The Nation *on Terrorism, Democracy, and September 11,

2001*. Ed. Katrina Vanden Heuvel. New York: Thunder's Mouth, 2002.

233–39. Print.

Because *The Nation* is the title of a magazine, it should not be underlined or italicized in the book's title as it would be when it is not part of the title; not underlining or italicizing it sets it off from the rest of the title of the book.
An article from a scholarly journal reprinted in an anthology:

Yolen, Jane. "America's Cinderella." *Children's Literature in Education* 8

(1977): 21–29. Rpt. in *Cinderella: A Casebook*. Ed. Alan Dundes. Madi-

son: U of Wisconsin P, 1988. Print.

An article from a scholarly journal reprinted in a critical edition of a work:

Gurr, Andrew. "*The Tempest's* Tempest at Blackfriars." *Shakespeare Survey*

41 (1989): 91–102. Rpt. in The Tempest: *Sources and Contexts, Criticism,*

Rewritings and Appropriations. By William Shakespeare. Ed. Peter Hulme and William H. Sherman. Norton Critical ed. New York: Norton, 2004. 250–65. Print.

An untitled excerpt of a chapter from a book reprinted in a critical edition:

Greenaway, Peter. ["Prospero's Books."] Prospero's Books: *A Film of Shakespeare's The Tempest.* London: Chatto and Windus, 1991. 20–25. Rpt. in The Tempest: *Sources and Contexts, Criticism, Rewritings and Appropriations.* By William Shakespeare. Ed. Peter Hulme and William H. Sherman. Norton Critical ed. New York: Norton, 2004. 325–31. Print.

A chapter from a book reprinted in a critical edition:

Marcus, Leah. "The Blue-Eyed Witch." London: Routledge, 1996. 5–17. Rpt. in The Tempest: *Sources and Contexts, Criticism, Rewritings and Appropriations.* By William Shakespeare. Ed. Peter Hulme and William H. Sherman. Norton Critical ed. New York: Norton, 2004. 286–98. Print.

Remember that when you have the title of a book, film, or play in the title of a work that is italicized or underlined, as in the preceding examples, you set it off by refraining from italicizing or underlining it.

PERIODICAL PRINT PUBLICATIONS

You typically need six main elements in a works-cited entry for a periodical: author (when provided), title of work, title of the medium the work appears in, and publication information for that medium, page numbers, and medium of publication. You can find the first five elements on the cover or contents page of the periodical and on the opening page of the article you are citing.

In works-cited entries for works from periodicals, list the following elements in order:

1. **Author:** Begin with the author's name, when provided, last name first, followed by a period. If there is more than one author, follow the same guidelines as for books.

2. **Title of Article:** The title of the article, in quotation marks, followed by a period within the final quotation mark comes next.

3. **Title of Periodical:** Next you will need to provide the title of the periodical, underlined or italicized, and not followed by a period.

4. **Volume and Issue:** For journals, include the volume number alone if the journal is continuously paginated throughout the volume year, or the volume number followed by a decimal and the issue number if each issue begins with

296   CHAPTER 13   Preparing the MLA List of Works Cited

page one (such as 19.3). Note that it is not necessary to write *V.* or *vol.* for volume. When there is only one number, your readers will assume that it is the volume number; when there is a number, a decimal point, and another number, they will assume the first is the volume number and the second is the issue number. (An exception is a journal that has issues only and no volume numbers—in that case, give the lone issue number in the same way that you would give a volume number.)

5. **Date:** When citing journals, list the date of publication in parentheses. Often, the journal will be published by seasons; in this case, you need only list the year. For all other periodicals, list the date (day, month, and year for a weekly magazine, and just the month and year for a monthly) followed by a colon. Do not enclose the year in parentheses the way you would a journal. Abbreviate the names of months except for May, June, and July.

6. **Page Numbers:** After the colon, you list the first and last page numbers of the entire article. Give the complete numbers for any numbers between one and ninety-nine, but with higher numbers you should shorten the final page number for numbers higher than one hundred if it falls within the same range, just as you would with articles found in anthologies. If an article does not appear on consecutive pages, give the number of the first page followed by a plus sign, such as 19+. To cite newspaper articles, you'll need to provide both section numbers and page numbers. When an article does not appear on consecutive pages, give the section letter if there is one and the number of the article's first page followed by a plus sign, such as A2+.

7. **Medium of Publication:** Follow the page numbers with the word *print,* capitalized and followed by a period.

8. **Pertinent Supplementary Information:** If you have any supplementary information to add, such as an article being part of a series, place it at the very end of the entry.

Sample Entries for Print Periodicals

20. ARTICLE FROM A JOURNAL WITH CONTINUOUS PAGINATION

Marks, Elise. "*Othello/me*": Racial Drag and the Pleasures of Boundary-
    Crossing with *Othello.*" *Comparative Drama* 35 (2001): 101–24. Print.

21. ARTICLE FROM A JOURNAL THAT BEGINS EACH ISSUE ON PAGE ONE

Sadoff, Ira. "Olena Kalytiak Davis and the Retro-New." *American Poetry
    Review* 35.4 (2006): 11–15. Print.

22. SPECIAL ISSUE OF SCHOLARLY JOURNAL

If you are citing more than one source from a scholarly journal that has published a special issue with a title, treat the issue itself like an anthology. Begin with the special issue's editor, followed by the name of the special issue. Add *Spec. issue of* before the name of the journal. Format the rest of the entry like a regular journal, but end with the inclusive page numbers of the entire journal. For articles in the special issue, cross-reference them to the edition the way you would multiple articles from an anthology (see #18).

> Haase, Donald, ed. *Jack Zipes and the Sociohistorical Study of Fairy Tales.*
>
> Spec. issue of *Marvels and Tales: Journal of Fairy-Tale Studies* 16.2
>
> (2002): 1–274. Print.

> Jones, Jane. "Jack Zipes and German Folklore." Haase 27–41. Print.

If you are citing only one article from a special issue, use the following form:

> Jones, Jane. "Jack Zipes and German Folklore." *Jack Zipes and the Sociohis-*
>
> *torical Study of Fairy Tales.* Spec. issue of *Marvels and Tales: Journal of*
>
> *Fairy-Tale Studies* 16.2 (2002): 27–41. Print.

23. ARTICLE FROM A WEEKLY OR BIWEEKLY MAGAZINE

You can tell whether a magazine is weekly or biweekly (published every other week) by looking at the date on the cover. If the day is supplied as well as the month, it is weekly or biweekly. Don't give volume and issue numbers for magazines.

> Kumin, Maxine. "Looking Back in My Eighty-First Year." *New Yorker* 1 Dec.
>
> 2006: 64. Print.

Occasionally a magazine that is normally published on a weekly basis will publish one issue a year that spans two weeks (as in the holiday season) and give two dates on its cover. When this happens, use both dates.

> Erdrich, Louise. "Demolition." *New Yorker* 25 Dec. 2006/1 Jan. 2007: 70–81.
>
> Print.

24. ARTICLE FROM A MONTHLY OR BIMONTHLY MAGAZINE

To cite monthly or bimonthly magazines, you need only provide months and years. For example:

> Douthat, Ross. "The Truth about Harvard." *Atlantic* Mar. 2005: 95–99. Print.

> Robbins, Alexandra. "Powerful Secrets." *Vanity Fair* July 2004: 119+. Print.

If a magazine that typically publishes once a month publishes an issue that spans two months, provide both months.

> Fallows, James. "Success without Victory." *Atlantic* Jan./Feb. 2005: 80–90.
>
> Print.

> Note: Monday through Saturday, the *New York Times* is usually divided into lettered sections, just like most other newspapers. However, sometimes the Saturday edition is continuously paginated from the first page to the last with no section numbers. Just use the page numbers of an article after the edition.
>
> The Sunday *New York Times* contains numbered sections. After the edition, give the section number preceded by the abbreviation *sec.*

25. NEWSPAPER ARTICLE

> Walters, Dan. "$400 Million a Big Deal? Not Really." *Sacramento Bee* 23 Oct.
>
> 2006, metro final ed.: A3. Print.

26. A SERIALIZED ARTICLE OR SERIES OF RELATED ARTICLES

Sometimes lengthy articles are serialized across more than one issue of a magazine or newspaper. If each installment of such an article has the same author and title (or just title, if there is no author), create a single entry. For journals, after the usual publication information, including page numbers, add a semicolon, and then follow with the same information for subsequent issues. For magazines and newspapers, use the appropriate dates (and section numbers, if applicable). End with medium of publication. If the different installments have individual titles, you'll need to create an entry for each. You may add supplementary information after the medium of publication to indicate that each article is part of the same series.

> "Gay Marriage Controversy Comes to Kern County." *Bakersfield Observer*
>
> 16 June 2008, A1;17 June 2008, A1–2. Print.

> Liptak, Adam. "Inmate Count in U.S. Dwarfs Other Nations." *New York Times*
>
> 23 Apr. 2008, late ed.: A1+. Print. Pt. 1 of a series, American Exception,
>
> begun 17 Oct. 2007.

> - - -. "Lifers as Teenagers, Now Seeking Second Chance." *New York Times*
>
> 17 Oct. 2007, late ed.: A1+. Print. Pt.1 of a series, American Exception,
>
> begun 17 Oct. 2007.

27. EDITORIAL OR OPINION PIECE

Editorials, both signed and unsigned, must be indicated as such to distinguish them from straight reporting and other types of articles in newspapers. This information follows the title of the piece. Use *editorial* if no authors are given, but refer to a signed editorial as an *opinion piece* because it is written by an individual columnist or guest contributor, not the paper's editorial board. (In your entry, do not underline, italicize, or enclose these terms in quotation marks.)

> Henderson, Noris. "Give Defense Reform a Chance." *Times-Picayune*. Opinion
>
> piece. 14 Oct. 2006, metro ed.: 7. Print.

28. REVIEW

Give the title of the review, followed by a period (if the review does not have a title, just put *Rev. of* and the title of the work being reviewed followed by a period). Write *Rev. of* and the title of the book, a comma, and its author (preceded by *by*); or the title of the film, a comma, and its director (preceded by *dir.*); or the title of the series, a comma, and its network. End with the medium of publication.

> Oates, Joyce Carol. "Dangling Men." Rev. of *Indecision,* by Benjamin Kunkel.
>
> *New York Review of Books* 3 Nov. 2005: 36–40. Print.

> Travers, Peter. "American Idols." Rev. of *Dreamgirls,* dir. Bill Condon. *Rolling*
>
> *Stone* 14 Dec. 2006: 132. Print.

> Friend, Tad. "The Paper Chase." Rev. of *The Office,* NBC. *New Yorker* 1 Dec.
>
> 2006: 94–100. Print.

29. CARTOON OR COMIC STRIP

Give the name of the cartoonist followed by the title of the cartoon if it has one, or the name of the cartoon strip if it is part of a series. Otherwise, write *Cartoon* or *Comic Strip*. Then give the publication information for its source. End with the medium of publication.

> Rees, David. "Get Your War On." *Rolling Stone*. 31 May 2007. 10. Print.

30. ADVERTISEMENT

Give the name of the product or company being advertised, followed by the word *Advertisement*. Follow with the publication information for the advertisement's source.

> Hypnôse by Lancôme. Advertisement. *Playbill* May 2007: 42–43. Print.

300   CHAPTER 13   Preparing the MLA List of Works Cited

WORKS-CITED ENTRIES FOR WORKS FROM REFERENCE DATABASES

In works-cited entries for articles you find in online databases, your entries should begin exactly as they would if you were working with an article from the print publication; however, you also need to include additional information about the online location of the electronic version you found. Provide information about the subscription database in the order listed next. If only the starting page number of an article is given, give the number followed by a hyphen, a space, and a period; if the database gives the total number of pages, as in 53(4), which means that the article begins on page 53 and is four pages long, you need to calculate the number of the article's last page (in this case you would list it as pages 53–57). If pagination is not available, use *n. pag.*

1. **Original Publication Information for the Article:** Follow the guidelines for the original print versions of journal, newspaper, and magazine, etc., articles.

2. **Name of Database:** Name of database (for example, LexisNexis), italicized or underlined, followed by a period.

3. **Medium of Publication:** The MLA previously recommended providing the URL of electronic sources, but its 2009 guidelines recommend omitting them. URLs are often unreliable because they may change over time or even according to different users and Internet sessions. Simply use the term *Web*.

4. **Date of Access:** Day, month, and year, not separated by commas, followed by a period.

Suppose you are planning on writing a paper about television, and you decide to look for articles on television history. You use your home computer to go to your library's online pages and look at the list of searchable archives and gateways to databases. You choose EBSCOHost, which gives you access to numerous online databases, such as *Academic Search Elite, Business Source Premier, EBSCO Animals, ERIC, GreenFILE, Health Source: Nursing/Academic Edition, Newspaper Source, MEDLINE, Psychology & Behavioral Sciences Collection, Religion and Philosophy Collection,* and various health- and business-related databases. You use "television" and "history" as your search terms in *Academic Search Premier,* limiting publication type to periodicals, and one of the articles you find looks interesting. It is called "What's Wrong with Television History?" and it is from the periodical *History Today.*

You decide to use this article. To do the citation, you start by reviewing how to do a work-cited entry for a periodical article. You start with the author, located near the top of the screen, under the article title, and then follow with the title, then the name of the periodical, not adding a period.

> Stearn, Tom. "What's Wrong with Television History?" *History Today*

There is quite a bit of information following the name of the periodical, including date, volume, and issue. Because your paper will be in MLA format, you realize you need to know if this is a magazine or a journal. The library has this article in the database, but no physical copy of *History Today*. You choose to download it in a Portable Document Format (PDF) file, and you see that the article begins with a brightly colored illustration of actors staging a Saxon battle. This type of illustration is typical of a magazine, not a journal. You decide to do a Net search for more information, and you type in "history today periodical." Your first hit takes you to an online bookstore that describes it as a magazine and shows a copy of a cover, which is also brightly illustrated and standard magazine size. You now know how to proceed, and you know that you need the date of publication, but not the volume or issue number. Because the article is from a magazine, you don't enclose the date with parentheses. You need to follow with the page numbers. You see "p26, 2p," at the end of the publication information, so you know that the article was on pages 26 to 27.

Stearn, Tom. "What's Wrong with Television History?" *History Today* Dec. 2002: 26–27.

Century

Now that you have the entry you'd have if you actually had the magazine, you need to complete it with all the information for the database. You give the database, underlined or italicized and followed by a period, and the name of the subscription service that provides access to the database, not italicized or underlined, followed by a period.

> Stearn, Tom. "What's Wrong with Television History?" *History Today*
>
> Dec. 2002: 26–27. *Academic Search Premier.*

Now all you need to do is add the term *Web,* followed by a period and then your day, month, and year of access, finishing the entry with the usual period.

> Stearn, Tom. "What's Wrong with Television History?" *History Today*
>
> Dec. 2002: 26–27. *Academic Search Premier.* Web. 30 Nov. 2008.

Following are more examples.

31. ARTICLE FROM A NEWSPAPER IN NEWSPAPER SOURCE

> Goldman, Tim. "Expecting U.S. Help, Sent to Guantánamo." *New York Times*
>
> 15 Oct. 2006: sec. 1:26. *Newspaper Source.* Web. 9 Oct. 2008.

32. ARTICLE FROM A JOURNAL WITH CONTINUOUS PAGINATION, EXPANDED ACADEMIC ASAP

> Goldstein, Gary B. "Did Queen Elizabeth Use the Theater for Social and
>
> Political Propaganda?" *Oxfordian* 7 (2004): 153 – . *Expanded Academic*
>
> *ASAP.* Web. 18 Jan. 2009.

33. ARTICLE FROM A JOURNAL THAT BEGINS EACH ISSUE ON PAGE ONE, ACADEMIC SEARCH PREMIER

> Susman, Jeff. "Harry and Louise Redux." *Journal of Family Practice* 55.4
>
> (2006): 276. *Psychology and Behavioral Sciences Collection.* Web.
>
> 21 Sep. 2008.

34. ARTICLE FROM A MAGAZINE, LEXISNEXIS

> "All on the Mind; Cognitive Enhancement." *Economist* 24 May 23 2008,
>
> U.S. ed.: n. pag. *LexisNexis.* Web. 20 Jan. 2009.

WORKS-CITED ENTRIES FOR INTERNET SOURCES

To cite online sources, list each of these elements, when provided, in this order:

1. **Author:** The work's or Web page's author's name if there is one, followed by a period.
2. **Title:** The title of the work, underlined or italicized, if the work stands alone, or enclosed in quotation marks if it is part of a series of pages on a site, followed by a period. Untitled works should be identified by a descriptive label, such as *Online posting* or *Home page,* and neither italicized, underlined, nor enclosed in quotation marks.
3. **Publication Information:** Original print publication information, if the work is reprinted and this information is provided (book titles are followed by periods, periodical titles are not).
4. **Site Title:** The name of the site on which the work is posted (unless the work stands alone), underlined or italicized, followed by a period.
5. **Publisher, editor, site sponsor, or Web Master:** This information is followed by a period. If not available, use the abbreviation *n. p.*
6. **Publication Date:** Provide the day, month and year, if available. If not available, use the abbreviation *n. d.*
7. **Medium of Publication:** As noted earlier, MLA no longer recommends providing the URL of the online source because URLs are often unreliable. Searching for Internet content using authors and titles is frequently more efficient than trying to use URLS, which may be obsolete. The MLA now recommends simply using the term *Web.*
8. **Date of Access:** The day, month, and year that you visited the site, not separated by commas, and followed by a period.
9. **Supplementary Information:** Include a URL only if your readers wouldn't be able to locate a source otherwise or if your instructor requests it; if in doubt, ask. If you do provide the URL, it should follow your date of access and a period and be enclosed in angle brackets. Sometimes you may need other information, such as naming a specific service, such as iTunes, if necessary to find a podcast. End the entry with a period.

35. NEWSPAPER ARTICLE PUBLISHED ONLINE

Murphy, Kim. "British Accuse Ex-KGB Agent in Poisoning Death." *Los*

Angeles Times 22 May 2007. Web. 22 May 2009.

36. AUTHORLESS ARTICLE ON AN ORGANIZATION'S WEBSITE

"China: Google Hints at China U-turn." Amnesty.org.uk. 8 June 2006.

Web. 11 June 2008.

37. ESSAY REPRINTED ON A WEBSITE

Orwell, George. "Politics and the English Language." *Shooting an Elephant and Other Essays*. London: Secker and Warburg, 1950. N. pag. George Orwell's Library. 24 July 2004. Web. 19 Apr. 2009.

38. ARTICLE FROM AN INDIVIDUAL'S TITLED WEBSITE

Shah, Anup. "War, Propaganda and the Media." *Global Issues That Affect Everyone*. Anup Shah. 31 Mar. 2005. Web. 11 Feb. 2009.

39. ARTICLE FROM AN ONLINE JOURNAL

Hollis, Erin. "Gorgonzola Sandwiches and Yellow Crayons: James Joyce, *Buffy the Vampire Slayer,* and the Aesthetic of Minutiae." *Slayage: The Online International Journal of Buffy Studies* 22 (2006): 11 pages. Web. 15 Mar. 2009.

(Pages are supplied for the preceding article because it is downloadable in PDF format.)

40. MATERIAL FROM PROFESSORS' WEBSITES

Cite material found on a professor's website in the same way you would cite other online sources. Include the course number and name (if available) and the name of the department and school at which the professor teaches. As with other website entries, only include the URL as supplementary information at the end of the entry if that is the only way your readers can find the source.

Hastings, Waller. "Motifs and Tale Types." *Fairy Tales*. Waller Hastings' home page.

English Department. Northern State University. N. d. Web. 11 Nov. 2008.

41. CARTOON PUBLISHED ONLINE

Marlette, Doug. "New York State of Mind." *Slate.com.* 2007. Web. 1 June 2007.

42. BLOG

Blogs (from "web log") are everywhere on the Web, and most are as worthless to researchers as someone else's daily diary or even a commentary scrawled on a bathroom wall. Nevertheless, blogging by mainstream journalists, scientists, educators, and others has been increasing over the years, and many important newsletters feature distinguished bloggers on their websites. Often these are people whose credentials you can evaluate, and they may provide useful perspectives. Just be careful—anyone can publish a blog, and rampant biases voiced with no editorial oversight are quite common. If you use a blog as a source, provide the pertinent information for the blog entry, such as the individual writing the blog, the title of the entry if there is one, the name of the blog, and *Blog.* Next, give the title of the blog itself, the title of the sponsoring organization if there is one, the date the material was uploaded (even if the actual time is provided, you don't need to include this unless it is necessary to locate the entry, as when someone has several entries on a given day but no titles), followed by a period, followed by *Web,* followed by your date of access.

Shachtman, Noah. "Nation's Spies: Climate Change Could Spark War." *Danger*

Room. Blog. *Wired Blog Network.* 23 June 2008. Web. Oct. 29 2008.

Sullivan, Andrew. " 'Disgrace,' Ctd." *Andrew Sullivan: The Daily Dish.* Blog.

The Atlantic.com. 19 June 2008. Web. 20 Nov. 2009.

43. PODCAST

Podcasts are an increasingly popular method for disseminating information on the Net and include a variety of sources, such as radio programs and college and university lectures. If you use a podcast as a source, provide the pertinent information for the type of material being podcast, such as the individual doing the podcast, the title if there is one, and *Podcast* followed by a period following the title of the work (or taking the place of the title if there is none). End with the usual information required in an online entry: the date the material was uploaded, followed by a period, followed by *Web,* followed by your date of access.

Podcast from a site's home page:

Fisher, Ian. "The Rome Bureau Chief on the Attack on the U.S. Embassy in

Athens." Interview. Podcast. *New York Times: Backstory.* 12 Jan. 2007.

Web. 13 Jan. 2007.

"Sexual Orientation Legislation." Podcast. *Today.* BBC Radio 4. Web. 1 Jan.

2007. Web. 12 Jan. 2007.

Podcast from an outside service:

Podcasts available exclusively through services such as Apple's iTunes Store present a different problem since they cannot be found through a unique URL or through a simple Web search. Instead, you must download the iTunes software to gain access.

"The Long Hard Winter." Podcast. *Nightline.* ABC News. 1 Jan. 2007. iTunes

Store. Web. 13 Jan. 2007.

44. YOUTUBE OR OTHER ONLINE VIDEO CLIP

The YouTube video-sharing website where users can upload, view, and share video clips is immensely popular, and it is where some viewers first see any number of clips, from moments on news and entertainment programs to commercials and personal video. Other Internet sites also offer clips. To cite a clip from the Internet, you will need to give the original broadcast information and the YouTube information, including the date of uploading and the posted user name of the uploader. Include your date of access before the URL.

1. **Title:** Begin with the title of the clip if there is one, and a descriptive label if there is not. Titles should be enclosed in quotation marks, but labels should not. Follow with *Video clip,* not italicized or underlined.

2. **Original Broadcast Information:** If the clip wasn't created by the uploader, provide the original broadcast information following the format for such entries.

3. **Site:** Indicate the site the video is uploaded to, underlined or italicized.

4. **Upload Information:** Provide the name or pseudonym of the person uploading the material if provided and the date of the upload if provided. Use *n. d.* if there is no date.

5. **Medium of Publication:** Use Web.

6. **Date of Access:** End with the day, month, and year that you accessed the clip.

> "Stephen Colbert on *The O'Reilly Factor.*" *The O'Reilly Factor.* Fox News
>
>   Channel. 18 Jan. 2007. *YouTube.* Rackjite1. 19 Jan. 2007. Web.
>
>   22 May 2007.

If you want to emphasize an individual in the clip, you may begin with that person's name.

> Pausch, Randy. "Dying Professor's Final Farewell." Multimedia Producer: Reda
>
>   Charafeddine. Reporter: Jeff Zaslow. *The Wall Street Journal* Digital
>
>   Network. Network. N. d. *YouTube.* Web. 10 June 2007.

WORKS-CITED ENTRIES FOR OTHER SOURCES

45. FILM, VIDEOCASSETTE, OR DVD

1. **Title:** The typical entry for a movie begins with the title, underlined or italicized.

2. **Director:** Cite the director (preceded by *Dir.*) after the film title.

3. **Pertinent Supplementary Information:** After the title, you may cite the producer, preceded by "Produced by" (not in quotation marks); screenwriter, preceded by "Screenplay by" (also not included in quotation marks), and the lead actors (preceded by *Perf.*) or narrator (preceded by *Narr.*).

4. **Distributor and Date:** Add the name of the distributor and the year of the work's release.

5. **Medium:** Indicate Film, Videocassette, DVD, or Laser disc. If you are citing any of the last three, you may also include the film's original release date before you give the information on its subsequent release in another medium.

> *Borat: Cultural Learnings of America for Make Benefit Glorious Nation of*
>
> *Kazakhstan.* Dir. Larry Charles. Perf. Sacha Baron Cohen. 20th Cen-
>
> tury Fox, 2006. Film.

> *High Fidelity.* Dir. Stephen Frears. Perf. John Cusack and Iben Hjejle. 2000.
>
> Walt Disney Video, 2001. Videocassette.

After the title of the film and its director and performers, the amount of information that you give in an entry for a film depends on its relevance. If the film is based on or suggested by a literary or nonfiction work of the same name, you can indicate this before the distributor. If the film and the literary work have the same title, simply write "Based on the [novel, short story, novella] by [name of author]."

> *Syriana.* Dir. Steven Gaghan. Perf. George Clooney, Matt Damon, and
>
> Amanda Peet. Suggested by *See No Evil* by Robert Baer. Warner Bros.,
>
> 2005. Film.

If the work of the screenwriter, director, or an actor is the primary focus of your paper, you may begin with this person's name, followed by his or her role, followed by the title of the film.

> Jordan, Neil, dir. *The Company of Wolves.* Perf. Angela Lansbury, David
>
> Warner, and Graham Crowden. Based on the story by Angela Carter. Pal-
>
> ace Productions, 1984. Film.

46. RADIO OR TELEVISION PROGRAM

Provide the information for these programs in the following order:

1. **Title:** Begin with the title of the episode or segment, enclosed in quotation marks.
2. **Program or Series:** Follow with the title of the program, underlined or italicized.
3. **Name of the Network:** Provide the name of the network, if there is one.
4. **Call Letters and City:** Provide the call letters of the local station if available and the local city, separated by commas and with a comma following.
5. **Broadcast Date:** Provide the day, month, and year the segment was broadcast, not separated by commas. End with a period.
6. **Medium of Broadcast:** Indicate whether the program was on the radio or television.

7. **Pertinent Supplementary Information:** Although not required, you can end with supplementary information if you believe it will help your readers.

> "Ghosts of Rwanda." *Frontline*. PBS. WGBH, Boston, 1 Apr. 2004. Television.

If you are focusing on the contributions of an individual, put that person's name before the title.

> Sedaris, David. "It's Catching." *Fresh Air*. Natl. Public Radio. WHYY, Philadel-
>
> phia, 9 June 2008. Radio. Excerpt from *When You Are Engulfed in Flames*.

47. SOUND RECORDING

1. **Primary Artist:** Begin the name of the person you want to emphasize, such as the composer, performer, or conductor, or the name of a group or ensemble.
2. **Title:** For a short work, use quotation marks. For a long work, use italics or underlining. **Other Artists:** Follow if appropriate with the names of other relevant individuals, such as singers, musicians, and orchestras and conductors.
3. **Manufacturer and Date:** Provide the manufacturer and release date. (Often only the year is available.) If no date is available, use *n. d.*
4. **Medium:** Indicate whether the recording is on a compact disc (CD), Long-playing record (LP), an audiocassette, or an audiotape.

> Waits, Tom, comp. *The Black Rider*. Perf. Tom Waits and Williams
>
> Burroughs. Island, 2 Nov. 1993. CD.

> LuPone, Patti, perf. "The Worst Pies in London." *Sweeney Todd: The Demon*
>
> *Barber of Fleet Street*. 2005 Broadway Revival Cast. Comp. Stephen
>
> Sondheim. Nonesuch, 31 Jan. 2006. CD.

48. INTERVIEWS

Use any of the elements that are pertinent in the following order.

1. **Person Interviewed:** Begin with the name of the person interviewed, followed by a period.
2. **Interview Title:** If the interview is part of a publication or program and has a title, add the title, enclosed in quotation marks, followed by a period. If it does not have a title or if you conducted the interview yourself, just write *Interview, Personal interview, Telephone interview,* or *Email interview.*
3. **Interviewer:** The interviewer's name may be added after *Interview with,* following either the title of the interview or the interviewed person's name if known and pertinent. You do not need to include your own name if you conducted the interview.

4. **Publication Information:** Include pertinent publication information, following the format for the type of source. If you conducted the interview, end with the date(s).

5. **Medium of Broadcast:** If the interview was broadcast on the radio or television, indicate this at the end.

Following are examples of interviews published in the online version of a newspaper, conducted through email, and conducted on a radio program.

> Jablonski, Nina G. "Always Revealing, Human Skin Is an Anthropologist's
>
> Map." Interview with Claudia Dreifus. *New York Times* 9 Jan. 2007. Web.
>
> 11 Jan. 2007.

> Olson, Laura. Email interview. 11 Jan. 2007.

> Whedon, Joss. Interview with Terry Gross. *Fresh Air*. Natl. Public Radio.
>
> WHYY, Philadelphia. 9 May 2000. Radio.

49. ORAL PRESENTATIONS

If you cite lectures, speeches, addresses, or readings, use any of the elements that are pertinent in the following order.

1. **Speaker's Name:** No prefix or title is necessary.

2. **Title:** Enclose the title in quotation marks; if there is no title, the descriptive label at the end of the entry will suffice.

3. **Meeting and Sponsoring Organization:** Provide what information you have about the occasion of the presentation and the sponsor.

4. **Location and Date:** Provide the name of the institution or building, followed by the city and the date.

5. **Form of Delivery:** End with a label that describes the mode of delivery.

> O'Hare, Denis. "Beyond Lies the Wub" by Philip K. Dick. Selected Shorts.
>
> Symphony Space, New York. 21 Oct. 2006. Reading.

> Moton, David. English 1A: Expository Composition. Bakersfield College.
>
> Bakersfield, CA. 22 May 2007. Lecture.

50. LIVE PERFORMANCE

1. **Title:** Live performances, comedy shows, concerts, plays, ballets, or operas, are treated much like films. Typically, begin with the title of the work. If there is no title, use a descriptive label.

2. **Author or Composer:** Follow with the name of the author or composer, preceded by the word *By.*

3. **Pertinent Supplementary Information:** Follow the author or composer with relevant information about the performance, such as the major performers (*Perf.*); the director (*Dir.*), the composer (*Comp.*); the choreographer (*Chor.*), and the conductor (*Cond.*).

4. **Production Information:** Next, give the company if provided, the theater, the city, and the date of the performance.

5. **Medium:** End with the medium—*Performance.*

> *Frost/Nixon.* By Peter Morgan. Dir. Michael Grandage. Perf. Michael Sheen
> and Frank Langella. Bernard B. Jacobs Theater, New York. 22 May
> 2007. Performance.

> *Edward Scissorhands.* Dir. and Chor. Matthew Bourne. Comp. Terry
> David and Danny Elfman. Perf. Sam Archer and Richard Winsor.
> New Adventures. Ahmanson Theater, Los Angeles. 31 Dec. 2006.
> Performance.

If your focus is a particular individual, you may begin the entry with that name.

> Poundstone, Paula. Stand-up comedy. Moore Theater, Seattle. 15 Nov. 2008.
> Performance.

51. PAINTING, SCULPTURE, PHOTOGRAPH, OR OTHER WORK OF VISUAL ART

1. **Artist:** Begin with the artist, if known.

2. **Title:** Italicize or underline the title of the work if provided. Otherwise, use a descriptive label, not underlined or italicized.

3. **Date:** List the year of composition; if unknown, use *n. d.* If an approximate date or range is known, follow by a question mark.

4. **Medium of Composition:** Specify the medium; be precise, for example, write "oil on canvas" rather than just "painting."

5. **Exhibition Title:** If the work is part of a temporary exhibition, add the name of the exhibition after the medium, followed by the exhibition dates.

6. **Location:** Name the museum, gallery, or other institution the work is housed in; if it is in a private collection, use "Collection of" (not in quotation marks) followed by the person's name or "Private collection" (not in quotation marks) if that information is not available or if the owner prefers anonymity.

Mapplethorpe, Robert. Untitled (self-portrait). 1972. Polaroid photograph. Polaroids: Mapplethorpe. 3 May 2008–7 Sep. 2008. Whitney Museum, New York.

Naso, Albert. *Rainstorm in the Amazon*. 2000–2001? India ink on paper. Private collection.

Picasso, Pablo. *Gertrude Stein*. 1906. Oil on canvas. Metropolitan Museum of Art, New York.

ANNOTATED BIBLIOGRAPHIES

What Is an Annotated Bibliography?

An annotated bibliography follows each works-cited entry with notes about the source. You annotate each entry with a few sentences that summarize what each source contains. You may also include evaluative information. A bibliography can contain more works than you actually use in your paper. Although *annotated bibliography* is the generally used term, some instructors may ask you to make an Annotated List of Works Cited instead; in this, you include only the sources that appear in your paper. You may also be asked to provide an Annotated List of Works Consulted, which includes sources that you looked at that may have helped you with background and context, but that you did not actually use in your paper. No matter what heading you use (based on what your instructor asks you to include), the principle for all of these lists is the same: give citations providing publication information so that your readers can find each source themselves if they choose, then follow each with a brief, informative annotation that may also include comments about what is useful in the source or how it stacks up against other materials out there.

Why Should I Write an Annotated Bibliography?

1. The most common reason, of course, is simply that it has been assigned by your instructor. However, this isn't just "busy work"; an annotated bibliography can help you write a stronger research paper. You read a source carefully and critically when you have to prepare an annotation, so it is a good idea to write the annotations as you read your sources and not wait until your instructor asks you to submit the assignment. Also, think of these annotations as works in progress—as you read more sources, you become more informed, and you become part of the ongoing conversation about your topic. You learn what experts see as the most important issues, what people are arguing about, and how they support and defend their own theories. Your growing knowledge can be reflected in your annotations. Many instructors want something slightly different when it comes to an annotated bibliography, so be sure to get details from your instructor before proceeding.

312   CHAPTER 13   Preparing the MLA List of Works Cited

2. Organization. Even if it is not a formal assignment, many researchers and students choose to complete an annotated bibliography anyway. Think of it as a tool for organizing and arranging your own material as you research. It helps make sure you capture all the pertinent information for your final works-cited page, and it helps remind you exactly which source is which. When doing a lengthy research project, you will go through dozens of sources on the same topic. It can get hard to remember which source is which, so these annotations will help distinguish your sources from one another.

3. Context. As noted earlier, you can put more than just a quick summary in your annotated bibliography. You can start the annotation with the summary of the material being covered, but then move on to evaluative comments, as well. Was anything unique about this source? What makes you want to use it in your paper? How does it compare with other research material you have found? Answering questions like these can help give your sources a better context.

Caution: Make sure that you find out what your instructor wants included in your final paper. Some instructors may ask you to turn in an annotated bibliography separately, but want the works-cited pages in your paper to be free of annotations.

How Do I Write My Annotated Bibliography?

1. You will begin your entry with a full MLA-style works-cited entry.

2. Begin the annotation on a new line, but do not indent any lines. Typically, you will include two to four sentences summarizing the source. For a book, you could either summarize the entire work or simply summarize the single chapter or article that you have chosen (but always check with your instructor for a preference here).

3. If you choose and your instructor approves, follow the summary with a brief evaluation of the source and discuss how it fits in with your research. If you prepare your annotations throughout the research process, this information can be used when you are writing the first draft of your paper.

4. Do not number or label your sources (such as source A or B). List them all in alphabetical order exactly as you would on an unannotated works-cited page. Also, do not place the works-cited information in bold or use a different type or color of font—there is no need to set if off in any way.

5. Skip a space between entries.

Below are two examples of annotated bibliography entries for a paper written by student Dianne Jeffries; it ties to the sample paper found on page 256.

Bagdikian, Ben. "Grand Theft: The Conglomeratization of Media and the

Degradation of Culture: 25 Years of Monitoring the Multinationals.

Multinational Monitor 26.1–2 (Jan–Feb 2005): 35–7. *Expanded Academic ASAP*. Thomson Gale. Web. 19 Oct. 2008.